THE INDIVIDUAL
AND
THE GROUP

Boundaries and Interrelations

Volume 1: Theory

THE INDIVIDUAL AND THE GROUP

Boundaries and Interrelations

Volume 1 : Theory

Edited by

Malcolm Pines

Tavistock Clinic
London, England

Institute of Group Analysis
London, England

and
President of the International
Association of Group Psychotherapy

and

Lise Rafaelsen

Gentofte Hospital
Hellerup, Denmark

PLENUM PRESS • NEW YORK AND LONDON

Library of Congress Cataloging in Publication Data

Main entry under title:

The Individual and the group.

   Proceedings of the 7th International Congress of Group Psychotherapy held Aug.
3-8, 1980, at the University of Copenhagen and sponsored by the International
Association of Group Psychotherapy.
   Includes bibliographical references and index.
   Contents: v. 1. Theory – v. 2. Practice.
   1. Group psychotherapy – Congresses. I. Pines, Malcolm. II. Rafaelsen, Lise. III.
International Congress of Group Psychotherapy (7th : 1980 : University of Copen-
hagen) IV. International Association of Group Psychotherapy. [DNLM: 1. Group
processes – Congresses. 2. Psychotherapy, Group – Congresses. W3 IN386 7th
1980i / WM 430 I634 1980i]
RC488.A2I5   616.89′152   81-17924
ISBN 0-306-40837-6 (v. 1)   AACR2

First half of the proceedings of the VII International
Congress of Group Psychotherapy, held August 3-8, 1980
at the University of Copenhagen, Copenhagen, Denmark

© 1982 Plenum Press, New York
A Division of Plenum Publishing Corporation
233 Spring Street, New York, N.Y. 10013

Printed in the United States of America

FOREWORD

Malcolm Pines and Lise Rafaelsen

The Seventh International Congress of Group Psychotherapy
organized in Copenhagen by the International Association of Group
Psychotherapy was one of the largest and most representative
congresses on this subject that has yet been held. Probably for
the first time we achieved the declared aim of the International
Association: that of bringing together representatives of the
different approaches to group psychotherapy in the same forum to
allow for communication, exchange, and development of our relationships. Previous congresses have been less representative and it
seems to augur well for the future of the Association and of it's
congresses that there was this strong force and wish for unification
and for exchange within the field of group psychotherapy.

The Congress theme, "The Individual and the Group: Boundaries
and Interrelations in Theory and Practice" was chosen because it gave
an opportunity once again to examine the very basis for group psychotherapy as theory and as practice. The basic theme, stated in the
opening papers by Professor Marie Jahoda and Professor James
Anthony, was replayed daily with new developments and variations
according to the theoretical position of each subsequent speaker.
The richness of development of this basic theme can only now be
grasped by reading through these papers for the design of the programme with its four concurrent sub-plenary papers did not allow
anyone to follow these different developments at the time. All the
plenary and sub-plenary papers are gathered in Volume I and we have
interspersed them with prepared discussions and with "free" papers
close to issues developed by the plenary papers. We have also included in Volume I the relatively self-contained section on
Therapeutic Community to complete the volume.

In Volume II we have brought together some of the contributions
to two major symposia, those on Psychosis and on Training and
Supervision in Group Psychotherapy. We have had to omit several
of these papers and it is hoped that separate publications will be
produced that take these symposia as their basis.   Our selection of
the "free" papers from the total of almost 500 papers presented at
the Congress is based upon a number of factors; originality, clarity,
the presentation of an international spectrum of opinion,
representation of different theoretical schools. The exigencies of
space also limited us to the publication of relatively short
communications apart from the Plenary Papers.

Our work in reading all these papers and in making the selection
has confirmed us in our previous impression that this Congress
achieved a high standard of theoretical sophistication. It helped
to build new bridges and to fortify some already built between
theory and practice and between different theories. What is true
for the individual cannot be untrue for the family or group. It is
also fascinating to gather some impressions of the way in which
group psychotherapy is developing in different parts of the world.
We are fortunate in having good representation from North and South
America and from the major European countries where group psychotherapy is strongly represented. We believe that the work presented
in these two volumes will contribute considerably to the spread of
information between these different geographical areas and schools
of thought and of practice and thereby maintain the impetus that
this Seventh Congress achieved and which we are confident that the
Eighth Congress in Mexico in 1983 will continue.

WELCOMING ADDRESS

Lise Rafaelsen, Chairwoman

Chief Psychologist
Psychiatric Dept., Gentofte Hospital
DK-2900 Hellerup, Denmark

It is indeed with the greatest pleasure and expectancy that
the Danish Congress Committee and I welcome you all here today.

When the president of the International Association for Group
Psychotherapy, professor Raymond Battegay, two years ago asked us
to arrange this Congress on their behalf, we felt it as an honour
and as a challenge.

With Dr. Malcolm Pines, chairman of the programme committee, we
immediately consented that the span should be wide, - geographically
and professionally. The theme: The Individual and the Group touches
upon so many aspects of human life and human thinking that no single
school of thought, frame of reference or field of practice can grasp
more than one perspective. So we made the choice of accepting the
immense diversity and dived into the large preparatory work, - the
results of which is now for you to judge.

We were optimistic, - an optimism which concerning the financial aspects proved too big. It was in 1978 and we soon realised
that the whole world's energy and economic crisis had made great
impact on foundations, banks, institutions, and research councils
from where we had expected economical support.

We received little, where we expected much, and nothing where
we had expected little, - and were harshly confirmed in the pessimistic notions that group psychotherapy is a new and somewhat doubt-
ful discipline, difficult to place between the humanities and the
sciences - and at one time we felt placed and left on the floor
between two chairs.

We survived, - thanks to all the support we received from you, by early registrations, - and also, the moral support, - made us try once again to seek new sources.

We certainly would have liked to be more generous in our invitations than to ask you to come and pay for yourself. But hélas these were our conditions !

———————

As you may see in the programme we did obtain support from many foundations and institutions and I wish here to express our gratitude to them all.

Explicitly I would like to mention the Danish Ministry of Education and the University of Copenhagen on which premises most of the congress takes place.

In Denmark the area of group psychotherapy is a newly ploughed field. We have not hitherto to any large extent taken part directly in the scientific exploration of group phenomenon or in the development of practices and methods. In dealing with interpersonal spheres we have tended to be more pragmatic. You only have to look at the well known agricultural co-operatives modelled all over the world. Our way as an old nation of farmers has been to utilize the interpersonal relations in one for everybody beneficial way rather than to explore and analyse them, - let alone using them for healing purposes.

So also the social welfare philosophy is a way of dealing with the individual and the mass in a practical way: by social changes the individual is treated, is secured its rights, by changing the social milieu the individual is hoped to thrive. We have tended to act outwardly rather than to turn inwardly. Hopefully we have come to a point now, when it is not a matter of either/or, but of one as well as the other.

If we leave the field of practical philosophy and turn to the poets, the speakers of the heart, the group has so often been conceived as the restricting agent, the enemy of the individual. I would like to read a short passage from H.C. Andersen's fairy tale "The Ugly Duckling":-
    The little duck has left his family and his neighbourhood as they treat him so badly, because of his ugliness. He arrives at a farmhouse where an old woman lives with her cat and her hen. With H.C. Andersen's own words: "In this house the cat was master and the hen mistress. They always said 'We and the world', for they thought themselves half of the world and much the better half at that. The duckling thought that there might be more than one way of thinking, but the hen would not hear of it.
    "Can you lay eggs," she asked.

"No." "Then be so good as to hold your tongue."
The cat asked: "Can you arch your back or purr ?"
"No." "Then keep your opinion to yourself when sensible people
    are talking." The duckling sat in a corner feeling most des-
pondent. Then he remembered the fresh air and the sunlight. Such
a desire to go swimming on the water possessed him that he could
not help telling the hen about it."

In this, the poet's notion of the group, there is no healing
powers. The theme is repeated again and again in the literature
and have I think not to be overlooked when dealing with group
therapy and its difficulties as being accepted as positively as
individual psychotherapy.

But now, we, of course, as professionals all know about projections, inner representations and group dynamics and are free to
go "swimming on the water."

It is my hope that by witnessing and taking part in this
congress, we shall join in the development of academic and scientific group psychotherapy.

Before ending this welcoming address I would like to tell
those of you, who do not know about Tivoli, - that it is an old
amusement park in the core of town behind solid walls. Inside these
walls you can find representations of many ways of thinking and
experiencing. The analytically oriented family therapist might
nod recognisingly when passsing or entering the spook train or the
underground caves with their monsters and feeries, and those
working with encounter techniques when seeing the bump-you cars,
those using mirror effect have a whole palace right there, and
those working with animals group-behaviour might enjoy the mice
circus. And for those just lingering natures there is a beautiful
garden filled with flowers and water fountains ... and just as the
walls of Tivoli for more than a century have contained these many
ways of thinking and being, - it is my sincere hope that the boundaries of the Congress will contain us all until we shall part on
Friday feeling enriched and fertilized by all we have shared.

OPENING ADDRESS

Raymond Battegay, M.D.

Professor of Psychiatry at Basle University,
Chief Physician, Psychiatric University Out-patient
Dept., Kantonsspital, Petersgraben 4, CH-4031 Basle

It is a great pleasure for me to open this Congress in a town
and in a country in which on one part the freedom of the individual
and his boundaries, and on the other part the interplay of free
groups in a democratic society are the two main constituents of the
state. It is not by chance that we meet in Copenhagen, Denmark, in
which in wartimes the population gave an example of a heroic behaviour and helped to save persecuted people even under the worst
conditions of occupation. We have a great admiration for this
country with its traditions of freedom and democracy.

In this atmosphere, the local committee under the chairwomen-
ship of Dr. Lise Rafaelsen has enabled this Congress to be held here
in such a well organized way. We owe to her and to her group all
our thanks. Together with this Danish group it is Malcolm Pines
with the Program Committee who have spent their time, their energy
and their intelligence for giving us such an eminent and thorough-
fully prepared program which offers a broad spectrum of group and
group psychotherapy approaches by the most famous researchers in
their respective fields. Already now I want to thank for all contributions coming from researchers from the most various countries
of the world.

In group psychotherapy we have under the aspect of "the individual and the group" to differentiate the psychological from the
sociological point of view. From the psychological aspect only
the individual is able to experience, not the group as a whole. We
could even say that in the psychology of each member, the group
does not exist, but only the group situation, (W. Schindler). Each
individual may have a group feeling and therefore extend his

narcissism on the single others and the totality. We can even say
that without the growing of what we would like to call a narcissistic
group-self in each one's fantasy, no group cohesion would result.
But this narcissistic group-self, this extension of narcissism on
to others, grows in each individual. There is no group spirit as a
primarily collective psychology, but only as a more or less parallel
feeling in each individual.

The fantasies of the participants may go into the same direction,
but it is only in the individual that such fantasies are possible,
not in the group as a whole. It is therefore not corresponding to
reality, when some authors (Argelander, Bion, Stierlin and others)
always address themselves to the group as a whole. The members must
feel narcissistically injured when they are taken only as particles
of the group, since in their experience they are individuals with
their own feelings, with which the others cannot totally participate.
A group psychotherapist who always speaks to the group in its
totality neglects the fact that individuals are forming the group,
and he traumatizes them, gives them no status and sets himself higher
than all others, since he is then the only well defined person in
the group. He furthers by that the regression of the participants.
I do not think that regression should be at any rate omitted in
the group members, but I think that it is better, the process of
regression goes on slowly after an initial stadium of explorative
contact. Only then the members can be led step by step to further
phases of group psychotherapy, such as catharsis, insight and -
last but not least - social learning.

From a sociological, interactional system approach however,
the group as an own entity exists. We examine the density and the
kind of interactions, the hierarchy of the group and the role of
the members in it. In this sociological view the individual is only
a part of the totality or even itself a system of interacting representations of objects of his individual life-history. The
individual, integrated in a surrounding system, must therefore be
observed and treated in its interactions. We would in this approach
in therapy try to change the interactional modus of a group and by
this also the attitudes of its members. If we do so, we have to
keep in mind that we are mainly acting in the sense of behaviour
therapy, deconditioning old and reconditioning new behaviour patterns
of the individual and not leading to an insight in the analytical
sense of the word.

Especially if we consider the group as a system and do not
respect enough the individual in its boundaries, but also in all
other group concepts, it is difficult to maintain confidentiality.
This point should always be discussed in the beginnings of group
psychotherapy, since each individual should have a right to expect
that what he says in a therapeutic frame, should be taken as his

secret also in a group, to which he opened it under the condition
that all members feel the obligation to respect his desire.

The theme "The Individual and the Group" gives us the occasion
to discuss about the interrelation between the individual, the group
and society. We certainly will have to contribute also from the
scientific side to the recognition of inviolable rights and of
dignity of each individual. Even if the group and society are seen
from a sociological point of view as systems, from a psychological
and human aspect the individual must remain within a framework of
a well defined legal order, with its freedom of decision and its
own responsibility. No system is thinkable which would declare
that the individual has totally to submit itself to the norms and
directives given by society and its protagonists.

Nobody else than group psychotherapists should be better able
to have in mind both, the individual with its rights, obligations
and responsibilities, and the group as a system of interdependent,
interacting men. They should therefore also make an effort to step
out of their treatment rooms and to have in mind the broader
dimensions of society with its interaction of groups. In one society
the group may be stressed in comparison with the individual, in
another society, the importance rather of the individual will be
seen. But regardless to the kind of political system, we have to
keep in mind that each human being in his own experience has his
expectations and hopes, his highs and downs, his own projects, but
also his sense of reality. Never a society can work in the long
range if it doesn't take care of these individual expectations on
one side and doesn't appeal on the sense of reality of its members
on the other side.

Each revolution in history came not only out of the fact that
the respective society neglected the social laws, but also that
the individual aspirations and hopes were not respected enough.
It is my sincere hope that this International Association of Group
Psychotherapy may not only contribute to more knowledge in the
field of group approaches and group psychotherapy, but also throughout the world to more respect for the group functions and for the
sake of the different societies as well as for the individuals who
must be able to feel free in each society. Only under this condition
each human being will have the impression that life is worthwhile
to be lived.

I now open the Congress and pass the floor to Dr. Malcolm
Pines who has done so much for elaborating an eminent program.

CONTENTS

C - Large Groups and Organisations

Part V - Clinical Perspectives

Part VI - Therapeutic Community Perspectives and Practice

Part VII - Basic Issues: Psychoanalysis and Group Psychother

INDIVIDUAL AND GROUP

Marie Jahoda

The University of Sussex, Science Policy Research Unit

Mantell Building, Falmer, Brighton, Sussex BN1 9RF

'Individual' and 'group' are terms which most people apply without difficulty to the affairs of everyday life; participants in this
Congress have, in addition, professional competence in their usage.
Given so much good collective common sense and specialist knowledge,
the only excuse for a non-expert in group work, like myself, to talk
about these terms is a subversive intention: to confuse an apparently
crystal-clear issue on the assumption that in matters of thought
agreement and harmony are not necessarily the best base for further
development.

Let me begin by pointing to a paradox in the human condition so
deeply ingrained in our existence that we hardly ever face up to it:
all experience, thought or feeling can occur only in an individual
organism equipped with an individual brain; short of science fiction
there are no collective organs which could provide identical psychological processes in different persons. We are all of us unique
individuals, conscious and sometimes proud of it. On the other hand
no experience, thought, feeling or achievement is conceivable as the
creation of a single mind. It depends on the past and present,
actual or implied, existence of others. Man is above all a species,
not an individual; but it is only the functioning of individual
minds which make the human collectivity possible. Language, culture
and all the other rules by which we live are achievements of the
species, not of individuals. But without individual minds, neither
language nor culture nor rules could exist.

However sharp the distinction in our common sense vocabulary
between individual and group, reflection shows that the one is in-
conceivable without the other. As Foulkes (1) says: ".....I shall

1

speak for convenience of presentation about the individual and the
group, although I believe that in practice these two can never be
separated and should not be considered even theoretically in isolation"
(p.47). They should not, but they are and 'for convenience' Foulkes
himself cannot abide by his own admonition.

The 'tension between the One and the Many' (2) is an age-old
problem in the history of thought. It underlies contrasting interpretations of history as much as political philosophies - the welfare
state versus unfettered competion of individuals, the emphasis on
the communal good versus individual freedom; and even such relatively
mundane affairs as the division of the social sciences; some, such as
sociology and anthropology (3) look at regularities in human affairs
without bothering about individuals, while branches of psychology take
the individual as the unit of study without its social context, each
approach sometimes aspiring to be the fundamental human science.
However heated the controversy between such contrasting views and
approaches, extreme positions are untenable, in the human sciences as
much as in politics. The fundamental paradox persists and in view of
it all priority claims break down; neither group nor individual came
first or is more important; they are indivisible in their essence
and consequences. While it would be foolhardy to ignore the common
sense incorporated in our vocabulary and confirmed by everyone's
experience which distinguishes so clearly between individual and
group, other language uses show that common sense is uneasy with the
sharp distinction. For most of us try to blur the sharp difference
in everyday language by attributing to groups and institutions things
that only individuals can do as when we say: parliament decides, the
group feels angry, the university takes responsibility etc. Of
course you could regard this as nothing but a convenient shorthand
for saying that members of the group judge or feel in certain ways.
But as often as not the group becomes a thing in itself, is reified
as if a group mind were as real as an individual brain where thinking
and feeling occur. When Eric Fromm (4) speaks of a 'sane society'
he invites a similar confusion. Sanity is an attribute of a person;
a society can at best be conductive to sanity, perhaps also to insanity, of individual minds.

What I take from this inconsistency between vocabulary and
language usage, developed over millenia through the collective wisdom
of individual minds, is that we cannot get away from the paradoxical
fact that individual and group are both, sharply distinct and indivisible.

So we must find a way of living with this paradox. It is
reasonably easy to do so in the spontaneity of daily life where
paradoxes do not bother us unduly because the full context of experience elucidates the appropriate meaning. But it is not so easy
to find a modus vivendi in the social sciences where inconsistencies

are out of order, at least to intention. The problem has preoccupied many good minds in many fields. The art historian Ernst Gombrich (5) for example, wondering how innovations in art styles come about, states the paradox thus: "We must acknowledge that it is individual people, craftsmen, designers, patrons, who are the subject of history, rather than the collectives of nations, ages, or styles, yet we must also recognise the limits of the individual and the strength of co-operative action in society and over time, for it is this aspect of human existence which entitles us to speak of evolution". (p.209). He deals with it by denying "the existence of all-pervasive laws which could permit us to explain any such development as an inevitable sequence of events". (p.211) Description rather than explanation is this art historian's modus vivendi. It is well to keep this way-out of inconsistency to mind as one looks at other social scientists who, in their great majority, aim at casual explanations.

Before doing so let me distinguish between two types of state-ment: statements about the full complexity of existence, and state-ments about concepts useful for investigating aspects of this be-wildering richness. The former recognise that in human nature individuality and collectivity are indivisible. Such statements are the province of poetry, philosophy, religion and some very private personal experiences. But science must simplify. Its task is not to make pronouncements about the essence of human nature but rather the effort - both more limited and more far reaching - to understand and explain aspects of the world in us and around us. Within this second type of statement, is it possible to look simultaneously at group and individual or do they have to remain separate centres of attention?

To answer this question one looks first at the research literature on the topic, which is truly enormous. A quarter of a century ago an annotated bibliography (6) on research concerned with individuals in groups contained 584 studies; it did not claim to be comprehensive but added new entries to a selection from a previous bibliography covering the period from 1900-1953 with 1400 titles. In 1969 a listing of relevant publications contained a staggering 5156 items (7). Even if I could claim familiarity with this enormous effort, I could not possibly summarise it here. Rather I shall select from my limited knowledge a few examples which, I believe, have some bearing on group therapy. This implies that I shall deal only with small groups where members meet face-to-face.

There are a great number of studies which focus on group pro-cesses without much concern about the individuals who constitute the group. Given Bion's (8) great influence in group therapy it is perhaps surprising that his well-known work, Experience in Groups is the outstanding example of a concentration on group processes to the virtual exclusion of concern with individuals. It is the group, not

We owe Dr. Jahoda much appreciation for her rich presentation including her lucid and challenging questions addressed to group therapists - all aimed at infusing clarity to a very complex yet important field of inquiry with major implications for the behavioural sciences as well as for individual and societal enhancement.

A COMMENT ON PROFESSOR M. JAHODA'S "INDIVIDUAL AND GROUP"

Earl Hopper, MA, PhD, MInstGrAn

Lecturer in Sociology
London School of Economics and Political Science
Houghton Street, London, W.C. 1., England

I am honoured to have been asked by Dr. Pines to discuss Professor Jahoda's paper "Individual and Group".   I have been a student of her work for many years, and I am grateful for this opportunity to say "thank-you".   She has contributed methodologically sound, theoretically informed, empirical research into problems which many have ignored.[1]   In other words, she has earned the right to warn of her "subversive intention: to confuse an apparently crystal-clear issue".   As a measure of her success, I confess that she has provoked a discrepancy between what I thought I knew and what I now think I know, and between certain polarities which are not quite dichotomous.

It is impossible to discuss this paper in depth in the allotted time of 10-15 minutes.   My comments must necessarily be brief - even cryptic.   However, I have written about these matters elsewhere, and they are under constant discussion in Group Analysis, a journal to which many members of the Institute of Group Analysis and the Group Analytic Society subscribe.[2]   Interested students and therapists are invited to consult this work.

Since the manifest statement of the paper before us has been put with such deceptive simplicity, it may be helpful to summarize its central thesis, as I see it.   The traditional understanding of the relationship between individual and group (which is itself an abbreviation for a more complex phenomenon), involves a fundamental paradox, some of the many implications of which are noted.   The resolution of this paradox is necessarily transitory, but it reflects upon and is a reflection of our political ideologies and practice, religious beliefs and rituals, moral and aesthetic values and judgments, the organization of scholarship and fields of knowledge, the conduct of

scientific inquiry, and, not least, our work as psychotherapists.
However, we are rescued from the possibly unproductive contemplation
of such profound issues by the recognition that through scientific
research during the past century, we have learned a very great deal
about the structure and process of groups, the effects of properties
of groups upon their members, the effects of properties of their
members upon groups, and about the effects of both upon both.   And,
yet, we are still constrained by the essence of this seemingly eternal
paradox; the gaps between meta-theory, theory, and data are large;
the literature is biased towards the group's influence upon the individual and away from his influence upon the group, which is often
conceptualized in terms of deviance; and basic methodological problems continue to confound us.   Thus, we are asked: to clarify the
relationship between group dynamics and group therapy; to realize
that the role of group therapist involves rights and obligations which
are usually granted to as well as taken by scientists, teachers,
doctors, citizens, friends, artists and priests; and to consider our
identities and intentions.

At the outset, we should register the fact that group therapy
has developed enormously since World War II.   Many of us feel convinced that our therapeutic work has improved and have a certain
degree of pride in referring to ourselves as group therapists.   However, we have contributed a paucity of good research on therapeutic
groups, and we remain unable to integrate in a satisfactory way the
lessons we draw from the different but related disciplines of group
dynamics, sociology, social psychology, ethology, psychoanalysis and
other schools of psychology, not to mention the various models available for the role of "helper".   Furthermore, our boundary problems
are exacerbated by the chronic disputes within some countries between
the medical and non-medical members of our profession, which at times
seem more vulgar than the language of clinical responsibility and
careful training would suggest.   Although the speed and scope of the
development of our profession have led to some of these difficulties,
this is not the level at which we have been invited to answer Professor Jahoda's questions, no matter how important and how much in need
of discussion such matters may be.

I would like to take note of three interrelated aspects of the
fundamental paradox, and comment on certain of their implications for
our theoretical and clinical work.   "Sociality" is of special impor-
tance.³   Individual human beings or persons differ from individual
human organisms.   Similarly, the human mind differs from the homo
sapiens brain, and human experiences from organismic sensations.
When groups and organisms are juxtaposed, it is possible to view a
group primarily as constraint; however, a person emerges from the
interaction between an organism and a group, and, thus, it is equally
valid to view a group as a facilitating and creative source of individuality.   Of course, a person is more than the sum of his past and
present relationships, but the existence of a psychic fact presumes

the prior existence of a social fact, and his organism is neither
causally antecedent to nor causally more important than his group
(although an organism and the organic aspects of a person have a
material basis, whereas a person, his psychological aspects, and his
society do not).[4]   Collectively, social systems differ from species
and populations, as do breeding groups from breeding aggregates.
Social systems also differ from aggregates of persons - for example,
crowds in a street.   Furthermore, a group represents only one type
of social system, and it is not always possible to generalize from one
type to another - for example, from an audience to a large group to a
bureaucracy.[5]   Thus, the human species, a human organism, a human
group or other type of social system, and a human being are distinct
but interrelated aspects of the same phenomenon.   Their boundaries
depend, at least in part, on the intentions and gestalt of an observer.

   All students of sociality must specify the level of abstraction
at which they have defined their problem.   Studies of groups require
at least two levels of abstraction, and studies of individuals at
least three.   In studying groups as such, it may be necessary to
ignore particular aspects of individuals, and in studying individuals,
particular aspects of their groups and their organisms.   In a sense,
individuals and their organisms are contexts for their groups; or, to
put it another way, group social systems are open to their biological
and psychological environments - more than are certain other types of
social systems.[6]

   In addition to meta-theory and theory proper, time is one of the
most important determinants of those aspects of a phenomenon which an
observer selects for further consideration.   It influences the scope
of observation and the limits to explanation.   In other words, it is
simply not possible to study everything at once.   All knowledge is
partial, and in the same sense that all phenomena have contexts, all
statements are subject to further qualification.   This is especially
true for phenomena whose boundaries are highly osmotic.   Nonetheless,
in any study there is a point in time when contextualization must stop.
Further changes to paradigms may be made subsequently, and by other
members of our community.

   This perspective would be acceptable were it not for "in-the-
beginning" problems, which always have religious, philosophical, moral
and political implications.   The inclusion of sociality within "the
sacred equation" has led to questions about first causes, moral relativity, free will and determinism.   For example, social systems and
human beings can only be changed by people, but it is difficult to
comprehend the moral basis for therapeutic or political actions within
a determined universe.   (Recent concern with the source of altruism
in human beings is a reflection of this more basic issue.)

   Solutions to such problems are various, temporary, and arbitrary.
They are imbued with established values and beliefs, and questions

about them will always lead to guilt, fear of punishment, and ontological insecurity.   The consideration of social systems and individuals as part of the "natural order" has led to the development of
the human sciences, including the study of group dynamics.   To some
extent science has alleviated feelings of guilt and fear of punishment with respect to these issues, but it has increased the intensity
and extent of ontological insecurity.   Furthermore, its general
methodology is a special source of frustration, and of paranoid and
depressive anxiety, mainly because it is necessary to work at such
high levels of abstraction and to ignore much of what is already known
and what is easily visible (as opposed to observable).

The actual findings of the human sciences may have made these
matters worse, because the more we have learned, the less compelling
and the more tentative our answers have become.   New data have forced
us to refine our questions, but it has become more difficult to make
qualitative distinctions at a common sense level of experience.   For
example, it is now reasonable to debate such issues as: whether projection or introjection is the first psychic act;   whether it is
necessary to project sensations which are said to stem from the death
instinct before it is possible to introject particular qualities of
external objects;   whether it is possible to introject such qualities
in their pristine form;   whether in the development of unconscious
phantasy instinctual impulses precede, follow or coincide with the
introjection of external objects;   and whether unconscious processes
originate within the dialectics of class relations within particular
social systems, or, for that matter, within the constraints of social
structures in general.   In fact, although we have learned more about
the importance of early relationships with external objects who possess certain qualities, we have also learned more about the early
perceptual activity of the human organism.

Thus, the hypothesis of an "original ego as an active agent" is
as reasonable as one of an "archaic ego as an organ of adaptation".
Although it is necessary to assume that persons are emergent phenomena, it is clear that a new infant strives to make sense of his experiences from the beginning, and seeks relationships with objects in
terms of both their own qualities and his perceptions of them, and in
terms of his instinctive needs.[7]   We have also learned that social
systems have emerged from breeding groups, and the latter from breeding aggregates;   yet, it has become clear that less sophisticated
species have what might be called societies and even cultures, and
that we must recognize within all species the contributions which are
made by the structure of their orgamisms to the structure of their
societies and cultures.[8]

At root, the general issue of the contributions which organismic
and social factors made to human nature is always linked to deeper
religious and political questions, our answers to which are likely
to shape the way we work.   Of course, such questions do not lend

themselves to scientific study, but science is based on axioms and
latent assumptions which influence the formulation of problems and the
conduct of inquiry. It is important that at least we are <u>clear</u> concerning where we stand.   Unfortunately, it is no longer in fashion
to discuss these matters directly, but I wonder if it is really necessary to avoid them so rigorously.   Are we afraid to risk our relationships with colleagues, and our own personal sense of conviction?
By comparison, the general methodological problems of "measurement"
and "causal circularity" are virtually unimportant, especially because
people will tolerate ignorance so long as they have a plausable explanation.   It seems to me that in this regard the members of our
profession are especially vulnerable.

Consider our preoccupation with analogies, and how this apparently intellectual enterprise stifles creative thought.   Naturally, all
sciences use analogies, especially during the early stages of their
development or when description is their main task.   However, in the
study of group dynamics and group therapy, analogies rule without regard for their degree of isomorphism or for the critical admonitions
of the past century.   I would suggest that this fixation, to use an
analogy, reflects the difficulties inherent in various aspects of the
fundamental paradox, as discussed above, but also the pervasive, ubiquitous anxieties associated with "in-the-beginning" problems.
People confuse identity and similarity with what seems to be a manic
sense of relief.

The most common analogies are with organisms, machines and persons.   Clearly, the underlying common factor is "system".   But this
observation is as banal as some of the work of systems theorists.
Whereas systems are neutral, the choice of analogy has important
implications.   For example, analogies with organisms always have a
conservative slant.   The powerful are always seen as the brains or
heart of the group, and the powerless as the genitals or stomach;
conflicts of interest are seldom considered, and it is always presumed
that the group originated from something which is sacred, at least in
the sense that it cannot be questioned.   Mechanical analogies are
often radical, but those who use them tend to disregard the sensations
and feelings of individual participants.   Curiously, they ignore the
limits to plasticity which are set by fundamental societal problems,
structural dilemma, and by the needs of human organisms.[9]   Analogies
with persons tend to ignore the variability and heterogeneity of
groups, and to neglect the highly osmotic boundaries between group
phenomena and individual participants.   For example, when a student
conceptualizes a group as a person, and, thus, one part as the id and
another as the superego, etc., he rarely allows for the possibility
that such functions can be shared and exchanged among the group's
participants.[10]

Clearly, the weaknesses of any one analogy are likely to be the
strengths of another, and vice versa.   Nonetheless, in the end, all

analogies must perish.[11]   The sooner we think in terms of theoretical
explanations, hypotheses and experiment, the more productive our intellectual work will be.   Of course, in saying this, I do not reject
the value of systematic illustration and case study.

A critique of all currently available work on groups should begin
with a specification of its analogies, intentional or otherwise.   For
example, a major flaw in Bion's work is the confusion of persons with
organisms, and, in turn, groups with persons.[12]   The source of this
confusion is his refusal to acknowledge the reality of social facts,
which, despite his early interests in politics, is based on his view
that object relations begin with the projection of phantasies which
originate from instinctual impulses.   Although this view avoids the
problems of reification, ultimately it leads to bizarre reductionist
assertions: for example, that through denial and splitting such institutions as armies and aristocracies originate from unconscious
basic assumption processes;   and that groups do not really exist, but
are phantasies which happen to be shared by an aggregate of individuals who are in a similar stage of regression.   In other words, the
"work group" consists only of individuals engaged in relationships
which pertain to the task at hand;   and the "basic assumption group",
only of individuals who share similar phantasies - including that they
are members of a "group".   Although Bion's work is in fact about
groups as such, and is, therefore, of special value to us, he claims
that it is really about individuals.   I have always been wary of
this underlying perspective because it suggests that sociological
studies of social systems and their cultures are produced by the mad
describing the mad - which may be true, but only in a particular
sense.

As a complementary perspective, the work of Foulkes warrants
special consideration.[13]   Through his distinctive concept of "matrix"
he avoids misleading analogies and the fallacies of reductionism -
although not, some might say, the fallacies of reification.   His
perspective is based on the view that social facts are real, and,
thus, he gives greater emphasis to the introjective aspects of object
relations.[14]   However, "matrix" was never defined with clarity and
precision, and has remained a residual category.   In fact, I wonder
if some of those who use the concept prefer to keep it ambiguous and,
thus, mysterious, in order to maintain an identification with their
Totem, and, in turn, a sense of exclusiveness.   In any case, despite
his intentions and claims to the contrary, a careful reading of his
work will show that Foulkes did not identify many properties of
groups at the social and cultural levels of analysis.

We may yet be able to integrate the theories of Foulkes with
those of Bion, and, hopefully, with those of others.[15]   Certainly,
this will be necessary in order to explain various aspects of creativity and innovation.   For example, whereas Bion's distinction between
work groups and basic assumption groups, combined with his reduc-

tionist view that groups as such do not really exist, <u>might</u> have
furthered our insight into such phenomena, equally, his views concerning pairing as a basic assumption, combined with the seductive creation of the role of Saviour, may have had an inhibiting effect.
Equally, although Foulkes' views concerning individuals within groups
make it possible to understand the individual as Hero, his concept of
matrix has not been developed sufficiently to permit the specification
of the group's response and contribution to this event.

Professor Jahoda is correct that we have neglected creativity
and innovation, and have tended to conceptualize them in terms of
deviance and pathology, although this may be more applicable to the
student of group dynamics than to the group-therapist - but perhaps
this is wishful thinking.   Nonetheless, it occurs to me that these
processes are closely linked to "in-the-beginning" problems; after
all, the notion of charisma as a source of social change refers to
the intrusion of "grace" into an earth-bound social system.[16]   Thus,
questions concerning creativity and innovation may arouse considerable
anxiety.   Familiar, simple analogies help to avoid anxiety, but when
they are of limited utility, it may be necessary to avoid recalcitrant
issues.   And, clearly, in the case of creativity and innovation,
which are only extreme examples of the effects of individuals upon
groups, the prevailing analogies are useless.

Of course, it might also be relevant to discover the sources
for research funds, and to see if countries and Foundations vary in
their research programmes.   Is it possible that government funds tend
to be allocated for studies of conformity?   I think that we have to
admit that innovation is both desirable and dangerous, and it may be
necessary for those in power to stress its pathological, inexplicable
and random qualities, however short-sighted this may be, especially
in light of current world events.

It will come as no surprise, given the drift of my comments, that
the preparation of this discussion was a source of some anxiety as
well as pleasure.   However, since the issues which Professor Jahoda
has raised are inevitable within Western schools of thought, I have
tried to respond to my anxiety in a creative way.   Nonetheless, she
has reminded me of how I have transformed what were once my acts-of-
questing into tentative answers of a kind.   I have been forced once
again to consider how I am able to maintain a sense of integrity among
my own roles as sociologist, group-analyst, psychotherapist, and
psychoanalyst-to-be, not to mention citizen and family member.

I imagine that in response to her paper, each person and each
generation may wish to reconsider their own positions concerning what
are in essence universal and eternal schisms and polarities.   Perhaps
no-one should be asked to contemplate these matters more than once,
but it falls to the lot of the psychotherapist and especially the
group-therapist to do so often.   Although ignorance and helplessness

are a source of frustration, they are also a challenge.   To see it
this way may increase our ability to contain despair and to offer
hope to our patients as we both struggle to endure and to transcend
the vicissitudes of our existence.

It is worth turning for help to the much neglected work of two
Danes.   The sociologist Svend Ranulf will remind you why the relationships between psychotherapists, both individually and collectively,
and institutions of authority, such as Church and State, are always
somewhat strained.[17]   He understood the signs which pointed towards
Auschwitz, and I am convinced that students of group dynamics should
renew their interest in these problems.[18]   The philosopher Soren
Kierkegaard will remind you that, for a thoughtful person, a leap to
faith may be necessary.[19]

Perhaps the proper attitude for both student of group dynamics
and group therapist is one of respect, wonder, awe and an awareness
that behind each new discovery is yet another mystery

REFERENCES

1.   For example, see one of her earliest contributions with
     P. Lazarsfeld and H. Zeizel, Marienthal, 1933.
2.   I have discussed these matters in more detail in a version of
     my lectures to the Institute of Group Analysis, London, and I
     am very pleased to learn that Professor Jahoda shares the same
     perspective, and that she defines the problem and sees its
     implications in terms which are virtually identical to mine.
     See "A Wider View of Groups", Group Analysis, November, 1976.
     I will refer below to other of my books and articles which
     pertain to this theme.
3.   This word has been introduced by Dr. Samuel Atkins, "A Psycho-
     analyst Looks at Man's Sociality", Psycho-analysis and Contem-
     porary Thought, pp. 115-150, 1980.
4.   For a recent review of the literature on this topic, see
     "Special Book Section", Encounter, March, 1978.   My own per-
     spective has been influenced by one of the traditions of the
     "Independent" or "Middle" Group within the British Psycho-
     analytic Society, as might be illustrated by M. Brierly,
     "Metapsychology and Personology", Trends in Psycho-analysis,
     London, 1951, and by the later work of J. Rickman on multi-
     person psychology.
5.   See Earl Hopper and Anne Weyman, "Sociological Aspects of Large
     Groups", in L. Kreeger, Ed., The Large Group, London, 1975.
     See also my Social Mobility: A Study of Social Control and
     Insatiability, Oxford, 1981.
6.   ibid.
7.   For a review of certain aspects of object-relations theory
     with special reference to groups, see C. James, "Chairman's

Position Paper", Panel on Object Relations Theory, VII International Congress on Group Psycho-therapy, Copenhagen, 1980. Dr. James would give the organism ultimate priority, whereas I would not.

8. For a review and critique of recent literature in this field, see M. Sahlins, The Use and Abuse of Biology, London, 1977. See also M. Chance and C. Jolly, Social Groups of Monkeys, Apes and Men, London, 1970.

9. See Hopper and Weyman, op. cit., and Hopper, op. cit.

10. For example, is it really feasible for Richter to conceptualize the working class of a community as its id? See H. Richter, Lernziel Solidaritaet, Hamburg, 1974.

11. I am grateful to my friend Dr. Walter Schindler for sharing Goethe's aphorism with me. It is interesting to note that in his own work he refers to group psychotherapy on the family pattern, but he does not say that all groups are families.

12. W. Bion, Experiences in Groups, London, 1961.

13. See the past issues of Group Analysis for a more detailed presentation of his ideas and references to his work.

14. In his consideration of the projection of archetypes on to the group matrix, his and Bion's work converge. I presume that each was influenced by Jung. I wonder if they were also influenced by work on dream screens and by The Tempest.

15. See Caroline Garland, Ed., "The Proceedings of the 'Survivor Syndrome' Workshop", Group Analysis, special edition, 1980.

16. See Max Weber, The Theory of Social and Economic Organization, edited by T. Parsons, New York, 1947. It is interesting in this connection to peruse such books as T.A. Buckley, The Dawnings of Genius, Exemplified and Exhibited in the Early Lives of Distinguished Men, 3rd edition, London, 1853, and R. Weiss, The Secret of Individuality, London, 1957, first drafted during the early 1930's.

17. Moral Indignation and Middle Class Psychology, London, 1938, and The Jealousy of the Gods and Criminal Law at Athens, Copenhagen, 1935. See also Earl Hopper and Marilyn Osborn, Adult Students: Education, Selection, and Social Control, London, 1975.

18. See Garland, op. cit.

19. For example, see his Either/Or

THE INDIVIDUAL AND THE GROUP AS SEEN BY THE THERAPIST

E. James Anthony, M.D.

Blanche F. Ittleson Professor of Child Psychiatry
Director of the William Greenleaf Eliot Division
  of Child Psychiatry
Director of the Edison Child Development Research
  Center
Washington University School of Medicine
St. Louis, Missouri (U.S.A.)

INTRODUCTION

At such times as this in my professional career, I see myself
awkwardly astride two worlds--the therapeutic world of the individual
and that of the group--and conscious of the precariousness of my position. Theoretically, practically and temperamentally, I am ready to
fall between the two and cultivate an "in-betweenness" that freely
acknowledges the assets and liabilities from both sides. Unlike
Buridan's Ass, I have been able to consider with clinical impartiality
the attractive opportunities offered by one and the other, taking a
little hay from each. In this, I am very much a child of my time,
reconciled to the inevitable controversies that punctuated the growth
of knowledge and praxis in the therapeutic field, and to resolve anti-
theses dialectically. I have learned to sleep comfortably and eclec-
tically with a variety of bedfellows, not all of equal worth and not
all to be embraced.

You do not have to be a shrewd observer to realize that the "I"
is strongly represented in this opening statement as if I needed to
affirm my individuality before launching myself into the world of
groups. Anyone who has undergone the arduous training of a psychoanalyst must be considered to have his primary investment in the individual and to be biased in this direction.

I have another problem comparable to the first: I received my
primary therapeutic training in the psychoanalysis of adults and sub-

27

sequently entered the field of Child Psychoanalysis. I have thus made
two transitions that have both necessitated theoretical and technical
reappraisals and revisions, one from individual psychoanalytic therapy
to group analytic therapy and one from adult psychoanalysis to Child
Psychoanalysis. Adult psychoanalysts wondered why I took up Child
Psychoanalysis since it was not, in their covert opinion, genuine
psychoanalysis, and psychoanalysts in general have wondered why I took
up group analysis since this was, in their overtly expressed opinion,
not even applied psychoanalysis. What was curious to me was that the
same reasoning was used to disregard both. Because of their immaturi-
ty, it was said that children lacked many of the qualities and attitudes which are held to be indispensable for carrying out an analysis:
they do not lie on a couch, they do not "free" associate, they do not
have an exclusive relationship to the analyst but include others such
as their parents, they do not develop a transference neurosis that
undergoes resolution within the period of analysis, and they do not
work through their conflicts and resistances. The same has been said
for group analysis or group analytic psychotherapy. Now, there are
child analysts and group analysts who accept these alleged limitations
as true and then attempt to overcome and counteract these difficulties
by substitutions, "parameters", technical modifications and conceptual
translations. On the other side, there are child analysts and group
analysts who refuse to recognize these differences and maintain that
all the phenomena encountered in the psychoanalysis of adults is found
equally with children and with groups. It is the analytic therapist,
they say, who makes his own restrictions, mostly from lack of courage
and confidence.

My own view is an in-between one, and I can do no better than
quote Foulkes on this matter:

>"Classical psychoanalytic concepts can be used with
>advantage in a group setting, but the operative processes
>are not identical with those observed in the individual
>psychoanalytic situation. The wholesale transfer of
>psychoanalytic concepts to a new field is particularly
>inadvisable when they have lost their original precision
>and are exciting controversy in their own field of origin.
>Even such concepts as transference and identification are
>in the process of revision, or tending to become confused"
>(Foulkes, 1965).

What Foulkes is cautioning against is the "wholesale transfer"
from the individual to the group context, but he is also pointing to
the fact that the field of psychoanalysis is itself undergoing rapid
change and that there is a real danger of borrowing concepts that are
already out of date. Some efforts to apply the theory and practice of
psychoanalysis lock-stock-and-barrel to the group has an old-fashioned
quality to it with dead-and-gone issues being brough to life again,
but anachronistically.

The theoretical tensions between the two worlds may be further aggravated by new developments. In individual therapy, the field has been sequentially transfused by new blood from the psychology of the ego, of identity, of separation-individuation, of the self, of narcissism and egocentrism, and of object relations, all of them emphasizing the individual, almost as if this individuality was a brand new discovery. From the group viewpoint, systems theory has entered the field and there has been a new and exciting look at the group-as-a-whole with its organizations, it communications, its informations, its processes, its ingredients, and its matrix of networks. Once again, there are strong attractions and opportunities from both sides, but the individual approach is strongly affirming individuality and the group approach is equally emphatic about the group. Despite this polarization, I, the individual "I", along with other group analytic therapists and group analysts, found it rewarding to take the in-between position. As I have mentioned, this is not without its tensions, but I like to think of them as creative tensions that may help to illuminate a whole spectrum of therapy ranging from the individual to the group.

THE TRANSITION FROM THE INDIVIDUAL TO THE GROUP SITUATION

The transposition of the individual into the group clearly has built-in resistances as the history of group psychotherapy well exemplifies. The truism that individuals are born into groups, live in groups, and die in groups overlooks some of the natural hazards occasioned by submersion in the group. This tends to be more so for artificial than for natural groups. The group cannot be taken for granted because of the inherent problems that it poses for the individual dispite his compelling need to be understood by and related to others.

It may come as a surprise to the Western listener that there is anything unusual in our experience of individuality, our sense of clear distinction between our beings and those of other people, our sense of boundaries between our personalities and theirs, and our belief in the value of human beings in themselves or, as Kant put it, as ends in themselves (Morris, 1972). A majority of the people in the world today have a relatively weak sense of the Self and in their languages there are no equivalents to this concept in contrast with the rich repertoire of words expressing communion with the group. Religious belief also plays a role in this. Faith in reincarnation excludes the notion of individuality in its Western connotation, since each person functions only as a carrier of a life within him that will be reborn after his apparent death, in another form. In fact, the exquisite element of inwardness and self-awareness manifested by the Westerner represents "an eccentricity among cultures" (Morris, 1972).

Historians have informed us that even in Western cultures, there has been as much struggle for individuality to emerge as for any particular human being during the course of his development which can be

summarized as a continuing struggle for individuation and identity
(Mahler, 1967; Erikson, 1950). According to Mahler, the psychological
birth of the human infant begins with endopsychic separation from the
dread oneness of symbiosis. Individuality can therefore be regarded
as a developmental achievement and never without accompanying vicissitudes. Historically, individuality had its birth at some time in the
12th century before the official rebirth of the renaissance. From the
evidence, it would seem that the lineaments of modern Western man,
free to express himself and to challenge authority, then entered the
human stage as a principle character. Thus history, culture and
development have all combined to create a very precious commodity that
could not therafter be easily sacrificed or relinquished.

The Freudian revolution did not postulate a serious dichotomy
between individual and group but the complexity of the individual was
greatly enhanced as compared with the individuality conceived of in
previous centuries. According to psychoanalysis, the individual
carries quite a package of universals into any group situation: a
universal symbolic language of dreams, myths, rituals and expressive
behavior; universal neurotic structures such as the Oedipal conflict,
sibling rivalry, castration anxiety, and so on; universal mental functions in terms of Conscious-preconscious-unconscious and ego-id-super-
ego trichotomies and mechanisms of defense; and universal fears and
fantasies regarding fundamental experiences like eating, excreting,
sleeping, reproducing and dying. All these universal propositions
generate meanings within the individual that are rich, detailed, concrete and idiosyncratic. This is indeed a formidable array of intro-
psychic propensities to bring to a group with others similarly endowed,
and so very likely to produce tensions.

This brings me to consider the different essential tensions that
are evoked when an individual enters a group and that may stimulate
progression or provoke disruption. Jahoda, in her presentation, has
mentioned the paradox involving "the one and the many," which is a
variant of the individual and the group. Other essential tensions
characterize the life of the group in that they involve apparent contradictory or even incompatible tendencies that seem to pull in different directions. Exposure to the group brings about an implicit
shift from the intrapersonal to the interpersonal, from the there-and-
then to the here-and-now, from the subjective to objective, from the
fantasied to the realistic, and from latent to the manifest. The
shift takes time to develop, is never complete and is always resisted
to a greater or lesser extent. Depending on the inwardness and out-
wardness factors, the inner directedness and outer directedness in
every group displays an idiomorphic configuration that alters with its
natural or therapeutic evolution.

FROM INDIVIDUAL TO GROUP THERAPY

The therapists reflect their culture as much as any individual

within it, and tensions between the individual and the group closely
reflect the orientation of the therapist.

Let me first give you an example from the culture. I will start
with the poet, Cummings (1958) who had this to say:

> "To be nobody--but--myself in a world which is doing
>   its best,
>   Night and day, to make you everybody else, means to
>   fight the hardest battle which any human being
>   can fight, and never stop fighting."

And here in similar vein, is von Keyserling stating that "man and
woman should never endeavor to be completely merged in one another;
the more intimate they are, the more strictly should they cherish
their own individuality." Here also is Montaigne (1957) remarking
that "it is absolute perfection. . . to get the very most out of one's
individuality" and H.G. Wells (1917) declaring that "to have free play
for one's individuality is the subjective triumph of existence, as
survival in creative work and offspring is its objective triumph."
In all these, we hear, loud and clear, the trumpet call for individualism. On the other side, we have Edmund Burke (1826-27), the orator,
announcing that "the individual is foolish," and Judge Learned Hand
(1954) speaks not only of the individual as helpless to affect the
march of civilization, but that he can very easily indoctrinate it
so that it is possible "to convert him into a fanatical zealot, ready
to torture and destroy and to suffer mutilation and death for an ob-
scene faith, baseless in fact, and morally monstrous." He goes on to
castigate unbridled individualism from which not Utopia but Bedlam
will emerge.

Therapists have the same reaction in work with groups. Some turn
away from it completely as antithetical to the therapeutic ideal of
helping the individual to realize himself most completely and effectively, and to this end, they envisage the group as a distracting and
unnecessary ambience. Those who undertake group work fall naturally
into three categories: those who treat the individual in the group,
those who treat the individual and the group, and those who treat the
individual by the group. Some group therapists, therefore, never make
the transition from individual to group; the individual remains in the
foreground of their therapeutic attention and the group provides
clearly a holding and facilitating background. Other group therapists,
of whom I am one, take a shifting bifocal point of view attending at
times to the individual and at times to the group, but progressively
leaving the treatment to the group. Finally, there are some group
therapists who completely disregard the individual and his idiosyncra-
cies as irrelevant to the therapeutic work of the group and address
themselves only and systematically to the group as a whole.

When the first type of group therapist comes into the group, he
brings with him his dynamic theories of the individual rooted in the

individual transference, the individual resistance, and the individual insight. The members understandably react individually to the
group therapist, maintain a one-to-one relationship to him, and
struggle for his undivided attention. At the other end of the scale,
the group rapidly adapts itself to being a group and nothing but a
group and the individuals strive to make themselves aware of the way
in which the group functions as a whole as well as in its different
parts. Eschewing, as they do, the individual psychology and psychopathology, the members take their cue from this and frequently respond
as representatives of the group or a subgroup within the group instead
of as individuals. As the members in the first type of group gradually become aware of the individual dynamics of other members, so a
member of the third type of group shows an increasing sensitivity to
group phenomena. Both have been influenced by the therapist's orientation and develop individual and group perspectives accordingly in
the same way as Freudian patients dream Freudian dreams and Jungian
patients dream Jungian dreams, as has often been alleged.

The transition from individual to group therapy can be viewed
both positively and negatively by the members. On the positive side,
the patient gratifies his gregariousness and his sense of belonging,
his feeling of "safety in numbers," his knowledge that there are
others like him "in the same boat" enduring similar human predica-
ments, the experience of having his wishes, fantasies and feelings
reflected in the mirror created by the group and the relief of finding that there are people like me; the discovery that others, not
only the therapist, can help to alleviate emotional suffering, the
finding of a new system of meaning within the group, a new cosmology
that built on intricate human relationships, and finally, the provision by the group of a rough male taste of reality that was not made
by us or for us but hits us in the face.

On the negative side, there is a manifest or latent fear of depersonalization or the loss of individuality and identity, and,
connected with this, a dread of fusion with the group symbolizing the
primitive pregenital mother or her breast, and lastly, there is an
apprehension over surrendering self control and risking regression.
The latter sometimes involves the experience of diminishing competence.
The more stable the group, the more continuous its existence, the more
goal oriented and task oriented it is, the more codified and structured
its sessions and generally the better organized it is, the less do
these primitive anxieties manifestly pervade the therapeutic circle.
The individuals feel more in control of themselves and view the group
as a friendly, helpful ancillary ego. Whereas mobs and crowds may
rapidly undergo primitive regressions and disorganizations, the
smaller therapeutic group is less given to contagious emotionality
and a significant lowering of intellectual functioning.

The therapist, too, may feel that he both loses and gains when
he moves from the individual to the group therapeutic situation. He

may experience a loss of control in the management of a patient that
has become Hydra-headed. The "logic of the Unconscious" is now multi-
plied by six or more and the ensuing material may seem more confused,
nebulous and non-sequential. There are, it would seem, too many
threads to follow. The absence of any systematic structural theory
to account for group phenomena undoubtedly leads to an over-reliance
on an intuitive understanding of process. The problem of shifting
one's theoretical orientation constantly from individual to group
(when one adopts an in-between therapeutic posture) can also muddle
the material still further. Another perplexing element concerns the
fundamental attitude to time and space within the group: should one
focus on the here-and-now of the group or on the there-and-then of the
individual, realizing the fact that "the group has no childhood."
The therapist transposing to the group, may also experience the dis-
comforts of direct exposure and recall that one of the reasons why
Freud retreated behind the couch was that he could not abide being
stared at! The reality of the group situation may also prove disturbing especially when the group develops what Slavson (1958) has
referred to as "reality saturation," the defensive flight into the
commonplaces of everyday life with a dearth of fantasy. If the
therapist is a psychoanalyst, he may find it especially cumbersome
to handle multiple transferences and not analyze one to completion.
Even at termination, he may feel that there are a lot of loose unresolved transferences floating about the group and settling in a dis-
concerting way on different group members aside from himself. This
may lead him to feel that in making the transition, he is moving from
depth to shallowness and experience some degree of narcissistic
dismay. Since shame is the more potent affect functioning in face-
to-face encounters than guilt, the therapist may not be accustomed to
the prolonged and detailed analysis of shame that often becomes a
group preoccupation.

On the positive side, the therapist may be relieved to find that
some part of his therapeutic burden is being shouldered by an increasingly therapeutic group and that he does not and should not try to do
all the work himself. As the group becomes less leader-centered and
more group-centered, the therapist may find himself becoming far less
active in clarifying, confronting and interpreting. Affects are
generally more easily available in the group and abreactive experience
may occur with greater frequency than in individual therapy. A huge
positive is the discovery of a new therapeutic world of the interpersonal which can often breathe new life into the tired and jaded individual therapist. As he moves back and forth from individual to group
psychotherapy, he will begin to find that his knowledge and experience
from each situation may enrich both the situations. He himself may
feel less isolated in his professional work and more confident in his
therapeutic abilities when he is successfully managing a group of
seven patients. He also is in a better position to assess the reality
sense of any particular patient, his reaction to others, and his
capacity to keep his narcissism within bounds. The group, in fact,

will furnish him with a different diagnostic picture of his patients.
Moreover, he will find that problems of power and rivalry are more
easily observed and treated in the group.

Group literature is replete with efforts to compare and contrast
the two modes of treatment (Battegay, 1974; Balint, 1962; Pines, 1980).
The individual and the group are inseparable, even if one chooses, for
therapeutic reasons, to ignore one or the other. As Redl (1974)
pointed out in his inimitable way, the individual patient is a
therapeutic illusion since there is always "a group beneath the
couch." One cannot exclude individuals in group therapy any more than
one can exclude the group in individual therapy. To my way of thinking, and this may have a touch of heresy about it, the individual
therapist, without a knowledge and experience of therapeutic groups,
is so much less of a therapist. A significant part of his therapeutic
skills will remain atrophied through disuse.

Some surprising comments have been made regarding the individual
and group approaches. For instance, Sander, comparing the treatment
of individual and family groups, speaks of the former as a psychology
of inner-directed, achievement-oriented and superego dominated Oedipus
and the latter as a psychology of outer-directed, consumer-oriented
and id dominated Narcissus. This highly condensed capsular account of
the younger and older psychologies makes sense to me only in stressing
the predominance of shame and preoedipal elements in group and the
predominance of Oedipal conflicts in the individual therapeutic situation. The outcome of the two modes of treatment is different in
Balint's (1962) opinion: the individual patient emerges as less
neurotic but not more mature, whereas it is vice versa with the group
patient. Battegay (1974) sees individual therapy as more thorough,
more concerned with content and more comprehensive in the insights
provided, while group therapy reaches greater emotional depths,
conduces to more adaptive behavior and fosters less dependency. It
is better equipped to foster real relationships. Individual treatment is maybe more subtle but group results, he claims, are impressive.
According to Pines (1980) each treatment modality is enclosed within
a therapeutic frame that creates a special illusion to which the
realities of the outer world no longer apply. Such a setting has its
"arrangements" specifically geared to facilitating the therapeutic
processes involved. Each setting creates its own system of morality
and each is governed by basic underlying fantasies. The changes
brought about are closely related to the processes operating in the
situation. In individual therapy, the Unconscious in part becomes
conscious with an increase in insight and in the group the patient
not only becomes less isolated but is more open and more expressive
of his feelings.

Clearly, one cannot compartmentalize these various factors and
there is a good deal of therapeutic overlap between the two treatments.
One can conceive of the patient leaving individual therapy with an

enhanced ego identity and group therapy with, in Erikson's terms, a
more effective group identity, but this is altogether too diffuse for
practical purposes. Scheidlinger (1980) seems to summarize an acceptable point of view. His theoretical stance:

> "stresses in the inseparability of individual and
> group psychological elements in their intrapsychic,
> interpersonal and group-as-a-whole contexts. I
> question the need for ascribing a theoretical
> primacy to any of these elements, which I perceive
> as a Gestalt, except where a group leader guided
> by his philosophy of what would be most 'curative'
> is moved by reality considerations to momentarily
> put stress on one or more of these elements in
> his planned interventions in behalf of individuals
> or of the group as an entity."

FROM INDIVIDUAL TO GROUP THEORY

In spite of all these considerations, there is still something
mystifying that occurs when the individual enters a group situation:
how does his individual repertoire of universals, discussed earlier,
become incorporated into the life of the group; how do his individual
concerns evolve into group concerns; and how does the group eventually
become represented intrapsychically? We can talk of all kinds of in-
ternalizing mechanisms such as introjection, incorporation, identification, assimilation, learning, mirroring, empathy, resonance, contagion, valency and learning but none of these mechanisms inform us how
something from the outside gets inside and remains inside. One can
use the physiological model of eating, digesting, assimilating, and
excreting to describe mental metabolism but our understanding is not
thereby increased. We can also think of it as the taking in of
selected perceptions and organizing them within the mind, but we still
do not know to what structures in the mental apparatus, as conceived
by psychoanalysis, the group percepts go. We may be forced to conclude that we need only to create an interpersonal theory and not an
intrapersonal one since, in its psychoanalytic form, the latter has
already had a general degree of acceptance.

A structural approach permits us to create a system and this has
several advantages. A structural model allows us to have manifest
and latent levels of operation, ongoing transformations and the possibility of making predictions when elements are submitted to modifying
experiences. Best of all, it helps to make immediately intelligible
something of the facts that confront us in our work. We can therefore look at the work of Bion as an attempt to provide some structural
theory although it is heavily indebted to Kleinian metapsychology, and
is therefore not altogether group-specific. Failing a structural
theory, we are reduced to making the most of process which may enliven
our clinical reporting but does not help in the generating of theory.

One can talk of mirroring, of myth-making, of the matrix, of the "reality of the stronger person," of play and participation, and group associations and basic assumptions and "central persons," all of which are descriptions of group process, but we cannot as yet pin these elements together in a structural theory. That is still to come. It took almost half the lifespan of Freud's psychoanalytic explorations before structural theory made its appearance and a new phase of psychoanalytic history began.

We do not know as yet what kind of groups bring about maximum change, what kind of therapist stimulates exchange or what loss of control, degree of regression, depth of therapy, in the service of the group, or variety of communication best brings about structural alterations in the individual.

It is possible that the new theoretical departures in the individual field--self psychology in relation to external as well as internal objects, object relations theory and separation-individuation theory will be successfully incorporated into a general theory of the group, but, at the present time, these are little more than promising possibilities, all of which have to do with the increased interest in preoedipal development.

Bionism may provide still another bridge between individual and group, since in both situations, deep regressions to the psychotic levels are alleged to occur if the group is allowed to stew in its own anxiety and secondary process communications are avoided. Words are regarded as preverbal sounds and any attempt to use them as rational communications must be avoided. They are to be given no more weight than the "bizzare verbalizations of the psychotic." It will be of interest to see to what extent Kleinian psychoanalysis will make greater inroads into the group field than Freudian psychoanalysis but currently, the classical approach is in the ascendancy.

If it is true that the group passes through successive individual-centered and group-centered phases, we need some form of conjoint theory to cover both aspects and different group therapists may use different combinations of individual and group theory. We may need to construct a variety of therapeutic models before we can embark confidently on such excursions into individual and group theory, unless, of course, one settles for experience and not insight.

The anti-analytic and the anti-group proponents highlight the essential tensions inherent in the paradox of the one and the many. The one side would insist a group cannot, in the nature of things, be psychoanalyzed; nor can the individual in a group be psychoanalyzed without creating a great deal of distortion and disturbance. The other side insists with equal passion that the group is not invested with any magical healing power that "such a belief in the group is sorcery, incantation (Wolf and Schwartz, 1971)." The essential tension

arising from such discrepancies and anomalies can be creative unless
the passions become excessive so that disruption results.

Let me use an analogy from the physical field (Devereux, 1940).
The behavior of two bodies in relative motion to each other can be
fully and precisely accounted for in terms of classical mechanics,
but not the behavior of three or more bodies, when approximations
become less and less accurate as the number of bodies increases.
Eventually, it becomes more efficient, economical and accurate to
ignore the individual bodies and to study instead the system in
terms of statistical mechanics. The question is therefore not at
what point individual and individual phenomena become irrelevant and
group and group phenomena all-important, but rather at what point
does it become more economical to use the group rather than the
individual as the frame of reference. One must also bear in mind
that there is an almost incredibly compendious and subtle dove-
tailing of individual and group processes with each intrapersonal
development mobilizing and reinforcing group responses. The objective
would then be not to determine whether any particular phenomenon is
"ultimately" an individual or a group one, but rather to analyze,
as precisely as possible, the interplay and mutual reinforcement of
individual and group factors involved. To quote Devereux (1940):

> "Discrepancies are best approached by determining the
> actual relationship between the divergent frames of
> reference with which the contending points of view
> operate. These two approaches study radically dif-
> ferent phenomena. The behavior of the individual,
> when seen as an individual and not in terms of mem-
> bership of a group, is understandable only within
> a specifically individual frame of reference and
> in terms of psychological laws. The behavior of
> a group, seen as a group, and not primarily as an
> aggregate of discreet individuals is understandable
> only in terms of a specific interactional frame of
> reference."

Devereux is here contrasting the individual with the large group.
In between is the small group, a transitional system between the individual and the large group, where the overall interactional pattern
is equally determined and equally understandable in terms of individual and group dynamics. One should not make determined attempts to
"reduce" group explanations to individual ones when one can employ
both in the therapeutic group. Bohr's concept of complementarity
would suggest that we can apply different and mutually exclusive but
equally truthful statements to the same phenomenon. If we were to
apply this to the group, it would seem that we could look at the
group "equally truthfully" in terms of individual theory, regarding
the group as a collection of individuals, or in terms of group theory,
regarding the individuals as a group. One would expect a genuine

complementarity between the individual and the group understanding
of any given phenomenon. The difficulty (or logical impossibility)
is to think simultaneously in terms of two different frames of reference, especially when the key explanations focus on quite different
elements. The legitimacy of transposing conceptual models pertaining
to the individual group and vice versa is certainly questionable, even
allowing for the fact that there are groups within the group, with
each individual carrying a representation of the group inside his
mind. It would be most sensible to conclude that the proper universe
of discourse for a group involves both individual and group frames of
reference with one or the other in operation within the therapist's
mind at different times during the course of treatment. At present,
it would seem to me that the successful group therapist would have
both frames at his command, using them with flexibility, sensibility
and understanding of the ongoing process. This is faute de mieux
in order to get started in the new field, but we would need to revise
it as soon as it fails to provide a sufficiency of explanatory power.

I would end with what must be the favorite quotation of group
therapists who daily experience the tensions generated by the individual and the group, the one and the many. It comes from the play,
The Cocktail Party, by T.S. Eliot in which the psychiatrist, Sir
Henry Harcourt-Reilly, says:

> "My patients
>
> Are only pieces of a total situation
>
> Which I have to explore. The single patient
>
> Who is ill by himself is rather the exception."

In my experience, every group therapist worth his salt resonates
to this empathically at many different levels.

References

Balint, M. and Balint, E., 1962, Psychotherapeutic Techniques in
       Medicine, Charles C. Thomas, Springfield.

Battegay, R., 1974, Group psychotherapy as a method of treatment in
       a psychiatric hospital, The Challenge for Group Psychotherapy:
       Present and Future, de Schill, S., ed., International Univer-
       sities Press, New York.

Burke, E., 1826-27, Reform of representation, Collected Works, Vol.
       6, Wells and Lilly, Boston.

Cummings, E.E., 1958, quoted by Charles Norman in The Magic-Maker,
       MacMillan, New York.

Devereux, G., 1961, Two types of modal personality models, in Study-
       ing Personality Cross-Culturally,B.Kaplan,ed.,Harper&Row,N.Y.

References (continued)

Erikson, E.H., 1961, Childhood and Society, Norton, New York.
Foulkes, S.H., 1965, Therapeutic Group Analysis, International
        Universities Press, New York.
Hand, Judge Learned, 1954, quoted by Justice Frankfurter, in New York
        Times Magazine, November 24, 1954, New York.
Jahoda, M., (see this volume)
Mahler, M., 1967, On human symbiosis and the vicissitudes of the
        individuation process, J. Amer. Psychoanal. Assoc., 15:710–762.
Montaigne, 1957, Complete Works: Essay, Travel Journal, Letters,
        newly translated by Donald M. Frame, Stanford University
        Press, Stanford.
Morris, Colin, 1972, The Discovery of the Individual 1050–1200, Harper
        and Row, New York.
Pines, M., 1980, The frame of reference of group psychotherapy, Group
        Analysis, 13 (1): 16–21.
Redl, F., 1974, Group psychological implications for individual
        therapy with adolescents, Psychosocial Process, 3 (2): 8–20.
Sander, F., 1980, Individual and Family Therapy, Aronson, New York.
Scheidlinger, S., 1980, Current psychoanalytic group theory, in
        Psychoanalytic Group Dynamics, Scheidlinger, S., ed.,
        International Universities Press, New York.
Wells, H.G., 1917, A Modern Utopia, Nelson Co., New York.

BEYOND THE INDIVIDUAL: THE RELATIONSHIP BETWEEN GROUP AND

SUBJECTIVITY IN A GROUP ANALYTIC PERSPECTIVE

Diego Napolitani

Societa Gruppo-Analitica Italiana (S.G.A.I.)

Via Vesio, 24, 20148, Milan, Italy

In common language the words 'individual' and 'group' indicate
two fundamental human experiences which, in their immediacy, are
placed in two orders of mental representations which are completely
different: the 'individual' is a thing, an object of our sensory
perception, which is characterized by its steadfastness in time,
beyond its expressive variability and the changes connected to its
growth, reproduction and deterioration.   Moreover, the individual
as regards the etymological definition, seems not to be divisible,
being the latin translation from the Greek 'atom' and it seems that
the principle of unity or of identity can be used for its understanding, passing thus from the physical sciences to biological ones.

On the contrary, the 'group' is not an object of our sensory
perception, because this only tells us something about single individuals but nothing about eventual 'ties' existing among them.   It
has no character of steadfastness, neither has it any objectively
definable borderline, it does not grow, nor reproduce itself and it
does not deteriorate according to natural laws, and it is defined as
a unity of parts, each of which can, at any moment, separate itself
and regain its own complete autonomy.

The immediate experience tells us that a group without individuals cannot exist, but not vice-versa: this fact induces a
logical description of the connection between individual and group
of the causal kind: the individual produces groups and science of
Man investigate this relationship in terms of needs, drives, individual necessities and of their group or social fulfilment strategy.

All this is, generally, conceptualized in terms of relationship

41

between nature and culture, or between structural components of the human condition, where biological data establish anyway the core of man's individual existence.   Perhaps we can consider as equivalent the certainty in which man moves considering the 'truth' of these data which are immediately sensitive and that certainty with which man has considered his centrality in the universe for thousands of years: the movement of sun and stars around the earth is a perceptual reality whose meaning, for thousands of years, was necessarily and exclusively entrusted to religion, mythology and poetry.   Beginning from Copernicus and Galileo up to the present day, science has been man's reflective process which mediates his perceptive data, makes them relative and arrives at the construction of new representations of the world, quite different or even contrary to those founded on immediate perception: it is the earth that revolves around the sun!

Biology sanctions the experimental criteria, which the concept of biological individuality is founded on: it consists of the data of common experience relative to the uniqueness of the features of human beings; but most precisely it consists in the fact that every individual is endowed with a genetic equipment of histocompatible antigens.   By this fundamental property of the individual, it is impossible to make a mixture of parts (either tissues or organs) among different individuals: every grafting goes fatally towards a degenerative process thanks to the recipient's histocompatible antigens, unless this antigenic inheritance is blocked either physically or chemically.   The grafting is therefore possible only by destroying, in an artificial and dramatic way, the biological individuality of the subject, whom the grafting is carried out on.

In the attempt to define the concept of psychic individuality, psychology, beginning with Freud, meets a process quite contrasting with that which characterize the concept of biological individuality.

Right from the early phases of his development, the human being shows an inclination to assume meaningful parts of relationships with others as constituent qualities of his own psychic identity.   Right from the beginning, the human being becomes by this process identical - he identifies himself - in a more or less extensive and stable way, with someone else's behaviour and wishes.

Subjectivity   therefore, from the beginning, immersed in a "transplanted" emotional and intentional tissue, with which it is initially almost totally confused, the subject can afterwards progressively distinguish himself from that confusion by means of his reflective capacity and his own symbolic creativity. We can therefore state that, while biological individuality coincides with the concept of identity (steadfastness of genetic store and rigorous uniqueness of the individual), psychological individuality results both from subjective components, expressed in terms of creative re-

flectiveness and from relational components, manifested as a continuity with others within its own internal experiential field.

If the biological grafting necessarily causes a complex organic
reaction of pathological kind - the rejection - the process of
identification, which can be metaphorically described as a psychic
graft, is the ground of that typically human and indefinitely open
phenomenon that is culture.

The identification process marks the borderline between man's
biological universe and the proper psychological one. Every event
which can be meant and somehow changed, regardless of the identification process, belongs to biology, its theories (e.g. the physiological pattern) and praxises (e.g. therapy). Every event which the
heuristic hypothesis of identification process applies to, belongs
to a science concerning the psychological individuality, considered
in strictly relational terms.

Interpreting facts occurring in one of the two fields, trying to
follow laws tested in the other field, alters the structure itself
of the scientific way of thinking. In this way we may run the risk
to be tempted to make up for the lack of a strict and coherent
methodology with poetic metaphors, faith acts, fabletelling or
ideologies.

Today psychoanalysis still carries the original Freudian ambition that psychology would have found its own scientific authority
only as long as it would be explained in neuro-physiological terms
attaining to the biological individuality, that is, it could find
only in the medical pattern its 'author', its 'patron'.

This confusing ambition has enormously increased the development of mythological thought within psychoanalytic movement (e.g.
the mythology of drives and the subsequent fixation of a medical
preconception in its praxis), and has opposed, on the other hand,
the coherent development of psychoanalytic theories concerning
linguistic, communication, creativity, in a word, culture.

In the psychoanalytic approach to collective behaviour (family,
communities, groups) the epistemological confusion between biology
and psychology makes things even more difficult and it lends itself
less easily to a mythic-naturalistic mystification. This becomes
evident as we consider that the psychoanalytic praxis with groups,
unlike that with single individuals, divides itself in a lot of
theoretical patterns and settings, often coming out from a further
hybridisation between psychoanalytic psychobiology and various
extrapolations from social sciences. Most of the authors are though
firmly anchored to individualistic biological preconceptions, and can
only therefore see in the complex group relationships the inter-

lacing of everyone's drives and mechanisms with others'.   That would
make them feel righteously belonging to a closed and self-reassuring
part of the psychoanalytic family that, borrowing the concept of
orthodoxy from religion, coined the paradox of a 'scientific orthodoxy' applied to psychoanalysis.   But this kind of faithfulness to
the origins is a real hindrance to scientific development of thought.

Bion and Foulkes are, among the psychoanalysts who devoted themselves to groups, those who most deeply, courageously and consistently
compared their creative thought with their common psychoanalytic
training, as their cultural matrix.   Both have reached, though
following different paths and ignoring each other at least officially,
very similar prospective conclusions: the human mind is, first of all,
part of a collective relational structure, that Bion calls protomental system, and Foulkes calls transpersonal system.   For both of
them, this fundamental quality of individual mind builds up in the
earliest age, when infant is not yet able to distinguish his Self
from his non-Self.   According to both, this experience of continuity
between inner and external world remains as a permanent frame of mind
that is re-established or displayed even in adult age under particular conditions.

One of these conditions is the group where, according to Bion's
language, the protomental system is restored and shows itself in
terms of basic assumptions, and, according to Foulkes' language,
the transpersonal system is re-established and shows itself in terms
of matrix and group network.

Both the authors clearly state the uselessness of conceptions
anyhow related to a sort of solipsistic structure of drives to understand these collective phenomena.   I think that their work leads
essentially to the hypothesis that the basic conflict is not between
nature and culture, but that it develops between opposite components
or polarities of the specific human experience: on one hand, the
experiential polarity of belonging to a mental collective or transpersonal system and, on the other hand, the experiential polarity of
subjectivity emerging as recreating uniqueness.

The polarity of belonging lies in the perpetuation in individual
consciousness of that complex of very often contradictory wishes,
values, precepts, intentions, in which infant finds himself plunged
coming into world.   Meeting this world, infant has not, initially, at
his disposal his own wishes or values: he is, by definition, lacking
in any automony.   His existence cannot be but heteronomous, i.e.
guided by another's 'nomos', and he gradually assumes this heteronomy
as his own property.

This appropriation of others' 'nomos' constitutes the primary
identification process, which is actively induced by parents through

every kind of educational manipulation; in this way parents lay the
foundation of transfer of cultural tradition, and, in terms of
child's individual experience, the foundation of belongings. This
infant's feeling is related, therefore, to an inner group growing in
him, before he is able to distinguish himself from it, to distinguish,
to recognise and to affirm his own order of wishes, in agreement or
opposition to the others'.

From this introjected world, from this group matrix, which represents the ground of every individual's psychic experience, subjectivity arises, in that slow and never ending individuation process,
which makes human life unique compared with every other living creature's one. The birth metaphor means here the separation of an
autonomous ego from an heteronomous ego, that is closely participating
to the transpersonal system of primary matrices.

This separation process bases itself on two pillars: the reflective recognition of the subjective Self compared with the non-
Self (that is, with the outer world and the introjected group matrix)
and the ability to keep these two levels of experience at the same
time united and distinct by creation and use of symbols. Symbols, I
mean, are not mental signs which simply take the place of something
else, but they are creative linguistic structures which mark the
borderline between infancy (lack of words) and adulthood, or build
up bridges between group matrices and subjectivity. Cancelling this
borderline or breaking these bridges, we have dissociation of the
two polarities of inner experience of man. We can observe the same
results, indeed, if symbols are assimilated in stereotyped traditional
ways of thinking.

This theoretical perspective overturns the order of the immediate experience I referred to at the beginning of this paper; an
individual is not an atomistic or monadic entity and, like autonomous
subjectivity, he is coming out from the group and not vice-versa.
Moreover, each individual, in that autonomous subjectivity, would not
have reason for making up or participating in social groups but for
the fact of pursuing realistic or work aims. We know that it is not
so, that not only most of the groups meet unrealistic needs, but that
each group forming itself for realistic needs tends perpetually to
acquire emotional features in opposition to realistic aims and to
become, e.g. according to Bion's point of view, 'groups in basic
assumption'.

These facts do not attain to autonomous subjectivity of each
individual forming a group, but to his belonging polarity, to his
group matrix, which finds self-confirmation and propagation ground
for its own primary cultural tradition by belonging to new - but
even ancient, indeed social groups.

starts with the family, kindergarten and school, and continues on into
the army, places of employment, profession, town and ultimately the
state.   Hospitals are certainly an added form of force which affect
the whole of man's totality, and which combine hope and salvation and
a way out of sickness and helplessness, but also anxiety and fear of
death.   There is no human condition in which man is so alone as in
illness.   The experience of feeling alone and threatened breeds the
need for human kindness and proximity, for gentleness and care.
These are the main needs for a hospitalized person.   But this need
for others, is a need for healthy and stronger people who can help.
The patient in hospital also has a strong need for privacy, silence,
peace and quiet, a need to hide his helplessness and illness.   There
is a feeling of embarrassment because of illness, a strong man is
embarrassed by illness or angered by it and himself.   In this mood,
he wants human presence.   A patient also reverts to memories and pines
for the outside world, he compulsively thinks about death and goes
through the feeling of death emotionally.   Illness, therefore, is
not just helplessness, it is also the power and condition of a profound awareness of oneself, of an ethical analysis and perception of
oneself.   Illness is also the hypostatization of the subject and
individuality, of character traits and inborn feelings. Psychotherapy,
especially group psychotherapy, must respect all this in the patient
to the maximum possible extent.

Group Psychotherapy also leads to the socialization of illness;
this is socialization of the deepest subjectivity, which means
emotionalness, traumas and irrationality.   In principle this artificial inversion of the phenomenon of illness is highly risky and uncertain.   For, psychoanalysis and an opening of the soul can provide
not only a way to shed light on syndromes and to go through a catharsis, but also can provoke lies. defensive lies, and, in a major
number of people, creative lies.

A person never gives the same story about an event or happening
when he is with more than one other person.   It is always different
to talk to a friend than to talk to someone unknown.   A single event,
a problem, an idea, is never presented in the same way at all times,
in all settings.   Man invents, turns around the facts, reformulates
what has been said, dramatizes, imagines: he translates facts into
fiction, with a view to emphasizing his story and giving it the
greatest possible affect.   Every man is a story-teller, i.e. every
man creatively "lies",and this can help him to rid himself of the
sick syndrome, but also to conceal and intensify it.   In psychotherapy work with groups one must never forget, first, the experience
of the church with confessions of one's sins, given in the deepest
of discretion, through whispers and in darkness before the representative of God;   second, the experience of public, moral, ideological
and punitive confession, before party, intern and concentration camp
collectives.

Our age and our generation can vividly remember the confessions and repentence of innocent people at court trials and in nazi and stalinist camps.

Therefore, the only humanistic psychotherapy is that which does not subordinate itself to any doctrine, or method, no matter how authoritative its protagonists and results may be, for there are few therapy results which can give us the right to be fully satisfied.

It would be bad for humanistic psychotherapy to become a form of medical engineering and routine expertise. What it must imply is true medical permanence and deep concentration on the invisible secrets of the human being and the roots of his pain and helplessness, imperfections and deformations. It should aspire towards an integral and creative approach to man, and not subject all patients to one single method, but rather choose and adapt the method to the patient and his personality. For, sickness and the personality are often not in a causal identity. That is why I suggest flexibility and narrowing down the therapeutic field of activity, well thought out and restricted criteria for choosing patients and especially reductive criticism of all methods, experience and principles of work with groups which enter psychiatry from ideological societies, forced collectives in totalitarian systems and associations.

In my opinion, group psychotherapy can be successful only if it is highly selective, and if it is run by strong, all round, professional and cultural people, and not by kind or ill-tempered authoritarians with or without their white coats. It is difficult to imagine a serious psychotherapy approach without having any knowledge of the true components which make up the human being.

As I understand things, the human personality is a dialectical whole of two fundamental dynamic, and essentially unharmonious, potentials. The individual, at the centre of which is the ego with its primary content and passions, and the collective, at the heart of which lies:

a) consciousness of dependence on others and of belonging to the human race, family, community, nation and mankind, this consciousness being genetically codified;

b) the emotional need for joining others at different philogenetic levels, which basically consists of various forms of love;

c) rationalization of the need for the collective, as a religious, ideological, pragmatic and self-seeking projection.

There is no social content in this dialectical interaction be-

tween the individual and collective, nor, by and large, is there
proportion or harmony. But, one thing is certain: the social,
historical and collective belong to the secondary and superficial
layers of man's structure, no matter how much one may believe and
claim that man is a "social animal" and genetic totality. Historically, and in our civilization he became such by virtue of existential
imperative. From the first stages of self-awareness to present-day
ontological and anthropological philosophemae and theorems, the basis
of the human drama has been the conflict between the individual and
collective, the personal and general in man and in the world.

All art, all religions, all of history about man proves this
to be so. The theory of alienation is derived from this point, a
theory which seeks to save man in his harmonious socialization, in
restoring him to his original "self".

This theory has had a major impact on our age, and we have no
reason to underestimate some of what it has taught us. Quite generally speaking, its underlying idea gave rise to the philosophy of
individualism and liberalism with its extreme consequences represented in Stirner's divination of egotism, Nietsche's idea of the
superman and Freud's instinct of death. Their ideas have served, in
our time, as the basis for the evolution of numerous currents in
the sciences, arts and philosophy.

And finally, we must ask: what is Man?

But man is also what he is not. What he has not manifested.
He is also all that we have yet to learn about him, and it would seem,
all that we will never know about him.

And it is here that the motives for eternal drama and tragedy
lie. I am in favour of developing and acquiring an active ethical
consciousness of the secret of man's being and uncertainty of his
potentials. For, psychiatry is a young science but it is an ancient
skill and spiritual act, an ancient activation of the soul as reflected in art, magic and miracles, which invented gods and made them
indispensable to man as long as there is pain.

BIBLIOGRAPHY

Abse, W.: Group-analytic Psychotherapy. Wright, Bristol, 1974.

Anthony, J.: There and Then and Here and Now. Inter. Jour. Group
          Psychother., XXV 2, April 1975.

Argyle, N.: Social Interaction, Tavistock, London 1976.

Butkovich, P., Carlisle, J. et al: Social System and Psychoanalytic
        Approaches to Group Dynamics - Complementary or Con-
        tradictory?   Inter. Jour. Group Psychother. XXV, 1,
        January 1975.

Cornation, M.:   Groupes et societe.   Privat, Toulouse 1969.

Fourier, Ch.:   L' attraction pass ionnes.   Pauvert 1967.

Fourier, Ch.:   Le Nouveau Monde Industriel et societaire.
        Flammarion 1973.

Fourier, Ch.:   L' ordre subversif.   Aubier - Montaigne 1972.

Fourier, Ch.:   Oeuvers completes.   Repr. de l' ed. da 1841-1845.
        Anthropos.   Tom 1-10. 1967.

Fourier, Ch.:   Theorie de l' unite universalle.   Anthropos.   Tom
        1-3 1972.

Fourier, Ch.:   Textes choisis.   Ed. Sociales 1953.

Fourier, Ch.:   Vers la liberte en emour.   Gallimard 1975.

Frank, J.:   Group Psychotherapy Research 25 Years Later, Inter. Jour.
        Group Psychotherapy, XXV, 2, April 1975.

Grotjahn, M.:   The Qualities of the Group Therapist in Kaplan,H. and
        Sadok, B.:   Comprehensive Group Psychotherapy, Williams
        and Wilkins, Baltimore 1971.

Home, H.:   Razmisljanja o transferu u maloj analitickoj grupi,
        Psihoterija, vol. V, br. 2, 1975.

Ivanov, N.:   Grupovaja psihoterapija-ezegodnike, Moskva, 1971.

Karasu, T., Bourgeois, M., et Meltzer, B.:   Idees et theories dans
        les Nouvelles Psychotherapies aus USA, Annales medico-
        psychologiques, 1977.

Krec, D., Kracfild, R.:   Pojedinac u drustvu, Zavod za udzbenike,
        Beograd 1972.

Libin, S.: Kolektivnaja psihoterapiji nevrozov, Medicina, Lenjin-
        grad, 1974.

Lifton, W.: Groups. Wiley, New York 1972.

Maslow, A.H.:   Toward a Psychology of Being, van Hostrand, New York
        1968.

Maslow, A.H.:Neurosis as a Failure of Personal Growth, Humanitas
        vol. 3, W.S. Sahakiana (ed): Psychopathology Today, Peacock,
        Illinois 1970.

May, R.: Angel, E. and Ellenberger, H.: Existence: New York 1958.

Osgood, E., Tannenbaum, H.: The Principle of Congruity in the Pred-
        iction of Attitude Change, Psychol. Rev., 1955.

Popovic, M.: Klinicka stacionarna grupna terapija. Psihijatrija
        danas 1977, 1:91–97.

Popovic, M.: Razvoj grupna psihoterapija. Psihijatrija danas.
        Beograd 1:5:14. 1978.

Proudhon, P.J.: Justice et liberte P.U.F. 1962.

Proudhon, P.J.: Oeuvres choisies. J. Bancal. Gallimard 1967.

Proudhon, P.J.: Oeuvres completes. Riviere (Devenir social). Tom
        6, 12, 13, 14, 15, 1962.

Proudhon, P.J.: Q'est ce que la propriete? Garnier. Flammarion 1966

Proudhon, P.J.: Textes choisis. Dallas. 1953.

Owen, R.: Textes choisis. Morton ed. Sociales 1963.

Rabin, H.: How to begin a psychotherapy group: Six approaches,
        Gordon & Breach, London 1976.

Rogers, C.: The process of the basic encounter group, Western Be-
        havioral Sciences Institute, La Jolla, 1966.

Saint-Simon, H.C.: Oeuvres completes. Reprod. de l' ed. du XIX
            siecle Anthropos. Tom 1–6, 1974.

Saint-Simon, H.C.: Physiologie sociale. Ed. G. Gurvitch 1965.

Saint-Simon, H.C.: Textes chosis. Ed. par J. Dautry 1951.

Slavson, S.: In the Beginning, Inter. Jour. Group Psychotherapy,
        XXV, 2 April 1975.

Spotnitz, H.: Comparison of Different Types of Group Psychotherapy
            in Kaplan, H. and Sadock, B.: Comprehensive Group
            Psychotherapy,Williams and Wilkins, Baltimore 1971.

Vassiliou, V., Vassiliou, G.: Variation of the Group Process across
            Cultures. Inter. Jour. Group Psychother. XXIV, 1,
            January 1974.

Walton, H.: Small Group Psychotherapy, Penguin, Harmondsworth 1974.

Yalom, I.: The Theory and Practice of Group Psychotherapy, Basic
        Books, New York, 1970.

THE HEALTHY AND THE UNHEALTHY FAMILY:

RESEARCH IN FAMILY INTERACTION*

Warren Kinston, Senior Research Fellow

Institute of Organisation and Social Studies
Brunel University
Uxbridge, Middlesex, U.K.

SUMMARY

The work of the Family Studies Group (Department of Psychological Medicine, Hospital for Sick Children, London, U.K.) in integrating a systematic research approach with the clinical development of family therapy is described. The various instruments developed and under methodological scrutiny include the Current Family State Assessment, Family Health Scales, Family Interaction Summary Format, Family Task Interview and Standardised Clinical Family Interview. The clinical method is a form of brief focal family therapy whose theory integrates objective description with subjective reports and historical details, and builds in a way of evaluating outcome.

This paper integrates and summarises a programme of research which has been developed within the Department of Psychological Medicine at the Hospital for Sick Children in London. The work was instigated and maintained by clinicians who constituted them-

---

* The work described in this paper has been carried out by the Family Studies Group in the Department of Psychological Medicine, The Hospital for Sick Children, Great Ormond St., London, W.C.1. U.K.

selves informally as the "Family Studies Group".   These include
Dr. A. Bentovim, Mrs. C. Burck, Mr. D. Evans, Dr. B. Lask,
Dr. P. Loader, Mrs. J. Stratford, and the author.

BACKGROUND

In 1973, two clinical trends - focussing on the family as a
unit and shortening therapy - coalesced in a new form of therapy.
In a weekly workshop, the method of "brief focal family therapy"
was developed, applied and systematically evaluated (Bentovim and
Kinston, 1978;   Kinston and Bentovim, 1978).   Both clinical and
research aspects of the work brought the primitive state of clinical
family description to our attention.   We wrote "Description of
families qua families was crude and simplistic in comparison with
the richness and complexity of description of the individuals".
(Kinston and Bentovim, 1978 p.140);   and announced our intention to
work at changing this state of affairs.

In the U.S.A. the gap between family researchers and family
therapists had been repeatedly noted (Framo, 1972;   GAP Report 1970)
but to little avail (De Witt, 1978).   It seemed to us that
clinicians needed to overcome their aversion to research methods
and commence systematic work.   By rooting this work in the attempt
to treat troubled families, it should be possible to obtain usable
knowledge.   Other workers have come to similar conclusions.
Epstein and coworkers also commenced from a model of family therapy
and developed appropriate methods of description and assessment
(Epstein et al, 1978).

There are a number of tasks which must be accomplished to
produce a coherent and comprehensive research programme which will
lead to clinically useful results.   These are:

      i)   recruitment of families;

     ii)   elicitation of family interaction;

   iii)   qualitative descriptions of interaction;

    iv)   quantitative ratings of interaction;

     v)   integration of research and clinical methods.

Each of these will be briefly reviewed together with an account of
the approach and contribution of the Family Studies Group.

RECRUITMENT

Finding whole families and inducing them to participate in a
research endeavour is not easy.   The methodological problems have

been considered in work with individuals (Stein, 1971). Typically researchers have easy access either to families labelled as psychologically disturbed or to non-labelled families, usually as part of their location within a treatment service or educational facility.

Volunteer families may be sought via advertising (Gottman, 1979; Riskin, 1976) or from natural community groups such as the Church (Lewis et al, 1976). These approaches lend themselves to personal and family bias (Rosenthal and Rosnow, 1975; Kokes et al, 1977). In studies of "healthy" individual volunteers the bias is in the direction of greater disturbance (Esecover et al, 1961; Edwards, 1968; Turner et al, 1969); while recruitment from a clinically labelled group may result in a healthier group volunteering (Carr and Whittenbaugh, 1968).

We have attempted to deal with this by recruiting consecutively or randomly from attenders at a variety of public service facilities which are a characteristic of the U.K. social services scene (hospital, clinic, school). The resultant bias is more geographic or social than personal and somewhat less relevant to our investigations.

This solution depends on a high rate of participation from those families approached. In an early study in 1976 we recruited 12 of 58 possible families, while in a 1979 study we recruited 17 of 19. Part of the reason for this improvement from 21% to 89% success may have been due to the different patient groups, but a great deal was almost certainly due to the increased attention paid to the minutiae of the recruitment method. Much so-called "resistance" or "opposition" on the part of the family came to look like sensible behaviour in the face of our poor communication, mishandling or plain laziness.

We have identified five components in our recruitment strategy.

1.   Obtaining full involvement and committment of the personnel with primary involvement with the family. This may be just one person (e.g. a Consultant Physician) but often includes others and it may take weeks or months to obtain. Family members automatically look for guidance and reassurance to these people and can pick up their views without explicitly asking. The family will not cooperate in time-consuming effort unless the research is clearly valued and understood by the people they know best.

2.   Conveying a "whole family" approach. The researcher must indicate his interest in and explain his need to see the whole family as part of a natural awareness of the

importance of the family as a unit.   Sometimes (as in the
Department of Psychological Medicine) this is part of the
orientation of the service facility, but in other cases
it runs directly counter to it.   Most people are aware of
the importance of their family and family life and rapidly
appreciate the approach.

3.   Taking practical problems seriously.   Our research cannot
     be conducted at the time and place of recruitment, and
     there is often difficulty in arranging a suitable time.
     We respect the difficulties involved and as well as
     offering some times, are agreeable to negotiating times
     to suit a particular problem.   We always offer to reimburse
     the costs of travelling to attend research interviews but
     do not reimburse the cost of time off work.   Letters for
     employers or schools are offered but rarely required.

4.   Simple written explanations and simple plans.   As
     researchers, we have sometimes been bemused and confounded
     by the practical complexity of our simplest studies.   How
     much more so is the subject!   It is necessary to devise
     simple straightforward explanations and directions to be
     taken home and discussed by all family members.   We make
     ourselves available on the phone for further enquiries.

5.   Repeated reminders and confirmation.   Attendance is improved
     if family members receive follow-up letters and telephone
     calls to confirm or remind them about appointments.   These
     contacts just prior to attendance can contain details of how
     to find the right reception desk - information which is
     unnecessary and confusing before this.   Phone calls should
     often be confirmed by a brief letter.   This is the only
     part of the recruitment procedure which can safely be left
     to a secretary.

     Much of the early work was concerned with the possibility of
systematic description, and was based on families coming for
psychological treatment (Kinston et al, 1979;   Loader et al, 1980).
To fulfil teaching responsibilities, these families were routinely
available for observation via one-way screens or videotape/CCTV.
In this work the interaction was elicited by clinicians as part of
their diagnostic and therapeutic efforts.

ELICITATION OF FAMILY INTERACTION

     In a research context, however, the eliciting of interaction
is a problematic issue.   Cromwell et al, (1976) reviewed available
techniques and found them to be mainly artificial family tasks based

on problem-solving, decision-making or conflict-resolution.   The
available "naturalistic" methods were generally unfeasible e.g.
observer participation of family meals (Dreyer and Dreyer, 1973);
home observation (Behrens et al, 1969).   There was no methodologically satisfactory research interview available despite the importance
attached to interviewing as a clinical and diagnostic tool (Ackerman,
1958;   Bloch, 1973;   Minuchin, 1974;   Glick and Kessler, 1974).

Family therapists had attempted to use a mixture of relevant
tasks for research purposes (Watzlawick, 1966;   Elbert et al, 1964;
Minuchin et al, 1978;   Lewis et al, 1976).   However, only Lewis et al,
(1976) gave any evidence for the reliability and validity of their set
of tasks.

We decided to develop two methods of elicitation and discover
the strengths and weaknesses of each.   One would be based on the sets
of tasks, and the other would draw on clinical interviewing.

The Family Task Interview (F.T.I.)

We aimed to produce a simple, easily administered, fully
standardised interview.   We wished it to be widely applicable
irrespective of the size, life-cycle stage, social class or
labelling of the family.

There were a number of issues which had to be faced:

a)   Administration by man or machine.   We found that
interviewer administration was less easy to
standardise than tape-recorded administration,
and that families were more comfortable with a
tape-recorder.

b)   Interview length.   Young children have difficulty
in participating beyond fifty to sixty minutes so
we settled on fifty minutes of tasks plus five
minutes for explanations on tape.

c)   Involvement of all or part of the family.   We
decided that all tasks should take place in the
same place and require all family members.

d)   Task complexity.   Complicated tasks block many
families from participating comfortably or at all
and tend to spoil standardisation.   We chose
straightforward tasks, worded as simply and
unambiguously as possible and requiring the minimum
of ancillary materials.

e)   Task variety.   Tasks should span a number of inter-
     actional areas and not over-emphasise verbal
     participation.   We settled on six tasks, five of nine
     minutes and one of five minutes.   Two demanded physical
     action.

f)   Family stress.   We aimed for a safe and supportive
     interview atmosphere and chose tasks to reduce the
     possibility that families might experience failure
     or persecution.

These criteria resulted in the construction of an Interview which
differed from those of other workers.   The tasks finally chosen
were:

1.   plan something together;

2.   build a tower with blocks;

3.   discuss likes and dislikes of each member;

4.   find a pattern in a deck of cards;

5.   express feelings and fantasy about an accident;

6.   explain a proverb to the children.

The Standardised Clinical Family Interview (S.C.F.I.)

Although a flexible approach by the interviewer is essential if
the family interaction is to be clinically relevant, it is necessary
to limit his clinical freedom in order to obtain sufficient standardisation.   We developed a semi-structured protocol which required the
interviewer to carry the family through a series of issues relevant to
family life.   As in the Task Interview, the bias is towards avoiding
unnecessary stress and allowing strengths to be revealed.

The S.C.F.I. consists of four phases:

Phase I: The Introduction (5-10 minutes).

           The interviewer meets each member personally and
           establishes the nature and rules of the interview.

Phase II: The Reason for Attending (2-15 minutes).

            The overt reason for attendance is discussed with
            emphasis on the family perspective.

Phase III: System Properties (30-45 minutes).

             The interviewer offers questions and probes about
             family life to stimulate interaction e.g. to-
             getherness, likes, roles, decisions, disagreements,
             discipline, extra-family relationships.

Phase IV: Conclusion (2-5 minutes).

The interview is ended, further arrangements made
and the family thanked for attending.

The technique of interviewing is a complex and important subject
(see Satir, 1967;   Minuchin, 1974;   Kinston, 1979) and therefore can
be no more than mentioned here.   Our research method requires a
clinician, already highly adept at interviewing whole families, to
undergo careful training.   For example, he must not lose role and
attempt to help or change the family, and he must take a far more
objective and formal stance than usual while still attempting to
facilitate informality and spontaneity in the family.   There are a
large number of procedural rules which have been developed to deal
with various contingencies which are likely to interfere with
standardisation.   Maintenance of the outsider perspective, a sense
of comfort, and control over the interview process do much to reduce
unnecessary anxiety in the family.

The interviewer must keep his focus on the family as a whole and
not get involved with individual members except in relation to the
family system.   For example, new topics are always addressed to the
whole family.   Specific measures to include the children are
necessary however.   Children need permission, encouragement and reassurance to regard themselves as important as parents from the point
of view of participation in the event.

Evaluation of Research Interviews

These interviews have now been piloted and evaluation is in
progress.   Some preliminary findings can be reported at this stage.

a)   Feasibility.   The S.C.F.I. is a difficult interview
to administer and it demands much training.   Content-
analytic studies are currently in progress to examine
deviations of the interviewer from his protocol and
rules.   By contrast, the F.T.I. has proved simple and
straightforward.   We have however found that a number
of families do not know what a proverb is.

b)   Acceptability.   Families tolerate both interviews well.
The apparent distress or disturbance of the family at
interviews is not reflected in their feed-back to us.
In general, families prefer the audiotape interview.

c)   Reliability.   The S.C.F.I. was administered to the same
group of 10 families on two occasions six weeks apart by
two interviewers (one male, one female).   Interaction
was rated using our Current Family State Assessment (v.i.).
There were no significant differences on almost all the
reliably rated categories.   There was also no order

effect (i.e. the score was independent of whether it
was made at the first or the second interview) and only
a small interviewer effect which was due to one interviewer stressing the importance of conflict-resolution.

d)   Validity.   The F.T.I. has been administered to a group
of clinical families   (Stratford et al, 1979).   This
revealed that it was deficient in exposing conflict.
Otherwise it both complemented and validated clinical
elicitation.   It proved especially valuable in exposing
the influence of the therapist on interaction.   Families
have received both the S.C.F.I. and F.T.I. but this data
is yet to be analysed.

QUALITATIVE DESCRIPTION OF FAMILY INTERACTION

Once the family is interacting, stimulated by either the
clinician or the researcher, the problem is how to describe what
occurs.   The descriptive categories chosen are determined by the
relevance to the purpose at hand and they must be generally understood and accepted.

We searched the literature and conducted experiments in which
family therapists described families as best they could.   From this
we developed a Family Interaction Summary Format and a guide to
clinical description (Loader et al, 1980).   This format is primarily
clinical.   It aims to be systematic, comprehensive, relevant, and
independent of the clinician's theoretical views.   With experience
in its use, it can be appropriately abbreviated and rapidly completed.

The Summary Format delineates eight conceptual groupings or
dimensions, each on a separate page.   These are: Atmosphere,
Communication, Affective Status, Boundaries, Family Operations,
Alliances, Parental Function, and Relation to the Environment.
Each of these are divided into subsections which act as an aide
memoire to description.   For example, the headings on the Communication page are:

- Comment on Clarity, i.e. communication of meaning,
    articulation, explicitness of content, verbal/non
    verbal congruence.

- How were themes and topics taken up, focussed upon,
    developed and changed?

- Describe the overall patterns of communication: the
    pathways, the noise level, the degrees of participa-
    tion, the conversational style.

- Comment on the giving and receiving of messages: the

frequency and nature of control (orders, demands,
requests, questions etc.), information exchange,
listening and acknowledgement, and space is left
for other comments.

QUANTITATIVE RATINGS OF FAMILY INTERACTION

When we commenced work, we doubted the value of much of the
communication between clinicians.   Our initial task was to find out
whether family therapists who wanted to and were assisted could agree
on the most commonly used categories of interaction.   We produced the
Current Family State Assessment (C.F.S.A.) by identifying about 30
categories and placing each on a 5-point ordinal scale with anchoring
definitions.   (Kinston et al, 1979).   We found that our raters
could produce very similar rating profiles of interviews and agreed
at a clinically acceptable level on many categories.   However the
reliability coefficients were not generally satisfactory for research
purposes and, despite much training, rater bias was a problem.   A
subsequent study using the C.F.S.A. revealed that formerly reliable
items were being rated unreliably (Loader et al, 1980).   Categories
such as Effectual Parental Coalition, Alliances, and Conflict
Acknowledgement which were derived from the clinical literature were
more reliably rated than categories which came from the research
literature such as Interruptions, Disagreement, and Intrusiveness.

We concluded that we could have little confidence in the assessment of a single rater using the C.F.S.A.   However, there were other
difficulties which stemmed from its non-clinical origins.   The raters
were asked to "rate what you see" and minimise inferences - a state of
mind that a clinician cannot adopt.   In particular the clinician
develops an overall assessment of the family and the C.F.S.A. did not
provide for this.   These deficiencies led us to develop the Family
Health Scales (F.H.S.).

In a pilot study we had attempted to obtain a clinical rating of
"overall family disorder" on a 0-100 scale.   We failed because of
complaints that the task was unrealistic.   We believed that our
clinicians had seen an excessively narrow range of families but that
a global rating was conceptually acceptable and useful to them if they
were given assistance in rating.   Assessment of physical health
requires the examination of many interlinked physiological systems:
in the same way family health was conceived as multi-dimensional.

In the midst of this work, Lewis et al, (1976) came to the conclusions from which we began.   Namely that family health is a
composite of many processes and that it is possible to distinguish
degrees of family health.   They studied both healthy and disturbed
families and found that experienced family therapists observed and
assessed family systems reliably.   Their work required only ranking
whereas we were concerned to use rating.

Family disorder, our definition ran, refers to abnormalities of communication, behaviour, relationships or atmosphere within the family as a whole, which are inconsistent with the intellectual, social or cultural status of its members and which are of sufficient intensity or extent as to interfere with its capacity to provide psychosocial protection and nurturance for its members and socialisation for the children. It leads to persistent suffering or disturbance in either its members or to those in contact with them or both.

The assessment of family disorder is a clincal matter: it must allow the clinician to use his ability to recognise defensive behaviour, or to weight particular pathological elements. Such assessment exists within a variety of theoretical viewpoints and we were concerned that our scales should be widely acceptable. Our first task was to select dimensions which could be considered in terms of a continuum of dysfunctional-healthy interaction. It seemed natural to think of optimal, adequate, disturbed and disrupted function and we chose 7 point ordinal scales with four anchoring descriptions. Each dimension is determined by judgement rather than an average and if the rater has insufficient information for any subscale or dimension it is simply omitted. The final score is the average of those dimensions which have received a rating.

Psychometric Properties of the Family Health Scales

Preliminary studies suggest that a reliable and valid global rating of family health is obtainable. Inter-rater reliability has been examined with rating from written descriptions of family interaction and from videotape. Spearman rank correlation coefficients have varied from borderline (.60 to .75) to acceptable (over .75). The work of Lewis et al, is supported in that all dimensions are highly correlated with family health (usually .80 or better). Our analysis also suggests that the Family Health Scales are specific and not merely reflections of individual disturbance - at least as measured by generally accepted indicators like the General Health Questionnaire for adult morbidity (Goldberg, 1972), the Rutter A Scale for school child morbidity (Rutter et al, 1970) and the Behaviour Check List for pre-school disturbance (Richman, 1977). Studies that are currently planned are estimations of construct and consensual validity and sensitivity.

INTEGRATION OF RESEARCH & CLINICAL METHODS

Our work stands or falls by whether it helps other therapists help families. While the methodological studies were being performed, the development of brief focal family therapy continued. Our descriptive effort was a useful input and permitted a far clearer distinction and description of observable interaction. We moved to a conceptualisation of "relevant surface action" i.e. overt interaction which is repetitious, circular, meaningless, difficult to stop and recognised by a clinician of any theoretical grounding as "pathological". We saw that such action had "depth meaning" based on the family's history. A focal hypothesis is developed to explain the presenting symptom, surface action, and depth meaning, and to act as a basis for intervention and a guide to criteria of improvement. This work will be described and exemplified at this Congress Plenary in far more detail by Dr. Arnon Bentovim and at a workshop run by Dr. Peter Loader.

We are currently developing a typology of family pathology based on the existence of the precipitating stress within the family of origin or procreation (Kinston and Bentovim, 1980). Outcome studies which will use the instruments described above should help us to clarify the nature of this typology and the prognostic implications of particular constellations of stress.

REFERENCES

Ackerman, N.W., 1958, "The Psychodynamics of Family Life", Basic Books, New York.

Behrens, M.L., Meyers, D.I., Goldfarb, W., Goldfarb, N., and Fieldsteel, N.D., 1969, The Henry Ittleson Center Family Interaction Scales, Genet. Psychol. Monog. 80: 203-295.

Bentovim, A., and Kinston, W., 1978, Brief focal family therapy when the child is the referred patient, 1. Clinical. J. Child Psychol. Psychiat. 19: 1-12.

Bloch, D., 1973, "Techniques of Family Psychotherapy: A Primer". Grune and Stratton, New York.

Carr, J.E., and Whittenbaugh, J.A., 1968, Volunteer and non-volunteer characteristics in an out-patient population. J. Abnorm. Psychol. 73: 16-17.

Cromwell, R.E., Olson, D.H.L., and Fournier, D.G., 1976, Tools and Techniques for diagnosis and evaluation in marital and family therapy. Fam. Proc. 15: 1-49.

De Witt, K.N., 1978, The effectiveness of family therapy. Arch. Gen. Psychiatry. 35: 549-561.

Dreyer, C.A., and Dreyer, A.S., 1973, Family dinner time as a unique behaviour habitat. Fam. Proc. 12: 291-301.

Elbert, S., Rosman, B., Minuchin, S., and Guerney, B., 1964, A method for the clinical study of family interaction. Am. J. Orthopsychiat. 34: 885-894.

Epstein, N.B., Bishop, D.S., and Levin, S., 1978, The McMaster model of family functioning. J. Marr. Fam. Counsel. 4: 19-31.

Edwards, C.N., 1968, Characteristics of volunteers and non-volunteers for a sleep and hypnotic experiment. Am. J. Clin. Hypnosis 11: 26-29.

Esecover, H., Malitz, S., and Wilkens, B., 1961, Clinical profiles of paid normal subjects volunteering for hallucinogenic drug studies. Am. J. Psychiatr. 117: 910-915.

Framo, J.L., (Ed.) 1972, "Family Interaction: A Dialogue between Family Researchers and Family Therapists", Springer, New York.

G.A.P., 1970, "The Field of Family Therapy". Vol. VII, Report No. 78.

Glick, I.D., and Kessler, D.R., 1974, "Marital and Family Therapy". Grune and Stratton, New York.

Goldberg, D.P., 1972, "The Detection of Psychiatric Illness by Questionnaire", Maudsley Monograph No. 21. Oxford University Press, London.

Gottman, J.M., 1979, "Marital Interaction: Experimental Investigations". Academic Press, London.

Kinston, W., 1979, "A reliable standardised clinical interview with the whole family". Working Paper of the Family Studies Group: London.

Kinston, W., and Bentovim, A., 1978, Brief focal family therapy when the child is the referred patient. II. Methodology and results. J. Child Psychol. Psychiat. 19: 119-144.

Kinston, W., and Bentovim, A., 1980, Creating a focus in brief marital and family therapy, in Budman, S., (Ed.) "Forms of Brief Psychotherapy", Guildford Press, New York, (in press).

Kinston, W., Loader, P., and Stratford, J., 1979, Clinical assessment of family interaction: A reliability study. J. Fam. Ther. 1: 291-312.

Kokes, R.F., Fremoun, W., and Strauss, J.S., 1977, Last subjects; source of bias in clinical research? Arch. Gen. Psychiatry 34: 1363-1365.

Lewis, J.M., Beavers, W.R., Gossett, J.T., and Phillips, V.A., 1976, "No Single Thread: Psychological Health in Family Systems", Brunner Maazel, New York.

Loader, P., Burck, C., Kinston, W., Bentovim, A., and Stratford, J., 1980, Family interaction: a guide to clinical description. (Submitted for publication.)

Loader, P., Kinston, W., and Stratford, J., 1980, Is there a "psycho-somatogenic" family? J. Fam. Ther. 2. (3).

Minuchin, S., 1974, "Families and Family Therapy". Harvard Univ. Press, Cambridge.

Minuchin, S., Rosman, B.L., and Baker, L., 1978, "Psychosomatic Families: Anorexia Nervosa in Context". Harvard Univ. Press, Cambridge.

Richman, N., 1977, Is a Behaviour Checklist for pre-school children useful? In: Graham, P., (Ed.) "Epidemiological Approaches in Child Psychiatry", Academic Press, London.

Riskin, J., 1976, "Nonlabelled" family interaction: Preliminary report on a prospective study. Fam. Proc. 15: 433-439.

Rosenthal, R., and Rosnow, R.L., 1975, "The Volunteer Subject", Wiley, N.Y.

Rutter, M., Tizard, J., and Whitmore, K., 1970, "Education, Health and Behaviour", Longmans, London.

Satir, V., 1967, "Conjoint Family Therapy: A Guide to Theory and Technique" (2nd Ed.) Science and Behaviour Books, Inc., Palo Alto..

Stein, K., 1971, Psychotherapy patients as research subjects: Problems in cooperativeness, representativeness, and general-isability. J. Consul. Clin. Psychol. 37: 99-105.

Stratford, J., Burck, C., and Kinston, W., 1979, Contextual factors
    in family assessment.   Paper presented to the London Forum of
    Family Therapy.
Turner, R.J., Zabo, L.J., Raymond, J., et al 1969, Field survey
    methods in psychiatry: The effects of sampling strategy upon
    findings in research on schizophrenia.   J. Health Soc. Behav.
    10: 289-297.
Watzlawick, P., 1966, A Structured Family Interview.   Fam. Proc.
    5: 256-271.

THE FAMILY AS THE MATRIX OF THE INDIVIDUAL:

GROUP PROCESS IN CHILD DEVELOPMENT

Dr. Melvin Muroff

17 Harcourt Road

Scarsdale, New York, N.Y. 10583, U.S.A.

It would be difficult to find anyone who disagrees with the
statement that the family is the matrix of the individual. Who
would doubt that the family affects our growth and development.
Most likely no one. Although it is easy to agree with this gener-
alization, there is a variety of opinions, theories if you will, as
to how it works. It is here that it would be difficult to find a
consensus. Perhaps, this is how it should be since the complexities
of human behavior make it impossible to understand all of it on the
basis of one point of view. Each of us perceives and understands
psychological functioning on the basis of our own prejudices which,
in itself, comes from that matrix which influenced us. The conceptual positon of this presentation developed from two distinctly
different, but not necessarily opposing, psychological theories:
psychoanalysis and group dynamics. Psychoanalysis has contributed
considerable data, although much of it is speculative, to our understanding of the internal process of the individual but it has not
been able to adequately cope with the problems of inter-personal,
social behavior. Group Dynamics, with its strict experimental
orientation, has advanced our knowledge of social interaction but
it does not include much data on intrapsychic functioning or child
development. Since each lacks what the other has, it seems reasonable and logical, to amalgamate both to discuss the family as the
matrix of the individual. The need to combine both becomes even
more evident if we recognize that "the family as a matrix" implies
group process and that "of the individual" suggests intrapsychic
phenomena. However, in order to consolidate the two, let us briefly
examine the unique contributions of each position relative to our
topic.

It is appropriate that we start with psychoanalysis especially since this year marks its 100th anniversary beginning with Freud's involvement with Breuer's report on the case of Anna O. As we know, Freud's interest in the nature of Hysteria propelled him to hypothesize and to explore the mysteries of the unconscious functioning of the mind. He carefully and symstematically evolved a theory of human development by analyzing patients' free associations and the latent content of their dreams. His purpose was to remove unconscious conflict caused by repressed instinctual drives and associated defense mechanisms. Freud was aware that the family, the environment, affected the development of the person and his psychosexual theory of child development was his explanation for the interaction between one's biological drives and the environment. We are all familiar with his age-fixed stages of child development: the oral, anal, phallic and the oedipal. The more the child is able to resolve his conflicts prevalent in each stage, the more he is able to differentiate reality. Any unresolved conflict in a given stage, leads to a fixation on that particular level and causes emotional conflict. Each stage of development has its particular biological drives and how they are either gratified or frustrated, determine a child's character structure.

Although Freud's early writings on instinct theory were revolutionary in his day, the time itself affected his thinking. This time matrix was deeply preoccupied with strivings for self-determination and all scientific investigations and models, were primarily concerned with a rigid Darwinian approach to isolating specific details in an effort to separate out one individual from the other. This molecular attitude pervaded even the political arena where each country was belligerently defining and defending its own individuality. It was a time when individuals were aggressively accumulating large fortunes and where individual power gave substance to such people like the railroad barons in America and to the banking house of the Rothschilds in Europe. Thus, the social forces of the day made it inevitable that Freud would also focus on the individual and his intrapsychic functioning. Perhaps the process of man's development requires that we first know about the individual's internal structure before we can understand how this unit, this individual, is affected by and interacts with, other units.

Freud's awareness of the fact that the family shapes and moulds the individual, is further emphasized in his later writings where he describes his group psychology. (Totem and Taboo 1912, Narcissism 1914, Mourning and Melancholia 1917, Group Psychology and the Analysis of the Ego 1921, and The Ego and The Id 1923). However, his position remained rooted to concepts of individual differences and to that of internal dynamics. Even today, many of us still may employ this approach: that of explaining and discussing the family matrix in the language of intrapsychic functions. For example, it is not uncommon to hear group interactions described in terms of: family ego, family projection, group transference, and so on. This

use, or misuse, of terms uniquely appropriate for describing one process to describe another, is not only unnecessary, but it frequently
tends to contaminate and to destroy the meaning of the first. It
is especially unnecessary since the second process has a meaningful
language and vocabulary of its own. Before proceeding further, let
us briefly consider the analytic view of the family as the matrix
of the individual as reflected in Freud's group psychology.

It is most likely that Freud would define the family matrix in
terms of his instinct theory since he uses his concepts of the ego-
ideal to explain his group psychology. This involves libidinal
attachments which, when not satisfied, leads to a sense of guilt due
to a fear of punishment or loss of love from the parents and then
later, this becomes projected on to others. The nature of the
group, the family, is determined by the libidinal attachments within
it. The process of identification with the leader and the empathy
of its members with one another, both tie the group together. The
family is described as having an innate mind of its own and its
growth pattern follows the rules which regulate individual development. All this takes place in the context of an unconscious, mystical continuous inheritance, passed on from one family matrix to
another. In many ways, Freud's mechanistic position states that the
family matrix is a negative influence and the healthy individual
continually strives to become independent from his early, primitive
group attachments. He was opposed to all group affiliations and to
any group memberships. He thought that the interests of the individual were opposed to his fellow man and to society. It is as
though every individual is an enemy of his family matrix, his culture. He suggests that perhaps the individual and his psychology,
is a more advanced level of development and group membership is a
regressive phenomenon; a reflection of one's inability to escape
from the "primal horde". Therefore, from this point of view, still
held by many, we might say that the family as the matrix of the individual, is a negative, regressive instinctual force which the individual must overcome if he is to be a whole person. Apparently,
it was difficult for Freud to cope with issues involving leadership and authority basic group dynamics concepts. Although his
personal difficulties certainly coloured his perception of the role
of the leader, Freud did recognize the existence and the importance
of such a position in the family matrix as well as its highly significant affect on the individual. He viewed leaders with a monistic,
negative attitude and he did not recognize that there are many
different kinds of leaders. For him there was only one type of
leader - the tyrant, the dreaded primal father. This father is the
family-ideal that negatively affects the individual by displacing
the ego-ideal in his ego. The leader is a person who needs to be
loved by the group members but needs to love no one but himself;
he is absolutely narcissistic. An identification with this leader,
the father, requires considerable ego modification, it determines
the ego-ideal and, subsequently, the quality of the super-ego. The

family shapes the individual by overwhelming the individual's ego by means of its parental ego-ideals. Then, through repression, the individual discards his original oedipal conflicts and develops a conscience. In this manner the individual's standards of conduct, self-control, and general conscience are determined by his emotional attachments to the parents. Social feelings rest on the foundation of these identifications with the parents and on the ego-ideals held in common with them.

Taking a macroscopic view of Freud's position, unjust as this may be, would show that when he elaborates his theory on intrapsychic development, based on biological need and shaped by the instinctual nature of the family, he is on relatively firm ground. His description of the first three years of child development is relatively accepted but he, and psychoanalytic theory in general, has difficulty in moving past this point. He is able to reveal significant insights into individual development to the point where the individual begins to be a social being and needs to interact with others. He is able to tell us how the family shaped and influenced the development of a superego and how it evolves from the ego-ideals and identification that the child makes with both parents. But, throughtout, his formulations indicate that there is no recognition of the fact that the family matrix is in itself a dynamic, viable process with a unique life of its own and one which has properties quite different from those derived from instinctual, biological drives.

Following after Freud, many analysts were aware of this short-coming in psychoanalytic psychology and men like Adler, Sullivan, Moreno, Foulkes, among many others, have attempted to correct this condition. They each proposed an analytic, social psychology to explain social behaviour after the formation of the super-ego, at the end of the oedipal period, and the third year of life. Still, each system lacks a coherent, and perhaps experimental, model to explain the socialization process coming after the third year. The difficulties in bridging the gap existing between the instinctual individual and the social individual remains unconnected. Although it is out of the realm of this particular presentation to discuss in depth any one position, an example of the more current social analytical position is seen by Foulkes.

Foulkes states that his approach to group psychotherapy is dependent on group process and psychoanalytic theories. For him free association is not possible in groups although free-floating discussions do develop. He calls the process of communication, when combined with the relationships in the group, a group matrix. He believes that there is an innate urge for people in groups to communicate and this is a force that brings and holds people together. Within each group there exists a "network" involving individuals with one another and where each is a reflection of the particular dynamics of his group. The leader, since he is not personally involved, is

described as being a conductor of the group somewhat similar to the
conductor of an orchestra. Transference exists but the quality is
different from that established in the one to one analytic situation.
Therapeutic groups develop their own psyche.

This extreme condensation of Foulkes' viewpoint is given to make
the point that present day analysts do use group process ideas. However, these ideas appear to be restricted to describing a process of
group psychotherapy. They do not have a conceptual model to explain
the dynamics of family group interaction and its effect on the individual. Another problem that exists, is that usually the ideas are
based on personal speculation about group process and, as such, do
not indicate the use of available experimental data in this area.
Therefore, if psychoanalysis wishes to study the family as the matrix
of the individual, it has to conceptualize a viable group process
model.

What does experimental group dynamics say about the family as
a moulder of the individual?   Although much has been written about
groups in the past years, the actual emphasis and experimentation
with groups started in the '30s with Kurt Lewin's publications. He
was not too concerned with the internal process of the person although he did accept the possibility of the existence of an unconscious. His experimental field theory concepts developed principles
which germinated the growth of group dynamics. He introduced a new
vocabulary to describe the effect that individuals have on one another. For example, power, the potential ability of one person to
get another to behave in a certain way. His topological psychology
emphasizes tension systems generally ignores the influence of maturation and heredity upon personality development. His significance
for us at this moment, is that he experimentally investigated the
importance of the group effect on the individual and indicated how
the scientific method can be used to study this phenomenon.

By the end of 1930, it was conclusively verified that a group
atmosphere exists and that it can determine the emotional state of
an individual. Conflict within the individual exists because he has
conflict with another individual. Conflict is not a consequence of
an analytic, historical problem reflective of an internal psychological fixation and retarding emotional development. The family as
the matrix, the moulder of the person, has properties of any group as
to its organization, its stability, and its goals. All this is considerably different from the organization, the stability, and the
goals of the individual in it. For the individual the family matrix
is a psychological, perceptual reality and its influence on him is
determined by his immediate psychological state. All this implies,
that to understand how the psychological properties of the family
matrix moulds the individual, we need to know how the individual experiences the qualities of this matrix. The psychotic individual
represents an interesting example of this view. From the observer's

vantage point, the patient is seen as being alone, isolated and withdrawn from others; he is not a member of any group.   A group process view would suggest, that the patient is in a group since his
fantasy life has an internal social climate which is populated with
imaginary people and with whom he is interacting.   The psychotic
patient develops his own family matrix and one to suit his immediate
phenomenological position.

     The principles of group dynamics would define the family matrix
as an atmosphere composed of a dynamic field of forces with discern-
able psychological barriers and tension systems.   The individual's
perception of this psychological atmosphere determines the quality
of his family matrix and, thus,its effect on him.   In this way, the
perceived atmosphere of the family matrix determines the development
of the individual.   The well known classical studies of White and
Lippitt give considerable insights into the effect the various atmospheres have on the individual.   They stress the fact that a group,
a family atmosphere is fundamentally determined by the quality of its
leader.   Generally, leaders develop one of three distinct types of
social climates: the laissez-faire, the autocratic, and the democratic.   Each of these environments give rise to significantly different behaviour patterns in its members.

     In a laissez-faire matrix the leader participates minimally and
he allows the group and the individual complete freedom to make all
decisions.   The leader is a non-participant member of the group and
does not, in any way, direct the process of the group.   (Somewhat
like Foulkes' conductor.)   Research reveals that the individuals in
this setting have minimal group ties, they emphasize play rather than
purposeful activity, and, when they are goal directed, generally
their performance was poor.   Also, it was found that there was little
group cohesiveness and direction among the individuals.   Moving from
research to application, how might such a laissez-faire family matrix
affect the individual?   Apparently, a person growing up in this environment would have extreme difficulty developing purpose and
direction in his life.   He would rather play than work and follow
rather than lead.   Possibly, these individuals would have difficulty
in forming close relationships with others and they would be looking
for an authority to give them structure.

     The autocratic leader is somewhat like Freud's tyrant, one who
is highly controlling and dictatorial.   He allows the individuals
minimal involvement in decision making and in knowing what direction
the group is going.   He is a strict overseer who is distant and does
not get involved with the ongoing task. The individuals in this autocratic matrix exhibit a high degree of animosity, hidden discontent-
ment, and considerable frustration.   They have a loss of individuality
and an increase of dependency.   Group interactions are primarily
hostile, aggressive, and with much scape-goating among members. They
work well, goals are accomplished and there is high purpose but only

as long as the leader is present. The group is cohesive while the
leader is there but disintegrates, members leave, when he is not.
An individual in this family matrix would tend to have a hostile
attitude, be suspicious, dependent on others to make his decisions
and lacking in intimate personal relations.   He would be aggressively self-seeking, stressing results rather than means, be immersed in
here and now solutions to problems and totally consumed with power
struggles.

All of us are most familiar with the democratic atmosphere.
Here the leader allows open discussion, objectively emphasizing fact
and understanding. Goals and objectives are developed by the leader
and the members. Structure is flexible and given by the leader
suggesting alternative ways for coping with problems.   In general,
there is a recognition of the importance of the individual contributions of each member in the group. Relating, co-operating with
others, understanding the social implications and importance of the
means to reach a goal, are all essential conditions of this matrix.
In this family atmosphere, the individual has the nutrients to develop
his potential with spontaneity and with minimal emotional conflict.
He is open to others, available to appreciate intimate contacts and
without defensiveness. Perhaps, what is most significant, is that in
this setting the individual develops self-reliance and confidence
and, can himself, become a group leader.

It is important to understand that there is a place for each of
these atmospheres. We need to be careful not to be too quick to make
any value judgments as to which is best. Each has its place and
particular value, depending on the purpose of the group. For example:
the autocratic system might be best for a work group where the purpose is to attain a specific goal. Some of us believe that a democratic approach is best for child rearing. The essential issue is
that group process theory suggests that there are three distinct
types of family matrices which influence the individual. The dilemma,
as suggested earlier, is that this approach, and many similar to it,
eliminates intrapsychic functioning and developmental states of the
individual. It assumes a point of view which insists on the importance of understanding in the here and now, how the individual receives
and integrates information about the social world and how this information affects behaviour. How can we resolve this dilemma? Can
we use this group approach combined with analytic thinking? Is there
a way to utilize the best of these two seemingly divergent systems?
Let us explore how the two might live together.

To accomplish our purpose it is necessary to use a group process model to describe child development. And, one which does not
do away with the psychoanalytic epigenetic approach but one which,
hopefully, adds to it. To do this it is necessary to consider that
the growth process, from birth on, takes place in a group setting.
In this, the intrapsychic process is influenced by how the child ex-

periences his world as a member of an interacting group. The departure from the traditional approach is made when we speculate how
the child experiences the quality of and his membership position in
the group. From this phenomenonological approach, most child development theories indicate that from birth, the child is in a field
wherein he is totally solipsistic, the center of the universe and,
in a word, the omnipotent leader. For him, he is not simply a member
of the family but its leader. In fact, at first, the child perceives
himself as being the only member, he is the group unto himself. Tension systems are only those which are inside of him and others, outside of him, are yet to be differentiated. Gradually, other members
come into focus but not as separate, distinct members outside of the
child's life space. In his group, from his experience, all group
members start from being a part of him and under his tyrannical control. In the first few weeks, and in the early months of life, this
infant-leader relates to other individuals as though they are there
for him. The other members of his group are there to take care of
him and his needs. We have adopted the custom to call such group
members Mothers. In this situation, this child-leader experiences
his life space as including all others as extensions of himself. As
he gets a few months older and further differentiation of his field
takes place, he experiences a further separation of self from others
but still, he remains the royal leader, the center of his group. At
this point, we might wish to change our topic to: the individual as
the matrix of the family!

As the core member of the group and, with all members being considered Mothers, the group interaction is primarily a one way street.
Up to approximately the third year of life, the child remains the
autocractic leader. Throughout, his omnipotent position is attacked
by other members but more often than not, in the usual course of
events, he sees himself as remaining the leader. During this period,
the usual group process task for the child, is to retain, at all
cost, his leadership position. However, by age three, and with much
resistance, he begins to recognize the autonomy of other individuals
who are in his field. Pressure and tension systems become evident to
him. He feels his power as leader threatened. Then, members of his
group do not respond as quickly or as often, to his every command.
The pressures within the field compel this child-leader to take cog-
nizance of the reality of the unique existence of other members within the family field. Primary narcissism must give way to reality
testing. From the group process position, the first three years of
child development can be seen as a process of not only relinquishing
the childhood narcissistic omnipotence but also as a time where the
child, in gradually accepting the differentiation of the self from
others, must allow others to be distinct members in his autocratic-
ally led group.

At age three, this task is usually accomplished but then a
significant change takes place in the child's territorial field. Up

until this time, the group was his. The gradual separation out of
members was tolerated and allowed. Other members were allowed into
his group on the basis of their acceptance of him as the leader.
There existed no members, or other groups for that matter, outside
of his own group. At three, the child can no longer deny that there
are others who are not members of his group and also, the reality
that there are other groups wherein he is not even a member. This
is a basic trauma for this child-leader especially since he experiences those others, those aliens, as potential invaders, threats to
his territorial space and his leadership position. It is hoped that
all understand that this does not happen all at once, but develops
gradually from approximately nine months of age and reaches its apex
at age three.

With the awareness that there are others who do not respond to
him as the caretaker-mother, members of his group, the child is
forced to cope with new pressures. The outside alien-individuals
are seen as powerful forces that directly tend to undermine his
authority and leadership in his own group. At this time, he experiences others, who are not original members of his group, demanding
entrance into his group. To make matters more difficult for him,
he does not have control over these invaders. Again, in our perception, we call these foreigners Fathers. A father is a stranger,
separate and distinct from the members of the child's group, one who
attempts to enter the child's territorial space without being invited
in. At age three, the child comes into direct conflict with another
authority and one that exists in reality. He then discovers the
weakening in his power. He has little choice about admitting this
new outside member: he is there. For the child this naturally leads
to a struggle for leadership and a painful awareness that this new
member is qualitatively different from the original members of his
group. The role of the father is to compel the child-leader to become cognizant of the reality that there are individuals, and groups,
other than the child's. The father, then, as an outsider of the
child's phenomenal world, represents external reality and authority.
He is there to challenge the child and to compete with him for the
leadership, the possession of the child's group and territorial
field. In a non-pathological situation, this new member is seen as
being very powerful and the child's solution is to align himself with
him, trying a co-leadership position. (Identification with the
aggressor). However, there cannot be a true co-leadership in a group,
since the experimental evidence indicates that in a group, one member
has the most power and, thus, the leadership. In instances where
both members have equal power, the group splinters into two or more
parts unless one member begins to dominate. In this struggle for
power, for the first time, the child must begin to form a truly
"social" interaction. At first he resists giving up his leadership
and this encounter is usually seen during the third and fourth years.
This fight over territorial space and the control of a group, is an
extremely critical event for the child. Its resolution determines

whether he will remain fixed at a three year omnipotent level or will
move on to further growth. It is essential that the new member be
seen as the leader and that he, the child, becomes a member of this
leader's group. If the child denies the existence of this new leader
and remains fixated, if not regressed, as the center of his group,
denying reality, he becomes unable to socialize. Perhaps this may
partially describe an autistic child, one who has an inability to
change group membership characteristics and position under the pressure of reality. This period of time, which most of us recognize
as the oedipal, calls forth the entire interplay of forces involving
competition, aggression, hostility, imitation and other adaptive
mechanisms. Using group process language to explain this social interaction, we would say that the oedipal situation is one which is
more than a struggle for the possession of mother. It is a crucial
battle for control over a group and territorial space wherein mother
is just another part of the overall situation. Further, this view
is not chauvinistic since it also holds true for the female child.

In this formulation the father's position is highly significant
since his role is to separate the child from his unreal, omnipotent
leadership position and primitive symbiotic ties with the care-
takers, mothers. How the child perceives the father-leader's authority will determine the quality of his potential contacts with others.
The father-leader is seen as the one who constructs the group atmosphere. The child from the ages of four to six, experiences and
responds to this leader's atmosphere and gradually gives up his omnipotent position to become a member of this leader's group. Hostilities
continue during this time and, hopefully, by the age of six, the
child begins to realize the reality that the territorial space which
he thought was his, actually never belonged to him. It is traumatic
for all of us to realize that if we are to have an identity, we can
not parasitically use the territory of others but must build and
develop our own psychological fields of power and control. (At this
time I would like to give clinical examples using the conceptualization of child development. However, due to the time limitation,
this must be done at another presentation).

Therefore, in summary, viewing child development from a group
process position, indicates that there is no primal horde from which
the child is trying to escape. A primal horde concept would have us
believe that the child is merely an ordinary member of an existing
group - which in reality is true. As this may be, from the child's
experience, he is the group and its leader. The issue is not the
escape from the group but the ability of the individual to become
differentiated while he is a member of the group. Further, differentiation is determined by the quality of his primary group membership. To a high degree, self-identity is correlated with the individual's position and affiliation within a group. A truly analytic
therapy would work through not only the intrapsychic developmental
traumas but also those related to the individual's loss of power
and center position in the family matrix.

CORRESPONDENCES BETWEEN THE PSYCHODRAMATIC THEORY OF CHILD DEVELOP-

MENT AND THE PROCESSES AND THERAPEUTIC GOALS OF PSYCHODRAMA

Gretel Leutz, MD

Moreno Institute of Psychodrama, Sociometry & Group

Psychotherapy, Uhlandstrabe 8,D-7770 Uberlingen/Bodensee

The psychodramatic method conceived by J.L. Moreno during the first quarter of this century is based upon a philosophic-anthropologic thought that has become increasingly important to new trends of modern psychotherapy.   Starting with the principle of empathic encounter and the phenomena spontaneity and creativity, Moreno undertook two steps revolutionary to psychiatry and psycho-therapy:

1.   He overcame individualistic unipolar thinking by replacing it with intersubjective multipolar approach, and thus laid the foundations for group psychotherapy.

2.   He turned the patient from the object of the scientist into the active subject - the co-participant in psychotherapy.

This theoretical progress during the second quarter of the 20th century consequently led to the development and differentiation of an equally new psychotherapeutic method, namely the triade Psychodrama, Sociometry and Group Psychotherapy.

After some introductory remarks concerning the general meaning of this approach I should like to outline how on the one hand it finds its expression in Moreno's "Spontaneity Theory of Child Develop-ment" and on the other hand in the psychodramatic process.   Further-more, I intend to refer to similar thoughts in modern psychoanalysis as put forward by KOHUT (1975) who, under the impression of a growing number of patients presenting a more or less new type of psychopathology - probably due to changed socio-economic conditions - calls for a new theoretical and practical approach to these patients.

I do hope that the comparison of the psychodramatic approach with Kohut's approach will open a stimulating and fruitful dialogue between representatives of both methods.

I. The intersubjective actional approach to psychotherapy

On this basis Moreno views men in permanent emotional entwinement, i.e. in interpersonal relations as well as in action and interaction.   Since healthy human relations and creative interaction are based on empathic processes, empathy occupies a central position in the psychodramatic method.   Moreno defines empathy as an one way emotional process directed from one human being to another.   In its reciprocal manifestation he refers to it as tele, two-way empathy. Both, empathy and tele, are irreducible phenomena aimed at reality (MORENO 1953 p. 311 - 318).   Empathy is especially evident in the relations of mothers to their babies.   It therefore stands to reason that Moreno gives it special consideration in the context of child-development.

Spontaneity as another irreducible phenomenon is also considered of major importance to child-development.   On the basis of these phenomena MORENO (1944) formulates the "Spontaneity Theory of Child Development".

II. "The Spontaneity Theory of Child Development"

In view of the intersubjective actional approach this theory describes human development as role-development.   MORENO (1964, p.II) states:

"Role-playing is prior to the emergence of the self.   Roles do not emerge from the self, but the self may emerge from roles."

In formulating role-development he (1964 p. IV)also refers to psychodramatic role-theory.   He defines role:

"as the functioning form an individual assumes in the specific moment he reacts to a specific situation in which other persons or objects are involved."

In contrast to psychosocial and sociological role-theories psychodramatic role-theory is not restricted to social roles.   It is broader and comprises all sectors of human life.   With regard to its position in science MORENO (1961, p. 519) says:

"The role-concept cuts across the sciences of man: physiology, psychology, sociology, anthropology and binds them together on a new plane."

Thus he considers the earliest actions of the newborn baby, as for instance the intake of food in interaction with the mother, as enactment of roles.   In speaking of "psychosomatic roles" of the child he avoids the term "sequences of behaviour", because in his view:

"Role is an interpersonal experience and needs usually two or more people to be actualized."   (MORENO 1964, p.184).

MORENO divides Child Development into two major parts, the First and the Second Universe of the Child.

The First Universe of the Child consists of the Matrix of All-Identity and the Matrix of All-Reality.

The Second Universe of the Child is characterized by the breach between fantasy and reality.   The differentiation between real and imagined things begins to take form.   From now on the child learns to live consecutively or simultaneously in both worlds.

The basic difference in role-development during these two major parts of development is expressed by the following statement of MORENO (1960, p. 83):

"There is enactment of role before the level of recognition and recognition of role before the level of enactment."

In the first stage of the First Universe of the Child, the Matrix of All-Identity, the child experiences himself and his environment as one; his actions and interactions with the mother as one event.   He cannot differentiate between himself and another subject or object.   The child experiences the mother as part of himself, carrying out functions, vital to his own life.   She thus becomes his auxiliary-ego.   (As we shall see later the principle of the auxiliary-ego is basic to psychodrama.)

During the Matrix of All-Identity, mother and child are warming-up to various actuality-states and by enacting complementary roles are forming "units of interaction" (LEUTZ 1974, p.40).   On the psychosomatic level the child's actual hunger and the mother's actual production of milk are merging in the process of breast-feeding, forming such a unit of interaction.

Corresponding to the unit of physiological function formed by the mother and child during pregnancy, which is to be considered the matrix of organic development, the unit of empathic interaction of mother and child after birth must be considered the basis of psychic and social development.   MORENO (1964, p. 64), therefore, calls it Matrix of Identity or Social Placenta.   It may be considered the primary model of all future tele-processes.

In the second stage of the First Universe of the Child, the
Matrix of All-Reality, the child begins to differentiate between the
persons and objects around him.   He recognizes representatives of his
environment, for instance his mother, toys, etc., but only when
directly confronted with them.   Now, in addition to the psychosomatic interactions, mainly psychological interdependences are
exerting growing influence on the development.   The child's psychological roles and interactions are predominantly inspired by and expressed in play;   for instance in showing and hiding objects, or in
hiding and seeking of the mother.   In this play her disappearance is
experienced as a loss, yet emotionally she is present non-the-less.
The threatening event is only semi-real.   This fact - as we shall
see later - finds its therapeutic correspondence in the semi-reality
of psychodramatic play.   In hide and seek the child's experience
sharply contrasts with the unsatisfactory experience of other
children whose mothers although physically present are emotionally
absent.

Another characteristic feature of play is the fact that mother
and child in the roles of the players as well as in their common joy
are experiencing each other as equals creating a pleasant state between themselves.   Their common play may be considered the primary
model of the confluence of empathy and spontaneity into creativity.

In both stages of the First Universe of the Child, the Matrix
of All-Identity and the Matrix of All-Reality, the child acts in
roles without knowing them.   As we already know "there is enactment of roles before the level of recognition...." (MORENO 1960,
p.83).

The development goes from primarily psychosomatic roles to roles
of more psychological nature.   They are shaped by the expectancies
and actions of the mother, especially by the manner in which she
enacts her roles in interaction with the child, thus exerting great
influence on his emotional and physical health.   Yet, it should
not be forgotten that the mother's enactment of roles is part of an
interaction in which also the child is actively involved.   In other
words, genetic factors - such as his sturdyness or subtleness - are
influencing his enactment of roles.   However, above all, this enactment is determined by his spontaneity as well as by that of the
mother.   In view of the great significance of spontaneity for the
development of the child within the framework of interdependence
between mother and child as well as for psychodrama-therapy (the
latter still to be discussed) we must now recall the definition of
spontaneity:

"Spontaneity is an adequate response to a new situation or a new
response to an old situation."   (MORENO 1953).

The Second Universe of the Child begins with his experiencing the breach between reality and imagination or reality and fantasy, as Moreno usually says. An increasing ability of abstraction provides the child with a new perception of the world and a new orientation. This is reflected in an equally new relation to the enactment of roles. From now on the child is able to recognize roles before enacting them:

"There is enactment of roles before the level of recognition and recognition of roles before the level of enactment."   (MORENO 1960, p.83).

The child must learn to live in reality as well as in imagination and to change instantaneously from one level to the other. In this he is even more dependent upon his empathy and spontaneity but also upon the empathy and spontaneity of the mother and other persons of reference.

If the child is enacting for the first time a heretofore only observed, i.e. recognized role, it is of utmost importance that the mother is able to engage adequately in an interaction appropriate to the new role of the child. If so, the experience of the mother's adequate and spontaneous reaction enhances the child's confidence in his mother as well as in his own spontaneity. This confidence in turn facilitates the enactment of previously merely recognized roles. Such accomplishments accompanied and mirrored by the mother's proud approval seem to be the primary model of adult self-confidence and self-approval.

I will not end these brief reflections on "The Spontaneity Theory of Child Development" without calling your attention to some cautioning thoughts with which MORENO (1964, p. 70/71) refers to the use of work - and time-saving mechanical devices in child rearing, especially during the First Universe of the Child. He states that the replacement of an auxiliary-ego, the mother, by auxiliary-objects cannot be without serious consequences.   For psychohygenic reasons he suggests that:

"homes and nursery schools should replace many of their auxiliary-object equipment by auxiliary-egos." (MORENO 1964, p.71)

In our time, when numerous children are consuming entertainment in splendid isolation - for instance, in front of television - these warnings and proposals are to be reconsidered.

III. Psychodramatherapy in connection with the Spontaneity Theory of Child Development

The Spontaneity Theory of Child Development and the psycho-

dramatic role-theory are important fundamentals of psychodramatherapy.   Depending on the exigences of various situations psychodrama can be applied in different forms, such as protagonist-centered,
theme-centered and group-centered psychodrama or as sociodrama.   Its
most frequent form, the protagonist-centered psychodrama, focusses
on the problems of one patient or client, we may say, on the individual in the group.   I shall now briefly outline the protagonist-
centered form of psychodrama because it best shows analogies between
psychodrama and the various stages of child development.

In the psychodramatic setting the group is the main locus of
encounter, of intersubjective togetherness, the stage-space the
locus of psychodramatic interaction.

Psychodramatherapy can be applied in terms of conflict-psychology
as well as in terms of self-psychology.   Under the aspect of
conflict-psychology it reproduces and treats actual and genetic conflicts; under the aspect of self-psychology it provides the patient
on the one hand with the resonance of other human beings missing in
his real life, on the other hand - i.e. in case of deficiencies in
the development of the self - with new growth-promoting possibilities.

We shall now look at psychodrama on the basis of our previous
considerations but also in view of the currently much discussed disorders of the self, i.e. in view of narcissistic disorders.

Let us imagine such a patient at the beginning of psychodramatherapy.   He may suffer from the feeling of meaninglessness and
emptiness, possibly combined with ideas of suicide.   Therapy may
represent his last attempt of survival.   In the group he may feel
equally estranged and isolated as in real life.   His tension,
anxiety and rage may cause a locked-up defiant attitude.   In his
retreat and depression he may feel as endangered as an abandoned
helpless baby.

What will happen to him in psychodrama?

Each session goes through three phases, the warming-up, the
interaction play and the closure.   The warming-up of the group as
well as of the protagonist is greatly dependent on the empathy of
the psychodramatist. It is decisive whether - like an adequate
mother during early stages of development of her child - he will be
able to sense the needs of his patient and to behave so that the
latter may become confident and open himself. If a conversation between the patient and the therapist or the patient and another
member of the group sets in, the issue will not be discussed much
longer. Instead, the psychodramatist converts the theme into
spontaneous play, in other words into psychodrama.   Beside events
of outer life also dreams and other intrapsychic events, can be

articulated in psychodramatic action, for instance by means of enactment of fantasy-images.

The beginning enactment of whatever theme, marks the onset of the second phase of the session. Psychodrama is never preconceived. It is unfolded by the spontaneity of the protagonist and shaped by the empathy, spontaneity and creativity of the psychodramatist. We know from child development, that "there is enactment of roles before the level of recognition...." (MORENO 1960, p. 53). The patient having become protagonist instantaneously experiences the following changes:

He no longer feels abandoned in his helpless condition, instead he has become the center of psychodramatic play. He finds himself in a "unit of interaction" with other members of the group, who are now acting according to his spontaneous directives, given by means of the psychodramatic technique of role reversal.

In addition he is also the focus of empathy of spectating members of the group.

In psychodramatic interaction we may well compare the protagonist with a newborn who according to a statement by KOHUT (1977, p.249 "is born powerful because a milieu of empathic self-objects is indeed his self."

We find a direct analogy to this consideration in the psychodramatic double-technique. In applying this technique a member of the group assumes the posture of the protagonist and mobilizes his empathy to the point where the border between ego and non-ego temporarily appears as non-existent; the double is able to verbalize, for instance, feelings of the protagonist, he himself is unable to articulate.

Psychodrama,being play, has the protagonist and the auxiliary egos experience all the portrayed situations under the aspect of semi-reality. Their experience, for instance, of the interaction of the present protagonist with the non-present enacted persons of reference, on the one hand is as real as in reality, on the other it is accompanied by the latent knowledge that the actors are not the real persons and that the played situation will end with the play. The experience of semi-reality in psychodrama corresponds to the important experience the child has in playing hide and seek, with the threatening situation experienced as semi-real.

The psychodramatic play is followed by the third phase of the session, its closure. The group members are still emotionally sensitized by the experience of the protagonist's psychodrama. They now relate to him with greater empathy than before, as initiates into part of his life.

Beside the perhaps pathologic reality of every day life, and
after the experience of the reproduction of an old traumatic reality
in the semi-reality of play, a new reality is now experienced in the
sharing and feedback.   The resonance of the group members to the
protagonist's psychodrama gives him the assurance that, also he, for
a change, is accepted - here and now - by other human beings who not
only are physically present but also emotionally in tune with him.
This further increases confidence.

The spontaneity in psychodrama has an analogous function in
child development; especially at the point of transition from the
First to the Second Universe of the Child.

For psychodrama not only takes place in the semi-reality but
also in the surplus-reality of play.   The surplus-reality comes into existence as soon as imaginings of the protagonist - for instance,
ideas of grandeur or inferiority - are not left in the patient's
imagination, but are converted into psychodramatic action. Fantasies,
future-projections, anxieties are concretized thus confronting the
protagonist with a heretofore non-existent reality, the surplus-
reality of psychodrama.   The enactment of real roles and events in
semi-reality as well as the enactment of imagined roles and fantasies
in surplus-reality are an expression of creativity.   Creativity in
itself always means broadening of a person's horizon and integration
into the world. It gives meaning to life.

IV. Correspondences between Psychodrama Therapy and a New Psycho-analytic Approach

The psychodramatic concept of health is based upon the presence
of empathy and spontaneity.   Both phenomena are prerequisites of
creativity, making life meaningful.   The concept of emotional disease
consequently is characterized by deficiency or loss of empathy and
spontaneity blocking man's creativity (MORENO 1964 Vol. I) therefore coined the term creativity neurosis.

In this context I should like to contend that psychodrama not
only suits the treatment of extra- and intrapsychic conflicts but
especially the therapy of the increasing Disorders of the Self in
the sense of Kohut, in other words, of narcissistic disorders. The
presenting symptoms consist in deficiencies of the phenomena which
characterise the psychodramatic concept of health, namely of empathy,
of spontaneity and of creativity.   These symptoms are felt as lack
of meaning - of interpersonal relations, - of joy, - of action and -
of responsibility.   During the past two decades patients suffering
from these disorders increasingly form the clientele of psychotherapists in industralized Western societies. Among psychoanalysts
KOHUT was the first to point to the fact that instead of the conflict-
ridden Guilty Man of previous decades. Tragic man, suffering from a

meaningless and unfulfilled life, more and more is seeking the help
of psychotherapists. Kohut simultaneously contends that these
patients cannot be helped sufficiently with the theoretical approach
and practical instrumentation of psychoanalysis. With regard to
psychoanalysis KOHUT (1977, p.238) says:

"True, we (psychoanalysts) tried to apply the theories that stood us
in such good stead with regard to the transference neuroses, man in
conflict, Guilty Man, also to this other level of human experience.
But I believe that we have not succeeded - indeed, I believe that by
relying on the classical conceptual armamentarium we could not have
succeeded. Classical theory cannot illuminate the essence of
fractured, enfeebled, discontinuous human existence:.....Dynamic-
structural metapsychology does not do justice to these problems of
man, cannot encompass the problems of Tragic Man."

KOHUT (1977, p.239) therefore calls for a new theory and
practice of psychotherapy adapted to the needs of these patients, for
a Psychology of the Self, the emphasis of which is - "and for good
reasons - more on the growth - promoting aspects".

He furthermore stresses the importance of empathy. According
to KOHUT (1977, page 253).

".....man can no more survive psychologically in a psychological
milieu that does not respond empathically to him, than he can survive
physically in an atmosphere that contains no oxygen. Lack of
emotional responsiveness, silence, the pretence of being an inhuman
computer-like machine which gathers data and emits interpretations,
do no more supply the psychological milieu for the most undistorted,
delineation of the normal and abnormal features of a person's psychological make-up than do an oxygen-free atmosphere and a temperature
close to the zero-point supply the physical milieu for the most
accurate measurement of his physiological responses......"

In view of Kohut's theoretical and practical challenge to
psychoanalysis in particular and to psychotherapy in general as well
as on the basis of decades of psychodramatic experience a future
dialogue of representatives of both methods may prove to be important
and fruitful. In this context I should like to refer again to
Moreno's writings regarding the pathogenetic effects of technical
civilization upon modern man during infancy as well as adulthood.

My presentations are an attempt to prove theoretically the
indication of psychodramatherapy in the treatment of the increasing
incidence of early - or narcissistic disorders. For, in accordance
with its concept of development and of health and by means of its
unique practice psychodrama aims at the development and restoration
of empathy, spontaneity and creativity thus also counteracting the
the traumatizations of our industrial civilisation.

THE APPLICATION OF FAMILY STUDIES TO PSYCHOANALYTIC THEORY

AND THERAPY

Samuel Slipp, M.D.

623 Park Avenue, New York, N.Y.10021, U.S.A.

INTRODUCTION

In recent years considerable development has occurred in extending psychoanalytic theory and technique to include patients
suffering from borderline and narcissistic disorders, depression, and
schizophrenia.   The paper presented today will utilize the knowledge
derived from family studies to understand the interplay between the
intrapsychic, inner world and the real, external world for these kinds
of patients.   The paper will be divided into two sections.   In the
first section, a theoretical position will be elaborated using object
relations theory as a bridge between the intrapsychic and interpersonal worlds.   In the second part of the paper, the treatment of
these sicker patients will be developed.

In his paper "Neurosis and Psychosis", Freud (1924) considered
that the conflict in neurosis was between the ego and the id, while
in psychosis it was between the ego and the external world.   Freud
wrote that in certain severe conditions the patient's ego can prevent
a psychotic break by undergoing ego distortions.   As Modell (1976)
points out, these distortions would be considered today as splitting
and loss of synthetic functions in the ego.   Freud's theoretical
frame of reference primarily focused on the ego's autoplastic response or internal adaptation to the environment.   The formulations
developed in this paper differ as follows: (1) in not focusing
primarily on intrapsychic factors, but on the interplay between the
intrapsychic and the environmental factors;   (2) these theoretical
formulations were drawn from my own direct observation and work, that
has been reported with these patients and their families at New York
University Medical Center and (3) the formulations are based on the

developmental theories of Jacobson, Mahler, Lidz and Winnicott.

The thesis will be developed that the patient's developmental
fixation is not simply the product of intrapsychic forces, as so
many psychoanalytic theoreticians consider.   Instead the family interaction itself interferes with normal ego development.   The thesis
will be presented that the interaction in the family corresponds to
and reinforces the patient's intrapsychic fantasy, his primitive
defenses, and his infantile cognition. The family does not present
an opposing reality to allow for the differentiation of fantasy from
reality. For example, how can a child give up splitting or the
belief that his anger will be destructive (the omnipotence of his
fantasies) if the family itself accepts and utilizes these in their
ongoing relationships? (A fuller description of this process is
contained in my chapter (Slipp 1980) in the book soon to be published
in memory of Edith Jacobson edited by Saul Tuttman).

To sum up my position: a distorted reality creates the distortion in the ego; or stated differently the family interaction,
by its very nature of corresponding to the child's inner reality.
prevents ego development and perpetuates the fixation. A second
thesis is also presented that the pathogenic interaction is not
limited to the mother-child dyad nor to early infancy.   Lidz (1965)
has similarly pointed this out, the trauma is panphasic. Thirdly, the
pathogenic family interaction sustains the developmental fixation
throughout childhood and into adulthood.   Lastly, the patient
gradually introjects this form of family interaction, and sustains
his fixation by establishing the same type of object relations with
others. He will select an object that fits and attempt to shape the
functioning of the object to correspond with the internalized world
of objects he has introjected from the family.

Drawing from my studies of the patient's family, specific
forms of projective-identification were found to occur which are
considered to produce specific forms of pathology. These have been
described in my previous papers for schizophrenia (Slipp, 1973),
depression (Slipp, 1976) and hysteria (Slipp, 1977). Projective-
identification is used by the parents to symbiotically bind and to
exploit the patient for the family's needs.   In treatment, these
patients attempt to recapitulate this process, doing to the therapist
what was done to them. They attempt to repeat the same parent-child
interaction in the transference-countertransference relationship.
The patient similarly uses projective identification to induce the
therapist into thinking, feeling, or behaving in accordance with the
patient's internalized objects. Originally in the patient's family,
external reality corresponded to the patient's intrapsychic processes.
In treatment, the patient attempts to distort, shape, and control
external reality again to fit internal reality. Methods of resolution
of the symbiotic relatedness through the use of the holding environ-

ment and the judicious interpretation of the countertransference are discussed.

Before proceeding into my theoretical work, a brief review of projective-identification is necessary, since it is a core concept used throughout this paper. The term was first introduced by Melanie Klein (1946) to describe the "paranoid-schizoid" phase of infantile development that she postulated. In order for the infant to preserve the good mother introject, which is essential for the ego's survival, the aggressive "bad" parts of the self are split off and projected into another person. Thus the "bad object" which threatens to destroy the ego from within, is projected out into another person so that it is possible to "control and take possession of the object."

Klein attributed these threatening bad objects to the death instinct, which I have not accepted. Also I have not used her developmental schema which is based on pathology, i.e. the schizoid and paranoid positions. My own preference has been for Mahler's (1968) developmental phases based on the separation-individuation process. In addition, I do not consider that it is always the bad part of the self or object that is split off and placed into another. For example, in depression I consider it is the good self that is projected by the parent into the child and the parent lives vicariously through identification with the child's achievement.

To summarize, projective-identification is used here, as in my previous work, to include: (1) a defense involving interpersonal relations; (2) a primitive (symbiotic) form of object relations; (3) a form of alloplastic manipulation and control of another; (4) a method of inducing pathology in another, and (5) as responsible for one type of countertransference, which has been termed objective or inductive. Other characteristics of projective-identification are: ego boundaries need to be fluid, so that an aspect of the self can be put into another. In addition, pressure is exerted to induce the object to think, feel, or behave in congruence with the projection. This form of manipulation and control of the object is accomplished through nonverbal (voice tone or bodily or facial gesture) forms of communication usually. For example, a narcissistic patient may speak in a monotonous unrelated tone of voice which may bore, distance, or put the therapist to sleep, as if the therapist were nonexistent. A close continuing connection with the object needs to exist so that the evoked behaviour in the object can be re-internalized through identification. In pure projection, firm ego boundaries exist, and the other is only perceived in terms of the inner feelings and images that are transferred, without efforts made to induce or control the other's behavior, feelings or thoughts.

THEORETICAL ISSUES

I shall first consider the topic of schizophrenia, and in

particular the issue of developmental fixation that results in the
lack of establishment in the ego of self and object constancy. Jacobson (1967) considers this lack as due to an insufficient neutralization of aggression, while others have considered that constitutionally
these patients have been born with a greater amount of aggression.
Both these explanations are on a purely intrapsychic level. Winnicott
(1965) on the other hand, explains this phenomenon in the interpersonal sphere, i.e. the interaction between mother and infant. When
the mother's responsive sensitivity to the infant's needs is "good
enough", the infant is able to maintain the illusion of omnipotent
control over the mother. This creates sufficient trust for the infant to internalize the good mother function. The infant then can
give up some control and utilizes a "transitional object" such as a
blanket or teddy bear. This transitional object serves as a substitute mother, to maintain the fantasy of fusion with mother and to
defend against separation anxiety. Further individuation and
separation occurs when the mother provides a "holding environment"
that contains the infant's aggression without retaliation or abandonment. Thus the child experiences that his hatred does not destroy
the object; enabling him to relinquish his omnipotence, and to
learn that the object has a separate existence. The child can thus
accept the object as constant and himself as separate and constant
also. When the mother is unresponsive during early infancy, Winnicott considers the above sequence of normal development does not
occur. These patients then attempt to recapitulate this mother-
infant relationship in treatment. They attempt to gain omnipotent
control over the analyst. There is a lack of differentiation between the self and the therapist, a predominence of projective-
introjective processes and the therapist is experienced not as a
separate individual, but as a gratifying good or non-gratifying bad
part object. In treatment Winnicott considers the therapist
functions as a "transitional object" and provides the necessary
"holding environment" to contain aggression that eventually leads to
self and object constancy, growth and development.

Khan (1963) extended Winnicott's usage of the term "holding
environment" from being limited to infancy to include the overall
caretaking functions of the parents in relation to their developing
child. Lidz's (1965) studies of families indicated that in schizophrenia, the trauma is also not limited to early childhood, but is
panphasic, and continuing throughout childhood. These families,
Lidz noted were unresponsive to the child's needs for nurturance
and personality development, and use the child to complete one of
the parent's lives. In the families of schizophrenics we studied
(Slipp, 1973) a specific form of family interaction was found which
was not responsive to the child's developmental needs, but to the
needs of the parents to maintain their marital relationship. The
empathic responsiveness of the mother to the child's needs, and the
provision of a "holding environment" to work through the child's

omnipotent destructive fantasies, as described by Winnicott, did not
occur.   Instead the child's omnipotent destructive fantasies are reinforced on a continuing basis by the parents' fear of the destruct-
iveness of their own aggressive impulses.   The parents were unable
to express and deal with their aggression.   Aggression was seen as
destructive to their self-esteem, survival, and to the marital
relationship.   Projective identification in these families occurred
with one or both parents projecting their bad self or bad parental
image into the child who was scapegoated.   Thus aggression could
be denied towards the spouse, who remained idealized as the good
object.   Essentially in these families the child learns that each
person's self-esteem and survival is determined by the other's behavior.   This has been termed by me as the "Symbiotic Survival
Pattern."   In the "Symbiotic Survival Pattern" the family reinforces
the child's onmipotent fantasies, or as Piaget (1954, 1963) terms this,
the preoperational, magical thinking of the child.   Piaget noted that
the young child uses the concept of magical participation in the
existence of external objects.   Objects are seen as coming and going
as a result of the child's own actions, schemata, wishes, or temporal
contiguity.   Objects are not seen as having an independent existence
outside the child's perception or action, and thus the child feels
in magical control of and responsible for their existence.   The family
continues to reinforce preoperational or omnipotent thinking, since
the child learns he is indeed made to feel responsible for the continued existence of the object, having to feel, think, and behave
in a certain fashion.   This prevents the differentiation of self from
other, and perpetuates fixation at the symbiotic phase of development.
It also renders each person both omnipotent and helpless, needing to
control the other as well as oneself.   Since this form of symbiotic
binding involves disqualifications and control of the patient's perceptions, thinking, feeling, and behavior;   the greatest amount of
disruption occurs in the ego of the child.

     Turning now to depressive illnesses, again one finds that most
psychoanalytic theories also stress intrapsychic causality.   In
Jacobson's (1971) theory of depression, she views intrapsychic
mechanisms as the primary etiological factor.   The strength of the
powerful parental image in the patient's superego is attributed by
her to the child's omnipotent fantasies.   Through the process of
splitting, division of the parental object occurs intrapsychically,
with the powerful parent incorporated in the superego and the deflated worthless parent incoporated into the self image.   In addition,
Jacobson considers the helplessness of the depressive as arising from
the intrapsychic idealization of the self, resulting in the child's
inability to live up to the high standards that he demands of himself.
In our studies of families with a depressive patient (Slipp, 1976), I
found in actuality that one parent was overly powerful and dominant
while the other parent was indeed weak and deflated.   Thus the actual
external familial power structure reinforced the child's intrapsychic

process of splitting. These findings are also described in the
clinical work of Cohen, Fromm-Reichmann, et.al. (1954) and the research of Lewis et.al. (1976). In addition it was noted the dominant
parent actually pressures excessively for achievement. Through projective identification of the good self image into the child, the
dominant parent can live vicariously through the child's achievements
and sustain his or her self esteem. The child functions as the
"saviour" for the family's social prestige. At the same time, the
dominant parent projects his bad, non-achieving self into the weak
parent, who is demeaned. A double introjection by the patient occurs,
with the dominant, punitive parent becoming incorporated in the
superego and the deflated weak parent in the bad self image of the
ego. The child internalizes the actual external pressure for
achievement, which become part of his good, achieving self image
(Jacobson's wishful self image). However, I also noted that in
addition to the pressure for achievement overtly, there is a covert
and simultaneous message to fail. Gratification for achievement is
withheld by the dominant parent, who is at the same time competitive
and jealous of the child's achievement and needs to maintain domina-
tion and control. The child is thus exploited and prevented from
becoming independent and strong by what I have termed the "Double-
Bind over Achievement". Instead the child is trapped by this no-win
dilemma; he loses whether he wins or fails. This double bind I
feel is responsible for the depressive's pervasive sense of helplessness. The rage that the child experiences can be expressed intrapsychically through masochistic self-punishment or depression. The
conflict can also be expressed interpersonally through an oppositional form of acting out. By partial compliance to both succeed and
fail messages, the patient can begin to achieve, but then withhold
gratification from the dominant parent by self-defeating actions.
In this way anger is expressed in a passive aggressive fashion and
some autonomy is preserved by the patient.

In my studies of families of women with hysterical and borderline personality (Slipp, 1977), I found that the fathers were
emotionally seductive in order to manipulate and control their
daughters to gratify the father's narcissistic needs. These fathers
used splitting and projective identification and projected the good
idealized maternal image into the daughter, and the bad maternal
image into the wife. The wife is then degraded and victimized,
tending   withdraw and to abandon her protective and nurturant
maternal role. The daughter thus complies to the father's demands
for a gratifying mother, and serves as a "go-between", to preserve
her parents marriage. (This family constellation involving an
Oedipal triumph was very accurately described by Freud (1905) in the
case of Dora). A dominant-submissive power structure thus was found
to exist, much like depressive and obsessive families. In addition,
there was a pervasive collusion among family members to deny perception, thoughts and feelings around certain emotional and sexual

areas, as well as a taboo against direct verbal expression. Because of this as well as the family's responsiveness to physical illness, there is a tendency to use somatic expression of conflict through conversion symptoms to transmit needs and emotional distress. Usually there is also a fantasy of rescue by a nurturant adult. Identification with both parents occurs, and the hysteric may shift back and forth between the manipulative, seductive, and exploitive role of the father or the role of the masochistic victim, like that of the mother. The more the daughters seem to identify with the dominant father, the more a hysterical personality seemed to develop. The more the daughters identified with the negatively perceived and victimized mother, the more a hysteroid, borderline personality evolved with depressive and paranoid features. Lidz (1965) found similar dynamics in the families of female schizophrenic patients, however in our study these patients were at the most diagnosed as borderline.

TREATMENT

Freud (1910) first mentioned countertransference in his paper, "The Future Prospects for Psychoanalytic Therapy", viewing it as a resistance in the analyst, interfering with the capacity for understanding the patient. Countertransference was defined as the analysts unconscious transference to the patient, based on his own unresolved intrapsychic conflicts and unconscious fantasies. Winnicott (1949) broadly expanded this traditional definition of countertransference, to include all the reactions of the analyst to the patient. He felt that with more disturbed, non-neurotic patients, countertransference difficulties were often based on objective reactions to the patient and not simply due to intrapsychic conflicts within the analyst. As a further development, Heimann (1950) recommended the use of countertransference as a therapeutic tool, that might serve as a better method for understanding the patient's unconscious than the analyst's conscious judgements. Little (1951) felt that with severely disturbed patients countertransference feelings could not be avoided and were always present. The countertransference that was provoked through projective-identification was often a repetition of the patient's relations with their parents. Little recommended admitting and interpreting the countertransference to the patient, after the analyst had resolved them for himself as far as he could.

Subsequently two papers were published by Heinrich Racker (1953, 1957) describing how the transference and countertransference each influenced the other. Not only did the patient's transference distort the perception of the analyst, but the analyst's countertransference also distorted his perception of the patient. In turn, this may influence the image that the patient has of the analyst. Racker further pointed out that if the analyst rejects his empathic responses and identifies with and acts out the internal objects that the patient projects into him, the analyst again recreates the patient's past trauma, and reinforces the patient's pathological fixation.

Bion (1959, 1970) pointed out the importance of the therapist serving as a "container" for the patient's projective-identifications. This provided the patient with the necessary safety and security essential for further growth. Balint (1952, 1968) also emphasized that during periods in which the patient was regressed, the therapist needed to accept and experience the patient's projective-identifications without acting them out or even interpreting them. Searles (1965) also considers that it is essential with more disturbed, non-neurotic patients to establish a controlled therapeutic symbiosis between the analyst and the patient. Searles considers that the ability to be open to the patient's projective-identifications; to function genuinely as a part of the patient and yet be separate enough to observe the analyze; allows the patient to differentiate self and object representations and to individuate. Similarly Kohut (1977) stresses the importance with narcissistic patients of their developing idealizing and mirror transferences, and the need for the empathic responsiveness of the therapist.

In working with narcissistic patients some controversy has arisen regarding the importance of interpreting the patient's aggression as against the holding environment. Modell (1976) indicates both are important, but that the timing of each is crucial for successful treatment. During the first phase, the narcissistic patient attempts to maintain the illusion of self-sufficiency by his nonrelatedness. Modell terms this phase "the cocoon". Others have used other descriptions, i.e. Volkan (1973) the "plastic bubble"; Guntrip (1968) a "sheet of glass"; while Giovacchini (1975) and Green (1975) have noted how the therapist may be treated as an inanimate object or as nonexistent. Kernberg (1975) reports that narcissistic patients may project their omnipotence into the analyst, idealize him, and fuse with him in the transference. Alternating with this, the patient may project devalued aspects of the self into the analyst, and attempt to demean him and render him helpless. Modell (1976) points out that the therapist needs to provide a holding environment without interpretations during this phase, since the patient does not have sufficient separateness essential for a therapeutic alliance. The therapist functions as a "transitional object", serving as an idealized object who is accepting and empathic toward the patient. This permits sufficient safety to permit further ego consolidation. In the middle phase of treatment, the emergence of rage occurs, which allows for further differentiation and the development of a therapeutic alliance. The therapist can then become more confronting and interpret the patient's grandiosity and fantasies of self-sufficiency. The third phase approximates a classical case with the emergence of a transference neurosis, although there is still the potential for regression to occur.

Langs (1976) offers some recommendations for detecting the therapist's countertransferential reactions. These may consist of uncharacteristic behavior with a patient, incorrect interventions, or deviations from the analytic framework. In addition cues may be obtained from the patient's associations, dreams, unexplained resistances, acute disturbances, symptoms, regressions, acting out, or disruption of the therapeutic alliance. Langs recommends self-analysis by the therapist to become aware of the countertransference. When derivative material from the patient suggests the countertransference, the therapist can acknowledge the patient's perception as correct thereby sensitively and honestly supporting the patient's reality testing.

Using our understanding derived from family studies, the countertransference may be helpful in determining the form of projective-identification the patient has employed. (This is the case only if the countertransference is due to the inductive or objective form and not due to the therapist's pathological transference). The patient will either attempt to induce the therapist into the omnipotent parental figure, or do to the therapist what the parent did to the patient. This provides the therapist with important clues concerning the transference and for reconstructing genetic material. By the therapist being open to experiencing what the patient probably felt as a child, the therapist can gain empathic understanding and consolidate the therapeutic alliance with the patient. In this instance the therapist processes the projective-identification differently than the patient. The therapist is not taken over by them nor does he act then out. Instead the therapist brings them out into the open for verbal discussion, to allow for emotional catharsis, understanding, and working through. Thus the present, here-and-now relationship with the therapist is not a repetition of the past, nor of other object relations that had served to reinforce the patient's pathological fixation. This allows for growth and change to occur.

Finally, once the patient overcomes his own resistance to change, it is important for the therapist to be aware that others in the patient's family may manifest resistance to his changing. Since the patient may have been the container for the projective-identifications of other family members, to disown their own conflict by placing it into the patient, the homeostatic balance of the family may become disrupted. Thus at the point where the patient is undergoing change, the therapist may need to recommend treatment for a spouse or other members of the family. This will prevent disruption of the patient's treatment or the development of pathology in another family member. The family member may be referred to another therapist, or may be brought in for conjoint family therapy.

SUMMARY

The contributions of family studies to the understanding of
intrapsychic and interpersonal dynamics is developed. Projective-
identification was found to be the primary mechanism used in the
family for the induction of pathology in sicker patients such as
borderline and narcissistic disorders, depression, and schizophrenia. The type of pathology that evolves corresponds to the
specific form of projective-identification by the parents of
certain split introjects into the patient. In schizophrenia this
is the parent's bad self or bad parental object, in depression the
good self, and in hysteria and borderlines the good parental object.
In treatment a recapitulation of this original parent-child interaction, involving projective-identification becomes manifest again
in the transference-countertransference interaction. The patient
attempts to establish a symbiotic relationship by attempting to
induce the therapist into feeling, thinking, or behaving in ways that
correspond to the patient's split internalized object. This is the
same mechanism that the patients experience with their parents. In
the patient's family, external reality correspond to the patient's
intrapsychic fantasies and cognition, resulting in fixation. In the
treatment situation, as well as in other important relationships, the
patient attempts to shape and control his external reality to fit
his internal reality. This serves to perpetuate the fixation. In
treatment, the therapist first provides a "holding environment"
which contains the patient's projective-identifiaations. Then when
sufficient differentiation of the self has occurred, and a therapeutic alliance established, interpretation of defenses, countertransference, as well as the transference is possible. In this way
the patient experiences an interaction which does not perpetuate
the fixation, is different than his own and his parents' reactions,
separates fantasy from reality, allows for individuation, ego
growth, and for change to occur.

BIBLIOGRAPHY

Balint, M. (1968) The Basic Fault, London, Tavistock.

Balint, M. (1952) Primary Love and Psychoanalytic Technique, New
York, Liveright.

Bion, W.R. (1970) Attention and Interpretation, London, Tavistock.

Bion, W.R. (1959) Experiences in Groups, New York, Basic Books.

Cohen, M.B.,Baker, G., Cohen, R.A., Fromm-Reichmann, F., and Weigart
E.V. (1954) An intensive study of 12 cases of manic-depressive
psychosis, Psychiatry, 17; 103-138.

Freud, S. (1924) Neurosis and Psychosis, Standard Edition 19: 149-153, London, Hogarth Press.

Freud, S. (1910) The future prospects of psycho-analytic therapy, Standard Edition 11: 141-151, London, Hogarth Press.

Freud, S. (1905) Fragment of an analysis of a case of hysteria, Standard Edition 7: 3-122, London, Hogarth Press.

Giovacchini, P.L. (1975) Self projections in the narcissistic trans-ference, International Journal of Psychoanalytic Psychotherapy 4: 142-166.

Green, A. (1975) The analyst, symbolization and absence in the analy-tic setting (On changes in analytic practice and analytic experience) International Journal of Psychoanalysis 56: 1-22.

Guntrip, H. (1968) Schizoid Phenomena, Object Relations, and the Self, New York, International Universities Press.

Heimann, P. (1950) On countertransference, International Journal of Psychoanalysis 31: 81-84.

Jacobson, E. (1971) Depression: Comparative Studies of Normal, Neurotic, and Psychotic Conditions, New York, International Universities Press.

Jacobson, E. (1967) Psychotic Conflict and Reality, New York, Inter-national Universities Press.

Kernberg, O.F. (1975) Borderline Conditions and Pathological Narcissism, New York, Jason Aronson.

Khan, M. (1963) The Privacy of the Self, New York, International Universities Press.

Klein, M. (1946) Envy and Gratitude and Other Works, 1946-1963, New York, Delacorte Press.

Kohut, H. (1977) The Restoration of the Self, New York, International Universities Press.

Langs, R. (1976) The Therapeutic Interaction, New York, Jason Aronson.

Lewis, J.M., Beavers, W.R. Gossett, J.T., and Phillips, V.A. (1976) No Single Thread; Psychological Health in Family Systems, New York, Brunner Mazel.

Lidz, T., Fleck, S., and Cornelison, A.R. (1965) Schizophrenia and the Family, New York, International Universities Press.

Little, M. (1951) Countertransference and the patient's response to it, International Journal of Psycho-Analysis 32: 32-40.

Mahler, M.A. and Furer, M. (1968) On Human Symbiosis and the Vicissitudes of Individuation, Vol. 1, New York, International Universities Press.

Modell, A.H. (1976) "The holding environment" and the therapeutic action of psychoanalysis, Journal of the American Psychoanalytic Association 24: 285-307.

Piaget, J. (1963) The Child's Conception of the World, Patterson, N.J., Littlefield Adams.

Piaget, J. (1954) The Construction of Reality in the Child, New York, Basic Books.

Racker, H. (1957) The Meanings and uses of countertransference, Psychoanalysis Quarterly 26: 303-357.

Racker, H. (1953) A contribution to the problem of countertransference, International Journal of Psycho-Analysis 34: 313-324.

Searles, H.F. (1965) Collected Papers on Schizophrenia and Related Subjects, New York, International Universities Press.

Slipp, S. (1980) The conflict of power and achievement in depression in forthcoming book to be published in memory of Edith Jacobson, edited by S. Tuttman, New York, International Universities Press.

Slipp, S. (1977) Interpersonal factors in hysteria; Freud's seduction theory and the case of Dora, Journal of the American Academy of Psychoanalysis, 5: 359-376.

Slipp, S. (1976) An intrapsychic-interpersonal theory of depression, Journal of the American Academy of Psychoanalysis 4: 389-409.

Slipp, S. (1973) The symbiotic survival pattern: A relational theory of schizophrenia, Family Process, 12: 377-398.

Volkan, V. (1973) Transitional fantasies in the analysis of a Narcissistic Personality, J. Amer. Psychoanalytic Assoc. 21: 351-376.

Winnicott, D.W., (1965) The Maturational Process and the Facilitating Environment, New York, International Universities Press.

Winnicott, D.W. (1949) Hate in the countertransference, International Journal of Psycho-Analysis, 30: 69-74.

FOULKES' NETWORK THEORY AND THE SCOPE OF GROUP ANALYSIS IN FAMILY THERAPY

Juan Campos-Avillar, M.D., Prof. Em.

Psychoanalyst and Group Analyst graduated from the
P.G.C.M.H. (New York)
Paseo San Gervasio 30, Barcelona - 22, Spain

There are very few group psychotherapists indeed that have contributed to the blooming modern development of group family therapy. There is an exception though, a true pioneer in the field. His main interest and publications in the development of Group-Analytic Therapy have resulted in that his ideas on family are not as well known by family therapists as they would deserve. I am talking of S.H. Foulkes. As early as the end of the forties he was already interviewing families conjointly for diagnostic as well as therapeutic purposes. It took him two steps, though, to overcome prejudices that had been imbued in him by his psychoanalytic training:
    1) To see people - strangers - jointly in a group;
    2) To see people - relatives with blood ties between them - at the same time and as a group.

His work with strangers, in a small group, led him to discover Group Analysis. The military hospital at Northfield and later The Maudsley, a teaching hospital, were to be the seeds of "therapeutic communities" the one and of the most creative schema on research, treatment and training in group psychotherapy the other. His work with families, although limited to family interviewing, was creative inasmuch as it led him on the one hand to conceptualize his "Network Theory of Neurosis" - one of the cornerstones of Group-Analytic Theory - and on the other to inspire his followers - mostly Robin Skynner - to set up the Introductory Course in Family Therapy, whose offspring is the Institute of Family Therapy (London).

The courage it takes for a psychoanalyst to move from the transferential sanctuary of the psychoanalytic situation into the open arena of conjoint family therapy and to overcome the ideological

resistances built up through his psychoanalytical training and
practice - mostly private practice - is something to be admired.
But to do so singlehanded, without the support of a group, and not to
fall into the trap of "systems" forgetting about the unconscious,
takes the stamina and the power of thinking that only very few men
in a century have. It is my tenet that the way - the analytic way -
that goes from psychoanalysis to family therapy cannot be taken
safely unless one uses the knowledge, the expertise and experience,
the stepping stone that Group Analysis provides. I shall try to
show this in the present paper and where it leads to.

The Coordinates of Therapy

All psychotherapy, all mental treatment - the one that uses
psychological means for treating the ills of individuals and groups-
is rooted in interaction, the interpersonal influence through expanding communication, of people belonging to diametrically differentiated social categories: therapists and patients, the ones who treat
and the ones who are being treated. In ancient days the ones who
treated were shamans, kings or priests, but they doctored the sick
of the tribe just the same.

With recognized expert knowledge and specialized training
today's professionalized psychotherapists are inclined to disregard
the fact that they belong to this part of the "tribe" that has been
invested with the "power to cure". The rest of the community, of
course, go to them for help when under distress, when they do not
find meaning for what happens to them and when they no longer know
what to do about it. That therapy - psychoanalysis, group therapy,
family therapy - is a valid response to treat the ills of the unsound
is a cultural artifact, an ideological position that changes - in
content - throughout times, but nevertheless it gives power to those
who are entitled to treat.

In this sanctioned role as expert it is the therapist who is to
set the limits of the therapeutic situation, the one to decide who is
to be in and who to be out of its boundaries, what is to be done and
said or not said and how within this social enclave. In this regard
modern psychotherapy does not much differ from traditional ways.
What was done then in the name of religion, superstition, for fear
of ghosts or to appease gods, today we do in the name of science.
The barrier between theory and practice, between technique and art
in psychotherapy is a very thin one and still less clear is which
one comes first. As a rule major theoretical breakthroughs have
followed technical innovations that, by the way, were discovered
by the patient more frequently than by the doctor. That was the
case for example with Freud's "free association", it holds true for
Foulkes' "free-floating discussion" and I would not be surprised
if it did not also for many a technique on which hangs the theorising
in modern family therapy. Witnessing the wide array of competing
theories and techniques in that field, contemplating the battles

between "psychoanalytical purists" and "systems purists", one cannot but wonder if family therapy is yet today something more than
a practice in search of a theory.

No doubt the insights gained from psychoanalysis are to be of
help towards theory building in family, as will be the ones that
come from systems, but jumping straight from individual dynamics
into systems without passing through the group will be helpful?
The tribe of therapists, the supposed agents of change, have their
own rules on how not to change themselves. Institutionalized theoretical blinkers more often than not lead them into blind alleys
and foreclose innovations which could have been of great utility.
That is exactly what happened to Freud in his battle with the family
business. After he had already discovered that "the natural opposition of the relatives to the treatment - an opposition which was
bound to appear sooner or later" - was so unsurmountable that it
provoked one of the most disheartened remarks of his career: "As
regards to the treatment of relatives (of patients in analysis) I
must confess myself utterly at loss, and I have in general little
faith in any individual treatment of them" (Freud, 1912), coming
to this paradoxical conclusion: "The external resistances which
arise form the patient's circumstances, from his environment (the
patient's relatives) are of small theoretical interest but of the
greatest practical importance" (Freud, 1917). For a person to whom
the theoretical understanding of clinical facts were of paramount
importance it is amazing that he could blatantly discharge these so
prominent clinical findings. How to explain that mishap without
entering deeply into Freud's biography and the vicissitudes of the
"Cause of Psychoanalysis" would be difficult. One cannot but wonder
what stopped Freud at the point of becoming the first family therapist after having treated Little Hans and spelled out in Totem and
Taboo the postulates that could have laid the foundations for a
systematic family theory and therapy. As Anthony points out in his
History of Group Psychotherapy, he had already stated: 1) that there
is a family psyche whose psychological processes correspond fairly
closely to those of the individual; 2) that there is a continuity
of emotional life in the family psyche from one generation to the
next, and, 3) that the mysterious transmission of attitudes and
feelings through generations is the result of unconscious understanding that makes the latent psychic life of one generation accessible to the succeeding one. Those principles were the cornerstone
for building a dynamic and developmental family psychopathology.
What then really stopped Freud at that critical point? Anthony suggests that it was Freud's intense interest in individual intrapsychic
conflicts - his own - that superseded everything else. By the same
token it could be said that they were his family problems or the
ones of his plexus - the psychoanalytic tribe - that impeded him to go
on. Nobody will ever know, but what is certain is that this
attitude of Freud's, addressed at keeping unpolluted the transference situation of psychoanalysis, was the base for the psycho-

analytic prejudice, which foreclosed for many years the psychoanalytic exploration of the family group.

Freud's views have to be contrasted with those of one of his
followers, Foulkes (1975), a few years later: "However, the psycho-
diagnostic value of those meetings (family sessions) can hardly be
overrated; while fascinating from a theoretical point of view they
are of great importance also from a point of view of a practical
method". Foulkes' fascination with the theme was the basis for his
Network Theory of Neurosis. However, he always thought that in
order to transform this knowledge into a powerful therapeutic tool,
some preconditions had to be achieved: "I have become more and more
convinced that the patient whom I see is himself only one symptom
of a disturbance which concerns a whole network of circumstances and
people. It is this network ... which is the real operational field
for effective and radical psychotherapy. Perhaps it would be more
correct to say it will be so in a future. This would be group
therapy in a natural group with the persons primarily involved in
the conflict themselves as members of the therapeutic group. Under
present circumstances it is very difficult to put such a multipersonal therapy into operation. It would be necessary for this work
that it could be shared by a team of therapists who would have to be
trained in both psychoanalysis and group analysis".

I am one of this generation of people that having come after
Freud and after Foulkes had a chance to be trained in psychoanalyis
as well as in group analysis. I fortunately took both. To my
disgrace however, in the country where I live and work neither the
State not the Compulsory Health Insurance System as yet consider
mental health and the training of mental health professionals to be
of their concern. Being mostly in private practice and private
research and teaching, my views and my experience will be tinted
by those unfortunate environmental circumstances, which, by the way,
are not by any means the best ground for the analytic treatment of
the family group. As a matter of fact, most of family therapy as
well as of group psychotherapy in contrast to individual psychoanalysis has developed from agencies, low-cost clinics, or hospitals
and were not privately paid for by the patients.

The Family and The Doctor: Perspectives of the treatment of the
family group.
      The family physician, this old institution that modern health
systems are trying helplessly to revive, was the primordial model
of family-doctor relations. All the tradition of medical care has
gone that way. The link between them, the cornerstone of that relationship, was the actual or possible sick patient. For the family,
their G.P., their family physician, is the one to whom they go for
help when one of their members is ill or who to ask for advice in
matters of health. For the doctor, on the contrary, his patient is
the one who he is treating and the rest are just the relatives. In

family therapy the nature of the relation patient-doctor, and
family-doctor becomes radically changed: the individual patient
vanishes or fades away while the family, as a whole, becomes the
patient - that is to say the basic unit for diagnosis and therapy.

This movement, from a conception of therapy centred in the
family implies a change that is to be resisted by both parties. It
means a threat to the old doctor as well as to the new patient: the
family itself. As far as the doctor is concerned, this movement goes
counter to what has been so far the "normal" development in medicine,
in psychiatry, in psychoanalysis and of all those new helping professions which were inpsired in the clinical medical model. The
tendency was towards polarization, to specialize progressively into
smaller fields of activity and in techniques each day more concrete.
To devote oneself to family therapy implies a de-specialization,
a re-generalization, to start with for which the professional is not
conceptually nor technically prepared and that on top threatens his
professional identity. For the family, this new outlook means also
a great change; unexpectedly it finds itself under the focus of
medical attention and, having lost the patient where they identified
their problem, is made to feel itself sick when treated by the doctor
that way.

Most likely this change in orientation will have serious implications in the organization and functioning of professionals and
services in the medical care of the future. For the time being the
most affected have been those which belong to the Psy-club and mostly
the ones in the field of mental health and social services. Balint's
(1957) observations regard the doctor's responses as an organizer
of the patient's offer of illness are applicable pari pasu at the
level of the family. There we know that the sheer medical examination, the labelling of the illness, the prescription of medication
for the symptoms offered by the patient is the most important single
fact in determining the doctor-patient relation, and the relation of
the patient with his own illness. The medical diagnosis and treatment of the identified patient offered by the family will equally
condition this patient's career as well as the attitudes the family
adopts regarding problems of communication, interaction and understanding or misunderstanding that concerns the whole family, and
of which the symptoms of the patient and the patient as a symptom
are result and proof of a failed attempt of resolution and expression.
Depending on the doctor's orientation and the way he understands and
reacts to the family problem, is how the family will try to solve
their own problem.

My purpose here is to examine the nature of the family-therapist
relation regardless if only one of the members is in therapy - in
case of individual psychotherapies or of group psychotherapies in
stranger groups - or if it is the whole family as a group which is
in treatment. My starting point is to consider the family network,

the <u>plexus</u> of the patient as S.H. Foulkes used to say - as a life
group that functions and reacts as a group, and my conviction that
when such a powerful change agent as the therapist impinges upon
the group, the latter cannot but react as a group. Family therapy
in a broad sense as understood by me, has as its function to clarify
with the aid of an expert and to work through a problem that was
previously defined by the family in terms of illness and health and
that affects the whole family. This problem, however, is not seen
with the same eyes from the perspective of the family as from that
of the therapist.

<u>The Family Illness Behaviour</u>
    When a family looks for a therapist, rarely if ever it thinks
that it is the family who is sick. They are in need of help, but it
is one of its members who is unwell, who is sick, or who makes them
all sick. He is the one who suffers and the others who suffer for
or because of him are just the relatives. In biological medicine
and dealing with just bodily ills, that may be true, or nearly true.
When we are dealing with "mental illness", or the functional aspects
of medical care, the matter turns out to be much more complicated.
The patient - diagnosed as such by the family - is the one who confronts them with a problem of behaviour. He doesn't know, nor does
the family, what has gone wrong with him. Self and mutual understanding and "common sense" has been lost. He is nuts, crazy, a
lunatic or just odd, has his or her ways, is nervous or even plainly
bad or perverse. He feels what he shouldn't, he doesn't think
straight, and he says or does things which are not proper. In sum,
he does not behave.

    These ugly patients do not inspire the same sort of sympathy
than the poor ones who are just plain and honestly sick. What those
of his kin expect from the doctor, what they want from him, is to
bring the patient back to his senses, make him behave, and if nothing
can be done since he is plainly crazy, grant the family permission to
disown him as a member, put him away, and even if it is to put him
into hospital, to get rid of him. In traditional psychiatry the
therapist makes the family's demands his own: he becomes an ally
of the relatives and gives his tratment to the patient, or else,
he takes over for the mistreated and midunderstood poor paitent and
crusades to free him from his wicked family. As in a battle, he
ends always by taking sides.

    In the case that the family finds a family therapist, they are
in for trouble. To start with, there is no agreement and most likely
they will end up by clashing. The medicalized, psychiatrized concept
with which the family diagnosed the patient is no fully held by the
therapist. He has his own mind as to patients and mental health.
What most modalities of family therapy do have in common is to have
transcended the individual model and to have adopted a psycho-social
one by which the family group is seen as a whole and where the family

becomes the basic unit for diagnosis, for therapy and for care. In
what family therapists differ is in the ways the family and its
problems are understood and, in consequence, are treated. Some of
them still think that their task is to treat the "sick patient", of
course with the relatives' help. Others, on the contrary, view the
family as if it were a single patient of which the patient is the
symptom. Finally, there are those who see the family in terms of a
group, where treating the group is treating all of them conjointly.

     Those of the first type are the most gentle. The are still
close to the shared medical model. Sooner or later they discover
that their assistants are of little help, that they rather sabotage
the treatment than cooperate. That is what led Sigmund Freud to
such a pessimistic view about the good intentions of the relatives.
The walls erected around the psychoanalytic situation were to protect the patient's analysis from the attacks of the relatives and
the force of the transference counteracts the resistance of the
family. But to no avail, they kept on breaking the contract and
putting their noses into it.

     Although the second group of therapists arrive by different
ways and rationales, depending on the conceptual frame of reference
from which they depart, there are several clinical findings that
force the therapist to think in family terms. Quite often a successful treatment and cure of the patient is followed by a family that
breaks apart or another relative who falls ill in turn. More frequent still are the cases that drop out of individual therapy under
the stress of family resistance. Both factors, plus the economical
problem implied in dealing with and luckily solving the problem of
treatment of the neurotic family by only one therapist and at the
same time, acted as a great stimulus for conjoint family therapy.
Not without reason, it was in public clinics or psychiatric institutions with limited manpower where the pioneers of family therapy
initiated their work. With those therapists, the family is taken by
surprise, has a shock. Not only they suddenly have lost their patient, but they have to start anew and clarify what their problem is.
Curiously enough, and regardless of the initial frustration and of
having lost the defensive role that the patient plays in family
dynamics, most of those families hold onto treatment. Very few of
them refuse as long as the therapist is convinced enough. That does
not mean, of course, that they drop their resistances by pure chance,
but now they are out in the open and can be dealt with by the therapist.

     The third alternative, the one proposed by Group Analysis and
which I adhere to, departs from another very different conceptual
framework and orientation. There is no need to isolate the patient
from the family in order to treat him. Neither is it unavoidable to
physically include the whole family, just because there is a patient
in the midst of them. You take the family as it comes. You listen

with equal attention to the one who talks as to those who are silent.
The mind is broader, it goes farther than what fits within a single
skull and under one skin. Regardless if it is a single individual
or the whole family who comes for treatment, you try to understand
what and whose problem it really is. You don't settle for appearan-
ces, you want the real thing. You try to clarify which is the network of disturbance and who are the people dynamically implied in it.
You carefully evaluate the resources for change present and try to
secure the cooperation of those who are able to contribute and who
agree to become part. This open attitude - analytic attitude - of
the therapist enables the family to join in. The problem originally
brought in terms of illness and health is redefined in terms of the
potential for change of the family group and of each of its members.
The free and honest discussion of the problem at all possible levels-
open as well as latent - is what makes possible to translate the
autistic message of the symptom into an articulate, conscious
(conscire = to know the other), shareable communication.

It is quite obvious that this is where the boundaries of the
therapeutic situation are and the degree of permeablility and flexibility of those boundaries is what makes the above described models
different. In the first, we have a group (therapist plus relatives)
treating an individual; in the second, the therapist singlehanded
is treating a group - the family; in the last, it is the group
(therapist cum family) which is treating itself, or better, who is
trying to understand and to solve the problem they have as a group.

S.H. Foulkes' contribution to the development of my family therapy
Foulkes' main concern was the understanding of psychotherapeutic
process and he saw the group as the most adequate tool to study it.
This is what led him into the development of Group-Analytic Theory.
His two most outstanding discoveries were the concept of Matrix and
the Transpersonal Network Theory of Neurosis. It was his conviction
that neurosis and other mental disturbances are of a multipersonal
nature, and that it is this network of communication and disturbance
that integrates the therapeutic situation, the object of treatment
that serves as base for all group analytic psychotherapies. When he
talks of life groups, of which the family is a prime example, he
takes care to clarify, however, that it is not kinship or blood links
that count but the psychodynamic bonds that hold the network together.
Such a network, in psychological terms, includes persons who are not
in the ordinary sense members of the family, which can as well include others of the proper family who are not implicated in the
problem at hand. It is trying to trace the boundaries of that active
psychodynamic network, how I came upon the main idea on which I have
been working for years. Foulkes' idea of plexus - short for complexus
- the intimate dynamic network which is of the therapist's concern,
pushed me to include in it the therapist himself when a family is or
has one of his members in therapy.

In what is meant by plexus, Foulkes (1975) defines it as "a relatively small number of people, which includes the family, who group themselves dynamically as the process of treatment proceeds around the central person - the patient - especially in connection with his conflicts which are significant for the disturbance for which he has come to consult us". And, he adds, "From the point of view of method it is at this stage important for us that we do not construct or anticipate such complexus of people and call them together for treatment. What happens is that we build up from what may be called the central patient, we then follow the psychodynamics as we become aware of them to a group of people around him who turn to have an essential connection with his basic conflict, symptoms and problems". In group-analytic diagnosis - like in group-analytic family therapy - the members of the plexus are seen in various constellations as the psychodynamic progress of the treatment commands. The individual patient - the central patient by family decision - is seen as the nodal point, merely a symptom in essence of a disturbance of the equilibrium in the intimate network of which he is part.

It becomes clear then that it is the plexus that is to be treated. But, as I have pointed out before, in the case of Freud, the therapist himself has his own plexuses - the one of his own family and the one of his professional network - and it is mostly through this last one that he is going to organize his practice and to do his task, boundarying the therapeutic situation according to them.

From my own point of view, every time that a member of a family consults a therapist, or more still, if he enters into treatment, the status quo, the equilibrium reached by his family, regardless of how unstable or pathological it was, gets unsettled. If we think in terms of the network of communication and disturbance, there is a major break of intimacy, a leak in communication and a brutal introduction of meaning through the boundaries of the family system with its environment, with the result that the family feels threatened. No wonder they resist. To me, any manifest disturbance within a bio-psycho-social system, at the same time that it shows suffering and pain it also is a cry for help, for health and has to be listened to and attended. Depending on how the social and professional environment responds to this call of the family, we will either help the individual, the family and society to solve their problem, or, instead, we will iatrogenically aggravate or perpetuate it. That is the way I think about "sick families" and "families in therapy".

The Family's Patient Career
My basic ideas are as follows. The family is a life group which remains in equilibrium and performs some task under some given conditions. At some point in its life cycle or because of an unexpected event, it gets out of balance and starts to show signs of suffering or dysfunction. One of its members starts with psychological or even

physical pain and his behaviour changes, or else within the family
start up some interpersonal conflicts between some or all of its
members. This can be just a temporal crisis or it can become absorbed in the family as a new way of equilibrium. They will cope with
it as they can. But, once their own coping resources are exhausted,
they will call for outside help; it could be a neighbour, a friend,
the extended family or a priest, a lawyer, a physician, who knows.
If they, or one of them consults a psychotherapist or if the advice
is to do so, the problem is reframed in psychological terms, becomes
psychologized. From that moment onwards, according to the response
of the therapist, the family homeostasis will take another route.
The family has as its function not only to generate, to foster and
to convey pathology but also a morphogenetic one: to generate growth,
maturation and change. A sheer diagnostic procedure or accepting the
proposed patient as such can as well make the family abdicate this
function or reinforce it in that direction. The expert's opinion
not necessarily has to be spelled out in words. It is enough to
accept one or to exclude another from the interview, as for confirming or challenging the structural arrangements and pre-established
dynamics or else to induce a positive or negative change in the
family system. That is why I think the first contact with the
family is paramount as it implies to be aware of the previous attempts
the family has been making so far at solving their problem.

Once treatment starts – just the same for one single member as
for all of them – and as long as he, she, or they are in treatment,
the family with the therapist or therapists constitute a group that
dynamically interacts. That can be formulated in terms of transferences–countertransferences, as in psychoanalysis, or in terms of the
changing family and personal matrix of the plexus as in group analysis, the truth is that the network of communication and transactions
within the socio-psychological group changes along with the degree
to which the unconsious conflict becomes conscious and they are able
to work it through.

When we are in conjoint treatment, and while we are in a session
the dynamics of this group are there to be seen. In between sessions,
by contrast, the family functions as an alternate group without therapist. The role of the latter is to become a sort of catalyst which
helps a new culture to crystallize, a culture where to say openly
on a verbal, symbolic level what otherwise would go through an un-
translated symptomatic level. The family gets healthier as long as
it achieves autonomy; as far as having activated its potential capacity for self-regulation and self-direction, it can dispense with
external help and containment. That is how, having learned to dialogue, it can assume anew its biological, psychological and social
functions and responsibilities regards the family group itself – and
each of its members – and regards the open community to which they
all belong.

Going back to the relatives' resistance which so much bothered
Freud for his individual centred psychoanalysis, in group-analytic
terms those external resistances become internal resistances of the
family plexus, or better said, interpersonal defenses against a threat
to change by just one of its members. What I want to stress here is
the importance that for the course of therapy is the fact that the
therapist be aware that under the couch of the patient in analysis
and around the circle of the small group of strangers who are in
therapy with him, there are hiding and flying the family members
they left home. In other words, all together they form a psychic
group that is being affected in their internal equilibrium and at
the level of the network of communication and disturbance by the
therapy that is taking place. Besides the difficulties that ignoring
that fact brings along, an eye should be kept on how and why the
relatives are being affected. Had Freud taken that into account,
maybe he could have thought, since it was hopeless to try to treat
them individually, to give them a chance by treating them collectively.

It is my conviction that many individual analysis or group
psychotherapies that fail, where the patient reaches a deadlock or
drops out of therapy without significant changes being achieved, do
so because the family network dynamics on diagnosis were not taken into
account. Of course, there are cases where with a successful treatment of the patient not only the patient but his whole family get
cured, but those cases are rare when they are approached without a
previous appraisal of the family context. It was just luck or sheer
intuition that they hit on the right patient, more frequently they
don't, and then one after the other or all of them at the same time
have to go into individual therapy. For not having proceeded to a
family treatment - most likely the right indication - or for having
chosen the wrong patient, the whole family becomes an "interminable
analysis" that goes on through generations of patients and analysts.

These considerations are of importance also for the conjoint
treatment of families. It has become customary in the field to
compulsively see the whole family together - at least those who
live under the same roof. Some family therapists go so far as to
refuse to see the family if some of the members are not present.
Regardless of how expedient and convenient ideally it could be, in
many cases it is not possible to have certain members present. Most
likely, it is internal conditions between members that foreclose the
possibility of the kind of frank, open deep and complete communication that is required from all of them. In those circumstances there
is no other solution than to exclude from therapy or from the meeting
that part of the family which is unfit, unable or unwilling to join
in the uncovering analytic process that is required for a group-
analytic family treatment. The solution is to concentrate on those
who understanding themselves and understanding the family can better
facilitate a change - that can be done with a group-analytic family

orientation even when only one patient is present. As a matter of
fact, in a consultation or in the first session with an individual
patient, that is what I mostly have in mind during the evaluation
phase.

There is one other reason why many family therapists abdicate
from treating the family analytically and feel compelled to move
into action methods and systems thinking. What is adduced is that
there is a cultural and social barrier between doctor and patient.
According to many, the low class populations who go to free clinics
and hospitals are unfit for an analytical approach. The culture of
poverty, of margination and hunger is not for talking and symbolic
thinking but for action and experiencing: that is why active techniques, interpersonal manipulation, and paradoxical interventions
are needed so much to change family systems. That may be quite
true, but it is not fair to reach these conclusions when not enough
time and dedication has been put into exploring the possibilities of
an analytic treatment of the family group. Foulkes said, as I
quoted above, that in order to put into practice such multipersonal
therapy – group therapy of the natural group – this work could be
shared by a team of therapists trained both in psychoanalysis and in
group analysis. Maybe the time is not ripe yet, since few therapists
are trained that way and still less had the chance of working with
families as a team. Until such time, however, it is useful to use
family interviewing with the group-analytic orientation here described, since it saves time and many hours of painful and useless treatment to individuals and families. Besides, it gives a chance to
re-orientate the course of treatment when either the therapeutic
modality chosen at the begining was not the most adequate one or else
when, because of the progress of therapy, the family dynamice are
changed and a shift of modality is required.

There is a word of caution, however, for those psychoanalysts
and group analysts who feel tempted to venture into family therapy
the group-analytic way. Try not to do it alone, by yourselves. It
is better to take the route with a team of colleagues. The mermaids
of action methods will tempt your analytic attitude and you can be
shipwrecked. Even with the help of your friends, the seas of family
therapy are stormy, and when you learn to navigate through them don't
expect that when you go back to the more calm shores of the couch
and the circle they will feel the same. Changing families in a
group changes the therapist as well. From now onwards when you deal
with individuals, even if in an analysis five times a week, you will
find yourself keeping an eye open to the phantoms of the family who
are haunting you both.

...And those who treat families ?

Along this presentation I feel I aroused more questions than I
found answers. I think I made quite clear which is my idea about
family health and the ways, in consequence, I think they should be

treated and why. I will try to share and reason with you some of my
experiences of the family as a member of the clan of analysts.

The first analyst I saw doing family therapy was Ackerman himself. It was at the end of the fifties at the Jewish Family Services
in New York. He was not as much into systems as the people of his
Institute are today. I had just started my psychoanalytical training,
was looking for a job and was going to be interviewed by Ackerman on
those grounds. Instead of interviewing me, however, he invited me
into a family session he was conducting. At the end of the session
I said to him: Thanks! I don't want the job! We both knew why.
I was not ready yet to get into family therapy.

I finished my training, first in analysis, then in group
analytic psychotherapy. I had had some experience with families,
but none in family therapy as such. I went home and there I found
myself in charge of a Psychiatric Unit in a Children's Hospital. I
could not avoid families any longer. Besides, there I set up a
training program following the lines of Foulkes' Outpatient Unit at
the Maudsley, the classical orthopsychiatric team approach - Child
Psychiatrist, Social Worker and Clinical Psychologist - which I had
taken in from America, in our Unit would not work. I was very very
analytic in those days; I think I still am, but in a different
way. We started to do groups of children on one side, of mothers
on the other, and of mothers and children together. With fathers
we could not run groups because they did not want to come, and before
we knew it we were interviewing families together. I say "together"
and not just "conjointly" because the therapeutic team plus the family
were all in the same group. What was started as a Child Psychiatry
Service after some years looked more like Family Psychiatry. Unfortunately, circumstances had it that I moved to the Medical School
to train physicians. In private practice, though, as a consultant
psychotherapist I had plenty of opportunity to do family interviewing.
What is more, it became practically my routine procedure to meet
patients for the first time. Some of those patients I treated in
conjoint therapy for a long time. Along with a growing familiarity
with the family and the use of this two-barrelled sort of thinking,
I dared to combine both methods: family group and individual analysis
with a member of the same family simultaneously. At one point, more
than half of my practice was in family groups. Most of the ideas
above exposed come from that experience. I must confess, though the
experience was exciting, it was painful as well. At one point, there
was so much crossfertilization between family and analysis that I
was tempted to give up analysis and get fully into family work.
Fortunately, I had my group-analytic friends from London to help me
out: The III Workshop in Group Analysis, January 1976, "Change and
Understanding", was dedicated to the theme of insight versus activity
techniques, and it gave me a safe ground to think through my problem
with the family. Today I am quite happy with what I do. What are
my conclusions by now?

1. Family interviewing as a diagnostic tool for the indication of therapy is a must.

2. The open field of conjoint or combined group-analytic family therapy is promising enough not to be shied away from by psychoanalysts and group analysts. Let us make sure that it doesn't apply to group analysis what Balint (1968) said happened to psychoanalysis in reference to group psychotherapy: "Although Freud himself adumbrated some allowing of the pure gold of psychoanalysis in order to make it suitable for the psychotherapy of broad masses, and although almost all of the pioneers of group therapy were trained psychoanalysts, we, as a body, refused to accept responsibility for its further development - in my opinion to the detriment of everyone concerned, above all of our own science. It is others who are now gathering a rich harvest in this important field and we have lost perhaps an irretrievable opportunity to obtain first-hand clinical observations on the psychodynamics of collectivities" - in that case of the family group I would say instead.

3. As a measure of security, this work should be done in teams, as I already said, but what is more, I think of teams of therapists not only out of caution but also for the sake of efficiency and for their own mental health they should apply to their own relations and as a group the same principles and outlooks they use with the families. I have done so as a consultant to "families" or "clans" of group and family therapists and I can tell you that it is helpful. I wish I had had that opportunity myself. On second thought, I think it would be still better if the team as a group of colleagues can discuss between them the work they jointly or separately do. Cotherapy is not the only answer. Besides, who can afford it, if not institutions or the State?

4. Psychoanalysts or group analysts have more families than ordinary people. On top of their family of origin and the one they constitute, by training and association they become part of the analytic family of the Institute. As Martin Grotjahn (1960) used to recommend, some family therapy with their own real families would do them a lot of good, and some group psychotherapy for the incestuous analytic family of analytic societies would do them no harm. Maybe that way we could find better ways to solve our "theoretical problems" by separating from the old family. That way the analytic family pathology will not be transmitted to their offspring. Just like in the real family!

References

Balint, M, 1957, "The doctor, the patient and the illness", Pittman Medical, New York.

Balint, M., 1968, "The Basic Fault", Tavistock Publ. London.

Grotjahn, M., 1960. "Psychoanalysis and the Family Neurosis",
        Norton & Co., New York.

Freud, S., 1912, "Recommendations to physicians..." S.E.XII, pg.120

Freud, S., 1917, "Introductory Lectures...", S.E.XVI, pg.459

Foulkes, S.H., 1975, "Group Analytic Psychotherapy: Method and
        Principles", Gordon & Breach Sc. Publ. Lt., London, pg.15

Foulkes, S.H., 1965, "Therapeutic Group Analysis", Int. Univ.Press,
        New York, pg.171-2

GROUP AND FAMILY THERAPIES: DISTINCTIONS

Stephen Fleck, M.D.

Dept. of Psychiatry, Yale University
25 Park St., New Haven, CT 06519

BACKGROUND

Group and family therapies are alike in some respects and these treatments are often referred to as if they were technically and conceptually the same, but there are differences between them that are more important than the similarities. It seems useful, therefore, to spell out and emphasize the differences.

Group treatment began in the realm of internal medicine with tuberculous patients who may not have been complete strangers to one another before entering group therapy but who were brought together in a sanatorium by their disease (Pratt, 1906). Subsequently the method was extended to other groups of patients formed on the basis of like medical, and still later, psychiatric or psychosomatic, diagnoses (Sadock, 1975). From the 1930s and 40s on, group therapy was significantly influenced by the pioneering work of Moreno (1975) in psychodrama and by Bion and his colleagues at the Tavistock Clinic (1961) in psychoanalysis. In the last two to three decades the concept of group therapy has expanded and now includes many forms of group-wide endeavors and methods to influence and change behavior or to enhance self-awareness as well as social comfort. Among these are groups engaged in transcendental sessions, in mass group meetings such as est, as well as many of the treatment programs developed for substance or food abusers of which Alcoholics Anonymous is the paradigm (Marmor, 1980).

This presentation, however, will be limited to consideration of psychiatric group therapy of families and of stranger groups brought together by a professional group therapist. Stranger groups

consist of members who are identified psychiatric patients who enter
the group by request or upon the recommendation of a mental health
professional, but only after having been screened before inclusion
in the therapeutic group. By and large, such group members can be
considered to be voluntary, coerced into participation primarily by
their pain and suffering and sometimes by failure in other treatment
efforts. This applies to patients not hospitalized, because hospitalized patients may not be able to refuse joining a therapy group.

In contrast to stranger groups, the family is a group that pre-
exists entry into treatment--and the family in which all members
enter treatment voluntarily is rare. Whereas there is no tangible
force that can coerce family members into participation, the authoritative message that for the sake of one family member's (the identified patient) welfare and treatment the entire family must be involved is more or less coercive, and minor children in a family may
simply be told that they must come to treatment (Boszormenyi-Nagy &
Spark, 1973; Skynner, 1976).

Family treatment is a more recent development than group therapy
and was probably first attempted in western societies in the 1930s
by Midelfort (1957) with families of schizophrenic patients. The
development of family treatment has two roots: one deriving from
the severe aberrations found in the family backgrounds of schizophrenic patients (Lidz, Fleck & Cornelison, 1965), and the other
stemming from child psychiatry where Ackerman (1958) pioneered the
concept that instead of seeing a patient in play therapy and having
the parents or other family members be treated individually by other
professionals, it might be more important and efficacious to observe
and treat the family as a unit. Families in which at least one child
is the primary source of complaint and clinical contact have become
the type of problem which has blossomed, even mushroomed, into the
field of family therapy. Stierlin et al. (1980) whose work spans
the two original strands of family treatment, Minuchin (1974),
Selvini (1974), and Skynner (1976) are all outstanding pioneers in
this particular field.

GROUP COMPOSITION AND TREATMENT DECISIONS

The composition of stranger groups is elective and usually
determined by the therapist/group leader or one or more coworkers.
Groups are often constituted according to preselected variables such
as diagnosis, age, sex or other demographic or psychopathological or
psychosomatic factors. The group members usually do not know one
another before they join the group. They may not all join at the
same time, although generally this would be desirable.

The decision to enter treatment in a stranger group is made by
each individual together with a professional such as an intake interviewer or with a dyadic therapist after a considerable amount of

psychotherapy or as a discharge recommendation after hospitalization.
Group members are usually under no constraints that prevents them
from opting out, except for their symptoms and possibly some external
(spouse or employer, etc.) demand for change or improvement but even
then members retain the option to leave the group.

The participants will have to evolve into a group for the purpose
of changing attitudes, psychopathological features, behaviors, and
improvement of social skills and comfort, etc. As an introduction to
the group, many therapists invite the members to state their particular goals in addition to informing their group peers of their reasons
for joining the group, their problems, their life histories--data
which become available for subsequent group discussions.

The family group consists minimally of two people, a parent and
a child, but usually three or more people--two parents and one or
more children. In addition, grandparents and collaterals and even
friends may be included if they are part of regular family life even
though they may not live in the same residence. In any case, they
are all "familiar" with each other; have long-standing relationships
which may well be pathological and even pathogenic; have developed
communication patterns that serve many purposes, possibly including
obfuscation and hiding information; and most importantly, it is a
group that exists under given biopsychosocial constraints which change
over time in an evolutionary cycle (Fleck, 1980a, 1980b).

The treatment decision for the family is very different, as
already indicated, and although a member can absent him- or herself
from treatment, he or she is still a member of the group. The family
members may, of course, all agree to participate in treatment, but
even if they do so "voluntarily" this decision relates to their
sense of family belonging--a complex mix of feelings, attitudes, and
family rules. Family treatment begins with a consideration of the
family's problems, not with informing each other about individual
backgrounds and complaints (Minuchin, 1974; Selvini, 1974; Stierlin
et al., 1980).

The issues raised by and involved in the absence of one or more
members are well known to all family therapists and are different from
absenteeism in the stranger group. That a member decides to absent
him- or herself is more important than the decision to come to treatment, because the absentee's behavior is often abetted, condoned, and
even desired by other family members. Absenteeism can constitute a
sabotage of family therapy. On the other hand, the rights of the
absent member and the reasons for missing sessions must also be respected, and while each absence may handicap family treatment, the
absentee may also protect his or her possibly precarious adjustment
and life pursuit. This situation may pertain in families with a
schizophrenic offspring where one or more siblings may have emanci-
pated themselves from their families of origin. They may reside at

TABLE I

STRUCTURAL & DYNAMIC ISSUES	Family Treatment	Stranger Group Therapy
Membership	Given; Preexisting	Voluntary; New (except in hospitals)
Composition	At least two generations; Often only one identified patient	Peers with regard to patienthood, often also age and diagnosis
Structure	Preexisting inverted triangles; Shared leadership	Pyramidal with one or more leader-therapists
Dynamics	Members seek linear relationships & identification with leader	Early group formation "against" leader, resisting identification
Conflicts	Preexisting; resolution is therapeutic and routine task	Arise in group and may illustrate individual problems
Goals	Change as unit, individuation and system competence	Individual and interpersonal changes
Outcome	Consolidation & functioning as unit Separation competence	Group dissolution Separation competence
GENERAL SYSTEM PARAMETERS		
Leadership	Therapist(s) & parents; Selective involvement with members	Therapist(s); Equidistant from members
Boundaries	Ongoing ego formation, intergenerational & family/community	Limited to sessions
Affectivity	Ongoing important parameter of family life	Issue in sessions only
Communication	Important tool and index in and outside treatment	Subserves therapy
Tasks and Goals	Geared to life cycle stage(s) in and outside treatment	Related to symptoms, psychopathology and relationships

some distance from the treatment center; they may have begun their own families; or may simply prefer not to be disturbed, however suggestive of pathology that may be. There are also potential advantages in dealing only with the critical triad of parents and a psychotic offspring.

If absenteeism occurs after treatment has continued for some time, both stranger groups and families must examine how they may have contributed to causing the dropout or in what way or manner they may have failed the absentee. In stranger groups, separation issues may be most important and useful and the group can decide in an essentially democratic fashion what, if any, efforts should be undertaken to induce the absent member to rejoin. On the other hand, the group may respect the dropout's presumed reasons for doing so (the person may indeed have attempted to explain them prior to leaving) or may decide that the group can function more effectively without the departed member. The separation is complete and final if either the group decides not to pursue the dropout or if the group fails in efforts to have the absentee member rejoin.

The family member dropout remains a member of the group and his or her absence remains a dynamic element in the therapeutic process even if no overt effort is made to have the absentee rejoin. Explorations by family members about the reasons and consequences of the member's absence, both with him and in therapy sessions without him or her, can and probably will continue indefinitely. If the family is one in which the index member was a scapegoat and this has been ameliorated or changed in family therapy, the therapist should entertain a high level of suspicion that the absent member has become the new scapegoat. Sometimes the dropping out of one or more children, especially of the index member, may serve as a message that the parents should be seen alone. This situation evolves fairly often from family unit treatment, especially if the symptoms or illness of the index member served to obscure or sidetrack basic marital problems or conflicts.

GOALS AND COURSE OF TREATMENT

Two treatment goals are identical in stranger groups and families: to further the individuation of the group members and to improve relationships and interactions with others. Whereas such individuation in stranger groups involves the freeing of ego functions from defensive inhibitions or distortions in group members who are likely to be either all adults (possibly of similar ages) or all adolescents; the members in the family group belong to two or more generations with a wide age range, and interaction patterns preexist and may have to be altered. In addition to furthering individuation, the treatment goals within the family also include those of helping members to assume appropriate familial roles and responsibilities consistent with individual and family life-cycle stages and to enhance family life as a unit for the present and the future.

Although the initial goal in the stranger group is group formation itself, the existence of the group is limited in time and space
to the meetings themselves and group formation subserves the individual hopes and goals for improved personal health. Once these hopes
and goals are achieved, or if it is realized that they are not at-
tainable, members leave the group which eventually dissolves. Unlike
the stranger group, the family is permanent whether they stay together physically or geographically. The treatment goals are related to
the triple family mission which is 1) to nurture, protect, and encul-
turate the young, i.e., to further the individuation of each member
of the family; 2) to improve the family's functioning as a group or
system; and 3) to provide society with adults who can participate
productively in the community's work and life. The second treatment
goal is the more important; i.e., to focus on how the family is operating as a system in the context of its evolutionary stage. Individuation and social adaptation outside the family are treatable in
other than group or family settings and meetings, but changing the
functioning of the family as a family requires the examination and
treatment of this unit in vivo (Fleck, 1980a). Table 1.

A SYSTEM APPROACH

The differences between stranger groups and families can be
drawn more clearly by examining the two groups in general system
terms. As clinicians we propose to view a human system along five
interdependent parameters: leadership, boundaries, affectivity or
sentient forces, communication, and the unit's task and goal pursuits
(Fleck, 1980b).

In stranger groups leadership is obviously vested in the therapist or therapists and leadership from within the group probably
arises in the form of a counter-leader; and such leadership, if any,
may shift among the members. The therapist/leader sets the boundaries, the meeting time, and place for the group. He or she addresses
affective or sentient relationships among group members for the sake
of analysis and even control when necessary; encourages communication,
paying particular attention to its quality and meaning; and leads in
the pursuit of the group's tasks and goals, to wit, the improvement
of the members' personal and interpersonal functioning. Group members
will develop transferences toward the leader as a parental figure and
usually more sibling-like relationships arise among each other. The
initial sense of group belonging may be expressed negatively by attacking the leader, because the easiest--one might say, the lowest--form
of group formation is based on some negative or hostile stance. In
group therapy this leader, indeed, gives very little and usually makes
demands which are neither explicit nor clear to the membership. A
stranger therapy group is probably the most difficult human group to
lead because the goals cannot be made explicit in that they are the

hopes and expectations (not necessarily conscious) of each individual. Unlike other human groups such as a business with the clear goal of making a profit or a military unit aiming at combat readiness, the therapy group has the mission to promote and abet personal growth which obviously cannot be so clearly defined even by the members themselves.

The family system is different because at each stage in the evolution of the family life cycle there are rather specific tasks and role performances to be accomplished, not only by the individual members but by the group as a functioning unit. While leadership in the family therapy setting itself rests with the therapist, it also resides in the parental pair or in other adults who at least function-ally may be a part of the family. Thus, whereas the leader/therapist in a stranger group may encourage the group as a whole to assume responsibilities and even leadership in a rather democratic fashion; family leadership remains with the older generation, except for a possible reversal late in the family life cycle when ageing parents become dependent upon their middle-aged children. Boundary issues in family therapy are not limited to the therapeutic situation. They involve the boundary management exercised by the adults with regard to individuation; that is, allowing and promoting a sense of self in the children throughout their early development, the regulation of the family/community boundaries which must be age-appropriate for the children and also must fit community expectations, and the establish-ment of the internal generation boundary which includes the incest taboo.

In the stranger group, affectivity which sometimes becomes an issue for group work, generally plays a minor role; in the family, affectivity is an important element in family therapy and in family life. In industrial societies where the nuclear family may be rela-tively isolated, this systems parameter becomes the major cohesive force for family existence. Affectivity is very much an issue in family treatment and it may be stated confidently that a disturbed family will demonstrate disturbances in their affective relationships.

Communication in the family is not only a tool for the therapeu-tic work, but also is an essential element in family life. The nature and modes of communication not only bespeak disturbances but also may help to create and perpetuate them--the most pathological examples being the amorphous and fragmented communication styles in the fami-lies of schizophrenic patients identified by Wynne et al. (1977). Among other communication disturbances are discrepancies between ver-bal and nonverbal communication, double-binding, and interfering with one another's freedom of speech or expression.

The fifth system parameter, task and goal pursuit, has only one pertinent part in stranger groups where only the group's therapeutic task matters; but in families it is a dual matter because the family

has its own tasks to pursue which are life cycle-stage related and
which are very much a focus for the therapeutic work. Beside
individuation, the ultimate goal in family therapy is to make the
system function better, not only in the context of therapeutic
sessions but throughout the members' lives. Figure I presents a grid
on which family functioning and performance can be scored (Fleck &
Quinlan, in press).

SOME NOTES ON PROCESS

The conceptual bridge between family and group therapies can be
said to have been established by Sigmund Freud. The first group any
human being becomes familiar with is the family. Freud's discovery
of transference, the keystone in psychoanalytic theory, has revealed
to us that all human relationships carry with them strands of our
earliest experiences, attachments, and conflicts. Thus, elements of
familial relationships, whether with parents and siblings or surro-
gates in these roles, enter into any human interaction, group therapy
included.

But this bridge also helps us to understand important differences. Whereas members of a stranger group can be expected to relate to each other primarily or at least modally as siblings might;
the relationships of individuals as well as of the group as a whole
towards the therapist or group leader may likely and usually carry
with them strands of the members' relationships to their parents.
Members of a family are obviously not all related like siblings although sibling rivalry across the generation line may occur in disturbed families at home and in each person's seeking recognition
and approval from the therapist(s).

The difference is especially marked in the early phases of group
and family treatments: in the srranger group, members may resist
the development of transference to the therapist even to the extent
of a negative-aggressive stance toward the therapist; by contrast,
in the family group, with the likely exception of the identified
patient, early transference manifestations often are competitive
attempts to be involved with the therapist. Thus, in the stranger
group, transference phenomena differ in that they often await some
opposition-engendered group cohesion ("You're not telling us anything, we don't have the foggiest notion what we're supposed to be
doing here"): whereas the familymembers behave rather centrifugally
and seek a dialogue with the therapist early on despite admonitions
not to do so ("Doctor, you must realize that my husband never takes
part in the disciplining so when Joe does these crazy things, it's
all up to me" or "They don't understand me, they have no right to
tell me when to be home").

Both groups bring resistance and ambivalence to the situation

producing centrifugal tendencies. In the stranger group these tendencies are covert--each member holds on to his or her secrets and
feels apprehensive and even ashamed to share intimate thoughts and
feelings. These diffident sentiments yield to or can be bypassed by
focusing on the leader in a groupwide attack, for instance. In this
way the group members can overcome the wish to leave the group or
resistance to forming it.

The family's sharing of secrets and withholding them from the
therapist, among others, does not start with therapy. Separation
may have been a wish or need for one or more members for some time
but was prevented by fused relationships in the family. Centrifu-
gality in disturbed families includes a child's wish to be grown up
and independent, a progression not perceived as threatening by well-
functioning families although they may feel sad about the impending
separation. Disturbed families are often not "grown up" with regard
to separation competence, among other aberrations. Often this
particular incompetence extends over several generations and is a
problem that may show in weaning difficulties, school phobias, and
narrowly drawn family boundaries. Therefore, separation mastery,
an issue that also arises in stranger groups with therapy termination,
is an essential family task which, if deficient, often must be addressed during treatment and becomes an issue again at termination.

Triangulation, i.e., diverting a dyadic issue or conflict by
involving a third person, is a common problem in family treatment and
pathological triangles are common in malfunctioning families. A typical pathological triad is parents who avoid conflicts and even
communication between themselves by focusing on or even stimulating
aberrant behavior in a child. Tri-generational triangles are also
often important in family malfunctioning. Families in therapy often
attempt to engage the therapist in such evasive maneuvers (Bowen,
1978).

OUTCOMES

As indicated previously, the stranger group serves only for as
long as the individual members believe that they can derive further
benefit from group sessions, even though the belief may be over-
determined by attachments formed during the experience or by having
become dependent on the group and the leader in particular. These
issues constitute separation tasks to be worked through by each
member and by the group together. By and large the stranger group
ends and dissolves when members decide that they have derived some
or all of the desired benefits from the therapy or that such a
desirable outcome will not eventuate and they want to stop trying.
Of course, groups also are dissolved for extraneous reasons such as
the leader or one or more members moving away (a common event in
academic settings).

Terminating family treatment is very different. Here the outcome is measured in terms of the family's functioning and performance as a group. Whereas this achievement may entail dissolution of the family as a tangible unit at certain stages, membership in the family in terms of role and hierarchial relationships cannot be terminated, only altered by death or a member moving away. Divorce, which may occur as a result of treatment or despite it, is a permanent separation or at least a permanent relationship change between the spouses. Divorce does not terminate, although it may severely alter, other intrafamilial relationships. Thus, the desired outcome of family treatment requires a reassessment of the family as a system which ideally would show a decline in deviancy scores on some family evaluation instrument such as the example shown in Figure I.

		0	1	2	3	4	5
		Not rated	Adequate or better	Somewhat deficient	Moderately deficient	Aberrant	Grossly aberrant
Leadership	1. Parental personalities 2. Parents' emancipation 3. Mutual support (+ coalition) 4. Power use + discipline						
Boundary Management	1. Mother-child dyad 2. Separation coping (ego boundary) 3. Generation boundary (intrusiveness?) 4. Family-community passages (rigidity vs. looseness; "rubber fence")						
Affectivity	1. Age-appropriate intimacy 2. Equivalency of family triads (e.g. scapegoating) 3. Tolerance for feelings 4. Unit emotionality (celebration or mourning)						
Communication	1. Clarity & respect for boundaries (speaking for oneself) 2. Confirmation and support (empathy) 3. Content responsiveness 4. Affect responsiveness 5. Verbal/non-verbal consistencies 6. Syntax 7. Contents (thought disorders, etc.) 8. Abstraction						
Task Fulfillment	1. Parental role complementarity 2. Nurturance and weaning (attachment-separation) 3. Enculturation 4. Peer relationship management 5. Unit leisure 6. Emancipation 7. Crisis coping 8. Tangible tasks & distribution						

Record Number or Name:_____

Date : - _____

From Yale Guide To Family Assessment
Copyright applied for 1980

Fig. 1. Interactional-Historical Systems Grid for Family Evaluation

Ackerman, N. W., 1958, The Psychodynamics of Family Life, Basic Books, New York.

Bion, W. R., 1961, Experiences in Groups, Basic Books, New York.

Boszormenyi-Nagy, I. and Spark, G., 1973, Invisible Loyalties, Harper & Row, New York.

Bowen, M., 1978, Family Therapy in Clinical Practice, Jason Aronson, Inc., New York.

Fleck, S., 1980a, The family and psychiatry, in: Comprehensive Textbook of Psychiatry, Vol. III, A. Freedman, H. Kaplan and B. Sadock, eds., 3rd edition, Williams & Wilkins, Baltimore.

Fleck, S., 1980b, Family functioning and family pathology, Psychiat. Annals, 10:17-35.

Fleck, S. and Quinlan, D. M., In press, Clinical family assessment.

Lidz, T., Fleck, S., and Cornelison, A., 1965, Schizophrenia and the Family, International Universities Press, New York.

Marmor, J., 1980, Recent trends in psychotherapy, Amer. J. Psychiat., 137:409-416.

Midelfort, C. F., 1957, The Family in Psychotherapy, Blakiston, New York.

Minuchin, S., 1974, Families and Family Therapy, Harvard University Press, Cambridge.

Moreno, J. L., 1975, Psychodrama, in: Comprehensive Textbook of Psychiatry, Vol. II, A. Freedman, H. Kaplan and B. Sadock, eds. 2nd edition, Williams & Wilkins, Baltimore.

Pratt, J. H., 1906, The "home sanatorium' treatment of consumption, Bost. Med. Surg. J., 154:210-216.

Sadock, B. J., 1975, Group psychotherapy, in: Comprehensive Textbook of Psychiatry, Vol. II, A. Freedman, H. Kaplan and B. Sadock, eds., 2nd edition, Williams & Wilkins, Baltimore.

Selvini, P., 1974, Self-Starvation, Chaucer Publications, London.

Skynner, A.C.R., 1976, Family and Marital Psychotherapy, Brunner/Mazel, New York.

Stierlin, H., Rucker-Embden, I., et al., 1980, The First Interview with the Family, Brunner/Mazel, New York.

Wynne, L.C., Singer, M.T., et al., 1977, Schizophrenics and their families: Recent research on parental communication, in: Developments in Psychiatric Research, J. M. Tanner, ed., Hodder & Houghton, London.

FAMILY PATTERNS IN PSYCHOANALYTIC GROUPPSYCHOTHERAPY

Jan van de Lande, M.D. Psychiatrist/Psychoanalyst

Medical Director Psychiatric Centre St. Bavo

Langevelderweg 27, Noordwijkerhout, Holland

Since 1968 I have continuously worked as a grouppsychotherapist. From 1968 to 1977 in the Youth Psychiatry Clinic "Amstelland" at Santpoort, Holland, and for adults and adolescents in private practice. From 1972 on - and I hope for many years to come - as a training analyst for grouppsychotherapy of the Dutch Society for Group Psychotherapy.

I also work many hours as a supervisor for grouppsychotherapy. At this moment I have 6 traininggroups a week, since my start in 1972 until now, up to a total of approximately 1300 sessions.

All those years and hours I have been working, without spending much time and thought to the working out of a frame of reference for myself, my trainees and co-therapists.

I felt quite comfortable with a psychoanalytic frame of reference, along the ideas of Bion and Ezriel, but most of all by Sigmund Foulkes with his statement: "Groupanalytic psychotherapy is a form of psychoanalytic therapy which takes as its frame of reference the group as a whole; and like all psychoanalytic therapy it puts the individual into the centre of its attention."

Though the book of Yalom was and is used by many Dutch students in grouppsychotherapy, personally I feel unsatisfied.

Following Malcolm Pines I like to integrate individual and social psychology into group analytic theory and I quite agree with his 8 propositions at the Amsterdam Congress on Psychotherapy in 1979, which I will mention now:

1. the essence of the individual is social, as he develops only in a social context and is defined as a person by this context;
2. neurosis and psychological disturbances in general have their origin in disturbed social relationships;

3. disturbed relationships develop from the unconscious forces of
   love and of hate. The neurotic, highly individualistic position
   is group disruptive in essence;
4. the resolution of the individual's conflict is possible in a
   social network, either that of the group in which the disturbance
   arises eg. the family or in a therapeutic group;
5. the symptom will be reactivated in the group, the symptom will
   be translatable into communicational processes. The person's
   world is actualized in the group context;
6. the healing properties of the group situation lie in the uncovering of the interpersonal disturbances and their resolutions in
   the relationships context of the group;
7. as each member of the group represents a deviation from the norm
   of the community to which all members belong, collectively they
   are the norm from which each one is a deviant;
8. the therapist's role is predominantly to be of service to the
   group as a whole.

Still, something was missing, was not fully stressed. Pines' references to the family were shimmering through but not worked out.
     Working all those years as a grouppsychotherapist with adolesc-
ents in a clinical setting, the importance of the "Wiederholungs-
zwang" - the repetitive compulsion - of familypatterns became more
and more clear.
     With adolescents you won't escape the situation that a group-
therapy is a challenge to them to repeat and repeat again every
familysituation, and to use the therapist for every role they need
in their staging the scene of home.
     There were times when I did 10 clinical groupsessions per week!
Of course there remained a difference between familytherapy and
grouptherapy and I didn't succeed in further integrating both forms
of therapy.
     When, in 1972, I started as a training analyst for the Dutch
Society of Grouppsychotherapy I was guided by Foulkes, Bion,
Whitaker and others.
     Many sessions and hours later I consider it wise to try to
state my present and own view on grouppsychotherapy.

     In general, I see the group as a platform on which people get
the opportunity to repeat certain patterns and concomitant emotions,
which originate from earlier group situations. This opportunity is
given to the people in a group by the use of all our technical
methods, frames of reference, the attitude, knowledge and behavior
of the therapists, the composition of the group etc.
     I chose 9 themes to show you how all this works together to
provoke this repetitive phenomenon. A provocation which is not
"really" needed, because this repetitive compulsion is present
intrapsychically in everybody, and has an essential survival value.
     Groupsituations which evidently have lifelong influences are:
the group in everybody's life, the primal familygroup; next the

extended familygroup and the various peergroups. In all the groups
people later willy-nilly belong to as work, church, sports, arts
etc., earlier groupphenomena are repeated.

These groupsituations provide emotional material which can be
brought into the open in grouppsychotherapy. These repeating processes, made recognizable by therapists and groupmembers, subject the
individual intrapsychic apparatus to mental stress. The ego struggles
against regression and sometimes fails, and the superego is put
under pressure when feelings of shame and guilt are made explicit.

Corrective emotional and social experiences become possible,
and may lead to changes in behaviour and feelings, at least when a
certain amount of insight in connections is recognized.

This is made possible, first of all, by the unravelling of the
specific transferences present in the group here and now. Distinction
has to be made between transference phenomena and the objective
reality in different groupsituations; insight in intricate connections is the purpose of therapy. Every groupmember is enmeshed in a
complex system of reality and transference. This intricate system
- this meatball - is frequently passed round the whole group; the
ball itself offers the owner only a small part of his possibilities
as a human being. It has become our function as therapists to take
this meatball to pieces, show the components, and try to make clear
how these parts interrelate and function in relation to the whole.

Whether or not people start to change their behaviour and feelings on the basis of this insight is not the purpose of grouppsychotherapy.

Therapy in the group is done by continuously changing the
context, the points of view and continuously shifting the interrelated systems.

My purpose is the development of understanding and insight in
what just now has passed as action and interaction. If this is
followed by a change of behavioural repertoir in relation to other
people, just fine. If a person has enough insight at his disposal,
why he does or does not do something, why he goes on repeating the
same behaviour, then a change in the behavioural repertoir may follow.

My purpose is not the same as that of many forms of experiential
grouptherapy: to facilitate the change of behaviour towards each
other, under the specific circumstances of the here and now.

The psychoanalytic frame of reference constantly refers to the
family of origin. Whenever psychopathological phenomena of more or
less serious nature are to be explained, in my opinion the family
offers the matrix.

The family - in whatever constellation - is of all groups in
one's past the most recognizable and of course the first group
that forms a pattern which leaves fortunate or inconvenient impressions in subsequent groupsituations.

In a psychoanalytically oriented grouppsychotherapy that tries
to understand and give insight into the patterns of the first and
later groupsituations in life - including the therapygroup - one
has to do with groupinteractions of all members at 3 levels.

First the petit niveau of the individual with his specific idio-
syncrasies and characteristics, also based on genetics and constitu-
tion who comes into action with another individual in the group.Their
interpersonal dynamics may refer to a pattern each of them has
absorbed and acquired in their primal group.

At the second level one is confronted with activities of the
group as a whole, based on and reducible to activities of a family
as a whole. As well as a family stands for more than the sum of its
component parts, the familymembers - so the group as a whole means
more than the sum of all interactions of all members. Every group
has its own specific way of behaving and creates its own ambiance.

Finally, all the interactions, at an individual level and those
at grouplevel, will reach a third and last level, when the group
as a whole - including the therapist - undergoes the influence of
and interacts with external reality. The last is certainly the case
in all training groups, where professional career and membership of
societies etc.,are at stake for group members and traininganalysts
as well.

The examples I will give, aim to illustrate how significant
groupsituations from the past, specially familypatterns, can be for
one's behaviour in groups. I encountered all these themes many times.
I first started in the traininggroups to give consistent attention
to these parallels. These groups count 8 psychotherapists in training, psychologists, psychiatrists, social workers and other disciplines that, for some of them, give access to the Dutch Society of
Group Psychotherapy. All have to participate in a trainee-group
for at least 48 sessions, 1½ hour once a week. Before starting I
ask them if they are prepared to stay in therapy as long as it will
turn out to be necessary for a favourable development of their
personalitystructure.

On this basis it's possible to work along psychoanalytic lines,
with full attention on the ongoing process and not on the compulsory
number of sessions. The groupmembers vary in ages from 25 to 55
years, and the groups are mixed in sex. Some of the groups I do on
my own, one with a cotherapist-in-training, and most of them I do
with a colleague psychoanalyst; this last form I prefer; together
we have developed, since about 8 years, a form of psychoanalytic group
rouppsychotherapy on the basis of a 2-therapist-system, in which both
both therapists are equal in training, experience and friendship.

I will describe some of the themes in a very compact way.

1. Sibling rivalry

It seems logic that the circumstances in a traineegroup are
favourable to promote rivalry and competition. The whole professional entourage (surroundings) however carries a big problem with

it. In our way of doing analytic grouppsychotherapy the groupmember
is almost forced to become a real patient and at the same time keep
his identity as a therapist-in-training.
Most remarkable is the eagerness to become a patient, and with the
others to bombard the therapist to be the real therapist in the group!
    It seems to me that in this way 2 important feelings are being
warded off:
a. if a trainee should feel himself more a therapist (as he really
   is), fear will come up to be at cross-purposes with the therapist,
   which might lead to severe punishment. As a child you are not
   allowed to be as big and clever as your parents, at least not to
   show it!
b. the trainee is afraid to experience a difference in love and
   especially in appraisal or even rating.
As a patient one is also judged, but the infantilism or regression
belonging to this is less feared and more accepted; a trainee is
more afraid of the appraisal as a therapist-in-spé, this might have
consequences for a professional career, although in Holland the
traininganalysts have no say in the selection for the next step in
the whole trainingprogramme.
    All this leads to a suppression of feelings of rivalry; they
refuse to criticize each other, or to evaluate; it strengthens mutual
loyalties from fear of letting each other down.
    It has to be made clear that every child in his family has
nursed the same fear of being loved less and judged differently from
the other children. A fear which is based on reality. Parents do
differ in their feelings towards different children. The realisation
of this fact is sometimes too painful and is repressed.

2. Sibling love

    Alternating with the rivalry and competition but less prominently
present, is the mutual love groupmembers can feel towards each
other. I'm not sure the conception 'sibling love' is as wellknown
as sibling rivalry.
    Although the members are together in the same group, sometimes
for years, it takes a lot of courage to be just nice to each other.
Of course they are interested in each other etc. but the expression
of a feeling of love is much less heard.
    On analysis the fear of intimacy is present, but especially of
intimacy in the long run: if we get too much attached to each other,
we'll lose too much autonomy.
    Ongoing analysis reveals the mourning over the loss of special
alliances in the family, or mourning over the fact of nót having had
such alliances but a lot of fantasies about them. One doesn't want
to be reminded of   what possibly is lost, or will be lost again at
the end of one's stay in grouppsychotherapy. A group ends as a family
ends. One leaves it.
    In anticipation of the finiteness of this relation, intimacy
and siblinglove will be kept at distance.

3. Leaving home

As was said before: the finiteness of the group is easily denied.
Anticipating the mourning, the group-members fall back on old
behavioral patterns similar to the old solutions in the adolescent
phase of life when one leaves home. This repetition of adolescent
behavior is easily recognizable: leaving the group with a quarrel
and displeased, or just sneaking off, or with a great deal of fuss,
or pretending that leaving the group doesn't affect you at all.

On analysis a second layer comes clear: the old fantasy returns
that, if one leaves the family there is a chance of never seeing
each other again. In real life this is solved by casual remarks about
coming home for dinner once in a while, or making arrangements about
who will do the washing. In traininggroups the warding off of this
fear is solved by making vague remarks about: we'll certainly meet
each other at congresses or in the Society for Grouppsychotherapy,
or by discreetly sounding the therapists about the possibility of
supervision when the group is finished.

Never to see each other again is a fantasy that has to be warded
off. One always risks that out of sight really means out of mind;
that parents and therapists are glad to get rid of their children.

4. New members

Repeating familypatterns becomes quite clear when the subject
of new groupmembers come up. Especially when you are able to work
along analytic lines in an open group. Two members leave our group
per half year, on an average. You might call these groups half-open.
When the group would have been closed - all members starting and
finishing at the same time - fantasies about successors, new children
etc. could not or hardly have been advanced. The half-openness helps
this process considerably.

All thoughts and fantasies around departure now are concomitant
with feelings and fantasies about new groupmembers.

Therapists are seen as pregnant when they announce new members.
The results are almost classic in our eyes: the speeding up of transference, heightened self-exposure and greater attachement to each
other. These processes become clear in the period just after the
departure of the older members and before the arrival of the new
ones. In this interregnum a feeling of solidarity and togetherness
springs up; almost literally an experience of being brothers and
sisters, threatened by pregnant parents.

Agressive fantasies towards parents-therapists are usually
worked under the table and as a defense we see projection.

Therapists are explicitly asked if they also find it boring
and difficult to start again with new members, to loose their grip
on the ongoing processes etc.

Groupmembers not only try to develop new bonds with each other,

but each of them directs himself fully on the therapists. Whatever
transferencefeelings still had to develop, now rise speedily.

All the experiences of having pregnant mothers, or not having
had them but fantasied about them; the experiences of the attitudes
of pregnant fathers; the special relation between each familymember
before the birth of a new child etc. Every groupmember makes haste
to raise these matters and come to a special bond with the therapists;
all members hurry in disclosing intimate matters, hidden fantasies,
feelings of shame and guilt. Confessions on the threshold.

All three symptoms speed each other up: selfexposure, togetherness, transference. This bomb has its agressive component as well -
as every bomb has of course - new groupmembers do not get a ghost
of a chance to feel themselves safe and comfortable in this closed
familygroup.

Some groupmembers even propose to leave the group untimely,
before the new ones arrive. They don't want to be confronted with
the new child. Quite a load of defense is offered. One doesn't want
to experience the feeling that a younger brother or sister could
become more important, or that the parents might never have loved
you, they take a new child.

In a family drastic shifts in relations take place between
parents and children right after the new baby is born. Rooms have
to be evacuated, nights are disturbed, love has to be shared, behavior
has to be adapted etc.

We experience the same things in a group: love and attention
of the therapists have to be shared with even more people, adaptation
is asked in place,theme and subject of the ongoing therapeutic
process, acquired positions in the group with members and therapists
have to be given up, at least put in the fridge. After some weeks,
sometimes a couple of months, the group has recovered more or less and
a new homeostasis is found.

5. <u>2-therapist-system is beneficial to parental transference</u>

Although this is obvious and present in the already given
examples, I would like to mention that the last word is not said
about the pro's and contra's of 1 or 2 therapists in a grouppsychotherapy.

I will shortly discuss the sex of the 2 therapists: man and
woman, 2 women, or 2 men. During my clinical work with several
disturbed adolescents I've been working with co-therapists of both
sexes. The last years however only with a man.

The advantage of a male-female pair is obvious and more in conformity with reality; there is no illusion of sexlessness, and
oedipal conflicts are easily prompted. As a disadvantage I see the
possibility of easily switching from one therapist to the other,
when sexual problems are under discussion. According to the sexual
relation with man or woman being more or less feared or wished for,
a selective use of the male or female therapist can be made. This
shift in engagement from one therapist to the other has to be sharply
watched and analysed.

The disadvantages of 2 therapists of similar sex are just as obvious. Psychoanalysts pur sang however object to all the emphasis on the importance of the real sex. With man and woman a psychoanalytic therapy is dependent on transference feelings. In principle these feelings are not strictly bound to the real sex of the therapist, but more to the projective fantasies. The chance to escape in engagement to the therapist with the most wanted sex is less great.

It is quite possible to achieve a meaningful tranferencepattern with 2 women or 2 men in a psychoanalytic frame of reference. At least I have learned to work succesfully with it.

But whatever goes for any duo or couple is the very good companionship between the two, based on love and understanding, including criticism and humour.

Nevertheless: in view of all the pro's and contra's I would be unjust to advertise these duos of similar sex!

6. Incestuous patterns

Bringing to light the incestuous familypatterns is one of the most difficult tasks in this form of grouppsychotherapy. The subject is getting closer for everybody when mutual relations between group-members and with the therapists are analysed more closely, with a focus on intimate feelings and fantasies.

Sometimes an intimate relation arises between groupmembers out-side the group. According to our code this relation has to be discuss-ed in the group.

It is not forbidden to have them, but they are highly undesir-able. All cases I have seen, led up to an untimely and premature departure of one of the partners.

It is of utmost importance to disclose intimate fantasies about each other, and to relate these to familypatterns. Fantasies about a relation with a groupmember, or having one in fact, even in a derived way: having a drink together, driving back home together etc. - are still far more easily discussed and analysed than fantasies about a relation with the therapist. Even dreams about it are reluctantly told. By being active in working out the relation with a groupmember, the fear around feelings of intimacy with the therapist is warded off. Brother-sister incest is chosen as a 'solution' for the repressed parent-child incest.

Next to these dyadic incestproblems we can make another related phenomenon recognizable at the level of the group as a whole. Mutual relations, even in fantasy have sometimes the function of keeping strangers outside. All love remains in the group, giving the group a feeling of a closed clan against the bad outside world. A function of incest frequently seen in families as well.

7. <u>Secrets in the family</u>

   The tendency of families to have secrets and to keep them from
the outside world threatens to be repeated in a grouppsychotherapy;
and with more ease in a grouptherapy wherein 2 psychoanalysts are
doing their utmost to let those familypatterns repeat themselves,
to give some insight in feelings and behaviour of the groupmembers.
   Inside the group we see the same loyalties towards secrets
develop as in the family. The difference between open and closed
secrets in the family (a theme well worked out by Christopher Dare)
is easily made identifiable in this form of grouptherapy.
   By 'closed' secret in the group we mean that some members of
the group share it, but not all. By 'open' secret we mean that all
members in the group share it - including the therapists - but not
the outside world.
   This is in conformity with the concept of open and closed
secrets in the family as Dare described them.
   We often see closed secrets in a group. Some members share a
fragment of their non-group life with each other, which gives them
a certain secret understanding; others drive home together, discuss
anything and everything and make deals to bring it yes or no in the
group. It is a first task of the therapists to make this closed
secret an open secret.
   Then, to start analysing the need to have those secrets: how it
works in helping to evade some dangerous themes, and furthermore
which reminiscences it calls to mind of closed secrets in the
various families.
   The continuation of closed secrets in a group can have a very
damaging effect, by making the group untreatable by its paranoid
attitude towards each and everybody. Open secrets are present as well
in grouppsychotherapy. Members and therapists do things together
which are not spoken of in the outside world. One of the most striking
examples seems to me the way the whole group lives in the mutual
understanding that the 2 analysts are the only real therapists, and
the groupmembers the real patients and have the right to feel and
behave themselves as such; while to the outside world these 'patients'
like to stress the point that it concerns a 'training'-group, where
they learn to become grouptherapists; the analysts also speak along
the same lines, when they describe their groups as: of course it is
<u>also</u> a traininggroup.
   Therapists and groupmembers try to keep an open secret of the
group, namely that this specific form of grouppsychotherapy is just
a normal therapy group, where you are wellcome with all your pains
and troubles and where you may be as regressive as you like, and
where you also may have secrets.

8. Educational aspects

In contrast to the above about the open secret in the group -
the training therapy being real therapy - seems to be the fact that
this group consists of young and old therapists with 2 trained and
qualified training analysts. One of the training aspects is the
need to identify yourself with the therapist. They want to become
qualified grouptherapists.

In my frame of reference of family patterns in grouppsychotherapy, I see a parallel with parents as educators. Parents are
not only libidinal objects but they are also models for the school
of life.

Therapists are not only objects ready for transference relationships, but also models to copy the art of therapy from.

Very notable is that almost all members have so much trouble
to bring that part of their identity - the nascent therapist, or
even the practicing one - into action at suitable moments. Questions
like: 'how would you yourself work this out in a group?', or: 'why
don't you pick it up, you're a therapist yourself?', are only
answered with difficulty. The next step is the question why. It
often appears that one rather renounces this responsibility and
prefers to sit put as a regressive patient. In analysis the parallel
becomes manifest with children in a family who have been given the
parental role too soon, and have to go through life as parentified
children.

Only after the working through of all these 'double ententes'
and parallels, it becomes possible to activate the hidden part of
their identities - the therapists -, and only then they can succesfully learn something of the doings of their training analysts.

9. Illness, birth and death

Three themes that can shake a family to pieces, but as such
they are only in a concealed way present in a group. Very severe
illnesses of groupmembers or therapists I never encountered in my
groups. If somebody told me in the interview before he starts in
a group, that he or she is suffering from a serious illness, I
would strongly suggest individual psychotherapy.

To bring fantasies about cancer and other deadly diseases to
normal proportions is sometimes such a heavy task, that the real
near death of a groupmember would lead to most complex forms of
defense and would overshadow all other themes.

Pregnancies and births have been present several times. From
the discussion of the wish to become pregnant and the fears and
fantasies around pregnancy and birth, a 9 month pregnancy in the
group of a growing group member in girth and importance, right up
to her return some weeks after birth.

Although in this case reality is overwhelmingly present, pregnancy has a far less threatening and process disturbing influence than severe illness or death.

It's no great achievement of course to get all groupmembers into action now, and to see how most of them in fantasies, thoughts and feelings repeat patterns from their original families.

The actual death of a groupmember I never experienced. Once I got the message of the untimely death (by heartattack while skating) of a groupmember, a year after he had left the group. At that moment, only one groupmember from the earlier period was still in the group. I thougt it unwise to bring it in.

Several times, in my clinical work I had to work through the suicide of an adolescent in a group. I could hardly keep myself and others on their feet.

Wellknown are the fantasies about the illness of the therapist when he is absent. Also the sometimes agressive fantasies at holiday time: plane-crashes and other disasters.

Less wellknown in grouptherapy is the uncertain feeling of guilt, when one of the groupmembers or the therapist is ill. Guilt, circling around the thought: weren't we too harsh for him or her, now causing illness? The same anxious feeling may withhold group-members to really attack each other: he could become ill, could die of it, become crazy or commit suicide.

Such fantasies can be brought to surface and reduced to well-known infantile fantasies, - sometimes strongly confirmed by the parents -, about the dangerous consequences of certain expressions and behaviour: your father will get a heartattack if you continue like that; you'll bring your mother to the grave; when you all think like that I had better kill myself.

After a very emotional session, wherein groupmembers got angry at one of the therapists, the next session one of them asked the therapist: 'you are looking very pale, are you ill or something, is everything allright?' This led to expressing all the fantasies once more about illness and death of parents by the hands of their children.

While leaving, the groupmembers sometimes express their thoughts about the future of the group they leave behind. As analysts we invite them to do so. It looks a lot like the making of a last will. About the further developments of everybody, who has to take care of whom, who will stay for a shorter or longer period in the group etc. Most of these fantasies are friendly and positive. Equally strong present are fantasies that the whole group - the whole family - will fare badly after your departure, the whole group will disintegrate, nobody can go any further without your presence, or alas, also: that you'll be forgotten from one day to the next.

The drink they take together in the little pub nearby after the last session of one of the groupmembers has all the character-istics of a funeral dinner, but now luckily in the lively presence of the dead familymember.

If my fellow therapists and I pay maybe more attention to these themes and aspects than others, we can partly explain this by being psychoanalysts and tend to give a maximum of meaning to family relations, partly by having worked in a youth psychiatry clinic where family patterns are so overwhelmingly present, and partly because we're also very alert on groupdynamics, with special attention to repeating patterns and phenomena.

The primal group pattern for us is the orginal family, how perfect or defective it might have been. This primal group pattern has the tendency to repeat itself in various new group situations.

Our tasks as analysts are to behave ourselves in such a way that changes are brought about in levels of interaction, that points of view are changed and that new contexts develop.

By getting insight in processes and repeating patterns of behaviour, individual members are given the opportunity to acquire new forms of behaviour, that may be more suitable to their personality structure.

If they are able to choose either to follow the family pattern or to bring about changes, then to me therapy is successful.

OUTLINING A SYSTEMIC - DIALECTIC APPROACH TO FAMILY

FUNCTIONING AND MALFUNCTIONING

George Vassiliou, M.D. and Vasso G. Vassiliou, Ph.D.

The Athenian Institute of Anthropos

34 Ivis Street, P. Faleron, Athens, Greece

The Systemic - Dialectic approach outlined briefly here is based on the evaluation of functioning of Anthropos and the therapeutic handling of his malfunctioning within the context of the natural system in the boundaries of which he lives, the family.

It stems from an epistemology which overcomes mechanistic thinking, cause and effect aetiology, attempts to understand a complex "holon" by understanding its parts and finally elminating the blind spots created by the assumption that the observer does not influence the observed.

It follows an epistemology that conceptualizes phenomena as processes. Following a transactional aetiology it attempts to understand first a complex "holon" and then try to analyze it in parts and understand them. It takes fully under consideration the transaction undergoing between observer and observed.

Anthropos (= the human being in Greek both male and female) is conceptualized as an Open System which exchanges with its environment information matter and energy. In this way he is viewed as the outcome of the transaction (mutual alteration) of the biological, psychosocial, sociocultural and socioeconomic processes operating within his boundaries.

These processes by establishing and maintaining channels of transaction give to the System an increasingly organized complexity and a negentropic (anotropic) direction. The psychosocial processes, as long as Anthropos participates in a family process, in a group process, undergo a constant differentiation of cognitions, emotions and patterns of transaction. This in turn enables Anthropos to con-

151

tribute to the differentiation of the group process itself and make
it more differentiated and therefore more effective in providing
boundarying. This is a process supporting the individual, strengthening his sense of reality, encouraging his efforts for the integration of experiences, accepting and understanding the other group
members and becoming accepted and understood by them, inviting further
individual commitment to the group effort.

Developments such as the above which are generated and nurtured
by the overall Group Process provide the needed opportunities for individual differentiation and growth. Self- esteem increases to
levels required for self-leading. From this point of view Anthropos
"Individual" and "Group Member" should be considered as two aspects
of one and the same process.

During such a differentiation Anthorpos is enabled to establish
the required direct and open communication with others during intra-
familiar and intragroup transaction. The result will be a dialogue
including each time a thesis, an antithesis and a synthesis. The
necessary requirements for the dialogue are availability, sincerity
and no intention to manipulate or exploit the other, characteristics
which build what we call trust.

An overlapping is created between people and permits them to
system with each other, to open up stimultaneously and permit a
mutual emotional - cognitive alteration to take place each time on
a level optimal to the furtherance and enhancement of their functioning. They both gradually discover and share what is plus or minus
for the living process, so their functioning will be firmly based
on operational values for living. It is not simply a summing process
whose outcome is the mere summative parathesis of views and opinions.

With the establishment of the dialogue a new system could emerge,
a Couple, which represents a higher level of organized complexity
since additional "channels" of transactions have been created and
must be maintained. We consider as such "channels" among other
things, the styles of self-esteem, the patterns of communication,
the rules of interpersonal conduct prevailing and the shared beliefs
(Virgina Satir, 1972).

Within the couple's boundaries partners will continue to grow
provided that their communication will remain open, sincere and
direct, so it will be enhancing the emergence of orderly, homeo-
dynamically regulated transactions of a complexity level which is
optimal to the differentiation of each partner. Under the circumstances the Couple as a system is ready for a new disequilibrium,
the addition of children. Provided that children will be raised
within the context of a family process which presents the characteristics required for functioning, growth and further differentiation

of both family and child, the child will become capable to create,
produce and share, to establish interdependent, co-operative relations
with others.

Two sub-systems are formed within the Family and function with
boundaries which should always remain clearly defined and maintained:
Parents and Children. However, during the development of the family
process, leadership is assumed at different times by different members.

The processes developing during family living present intrapersonal, interpersonal and multipersonal aspects. This is illustrated
by the very developments in the field of family therapy: from the
work on the psychodynamics involved (Ackerman, 1966), to the work on
the communication patterns prevailing (Watzlawick, 1967), to the
work on boundary structuring (Minuchin, 1974), to the work involving
Extended Family relations (Borszomenyi-Nagy, 1973, Bowen, 1978), to
the conceptualization of Family Therapy as education for change
(Satir, 1972), the gradual extention of the field along systemic
lines involving more complex levels of organization is obvious.

When malfunctioning prevails it remains originally masked, disguised under different "complaints". For instance the Mother of
family 'A' having father, mother and three sons, 16, 14 and 8 years
old respectively, calls and complains that "our children are constantly fighting with each other".

The Diagnostic Family Interview though reveals that under this
mask there is a considerable disturbance in relational patterns.

Mother has a close, intimate, reciprocal relation with her third
son. With this son she tries to find the support, the strengthening,
the acceptance and the positive affect she needs.

This mother and third son relationship is the dominant one in
the family.

As a result, first and second son remain isolated.

Mother and third son are crossing the boundaries of their respective subsystems. This breeds, of course, antagonism. Father
antagonizes the third son for occupying mother's attention. The
first and second son antagonize their younger brother for mother's
favours. This creates a constant fighting between the three boys and
provokes disciplinary, very punitive interventions from father who
fights all three boys.

Mother attempting to buffer the situation plays a protective role
which places everybody in a bind. She behaves for instance like saying to the father "I will protect you preventing you to become un-

just to your children. However, I will simultaneously prevent you
from realizing that I myself create the situation which forces you
to become punitive."

Obviously the patterning of relations of this family needs restructuring. A working relationship should be established and maintained between father and third son. Father should be trained to
relate with the three boys as one sub-system, with the Mother learning
respectively to do the same. The three boys should be trained and
assisted to proceed and structure the boundary of their own sub-
system.

Father and Mother should be trained and assisted in structuring
the boundary of the parental sub-system. One is confronted here with
a demanding therapeutic and educational task.

After the Diagnostic Family Interview one has to proceed, to
plan at the indicated periods of time (a) further family sessions
combined with (b) sessions of the sub-group of siblings and (c) of
the parental sub-group.

Intervening strategically along the lines of the described sub-
systems, we shift the focus of intervention from one member of the
family to another and level of intervention from one sub-system to
the other and to the Family System as a whole, so we can achieve the
required restructuring most effectively, (multilevel-multifocal
intervention).

The approach according to which this intervention is applied
(Vassiliou, 1977) calls for the full consideration of all the processes involved in family transaction, the socio-cultural and socio-
economic included. For this reason troubled couples are invited to
workshops which study the transition of family living from traditional
patterns of transaction, roles, values and ideologies to the ones
needed for adjustment in the technologically developing milieux.

During these workshops the extensive application of Action
Techniques leads, in a laboratory-fashion, to a final integration.

The combination of the described groupings generates between
family members the transaction optimal for therapy and growth.

BIBLIOGRAPHY

Ackerman, N., Treating the Troubled Family, New York, Basic Books,
          1966,

Boszormenyi-Nagy, I. and Spark, G.M., Invisible Loyalties, New York,
          Harper and Row, 1973.

Bowen, M., _Family Therapy in Clinical Practice_, New York, Jason
        Aronson, 1978.

Minuchin, S., _Families and Family Therapy_, Cambridge, Mass, Harvard
        University Press, 1974.

Satir, V., _Peoplemaking_, Palo Alto, Calif: Science and Behavior
        Books, 1972.

Vassiliou, G. and V., _Outlining a Dialectic-Systemic Approach
        Concerning Functioning and Malfunctioning of Anthropos
        and His Suprasystems_, The Athenian Institute of
        Anthropos: T.R. XXII, 1977.

Watzlawick, P., Beavin, J.H. and Jackson, D.D., _Pragmatics of Human
        Communication_, New York, Norton, 1967

SYSTEMS CONCEPTS IN GROUP AND FAMILY THERAPY

Claus B. Bahnson, Ph.D., Professor of Psychiatry

Jefferson Medical College, Thomas Jefferson University

Philadelphia, U.S.A.

Systems theory plays a significant role for the development of group and family theoretical concepts. Obviously, both groups and families constitute systems, but systems thinking has hardly had a full impact as yet on a generation of therapists who have trained under the aegis of psychoanalysis or behaviorists who mainly have focused on individual intrapsychic process or behavior - which does not obliterate the fact that the individual all by himself also is a "system".

The development of systems theory has not taken place in a vacuum, but has grown out of theoretical developments in physics, philosophy, psychology, sociology and biology, where limited inter-actional concepts have served as precursors to the meta theoretical framework of systems theory. From gestalt theory - as exemplified in the logo of this conference produced by our beloved late Prof. Edgar Rubin - we learned that in perceptual processes we cannot account for the apperception of the whole on the basis of an additive amassing of perceptions of the elements or parts. This was the essence of the pioneering work of psychologists such as Köhler, Wetheimer, Rubin, Katz, Goldstein and other original gestalt thinkers. In mathematics and physics, Einstein's and Heisenberg's relativism and Bohr's complementarity thinking put an end to a simplistic con-cept of a Newtonian reality, which also had been questioned previous-ly by the continental philsophers, including Kant, Spinoza, Hegel and Schopenhauer. In sociology and economics, scholars such as Marx, Weber, and Parsons pointed out that the fate of the individual social or economical "element" was dependent on the characteristics of the whole system, thus introducing relativistic and systems concepts in the social and economic sciences. Systems theory grew in a societal climate where elementarism, through isolated

study of events of individuals, became too limited and ineffective
for the understanding and prediction of behavior of such part processes or individuals. Not only were concepts of gestalt or systems
introduced within single disciplines in order to account for the behavior of subsystems, but interdisciplinary systems were recognized,
e.g. in psychsomatic medicine, simultaneously physiology and psychology, or in social psychology where concepts such as alienation included both economic and psychological components. Similarly, Pareto
pointed toward the structural isomorphism between biologic and economic theories.

Formal systems theory as formulated particularly by von Bertalanffy, but also by scholars such as William Gray, James G. Miller,
Roy Grinker Sr., Gregory Bateson, Albert B. Scheflen and Kenneth
Boulding, only to mention a few, thus has developed into a meta
theoretical framework linking part systems, described on the levels
of different disciplines, into a larger framework. Based on the
isomorphic thinking which guides our human formulation of the processes observed on different conceptual levels (e.g. physiological,
psychological, social) an integration of these part processes has
become possible that allows for the achievement of a wider vista on
the meta-level than can be achieved from the observation posts of
the sub-systems and at intradisciplinary integrative levels.

Two main developments have taken place, one related to the
effect of increased communication among scholars and therapists,
resulting in a stepwise reduction or discarding of some of our many
sets of blinders, the second related to what is becoming a more and
more obvious fact, namely that it is the same human mind and brain
that approaches observations in different disciplines, and that it
therefore should be no great surprise that theoretical formulations
in different subject areas show marked Isomorphism. Systems theory
thus moves the focus from the "elements" of observed"realities" - in
the sense of the naive realist - to a conceptualization in which one
is aware that the observer, as the phenomenologists and existenial-
ists have pointed out, is the creator and originator of his observations and formulations. We have come to the humble realization
that we cannot tap "reality" or "truth", but that we must create our
own worlds; and we cannot get rid of our last set of blinders, i.e.
the specific limitations and characteristics dictated by the structure
of our own minds and nervous systems.

However, the great strides that have resulted from the advent
of systems theory, and that were set in motion on the basis of our
impatience with the inadequacy of mechanistic thinking, are
characterized by an emphasis on systems versus reductionism, interaction versus isolation, the mutual influence of participating parts,
and interdisciplinary studies and interactions necessitating supraordinate conceptualizations. A special consequence of the systems
thinking in psychology and biology is the revelation, expressed e.g.

by Gordon Allport or the biologist, Paul Weiss, that human and other
living systems are "open systems" rather than closed and entropic
systems as are those in classical physics. Of course, the interesting
question is now whether advanced physics will come to the conclusion
that negative entropy characterizes also the universe at large. The
concept of negative entropy in biological and group systems is significant since it implies growth and change rather than a continual
seeking towards homeostasis and equilibrium.

Systems theory was developed in a climate of controversy between
mechanistic and vitalistic points of view. By developing an integrative supraordinate meta system, systems theory superseded this
dualistic battle between "antecedent" and "teleologic" causality and
integrated these concepts as subset-theories representing complementary part solutions. Systems theory also clearly opposed the
older concept of linear causality and replaced it with the concept of
mutual integration of multiple variables representing the total
gestalt.

The development from "linear causality" to systems concept of
causality ensued through the development of "circular causality" as
developed by cybernetics by Norbert Wiener in his mathematical model
slated to encompass organized complexity. Shannon, in his mathematical theory of communication, and Ashby, in information theory,
fulfilled similar intermediary tasks. Cybernetics, running parallel
to S-R theory, provided the intermediary step from simple linear concepts of unidimensional causality to the complex formulations of
systems theory, conceptualizing organisms as organized gestalts
characterized by wholeness, multivariable interaction, and negentropy.

Von Bertalanffy emphasized that open living systems are never
characterized by the second principle of thermodynamics in physics,
reflecting chemical or thermodynamic equilibria, but in contrast,
represent steady states of balanced tensions. Even the steady states,
or homeostasi, are questionable in light of the systems theoretical
emphasis on evolution and open systems. Instead of the entropy in
physics we introduce the negentropy of living systems. Von
Bertalanffy, in concert with Piaget's formulations, hypothesized
progressive differentiation, progressive segregation, and progressive centralization in individual and group system. He also
introduced the concept of anamorphosis - the transition towards a
higher order - as a principle of psychological development. Karl
Menninger, similarly, introduced the concept of heterostasis in open
human systems in contrast to the older homeostatic concept, emphasizing that human development, both individually and in groups, reflects a progressive moving away from the status quo.

Systems theory also necessistated a replacement of the mechanistic model in personality theory,substituting for drive and
learning theories, conceptualizing man as a robot, with the concept

of a dynamic hierarchical order of parts and processes. Systems
theory also contributed to replacing the learning theory concept of
man as an "empty box" (tabula rasa) in which the "internal processes"
reflect hypotheses projected on to the person by the observer, with
a concept akin to phenomenology in which internal activity and
spontaneity of the open system is characteristic of the autonomous
behavior which precedes reactions to external stimuli. "There is
nothing new under the sun", Albert Scheflen has pointed out that
systems theory has reverted to a naturalistic approach which is as
old and classical as the study of nature, in contrast to the isolated
elementarism of the nineteenth century.

As a person working both with individual and family systems, I
have produced my own version of systems theory represented on
Figure 1.   The different loops represent different levels of observation on different systems interactional levels. A basic concept
is that the level of observation and the inclusiveness of phenomena is
an arbitrary choice dependent on the observers' interests and
leanings. However, the higher level of organization to the left in
the figure are in some ways hierarchically higher than those towards
the right, although that, again, is a matter of axium and dogma.
The reason that one may think of a hierarchical elevation going from
right to left is simply that we move from the micro- to the macro-
cosmos in the figure; but it is admittedly arbitrary whether or not
that should be called a higher order. The phenomenon is most clearly
visible when considering the transition from the individual to the
family or group system in which the individual clearly is a part of
the family or group, although the family or group is not necessarily
more complex or encompassing than the individual, but rather operates
and is observed on, different levels of description. As a matter of
fact, as we move from "lower" to "higher" hierarchical levels, there
is a clear shift in lexical and conceptual description of the phenomena, but not necessarily characterized by an increasing complexity,
since the description of physiological phenomena can be as complex
as - or more complex than - the description of e.g. group behaviors.
However, in terms of the micro-macro concept, the inherent complexity
obviously grows as we move from the small to the large, since the
large is composed of the small, and it may be that it is the limitations of our human conceptualization of complex phenomena that simply
tend to reduce the perceivable complexity down to a certain constant
that then may characterize formulations on any level. That, however,
would not change the basic concept that complexity will increase as
we move from the micro focus to the macro concept, as we also see
when we compare experience in individual versus family systems.

Family Therapy

Let us now look at the evidence for systems processes in the

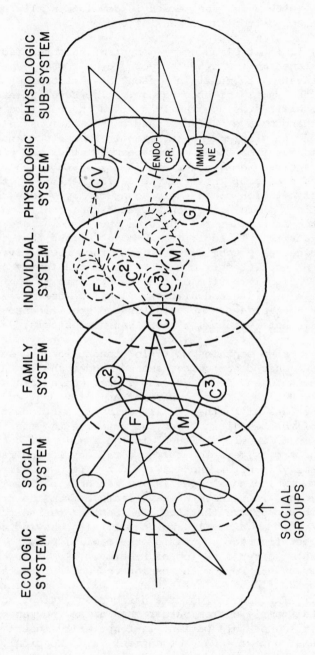

Figure 1. Alternative systems levels

family and in the group, starting off with the family as a special
group, because the family is that system most adjacent to the individual system with which the person is developmentally and
historically enmeshed from the moment of conception.

The family is in itself a complex system characterized by
developmental stages moving from the young dyadic family, through
triadic and quadratic, to multiple person interactional systems
already within the family of procreation.   The developmental time
dimension is significant since family systems changes take place over
time with the changing age variables and constellations related to
individuation of the single members. Family therapists know that,
relatively independent of the specific personalities and problems
characterizing a given family, certain family systems behaviors
develop at given stages of the family's development, e.g. the enmeshed procreative fusion of the very young family versus the problems of separation, differentiation and loss characterizing the
family at a later stage when the children have become late adolescents or young adults. In addition, we have learned that tri-
generational processes predominate, so that the procreative family
cannot clearly be separated from the system of the family of
orientation. The family system of the grandparents is contiguous
with the system of their grandchildren. Thus, we are never talking
about "a family" but always about a given and specific progressing
family process in heterostasis, rather than homeostasis.

The family system contains multiple transactions on several
levels, including shared economics, shared needs, shared culture,
shared coping methods and defenses, and shared goals, ethics and
styles. Because the very tender years of an individual are spent
in close transactions with other family members, particularly the
parents, many of the behaviors which characterize the constituent individual later in life, are "learned" in the family and cannot be
understood without consideration of the total developing family
system.   The family is often characterized by its own "development
level" of needs, including all the family members, particularly in
centripetal enmeshed families. We have learned from the treatment
of schizophrenic youngsters that the treatment of the so-called
"designated patient" as a single individual, after having removed
this family member from the context of the family, only to let the
individual re-enter after a period of treatment, leads nowhere, because the family system forces the designated patient to take on
many of the symptomatic behaviors after the patient returns to the
family context.   In other words, the designated patient acts as a
part of the total family system rather than as an independent
operational unit. When this patient is temporarily inserted in a
different systems context (e.g. a treatment unit, hospital, or therapeutic group) his dynamics and behavior can be modified and even
developed. But by returning the patient to the original system of
the family, the old problems tend to reoccur.   Therefore, it has be-

come necessary to treat the total family system rather than the individual. As it has been pointed out by many scholars, the variables
which we use for conceptulization of the family process are not
identical with the intrapsychic variables with which many of the
current generation of therapists have grown up. Although there
clearly is an isomorphism between the conceptualization of the individual and of the family, with several overlapping variables such
as communication, affective expression, degree of isolation and repression, etc., there are other variables that characterize the
family system better than the individual system, such as the concept
of centrifugal versus centripetal relationships. These characteristics of the family system have profound consequences, not only for
the cohesion or diversification of the family system itself, but
also for its members, later in time. I have formulated in a simplified fashion the typical developmental family characteristics
associated with centrifugal and centripetal systems and have related
these family characteristics to the "choice of illness" later in
life of the family members (Figures II to V)

In the family, the behavior of one member transacts with all
others, and the family behaves as an organism with the different
individuals serving as parts. This is clearly observable with regard
to shared needs, on a given developmental level, of different family
members, in the sense that if certain needs are expressed or "acted
out" by one family member, this expression serves to satisfy most,
if not all, other family members' needs in this particular area.
Therefore, we often see that if the expression of needs, e.g. sexual
needs in a teenage child, is being diverted or inhibited during the
therapeutic process, then one of the adults will "take over" and
express this need in lieu of the child - or vice versa. A similar
situation pertains to shifts in ego defenses, e.g. when one family
member projects in a paranoid fashion, and the others are served
thereby. When the paranoid defenses are alleviated or changed in
this family member, then the paranoid mechanism is taken up by
another family member, indicating that defenses and regressive man-
oeuvers also are shared among family members. Guilt and loyalties,
belonging to the "conscience aspects" of psychological functioning,
also are shared in families, so that when the loyalty or retribution
is expressed by one, other family members may not feel compelled to
replicate this function. Often one Minister, Rabbi, or Priest in
the family will put the minds at ease for all the others.

Due to this system sharing, treating the whole family as an
organism prevents the error of modifying one part without regards
to how this part - or person - fits into the functioning of the
total family. Thus, the goal of change in the family communication
and family assignments of different functions to the constituent
members may permanently change the conditions that provoked a regressive disease in one family member, thus producing a permanent

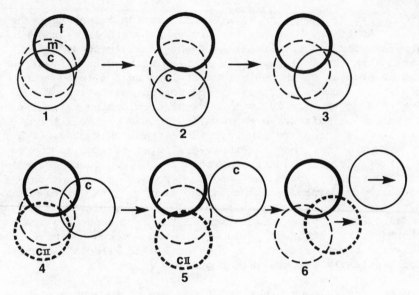

Figure 2.   Normal family development

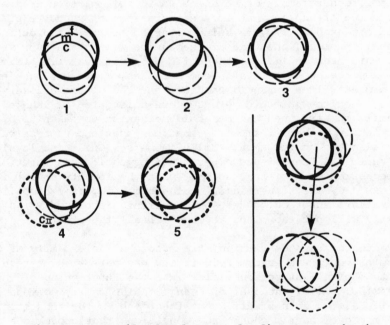

Figure 3.   Family development leading to psychosis

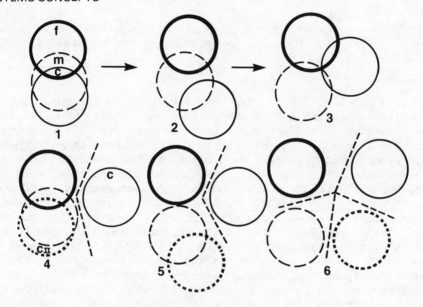

Figure 4. Family development leading to borderline states

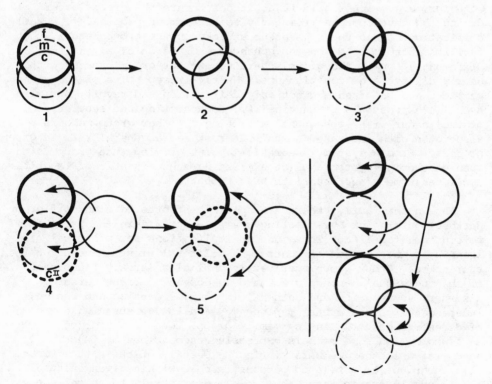

Figure 5. Family development leading to somatization

result through a shift in direction of the projected development from
the point of intervention in the nuclear, or the extended family.

Group Therapy

The group is different from the family in many respects. The
treatment group if of a more short-lived character; usually is composed of individuals of approximately the same age; has not had
longitudinal personal experiences in common (except in very special
groups); and probably are placed higher in the hierarchy of systems
as we move from the individual, through the family, to society at
large. However, the group also has many characteristics in common
with the family, and just as the human organism can be described as
an integration of sub-systems efficiently working together for the
common goal of survival, also groups of human organisms can be understood as systems that partly submerge individual needs in order to
create jointly a new larger system for enhanced survival in the
larger social and environmental setting. Although the co-living
of treatment groups is of shorter duration than relationships in
the family, many regularities occur in the group rather independent
of the particular characteristics of its members. Slater, Yalom,
Foulkes, Pines and others have described the regularities of group
behavior, e.g. with regard to attitudes toward the group leader
during the developments from early to late group process. The early
"deification" of, and the subsequent attacks on the group leader, that
facilitate group cohesion and enhanced expression of affect and
differentiation in the group, characterize the group process with
nearly all types of constituents. Nearly irrespective of the given
participants we often see not only deification and revolt, but also
symbolic expressions of cannibalism, decathecting and secularizing
of the leader with subsequent cathecting of other group members
associated with increased sexual interest, as a general rule in group
process. From a systems theoretical point of view, the group is an
open developing system and not expressing a homeostatic or repetitive
cycle, as some group theorists have thought.

As in the family, there are specific efforts to fight off group
death by pairing or by selecting a new leader within the group as if
to continue its life. The stunning implications for political
leadership and changes of control in political groups have often been
overlooked. Other group therapeutic variables largely independent
of the individual members are the development of trust versus
distrust, spontaneity and authenticity versus caution and facade,
independence versus mutual dependence, and low versus high degree
of defensiveness. As in the family group, the therapy group functions
as a whole with some members expressing unconscious or functional
needs for all other members within the Gestalt of the group. Thus,
also in groups of unrelated persons, albeit within given cultural
sub-groups in our society, the group members truly function as a
system which has its own developments and laws that determine the

group behaviors of the single constituent. That does not mean that
the single personalities do not influence the group process, but it
is within the framework of the macro structure of the group process
that these variations may occur.

Psychosomatics

Systems theory has had a significant impact on psychosomatics
and psychobiology because it has provided a formal framework within
which the psychosomatic conceptualizations can be described without
regressing to reductionistic and mechanistic linear concepts, as
for example by describing experience as an epiphenomenon stemming
from physiological process, or, vice versa, conceptualizing physiological events as "results" of experienced stress phenomena. Systems
theory provides a paradigm which allows us to integrate physiological
and experiential phenomena within one meta system, permitting the
formalization of e.g. my psychosomatic complementarity concept within a meta theoretical structure. The alternative of regressing
either along the physiological developmental or the behavioral
developmental axes can be linked to particular defensive strategies
which, again, are interlocked with the fate of the family's development and solution for drive discharge many years prior to the event
of the illness. It is then no longer a question of whether the hen
or the egg came first, but the graduation to a supraordinate construct including the developmental process all the way from the in-
ception of the egg to the "old hen". It is no longer a question of
whether the physiology or the psyche comes first, but a meta construct allowing for a simultaneous conceptualization of these levels
of observation and expression, even allowing for prediction of behavior interlocking both.

Conclusion

Systems theory, then, is the broader meta concept encompassing
such as the individual, the family, the group, and psychosomatic
process. Systems theory encompasses theoretical formulations on
different levels of conceptulaization and focus, e.g. the personality
sub-system; the total individual as a system; or the family or group
as a system. These systems have an interface or transaction with
each other in the sense that, as Grinker has pointed out, what is
hierarchically a higher gestalt seen from a lower level of sub-
systems now becomes one of the "elements" which is integrated into
the gestalt of the supraordinate system. For example, the perception of the individual as a system represents an integration and
hierarchical co-ordination of several sub-systems, including personality and physiological sub-systems; but at the same time this
individual system forms a part of the gestalt of the family system,
etc. This introduces the concept of relativity of the organization
of observations and data. Therefore, we will need in the future a
transactional lexicon or syllabus for the translation among different

systems subsets, such as the translation from individual to group
formulations, both relative to their set of observations and transactions.

General systems theory makes it possible to work with multiple
factors in interaction and with the complexity of the results of
these interactions - presenting us not with an either/or, but with a
both/and solution, reflecting the complementarity between different
part choices of variables (observations) and between different
formulations of dynamics from different hierarchical levels. Not
only have we been forced to become humble, considering the relativity
of our formulations, but we have also approached a system which
possibly may reintegrate into an encompassing meta theory, observations and formulations which previously represented separate and
isolated views.

THE PERSON AS EXPRESSION OF THE GROUP

Romano Fiumara

III Clinica Psichiatrica Universita

Roma, 00191 Viale di Villa Massimo, 47

To start with definitions, "persona" was the name given by the Ancient Romans to the mask usually worn by the actors in the theatre, so we could say it is most meaningful in the sense of actor, or character.

But in psychology the term is not often used, and in any case not with this meaning (except in the case of the Jungian school, to be discussed later).

For my own part I have resorted, in a perhaps banal, perhaps provocative style of work, to the definitions to be found in the Italian dictionary, and have chosen the following.

In this dictionary (1969), under "person", we can find the above mentioned actor's "mask" of Latin use, followed by a definition of "person" as the individual, whether man or woman. The same dictionary defines "personality" as the quality of the person, or the complex characteristics which distinguish that person from others.

So we have "person" as mask and as individual who, by means of his/her personality, is distinguished from others.

At this point another problem arises which is of great relevance for any analysis of group phenomena: the relationship between the single person and the group, between individual and collective, where we can perhaps find the root of all the problems of human existence, if it is true that a Dasein is always a Mit-Dasein.

The problem as such has obviously been of interest to the field of philosophy, or more exactly epistemology, where we find a parti-

cular interesting enquiry conducted by Karl Popper, together with
equally illustrious Noble prize-winning neurophysiologist, John
Eccles, the inquiry resulted in the volume "Self and its brain"
(Popper K., Eccles J., 1977). A concrete attempt at combining philosophical and scientific investigation.

Popper developed a philosophy of "three worlds" of which the
first is the material world, both organic and inorganic, thus including biology, the human body and brain, and all the machines and
goods manufactured by man; and the second is the world of conscious experiences, not only the awareness of our immediate perceptions, but also our memories, imagination, thoughts. Finally,
the third is the world of objective knowledge, which includes the
objective contents of the ideas implicit in artistic and scientific
expression.

In brief, world 1 is the physical world, world 2 the world of
consciousness, world 3 the world of culture.

Eccles' knowledge contributed towards neurophysiological
assumptions, and a plan was drawn up which included cerebral
structures and the interaction which they establish with world 2
(consciousness) and world 3 (culture).

An interesting factor of Eccles' plan is the distinction of
world 2 (consciousness), into three levels; external sensations,
or perception through the receptive organs, internal sensations, and
finally a third level pertaining to a cerebral entity which forms
our very basis as beings capable of conscious experience throughout
our lives: the Self. In the Italian translation this entity was
indicated as "pure Ego".

Of all Popper and Eccles' conceptualizations I would emphasize
the constantly circular relationships between worlds 1, 2 and 3,
pivoting on a central entity founded on these relationships, the
"essence" of the individual, the Self according to Eccles.

The problem of interaction between individual and group, one
and many, single and environment, can also be seen from another
angle - for example by shifting the accent to another philosophical
standpoint that is genetic epistemology.

Now, within the perspective of genetic epistemology, Michael
Lewis and Jeanna Brooks-Gunn (1979) have recently published the
latest studies on social cognition and the acquisition of Self.
From this research, carried out with the aid of the mirrors, videotapes and drawings, it is evident that social cognition necessarily
includes a knowledge of the Self. This knowledge, which appears
very early on in the child (not later than the first year of age),
is fundamental for active development.

The above-mentioned authors emphasize the dualistic character
of the Self, in the distinction between Self as subject and Self as
object.

From what we have said so far we can conclude that, whether man
is seen as a passive subject in his relationship with reality, or as
an active agent, the basis of a progressive organization of the person is represented by the Self.

Let us now consider another standpoint, in which, we perhaps
feel more at ease, that is the psychoanalytical theory.

The terms Ego and Self are common in analytical literature, but
their use faces two difficulties: the first is conceptual, in that
the two terms are not clearly separate, and the second is semantic,
since an unvarying criterion as to how to define the word "Self"
does not yet exist. The question of the psychoanalytical concept of
the Self begins explicitly with Hartmann, who distinguishes between
the Ego, as a psychic system, and the Self, as a concept referring
to the Self proper. But even today, almost 40 years later, the
question doesn't seem to me to be completely resolved.

It has certainly been closely examined by many authors, from
Paula Heimann to Edith Jacobson, from Melanie Klein to Winnicott,
from Erikson to Guntrip and Kohut and many more; they all would be
worthy of comparison and discussion, both for the specific meaning
each has given to these terms, and for the place given to these terms
in the theoretical model used to elucidate the dynamism of the psyche.

But this is not the place to make such an attempt, particularly
since those who have tried have inevitably ended up by adopting
systems of their own, as for example Leon and Rebecca Grinberg (1975),
who, after a survey of psychoanalytical concepts regarding the Self,
concluded by proposing their own personal concepts of Ego, No-Ego,
Self, No-Self and unconscious fantasy of the Self and the Ego.

And if we add here the concept of Self as proposed by Eccles and
Popper, or of the existential Self and categorical Self as proposed
by Lewis and Brooks-Gunn, we find ourselves with a veritable Tower of
Babel.

And at this point, not so much for the pleasure of contradicting
myself and adding confusion, but in order to clarify my working
references, being of Jungian training myself, I shall briefly mention
a few basic concepts of Jungian theory as recently systematized by W.
Whitmont (1969). In this approach the terms Ego and Self acquire a
very special meaning. As we know, the term "complex" was first in-

troduced by C.G. Jung to indicate the basic structural element of the unconscious. It is made up of a group of associations with a powerful emotional charge, which is autonomous, and can be activated or developed by subsequent individual experiences of a similar affective tone.

Contrary to the opinions of other non-Jungian authors, the complex is not therefore pathological in itself, indeed; since it forms the basic structure of our psychic make-up, we should perhaps call it the healthy part. It becomes pathological only to the extent that its original genetic core, or "archetype", is deviated and distorted by means of the conflictual contents derived from the individual's personal life. According to the terminology introduced by Whitmont, these conflictual contents, pertaining to the subjective personal unconscious, make up the "shell" of the complex, while its "core" is formed by the archetype.

At the level of personal identity, we could propose the consideration of an "identity complex" which we assume functions like every other complex.

And, according to Whitmont's schema, what we usually understand as Ego represents in fact the shell of the above-mentioned identity complex; its archetypal core, as the all-inclusive unit of all the individual's real potential, makes up the Self.

This approach, which distinguishes in complexes a shell pertaining to the personal unconscious, and a core pertaining to the collective unconscious, could be very useful in indicating a way of integrating Freudian and Jungian metapsychology. In effect the past, whether ontogenetic or phylogenetic, never ceases to influence the present, even if analytical psychologists have above all persisted in the phylogenetic influence, and psycho-analysts have emphasized ontogenesis.

Here I would directly connect to the personal identity complex the way another Jungian author, Erich Neumann (1953) treats the question.

Neumann's basic assumptions are, in brief, that the psyche, as Gestalt theory has shown, has a field character, and, on the other hand, that any sort of knowledge is always a field process, of a relative nature, only associable to the type of cognitive system which is effective at the moment of knowledge.

Starting from this premise, Neumann distinguishes 3 levels or fields of knowledge, the most superficial of which is our familiar Ego-cognition. Quite apart from this conscious level of the personality, two other, subsequent fields of knowledge can be observed

in the schema adopted by Neumann, the archetypal field and the field
of the Self.

The Self thus appears as an unconscious entity more profound
than the world of archetypes, which it organizes.

The relationship between the fields of Self and conscious Ego
follows a Self-Ego, Ego-Self axis, which is the central axis of
becoming conscious which constitutes personal identity, and which
promotes the phenomena of form organization and thus general cognitive
processes.

As the archetypal field becomes gradually unfolded, activated
by experience and personal history, so the archetype becomes evident.

On the basis of these preliminary remarks we can now turn to
the specific function of the group.

In the progressive working out of a personal identity, and the
correlated structuring of the Ego as centre of the field of consciousness, the group can be said to have priority over the individual.

This statement, in the light of what we have said so far,
appears tenable in the first place if we admit that the child is
born equipped with a series of archetypal potentials, which we can
consider as the basic "starting-group" in the gradual process in
which he defines himself as single and distinct from others. And
as such the child gets the feeling of himself in the realm of consciousness. This argument is reinforced if we admit that, as the
archetypal potentials are progressively revealed, the social group
the child belongs to will provide him with the necessary experiences
to empathically create the space for this opening-up process: in
this sense the external group educates (ex-ducere), in the sense
that it makes the internal "group" emerge. This is equally true if
we consider the mother's actions alone in the sense that she represents the group "norms", and transmits them to the child.

Anyway, dealing with the subject of the Self, in purely Jungian
terms, we can see that it is not very far removed from the one proposed by Douglas Levin (1969), of definite Freudian faith, who published a paper entitled "The Self: A Contribution in its Place to
Theory and Technique". A plenary session of the International
Congress of Psycho-Analysis in Rome was devoted to the same theme.

Levin, in brief, like Hartmann, sees the Self as a fourth
psychic agent, next to the Ego, Super-Ego and Id, and he elevates
it functionally, to the position of great reservoir of libido, from
which libidinal energy can be extracted for the purpose of object

relations, like the pseudopods of an amoeba. (This, then, corresponds to the Self, and not to the Ego or Id, as Freud stated in
"Outlines of Psycho-Analysis"). On the other hand the Ego, according to Levin, should be considered as the great system of mental
functions and a central control.

The discussion at the Congress showed contrasting opinions.
Kohut (1970), who was also the moderator, summarized the session by
assigning to the Self the function of "organizer of the Ego's
activities".

In any case, I should personally like to underline the need,
agreed upon by all, of admitting to a Self, and of giving this Self
functions of Ego-organizer, and placing its genesis at the moment
of the child's earliest relations with its mother, whose function as
"good enough", to quote Winnicott, is essential for assuring a
normal presence and cohesiveness of the Self. All in all, it seems
to me that, starting from different points of view, the existence
of an Ego-Self and Self-Ego axis is admitted even by Freudians.

And at this point I believe it is irrelevant to give the Self
a specifically Jungian connotation, since we have to consider that
specific experiences of relationship of mirroring oneself in the
mother and the environment, are necessary: they empathically echo
the potential archetypal roots of the individual.

I should like to stress, though, that the experience with the
mother can still be considered a group experience, since the mother
is in effect the mouthpiece for the group laws.

And if we then admit, that with its mother the child premature-
ly experiments with other people's presence, if only of the members
of his immediate family, so it seems to me essential to admit that
the individual is always an expression of the group. The group,
in effect, plays a fundamental part in the definition of the Self,
and on this basis it can be supposed by the Ego as the agency of
the individual's cognitive and decisional functions.

Everything we have said so far can be best utilized in group
psychotherapy, and particularly in group analysis.

So if we briefly consider the practical and theoretical foundations of group analysis (I would personally restrict this term for
S.H. Foulkes (1976), just as psycho-analysis is used in direct
reference to Freud), these foundations appear to be centred around
two focal constructs, one of which represents the credit given to
the group as a fundamental therapeutic agency, while the other, as
the essential therapeutic tool, represents free participative
communication in the group context. Here it seems appropriate to
quote Foulkes' statement concerning the participants in a group

analysis: "They collectively represent the norm from which each of them deviates".

The group therefore appears to correspond to an organizing, regulating "centre" or "system", to which the single components are related, for the purpose of naturally modifying their behaviour patterns.

To sum up, adopting a systems approach, the therapeutic group is a system, an open system, and the individuals participating in the group are sub-systems, on Foulkes' side. On Jung's side we have the Self as super-ordinate model which creates and maintains order in "the man" system, where complexes and archetypes can be considered sub-systems. And, if we consider the concept of the Self as an Ego-organizer tenable also in the Freudian school, this analogy (Self = group) becomes always sustainable.

The above-mentioned theoretical analogies become even clearer at a clinical level, which brings me finally to introduce one example, taken from my clinical practice at the Psychiatric Clinic at Rome University.

I think it is correct to inform you that the group I am speaking of started as part of a research project concerning the genesis of obsessive thought. The group is composed of 10 participants, equally divided between the sexes, of a similar cultural background (all, except one,having graduated from senior high school), of ages ranging between 23 and 35.

Most of the participants (8 of them), were clinically diagnosed as obsessive neurotics: the remaining 2 were clinically considered as cases of character neurosis with hysterical symptoms.

Six out of the 8 obsessive members were under pharmacological treatment.

The group was conducted in co-therapy. At the end of each session the interactive chronogram was jointly compiled, in accordance with Murray Cox's instructions.

Attendance at the group was particularly stable, the average never less than seven.

The conscious intent, previously agreed upon by the two thera- pists, was above all to encourage free communications between the members, sending back to the group any message or request addressed to the therapists.

And, if the therapists did intervene with an interpretation, it was simply with a view to emphasizing the appearance of resistances

or defences which were obstructing the free flow of communication.
Within these limits, any dreams that were brought up, were not given
particular attention, nor were repressions into the past encouraged.

At the end of the 15th session, the first conductor had intervened a total of 30 times, thus averaging twice a session, with a
total average, considering the number of verbal interactions among
members of the group, of approximately 5%. The second conductor had
intervened only 4 times in all.

In a limited description which may not do justice to the immense
variety of events that took place in the group, I think I can briefly
state that the group was above all used by the single members as a
"good enough" container of their respective differences, in the sense
that each one, in the group atmosphere, could make use of the group
matrix as a temporary membrane, while forming their own personal
membrane, which I think is comparable to the concept of Self.

In this sense, if the group membrane is sufficiently sound, the
individual may abandon his false-Self, re-elaborating the damages,
suffered previously during his attempts at building up a Self.

And in this connection I should like to quote a clinical example chosen from many similar ones, the case of Gino.

As the group progressed, he, a young 23 year old, had been
silent for many sessions, and declaredly sleepy, which is a way of
hardly participating, and showing a kind of evasive and unassailable
resistance.

Then, in the 11th session, taking advantage of questions raised
by some of the participants about another member's absence, the
conductor noted, with specific intent, that there are "present members
who are also absent", and everyone's attention naturally turned to
Gino, who was warmly invited to state his case. The invitation had
the quality of being warm, that is it generated a sufficient degree
of warmth to allow Gino not to go on being silent and reserved, but
to open up creatively. In this particular session, too, Marina was
missing. She was felt by many members as being the "Great Mother",
paralyzing in her silence. So Gino, situationally deprived of a
concrete frame of reference for his experiences and fantasies of an
inhibiting mother (as he later states), was temporarily able to un-
tie himself from this mother image and make use of a substitute,
perfectly fitting mother, the group. An attempt at substitution of
a primary experience. In this attempt Gino expressed himself at
last. As a metapsychological introduction to the material offered
by Gino, I should like to quote a brief outline summarized by
Malcolm Pines (1980): "These themes of narcissism and self and
object representation are intimately entwined. They are twins. The
theme of twins and the emergence of twin phantasies in analysis, and

and the significance of twins in mythology has been traced by Otto
Rank. The twin is a form of double just as the mirror reflection is.
The double, the twin, symbolizes the second self whose existence is
shown by the shadow in the reflection. Man's first concept of his
soul is related to the shadow, to which reverence is paid in religion
and taboos. Powerful taboos are based on the need to protect the
shadow from harm being done to it".

In Gino's case we were dealing not merely with a twin, a double,
a narcissistic mirror reflection, but indeed with a Siamese twin.
He in fact declares to the group members his conviction that he was
born with a Siamese twin brother, who was taken away from him.
Suffering from obstetric paralysis in his left shoulder, he maintained that this was proof of the fact that he had been connected
to his twin by the right hip, and to compensate for this disjunction
on the right side, a deliberate wound has been inflicted on his
left side as a compensatory measure.

This delusional conviction was decisively criticized by all
members of the group, and Gino was gradually led to agree with the
criticism and accept the fact that we were not dealing with reality,
but fantasy.

In this sense it seems that the group matrix can pave the way
to a real psychic birth, that is no-one wants to force Gino not to
be what he is and deny his own history; he is simply invited to
distinguish fantasy from reality, as a first attempt at fixing his
own individual boundaries.

In the 14th session, after the usual silence following the
conductor's arrival had been commented on, (the conductor being
called "the professor" by group members) and after they had talked
about the difficulties some members had had in facing school exams,
Gino was invited to speak. Sonia, a teacher, drew his attention to
the fact that she participated by expressing opinions about the
others, while Gino had spoken only once, and only about himself,
not others. Gino justified himself, talking about his state of confusion, his mislaid identity, his lack of sense of time, and his
impression that the group had been set up especially for him. He
speaks, too, about his experience with his mother, who had never
taken enough notice of him, of having been treated in the family
like a big baby, left to himself, like an open hospital where he
fell down the stairs and was burnt several times.

All the other members challenged his idea that the group was
made for him. "We were all made for each other".

Accepted by the group that disputes with him, but doesn't refuse him, Gino tells them about visions he had had, and murder

fantasies. He tells them that after the last session he had gone up
onto the Gianicolo Hill, where a cannon shot is fired every day at
noon, and having become aware of an old man going around too close
to him, he had imagined pushing him down the hill.

The conductor's subsequent remark aimed at connecting the
various events of the session: "I wonder if Gino, with a clarity he
doesn't admit to owning, wasn't trying to show us what happens when
we use silence: loss of personal identity for the impossibility to
compare, loss of the sense of time, illness as the only form of
identity. And the silence comes perhaps from a fear of letting out
the Siamese twin, which perhaps we all carry hidden inside. And
then from the silence come aggressive and murderous fantasies too".
The impossibility, then, of expressing the Siamese twin leads to
confusion and the consequent impossibility of forming a boundary of
the Self, and at the same time an atmosphere of fluctuating aggressiveness, which, as in Gino's case, led him to homicidal fantasies
towards an old man tending to invade a vital space defined by a
still too fragile Self-membrane. The image of the old man may
correspond to a father image, or Super-Ego image of the "professor"
who inspires fear of the exams. In an exam, one can only make a
correct, consequential statement, not a wrong one, a private shadow-
twin. After all, the father professor who inspires fear forbids
the expression of the shadow-twin, who is thus kept split off and
feared, weakening the sense of Self by provoking further splits and
silences. Gino would like to push the father professor who in-
trudes into his space down from the parapet where the cannon is,
which, by firing, creates a deafening silence. In this session Gino
took advantage of the last few minutes to tell the group that his
"normal" brother had told him everyone would like to be in his
situation, (Gino doesn't work any more because he is considered
mentally ill) showing that he understands nothing about Gino's
condition. And Gino remarks: "Well, am I crazy or are other people?"

In this sense Gino, reinforced by an incipient and lively sense
of Self, tries to reverse the Super-Egoic social norms which distinguish the "crazy" from the "sane". In reality the therapist
"professor" who lets the group speak, is not connected to the one who
inspires only silence, he is a valid twin to be ultilized. In
theoretical terms, to allow, or better, stimulate into action group
communication - according to Foulkes' method - fosters the formation
of a group"membrane" and at the same time "individual" membrane:
the Self, the authentic subjectivity of the individual. So the
person is an expression of the group.

In the session immediately following the one described above,
Gino's car is parked next to the therapist's. And in the session
that followed Gino showed, we can say, a further strengthening of
the Self, deciding not to take medicine any more because they
"weighed on his stomach".

All this material could be brought to a more abstract expression by resorting to systems concepts, and to physics: in particular to thermo-dynamics of open and closed systems.

In this connection it may be worth recalling that physicist Brillouen (1953), has mathematically demonstrated the equivalence between negative entropy and information.   For a full demonstration, see Brillouen (1953).

In conclusion, I personally believe that mental illness, in its broadest significance, is the expression of a close and therefore defective system of communication, whereas health and recovery can be found in the opening of the system.   I strongly believe moreover that group-analysis is the most effective therapeutic technology which can open a closed system because a group analytic situation is the very place in which the equivalence between negative entropy and information can be implemented and utilized to construct or to strengthen the Self of the individual.

And perhaps this same technology could be successfully used in the treatment of organic illness, and not only of psychosomatic ones.

The group is always before the person, the healthy person and the ill person. It is the group which expresses the Self or the person.

REFERENCES

Brillouen, L., 1953, The Negentropy Principle of Information,
     J. Applied Phys., 24:1152
Cox, M., 1974, The Group Therapy Interaction Chronogram, Br. J.
     Social Wk., 3:238
Fairbairn, W.R.D., 1955, Observations in Defence of The Object Rela-
     tions Theory of the Personality, Br.J.Med.Psychol., 28:144
Fordham, M., 1976, "The Self and Autism" Heinemann Ltd., London.
Foulkes, S.H., 1975, "Group Analytic Psychotherapy. Method and
     Principle," Gordon and Breach, London.
Grinberg, L., and Grinberg, R, 1975, "Identidad y cambio," Editorial
     Nova, Buenos Aires.
Kohut, H., 1970, Discussion on the paper: The Self: a contribution to
     its place in theory and technique, Int.J.Psycho.Anal. 51:38
Langer, J.,1969,"Theories of Development" Rinehart & Winston Inc.N.Y.
Levin, D.C., 1969, The Self: a contribution to its place in Theory
     and Technique, Int.J. Psycho.Anal., 50:41.
Lewis, M., and Brooks-Gunn, J., 1979, "Social Cognition and the Ac-
     qusition of Self" Plenum Press, New York and London.
Napolitani, D., 1980, Beyond the Individual, Group Analysis, 13:12
Neumann, E.,1953, Die Psyche und die Wandlung der Wirklichkeitseben.
     Ein metapsychologischen Versuch, in "Eranos-Jahrbuch XXI",
     Rhein Verlag, Zurich.

Pines, M., 1980, Psychotherapy of the borderline and narcissistic
      disorders.   (Unpublished paper).
Popper, K., and Eccles, J.C., 1977, "The Self and its Brain" Springer-
      Verlag, Berlin.
Whitmont, E.C., 1969, "The Symbolic Quest" Barrie Brooks Ltd., London.

ROLE AS A BRIDGE CONSTRUCT IN UNDERSTANDING

THE RELATIONSHIP BETWEEN THE INDIVIDUAL AND THE GROUP

Yvonne M. Agazarian, Ed.D.

1831 Chestnut Street
Suite 802
Philadelphia, Pa. 19103

Before the 1960's the similarities between the group and individual dynamics were more in focus than the differences. In the exponential explosion of different kinds of group formation, after the 1960's the differences became increasingly important, particularly in regards to the impact that group dynamics had on the individual's social role.

Take, for example, the role of the hippy in the 1960's. To explain hippy behavior in terms of a role in the large group system makes much more sense than to attempt to explain it as an expression of individuality. We, in this room, probably feel ourselves immune from the kinds of groups that elicit the kinds of role behaviors that the hippy groups elicited. It may even be that most of us believe that even if we do join a group with behavioral norms that are deviant to our own, we would still maintain our individuality to the point that we would choose what role to play. This idea is supported by the findings that the ability to resist group pressure is related to ego strength (Alper) and then brought into question again when it is noted that the ability to maintain ego function without regression in a group is a function of the group norms as well as group pressure. It is suggested, therefore, that for each of us, the group defines the probabilities of our behavior.

Thus, as a member of a Hari Krishna group we would shave our heads to a top knot, wear a saffron robe and chant. In a Moonie group we would work eighteen hours a day begging for funds. We would proselitize in an EST group, drink death in a Jones group; napalm, rape and murder in a Mailai group.

It is my intention, in this paper, to explore the concept of role as a function of the group-as-a-whole, and to hypothesize that

the behavior of a person in a group has more to do with the group
than it does with his individuality. In other words, that group
role is a function of group dynamics. Therefore, in group psychotherapy, the therapist's primary focus is the group as the intervening variable in therapeutic change.

When role is defined as a property of the group, then role
prescriptions are filled, sometimes by individuals, sometimes by
sub-groups and sometimes by identifiable clusters of behavior that
are a group property and serve a role function, although they appear
independent from all individual members or sub-groups. These group-
role dynamics are a manifestation of the invisible group.

THEORY OF THE INVISIBLE GROUP

In my presentation of the Invisible Group, let me first define
what it is not, by defining the Visible Group. The Visible Group
exists in space and time -- its meetings are scheduled, for a
specific duration in a particular place; it has members who are
present and can be counted, and whose seatings can be charted. The
Visible Group has a descriptive identity implying structure, goals
and/or populations like; a long-term or short-term, open-ended or
closed therapy group or training group or work group. Information
about the Visible Group is public. It can be acquired by observation
or by asking.

It is the Visible Group that the individual patient joins,
experiences, and labels as his psychotherapy group. For the majority
of group psychotherapists, the Visible Group is the group whose
process they watch, whose dynamics they seek to understand. Most
significant of all, perhaps is the fact that it is not necessary to
have a group theory in order to make sense of the Visible Group
process or to explain the Visible Group dynamics. It is only
necessary to observe, describe and use common sense.

The Invisible Group, on the other hand, cannot be seen. It can
only be inferred from behavior and must be defined by theory. The
first formulation of the Theory of the Invisible Group will be
published in February in the book of that title which I wrote with
my co-therapist, Richard Peters. Presented here are those aspects
of the theory that are necessary to the understanding of roles.

In formulating the theory of the Invisible Group I have applied
General Systems Thinking to groups. General Systems Theory has
obvious advantages, including compatability with psychoanalytic
theory and the potential for refining the work already done in
Gestalt and Field Theory.

In Field Theory, Lewin defined a person's Life Space as a "map"
of the world-as-the-person-perceives-it in relationship to his goal.

(For our purpose, we define goal as both conscious goals and as unconscious goals.) The individual is located within and moving
through this "Life Space." By looking at the "map" of the Life
Space, it is possible to predict the most probable path that the
person will take to the goal. Lewin expressed this as "behavior is
a function of the Life Space;" or "behavior is a function of the
interaction between the person and the environment as it exists for
him."

The Life Space represents, therefore, the conceptual map of the
person's perceptions of himself and of his environment. Perception
is defined as the ability to integrate discriminations of similarity
and difference. Integration is defined as organization by the principles of reality and irreality.

It is to be noted here that the psychoanalytic constructs of
conscious, pre-conscious and unconscious, are, for the purpose of
this theoretical schema, subsumed in the system components of reality
and irreality. The reality component corresponds to the ego, the
irreality component to the id and the archaic super-ego.

Organizations at the level of reality are subject to the secondary process laws of reality testing and are oriented in time. Thus
at the level of reality there are the ego functions of memory (past)
data collection (present) and prediction (future). Organizations at
the level of irreality are subject to the laws of primary process and
secondary process and are not necessarily oriented in time. Thus, at
the irreality level, past memory and future predictions are not
necessarily oriented in time. Thus, at the irreality level, past
memory and future predictions are not necessarily differentiated from
present data collection, and may be perceived as present, hence
projection.

Role behaviors that reflect the irreality organizations of
perception are likely to reflect the wishes and fears of the person,
and to serve as outputs to the environment that carry that information.
This, in contrast to role behaviors that are reflective of greater
reality orientation.

Group-as-a-whole dynamics are a function of the interdependence
between the Individual and the Group. The theory of the Invisible
Group defines four systems: two seen from the Individual perspective
and two seen from the Group perspective. The first system from the
Individual perspective is the Person system. Output behavior from
the Person System is defined as the Person Role, which is expressed
by the Life Space equation ($b = f(P,E,)$. The member system emerges
when group is the environment that is perceived, and the output of
the member system is the member role. Member system role behaviors
also have a potential for clustering with other compatible behaviors.
From the Individual perspective these clusters represent interactive

role relationships and/or sub-groups. From the group perspective,
these clusters of behavior represent a role for the group. It is by
de-coding the information in these behaviors that the group system
can be deduced.

Maturation of a system leads to increasing differentiation in
both the structure and the function of the system. This process is
reflected in the development of the group-as-a-whole. Fixations and
regressions occur in the process of group development. Resolutions
of these, as well as the maturational process itself, result in
changes in the "reality" discriminations of the group-as-a-whole
system which entail similar changes for all the sub-systems in the
hierarchy. The reverse is not true, however. A change in a sub-
system's discriminationary organization does not affect systems
further up the hierarchy. It is for this reason that group-as-a-
whole interpretations which successfully influence the development
of the group are therapeutic for each individual in the group,
whereas individual interpretations will not change the group-as-a-
whole.

I intend to examine this argument in the light of a real episode
that occurred in a psychotherapy group.

A member, Ann, returns from vacation shortly before the therapist
herself is about to take her vacation. Ann announces to the group
that she is going to leave the group. The group asks for her reasons.
Ann says that she feels that the group takes energy away from the
relationship with her lover. "They don't talk together the way they
used to..." The group expresses polite regret at her decision. The
tone of the group is flat, remote, uninvolved.

INTERPRETATIONS

Individual interpretations focus on the individual perspective
and group interpretations focus on the group perspective.

An individual interpretation is in the service of individual
development with a focus on either transference or resistance,
designed to induce insight into the individual dynamics of particular
member and for any other member whose dynamics are in resonance.

A group interpretation is designed to produce insight into the
resistance, fixation, regression or repetition in the group dynamics
that serve to interfere with therapeutic group development. When
insight occurs at the group level, insight potential also exists for
the individual group members.

INDIVIDUAL INTERPRETATION

Individual interpretations are of two kinds: 1) Person-role

interpretations -- those that focus on intra-person dynamics and
2) member-role interpretations -- those that focus on inter-personal
dynamics.

To illustrate, let us trace the journey of Ann, as she entered
the group as a new member.

Even before Ann joined the group, her "member" system had begun
to emerge from her "person" system. In other words, a new focus of
awareness had begun to exist for her; her expectations, her wishes
and her fears of "the group" had become mobilized. These expectations
were determined by her past psychological experience with significant
people and with other groups.

As a "person" she enters the group with all those behaviors that
she usually uses in new situations, that have worked for her in the
past. As a "member" she will select those behaviors which seem
appropriate to the group situation as she sees it. The situation as
she sees it probably has more to do with her irreality expectations
than with the real group that exists.

Ann's person-system output are the person-role behaviors that
are a function of her perceptions of her general environment. Ann's
member-system output are the member-role behaviors that are a function
of her perceptions of the specific group environment. $(b_p = f(P,E))$ vs,
$(b_m = f(P,GE))$. How closely the preception of the group environment
approximates the real group will depend upon the reality/irreality
discrimination/integration organization of her preceptual system.

INDIVIDUAL PERSON-ROLE INTERPRETATION

Two years ago Ann left a group and never returned when I went on
vacation. At that time she substituted group with a sequence of
lovers. This time, when she separated from me to go on her vacation,
she again felt abandoned by me; and again her impulse is to abandon
and turn to a surrogate mother before I can abandon her again. A
person role interpretation would focus on Ann's psychodynamics,
like: "Ann, you are again attempting to abandon before you are
abandoned." This individual "abandoning" interpretation takes into
account Ann's person-role dynamics: her basic depressive position,
the separation anxiety that she feels, her terror of being passive,
her early history as a runaway from a sequence of foster homes, and
her later history as a bi-sexually acting-out teenager, and a runaway from reform schools.

INDIVIDUAL MEMBER ROLE INTERPRETATIONS

A member interpretation takes into account the way in which
Ann's dynamics are expressed in her behavior in the group. In this

case, the relationship between Ann and the group repeats, for Ann, the alienation she experienced in relationship to her withdrawn and narcissistic mother. Ann's approach to the group has been typically mercurial, passionate, seductive and dramatic. The group's response to Ann has been more typically supportive and holding. In this instance, however, the group is withdrawn, disinterested and polite.

A member interpretation would point out to Ann how she was repeating in the group her earlier relationship with her mother, and her typical solution to the stress of it, which is to threaten to leave for a more satisfying relationship. "Ann, you and the group are re-playing your rejection of your mother for another, and her disinterest in what you do."

What makes a member-role interpretation significantly different from a person-role interpretation is that a member interpretation takes into account the interpersonal as well as the intra-personal dynamics, and points out the reciprocal role relationships that have been elicited by the member,in the group.

What made this episode remarkable, in this particular group, was the phenomenon of regression, for both Ann and the group. When Ann first entered the group, she engaged in what I call the self-fulfilling prophecy. The self-fulfilling prophecy is the repetition and reproduction of early conflicted relationships. This is a common phenomenon in groups as individual members tend to recreate, with the unconscious help of the group, a repeat of unresolved events that occurred in childhood.

Successful repetition requires reciprocal role relationships, in which the group produces the behavior that is needed to reproduce the original conflict. The self-fulfilling prophecy appears in group very much like a play, in which the patient is the script-writer, the producer, the director and the protagonist while the group are the supporting cast.

This group, however, is an experienced, open-ended group which has, over its years of life, seen many members come and go. This group is in fact usually very attuned to the self-fulfilling prophecy and had in fact already worked successfully on Ann's when she first joined. This made it all the more remarkable that such an obvious and dramatic regression was in force without any apparent awareness on the part of either Ann or the group.

GROUP INTERPRETATIONS

To make an interpretation from the group perspective one asks oneself what role the person is playing for the group. Notice the shift in perspective. At the individual level one asks what role is the group playing for the individual. From the group perspective one asks what role is the individual playing for the group? It is in this sense that role is a bridge construct in understanding the individuals' relationship to the group both from the individual perspective and from the group perspective.

It is from the group perspective that Foulkes writes; "...the individual patient and his disturbance is only a symptom of the conflicts and tensions within his group..." (Foulkes, 1965, p. 291).

There are two kinds of group interpretations: 1) group-role interpretations that focus on role as a voice for a group dynamics, and 2) group-as-a-whole interpretations which focus on the developmental dynamics of the group.

Before I give examples of these two kinds of group interpretations it is important to lay a brief foundation of developmental group dynamics which are the matrix against which the group-as-a-whole interpretations are made.

Six phases are germaine to the development of group (Bennis & Shepard). These are: Phase 1, flight and Phase 2, fight, which express dependency on the therapist in the flight/fight mode; Phase 3, the authority issue in which there is a pseudo-resolution of dependency; Phase 4, the phase of enchantment which expresses dependency in the pairing mode with group as object; Phase 5, a regression to the depressive and schizoid paranoid positions in the phase of disenchantment and Phase 6, the phase of consensual validation which is the work mode of a mature group.

In each phase, the "irreal" Basic Assumption Group goals, flight-fight, dependency and pairing are in conflict with the "real" maturational work goal. Role behavior represents forces in relationship to these two oppositional goals. This group was a mature group, in that it had worked through the phases of group development and was thus capable of both mature work, and also regression to the dynamics of any of these phases in the service of that work.

Throughout all phases of group development and in the regressions that occur in the service of development, the therapist is most often the container of the archaic roles: that of benevolent, nurturing figure upon whom group survival depends and that of the malevolent withholding figure by whom group survival is threatened. Individual members, sub-groups and the group as-a-whole, however, are also used by the group as the container for those constellations of dynamics that are denied, projected and/or displaced. It is in this sense that one asks, what role is Ann playing for the group? In other words, what particular aspects of the group-as-a-whole's dynamics are being denied and displaced onto Ann or projected into Ann.

GROUP ROLE INTERPRETATIONS

A group-role interpretation will focus on the group's dynamics, understood in terms of the group's present reality and/or irreality. The present reality of this group is that I, the therapist, am shortly to leave for vacation. The group, in refusing to react to Ann's threatened departure, is displacing onto Ann its own denial of concern at my impending departure. What is more, Ann's threat of leaving fulfills both the fantasy of revenge and the wish to be the active rather than the passive partner in separation: The regression in the group's ability to recognize the self-fulfilling prophecy nature of Ann's role, serves the purpose of retreating from work to the defensive alienation of the phase of disenchantment and the intellectualization and isolation of the flight phase. In both of these phases, dependent rage is denied. Thus, the group is passive, Ann is active; the problem is Ann's and not the group's; and there is involvement neither with Ann nor the therapist.

Group-role interpretations would be along the lines of "What is Ann voicing for the group?" or "The group is stuffing Ann full of the feelings it wishes to disown -- what are those feelings and what are they about?"

This last interpretation is most clearly a container interpretation. In this particular context, a group-as-a-whole version seemed preferable, in that there existed in the group a history of using the empty chair, either actual or threatened, an escape route for dynamics that have not been worked through.

GROUP-AS-A-WHOLE INTERPRETATIONS

Group-as-a-whole interpretations essentially deal with those dynamics that are related to group development, and thus effect the kind of group that the group can become.

This particular group, earlier in its history, gained insight into their use of a scapegoat as a way of separating from the group both the unacceptable feelings and the member who was the container of those feelings. Thus, this group had been skillful at avoiding the analysis of its schizoid-paranoid layer, by extruding first one, and then a second member, both of whom experienced an aggravation of paranoid responses before they left the group. In the process of gaining insight into and working through these two group events, the group became alert to the scapegoating of individual members.

Groups, however, are infinitely resourceful, much as individuals are. With greater sophistication and insight, the group stopped nominating and expelling a scapegoat. The scapegoat solution was replaced by a different solution: that of "the empty chair." When dynamics conflicts in the group were not worked through, it would

happen that one or another of the group members would be absent from
the group, always with some plausible excuse. What is more, in the
absence, this absent member consistently acted out for the group,
the dynamics that the group was avoiding. The effect of this rota-
ting "empty chair" was to relieve the group of tension. Once again
the group gained insight into the function of the empty chair, the
acting out stopped. What followed was yet another compromise solution: that of the "leaving member." The "leaving member" role
provided a method by which the group tension could be contained
within the group and not acted out, but also not analyzed. The
leaving member represented, for the group, a symbolic "emptying
chair" as a "way-out" for whatever group issue was being avoided.
In its simplest form, the "leaving member" role was played by an
individual group member, as it is in the example of Ann. In more
complex forms, the "leaving member" was represented by a sub-group
or by the whole group suggesting that the most direct way to
therapeutic cure would be to terminate the group and thus, their
dependency.

The use of the dynamic of "the leaving member" was therefore
not a new phenomenon for this group. It was, however, new for Ann,
a relatively new member to the group. To interpret the "empty chair"
solution would make sense to the group, but probably not to Ann.

However, I did make a group-as-a-whole interpretation, thus:
"This group is in the process of once again arranging for an empty
chair so that the feelings about the therapist can be evacuated from
the group." This interpretation did open the group up for work.
The group recognized an old mechanism for denying dependency.
Individual members worked on their rage and grief at abandonment.
Against the matrix of this work it was possible to make a series of
individual interpretations, including one to Ann about feeling
abandoned when she separated for her vacation. Using a group-as-a-
whole insight as a matrix against which individual interpretations
could be made later was particularly important in that, for some
individuals in the group the relevant work was the ability to
experience the grief and rage of separation without denying or displacing the feelings, whereas for others, permitting the re-es-
tablishment of a relationship when the therapist returned was the
focus.

Let me again underline the relationship between the dynamics
of the individual and group roles. The individual, by denial,
displacement or projective identification, induces a reciprocal role
response from the group in the service of the repetition compulsion
whose source is a fixation in individual psychodynamic development.
So the group, by denial, displacement or by projective identification,
uses the individual as a container for those dynamics that are not
yet integrated into the developing group system, and which, if
uninterpreted, may form the nuclei of fixations in the development

of the group which in turn will serve as a source of compulsive
repetitions in the life of the group.   The dual perspective of role
is therefore necessary if the group therapist is to make interventions that facilitate group growth.

Thus, just as it is necessary to know the dynamics and history
of the individual member to make individual interpretations that
result in insight on the individual level, so it is necessary to
know the dynamics and history of the group to make group interpretations that result in insight at the group level.

THE VOICE OF THE GROUP

How does one apply this theory in practice?   My suggestion
would be to learn to listen and understand the voice of the group.

As clinicians, whether psychotherapists or psychoanalysts, we
are used to listening with our third ear to the voice of our
patients' unconscious, expressed through their words.   What is
known as our third ear is, in fact, a certain sort of listening that
we have learned to do formally by listening with a certain sort of
selective attention.   We pay but little attention to the manifest
content and a lot of attention to the latent content, for example.
Before Freud's theory of instincts and the unconscious, there was no
way of formally organizing our intuitive understanding of the latent
content into a theoretical framework that was useful in individual
therapy.   This is not to suggest, of course, that many people
before Freud did not effectively organize what they intuitively
understand by listening with their third ear.   The Greek myths and
Shakespeare's plays attest to that.

The same is now true for our intuitive understanding of the
voice of the group.   Intuitive we are.   We do not yet however have
a commonly accepted theoretical framework that is useful in group
psychotherapy.   We do have a head start in that listening to the
voice of the group requires the same utilization of our free
floating attention as accompanying our patient through the therapeutic hour requires.   What is different is that whereas in
individual therapy our focus is on the patient's unconscious (and
its relationship to the collective unconscious, if we are Jungian)
in group psychotherapy our focus needs to be not only on the patient
and the patient's unconscious but also on the group and the
equivalent of the group unconscious.   This is where the concept of
role is a useful bridge construct.

SUMMARY

The construct role is presented as a key concept in applying
the Theory of the Invisible group to the understanding of behaviour
in small and large psychotherapy groups.

The Theory of the Invisible Group defines four Hierarchically related systems: the person system, the member system, the group-role system and the group-as-a-whole system.

Each is a system with boundaries and components that differentiate it from the other three systems. The boundaries between each of the four systems are potentially permeable to the outputs from each of the other three systems, and each one is therefore capable of being modified by any one of the other three systems.

In addition, each system is capable of being defined by an equation representing the Life Space. The Life Space equation for each system therefore defines the behavioral output of that system. Since we have defined system outputs as roles in these life space equations, role and "system output" are synonomous terms. All systems (and their particular life space equations) are related hierarchically in terms of levels of abstraction. Finally, because according to the principle of isomorphy each system shares basic structural features and the same laws of operation, increasing one's understanding of any one of the systems will increase one's understanding of every other.

Each system has a component of reality and a component of irreality. The irreality and reality components are interdependent: a change in one influences the other. Outputs from each system are defined as communication behaviors or roles. Roles convey information that reflects the reality/irreality organization of the system (b = f(L. Sp.) (Which is directly related to the system goal). Outputs from a system are potentially inputs to other systems. Thus system outputs potentially contribute to the reality or irreality organizations of all other systems.

When defining the individual systems it was noted that reality communications followed the laws of secondary process, and reflected the conscious, ego-oriented goals of the system, and that irreality communications followed the laws of primary and secondary process and represented the unconscious, id-oriented goals of the system. This same structure and function characterizes group system outputs. Outputs from the irreality group-as-a-whole component represent roles in relationship to basic assumption group goals, and reality outputs represent roles in relationship to work group goals.

It will be noted that each system is a sub-system of a larger system. For our purpose, we have defined four levels of the hierarchy. However, it should be noted that the group-as-a-whole system in its turn has a role and can contribute to the reality/irreality orientation of the organization or society (a clinic, perhaps, or a Community Mental Health System) of which it is a part.

Thus, we have analysed the episode of Ann in terms of the

dynamics of four systems, expressed in roles. Ann's person-role repeated her pattern of running away; her reciprocal member role contributed to a mutual rejection pattern familiar to her and other members; from the group perspective, she was the voice of the group in a group-role of rejecting rejection; and finally her "emptying chair" served as the container role for the denied dependency of the irreality group-as-a-whole.

Conceptualizing group in terms of four systems permits the therapist to choose which level of role to influence. Roles represent reality and irreality forces in relationship to system goals. By choosing to influence the role at the level of the group-as-a-whole, the therapist potentially influences the level of reality in all sub-systems.

Reference: Y. Agazarian and R. Peters. The Visible and Invisible
            Group. International Library of Group Psychotherapy
            and Group Process, London, Routledge & Kegan Paul (1981).

INTERACTIVE CONCEPTS IN PSYCHOANALYTIC
DEVELOPMENTAL PSYCHOLOGY: THEIR
RELEVANCE TO THE INDIVIDUAL/GROUP LINKAGE

Victor L. Schermer, M.A.

Suite 702, 1831 Chestnut Street
Philadelphia, Pa. 19103
U. S. A.

This paper is an attempt to show how psychoanalytic concepts
which originated within a mentalistic framework have become increasingly interactive in their meaning and implications, and that
therefore they are more congruent with theories of group process
and development than the point of view which regards the organism
as a relatively closed psychophysiological system whose exchanges
with the environment serve solely the functions of drive reduction
and survival. The term "interactive," borrowed from Robert Langs,
is used here to imply a full and rich open-systems interchange with
the environmental context and with significant others, involving
simultaneous autoplastic and alloplastic changes, or in Piaget's
terms, assimilation and accommodation.

Robert Langs (1976, 565 ff.) first used the term "interactive"
to refer to particular field characteristics of the psychoanalytic
dyad. The use of that term in this paper is founded upon Langs'
integration of the internal and the interpersonal spheres. The
term "interactive," as a complementary formulation to "intrapsychic,"
shall be used to include the following processes: (1) communication
and motility, (2) reciprocity, that is, the mutual activation and
reinforcement of responses and mentation between two or more persons,
(3) self-initiated activity in interplay with activity stimulated
by the drives and by the environment, and (4) boundary systems for
creating a distinction between internal and external events out of
a relatively non-differentiated state. (These processes reflect
the negative entropy of living systems as opposed to the closed
physical system which tends to dissipate energy and information
over time. There are relatively closed systems within living systems, for example the action of the circulatory system over a
short period of time. Also, living systems may be short-circuited

193

into closed systems creating thereby a pathological condition.   In
this author's opinion, such systems paradoxes are responsible for
many of the inconsistencies of psychoanalytic theory.)

Groups appear to incorporate in their evolution certain interactive characteristics of the child, first in relation to its
mother, then to its nuclear and extended family, and finally in the
peer group.   Robert Boyd (personal communication, 1980) has suggested that this is just what should be expected, since as he says,
"the social system comes into being at the first meeting of the
group.   It's unique identity is developed over a series of transactions, as the life of the group progresses."

Regarding treatment, the psychotherapy of borderline, narcissistic, and characteriological disorders requires that the group
therapist pay increasing attention to interpersonal relations, their
connection with internalized object relations, and the "holding context" of the group-qua-group.   Ganzarain (1977), for example, has
pointed out the significance of boundary conditions in the working
through of pathological object relations in group psychotherapy.
In order to accomplish reconstructive goals, the shift from a purely mentalistic to an interactive psychoanalytic metapsychology must
be made explicit and definitive.   The relationship between the individual and the life of the group is markedly altered in the light
of changes in psychoanalytic constructs as they incorporate new
findings from the consulting room and from the study of child development.

What follows consists of three parts.   The first is a focused
review of the history of psychoanalytic theory.   The author hopes
here to show that the closed systems principles of psychic determinism and conservation of psychic energy, derived from nineteenth
century physiology and Herbartian associationism, while still useful in some ways, are not valid in the wider scientific sense (cf,
Amacher, 1975 and Ellenberger, 1970 for scholarly studies of the
origins of Freudian theory).   The second part is a reconceptualization of some psychoanalytic constructs in interactive terms.   The
third part of this discussion involves the relevance of interactive
constructs to the group situation.

Changes in psychoanalytic theory

Psychoanalytic constructs, as is well known, were originally
patterned after the model of nineteenth century Helmholtzian physics, which Freud inherited from his research in Brucke's physiolo-

gical laboratory, a closed system model based on the priciple of
conservation of energy, which Freud used literally in the Project
for a Scientific Psychology and then metaphorically in The Interpretation of Dreams to develop a model of the mental life and particularly of dreams and of hysteria. The shift in Freud's thinking from
a literal to a metaphorical concept was both subtle and ambivalent
and has great implications for group psychology and other disciplines.
The use of this model served the purpose of organizing disparate
data within a coherent scientific frame, but from the outset there
were violations of the theory which required amendments, particularly
to account for rational thought (secondary process) and the profound
influence of one human being on another via the transference. That
is, the mental apparatus followed not only the principle of tension
reduction but also of adaptation to reality and of an intense bond
with another person which in its earliest form served the purpose
of ego delay, i.e. the negative entropy of living systems. An additional principle, that of psychic determinism, Freud derived from
Herbartian psychology, which held that all ideas are linked to
one another through associative connections, some of which were not
immediately available to consciousness. But there was a paradox
implicit in the notion of psychic determinism. If ideas are influen-
cable only by other parts of the psyche, how can new ideas enter
the system? How can there be growth, development, and change? Freud
was forced to repostulate the obvious: the existence of apparatuses
of consciousness and perception which established contact with the
external world. Freud's compromise between an open and closed system
theory was developed in the instinct theory by contending that an
instinct had not only a source (energy) and an aim (direction) but
also an object, something outside the infant which acted as a source
of gratification.

Nonetheless, Freud continued to emphasize the closed system model in the pleasure and constancy principles and in the role of the
archaic, the internal, and the intrapsychic in his psychological investigations and therapy. Combined with a very powerful philosophical orientation and key principles of interpretation, this approach
proved forceful in uncovering the darker, hidden side of human nature in a systematic way.

The subsequent structural model was partly an attempt to give
an even greater range to the role of unconscious processes (now the
process of defense could be unconscious) and partly, via Anna Freud's
Ego and the Mechanisms of Defense (1946), to allow more fully for
the individual's need to adapt to the external world. Not incidentally, this shift occurred in conjuction with the emergence of
child analysis and of the analysis of the character disorders.
One now had a concept of an organism possessing mechanisms for adaptation to external necessity. The focus in treatment became geared to

correcting the faults in such mechanisms.

Shortly thereafter, with the work of Hartmann, Kris, and Lowenstein, there was a definite break in the continuity of psychoanalytic theory. The concepts of epigenetic development, adaptation, and apparatuses of primary autonomy with a conflict-free sphere established two separate but related psychoanalytic psychologies: an ego psychology and an id - superego, or conflict, psychology. The mental apparatus of the infant was now seen to be highly susceptible to maternal and cultural influences (cf. respectively the work of Spitz and of Erickson). The ontogeny of pre-Oedipal mental life could now be systematically explored, it becoming more and more clear that the infant is involved in a complex dyadic system in which the mother is more than a need-satisfier.

In the meantime, through the influence of Melanie Klein, Winnicott, and others, a separate stream of psychoanalytic investigation developed: object relations theory. In this approach, the impact of the external world and particularly the mother is stressed from the moment of birth, in both the real interaction and the primitive fantasy life of the infant and (one might add in agreement with Harold Searles) the primitive fantasies and reveries of the mother. It became clear that in the symbiotic exchange within this dyad lay the formative base of future object relations and psychic structuralization.

As a result of such perspectives, a paradox evolved in which the deepest portions of the psyche (the ones which in the early metapsychology were totally inaccessible to environmental influence) were seen to be formed partly by the environment, and this is most eloquently expressed in Hans Loewald's paper "On motivation and instinct theory," (1971) in which he developed the idea that the id itself is a consequence of the impact of an object on the nascent mind! That is, Loewald contended that the id does not exist innately or biologically, but is the agency which forms mental representations of biological states as a result of the presence and ministrations of the maternal object. This crucial reconstruction of psychoanalytic theory integrated thirty-two years of post-Freudian ego psychology and object relations theory. At this juncture, the mind and more specifically the deep unconscious has become truly an open system, for its very existence and structuralization derives from its interaction with and early lack of differentiation from the environment. (It may be interjected here that the group itself is such an environment and that the notion of a primitive group mentality or matrix makes much more sense in the context of this revised metapsychology than it does under the earlier closed system model.)

With this fundamental change in psychoanalytic theory, the way had been paved for a fully interactive view of development, of pathology, and of treatment. Yet the resistances to change are strong. Meissner (1979) finds Balint's (1950) seminal notion that psychoanalysis might be a "multi-body psychology" a "troublesome question." In the review presented here, Balint's insight is neither troublesome nor any longer a question. Psychoanalysis is, indeed, a multi-body psychology.

Interactive constructs in psychoanalysis

An interactive construct has been defined as one which incorporates relationships between the inner world and external reality, between organism and environment, or between persons. Such constructs may refer to an interface or boundary, a correspondence or analog, a lack of differentiation between the two (an original unity), or a mutual impact. Interactive constructs are far from being organized into a unified perspective. However, this does not severely limit their usefulness in understanding groups. Indeed, it is precisely such constructs that help to explain the relationship between the individual and the group within a contemporary psychoanalytic framework.

As examples of psychoanalytic interactive constructs, which represent a multi-person psychology relevant to the group situation, the focus here shall be on the work of the Kleinians, of D.W. Winnicott, of Margaret Mahler, and of Otto Kernberg and Heinz Kohut. Other emphases and conceptualizations of the problem are possible, the task at hand being to re-think psychoanalysis as an interactive psychology. No attempt will be made here to elaborate on the work of the above psychoanalysts, but rather to show how each embodies interaction in his point of view.

The work of Klein and her students, especially Bion, is highly controversial, especially with regard to technique and to mentation during the first year of life, but the heated arguments should not obscure for us the insights which Kleinian theory has to offer. Grotstein (1978) correctly points out that although Klein couched her ideas in the language of the life and death instincts, hers is also a theory of how the infant communicates via fantasy with the outside world, particularly the mother. The present writer will suggest that this understanding of Klein as a communications theorist is congruent with Jean Piaget's careful thinking and research on the infant's thought processes during the sensori-motor operations stage.

Klein pointed out, in what she eventually referred to as the "paranoid-schizoid position," certain primitive, psychoticlike fantasy-defense configurations in which the infant puts some painful or destructive part of itself into the mother and identifies it with her (1952). This temporarily protects the infant against the full, devastating impact of the painful or harmful stimulation. The present author, with Charles Ashbach (1978), has suggested that the repetition of this process is the modus operandi of early and primitive group formation. The term projective identification is sometimes used to refer to such processes.

Klein implicitly recognized the sensori-motor feedback loops involved in putting inner fantasy contents into the mother. She showed how the infant creates an inner and outer reality in this way, and how he looks and manipulates to see whether the mother contains these contents and how she contains them. The exploratory and curiosity drives are essential and innate, and the environment is modified along with the projection.

One can see how such a process of conscious and unconscious feedback loops operates in group as a simultaneous modification of self and group with each action taken by a group member.

The reciprocal interactions and communications implicit in the Kleinian perspective reflect a major change in psychoanalytic thinking. Consider that, for Freud, the function of motility is at first discharge, then the bringing closer of the need-satisfying object, and only by a long and circuitous route, the exploration of reality. For Freud, too, the perceptual apparatus is essentially passive and is well illustrated by the Wolf Man's reconstructed experience of the primal scene. The focus there was upon the reception of the event in the perceptual and memory systems. No attention was given to the powerful interpersonal dynamics which must have taken place between Freud and his patient during the process of discovery. From an interactive point of view, the memory (or reconstruction) would be seen in the context of an ongoing relationship. This is precisely the shift in perspective which is required of the group therapist in his comprehension of mental phenomena within the group matrix.

For Klein and for Piaget, motility is an integral part of the infant's earliest self-initiated attempts to discover "reality." Bion elaborated this notion further in the concepts of "container and contained" (1975, pp. 72-82), and the "thinking couple" (cf. Grotstein, 1979), in other words the creation of boundaries, objects, spaces, and contents in the internal and external worlds. For Bion, in a way which is surprisingly reminiscent of Loewald's formulations, thoughts <u>originate</u> from the containment by the mother's breast (to which one must add, her personality) of those protomental biological events which Bion in his later writings referred to as Beta elements. Bion further had previously (1961) raised the intriguing question of how thoughts are created in a group.

In brief, we have in the thinking of Klein and of Bion the basis for a study of primitive mentation which requires interaction for its development. We are no longer dealing with an organism conceived as an isolated mind-body unit with the mind reified as a thing, but with an individual who evolves a fantasy life and an ego through communication and action into an expanding external world and who stimulates for feedback other human beings and objects in that world. This from the moment of birth of the individual and of the group.

Winnicott (1953) viewed interaction in a somewhat different way from Klein through his concept of the "transitional space." Without reviewing this well-known concept, let us look at it from a systems-theoretical perspective. This is a boundary region which mediates and integrates two configurations of objects: initially mother and infant, then fantasy and reality. The transitional space is at once subjective and objective, in the mind and in objective reality. The space is initially formed through the infant's anticipation followed by the actualization of the maternal object, is expanded via the transitional object, and culminates developmentally in play and cultural sublimations. What is characteristic of this transitional region is the co-ordination of inside and outside. In modern computer language, this region consists in the creation of analogs which, high-lighted by the child's discovery that he can use a blanket or a doll to obtain the same sense of comfort that he does from mother, makes for some correspondence between the inner life and external reality. Despite his primary interest in the boundary region, rather than, say, intraphysic structure, Winnicott dealt with a crucial aspect of human development which constituted his singular contribution to the field. It must be kept in mind that, although we may find the most primitive and outlandish creatures at the bottom of the ocean floor, evolution proceeds more slowly there than at the beaches, the transitional space between land and sea. So Winnicott's is essentially a psychology of growth and change at the boundary.

It can be noted here that we can by extension define an aspect of groups which has hitherto received insufficient attention. This is the creation in the group matrix of analogs to the inner life as well as the establishment of mental models in each individual of group fantasies and realities as a function of his or her parti-

cular vertex of perception. We have located a particular type of
boundary: one which mediates between individual and group life
through the creation of analogs.

Margaret Mahler's is perhaps the most extensive study of the
mother-infant dyad in the history of psychoanalysis (cf. Mahler,
Pine, and Bergman, 1975, for a detailed overview). The present author, with Charles Ashbach, has formulated a theory of group development based on Mahler's theory of symbiosis/separation-individuation.
The separation-individuation process has been studied by Mahler from
two perspectives: the observable interaction of the mother and infant, particularly as the latter acquires increasing motility and
tolerance for separation from the mother, and the internalized
structures and self- and object-representations which the child
acquires in the process.

Mahler's work suggests that there is a reciprocal developmental relation or interdependence among maturation, interpersonal behaviors, and internalized object relations. For instance, the
child's ability to maintain a constant object representation of
the mother facilitates its ability to spend increasing amounts of
time away from mother and allows for a successful resolution of
the rapprochement subphase. Conversely, the child's maturation of
the libido and of motoric capacities along with the mother's appropriate responsiveness, normally thrusts the child out of the symbiotic orbit into situations which facilitate and require the development of object constancy. The parallel to the evolution of groups
seems to the present author to be quite striking. As groups increase their "motility," we observe thrusts away from a leader-
centered group which increasingly require that the group have a
constant image of itself and of the context.

Finally, we must look briefly at the study of narcissism.
In order to account for pathological narcissism, both Kernberg (1975)
and Kohut (1971) have postulated a grandiose self, a primitive and
relatively undifferentiated version of the self which Kernberg views
as defensive and Kohut as fixated at an early stage. This self
takes the external world as a mirror, as a source of supply, and as
a way of maintaining cohesion during impending fragmentation.
Again, it is interesting to notice how the group as maternal entity
is used in this way both in small groups and large social systems.)
Here we have a condition in which Kohut and Kernberg agree that a
lack of differentiation between subject and object exists. Kohut
speaks of a "self-object," a structural entity to which he ascribes
particular significance in the development of narcissism. Kernberg
refers to self-object-affect units as the earliest internal regu-
lators of tension-states (1978). We may thus speak of narcissism

as an interaction between self and object prior to their complete
differentiation. In this condition, the world as introjected is
cathected as part of the self and derives its perceived atrributes
from the self. This is an interactive concept of narcissism in
contrast to the view which regards narcissism as a de-cathexis or
lack of involvement with the external world.

The relationship between the individual and the group

Thus far, the emphasis has been on psychoanalytic theory, its
movement from a closed system to an open system formulation, and
the development of constructs which are interactive as well as intrapsychic. It seems to the present writer that this change which
has stolen upon us without our full appreciation of its implications,
calls for a radical re-thinking of psychoanalytic theories of group
life. Here, one can only begin to appreciate the dimensions of such
a task.

From the vantage point of the closed system model, the life
of the group is entirely encompassed by the satisfaction of individual needs, drives, instincts. The group and its members are objects of instinctual gratification for the others, and their intrapsychic processes are independently determined by individual unconscious dynamics. Psychological processes are relatively isolated
from the group system. When we look at a group from this perspective, we try to see how the members meet each others' infantile
needs.

The tripartite structural model and the dynamics of the Oedipal Complex and the "family romance" allowed for a more sophisticated object relations formulation of groups, delineated by Freud
in his Group Psychology and the Analysis of the Ego (1921). Pre-
Oedipal and Oedipal attachments and identifications are the moti-
vators of group life, or in other words mutual and parallel transferences are the basis of group cohesion and of the group dynamic.
Freud clearly recognized the existence of an entity called a group
and he proposed to explain its characteristics on the basis of
transference and identification.

Several examples of group theories based on this formulation
may be given. Whitaker and Lieberman's (1964) concept of the group
focal conflict and Ezriel's common group tension (1973) express a
movement towards a commonality of transference and of internal
dynamics consistent with Freud's notion of a mutual identification
with the leader, and by extension, a fantasy object called the group.

Bennis and Shepard (1956) emphasized the group resolution of the Oedipal Conflict as a major turning point in the life of the group. They introduced the concept of role differentiation, an element not present in Freud's formulations.

From a therapeutic standpoint, Wolf and Schwartz (1962) evolved a by now classic model of group therapy as "couch analyses" in parallel, with the added advantage that the members could observe each other being analyzed and learn from that experience. Kauff has correctly pointed out what different technical recommendations follow from such a model in contrast with those which emphasize maximum interaction of the membership.

The key problem that the present writer sees in the therapist treating the members from a primarily intrapsychic perspective is that the group never gets beyond a stage of what Piaget refers to as parallel play. That is, since they are regarded separately by the therapist, the participants rarely establish any significant contact with each other. (Note: It was pointed out at the Congress that the present author's interpretation of Wolf and Schwartz' conceptualization of group therapy as emphasizing the intrapsychic other than the interpersonal may be erroneous. If so, it is a not uncommonly held view and may be in need of clarification.) The Tavistock model and Foulkes' group analysis have done much to correct this situation. To some extent however, group-as-a-whole approaches can cause the therapist to selectively inattend to individual dilemmas as they are projectively identified into the group container. The interactive viewpoint encourages equal attention to the individual and the group.

What are the implications of an interactive, multi-body psychoanalytic model for group theory and psychotherapy? It seems to this writer that such conceptualizations lend themselves towards an extension and elaboration of already extant approaches as well as to a major reconsideration of both individual and group in which they are subsumed under a supraordinate construct of species-specific integration of somatic, mental, and group phenomena. These points can be developed further.

Bion's basic assumption states, for instance, can be expanded and operationalized by considering their connection with the interactive aspect of Kleinian theory. The group is initially objectless and the members constitute an object by reverting to primitive fantasies which are placed into the group through action and communication. The feedback from such fantasies is perceived somewhat differently by each member, creating roles within and valences for

particular group configurations. Bion did not however, carry this
concept far enough. For example, he did not show how each basic
assumption state transforms the group into a container for part and
whole objects nor did he specify when the group is in the paranoid-
schizoid or depressive position, and there is also some question
as to whether the pairing assumption is pre-Oedipal or Oedipal in
character. Nor did Bion allow for the evolution of groups towards
higher levels of development, a shortcoming which has been addressed
by Gibbard (1974) and by Shapiro (1977). Most importantly from
the point of view of psychotherapy, Bion made no effort to deal
with the very essence of projective identification in a group,
specifically the reciprocal modifications in the member's internal
objects and self-representations and the group's collective fantasy which constitutes the group as an object, in Piaget's terms
the modification of the individual and the group through mutual assimilation and accommodation. He thus omitted an explanation of the
therapeutic potential in a group, namely the modification and reconstruction of pathological object relations within the ego.

     Time does not permit the elaboration of how other inter-
active constructs might be applied to current models of group
therapy and group psychology. One must discuss briefly the more
radical implications for the relationship between the individual
and the group. Freud laid the groundwork for such a discussion by
hypothesizing a group psychology a _fortiori_ to the psychology of
the individual (1921, pp. 122-128). This constituted an awareness
on his part of the necessity for a multi-body or interactive framework for psychoanalysis.

     The patently observable and obvious fact that a group consists
of individuals who come together for one or another purpose ob-
scures the deeper awareness that individual development occurs in
the context of groups and that a portion of the individual psyche is,
in effect, a group mentality. Freud saw this portion in the super-
ego, but as we have been suggesting, the entire process of development is interactive. Colman (1975) has said that the infant's first
awareness of a group world occurs in the symbiotic phase, where the
oneness with the mother contrasts with the separateness of others
who hold, play with, are visible to the infant. This sense of things
is revived in the adult's experience of the group as a one-ness
(the symbiotic maternal object) and as simultaneously a collectivity of significant others.

     The potential for "grouping" now seen to exist embryonically
from the moment of birth is as much a part of the human mind as is
the somatic base and the cognitive-affective "mental life." The
more one ponders this problem, the more one is forced to conclude

that the concepts of individual and group are as much personal
constructs used to maintain a sense of identity, as they are scientific constructs.

A group is as somatic, if you will, as a need for an impulse.
This is an ethological and cultural-anthropological perspective.
It is just as instinctive for higher organisms to form flocks as
it is for them to forage for food and to reproduce. The biological
base does not stand in contrast to the social matrix but is integrated with it. The correct distinction is functional, not-biolo-
gical-versus social. That is, one must observe whether a particular bit of behavior is oriented towards, say, nurturance or sex or
the establishment of a social system.

The self differentiates out of a primitive group matrix as
as much as it contributes to it, just as it differentiates out of
and contributes to somatic processes. What is true of the self
is also true of the dyad, as both Bion and Kernberg have suggested,
and also of the family. The differentiation of selves, couples,
and families from the social matrix is clearly evident in the transition from adolescence to adulthood.

An interactive psychoanalytic metapsychology is of necessity
a group psychology, a psychology of internalization and externali-
zation across various boundaries.

Theory and observation of groups, then, must address themselves
to the question of what differentiates out of the mass and what is
being repeated in this process. Rather than take the individual for
granted, one has to inquire into the types and characteristics of
boundaries that are formed in group evolution. Paradoxically, it is
only rarely that groups consist of fully individuated persons, and
only as the outcome of intensive and extensive developmental processes.

The nature of group psychotherapy needs to be reconsidered from
an interactive point of view. Rather than changing people's minds
we are changing their interactions, or more specifically and to review, their fantasy and defense communication patterns, their transitional space, their internalization processes, and their experience
of symbiosis in which others are a part of themselves. In the point
of view being presented here, changing interactions, not superficially but deeply, is tantamount to modifying unconscious and internalized object relations. Our simultaneous research and psychotherapeutic efforts need to be directed to learning what group configu-

rations and patterns of development lead to lasting therapeutic gains. This is quite a different task from the one which prevailed when group therapy was regarded as a form of applied psychoanalysis, when the individual was regarded as a closed-system, a psychobiological isolate whose formative object relations were regarded as purely need-satisfying.

References

Amacher, P. Freud's Neurophysiological Education and Its Influence on Psychoanalytic Theory. Psychological Issues, V. 4, #4 (Monograph 16), 1965.

Balint, M. Changing therapeutic aims and techniques in psychoanalysis. Int. J. Psycho-Anal., V. 31, 1950, 117-24.

Bennis, W. and Shepard, H. A theory of group development. Human Relations, V. 9, 1956, 415-437.

Bion, W. R. Attention and Interpretation. London: Tavistock, 1975.

Colman, A. Group consciousness as a developmental phase. In Colman, A. and Bexton, W., eds. Group Relations Reader. Washington, A.K. Rice Series, 1975, 35-42.

Ellenberger, H. The Discovery of the Unconscious. New York: Basic Books, 1970.

Ezriel, H. Psychoanalytic group therapy. In Wolberg, L. and Schwartz, E., eds. Group Therapy: 1973. New York: Intercontinenal Medical Book Corporation, 1973.

Freud, A. The Ego and the Mechanisms of Defense. New York: International Universities Press, 1946.

Freud, S. (1921) Group Psychology and the Analysis of the Ego. Strachey, ed. Standard Edition of the Complete Psychological Works of Sigmund Freud. V. 18, London, Hogarth Press, 1955, 67-145.

Ganzarain, R. General systems and object relations theories:
    their usefulness in group psychotherapy. Int. J. Group
    Psychotherapy. V. 27, #4, 1977, 441-56.

Grotstein, J. Freud and Klein: Divergences within a Continuum.
    N. Y., Psychotherapy Tape Library, 1978.

Grotstein, J. Who is the dreamer who dreams the dream and who is
    the dreamer who understands it. Contemporary Psychoanal.,
    V. 15, 1, 1979, 110-169.

Hartman, J. and Gibbard, G. Anxiety, boundary evolution and social
    change. In Gibbard, G., Hartman, J. and Mann, R., eds.
    Analysis of Groups. N. Y.: Jossey-Bass, 1975.

Kernberg, O. Borderline Conditions and Pathological Narcissism.
    N. Y.: Jason Aronson, 1975.

Kernberg, O. Object Relations Theory and Clinical Psychoanalysis.
    N. Y.: Jason Aronson, 1978.

Klein, M. Notes on some schizoid mechanisms. In Riviere, J.,
    ed. Developments in Psychoanalysis. London: Hogarth Press,
    1952, 292-320.

Kohut, H. The Analysis of the Self. Psychoanalytic Study of the
    Child Monograph #4. New York: International Universities
    Press, 1971.

Loewald, H. On motivation and instinct theory. Psychoanal. Study
    of Child, V. 26, 1971. 91-128.

Mahler, M., Pine, F., and Bergman, A. The Psychological Birth
    of the Human Infant. New York: Basic Books, 1975.

Meissner, W. Internalization and object relations. J. Am. Psy-
    choanal. Assn., V. 27, 2, 1979, 34.

Shapiro, R. Psychoanalytic Knowledge of Group Processes. Panel
    Presentation. Fall Meeting of the American Psychoanalytic
    Association, 1977.

Winnicott, D. Transitional objects and transitional phenomena:
    a study of the first not-me possession. Int. J. Psycho-
    Anal., V. 34, 1953, 89-97.

Wolf, A., and Schwartz, E.K. Psychoanalysis in Groups. New York:
    Grune & Stratton, 1962.

GROUP AND INDIVIDUAL BOUNDARIES IN GROUP PSYCHOTHERAPY:
THEORETICAL AND TECHNICAL CONSIDERATIONS

Aaron Stein, M.D.

Clinical Professor of Psychiatry, The Mount
Sinai School of Medicine, City University of
New York, N.Y., 1140 Fifth Avenue, New York,
N.Y. 10028

Boundaries define and establish individuals and groups
(and organizations) and help to maintain them. To give some
examples: The City University of N.Y. loosened its boundaries
to include The Mount Sinai School of Medicine. The Mount Sinai
School of Medicine included the CUNY affiliation by extending its
own boundaries. However, it maintained the boundaries of who
should be admitted to the medical school, who should leave and
it also defined its function as the training of medical students.
The individual medical student included in his own individual
self boundaries the medical school and the university affiliation
but largely maintained his identity and function as a student in
the medical school. These examples could be further elaborated on,
but they illustrate the significance and some of the effects of
boundaries.

THE USE OF GROUP AND INDIVIDUAL BOUNDARIES TO ESTABLISH
THE GROUP AND DEFINE ITS FUNCTION IN GROUP PSYCHOTHERAPY

Similarly, in group psychotherapy, defining, maintaining and
changing group boundaries are involved in establishing the group,
its membership (who enters and leaves) and in defining the group's
function.

In establishing the group, the decision as to what kind of
group will be set up is the first step. This is decided by the
leader, the sponsoring organization, the organizational set-up
and the requirements of the environment or the external
situation (Astrachan 1970, 1975). The type of group decided upon
involves setting up boundaries as to time, type of leadership,
the nature of leadership interventions and member participations.

Examples of such boundaries determining the type of group are:
Psychoanalysis in groups, psychoanalytically oriented group
psychotherapy, supportive group therapy, group counseling, group
guidance, gestalt groups, psychodrama, various self-help and
growth promoting groups including groups for the treatment of
addiction. Taking this last, groups for the treatment of
addictions, the decision to set up such a group involves setting
up group boundaries that exclude non-addicts and exclude treatment methods not focused upon relieving addictions.

This last point relates to the setting up of boundaries as
to who enters or leaves the group, and this also helps to establish
the kind of group. Only addicts or aged people or adolescents may
be included or colitis patients or patients with asthma or those
with marital difficulties, etc. may be included in the group and
others excluded. Or, only non-patients who wish to enhance their
growth potential may be included and patients may be excluded.
On the other hand only patients - those who need and acknowledge
their need for treatment - are included in certain groups and the
kind of patients also determines the kind of group: schizophrenics,
patients with affective disorders, borderline states, character
disorders or neuroses.

Time boundaries are also used to determine the kind of
group - short term Tavistock groups, encounter groups, marathon
groups and counseling groups dealing with specific problems;
these are all short term. Long term groups are those involved
in psychoanalytic or dynamic group therapy, to cite a couple of
examples. Time boundaries and the boundaries related to the
goal or task of the group determines who leaves the group. In
a short term group, for parents of blind children, all members
leave at the end of the 8 or 12 week period. In open ended
psychoanalytic and group dynamic groups, patients leave and
enter as the goals of treatment are accomplished, or when it is
clear they are not suitable for the group and cannot achieve the
goals they need.

The task of the group, its function or the purpose for which
it is set up is defined by boundaries set up by the leader,
and also by the members agreeing to join the group for the
stated purpose - the group contract. Some of this has been
indicated above. Patients with mental and emotional difficulties
agreed to call themselves patients and enter the group for the
purposes of treatment of their illness. Non-patients need a
different goal and a different type of group, as, for example,
a group of professionals and executives or students agreeing to
work with and enter into a Tavistock type of group in order to
study group dynamics. The use of group boundaries to define the
task of the group is one of the most important functions of the
group boundary.

THE DEVELOPMENT AND MAINTENANCE OF THE GROUP BY UTILIZATION OF
GROUP AND INDIVIDUAL BOUNDARIES

The utilization of boundaries, group and individual, by
the leader and the members maintains the group and helps the
group interaction develop and pass through various phases.
Both the leader and the members use individual boundaries and
group interaction and function.

Taking the leader first, the boundaries he establishes for
himself in relation to the members and the group function
determines the type of group, its maintenance and function, as well
as the transference manifestations, and the development of regressive changes in the group interaction and in the members.
One extreme is the Tavistock group where the leader sets up
strong boundaries, limiting his relation to the group interaction
and to the members by limiting his interventions to transference
to the leader interpretations. This leads to a leader centered
group (which remains in the first or dependent phase of the
group's development) and to focusing the work of the group on the
group interactions and not the individual member's reactions or
needs. In this type of group and related types, like the group
dynamic group where the leader sets up similar interventions
limiting boundaries on his participation, regressive phenomenon
are elicited, often to an intense degree, both in the individual
members and in the type of group interaction.

The other extreme would be some of the problem solving,
gestalt, existential, and encounter groups where the leader
breeches his self boundaries and becomes an active participant
with the members of the group and joins in the intense emotional
interactions of the group. The advantages and dangers of this
type of individual boundary loosening by the leader has been
discussed elsewhere (Astrachan 1970 and Yalom & Lieberman, 1971).
Manipulative pressure to remove defenses and individual ego and
self boundaries lead to regressive changes in the members and
in the type of group interaction.

Within these two extremes the leader needs to establish
boundaries for himself and for the group in order to maintain
the group and facilitate the group interaction necessary to
achieve the group task. Perhaps the most important boundary is
the one the leader sets for himself to limit his participation
and personal involvement in the group so as to establish and
maintain a "group centered" attitude in leading the group. While
this group centered attitude will vary with the type of group
and the personality of the leader, it is the most potent factor
in facilitating the phases of the development of the group
interaction. These three phases are: 1. The phase of dependency;
2. The phase of interaction; 3. The phase of independent

participation in the work group for self-investigation and change in growth. The group centered attitude of the therapist helps to inhibit the transference manifestations directed towards him and divert these towards the group members, paving the way for the intense member-to-member interactions of the second phase of the group development. By setting up the boundaries of limiting his interventions to group centered ones, the leader denies gratific- ation to the unconscious wishes of the members to be nurtured and facilitates the regressive changes in the members from object choice to identification. This enables the emotional ties to be set up that lead to the member-to-member interaction and also permits the emergence of ambivalent and aggressive attitudes towards the therapist. Some of these are primitive transference manifestations but they prepare the way for the emergence of the separation - individuation phase of the group members' relation- ship to the therapist.

Finally, and technically this is the most important, the boundary of the group centered attitude of the leader, enables him to intervene and facilitate group interactions thru "here and now" and particularly "group as a whole" interpretations. These interventions are most effective in dealing with the resistance - the maintenance of rigid boundaries by the members of the group to avoid interaction.

The leader also has to set certain other boundaries to maintain the group and facilitate the group interaction. Absences and lateness are called to the attention of the group members; the preservation of confidentiality, dealing with scapegoating, sub-groups and deviant members - all by means of group centered interventions - maintain the group and expedite its work. The assimilation of new members and the leaving of members who are unsuitable or who have completed the task are used in group centered discussions by the leader to define the group boundaries and the group task.

Turning now to the members of the group, they help to establish the group by accepting the group boundaries and the group task - patients in a therapy group or students in a Tavi- stock group - by attending and participating. They help to maintain the group by working within the conditions or boundaries that are established - maintaining confidentiality, discussing their own problems, giving feedback to and interacting with the other members.

The most important boundaries the members set up stems from the group centered attitude of the leader and are related to the diversion of the transference manifestations from the leader to the members and also to the regressive change in object choice to identification. This change in the relationship to the leader

and sharing him as an ambivalently seen identical object leads
to a series of identification thru introjection. In one sense,
the members set up boundaries to limit their interaction with the
leader and at the same time they loosen ego boundaries to
regressively identify with him and with each other. By identifying
with the leader and each other, they break through the boundaries
of self and ego identity and regress to more primitive introjective identifications.

These identifications, with the leader and each other,
help to establish the emotional ties in the group. They also
lead to transference manifestations in the group when the members
turn to each other and interact in the second phase of the group
interaction. Aggressive and primitive transference manifestation
also appear - projective identifications, splitting, fantasies
related to ambivalently perceived part objects, etc. (Kernberg
1976). These are all examples of the regressive loosening of ego
boundaries and of a return to the more symbiotic phase of object
relations.

During the second phase of member-to-member interaction,
individual characterological traits are shown by the members -
aggressive, passive, hysterical, masochistic, etc. These
represent individual rigidly maintained ego-syntonic boundaries
which are used to resist interacting in the group. Similarly the
group members unite, each in his own characteristic way, to set
up various types of group resistance - silence, acting out,
scapegoating, subgrouping - all again representing defensive
group boundaries set up in the service of resistance.

While these rigidly held individual and group boundaries
are part of resistance to participation in the group interaction
they bring out and clearly make evident characterological traits
which, even though they may be egosyntonic, are pathological in
that they divert energy from and interfere with effective interpersonal relationships and functioning. Such character traits are
seen more quickly and clearly in group therapy than in individual
therapy. They are thus exposed more clearly and are more accessible
for therapeutic intervention. The deflection of the transference
manifestations and the group as whole interventions by the therapist help the group members to investigate and deal with these
characterological difficulties very effectively in the group therapy.

The same is true of the primitive transference manifestations that occur in the group - identification, projective
identification, ambivalence and derivatives of incorporative
and projected oral, anal, phallic, etc. fantasies. They are the
result of regressive changes in the individual members and the
cooperation of the members in setting up regressive group interactions in the service of resistance. The individual members

PSYCHOSOCIOLOGICAL COMPROMISE FORMATION AS THE CHANGEOVER

POINT BETWEEN INTRAPSYCHIC AND INTERPERSONAL RELATIONSHIPS

A. Heigl-Evers and F. Heigl

Moorenstrasse 5, Lehrstuhl für Psychotherapie

4000 Dusseldorf 1

Carl Friedrich von Weizsacker once (1977) pointed out that Freud demonstrates a special kind of Midas effect in that for him, truth is transformed into intrapsychic causalities and structures. Moser noted (1978) that psychoanalysis has never produced a theory of inter- action; and as early as 1962, I.A. Caruso (1962) warned psycho- analysis against reducing the sociological to the psychological. Recently (1979) T.H. Ogden devoted some critical thought to the fact that psychoanalytical theory suffers from a lack of terms and con- cepts to describe the inter-relationships between intrapsychic phenomena such as thoughts and emotions and external phenomena such as interpersonal relationships. What is meant here is the reality of the other person in an object relationship, an interpersonal relationship on the one hand, and the representation or image of this person on the other.

Freud included sociopsychology in individual psychology when he wrote in 1921: "Im Seelenleben des Einzelnen kommt ganz regelmaBig der Andere als Vorbild, als Objekt, als Helfer und als Gegner in Betracht und die Individualpsychologie ist daher von Anfang an auch gleichzeitig Sozialpsychologie in diesem erweiterten aber durchaus berechtigten Sinne."(1). (GW Bd. 13, S.73) Conversely, Foulkes (1964) developed the thesis (p.172) that individual analysis should

---

(1) "In the mental life of the individual the other very often
    appears as a model, an object, a helper and as an enemy. For
    this reason, individual psychology is, from the very beginning,
    social psychology as well in this extended but thoroughly
    justified view (Author's transl.)

be looked upon as a form of group therapy because it shows up - in
transference - the conflict ridden relationship of the individual to
society.   Here, then, the opposite position is taken: individual
psychology, as represented by individual analysis, is reduced to the
sociopsychological phenomenon of the group.   It appears to us that
both these should be viewed critically; they are, after all, both
based on the assumption that individual psychology and social psychology are basically the same thing.   We maintain that there is a
difference between objects that are merely phantasized - object
representations - and actual concrete objects or reference persons.
The latter, unlike the former, have a reality of their own and thus
cannot be anticipated in the same way that internalized objects can
be anticipated (cf. Heigl-Evers 1978, p.37).

Representations of objects do, however, have an effect on
objects that are actually present; in other words, the individual
is influenced in his interaction with real reference persons by the
representations and phantasies that he has developed of then or that
he associated with them by transference.   Thus the representations
of an object can also have an influence on the behavior of this
object.   This is especially true of the relationship between mother
and child: the infant exerts this kind of interactional influence
when, out of a vague phantasy of something bad in connection with
some failure in internal "interaction" it begins to cry loudly and
in so doing signals for the mother - the corresponding real object -
to come, thus causing her, possibly under the pressure of guilt
feelings, to fulfill the child's needs.   This is a case of projective
identification, a mechanism that was first described by Melanie
Klein (1955, p. 311f.).   "Projective identification is bound up with
developmental processes arising during the first three or four months
of life (the paranoid-schizoid position) when splitting is at its
height and persecutory anxiety predominates.   The ego is still largely
unintegrated and is therefore liable to split itself, its emotions
and its internal and external objects, but splitting is also one of
the fundamental defences against persecutory anxiety.   Other defences
arising at this stage are idealization, denial, and omnipotent control
of internal and external objects.   Identification by projection
implies a combination of splitting off parts of the self and projecting them on to (or rather into) another person.   These processes
have many ramifications and fundamentally influence object relations."

Ogden (1979) also addressed himself to the concept of projective
identification, in which he sees the possibility of establishing
the above mentioned, neglected relationship between intrapsychic
phenomena and those of external reality.   He uses the term projective
identification in the sense of a group of phantasies and corresponding object relationships that are related (1) to the self's
desire to rid itself of certain aspects, (2) to the projection of
such unwanted aspects onto another person and, finally, (3) to the
reinternalization of a modified version of that which has been ex-

cluded (Ogden 1979, p. 357). Seen in this way, projective identification contains three phases or aspects, which form a psychological
unit: in the first phase the projector phantasizes that he frees
himself of an aspect of his self and projects this aspect in a controllable way onto another person. In the second phase the projector exerts pressure by means of interpersonal interaction on the
recipient of his projection in such a way that the recipient is
made to experience feelings that are congruent with the projection.
(The feelings of the recipient cannot actually be identical with the
projected feelings, but only congruent with them.) Finally, in the
third phase, the recipient processes the projection psychologically
and behaves accordingly in the interactions. In this way a modified
version of that which has been projected becomes available to the
projector for re-internalization (Ogden, p.371).

Thus this conception takes into account that the projective
phantasies of the subject have an effect upon real external objects
in a sequence of externalizations and internalizations. In this way
then, a first step has been taken to conceptualize the communication
process between subject and object. This represents a departure
from psychoanalysis merely as a theory of the subject system. In the
second phase of projective identification as described above an
interpersonal-interactional process becomes observable and describ-
able - a process that is directly determined by both of the involved
subjects through intrapsychic mechanisms and structures that are
comprehensible indirectly by means of observation and the resulting
conclusion formation process.

The distinctively new aspect that Ogden adds to the concept
of projective identification - an aspect that extends beyond the
subject system to include the communication process - is the pressure
exerted on the recipient of the projection in interpersonal interaction - pressure aimed at making the recipient himself experience
the emotions associated with the projected phantasies. Grinberg
(1973) who has concerned himself with projective identification in
connection with group processes, speaks of introjection of the projected aspects on the part of the recipient.

He describes how the recipient of a projective identification -
in particular the analyst in a therapeutic dyad - can process it.
When he unwittingly becomes the object that is projected onto him,
when he experiences himself as such, then a projective counter-
identification takes place. In such a case, then, the recipient
of a projective identification under the interpersonal-interactional
pressure described by Ogden has himself identified with the projected object, i.e. he has unconsciously succumbed to this pressure.
Pressure and counter-pressure in the projective identification and
counter-identification might be motivated in the following way: if
one gives in to the pressure, one is at one with the other, whether
it be an individual or a group; one takes on the manner and pace

of the other. This can only mean, however, that the recipient of the
projection has produced phantasies of objects and their related
object relationships in his own psychological development that are
similar to those of the projector and that he is in a regressive
state of mind at the moment of reception. On his part, the projector
will be inclined to adapt himself in the interpersonal-interactional
process to a congruently behaving recipient in the interest of confirmation and reinforcement, because in this way the effect that the
projector unconsciously wants from a projective identification -
ridding himself of undesired aspects of his own self and, at the same
time, keeping them alive in another - is optimally realized. In
such a case, the process Ogden refers to as a processing or meta-
bolizing of that which is projected does not take place. That which
is projected is, rather, re-internalized in its unaltered form, i.e.
it now has to be kept separate - by means of projective identification - from the experience of the person who is doing the projecting.
In this connection, a defensive manoeuvre takes place in the recipient
as well. When defensive manoeuvres become enmeshed with each other
in interaction, a stagnation is produced from the standpoint of the
therapeutic process. This may be observed frequently in individual
treatment and especially in group processes, since in the latter's
projective identification and counter-identification occur again and
again among the group members in particular.

     We have referred to the result of such projective identification
and counter-identification in group processes as psychosocial compromise formation. According to the definition that we have given
(1973, 1975, 1979), the formation of psycho-social compromises in
small groups are relatively permanent, interpersonal manifestations
of the pathogenic, intrapsychic dynamics of conflict - configurations
of the way the partners of interaction relate to one another in the
sense of averting mutually experienced latent conflicts. They help
to cope with dangers stemming from intrapsychic conflicts of the
individual that threaten relationships. The psychosocial formation
of compromises represents an attempt to conceptualize a process
leading from internal psychological reality to interpersonal reality
- a process determined by the fact that intrapsychic compromise brings
about an interpersonal, psycho-social compromise.

     In the following section, we would like to show with the help
of a casuistic example how projective identification in small groups
can lead to psychosocial formations of compromise. It is our intention to demonstrate how intrapsychic elements in a sense extend
into interpersonal interaction: how the communication from unconscious to unconscious that was postulated by Freud is actually
realized interactionally or psychosocially (GW Bd. 8, 1913, p.445).

     The case in question is one involving a group process within a
study group, into which we were able to gain insight in two ways:
(1) one of the participants, whom we shall refer to as Heinrich, was

in individual psychoanalytic treatment with one of us and (2) the
group leader, whom we shall call Katrin, reported to us about the
progress of the group in connection with our function as group
dynamics supervisors.

The group was composed of people involved with social work who
were continuing their training.   At this point - at a weekend
seminar - they were reporting on and discussing the content and progress of the seminars they had had up to that time.   The group consisted of two regional sub-groups from the southern and western parts
of the Federal Republic of Germany, each of them having 6 to 7 members.
The meeting itself took place in Karlsruhe.

Heinrich, the participant in question, drove the distance of
about 250 km (156 miles) to Karlsruhe alone, on a sunny weekend,
after
having spent a week in which he had had so much work to do that he
had been forced to leave much of it unfinished. Both before and
during the drive he was in an extremely bad mood; one might go so
far as to say that he was filled with dysphoria.   He felt that it
was unreasonable for him to have to make this trip: for one thing,
he was overworked, but what was even more important for him was his
(mistaken) belief that in comparison to the other participants, his
competence in the subject matter to be discussed was vastly superior.
Thus he was not expecting to profit from the seminar professionally;
on the contrary, he assumed that the others would be placing one-
sided demands on him and exploiting him.

Individual analysis showed that Heinrich's notion of being
suppressed and exploited stems from his own unwanted inner impulses,
phantasies and feelings. The effect of these impulses is that he
tries to humiliate others, to force them to accept his conceptions,
to pressure them into producing what he wants. These strong sadistic
suppressive impulses are in conflict with Heinrich's ideas of integrity and respect for others. For this reason these phantasies and
feelings, which represent a threat to the integrity of his self, are
located by Heinrich in others, i.e. they are projected into others.
It is a case of projective identification involving, among other
things, the phantasy that the projected content takes possession of
the recipient. A phantasy of this type would, in this case, imply
not only that Heinrich's colleagues in the study group are safistic
oppressors, but also that they suffer from the conflict that arises
between these impulses and their own ideals.

By transporting his anal-sadistic suppressive tendency into the
other members of the study group, Heinrich has, for his part, rid
himself of the attending internal pressure. He is no longer at the
mercy of the pressure of inner demands associated with aspects of his
self, i.e. the above mentioned anal-sadistic suppressive tendency.
This pressure of inner demands is now active in the others; the others
are now subjected to pressure of this kind, which they in turn direct

toward others, including Heinrich.   As a result, a power struggle
with real objects develops in the subsequent interpersonal interaction.

For Heinrich this represents a liberation in the sense that he
is no longer the object of archaic, rigid impulses of his will.   In
his childhood such impulses had caused him again and again to want to
tear himself to pieces in a kind of fit like a hobgoblin - to threaten
to get so mad that he would burst when he did not get his way, so that
his environment called out in a comical, ironic way: "poor ol'
Heinrich is dying."

In the course of the discussion with the other group members
Heinrich developed the view that they should all be ashamed of their
insignificant contributions; that the things they had to say were
patently ludicrous. In his phantasy Heinrich saw everyone as being
subject to his own anal standards. He himself had rid himself of
these standards in the manner described above.

The pressure exerted by Heinrich in interpersonal interaction
in connection with his projective identification took on the following
form: 2) Heinrich disqualified whichever group member was speaking
in a manner that was more non-verbal than verbal, i.e. by means of
intonation and a hectic way of speaking, with comments such as the
following: "Have you at least thought of that?!" - "Well, everybody knows that!" - "What do you mean by that?!" - "I just wonder what
you're getting at." These are all rhetorical questions of a generally
disqualifying, critical tendency toward the other person. If one
continually devalues or disqualifies the other members of a study
group in this way they will muster all their authority, competence
and possibilities of professional self-assertion and try to bring
all this to bear. The underlying motivation and the style in which
this is carried out vary. In this group it became evident that the
other group members very stubbornly and inflexibly clung to their
experience and used elaborated technical jargon without seriously
responding to Heinrich's arguments. Experience and terminology were
presented as irrefutable authorities that could hardly be called into
question. In this way Heinrich was to be bereft of power and held
down.

After a certain period of time a change in the style of the discussion became apparent, which leads one to suspect that a processing - a kind of digestion - had taken place in the recipients:

---

2) According to our observations, the interactional pressure described by Ogden is generally carried out in the form of non-
   verbal signals such as intonation, rate of speaking, expression
   of face and gestures.

the others started dealing with Heinrich's factual arguments in a
friendly way but they continued to gloss over them; they were still
not seriously taking his arguments into consideration. For Heinrich
the others have now become oppressors who will not give him a chance
to get up. A struggle that first took place within him has now been
transposed to the external world. In this way Heinrich experiences
a verification of the content of his projective identification; it
is apparent to him that the others are sadistic oppressors.

At this point the question arises as to the manner in which
Heinrich's projection was psychologically processed by the group of
recipients. Ogden points out that in this connection forms of
defense and other processing may come into play that are different
from those present in the projector. Thus there may be attempts to
integrate with their own personalities the phantasies and feelings
activated by a process of induction. They might try, for example,
to deal with these feelings and phantasies by means of understanding
or sublimation.

As described above, the recipients developed a new mode of discussion at this point - a kind of jude style. This style is
characterised by the nodding approval given to Heinrich's contributions to the discussion, by their polite, friendly reception, but
also by an unwillingness to respond to their content in any detail.
Thus a polite, flexible form of suppression took place of the more
rigid anal-sadistic devaluation brought about by the stubborn insistence on the authority of experience and professional jargon that
had gone before it.

The result of all this was a veritable tidal wave of anger and
anxiety in Heinrich. The very phantasies and feelings of anal-
sadistic dominance that he had tried to rid himself of by means of
projective identification were now being thrown back at him in a
radically altered form that was not readily recognizable to him,
though the basic quality of suppression remained unchanged. At this
point it should be mentioned that at about the same time as this
experience, Heinrich told the following dream in analysis: "I was
in a circle of several people - there were about 8 or 10. I had my
arms outstretched, at about shoulder level. Another person or
several other persons in the circle took my hands - with my arms
still in this position and there was a contest to see who would be
able to press the other person down; who would be able to make the
other person smaller. Somehow it was clear to me that I would lose.
I wanted to get out of the circle and had mixed feelings of anger
and anxiety. I woke up with this mixture of anger and anxiety
and felt at the same time a headache and strong muscular tension in
the shoulders, neck and upper arms." In the analytic session following this weekend Heinrich remembered a regularly occurring childhood
situation: he is sitting - at ease and with a certain amount of en-

joyment - on the toilet, until he hears his father coming, who shakes
the door and wants to come in. As his father approaches he senses
that everything is getting cramped inside him: his father denies him
his peaceful sanctuary, his relaxed, pleasureful, productive activity.
He also reports having experienced a similar inner cramp, together
with anger, as a schoolboy, when his father asked to see tests that
he had written in class and demanded that he make the best grades in
his class. It was also the father, by the way, who took care of
Heinrich during his first year of life while his mother was ill and
who carried out toilet training when Heinrich was only 9 months old.

The defensive function of his projective identification was now
questionable for Heinrich. He could no longer use projection to discharge his conflict - and anxiety-ridden anal-sadistic phantasies and
feelings onto his so friendly seeming colleagues, nor was he able to
keep these experiential qualities alive in the others in his usual
way, i.e. via identification. It was thus inevitable that he would
be exposed to increased pressure from the anal-sadistic feelings
gathering inside him, together with the fear of being put down or
expelled by the group if he should put these feelings into practice.
On the other hand, the (for him) unusual processing of such impulses
on the part of the recipients - a friendly, polite suppression and
put-down of one's discussion partner - opened up a possibility of
reinternalization which was so new to him that he was not able to
carry it out spontaneously.

His oppression became so strong at that point that he sought
release - thanks to the functioning of his realistic ego components -
by means of a temporary spatial separation from the group. He used
a conventional excuse to leave the room, i.e. he withdrew from the
interpersonal-interactional field and concentrated on himself; he
tried to process the conflict that had been mobilized all by himself.
This conflict consisted, on the one hand, of anal-sadistic impulses
to disqualify and subdue the object and, on the other, a need to be
together with, a sense of being part of the object. At the same
time, Heinrich was also affected - during the processing phase -
by experiences of interpersonal interaction on the periphery of the
actual study group session. When he had arrived at the location of
the meeting after the tiring drive described at the beginning, he
had been greeted by a fellow participant - Jochen - in an unexpectedly friendly way - so friendly, that he was at first only
suprised, but then pleasantly moved. Another interactional influence
consisted in the fact that Heinrich had always been on friendly
terms with Katrin, the group leader, and did not have to fear any
real threat on her part. In addition, as a result of previous
experience with the members of this group, Heinrich could be sure
that they would not reject him in the end; that they would never
totally deny his competence - especially since he was considered to
be the spokesman of one of the two subgroups.

Upon returning to the meeting room after almost a quarter of an hour Heinrich was able to reinternalize the phantasies and feelings he had projected in the form offered by the recipients and - in addition - to carry out a sublimation.

When Katrin, the discussion leader mentioned above, summarized majority opinions, which Heinrich did not share, he made the following commentary with a slightly ironic intonation: "Vox majoritatis non est vox dei". The success of this comment was very striking: all of the members of the group laughed out loud. In complete contrast to the proceedings up to this point a humorous mood prevailed for a short time, encouraged, in particular by Katrin and the influential group members Jochen and Kurt, who are especially receptive of witty apercus.

Katrin, who up to this point had generally been the spokesman of the majority opposed to Heinrich, took up this ironic statement and turned the floor over to him: "Heinrich is of the opinion that the voice of the majority is not the voice of truth - maybe we should listen to what he has to say." As Heinrich started in his characteristic manner - to make an extended speech, one of the parti- cipants placed the microphone of his tape recorder in front of him. In reply to Heinrich's puzzled question as to the meaning of this, he laughed: "If you're going to start with your first, secondly, thirdly, we have to get it down on tape."

Thus, for the first time, Heinrich had an opportunity to present his point of view concerning the matters being discussed somewhat more thoroughly. After this Jochen adapted himself to Heinrich by turning to him,whenever he was obviously not in agreement with Heinrich's opinion, making a little bow and saying something to the effect of "What does the expert think?" or "If I may be permitted to ask the expert a question".

During the further course of the discussion, Jochen applied this approach to everyone whose opinion he did not agree with in a particular instance. He combined some variant of the question "What does the expert think?" with the ironic reverence of a slight bow in the direction of the person spoken to. Now almost all of the participants in the discussion started using this style of expression - with individual variants - so that the participant whose opinion one did not agree with was not addressed directly but by means of a polite formula. Thus a psychosocial compromise formation was develop- ed which might be described as a "mutual ironic, witty reverence among experts". Dynamically speaking, this represents the cancellation of a defusion of instincts, a naked power instinct without libidinal needs, a mixture of the two as a form of friendly, ironic criticism or critical, ironic friendliness. What this means from the standpoint of the object relation theory (Kernberg 1976) is: (1) the splitting

of a primitive ego state of Heinrich's with the accompanying projection of a sadistic-exploitative self/object representation -
where the self/object boundaries are permeable - onto the group as
a collective object; (2) the deposition of such unwanted aspects
in himself onto the members of the study group by means of interactional, non-verbal pressure; (3) the processing or "digestion"
of the discharged impulses by the group members in the form of a
sublimating alteration of the non-verbal impulses mentioned above
and finally (4) the sublimating reintrojection, i.e. internalisation
of that which was originally projected but which has already been
changed by the others into a new ironic form.

Psychosocial compromise formations as points of changeover from
intrapsychic to interpersonal relationships protect the individual
group member from a loss of a sense of belonging and the group as
a whole from disintegration or the loss of members; that is to say
they strengthen group cohesion. This protective function is based
on the processing of anxiety - cathected instinctive impulses by
means of projective identification - with the accompanying interpersonal-interactional exchange between subject and object - in a
way that reduces anxiety.

Seen in this light, psychoanalysis is not merely representational psychology, a psychology of the subject, but also a psychology
of the unconscious components of real interpersonal relationships.
This is, then, a reply to the criticism of v. Weizsacker, cited at
the beginning of this paper, to the effect that for psychoanalysis,
truth can only be represented in terms of intrapsychic causalities
and structures. In our opinion, however, this does not mean that
psychoanalysis is a theory of interaction or a psychology of human
interaction. Psychoanalysis can only describe a part of human
interaction - that part, namely, which is conditioned by projective
identification with its three phases or aspects.

REFERENCES

Caruso, I.A., Soziale Aspekte der Psychoanalyse. Stuttgart;
        E. Klett, 1962, p.1.

Foulkes,S.H., Therapeutic Group Analysis. Allen and Unwin, 1964.

Freud, S., Die Disposition zur Zwangsneurose. (1913) Gesammelte
        Werke, vol. VIII, London, 1943, 442 - 452.

Freud, S., Massenpsychologie und Ich-Analyse (1921) Gesammelte
        Werke, vol. XIII, London, 1940, 73 - 161.

Grinberg, L., Projective identification and projective counter-
        identification in the dynamics of groups. In Wolberg,
        Schwartz (Ed), Group Therapy 1973, An Overview. Inter-
        national Medical Book Corporation, New York, 1973, p.
        145 - 153.

Heigl-Evers, A. and Heigl, F., Gruppentherapie; interaktionell -
        tiefenpsychologisch fundiert (analytisch orientiert) -
        psychoanalytisch. In Gruppenpsychotherapie und
        Gruppendynamik, vol. 7, Gottingen 1973, 132-157.

Heigl-Evers, A. and Heigl, F., Zur tiefenpsychologisch fundierten
        oder analytisch orientierten Gruppenpsychotherapie
        des Gottinger Modells. In Gruppenpsychotherapie
        und Gruppendynamik, vol. 9, Gottingen 1975, 237-266.

Heigl-Evers, A. and Heigl, F., Die tiefenpsychologisch fundierte
        (analytisch orientierte) Gruppenpsychotherapie.   In
        Die Psychologie des 20. Jahrhunderts, vol. 8,
        Zurich: Kindler, 1979, 802-811.

Heigl-Evers, A., Konzepte der analytischen Gruppenpsychotherapie.
        Gottingen: Verlag fur Medizinische Psychologie im
        Verlag Vandenhoeck und Ruprecht, 1978.

Kernberg, O.F. Object-relations theory and clinical psychoanalysis.
        New York: Jason Aronson, 1976.

Klein, M. and Heimann, P. and Money-Kyrle, R.E., New directions in
        psycho-analysis. London: Tavistock Publications, 1955.

Moser, U., Affektsignal und aggressives Verhalten. Psyche, 1978,
        32, 229 - 268.

Ogden, T.H., On projective identification. International Journal
        of Psychoanalysis, 1979, 60, 357-373.

Weizsacker, C.F., Gesprach mit Sigmund Freud. In v. Weizsacker,
        Der Garten des Menschlichen. Beitrage zur geschicht-
        lichen Anthropologie. Munchen/Wien: Hanser, 1977,
        p. 272.

THE IMPLICATIONS OF ECOLOGICAL CHANGE ON GROUPS, INSTITUTIONS AND
COMMUNITIES — REVIEWING A THERAPEUTIC COMMUNITY EXPERIENCE WITH
OPEN-SYSTEM THINKING

Harold Bridger

Tavistock Institute of Human Relations
Tavistock Centre
120 Belsize Lane
London NW3 5BA

Out of this personal, historic description some key principles
and dimensions will be drawn which affect the purpose and functions
of therapeutic communities and institutions when considered as part
of and interacting with the wider society.   I will also try to
distinguish such principles and dimensions from those which govern
a community or institution endeavouring to operate as a relatively
'closed system', i.e. one regarded "as sufficiently independent to
allow most of its problems to be analysed with reference to its
internal structure and without reference to its external environment."[1]   In effect, I am distinguishing the more limited therapeutic
community based on established firm boundaries between it and its
environments from one conceived and developed as an open-system.

The experience to be revisited was, as far as I am aware, the
first attempt at actually creating a therapeutic community as an
open-system by intention and not just by accident.   It was conducted during World War II and developed as an integral part of the
Army's medical operations.   I shall be reviewing that endeavour,
however, with the insights, knowledge and experience of the 36 years
which have followed that beginning.

The country-at-war emphasised an environment which, at one level,
could not be denied by the professional staff and patients of a
hospital.   Yet returning people to health in that hospital setting
posed quite considerable problems and difficult decisions for both
staff and patients.   All were military personnel with the
professional staff in various therapeutic roles.   The paradoxical
issues were not dealt with explicitly but appeared in various

stressful and rationalised forms such as when decisions were made
concerning the return of men to the armed forces or to civilian life.
Correspondingly, it was important to consider how far the professional
staff member's own purpose, values and approach to treatment was
affected by that environment and by organisational aims and functions.
In the community and organisational life of today those choices, problems and decisions may not appear so sharply, but they are just as
real and critical.   In fact, the personal and organisational issues
are even more fundamentally difficult today than in 1939/45.
Dilemmas of values and standards, environmental uncertainties, overall
complexity and increasing inter-dependence are always besetting our
thinking, planning, decisions and actions.   In a word, the
environment today can be acknowledged just as well as a war-climate -
but much more easily denied.

ANTECEDENTS

Wilfred Bion's Northfield Experiment

While Bion and Rickman were developing their ideas with their
colleagues at the War Office Selection Boards [2,3,4,5,6] and exploring
their implications for therapy and training, some serious problems
were affecting military psychiatric hospitals dealing with break-
downs in battle and in Units.   It was being discovered that the
automatic withdrawal of psychiatric casualties back to base and
then to hospital seemed to be associated with a growing high
proportion of patients being returned to civilian life.   It was as
if "getting one's ticket", as it was called, had replaced one of
the objectives of hospital treatment, which was to enable healthy
officers, NCOs and men to return to the Army.   Even at one of the
largest hospitals, Northfield Hospital (800 beds) near Birmingham,
where the military medical staff who had been appointed to head
wards and develop their own treatment methods were highly qualified
psychoanalysts and psychiatrists, the Rehabilitation Unit to which
patients were transferred for review before leaving for the Army or
"Civvy Street" seemed to have no better statistics than the rest.

Wilfred Bion was appointed to the command of the Rehabilitation
Unit at Northfield to develop his own approaches to the problem,
based on the learning and experience gained in WOSBs.   He undertook
a double role as Officer Commanding that Unit, and as psychiatrist
helping his men to face the working through of issues following their
treatment and to make decisions about their future - including that
of returning to military duties or civilian life.   Returning to the
Army might, of course, contain various possibilities including
changes of role, unit and conditions of work.   Inevitably either
course entailed confronting not only the conscious and unconscious
attitudes and desires of individuals, but the values and norms
which had been established in the Rehabilitation Unit and Hospital

over time.   It is clear from many accounts that the notorious
indiscipline, slackness and untidiness of the Unit which Bion took
over was one form of showing him and the Review Panel how unsuitable
it was for returning any of its members to the Army!   T.F. Main[7],
in the First Annual Lecture founded in memory of S.H. Foulkes, gives
a lively description and goes into some detail on Bion's approach to
his Unit.   He omits, however, one key factor in the situation which
leads him to ascribe Bion's departure ("sacking") after only six
weeks of work with his Unit, to the inability of the Commanding
Officer of the Hospital and his professional and administrative
staff* to tolerate the early weeks of chaos which accompanied the
self-management and functional leadership responsibilities demanded
of the Unit by someone who, as the men were trying to insist, should
have taken over those responsibilities himself.   Main was only
partially correct.   Bion was essentially facing his Unit and the
Hospital professional staff with the task and responsibility for
distinguishing between their existence and purpose as a military
organisation and their individual inferences (in the majority of
cases) that health entailed a return to civilian life.   In addition,
more fundamental issues were at stake, as I will hope to show later.

The degree of success Bion achieved in that six weeks amply
demonstrates not only the validity of the principles he and Rickman
had evolved but said even more for the 'double' professional approach
he had employed.   He was in uniform, an officer in the organisation
(i.e. the Army) confronting his men with the state of their Unit and
morale;   he was also a professional psychiatrist consulting with
these same men in assessing their health and direction of choice
during a time of the nation at war.

Two of the critical lessons to be derived from his "sacking",
however, which I was later to define when succeeding Bion to the
command of the Rehabilitation Unit at Northfield and making my own
analysis of the situation, were:-

(a)   That while he had established his own professional
       and technical approach to the situation and the Unit,
       he had not sufficiently appraised the effect it
       would have in its contrast with the psychiatric and
       organisational approaches of all the other psychia-
       trists and administrators (including the Commanding
       Officer) in the hospital.   In my personal discussions
       with him between the time of his leaving and my
       appointment, it became clear that Bion's philosophy,

---

* Actually by no means all the staff were of the Commanding Officer's
  mind at that time.   Some who were interested in Bion's work and
  that of the Selection Boards, understood this better than others.
  The 'chaos' reason alone, however, would never have occasioned
  the "sacking";   the rest of the hospital was far from peaceful!

value system, technical and organisational appreciations
were poles apart from those of others such as Foulkes
and Bierer, who were operating under quite different
principles and values.   This was not to say that it was
Bion v. the rest.   There were differences between the
others' approaches too but, in general, they were consistent in their aims of fulfilling the expectations,
resources and future life needs of the individual
regardless of hospital, army or war needs.   I can well
remember the expressive comments with which both Rickman
and Bion voiced their total disagreement.   It was
encapsulated in an experience which they had had when
given the opportunity of observing Foulkes in a first
group session.   Foulkes had opened that session by
saying "I want you to look on me as you would the
doctor in a white coat and not as someone in uniform".
In addition, Foulkes at that time utilised the group
approach more as a way by which the work with any one
individual could be observed and reflected upon by
the others.   It was a setting rather than having a
dynamic life of its own in the Bion/Rickman sense.[8]
Later, after my appointment, I was able to enlist
Foulkes's collaboration in working with actual activity
groups - and then the strength and persistence of the
forces operating towards the attainment, distortion
or avoidance of group goals demonstrated their
relevance to him.   But I will be referring to this
development later.

Referring back, however, to Bion's quite distinctive
approach in conceptual form and in professional/
technical practice, it is no wonder that a high degree
of rivalry and even less desirable emotions were
fuelling the hospital climate at that time.

In effect, therefore, the introduction of change
processes requires a search for common understanding
of both purpose and methods.   While only a few of
the likely consequences of any such change might be
predictable, it is important to engage in exploring
the implications of any steps envisaged even if
the outcome is unknown.   It is equally important
to set up the equivalent of a forum or "mini-
scientific society" in which a collegiate climate
can be established in exploring common problems
and different ways of approaching them and resolving
them.   It is necessary to have that opportunity
of adapting to change under conditions and in

circumstances which are "good enough" (to use Winnicott's term) to effect the transition.

(b) That while Bion was fully aware, both in his organisational role and in his professional one, of the central importance of the country at war as a critical environmental force which had implications for the internal worlds and defences of his men, he neglected - and was indeed somewhat disparaging of the more immediate environments of the hospital and traditional reactions of the bureaucratic aspects of the military machine.

The Commanding Officer at that time was, by profession, a psychoanalyst who perceived his task as maintaining co-operation between the professional and administration functions in the hospital. Bion, in contrast, really demanded that the external organisation as the environment of his Unit, should stand and tolerate the forces and pressures which his efforts and ideas might release in the struggle with his Unit and with the hospital mission he was endeavouring to fulfil. He expected people to see for themselves that what was happening was, in essence, a microcosm of the tasks and problems facing military hospitals as a whole. As a Major commanding tanks in the first world war and a psychiatrist in the second, Bion showed his own range of capabilities. He could also, however, expect too much of his wider environments. In addition, he did not recognise, or perhaps not accept, that it was equally his business and part of his task to take these environments into account, just as much as he had taken the Army and the country at war so very seriously. In passing, and without taking one iota from his great insights and creative work, I believe that Bion was not at ease with the group as an open system, i.e. he was not at home with what I have referred to as "the implications of ecological chage in groups, institutions and communities". In this respect neither were Foulkes and Bierer, who were less so - it was not in their philosophies or compass.

While all three, and others at Northfield and since, showed high regard for the immediate environment of the individual, they differed, depending on their values and perceptions of the therapeutic task, in the way they used that environment of the group, and in the expectations and demands they expressed in the context of the wider environments.

The Second Northfield Experiment - The "Therapeutic Community"

I. Orientation.   So far as I am aware the term "Therapeutic Community" was first coined in connection with this second experiment which I initiated over the period 1944/45.   Over the course of time an increasingly large number of people contributed to its development, not least the transient population of officers, NCOs and men who learned to take responsibility over time for their own return to health, and in so doing, found that the process of creating and developing the community was a critical constructive ally for the various disciplines and resources available to them.

Following Bion's departure from Northfield, the possibility of my taking over the role of commanding the Rehabilitation Unit was raised.   It was recognised that I was not a psychiatrist or a psychologist but had held a command, was an educationalist and teacher by profession, and had extensive experience of the various approaches developed at the selection boards.   I had been seconded originally to understand more of the group and organisational processes and, although it was not remotely like the field command from which I had come, here was the chance to test out the ideas and experience I had gained in an organisation with a very different mission!   In one sense I welcomed the opportunity and challenge; in another sense I was quietly terrified, since I had no idea of what a mental hospital was like and felt, as in all such changes, as if I had been suddenly deskilled.

My actual posting was to take place only when the last Commanding Officer had been replaced by a Medical C.O., professionally a pathologist, but with regular army command experience.

In the meantime, I was to be given the chance of acclimatising myself by visiting a selected number of other military psychiatric hospitals, the opportunity to meet and talk with a variety of people who I felt might be able to help my orientation.

My discussion with Bion, as I have already intimated, led me also to consider working in some dynamic form with the institution as a whole while also being prepared to consult and collaborate with those parts of the organisation which showed a readiness for responsibility in attempting to achieve the health of an enterprise however small, or to create some entity which could grow.   I therefore decided to adopt what I called the 'double-task' approach but with one task located with the hospital as an institution and with the other task at the level of those parts which showed leadership in developing some relevant creative work.   This leadership had also to include a readiness to perceive, reflect on and review the way that group or part was working.

2. Entry and Joint Planning.   I reported to the C.O. of
Northfield with some trepidation, wondering whether some of the half-
formulated ideas would ever take root, let alone bear fruit.   Tom
Main, in his account[7], writes that we arrived about the same time.
Actually he arrived quite some time later to replace the two
divisional psychiatrists Emmanuel Miller and Alfred Torrie, who had
already given me every support in getting the design started.   The
new C.O. and I had, together, to settle down, to meet the professional
staff of the different disciplines and learn about the hospital as
a whole.   Foulkes and others invited me to observe their group
sessions; I had discussions with nurses, social workers, administrators, occupational therapists and indeed every section of staff
in the hospital including building and maintenance engineers.
Learning about the various systems and the roles of those who
operated them in whatever form or level, certainly allowed me to
appreciate the prevailing and distinctive and indeed conflicting
cultures.   Obviously I could not know at this early stage how
they all hung together, but it was important even to experience the
confusion of a newcomer and gain some sense of what the whole place
was about.   I had learned, for example, that whilst devolution to
wards, in almost every respect, had its advantages, the atmosphere
of "live and let live", of some wards being more privileged than
others in different ways, of undercurrents and 'politics' within
and between the various functions of professional and administrative
staff and so on, left much to be desired.   It was agreed that I too
would have a double role: I would assume command of the Rehabilitation Unit but also undertake a role involving special responsibility for the 'hospital as a whole' in a social sense.*
I proposed that my role should be that of Social Therapist to the
'hospital as a whole', thus distinguishing it from my Unit command.
The respective offices for myself and my two staffs would also be
distinct and separate in the hospital.[9]   In particular I proposed
a drastic reformulation in the hospital layout.   Influenced by the
Peckham experiment[10] and recognising the 'social gap' in ward,
professional and administrative relationships, I suggested, without
necessarily reducing the number of beds, that the ward in the very
centre of the hospital be cleared and named "The Hospital Club".
A meeting of representatives from each ward to explain the move and
suggest they discuss equipment and organising methods was to be the
only other positive action regarding the Club itself.   My Social
Therapy office was, however, close by and so were the offices of my
staff related to that role.   I explained that I wished to create
some identifiable equivalent of the 'hospital as a whole with its
mission' and this would be represented by, for example:

---

* In "today's terms" this would be more akin to the organisational
  development (OD) role than the personnel role.

• Staff seminars to explore and discuss what was intended
and what the implications were likely to be.

• Independent professional discussions according to the
particular discipline or function - e.g. psychiatrists,
nurses, and so on.

• Ward meetings when requested for exploring the implications
of external effects and the impact of internal stresses
in the wider environment.

• The Hospital Club with its deliberate emptiness but
allocated space for potential development, also
represented the patient's own personality and social
gaps within his 'life space'.

• Greater emphasis to be placed by all activity supervisors
on changing the pattern of relationships with patients
to one of watching for initiatives on their part and
responding to them.   Previously the effort had been
more in the direction of teaching skills and well-meant
instruction-centred methods.

After very full discussion and when the various steps were
agreed, the series of staff discussions were begun and gradually, over
a period, the empty Hospital Club made its presence felt.   It took
a little while for the representatives' meeting to be arranged - not
because of finding appropriate people within the wards but because
everyone knew amongst other inter-ward considerations that one of the
main matters for discussion would be what each ward might contribute
from their "recreational armoury"!   Already, however, in the intervening period between the official opening and the date of the
meeting - talk and feelings were beginning to flow within and between
wards.   The various staffs ranged in their attitudes from the highly
sceptical to equally highly interested members.

Nothing happened at once or symmetrically.   Growth was horti-
cultural and the activity patterns across the hospital were much more
tree-like with branches in all directions, rather than representing
any tidy ordered curriculum or programme.   Even when an eventual
richness of societal endeavours became established, perhaps then to
fall into decline, to be abandoned or wrecked and then rebuilt,
depending on the population and the different needs or states of
illness, there was never any time or chance to say "Now we have
arrived!"   In that sense the therapeutic community as an institution
became far healthier than many businesses/organisations.   The
individuals comprising the former might be sick, mad or bad; those
of the latter might be sane and physically healthy but institutions
are not the same as the sum of the individuals comprising them - and
we were continually learning and relearning this at Northfield.

A much fuller and detailed account is contained in the Menninger
Clinic Bulletin (Vol.10, No.3, May 1946) - attempting, inadequately,
to give a review of the community's state only eight months after its
beginning.

Returning to the Club, the cumulative awakening of interest
eventually led, not to a meeting of ward representatives to reach
some businesslike arrangement mutually agreed, but to a protest
meeting which I was summoned to attend.   The protest, with full and
prepared arguments, was to ask why we were wasting public money and
space in wartime - money and space that could be put to so many good
uses!   I agreed and suggested that we work out what could best be
done with it and how, since it was ours to do with as we wished.
And we certainly could use it for the war effort quite directly.

Without giving a blow by blow account it is difficult to convey
the tremendous energy and directive ability which can be generated
when it is possible to find the transitional setting/experience
through which the insights of therapy, derived from their treatment,
could be allied with social purpose and satisfaction in identifying
with institutional forms, infrastructure and activities.   By the
same token, of course, in such a society the growing Club and its
facilities (which eventually won the day against other proposals)
was equally frequently damaged, despoiled and even smashed up on
occasion.   Perhaps one of the most critical and probably the most
important boundaries crossed in the development of the therapeutic
community was when the apparently inevitable ebb and flow of social
change led, more positively, towards serious patient-community
efforts in those "recovering".   A critical step forward was made
when they began to share responsibility for those entering the
Admission Ward and to care, in the earlier phases, for those who
might benefit from empathy and the experience of those who "had been
through it" themselves.   The growth and development of the hospital
newspaper, the external schools' repair teams and many others not
only facilitated the interaction between outer society and inner
struggles towards health, but were themselves 'workshops' for self-
review for the forces and emotions affecting the life and work of
the groups.

I have said little so far about the staff groups but they too
developed many different directions of interest and enquiry.   For
example, the nurses, in particular, explored over a long period the
nature of their role in such a therapeutic community.   Previously,
they would all have been able to work according to the principles
governing hospitals accepting patients with physical illnesses
despite the fact that there was only one medical ward as such in
the place.   Now, there emerged the problem of discovering the role
of the nurse in a therapeutic community institution - where only a
few patients were in the ward all day - let alone in bed!   Their
patients were out in Birmingham schools (learning as well as doing),

repairing toys at a department store stand to develop cash for
charity or hospital activities, in the car factory opposite the
hospital, in the Club, etc., and in many additional types of treatment sessions with psychiatrists.   There was only one way - for the
nurse to learn more and to be with her patients in a different role,
and where they were.   Above all the force-field of therapeutic
functions could be more clearly seen to have changed.   The therapeutic task now involved far greater inter-disciplinary practice of
all kinds.   The Admission Ward became a joint patient/staff project;
skill and creative activities became media for therapy in groups at
work; hospital and environmental endeavours involved collaboration
between professional therapeutic staff and social practitioners from
a variety of functions.   A few months before the boundaries between
them had been distinct and their tasks regarded as separate.   And,
in turn, the greater the orientation of the hospital to the core
mission, the more ready the Rehabilitation Unit was to face its own
purposes and decisions of its members.

When Tom Main arrived, the psychiatric scene developed still
further.   He showed his support for the developments taking place
and his own enthusiasm and skill with his colleagues enabled many
steps forward to be taken.   This change was perceived in our daily
meetings with the Commanding Officer and when there really were
explosions in the course of community growth, we were able to develop
a strong collegiate group to work things through.   What was demonstrated over the course of time was the need to gain sanction in
appropriate quarters through collaborative work and inter-disciplinary
competence.   The development of key resources within a system to
appreciate and share perceptions with consultative initiatives from
without is an ongoing necessary part of any dynamic community -
whether with a therapeutic mission or another.   To balance and
optimise the forces and resources from within and without is the
strength of the open-system approach.[11]   The price we pay for that
is the increased demand on inter-dependence and the management of
complexity, conflict and uncertainty.   With the relatively closed
system the price we pay - much more, particularly today, than in
the 1940s - is really exemplified by what happened to Bion at
Northfield - and to others elsewhere.   One method is not good nor
the other bad.   Depending on the characteristics of the institution,
its mission, people, methods and technologies, values and standards
etc., within its various relevant environments, there is a price or
cost for any particular choice made in the way it is run, structured
and developed.   We cannot have the choice or option without the
price that goes with it.

REFERENCES

1. F.E. Emery and E.L. Trist, The causal texture of organisational
        environments, Hum. Relat. 18:21-32, (1965).
2. W.R. Bion and J. Rickman, Intra-group tensions in therapy. Their
        study as the task of the group, Lancet, 2:678-681, (1943).

3. W.R. Bion, The leaderless group project, Bull. Menninger Clin.,
        10:77-81, (1946).
4. J.D. Sutherland and G.A. Fitzpatrick, Some approaches to group
        problems in the British Army, Sociometry, 8:443-455, (1945).
5. B.S. Morris, Officer selection in the British Army, Occ. Psychol.,
        23:219-234, (1949).
6. H. Bridger and R. Isdell-Carpenter, Selection of management
        trainees, Industr. Welf., 29:315;177-181, (1947).
7. T.F. Main, First Memorial Lecture S.H. Foulkes, Institute of
        Group Analysis, London, (1979).
8. W.R. Bion,"Experiences in groups," Tavistock Publications, London,
        (1961).
9. H. Bridger, The Northfield experiment, Bull. Menninger Clin.,
        10:71-76, (1946).
10. I.H. Pearse and L.H. Crocker,"The Peckham experiment," Allen and
        Unwin, London, (1943).
11. H. Bridger, The contribution of organisational development at
        the level of the whole organisation, in: "Organisation
        Development in Europe," K. Trebesch, ed., Paul Haupt Verlag,
        Bern, (1980).

BIOLOGICAL SYSTEMS ANALYSIS OF MENTALITY

M.R.A. Chance, D.Sc. and Romana Prokopiw

Sub-Department of Ethology, University of Birmingham
Uffculme Clinic, Queensbridge Road, Birmingham, UK

As a biologist looking at psychiatry today, I find the most surprising thing is the lack of any clear idea of what constitutes a cure. The definition of mental health has only recently been attempted. So I want to suggest two things.

The first is that not until we have a clear idea of what constitutes mental health can we be in a position to know how to go about tackling so-called mental illness systematically. A century ago, or more, Claude Bernard, the physiologist, saw medicine in the same position as psychiatry is today when he wrote: "We shall never have a science of medicine as long as we separate the explanation of the pathological from the explanation of the normal vital phenomenon." Bruno Bettelheim, the psychotherapist, clearly sees that this now applies to psychoanalysis when he says: "When psychoanalysis is applied outside the limits of psychotherapy various hazards may appear if its original points of departure, and its continual emphasis on the morbid and pathological, are not tempered by equally careful attention to the healthy, the normal, and the positive." It was the laying bare of the anatomical, physiological and biochemical structures that eventually laid the foundation for cures in the now successful aspects of medicine.

The second point I want to suggest is that we need to describe the structure of mentality in order to understand the way to a correct definition of the problem. Adolph Meyer was more right than wrong when he asserted that "there are no mental diseases, only characteristic reaction patterns to stress." Vaillant wrote up the Grant Study, which, for all its imperfections, is the first longitudinal study of a group of healthy graduates through their middle

249

life to old age. Vaillant concluded that the nature of a person's
reactions to stress determines whether or not his condition deteriorates to mental disorder or enables him to continue in mental
health.

So I feel justified in concluding that as soon as possible we
need to find out what constitutes a healthy mind, and for that we
need to know the structure of the mind. As I shall show, the recognition of man's deep biological commitment to social life makes
the task of defining mental structure essentially one for collaboration between group psychiatrists and ethologists, provided they can
agree at the outset that man's mind is an information processing organ.
In The Evolution of Consciousness, John H. Crook concludes: "Information processing is the prime function of 'mind' - its organic role."
What we need for the task of defining a healthy mind is, therefore,
to draw up from relevant existing studies a picture of mind as an
information processing structure. Crook takes the definition of this
structure a stage further when he writes: "The cognitive apparatus
with its subjective aspect is, above all, concerned with the manipulation of information governing the context of the organism in
relation to the environment through the flexible expression of
evolved strategies."

The uniqueness of man is that he has taken this strategy of
behaviour to its limit by evolving an organ for the processing of
information from every source, but especially from the environment.
This is his intelligence. To understand how this has come about
we need to realise that to do this man's mind has become a systems-
forming organ. That is to say, the mind is an organ that can construct, out of ideas, concepts and other aspects of thought, a
planning capability, a strategy producing, creative system. So,
first of all, let us be clear about what a system is. For systems
are a result of a biological property, namely that of combinatorial
competence. (The ability to create, stabilize, or destroy systems
is what an organism does).

Hall and Fagen, in a paper called The Definition of Systems
make clear that a system consists of objects with attributes which
cohere. The relationships that are brought about by this coherence
not only tie the system together, but create the conditions from
which the properties of the system arise. All objects relate to
one another in the universe in some way or another, but the importance of the concept of a system is that within an environment a set
of objects can be seen to cohere and interact in such a way that
their attributes define the nature of the system, and may create
properties which the system alone manifests. The coherence of a
social group is just such a system, since it brings about relationships which are generated by the coherence of the individuals making
up a group. The coming together of objects to form a system is

called 'systematization' and any tendency of the objects to fall apart is called 'segregation'.   These two fundamental aspects of a system, are, in biological systems, in balance with one another. Biological systems also develop sub-systems, through a process called differentiation, for example, the differentiation of organs within the body during development.

Intelligence is an integrated system.   The behaviour of a simple vertebrate is, however, not integrated, but, as Claire and Bill Russell showed a quarter of a century ago in their book Human Behaviour: A New Approach, the behaviour of simple vertebrates is very largely made up of a bundle of separate signal-response units. In these units, inbuilt filters sift the information from the welter of environmental stimuli and trigger fixed-action stereotyped responses, which are then guided by orienting mechanisms.   Since, moreover, sensory awareness is restricted in the primitive vertebrate to single-sense modalities, the system remains one for triggering responses rather than for being informative.

Recently, Harry Jerison, in his book The Evolution of the Brain and Intelligence, by noting the periods in evolution when the mammalian brain has enlarged, has provided an explanation of how incoming sensations have been integrated to produce an awareness of the nature of an object separate from its background.   A build-up of information about the nature of an object is achieved in part by locating it as precisely as possible in the environment.   The primitive vertebrate detects the exact location of an object through smell and hearing "triangulation" procedures: that is, it finds out the direction in which the object seems to be, moves to another place, and relocates the object from there.   The animal correlates the two different directions at which the object appears with the distance the animal itself has moved to fix the object's location.   The location, and hence concept, of the object, is thus contingent on the animal's own movements.

Later, with the mammals' (particularly primates') development of social life, the contingency component of awareness was elaborated to give self-awareness.   Then in man's ancestors, during the hunter-gatherer phase, this ability to conceptualize became elaborated into strategy-synthesising competence.   Finally, in modern man, awareness contingent upon the individual's own behaviour appears in the first six months of life, in the infant's relationship with the mother. The emerging intelligence of the infant is constituted of behavioural strategies as well as conceptual competence, both contingent on the infant's behaviour. This intelligence later becomes objectified in language.

The active pursuit of information, which leads to intelligence, varies according to the type of animal.   Desmond Morris (Symposium

of the Zoological Society of London, 1963) has pointed out the importance of the fact that species differ with respect to their degree
of specialization. At the one extreme, the specialist possesses a
structure and behaviour which confine it to a relatively narrow niche.
At the other end of the spectrum, the structure and behaviour are
more versatile and allow the animal to exploit a much greater array
of enviromental conditions.   This is the opportunist. Let me quote
from Desmond Morris:

> The great behaviour differences between extreme specialists
> and extreme opportunists lies naturally in their exploratory
> activities. We may speak here of neophobic and neophilic
> dualism. Neophobic behaviour, the fear of the new, exhibits
> itself most strongly in the specialists. It has been
> strengthening itself phylogenetically in these cases;
> channelling them into their one track existences, but it
> also operates ontogenetically. The specialist animal has
> a low level of curiosity; exploration occurring only when
> it must. A well-fed snake, lion or eagle, relaxes. With
> the opportunists, however, what we call neophilic behaviour,
> the love of the new is the prevalent tendency and every-
> thing is investigated in case it will provide yet another
> string to the bow of survival.

The high curiosity level of the opportunist provides the basis not
only for the operation of intelligence, whereby a vast reservoire
of experience is built-up, but for the expansion of intelligence
during the life of the individual.

In the resolution of a problem, the animal will be able to
exploit the returns from earlier curiosity, but the problem may
present a threat, so an ability to solve problems also means that
the animal has to build up an ability to stay with a problem by post-
poning action, where possible, until it has come to understand what
is going on. This, by definition, involves suppression of escape.
Such an ability is reinforced in the social environment by reflected
escape towards the dominant centre, and forms the linchpin of the
system of cohesion which keeps individuals together in an agonic
society.

Two modes of social existence have evolved amongst the primates.
Agonic cohesion, as seen in the societies of the baboons and
macaques, evolved be. ase of the continual threat to members of the
society from predators in open country where refuges are scarce, and
individuals receive protection by remaining close to the dominant,
centrally-placed individual, usually a male or two, who possess low
thresholds of aggression and so are periodically provoked to be
aggressive to other members of the group. Consequently, individuals,
other than the dominant, in this type of society, have a persistently

high arousal level, providing them with quick release of responses whereby they can equilibrate quickly. That is to say, they can adjust the distance between themselves and the dominant individuals, submit, displace the aggression onto lower-ranking individuals, defend themselves, or, by subtle alliances, counter-threaten, and so in these ways make an adjustment to the sudden disruption of their life. In this way they also avoid punishment. Because of the potential threat, the individual's attention is continually deflected towards high-ranking individuals who come to expect this attention. Much effort is spent in seeking high status and in reacting to the diverse patterns of social re-arrangements continually going on. As a result, the individual's attention, and the operation of his intelligence, is confined to social matters where response categories are fixed, and predominant attention is not free to be transferred to less immediate matters.

Hedonic societies, however, cohere because of the rewards of social contact; this contact brings a lowering of arousal and consequent flexibility of the behaviour, thereby freeing attention. Periods of socialization are followed by periods in which the exploration of the physical environment can lead, under appropriate circumstances to the invention of new solutions to old problems. Then, the newly invented strategies provide individuals with the ability to tackle new problems, as demonstrated by Emil Menzel in his study of groups of chimpanzees. In an agonic society, the restrictions of solutions to a fixed number of strategies drastically slows down the incorporation of new information and the expansion of awareness. In an hedonic society, where display is the basis of social cohesion, and the exploratory faculty the basis of awareness, social contact is a reward which simultaneously reduces arousal and makes the individuals aware of each other. This means that social cohesion fluctuates, and, when it is relaxed, allows arousal to be contingent on the effects of attention, rather than as in the agonic society, where attention is restricted by the existence of high arousal.

The relationship between arousal and attention is, therefore, reversed between the two modes. In this way, among primates, the operation of intelligence has become contingent on social contact. Nevertheless, the two modes we have been describing are at one and the same time properties of our mind, and also of our social relations. This means that changes in one are reflected in the other.

Intelligence has always guided the behaviour of an animal at the level to which the species has evolved. That this does not always happen in man is due to the operation of the agonic mode in man's mentality. Individuals, during their upbringing, pass through phases when their social relations are of a predominantly hedonic or agonic nature. As Pearce and Newton, in the Conditions of Human Growth,

pointed out, the relationship between a mother and a child, which is
dependent upon the mother, can either be a validating, responsive,
cherishing relationship, predominantly hedonic in nature, or, at a
different time, a denying, agonic type. The strategies which are
appropriate for the local and temporary requirements of an agonic
phase become fixed in the mind. These strategies, then, are incorporated as differentiated, fixed, sub-units of the personality. They
are used as stereotyped responses in defensive situations resembling.
those for which they were originally devised. Clearly, to put the
intelligence in control of the personality, these sub-units must be
exposed to scrutiny and their restrictive influence on a person's
ability realized. Then they can be de-differentiated, and the overall flexibility of the personality re-established under the control
of the intelligence. This should be the goal of therapy.

In therapy, staying with the group when the individual mind is
in the agonic mode involves suppression of escape from the group.
This, as we have seen, creates the pre-conditions for problem resolution. The acceptance and support of the individual by the group
reduces the individual's level of arousal and his tendency to escape.
This, in turn, makes him capable of staying with the problem, as in
the hedonic mode.

If establishing intelligence in control of the personality is
seen as a goal of therapy then clearly the person's mentality must
be transferred to, and firmly imbedded in, the hedonic mode. As
we have seen, this requires re-establishing this mode in the person's
social relations. This, then, is the biological rationale of the
group psycho-therapy movement.

REFERENCE LIST

Bernard, C. 1957. An Introduction to the Study of Experimental
        Medicine. (p. 146) Dover, N.Y.

Bettelheim, B. 1960. The Informed Heart. MacMillan, New York.

Meyer, A. In Adaptation to Life by Vaillant

Vaillant, G.E. 1977. Adaptation to Life. Little, Brown & Co.,
        Boston.

Crook, J.H. 1980. The Evolution of Consciousness. Clarendon Press.
        Oxford.

Hall, A.D. and R.E. Fagen. Definition of Systems. A General
        Systems Year Book of the Society for Advancement of General
        Systems Theory. Eds. Bertalanfly, Von L. and Rapport,
        A. Vol. 1 18 - 28. 1956

Russell, C. and W.M. S. Russell. 1961. Human Behaviour: A New
    Approach. Deutsch, London.

Jerison, H. Evolution of the Brain and Intelligence.   Academic
    Press, London 1973.

Morris, D. 1964.   The response of animals to a restricted environ-
    ment. Symposium Zoological Society, London. 13: 99-118

Chance, M.R.A. and C. Jolly.   Social Groups of Monkeys, Apes and
    Men.   E.P. Dutton & Co. N.Y. and J. Cape London 1970

Chance, M.R.A. and R.R. Larsen (Eds.) 1976.   Social Structure
    of Attention.   John Wiley.   London and New York.

Chance, M.R.A.   The Infrastructure of Mentality In: Ethological
    Psychiatry: Psychopathology in the context of Evolutionary
    Biology.   (Ed) M.T. McGuire and L.A. Fairbanks.   Grune
    and Stratton.   N.Y. 1977.

Menzel, E.W. Spontaneous Invention of Ladders in a Group of Young
    Chimpanzees.   Folia Primate: 17 : 87-106, 1972.

Pearce, J. and S. Newton.   The Conditions of Human Growth.   Citadel
    Press, New York, 1969.

BOUNDARIES AND BOUNDARYING: A SYSTEMS PERSPECTIVE

Helen E. Durkin, Ph.D.

7 Fairview Road, Scarsdale, New York 10583, U.S.A.

The Changing Paradigm

Boundaries play an increasingly dynamic role in the clinical management of individual and group relationships. I plan to present a case illustration, but because most of what we know about boundaries and the boundarying process comes from general systems theory, I thought it might be a good idea to put the topic into its systems context and try to show why and how GST can add substantially to the effectiveness of the current "group therapies".

Edgar Levinson (1971) had made the point that "paradigms are time and space bound", and indeed time seems to have caught up with the psychoanalytic paradigm. It has revealed certain theoretical inadequacies, and their consequent clinical deficiencies, the worst of which I am sure you will agree, is actual change of behaviour does not, as had been expected, regularly follow insight. This is particularly true of our narcissistic and borderline members.

Both thoughtful psychoanalysts and their severest critics have attempted to overcome these shortcomings. But the ensuing con- flicts have not yet produced higher levels of integration, and simply combining their ideas would lead only to a "patchwork" theory of group therapy. During the sixties therefore, we were searching for a way to incorporate the most valid of these findings into traditional group therapy. What we really needed, in my opinion, was a supra- ordinate theoretical framework which could accommodate the new ideas and at the same time bring us into the mainstream of modern science.

Meanwhile general systems theory had come of age and appeared

257

to be worth investigating as a possible solution of our predicament.
Spurred on by the fact that the cybernetic branch of general systems
theory had already generated a systems-orientated family therapy, we
formed a task force to investigate the possibilities for group
therapy.

Systems Concepts

    We learned that systems thinking had come into being because,
after quantum mechanics and relativity theory had expanded our
scientific horizons, many leading scientists began to focus on the
organisation rather than the content of whatever phenomena they
were studying. They made a distinction between complex organized
phenomena which are the product of their interaction, and the
simpler sums or aggregates which interact additively. They made up
intensive study of the "organized complexities" and began to call
them systems.   A system was defined by von Bertalanffy as "an
order of parts and processes standing in dynamic interaction (1968).
Finally they proceeded to identify the basic structural features of
systems in general and to codify the laws by which systems operate.
This comparative study of the entire spectrum of systems introduced
a whole new order of knowledge about the interrelationships among
systems and their modes of interacting.

    It was to be expected that such discoveries, at the cutting
edge of science would engender a host of new structural hypotheses
and techniques, which would be applicable to most fields of science.
Why not, then, to group therapy? We were excited by the notion
and continued our investigation with enthusiasm.

    We had begun by examining the application of cybernetics to
family therapy but the literature did not, at the time, have anything to say about individual or intrapsychic systems, which I,
as an analytic group therapist, considered essential.   Moreover,
they dealt chiefly with the effect of the family system on the
behaviour of its individual members, whereas what we needed most
was to know how to form new systems.   For therapy groups are composed of strangers. They begin as aggregates and one of the
therapist's primary tasks is to help them organize themselves to become a suprasystem which can then serve as a valuable partner in the
group therapeutic process.

    A number of us found an excellent and indeed a very stimulating
solution to the problem, in von Bertalanffy's new model of living
systems, which highlights the notion that every living system, no
matter how dysfunctional, has the inherent (phylogenetically programmed) potential to restructure itself. Given some assistance
living systems are able to increase their autonomy. The structural
features which make this possible are their permeable boundaries

and the fact that they have the capacity to open or close them. It
is for this reason that living systems can exchange matter/energy,
and information with one another and so regulate the rate and volume
of these exchanges. They can maintain their own stability by excluding excess input, and they can restructure or transform themselves by importing energy and information. Moreover as the process
of opening and closing their boundaries is carried out consistently
over time, they develop a new phenomenon discovered by von Bertalanffy
which he called "fliessgleichgewicht". It is a dynamic or "flux" as
opposed to a static, equilibrium produces a steady state
which permits them to maintain a stable identity while progressively
transforming themselves. This robust view of living systems is very
heartening to the therapist. It has certainly inspired me to deal
more firmly and effectively with the ever-frustrating "repetition
compulsion".

Some Clinical Implications

But the therapist must keep in mind that therapy groups are composed of members, who in the course of their earliest exchanges with
their parental systems, have become to varying degrees dysfunctional.
Their potential for managing their own boundarying process has
usually been impaired. Their boundaries tend to lack clear definition.
They may be too open or too closed, and in the wrong times and places.
Consequently their ability to communicate is poor.

The Boundarying Process: A Systems View of the Therapist's Function

Let us suppose now, that you want to take advantage of this
structural point of view and of the additional information it puts
at your disposal. How would you go about it? Our task force members
did it in a number of different ways and you too will find that
there is room for diversity. Today I am inviting you to examine my
own adaptation with me. I adopted an overarching systems theoretical
framework, but continued to employ analysis as the critical conceptual subsystem. In that way I am able to put the flesh and blood
of content on the skeleton of structure.

In order to formulate a working hypothesis for changing systems
structure I took my cue from the way normal systems do it by employing boundary opening and closing. I made the assumption that
the therapist may temporarily assume responsibility for monitoring
the group, the individual and the intrapsychic boundaries. I intervene to facilitate change only when one of the systems in the group
interaction seems to be mismanaging one of its boundaries.

As I tested out the new boundarying technique I found that both
the group members and I could intuitively spot dysfunctional exchanges and boundaries, in much the same way that one can detect

preconscious conflict and motivation. I am sure that perceptive
therapists of any "denomination" will be able to do the same because
there are many signals. For instance, if a group or a member seems
flooded with excess feelings, thoughts, or activity, or appears to be
in a confused state, I listen with especial care to find out which
of its boundaries needs to be closed. If none of the members picks
it up, I intervene to facilitate its closure. If I have succeeded,
the system in question will be calmer and become more selective in
its exchanges. If, on the other hand, I have been able to catalyze
a given system's potential for opening one of its dysfunctionally
closed boundaries, I shall be able to observe that a transformation
has occurred which will be directly reflected in new behavior, or
as we say in systems language, in its mode of interacting. In other
words, if the group therapist systematically uses the interaction
to catalyze their potential for boundary management, the three
systems will gradually move toward structural autonomy.

How to Facilitate Boundary Change

        So much for the new technical principle of boundarying. You
must be wondering how one "facilitates" boundary opening or closing.
Well, when we first faced this problem, we began by scanning the
whole array of already familiar techniques to see if they could
serve the purpose. My own experience had often proved that a
correctly timed transference interpretation can open the intrapsychic boundaries to a flood of recollections, or close them to
impulses to act out. Yet it had become evident that when boundaries
seem intransigent, the more dramatic experience of gestalt exercises,
encounter techniques or role-playing may be more successful in
opening them. On the other hand ego psychoanalytic and certain
transactional techniques serve the equally important task of closing
boundaries to increase stability and identity.   Thus GST broadens
our perspective and increases our technical options. We need no
longer be confined to the techniques of a single approach.

        Meanwhile Bill Gray and Jim Durkin suggested another way to
facilitate boundary change in order to bring about transformations.
In constructing their GST models of group therapy they gave special
attention to the flow of the emotional and cognitive processes which
are organized by the boundarying process. They both observed that
genuine spontaneous emotions tend to open boundaries. Jim added
that cognitive input tends to close boundaries. He made the obvious
but often ignored point that both emotion and cognition are
essential in practice because emotional flow is evanescent and
cognitions are needed to give the transformation they generated,
stable form and durability.

        This work confirmed my own experience. I formulated the working
hypothesis that in the case of human individual and social systems,

spontaneous emotions (in contrast to those which serve the defences)
carry enough energy to stimulate new action, while cognitive processes convey information which forms new boundaries or maintains old
ones. Here then is another way to facilitate structural and behavioral change.   My hypothesis has been clinically productive but
I believe that current neurophysiological research will soon provide
us with more precise information about the neurological correlates
of emotion and cognition.

We have far from exhausted the clinical implications of systems
theory but its broad structural viewpoint and new information will no
doubt stir the imagination of creative therapists and you too will
make new hypotheses and design new techniques. That is what happened
among our own members. So the field is wide open to new applications
of GST and I hope that many of you will give it further thought and
contribute to our fascinating project.   If you are interested,
please get in touch with me.

Introduction to the Case Illustration

Perhaps a concrete example will clarify what I have said about
the role of boundaries and boundarying in the clinical management
of individual and group relationships. It illustrates the way that
facilitating boundary opening/closing leads to transformations and
behavior changes which gradually increase the autonomy of the
systems involved.

Because most authors have dealt with the effect of the group
on the behavior of its individual members, I decided to show that
the reverse also happens; that changing the structure of one individual member or of her intrapersonal organization also brings
about these changes in the other members and in the group as a whole.

The Presenting Problem

Marge, a young woman of twenty-six came for help because she
had just broken off with still another man who had treated her
"shabbily". She said she felt hurt, angry and powerless. Within
minutes she complained about her mother in exactly the same words.
She said she had always been her mother's favourite but had experienced her as intrusive and felt she had to keep fighting her to
avoid being completely controlled.

Comparative Diagnosis

The Psychodynamic viewpoint

Marge had clearly never completed the process of separation and
individuation. Identity problems remained but she exhibited focal

ego strengths, such as competence at work and persistence in reaching
her own goals. I saw her not as borderline but as orally-regressed
with strong self-defeating tendencies. She suffered from her repeated re-enactments of her split transferences to the good and the
bad mother of infancy and of an aborted oedipal transference. She behaved submissively with significant others, gave them lip-service,
but acted out her inner defiance - which was exactly how she provoked
mistreatment.

From the Structural Viewpoint

Marge had been unable to shut out her mother's persistent need
to regulate her feelings, thoughts and behavior. Consequently she
never developed adequate control of either her interpersonal or her
intrapsychic boundaries. No wonder then, that she possessed no firm
sense of her own identity. In close relationships she frequently
opened up so extravagantly that she ruined them. In the group where
opening up would have helped her, she tended to remain closed unless
prodded. Moreover her repeated re-enactment of mechanized transferential modes of interacting interferred severely with her inate
capacity to change and grow.

The Psychodynamic Aspect of Treatment

During the first year or so I saw Marge individually. It soon
became clear that she was bound to keep me in the role of the
nurturant mother. Unlike most patients she experienced my analysis
of her relationships with her parents and her boy-friends, as a
caring act. She even welcomed my, of course, very gentle attempts
to help her become aware of how much she provoked mistreatment. I
let this transferential attitude be, but was careful not to play
into it. As a result her week-end battles with her mother abated
somewhat and she began to choose less sadistic men. These were,
of course, transference results but they served to make her feel she
was able to change her "fate". The next phase of treatment consisted mostly of analysing those transference re-enactments which
dominated her outside life. I could only very gradually touch on
her transference to me and then only enough to prevent the formation
of a fully idealized transference.

The Intransigent Marital System

When she finally married Don, they quickly set up a two-way
mutually withholding parent/child relationship. Although they both
wanted to be loved neither dared to give or receive love freely.
They were desparately afraid of being sucked into each other's
orbit which was how they had experienced their mothers. Their modes
of interacting dovetailed of course. Marge expected to be loved
but repeatedly provoked rejection and Don, who even as a child, had

vowed never to be like his hysterical incompetent mother, kept his
feelings very low key and presented a strictly logical facade.

Afraid of being controlled, each attempted to control the other.
Consequently they fought over everything. For instance, Marge took
his rare affectionate gesture as the prelude to a "sexual attack".
He would give her reasonable arguments in turn. His cool cover-up
served to avoid his growing anxiety and his anger, but that only made
her press harder until at last he simply withdrew. When they did
actually make love, Marge would, as soon as she felt herself yielding, accuse him of being either incept or manipulative. That would
end the encounter with Marge feeling rejected and helpless while Don
felt injured because his "best efforts had been grievously misunderstood."

Marge did get Don into treatment with me but it seemed impossible analytically to turn her excellent facility for insight into
new ways of behaving in this critical area of her life. I invited
her to join a group because I thought that if she heard the other
members rake me over the coals without losing my good will, she
might risk projecting the bad mother image on to me. Moreover experiencing her transferential patterns of interacting with others
could be expected to be dramatic and experiential enough to activate
behavior change.

The Group Interaction

At first Marge kept a tight control of her boundaries. Her only
input into the interaction was very perceptive but concerned their
feelings and behavior rather than her own. But they liked her
sensitivity and soon got her at least to talk about her troubles with
her husband. They then joined in more openly and gradually began
to express feelings toward one another. Ralph, one of the more
masochistic men, sensed Marge's essential unavailability and began
to be attentive to her. As expected she responded with apparent
warmth but as soon as he described his sexual fantasies about her,
Marge turned to someone else and changed the subject. The others
noticed how upset he was and the entire interaction changed to a
lively exchange of very personal feelings interspersed with a
number of insightful comments.

They were clearly not ready to come to grips with sexual
feelings. Instead Marge's ability to get in touch with her own and
others much more primitive feelings led them into an exploration of
their infantile feelings and experiences with their preoedipal
mothers, which lay at the base of the sexual problem.

After a while, however, it seemed to me that Marge was beginning to use her insight to perpetuate her masochistic defences and

to become increasingly entrenched in her investment in pain and
suffering. This began to hold back the group as well. At some point
I decided that talking on the content level was not going to change
either her behavior or theirs. I decided it was time to change to
structural interventions which addressed her (or them) as a total
person instead of analysing a part and attempted to catalyze her
potential as a living system to restructure herself and take the
action of using her insight for instead of against herself, I waited
for an opportunity.

    In the very next group session, Marge complained that she was
"tired of jumping through Don's hoops". Before long Elly interrupted her saying, "You know, Marge, I've never heard you say one
good thing about Don": Marge was nonplussed, her seemingly static
equilibirum was shaken up. She looked perplexed and after a minute
said, "Oh - but I thought - I thought - you all knew I - I love him."
After an unhappy silence, I said, "You know Marge, I think you have
a hard time closing your boundaries against anyone who really gets to
you, like Don and your mother."   Marge: "Yeah, ...but why....does
Elly think I don't love him?" Pete, who had previously identified
with her confusion offered an answer: "I think you keep getting mad
at the very ones you love." Her whole demeanor and tone of voice
changed. She said spontaneously, "My God - it's true: I was never
able to keep my mother out from under my skin ... whenever I tried to,
I felt guilty - but mostly I complied and got furious. I keep doing
that with Don .. damn it .. who needs it? Because of her manner I
felt the "new" thoughts and feelings had really penetrated her now
open boundaries.

    Because of other intrapsychic boundary complications, she was
not yet ready to change her behavior toward Don, but the next weekend her behavior with her mother changed drastically. The first time
her mother made what Marge felt as an unreasonable demand, she simply
answered with a firm refusal, and avoided getting into the usual
argument about it. When she told us about it in the next session
she expressed surprise that her mother had actually respected her
stand, and we all laughed at how much her mother had changed since
treatment began.

    Wanting to help her stabilize the new mode of interacting which
seemed to reflect a structural transformation I gave her some
positive feedback saying, "It seems you can_ manage your own
boundaries!" Her manner changed again. Her slow ... thoughtful
speech with its many pauses indicated to me that she was really
processing the new input. She went on, "Mm.. Ye..es .. It just ...
never dawned on me ... I always ... always ... thought ...I was
terrified ..... if I closed her out ... she'd never ... ever ...
let me in again .... But she wouldn't dump me ... My God ...
I can hardly believe it ... I'm really in charge ... of myself ...

yes myself ...   Again I said, "Why not, they are your boundaries."
She grinned. All hesitation was gone now. She clapped her hands
and said laughing, "Wow, I feel like my own person for a change!"

The Group Transformation

In the next group session Marge tried out her new behavior with
me. At one point she interrupted me saying firmly, "Please stop
talking; there is something else I want to say." My silence and
friendly smile served again as positive feedback. The other members
had watched me carefully out the corners of their eyes, and reading
no danger signal, congratulated her on her changed behavior. It
was not long before they too became more openly angry, and some of
them began to work out their negative transferences toward me - and/
or to other group members. For example, Ralph whose problems reson-
ated with Marge's, finally stopped casting me in the role of the controlling mother. At the same time his relationship with his current
girl improved enormously.

Moreover, the structure of the group as a whole underwent a
marked transformation. As their interpersonal boundaries opened,
the group boundary closed. As a suprasystem it managed it's own
boundary function and developed a flowing equilibrium so that for a
time there was little need for interventions from me. Each of the
three group systems seemed to be moving simultaneously toward increasing its own autonomy.

Conclusion

For Marge, as for some of the others, the most important result
of closing an external boundary was that it enabled her to open
another crucial intrapsychic boundary which had blocked her normal
spontaneous sexual responses for a long time. It was she who was
then able to lead the group into its next phase. Having explored
their confusing ambivalent ties to the mother of infancy, and resolved their problems of separation and individuation to a large
extent, they were able to deal with their varying oedipal difficulties in the group interaction and gradually to restructure their
sexual patterns of interacting.

In the meantime Don had worked out some of the problems which
had reinforced Marge's dysfunctional behavior and for the first
time they were able to risk experiencing tenderness and sex together. There was a genuine turnabout in their marriage. As further
evidence of their mutual structural and behavioral transformations,
Marge had a baby. Moreover, they were able to deal quite well
during their summer vacation, with the expectable moments of regression and despair during the pregnancy. There was some further
working through to be accomplished but treatment was nearing its end.

What the Case of Marge Illustrated

1.   It familiarizes the reader with systems at three levels of complexity, in interaction - the group suprasystem, the individual system,
and the intrapersonal subsystem.

2.   They constitute a small hierarchy of interacting wholes which
are isomorphic, obey the same laws of operation, and exert a mutual
influence upon one another.

3.   It distinguishes between structure and content in diagnosis and
interventions.

4.   It illustrates that in the case of human individual and social
systems, energy and information are conveyed in the form of the
members' emotional/cognitive modes of interacting.

5.   It demonstrates that the therapist may assume responsibility for
monitoring the intrapersonal, the interpersonal, and the group
boundaries and that he can facilitate transformations at all three
systems levels to the end that they can move harmoniously toward
autonomy.

BIBLIOGRAPHY

Bertalanffy, L. von 1956, General Systems Theory, General Systems
            Yearbook //1 p. 11o ff. The Society for General
            Systems Research, ed. Anatol Rappoport.

Bertalanffy, L. von., 1967 Robots, Men and Minds. Brazillier, N.Y.

Bertalanffy, L. von, 1968, General Systems Theory, Brazillier, N.Y.

Durkin, H., 1972, Group Therapy & General Systems Theory in
            Progress in Group & Family Therapy, Ed. C. Sager & Helen
            Kaplan. Bruner Mazel, N.Y.

Durkin, J., 1980 Boundarying Structure of Autonomy in Living Groups.
            General Systems Yearbook. The Society for General Systems
            Research, ed. Anatol Rappoport.

Durkin, J., 1980 7th Annual Bertalanffy Lecture. The Proceedings
            of the 24th Annual North American Meeting in 1980, San
            Francisco. Ed. H. Banathy by The Society for G.S. Research
            1980.

Gray, W., 1873 Emotion/Cognitive Structures, General Systems Year-
            book Vol. XVIII.

Gray, W., The Evolution of Emotional/Cognitive and System Precursor
     Theory.   Ed. Jim Durkin.   Bruner Mazel, N.Y.

Haley, J., 1973, Changing Families, Grune & Stratton, N.Y.

Levinson, E., 1972, Fallacy of Understanding, Basic Books, N.Y.

Miller, J.G., 1965, Living Systems, Basic Concepts
     Behavioral Science, 10 p 193-237.

Watzslawick, P., 1967, Pragmatics of Human Communication.
          W.W. Norton, N.Y.

GROUP DYNAMICS: A MODERN REDEFINITION OF THEIR THERAPEUTIC SIGNIFICANCE AS BOUNDARY PROCESSES

Morton Kissen

Associate Professor
Institute of Advanced Psychological Studies
Adelphi University, Garden City, N.Y. 11530

Group dynamics have not always been viewed as having a positive influence upon the group psychotherapy process. During the last 35 years, a number of significant systematic changes have occurred in both the conceptual delineation of group dynamics and their technical use in the form of specific interventions with groups.

In the present paper, I will develop a conceptual definition of group dynamics that views them as "boundary processes" having tremendous practical significance for the therapeutic potential of a given group experience. Both general systems and object relations concepts will be emphasized in my presentation. Despite the heavily theoretical emphasis of these two conceptual approaches, I will always be setting my sights upon the more practical significance of this conceptual excursion for the decision-making needs of the group therapist who must somehow say or do something in his work with groups.

I will begin by offering a fairly traditional definition of group dynamics. I will next broaden and deepen this definition by placing group dynamics within a historical frame-work that traces the gradual evolution of a modern general systems model for understanding group dynamics and for implementing that understanding in the form of specific interventions with groups. My historical presentation will particularly focus upon three systematic positions that have been outlined with regard to the understanding and therapeutic use of group dynamics over the past 35 years.

The first systematic position high-lights the noxions, anti-therapeutic aspects of group dynamics and views them essentially as impediments and obstacles to the goals of the group therapist. The

second historical approach to group dynamics involves a rather
radical shift away from the view that they are obstacles, and instead, depicts them as the very heart of the matter during the group
treatment process. As a matter of fact, according to this second
view-point, nothing else other than group dynamics has any true
therapeutic significance in work with groups. The third systematic
view-point about group dynamics involves a transition toward an
understanding of them as very significant boundary processes having
both general systems and object relations characteristics. This
third and most recent definition of group dynamics both holds on to
the emphasis in the second historical approach upon the very central
therapeutic significance of group dynamics and yet, paradoxically,
frees the therapist to temporarily neglect them in his specific
treatment interventions.

Throughout my historical presentation, I will be contrasting
the vertical approach to group intervention in which a particular
group member is singled out for more intensive confrontation with
the horizontal approach in which a substantive sub-group or perhaps
the group-as-a-whole is focussed upon by the group therapist. I
will offer a number of concrete illustrations of specific group
interventions to highlight the practical implications of the three
historical and conceptual approaches that I am tracing in this
paper.

A Functional Definition of Group Dynamics

Let us begin by establishing a functional definition of group
dynamics that has some practical implications for work with psychotherapy groups. It is safe to assume that every group moves through
a number of dynamic phases as it evolves toward becoming a more open
therapeutic system. These dynamic moments in a group's history need
not be viewed, at least initially, as either facilitating or retarding the group's progress toward its therapeutic goals.

Certain typical group dynamic events have been repeatedly
noted in the group psychotherapy literature and have been given familiar labels such as scape-goating, pairing or group rebellions.
Bion, in a number of writings (1952, 1959) has described the shifts
back and forth by a group between irrational basic assumptions of
fight-flight, dependency and pairing all of which contribute to a
less realistic and more emotional and motivationally over-determined
group atmosphere.

Basically, these highly motivational and emotional group
processes for Bion are the heart of the matter and must be actively
focussed upon by the group therapist. Indeed group dynamics can be
defined as those highly emotion and motivation-laden interactive
moments in a group's development which have very great functional
significance for the practical intervention strategy of the therapist.

A group that is in a <u>fight-flight</u> phase must somehow be attended
to by the therapist. He may decide to approach his group that is
busily engaged in victimizing a particular member either <u>vertically</u>
(by addressing the latent psycho-dynamics of the victim, i.e., his
need to gain the attention of the over-all group by provoking anger
and attack from the other members) or <u>horizontally</u> (via a typical
Bion-Tavistock oracular pronouncement with regard to the fact that
a victimizing interaction is taking place in the group). Somehow,
however, a group dynamic event requires some form of action or
intervention from the therapist.

Thus, the functional definition of group dynamics that I would
like to articulate contains an inherent emphasis upon them as highly
motivational interactive processes that are significant <u>signals</u>
or <u>cues</u> to the therapist for the necessity of some form of horizontal or vertical group intervention. Group dynamic events require
some form of response by the therapist.

In the next section of my paper, I would like to outline three
significant phases in the recent history of the group psychotherapy
movement. Each of these phases has been associated with a
different functional definitions of group dynamics having practical
implications for the choices available to the group therapist.

The First Phase: Group Dynamics as a "Distraction" to the Therapeutic Process

The first historical phase emphasizes the rather early notion
that the task of a group therapist is the same as that of an individual therapist. The only difference between individual and
group treatment, according to this view-point, is that the latter
just happens to take place in a group setting. Thus, all a therapist who works with groups need do is focus in a relatively systematic and comprehensive fashion on the psychodynamic and therapeutic needs of each individual member of his group. Individual X
may therefore require some interpretation of her unspoken resentment or competitive feelings toward the leader, who represents, at
an unconscious level, her ambivalently loved father. Individual
Y, on the other hand, may require an interpretation with regard to
her much dreaded affection feelings toward the leader who unconsciously represents a potentially abandoning mother figure.

The basic intervention strategy is a <u>vertical</u> one with the
sole focus being upon intra-psychic issues having transferential
significance for the interation of individual group members with
either the group leader or particular other group members.

This treatment model with groups is largely articulated in the
writings of Alexander Wolf and Emanuell Schwartz (1955, 1962). Wolf
and Schwartz emphasize an almost totally <u>vertical</u> model of therapeutic

intervention in which group dynamics are viewed as mere distractions
and obstacles to be over-come by the therapist in conducting his
group. Highly emotional and motivated interactive behaviour involving diverse segments of the group distract the therapist from his
essential task which is to analyze the internal dynamics and transference reactions of individual members. The therapy process just
happens to take place in a group context - in part to maximize the
number of individuals who can be reached therapeutically.

It can be assumed that much of the "bad press" and critical
reactions to the burgeoning group psychotherapy movement stemmed
from this historical period in which groups were viewed as mere
vehicles for increasing the number of patients who can be intrapsychically and vertically treated. The tendency to ignore group
dynamics and to focus almost totally upon individual psychodynamics
led to a noticeably cynical and superficially rationalized attitude
for justifying the placement of people into groups for therapeutic
purposes.

The Second Phase: Group Dynamics as the "Heart of the Matter" during Group Psychotherapy

The second historical phase was ushered in by the writings of
Bion (1952, 1959) with regard to the central significance of group
dynamic events such as fight-flight, pairing and dependency interactions during a group's development. Bion essentially reversed
the treatment approach espoused by Wold and Schwartz in his emphasis
upon the focal significance of group dynamics as signals to the
therapist of the need to formulate some form of appropriate group-
as-a-whole intervention.

The therapist, according to Bion, must approach these group
dynamic events as especially significant bits of interactive behaviour requiring some form of objective observational pronouncement.

The Bion approach has recently been, integrated with Ezriel's
(1950) approach to the study of common group tensions. John
Borriello (1976) describes a treatment model largely stemming from
the work of Bion which he labels the "therapist-centred group-as-a-
whole approach." In this model, he emphasizes the restriction of
the therapist to group-as-a-whole interpretations in confronting
a given group with its underlying basic assumptions. Thus, during
a fight-flight phase, the leader might say to his group - "You have
decided to ignore each other and fight with me because of your fantasy that I am persecuting you." During a dependency phase, the
leader might say something to the effect - "You all seem to feel
that I am a powerful magician who can cure all of your ills."
During the pairing phase, the leader might comment - "It seems

that everyone is enjoying the discussion taking place between
member X and member Y."

Of course, eventually, the therapist must focus upon the individual group members and their unique modes of responding to the
common group tension or basic assumption environment that has occurred as a central event in the group. Thus, the therapist might
note that individual X characterologically responds by withdrawing
and becoming depressed whereas individual Y characteristically
responds by attacking the leader or individual Z. Such a subsequent individual focus, however, is a mere after-thought to the
more essential intervention which is of a largely horizontal and
group-as-a-whole nature.

It is interesting that those who have totally relied upon
the Bion-Tavistock model in their group therapeutic work have been
able to report powerful therapeutic changes despite a tendency to
deliver their pronouncements in a stuffy, pompous and noticeably
oracular manner.

Group dynamics are thus the most central issues for the Bion-
Tavistock approach. They can neither be neglected nor ignored and,
if anything, need to be continuously focussed upon in the form of
group-as-a-whole interventions. The emphasis is upon an almost
totally horizontal attention on the part of the leader to these
highly motivational group interaction processes.

The Third Phase: Group Dynamics as "Boundary Processes" having
Object Relations Characteristics

During the latter part of the second historical phase, a
gradual disillusionment began to occur with the Bion-Tavistock
group dynamic model. The stuffy and pompous oracular pronouncements delivered by Bionian therapists were beginning to be seen as
overly mechanized and lifeless forms of group intervention. Individual group members and exciting, emotionally significant interactions between pairs and small sub-groups were somehow being overlooked so that the total group theme could be illuminated by the
therapist or group conductor as Foulkes (1957) preferred to call
the group leader.

More and more therapists began to view the group-as-a-whole
approach espoused by Bion as a charicature of group psychotherapy.
Many members of therapy groups, T-groups, and work-shop groups
became disenthralled and unhappy with this form of intervention that
seemed to move the group so far away from the emotionally vibrant
interactions taking place within more discrete segments of the
group. For example, member X might be struggling to express some
extremely conflict-laden feelings toward member Y by moving to
touch and embrace her and the leader would make some sort of state-

ments such as - "These two members are acting out a conflict that
every member of the group is feeling."

While this form of intervention may be objectively correct, it
was seen as having an intellectually stultifying effect upon an
emotionally significant group interaction. Of course, this form of
intervention may generate a great deal of angry feelings directed
at the leader and perhaps the opportunity to work through some negative transference distortions. On the other hand, these angry
feelings are being provoked via an artificial contrivance which
appears as a distraction to the ongoing emotionalism inherent in
the interaction between two peer group members.

In terms of general systems theory which is beginning to be
popularized through the writings of Helen and Jim Durkin (1973,1974A,
1974B), this form of group intervention has certain boundary properties which may be classified as system-closing rather than system
opening. Jim Durkin, in particular, has classified group dynamic
processes in terms of their boundary regulating and structual
characteristics. He distinguished a rigid form of emotional fore-
closure which he labels summing from a more open, flexibly emotional
mode of group interaction which he calls systemming.

Thus, the typical Bionian group-as-a-whole pronouncement seems
to involve the introduction of a highly cognitive boundary closing
structure into a potentially open boundary system. Indeed, since
the goal according to General Systems Theory is to facilitate relatively flexible opening up of group boundaries and movement toward
the so-called organic living system, the group-as-a-whole form of
intervention was seen as having just the opposite effect.

In certain ways, the new general systems model viewed group
dynamics with the same suspiciousness as did Wolf and Schwartz
during an earlier historical period. Jim Durkin (1974B) alluded
to the excessive interest on the part of group psychoanalysts with
the relatively intellectual pursuit of the "secret meanings"
underlying group dynamic processes. He contrasted such an approach
with a more structural treatment model. The newer model emphasized
a focussed attention upon formal properties within the group such
as the boundary regulating functions within the group members inherent in their comfort or discomfort with emotionally open systems
communications.

The General Systems model, in many ways, introduced an over-
valuing of feelings over more cognitive modes of communication -
perhaps in part as a corrective to the seemingly over-intellectual
Bion-Tavistock intervention model. In a recent paper (1980), I
explored this aspect of the systems approach which is paradoxical,
in light of the heavily intellectual and complex philosophical
arguments underlying General Systems Theory.

I do feel, however, that the truly innovative aspect of the systems approach is its contribution to a modern functional re-definition of group dynamic processes. A contemporary definition of group dynamics conceptualizes them as boundary processes in-herently having neither <u>summing</u> (<u>closed system</u>) characteristics nor <u>systemming</u> (<u>open system</u>) characteristics. The functional properties of group dynamics remain their highly emotional and motivational characteristics and the fact that they require some form of thera-peutic response from the group leader. It is the response of the leader that is most essential in creating either a more organic living system or an emotionally barren closed communication system within the group.

Once group dynamics are seen as structural boundary processes that may be potentiated in the form of either an open or closed system then the leader's true functions as "catalyst" (Durkin, 1973) or boundary-regulator for the group can be exposed and illuminated. Although General Systems Theory has been previously described as a "theory in search of a technique" (Durkin, 1974), a number of very specific group strategies can be generated from this approach.

The boundary regulating function of the leader in response to group dynamic signals from his group may move him in either a boun-dary opening (systemming) or boundary closing (<u>summing)</u> direction, depending upon his perception of the overall shape of the group and emotional communicative needs of the group members. As Kernberg (1975) has recently noted, the systems properties of a group leader's therapeutic intervention must be explored through an empir-ical validation of its emotional impact upon the group. Both <u>vert-ical</u> (individual-within-the-group) and <u>horizontal</u> (group-as-a-whole) forms of intervention have specific types of boundary properties which may either open up or close off an organic living system with-in the group.

<u>Vertical</u> forms of intervention may have either a pre-oedipal or more advanced oedipal character depending upon structural boundary features that exist within the group. Similarly <u>horizontal</u> forms of intervention too may have either a pre-oedipal and depen-dency-enhancing character or a more advanced oedipal (self-assertion and competition-enhancing) character. Much depends upon the systems properties of group dynamic responses of individual members and the group-as-a-whole.

In a recent work-shop that I conducted with a group of mental health professionals, I presented the group with a formulation that a conflict existed within the group between those who would like to act out and live out certain strong feelings of intimacy and physical attachment and those who were fearful of such an emotional sharing and prefer to keep topics and group interactions on a more intel-lectual and emotionally insulated level. My intervention had the structural properties of a horizontal summing (and hence system closing) operation and yet it had a different effect on particular group members. Some did indeed experience it as an overly intellectualized statement which essentially cut off feelings. Others, however, paradoxically, experienced it as a creative formulation which allowed them to open up and get in touch with many feelings that were previously unavailable.

In many groups that I have conducted, I have alternated my interventions from a more horizontal, group-as-a-whole mode to a more vertical and individual-within-the-group mode and have found both system opening and system closing boundary responses to occur.

In general, I have found the paradoxical form of interventions (Goldberg, 1977) and the so-called paradigmatic interventions involving irony, irrationality, obtuseness and playful use of absurdity to be the most conducive to the creation of an open and living group system. Ormont (1964, 1968, 1969) has described a number of paradigmatic techniques such as joining the group resistance which utilize irony and paradoxical humor to open up an emotionally stagnant and pre-oedipally fixated psychotherapy group.

Ormont has been able to by-pass the horizontal mode of intervention and to concentrate solely upon individual group members and yet take into account significant dynamic tensions within his groups. Thus, he describes a passive and largely depressed and masochistic group who were allowing a particular member to dominate each therapy session with a series of jokes and clowning interactions. Ormont's intervention ignored the resistant group-as-a-whole and was directed at the clowning group member with the following statement - "Why don't you get the other group members to pay you for your entertainment work." Ormont had decided to join the group resistance and to utilize a paradigmatic mirroring technique to exaggerate it in the group. The use of irrationality paradoxically led to a more emotionally meaningful form of communication by the previously silent and passive group members.

A modern functional definition of group dynamics as boundary processes thus frees the therapist to deal with them in a variety of creative ways a number of which may even outwardly ignore the behavior of the group-as-a-whole. Object relations principles can be effectively integrated with general systems principles in determining a particular intervention response to a given group dynamic process. Once group dynamics are seen as boundary processes, the leader is free to explore the object relations inherent in these dynamics via a focus upon sub-systems, systems, or supra-systems transactions taking place within the group. The intervention itself may be offered in either a vertical or horizontal fashion.

As an example, a resistant group of overly passive and depen-

dent individuals can be dealt with in a variety of ways. The entire
group can be informed of its magical wishes to have a leader who
actively performs tasks that individual members are too weak to per-
form. A particular member who seems relatively active can be focussed upon and asked to diminish his activity level since it doesn't
actually pay off in the long run (paradoxical or paradigmatic intervention). The leader can remain passive and inert himself (in
a sense, mirroring the passivity of the group members). The leader
can actively engage one of the slightly more active and emotionally
visible members in an extended dialogue and interaction (thereby
creating envy and competitive Oedipal feelings in the other members).
The leader can focus upon a pairing interaction between two members
who evidently are engaging in a cozy, dependent relationship of
great passive interest to the other members of the group. Finally,
the leader might work with a particularly dependent member on his
wish for the strong father figure he never actually had.

Each and every one of these intervention strategies are valid
and potentially quite effective as long as the boundary properties
of the original group dynamic which served as a signal for the
leader's response are comprehended.

The object relations tendencies underlying particular projective identification (Ganzarain, 1977, Malin and Grotstein, 1966)
and proxy-evocation (Wangh, 1962) interactions within the group
can be effectively approached from a sub-system, system or suprasystem direction as well. Thus, a group that is fearful of losing
control over emotion and "going crazy" may become preoccupied with
a particular member who appears to react in what seems to be a strange and unacceptable manner. The leader may once again address
the entire group via a formulation of their unconscious dread of
losing control, address the individual member in a supportive or
paradoxical fashion or explore the feelings of a particular pair
who are attempting to escape from the situation via a neutral
discussion that essentially ignores the behavior of the apparently
disturbed member. The primary issue is that the leader be alert
to the projective identification and role suction processes underlying the group interaction.

In summary, I am re-defining group dynamics as boundary
processes having distinctive systems and object relations properties. My historical analysis has led to a modern functional definition of group dynamics as communicative signals requiring some
form of intervention or response from the therapist. The boundary
properties of both the original group dynamic process and the
leader's ultimate response need to be articulated from a systems
vantage point. The most effective and systems opening forms of
intervention require a solid comprehension and grasp on the part of
the therapist of the significant dynamic processes occurring within
the group.

REFERENCES

Bion, W.R., Group Dynamics: A review. International Journal of
    Psychoanalysis, 1952, 33, 235-247.
Bion, W.R., Experiences in Groups. New York: Basic Books, 1959.
Borriello, J., Leadership in the therapist-centred group-as-a-
    whole psychotherapy approach. International Journal of Group
    Psychotherapy, 1976, 26, 149-162.
Durkin, H., Catalysing self-regulatory processes in group therapy.
    Group Newsjournal of the Eastern Group Psychotherapy Society.
    Nov. 1973, 1-4.
Durkin, H., The evolution of a new group therapy model: The role
    of the therapist in systems theory. Group Newsjournal of the
    Eastern Group Psychotherapy Society. July 1974A, 1-15.
Ezriel, H., A psychoanalytical approach to group treatment. Brit-
    ish Journal of Medical Psychology, 1950, 23, 59-74.
Foulkes, S.H., Group-analytic dynamics with specific reference to
    psychoanalytic concepts, International Journal of Group
    Psychotherapy, 1957, 7, 40-52.
Ganzarain, R., General systems theory, object relations and their
    usefulness in group pscyhotherapy. International Journal
    of Group Psychotherapy, 1977, 27, 441-456.
Goldberg, C., Therapeutic Partnership, Ethical Concerns in Psycho-
    therapy, New York: Springer, 1977.
Kernberg, O.A., A systems approach to priority setting of inter-
    ventions in groups. International Journal of Group-Psychothe-
    rapy, 1975, 25, 251-275.
Kissen, M., General Systems Theory: Practical and theoretical
    implications for group intervention. Group, 1980, 4, 29-39.
Malin, , and Grotstein, ., Projective Identification in the
    therapeutic process. International Journal of Psychoanalysis,
    1966, 47, 26-31.
Ormont, L., Establishing the analytic contract in a newly formed
    therapeutic group. British Journal of Medical Psychology,
    1964, 85, 333-337.
Wangh, M., The "evocation of a proxy." in R.S. Eissler et al. (Eds)
    Psychoanalytic Study of the Child. New York: International
    Universities Press, 17, 1962, 451-469.
Wolf, A., and Schwartz, E.K., The psychoanalysis of groups: Impli-
    cations for education. International Journal of Social Psy-
    chology, 1855, 1, 17-24.
Wolf, A., and Schwartz, E.K., Psychoanalysis in Groups. New York:
    Grune and Stratton, 1962.

PERSONAL BOUNDARY MANAGEMENT AND SOCIAL STRUCTURE

Les R. Greene

Department of Psychiatry
University of California at Davis

In one of his last published works, the late A.K. Rice
advanced two propositions regarding the nature of the individual's
dynamic relationship to a social collectivity (1969). One of these
tenets held that group membership inherently involves the potentia-
tion of primitive, latent anxieties around the preservation of ego
identity, that is the sense of self as a familiar, integrated and
demarcated entity. As a corollary, Rice posited that the capacity
for joining in the rational, task-oriented activities of a group was
directly limited by the extent to which the individual needed to
defend against these archaic threats to the integrity of self
boundaries. Rice's insights into these group-induced processes of
regression and primitivization which affect the participant's self
concept have served as an important aspect of the theoretical
elucidation of the interface between the personality system and
social system. The present paper, incorporating recent contributions from such diverse areas as developmental psychology and object
relations theory, aims at expanding upon and further articulating
the self boundary issues attending participation in group life.

PERSONAL BOUNDARIES

It seems appropriate to start this work with some comments
about a boundary construct as it has been developed in personality
theory, although the reader is referred elsewhere for more thorough
reviews of this concept (Fisher & Cleveland, 1968; Landis, 1970).
Beginning with Federn's extensive introduction (1928) of the concept
of ego boundaries, theorists within ego psychological (Blatt & Wild,
1976; Jacobson, 1964) and object relations (Kernberg, 1976) frameworks have considered the essence of the earliest stages of ego

279

formation to be the acquisition of the capacity for making ever more
subtle cognitive distinctions. From an objectless, undifferentiated
state of autism in which the infant is unable to distinguish between
internal needs and external reality, an initial set of psychic
differentiations is gradually developed. These rudimentary demarca-
tions derive from the infant's repeated experiencing of a sequence
of bodily frustration and tension and the gratification of these
somatic needs via the ministrations of an external agent. Memory
traces of these alternating sensations and perceptions become the
basis of the earliest intrapsychic distinctions, consisting of
globally experienced affective states of "good" and "bad", a vaguely
felt temporal sense of "before" and "after", a shadowy spatial sense
of inside and out, and, most critically, a burgeoning awareness of
self and nonself. These fundamental boundary formations pave the
way for more complex, reality-based differentiations. Very gradually,
primitive images of aspects of self which are partly fused with and
in crude, diffuse emotional relation to partial images of the mother
evolve into clearly differentiated and relatively stable representations of a unified and integrated self and complex, realistic and
whole objects, i.e. self and object constancy.

The ontogeny of psychic structuralization, in general, and
object relations, in particular, are viewed as internal processes
which are intertwined with and reciprocally related to a progression,
termed separation-individuation (Mahler, 1968), involving the
infant's increasing psychological independence from his mother.
Even under optimal environmental and constitutional conditions, these
mutual developmental sequences are inherently fraught with marked
ambivalence and anxiety. Each step toward intrapsychic differentiation and interpersonal separation, before the attainment of self and
object constancy, is welcomed for the sense of autonomy, freedom and
mastery which it affords, but is simultaneously feared for the
accompanying threats over abandonment, isolation and loss of object
love. Fixation at or regression to developmentally early phases of
partially merged, symbiotic relatedness can preserve or re-activate
feelings of total security and omnipotence, but can evoke terrors
over the annihilation of the sense of a separate self through engulfment by the symbiotic partner.

Increasingly, the developmental literature depicts the infant
as having the innate capacity to cope with and defend against these
conflicting, contradictory wishes and fears by means of a variety of
preverbal, distance-regulating behaviors such as eye contact and
bodily orientation (Beebe & Stern, 1977; Freedman, 1977). Rather
than being in passive communication, the infant is regarded as
actively engaging in a series of repeated separations from and re-
unions with his mother in order to modulate his anxieties. These to
and fro, regulatory behaviors, which are finely attuned to the
mother's own engagement-disengagement behaviors, are considered
universally needed coping mechanisms which significantly facilitate

the diminishing of psychological dependence and the building up of
stable and differentiated self and object representations. An
important implication for group psychology is that the distance-
regulating features of the actual relationship between the infant
and his mother are thought to be internalized and contained in the
earliest self-other introjects. As Beebe and Stern speculate,
"...what is internalized includes mutually regulated sequences of
maternal-infant actions with a particular temporal patterning. It
is important to note that since the infant is in a dyadic system in
which the behaviors or action-schemes are potentially so intimately
meshed with the mother's, one aspect of what becomes internalized
in the first object-relation is a 'time-frame of connectedness' or of
mutual responsivity" (1977, p. 52). Stated somewhat differently,
the structural properties of the actual mother-infant dyad, particularly the degree to which the dyadic interactions respect of
obfuscate the integrity of the separate personality systems, are
mirrored in the infant's earliest self-other internalizations
(Fisher & Cleveland, 1968).

An additional and related notion pertaining to these primitive
representations of self and mother is that of individual differences.
Both constitutional factors, including the infant's sensitivity to
and tolerance of frustration, and environmental conditions such as
the mother's own conflicts over handling of separation and loss
(cf. Masterson & Rinsley, 1975) affect the intensity of the several
anxieties encountered during the subphases of separation-
individuation. Moreover, observational evidence suggests a wide
spectrum of individual styles in coping with these anxieties (Pine,
1971; Sroufe & Waters, 1977). Some infants and toddlers cope primarily through consistent behavioral attempts to foster and prolong
symbiotic closeness, while others seem to require exaggerated self-
other distance and differentiation. Still others seem to alternate,
perhaps in response to qualitatively different threats, between
excessive clinging and rigid boundary-reinforcing behavoir. It
seems to follow that the earliest introjects vary across infants as
a function of the salience of anxieties and preferred coping styles
occurring during the repeated separations from and rediscoveries of
the mother. That is, the set of primitive introjects of self in
relation to mother should differ from individual to individual in
terms of the balance and predominance of needs and regulatory
behaviors reflecting fusion and differentiation. As will be elaborated later, this postulate also has important implications for the
individual's relationship to a group.

In normal development, the role of these archaic introjects is
diminished through their integration into more mature identifications, these, in turn, consolidating to form relatively realistic,
stable and enduring representations of self and the object world.
Failures to negotiate and resolve the stresses of the early phases of
separation-individuation, however, preclude the attainment of these

permanent and differentiated concepts of self and others. Under
these conditions, the primitive object relations remain more salient
and have a greater impact on subsequent psychological functioning.
Without the capacity to experience self and others as viable, independent and interactive entities, earlier modes of object ties,
involving infantile needs for merging and exaggerated differentiation,
persist. The reliance upon these early self-other introjects serves
compensatory and restitutive ends, providing some measure of self-
preservation, either through fantasies of fusion with a protective,
all-good mother or through images of an impenetrable, invulnerable
self. As Silverman has discussed (1979), these primitive, reality-
distorting self concepts can serve a wide range of defensive needs.
In the case of merging fantasies, such needs include the magical
sense of continuous oral supplies, feelings of complete protection
from threats over object loss and the denial of aggressive wishes
toward the symbiotic partner. In similar fashion, a hypercathexis
of boundaries encircling some aspects of self can serve a variety of
defensive needs.

In the context of failing to achieve self and object constancy,
these early object ties and archaic needs have been directly implicated in several forms of psychopathological conditions. For
example, the blurring of independent perceptions and ideas in
schizophrenia (Blatt & Wild, 1976) or the polarized, exaggerated
distinctions manifested in paranoid and borderline states (Kernberg,
1976) are viewed as conceptual concomitants of the activation of and
reliance upon these primitive internalizations.   To a lesser degree,
disturbances in the development of well delineated self and object
representations and the consequent reliance upon primitive self-
object introjects have also been discussed in connection with
neurotic disorders (Fierman, 1965) and characterological problems
such as the overdifferentiated and underindividuated personalities
(Lewis, 1958).

A number of theoretical issues regarding the role of these
archaic representations in psychopathology have yet to be resolved.
It is not clear, for example, whether the pathological blurring or
rigid reinforcement of boundaries reflect developmental fixations
at or dynamically motivated regressions to early subphases of
separation-individuation (cf. Blatt & Wild, 1976; Witkin, Dyk,
Faterson, Goodenough & Karp, 1962; Silverman, 1975). It may be that
the activation of primitive object relations occurs via both
mechanisms with different resulting symptomotology. A second,
related question concerns the interrelationship between needs for
fusion and needs for differentiation. Normal development implies a
gradual diminution and renunciation of symbiotic needs in favor of
increasing autonomy and individuation, that is one continuum
anchored by the polar opposites of fusion and differentiation. In
the service of defensive, restitutive aims, however, there is likely
a more complex intertwining of merging and separation needs than can

be accounted for by a unidimensional continuum. Paranoid schizophrenia, for example, can be conceptualized as a state in which there
is simultaneous activation of primitive object ties reflecting both
needs for fusion and needs for rigid self-other boundary fortification
(Blatt & Wild, 1976). There is growing research evidence, moreover,
which further suggests that fusion and differentiation are not aspects
of one developmental continuum. Several measures have been con-
structed, such as the body image boundary scales (Fisher & Cleveland,
1968), the ego boundary scales (Landis, 1970), and the Boundary-
Fusion Test (cf. Greene & Geller, 1980), all of which purportedly
assess two dimensions: proclivities for the blurring of self-other
boundaries and preferences for the reinforcement of self-other
distinctions. Empirical evidence to date indicates that these
dimensions are not consistently correlated with each other, supporting
the view that needs for fusion and for differentiation reflect two
separate lines of development. While it is beyond the scope of this
paper to do other than name some of these unresolved theoretical
questions, the point remains that there is basic consensus regarding
the influence of archaic introjects which reflect both needs for merging and for self-other distance in several forms of psychopathology.

THE ROLE OF PERSONAL BOUNDARY MANAGEMENT IN GROUPS

These conceptualizations regarding the ontogeny of psychic
representations of self and others can now be applied to elucidate
further those regressive phenomena occurring whenever a person joins
a group. The task involved in the transition from singleton status
(Turquet, 1975) to group membership involves the development of
object ties with all the other group participants. Intrapsychically,
mature object relations involve the attaching of drive cathexis to
newly formed object images which closely correspond to the external
objects in the current social setting (Saravey, 1975). This process,
in turn, requires the continuous and extensive reality-testing of
the fit between pre-existing representations and the actual
personalities of the present group members in order to form
relatively accurate new object images (Main, 1975; Saravey, 1975).
That is, to relate realistically to others in the present is to
discover, painstakingly, how they match and differ from specific
object representations built up over previous relationships. In
reciprocal fashion, each group member also needs to participate in
the reality-testing endeavors of all the other group members. The
multiplicity, specificity and complexity of object relations to be
established and the pressing need to form immediate ties create the
conditions for the regressive processes typically observed in group
life. These processes consist primarily of a shift in cathexis from
developmentally mature representations of self and others to earlier,
less differentiated and less integrated introjects and identifications, mostly involving the self in relation to the preoedipal
mother. In essence, there is a re-activation of simplified psychic

representations of aspects of self and others which are linked by
crude and diffuse affective states of "good" and "bad", representations originally formed during the subphases of separation-
individuation. Individually and collectively, group members can
then externalize some of these primitive object images onto different
group targets, such as the group leader, and thereby create a
simplified emotionally dichotomous world of good and bad part objects
with which it is comparatively easy to relate.

The cost of relying upon these expedient, albeit fantastic,
object ties is a resurgence of anxieties over separation-individuation. Several authors have proposed that the group-as-a-whole
becomes preconsciously equated with the preoedipal, symbiotic
mother; that is, the group entity becomes projectively endowed with
primitive representations of the symbiotic mother (Bion, 1959;
Durkin, 1964; Gibbard & Hartman, 1973; Scheidlinger, 1974; Slater,
1966). As a consequence, the relationship to the group entity is
considered to recapitulate the anxious, conflictful experiences
attending the developmental sequence of separation-individuation.
Analogous to the ambivalence and ambitendencies of the infant, the
group member must cope with contradictory wishes and fears of the
so-called fusion-individuation dilemma. Partial merging with the
collectivity, via diffusion of personal identity and temporary
disolution of ego boundaries, is yearned for, but also dreaded
because of threats over the total loss of a sense of separate self.
The preservation of personal identity is also ambivalently held.
Separateness implies autonomy and the freedom to pursue one's own
goals, but is accompanied by threats over isolation and abandonment.
The ultimate survival task for the group participant is to master
these ambivalences and anxieties and to re-establish viable self
boundaries which will permit both a sense of personal uniqueness and
unity with the group. In fact, it has been postulated that the core
motivation for joining any collectivity may be precisely to re-
experience and repeat the developmental sequence leading from
relatively fused and amorphous self-object ties to the establishment
of a clearly delineated and stable set of self and object representations.

While all social contexts have the potential to evoke threats
over self-preservation, there is considerable variation across
settings and within settings over time in the nature and salience
of these primitive anxieties. One major determinant in the modula-
tion of these archaic threats is the social structuring of a
collectivity. At one level, group structure refers to those
rational and manifest divisions of labor and authority which demar-
cate a group from its embedding context and which lead to the
formation of differentiated work roles. However, it is primarily
at a less conscious or "fantasy" level where social structural
properties serve to regulate concerns over the loss of self through
engulfment or isolation. Introduced by Bion (1959) and elaborated

upon by others (Jacques, 1974; Miller, Rourke, Davis, Howenstine, Morrison & Reed, 1978), this latent social structure designates those irrationally-determined arrangements and patternings within the group which are designed to satisfy participants' needs not met in the service of rational work activity. This covert structuring dynamically derives from the group-wide activation of primitive object relations which are collectively "pooled" and externalized onto the more rational elements of social structure. As stated earlier, because these externalized contents are relatively crude relations of self to part objects which are invested either with libidinal or aggressive drive derivatives, a simplified world of good and bad, ideal and devalued dichotomies is superimposed upon the manifest social structure. This fantasy structure serves a variety of emotional and defensive needs. Role relations are rendered considerably less complex; members can readily identify with each other by projecting "badness" onto commonly agreed upon objects. Precisely because the archaic representations contain self-other boundary-regulating properties, their activation and deployment in the current group context defensively functions to regulate anxiety over loss of personal identity. As exemplified by Slater's (1966) analysis of the vicissitudes in the prevailing fantasy structure, members can regulate the permeability of self boundaries, on a group-wide basis, by projecting onto the group entity object ties which emphasize either fusion or separation images. In sum, the same regressive forces which induce primitive anxieties over loss of viable self boundaries also create the conditions for primitive defensive and compensatory operations based on the socially shared activation and enactment of early self-other introjects.

The specific fantasied structure operating in a group context at any moment is multiply determined by several factors. The personalities of the members, their wishes, needs, previous intro- jects and identifications, will significantly influence what will be attributed onto the group (Ezriel, 1950). Also, the manifest social structure, that is the rationally determined divisions of labor and authority, seems to affect the nature of the fantasied social relations (cf. Miller, 1977). Group settings overtly structured in different ways tend to evoke different primitive anxieties and fantasied structures. This phenomenon has been explained on the basis of the notion of the structural similarities between the current group setting and early mother-infant interactions; the more the overt structuring of a social setting corresponds to patternings of the primordial mother-infant dyad which originally evoked situation-specific concerns and images, the more likely those par- ticular fantasies will be transferred onto the group (Newton, 1973). Applying this analogy, the more the real structure of a group resembles the caretaking pattern of an over-protective, symbiosis- fostering mother (cf. Masterson & Rinsley, 1975), the more likely should concerns over fusion predominate among group participants.

Concretely, a group structured so as to minimize exchanges with the
environment and to obscure differences in roles among participants
would seem to correspond to the patterning of a symbiotic mother-
infant matrix and should tend to "pull" for images over fusion and
engulfment. Other real social structures should facilitate the
superimposition of fantasied relations emphasizing separateness and
distance. It could be conjectured that the more the manifest
structures correspond to mothering patterns which fail to mediate
and organize external reality - patterns considered to give rise to
the pseudoindependent, overdifferentiated personality (Horner, 1975;
Lewis, 1958) - the more that these concerns over separation, fragmentation and isolation should prevail. A group characterized by
frail external boundaries which insufficiently regulate exchanges
with the environment and divided internally in an overly rigid and
poorly integrated fashion would seem likely to facilitate the
activation of isolation imagery.

As Jacques has formulated (1974), vicissitudes in the underlying
fantasy structure of a group can occur as a function of the ascendence
of different needs and wishes among the social participants as well
as through changes in the overt social structure. From the perspective of the individual member, what must be underscored is that
the prevailing socially-constructed fantasied relations are compromise
formations or "common denominators" (Ezriel, 1950) shaped to a large
degree by the confluence of the predominant tensions and needs within
the entire membership and the rational structuring of the social
setting. As a consequence, the operating fantasies may only partially
meet an individual's particular defensive needs. Take, for example,
a setting in which the salient social fantasy fosters a sense of
oneness (Silverman, 1979; Turquet, 1975) or utopia (Gibbard & Hartman,
1973) among the members as an operation designed to avoid aggressive
impulses within the group. This defensive structuring may serve well
the needs of those whose early internalizations reflect proclivities
to blur self-other boundaries. This same group defensive solution,
however, might exacerbate anxiety among those members whose early
introjects reflect preferences for sharp self-nonself distinctions.
Based upon the assumptions that primitive self-object ties containing
preverbal, boundary-regulating properties are internalized and retained as a fundamental layer of psychic structure and that these
early introjects are activated and projected onto the current social
field, including the group entity, it seems reasonable to posit that
individual efforts would be directed at creating a social structure
which replicates the personally preferred structural ties of the
primordial self-mother dyad. Each participant can be viewed as
projectively attempting to superimpose upon the manifest social
structure a unique set of fantasied relations which, among other
defensive purposes, will serve to attain the preferred degrees of
experienced fusion and differentiation

It may be useful in this theoretical context to adopt and

extend Bion's (1959) construct of valency, a notion referring to personal proclivities for joining with others in promoting specific emotional and cultural climates. In addition to his postulated valencies for emotional states of fight-flight, dependency and pairing, themselves considered group means for varying degree of self-other differentiation (Slater, 1966), participants may be differentially predisposed for groups fostering even more extreme degrees of merging and separation. That is, settings may be differentially attractive to members as a function of the degree to which the prevailing socially-shared fantasies blur or reinforce the boundaries demarcating a sense of self. Returning to Rice's propositions pertaining to threats to personal identity which intro-duced this paper, the construct of valency may have important implications. It seems meaningful to propose that the greater the congruence or fit between the group defensive solution for coping with threats to personal identity and the individual's preferences for regulating degree of self-other differentiation, the lower will be the experienced anxiety and, consequently, the greater should be the commitment to work on group tasks. Conversely, the less the correspondence between the fantasied self-other relations shared by the group membership and the individual's unique schemata, the more should the individual be diverted into using personal defensive strategies in coping with threats to self-boundaries. As Edelson points out (1970), what constitutes conditions of safety for some participants may collide with the defensive needs of other members, resulting, in the extreme, in their taking flight from the group.

EMPIRICAL INVESTIGATIONS

We've recently initiated a series of quantitative, empirical studies to investigate the effects of these postulated preferences or valencies for fusion and individuation experiences in groups of varying social structure. If the research literature bearing upon psychoanalytic constructs is sparse (cf. Luborsky & Spence, 1978; Silverman, 1975), it is practically nonexistent with respect to notions pertaining to a depth theory of groups. The brief description of methodology and results which follows is intended chiefly to serve as a catalyst for futher systematic research in this area. Similar to Silverman's (1975) contentions about the importance of experimental work in the validation of psychoanalytic constructs and formulations, we feel that quantitative research on depth group conceptualizations is a necessary supplement to the insights and hypotheses generated in the course of clinical work in groups.

This initial set of studies (Greene, 1976, 1979, 1980; Greene, Morrison, & Tischler, 1979, 1980a, 1980b; Greene & Rosenkrantz, 1980; Rosenkrantz & Greene, 1980) have all been implemented in the context of Tavistock group relations conferences, educational events which

offer opportunities for experientially based learning about group
phenomena (Rice, 1965; Rioch, 1970). Because of the relative
control and constancy of variables across these conferences, they
seem to lend themselves well to experimental investigation. In
addition to the same definition of task and general equivalence of
membership characteristics across conferences, the role behavior of
the group leaders, or consultants, is tightly "scripted." Following
a psychoanalytic paradigm, consultants restrict their interventions
primarily to the clarification and interpretation of group-as-a-
whole phenomena occurring in the here-and-now. While departures
from leadership role requirements can never be completely eliminated,
the Tavistock model does seem to ensure considerable comparability
in leader behavior across conferences. Thus, on several major
parameters, these conferences can approximate the precision of
laboratory conditions in which a few selected variables are isolated
and manipulated for systematic study. A second crucial feature of
Tavistock conferences, in contrast to other social psychological
experimental contexts, is the level of affect and depth of process
evoked therein. The stripping away of the institutional supports
and anchors, such as dependency gratification by the leader and
explicit rules and roles, readily evokes intense group-induced
anxieties and social defenses which might otherwise be masked or
mitigated. In essence, their approximation to laboratory controls
and their power to evoke "real world" affects combine to make these
conferences particularly well suited for systematic research on
depth group constructs.

Our initial studies can also be characterized by their use of
nonverbal behavior as a primary dependent variable. Based upon the
increasing appreciation of the instrumental role of nonverbal
behaviors in regulating fusion and differentiation in primordial
self-other relations and the theoretical notions regarding the
activation of these primitive object ties in group life, it follows
that the investigation of such behavioral variables as eye contact
and body orientation could serve as projective-like measures of the
individual's fantasied relations to the group.

Our preliminary findings have been quite encouraging. The
data have tended to support the formulations about the confluence
of social structural parameters and personal preferences or
valencies for controling self-other differentiation upon the
individual's participation in the group. In general, the results
support the view that members with differing needs and preferences
in regulating self-other boundaries are attracted to different kinds
of groups; moreover, this differential affinity seems to depend upon
whether the setting will facilitate or interfere with the establishment of fantasied relations which serve the participant's
particular needs for fusion and separation.

Two of the studies can best illustrate these data. In one

project (Greene, 1980) we examined the behavioral reactions of
conference members across two small group contexts differing in
formal structural properties, namely self-study groups and groups
involved in intergroup activity (cf. Astrachan & Flynn, 1976). The
external boundary encircling each of the self-study groups is
comparatively more impermeable than the boundary demarcating each
group in intergroup activity; at the same time, the self-study
groups are less internally differentiated than the small groups in
intergroup relations. These considerations of differences in
manifest structure led to hypotheses that images and concerns over
fusion and engulfment would prevail in the former settings while
threats and images around separation would predominate in the
intergroup contexts. By preassessing the members on the Boundary-
Fusion Test, a questionnaire said to tap idiosyncratic preferences
in managing self-other boundaries, we further hypothesized that the
self-study groups would be more attractive to those participants
with high fusion needs or minimal needs for self definition, whereas
the intergroup context should be favored by participants with minimal
needs for fusion and strong valencies for self boundary fortification.
From videotapes of these group settings, we extracted 22 nonverbal
behaviors which have been regarded in the research literature as
motoric means for controlling self-other distance and differentiation. Statistical analyses revealed that these engagement-
disengagement behaviors varied across group settings and across
members in the hypothesized directions. The data showed, first,
that there was more self-other distancing and reinforcing of self
boundaries in the self-study groups, consistent with the view that
these were compensatory maneuvers necessitated by the threats of
fusion in these settings. Moreover, interactive patterns were
obtained revealing that members who prefer to blur self boundaries
seemed comparatively more involved vis-a-vis the self study groups,
while those who cope via a hypercathexis of boundaries seemed to be
more engaged in the intergroup settings.

In a followup study (Rosenkrantz & Greene, 1980), we examined
the same set of distance-regulating behaviors across study groups
which were led either by male or female consultants. Our understanding and interpretation of recent theoretical and empirical
contributions on the effects of gender in groups (cf. Greene,
Morrison, & Tischler, 1980b) led to the assumption that female
leaders were more likely to serve as repositories for projected
aspects of symbiosis-fostering maternal images, whereas male
leaders might more likely be projectively endowed with more
developmentally advanced object representations reflecting greater
differentiation of self from other. On this assumption that the
real differences in contexts would support different social
fantasies, it was hypothesized that the two groups would be
differentially attractive to members as a function of their preferences for regulating self boundaries. Consistent with this
expectation, the data revealed that members who tend to blur

self-other boundaries were comparatively more involved in female-led groups while those who sharpen cognitive distinctions found the male-led groups more involving.

These data seem to support our formulation regarding the congruence between an individual's preferred level of self-other differentiation, postulated to derive as a residue from early inter-actions between the infant and mother, and social structures which can sustain specific kinds of social fantasies. The results suggest that engagement behaviors increase and disengagement and distancing behaviors decrease when there is a fit between the personal and social means of defending against threats to self boundaries. While going beyond the data, it does not seem unwarranted to conjecture that capacity for rational work on group tasks also increases with the degree to which social fantasied relations are consistent with the idiosyncratic needs for fusion and differentiation of each group participant.

In more general terms, the findings to date seem to underscore the importance of a group theory which incorporates both individual and social perspectives. The obtained interactive patterns of distance-regulating behaviors could not be accounted for from an exclusive group dynamics or personality framework. Unfortunately, Scheidlinger's (1960) lament of several years ago about the tendency toward reductionistic thinking in group psychology still holds somewhat true today. However, recent advances in object relations theory, particularly its integration into psychoanalytic structural theory (Kernberg, 1976) which thus provides a compre-hensive framework for conceptualizations about the activation of both primitive and mature self and object representations, should serve as a model and impetus for more complex theory building of the individual-in-the-group. From the point of view of the individual participant, immersion in a group can be regarded as involving the activation of a developmental hierarchy of internalizations, from the primitive and earliest introjects to advanced partial identifications, as well as a developmental range of anxieties and defensive operations. Anxieties in groups can range from archaic threats over loss of self boundaries, to intermediate concerns over the management of ambivalence toward authority, to Oedipal-level concerns over mastery and competence. Ultimately a depth theory of the individual-in-the-group must be sufficiently broad so as to encompass those personal and social factors which give ascendency to a particular level of anxiety and defensive maneuver. Many aspects of the interface between the individual and the group are still largely unknown. What, for example, are the social and psychological determinants of an individuals member's choice of defensive solution? What socio-psychological factors lead to the individual's joining in relatively primitive social defenses versus his "cooperation" in mature, socially shared coping patterns versus his reliance upon strictly personal strategies? Our systematic and ongoing efforts at examining the interface between the individual and the group in terms of fusion-individuation concerns reflect but one of many similar confluences of personal and social factors upon group participation. Clearly, the continuing, judicious application of advances in objects relations theory and in psychological constructs of the self as well as a greater number of experimental investigations would seem to be two vital factors in the future development of a comprehensive theory of the individual's relationship to a group.

REFERENCES

Astrachan, B. M., and Flynn, H., 1976, The intergroup exercise: A paradigm for learning about the development of organizational structure, in: "Task and Organization," E. J. Miller, ed., Wiley, New York.
Beebe, P., and Stern, D. N., 1977, Engagement-disengagement and early object experiences, in: "Communicative Structures and Psychic Structures," N. Freedman and S. Grand, eds., Plenum, New York.
Bion, W. R., 1959, "Experiences in Groups," Basic, New York.
Blatt, S. J., and Wild, C. M., 1976, "Schizophrenia: A Developmental Approach," Academic, New York.
Durkin, H., 1964, "The Group in Depth," International Universities, New York.
Edelson, M., 1970, "Sociotherapy and Psychotherapy," University of Chicago, Chicago.
Ezriel, H., 1950, A psychoanalytic approach to group treatment, British Journal of Medical Psychology, 23:59-74.
Federn, P., 1952, "Ego Psychology and the Psychosis," Basic, New York.
Fierman, L. B. (ed.), 1965, "Effective Psychotherapy: The Contribution of Hellmuth Kaiser," Free Press, New York.
Fisher, S., and Cleveland, S. E., 1968, "Body Image and Personality," (2nd. Rev. ed.), Dover, New York.
Freedman, N., 1977, Hands, words, and mind: On the structuralization of body movements during discourse and the capacity for verbal representation, in: "Communicative Structures and Psychic Structures," N. Freedman and S. Grand, eds., Plenum, New York.
Gibbard, G. S., and Hartman, J. J., 1973, The significance of utopian fantasies in small groups, International Journal of Group Psychotherapy, 23:125-147.
Greene, L. R., 1976, Body image boundaries and small group seating arrangements, Journal of Consulting and Clinical Psychology, 44:244-249.
Greene, L. R., 1979, Psychological differentiation and social structure, Journal of Social Psychology, 109:79-85.
Greene, L. R., 1980, On fusion and individuation processes in small

groups: An empirical investigation of the effects of personal
and group boundaries, manuscript submitted for publication.

Greene, L. R., and Geller, J. D., 1980, Effects of therapists'
clinical experience and personal boundaries on the termination
of psychotherapy, Journal of Psychiatric Education, 4:31-35.

Greene, L. R., Morrison, T. L., and Tischler, N. G., 1979,
Participant's perceptions in small and large group contexts,
Human Relations, 32:357-365.

Greene, L. R., Morrison, T. L., and Tischler, N. G., 1980, Aspects
of identification in the large group, Journal of Social
Psychology, 111:91-97. (a)

Greene, L. R., Morrison, T. L., and Tischler, N. G., 1980, Effects
of gender and authority on perceptions of small group co-
leaders, manuscript submitted for publication. (b).

Greene, L. R., and Rosenkrantz, J., 1980, Personal boundary
regulation in the large group, manuscript in preparation.

Horner, A. J., 1975, Stages and processes in the development of
early object relations and their associated pathologies,
International Review of Psychoanalysis, 2:95-105.

Jacobson, E., 1964, "The Self and the Object World," International
Universities, New York.

Jacques, E., 1974, Social systems as a defense against persecutory
and depressive anxiety, in: "Analysis of Groups," G. S.
Gibbard, J. J. Hartman, and R. D. Mann, eds., Jossey-Bass,
San Francisco.

Kernberg, O., 1976, "Object Relations Theory and Clinical Psychoanalysis," Aronson, New York.

Landis, B., 1970, Ego boundaries, Psychological Issues, 6.

Lewis, H. B., 1958, Over-differentiation and under-individuation of
the self, Psychoanalysis and the Psychoanalytic Review, 45:
3-24.

Luborsky, L., and Spence, D. P., 1978, Quantitative research on
psychoanalytic therapy, in: "Handbook of Psychotherapy and
Behavior Change," (2nd ed.), S. L. Garfield and A. E. Bergin,
eds., Wiley, New York.

Main, T., 1975, Some psychodynamics of large groups, in: "The Large
Group: Dynamics and Therapy," L. Kreeger, ed., Constable,
London.

Mahler, M. S., 1968, "On Human Symbiosis and the Vicissitudes of
Individuation," International Universities, New York.

Masterson, J. F., and Rinsley, D. B., 1975, The borderline syndrome:
The role of the mother in the genesis and psychic structure of
the borderline personality, International Journal of Psychoanalysis, 56:163-117.

Miller, J. C., 1977, The psychology of conflict in Belfast:
Conference as microcosm, Journal of Personality and Social
Systems, 1:17-38.

Miller, J. C., Rourke, P. G., Davis, G. H., Howenstine, R. H.,
Morrison, T. L., and Reed, H. D., 1978, "Reparation and Change:
Psychological Aspects of Social Innovation," CEGO, Washington,

D.C.

Newton, P. M., 1973, Social structure and process in psychotherapy: A sociopsychological analysis of transference, resistance and change, International Journal of Psychiatry, 11:480-509.

Pine, F., 1971, On the separation process: Universal trends and individual differences, in: "Separation-individuation," J. B. McDevitt, and C. F. Settlage, eds., International Universities, New York.

Rice, A. K., 1965, "Learning for Leadership," Travistock, London.

Rice, A. K., 1969, Individual, group and intergroup processes, Human Relations, 22:565-584.

Rioch, M. J., 1970, Group relations: rationale and techniques. International Journal of Group Psychotherapy, 20:340-355.

Rosenkrantz, J., and Greene, L. R., 1980, Effects of psychological differentiation and leader gender on participation in small groups, manuscript in preparation.

Saravey, S. M., 1975, Group psychology and the structural theory: A revised psychoanalytic model of group psychology, Journal of the American Psychoanalytic Association, 23:69-89.

Scheidlinger, S., 1960, Group process in group psychotherapy: Current trends in the integration of individual and group psychology, American Journal of Psychotherapy, 14:346-363.

Scheidlinger, S., 1974, On the concept of the "mother-group", International Journal of Group Psychotherapy, 24:417-428.

Silverman, L. H., 1975, On the role of laboratory experiments in the development of the clinical theory of psychoanalysis: Data on the subliminal activation of aggressive and merging wishes in schizophrenics, International Review of Psychoanalysis, 2:43-64.

Silverman, L. H., 1979, Two unconscious fantasies as mediators of successful psychotherapy, Psychotherapy: Theory, Research and Practice, 16:215-230.

Slater, P. E., 1966, "Microcosm: Structural Psychological and Religious Evolution in Groups," Wiley, New York.

Sroufe, L. A., and Waters, E., 1977, Attachment as an organizational construct, Child Development, 48:1184-1199.

Turquet, P., 1974, Leadership: The individual and the group, in: "Analysis of Groups," G. S. Gibbard, J. J. Hartman, and R. D. Mann, eds., Jossey-Bass, San Francisco.

Turquet, P., 1975, Threats to identity in the large group, in: "The Large Group: Dynamics and Therapy," L. Kreeger, ed., Constable, London.

Witkin, H. A., Dyk, R. B., Faterson, H. F., Goodenough, D. R., and Karp, S. A., 1962, "Psychological Differentiation," Wiley, New York.

DO BOUNDARIES EXIST?

A TRANSPERSONAL APPROACH TO PSYCHOTHERAPY

Pierre Weil, PhD

Professor of Transpersonal Psychology, Dept. of Psychology

Federal University, Belo Horizonte, Brasil

In our daily life and following our common sense, our being is
constantly in contact with boundaries: physical ones, like the skin
which separates our body from the outer world, or the walls of my room;
emotional frontiers which many times makes us unable to reach or feel
each other in our object relations or even ourselves; mental barriers
which impeach knowledge or to apprehend the whole reality, cutting it
all the time into little pieces or fragments through perception and
language; Boundaries between conscious self and unconscious; barriers
of human regression and evolution.

Two major contemporary scientific events are questioning the
actual existence of such boundaries. One is the discovery of the
hologram in modern physics, the other is the description by transpersonal psychology of a state of consciousness in which all barriers
are dissolved: the state of Cosmic Consciousness.

Questioning formal logic

Since the researches of Max Planck and De Broglie showing that
a particle is at the same time matter and energy, the basic principle
of non-contradiction of classical formal cartesian logic, has been
seriously shaken. Today it is necessary to create a new logic
which includes on the same time contradiction and non-contradiction.
This is what Stephen Lupasco (1) has done, showing that there are
common laws between what he names the three matters: Physical,
Biological and Psychic; these laws are the laws of energy, of trans-
finite movement of potentialisation of heterogeneity, and actualisation of homogeneity and actualisation of heterogeneity and
potentialisation of homogeneity.

The Whole and the Parts

These last ten years, a new contradiction has been discovered in modern physics; it is the propriety of holographic shapes (2, 3, 4). A hologram is a photographic shape through which you can project in space any object in three dimensions; if we cut this shape in two, four or six parts, each part projects the whole figure in three dimensions. The physicist David Bohm (5) has built a new theory of the universe based on this fact: the holonomic theory; following this theory, the whole programming of the universe exists in each of its parts. The neuro-physiologist Karl Pribram (6) produced a holographic theory of the brain; the brain, like the Universe, is a hologram; it is the unique explanation of the fact that one part of the brain takes over the function of another injured part, without any apprenticeship.

This principle, following which the whole is in the parts, and the parts are in the whole, is also in flagrant contradiction with formal logic. And if this is an actual fact, there are no more boundaries in the universe, and consequently nor in Man.

This is also what the French physicist Charon (7) explains in his "Theory of complex relativity"; following his researches, what we name the "spirit" is contained in all the sub-atomic particles in another space-time dimension; all these billions of particles of ourselves are instantly connected with all particles of the universe and contains past and future programmings, eliminating the boundaries of time and space.

Relationship between States of Consciousness and Reality

So where are these boundaries? The answer of transpersonal psychology, is that these boundaries exist only in our mind, which is, as Piaget (3) showed a product of interiorisation of the outer world through our five senses; transpersonal psychology, specially inspired by eastern psychological experiences of other states of consciousness, indicates that boundaries exist only in our waking state of consciousness; there are other states of consciousness in which are experienced other kinds of realities.

We summarised this principle in one formula:

$$\boxed{ER = f\ (SC)}$$

Experience of Reality ER is function f of the State of Consciousness SC we are in. (9)

As Charles Tart (10, 11) showed this principle constitutes a

revolution of paradigms of our contemporary science which is a
science limited by the waking state of consciousness; it must be
possible to build other sciences based on other states of consciousness. The underlying paradigms of our modern science is that we can
only accept as "reality" what is controlled by our five senses and by
our reasoning.   As we showed briefly above, modern physics is
questioning seriously not only our reasoning based on an obsolete
system of logic, but also our five senses.

For instance, complicated apparatus is necessary to detect or
measure the presence of normally unseen energies, like x-rays or
cosmic rays.

Cosmic Consciousness

In the beginning of this century, a Canadian psychiatrist, R.M.
Bucke (12), analysed testimonies of mystics, saints and also common
people of all cultures, times and religions of the world; through
content analysis, he found that there are some common points in the
descriptions of this special state of consciousness; he named this
phenomena; Cosmic Consciousness.

William James (13) also describes special state of consciousness in his well known book: Varieties of Religious Experiences.
Like C.G. Jung (40) he had his own cosmic experience.

Experimental Approach

With the creation of transpersonal psychology, under the influence of Ch. Buhler, Abraham Maslow, Allan Watts, Arthur Koestler,
Victor Frankl, Antony Sutich, Michael Murphy, James Fadiman,
Stanislaw Grof, many workers have made such content analysis and
experimental approaches of the cosmic consciousness phenomena.
(Specially Deikmann (14), Prince and Savage (15), and Pahnke (16).)
In our own research (17), we analysed 153 narratives gathered from
groups of dream, pre-death, meditation, drugs, psychosis and
fortuitous experience.   1803 phrases were classified and codified,
and from these, 107 different classes of answers were extracted.

Here are the first ones, in order of statistical classification:

Categories	%
Encounter with being in other dimension	67.44
Vision of an indescribable light	62.79
Out of body experience	53.48
Coming back to daily experience	44.18
Vision of immaterial objects	37.20
Communication with a being in another dimension	30.23
After effect of depression and sadness	30.23

<u>Categories (continued)</u>   %

Happiness and bliss during the experience	30.23
Sensation of flying	30.23
Time-space transcendence	30.23
Hearing unmaterial sounds	27.90
Comparison between the two kinds of reality (Waking and Cosmic)	27.90
Loss of fear of death	25.58
Sensation of weight after coming back to the physical body	25.58
Desire to remain in and not come back to daily reality	23.25
Feeling of deep peace state	23.25
Immediate knowledge through direct revelation of cosmic reality	23.25
Description of coming back to the body	20.93
Noetic feeling, that the experience is actual	18.60

Through factor analysis (41) of a special questionnaire, we found four underlying factors of cosmic experience:

- Transcendental phenomenas

- PSI phenomenas (Extrasensorial ESP and Psychokinetic PK)

- Affective phenomena

- Perceptive phenomena (Proprio and exteroceptives)

Specially the two first ones, and the majority of descriptions we listed above, are an indication of existence of some hidden function on functions in man, which can help him to transcend the barriers of his own mind and five senses. This is also what the School of Rhine of Duke University is demonstrating through their well known and highly developed researches into Parapsychology; (18) Psychotherapy can no longer ignore the results of these researches, specially because they are questioning the "pathological nature of many psychotic" symptoms and of psychopathological nosology (19).

Dissolution of Physical Boundaries in Psychic Healing in Brasil

In Brasil we have observed, in afro-Brasilian and Indian healing rituals, a very exciting process of psychological and somatic cure. Sensitive people, in trance state, can manifest in their own body, two or three minutes after entering into deep trance state, any psychological or physical manifestation of a patient.

For instance, he can manifest skin diseases, asthma with actual mucus secretion, electroshock manifestation in the case of a recent electroshocked schizophrenic patient, circulatory disturbance, and so on; he can also manifest verbally the main desires

and anxieties or hostility of the patient; he can even manifest
agression or resentments of a patient's family, friends or competitors.
The process is very similar to psychodrama's auxiliary ego in the
function of double or antagonist, with an essential difference: here
the auxiliary ego is completely unconscious (which state can be
easily proved by physiological checking) and does not know nothing
about the patient and his life. We have personally observed hundreds
of such manifestations; they show that there are no interpersonal
space boundaries. Those facts may have, after specific researches
and investigations, a profound repercussion not only on medicine and
psychotherapy but also on epistemology. Many questions have to be
answered, like for instance:

    - How is the programme of the disease of one body communicated
to the body of the sensitive?

    - What are the curative factors; how for instance, are negative
feelings of symptoms "metabolised" in the body of the sensitive?

    - What is the mechanism which makes epileptics, when trans-
formed in sensitives and healers, seem to be completely cured of
their "Disease"? The same question can be done for many named
"Schizophrenics". Mircea Eliades demonstrated the existence of
these facts in 70% of Shamans. (20)

Is Psychosis a "Disease"?

    Transpersonal psychology begins to give some hypothetical
frameworks which are questioning the nature and usefulness of the
medical term "disease", specially in case of psychosis. It seems
that psychotic crisis is in reality a trance state, an altered state
of consciousness in which other forms of reality (parapsychological
and transpersonal) are experienced,without any understanding of it
by relatives and medical or psychological assistance. As Maslow
showed, there is a repression in our society of manifestations of
peak-experience; like Freudian sexual repression, this kind of
repression may be responsible for what we name Psychosis. Jung in
his whole work (21), and specially R. Assagioli (22), insists on
the malevolent consequences of ignorance and repression of higher
states of consciousness.

Questioning other kinds of Boundaries

    There are many other aspects of classical psychopathology and
views of boundaries, which are questioned by transpersonal psychology; one of them is the frontier between consciousness and un-
consciousness. The other one is the problem of the frontiers of
regression, which underlies the problem of the beginning of the
Self and the existence, and nature of intrauterine and preuterine

memories;   and finally, there is the problem of limits of the evolution of the adult.

We will conaider these essential problems;   here it is only
possible to give a summary;   you will find more information in the
bibliography

The Boundary between Conscious and Unconscious. Does the "Unconscious" Exist?

Transpersonal psychology is essentially concerned with States of
Consciousness (10, 11). Specially inspired by the different kinds of
Yoga approaches (2, 3) of human consciousness, we can distinguish
four main states of consciousness:

- Waking State which brings physical body into relationship
with the physical world, through our five senses and the control of
our reasoning. In this state we emit predominantly Beta electro-
encephalographic waves.

- The Dream State of Consciousness, in part well known to
classical psychoanalysis, which connects our sub-system of subtle
energies, like our emotional life and imagery with subtle energies
of the universe. During this State of Consciousness we emit predominant Theta waves.

- The Deep Sleep State of Consciousness, in which the relationship of our consciousness with the physical world of gross energy
and the subtle energies is totally cut off. In this state of
consciousness we emit predominant Theta waves.

- The Cosmic State of Consciousness, which we described briefly
above, in which individual consciousness of self and universal self
are experienced as one. In this state of consciousness also
Theta waves are predominant. It is interesting to observe that these
kind of waves are the same in terminal states of existence, intra-
uterine life and sleep.

In relationship to the matter of boundaries between Conscious
and Unconscious, Transpersonal Psychology lead us to change these
concepts;   following these experiences, there is no Unconscious-
ness;   Consciousness does always exist in the four states we
described above. What we name "Unconscious" is the result of a
veil between each of these states, which makes us forget, when we
are in one of these states what happened in the other state.   Only
in Cosmic State of Consciousness does this veil disappear totally;
from this point of view, the waking state of Consciousness is very
limited.

So, following Transpersonal Psychology, Consciousness is always present; as Assagioli (22) has shown, the Self has the property of identification with our body, our emotions, our mind, our dreams, and our roles; when this occurs, consciousness is centered only on some figure which is proper to the specific state we are in. In Gestalt perspective, when we perceive the figure, the background does not exist anymore for our consciousness; but the consciousness is always present.

Boundaries of regression and evolution. The problem of the beginning and the end of the Self

As we know it, the concept of regression has been emphasised by Freud (24); for him it was a return of the libido to previous phases of it's development, under the influence of great obstacles which block instructual discharge.

As Laplanche and Pontalis (25) show, it is a reply of what is "written". Three kinds of regression are described by Freud; Temporal (with specific focus on the object and libidinal developmental stage, and/or ego development; Structural which is related to the form of expression of the regression, and the Topographic.

In this brief summary, we will speak more about the Temporal or chronological aspect, nevertheless recognising that it is not easy to separate entirely these points of view. Our focus is on the limits of this regression. We have extensively treated this matter in one of our last books (26). The conclusion of this analysis is that there are no boundaries of regression. We describe the works following stages of regression; inspired by the works of Freud, Rank (28), Ferenzci (29), Leboyer (30), Grof (31, 32), Prince and Savage (15), and others.

1. Post-Uterine Level

This level of regression includes the Freudian Psychodynamic levels of regression like the phallic, anal, oral, which are well known by classical psycho-analytical psychotherapies.

2. Intra-Uterine Level

Our own experience in Psychodramatic rebirthing with which Anne Schutzenberger (32) and other authors have worked (33) for twenty years, shows that there exists intra-uterine memory; all bodily reactions and emotional disturbances of birth can be reactivated and abreacted in special therapeutic frameworks. This is what Grof names the Rankian level of regression (31).

But regression does not stop here. Following Stan Grof's psychedelic experiences of Psychotherapy (32), there are four "basic perinatal matrixes" (BPM). The first one is specific to the primal union with the mother, the second one is related to the antagonism with the mother and corresponds to the contractions in the closed uterine system; the third one is characterized by synergism with the mother through which the propulsion through the birth canal happens, and finally the fourth BPM is characterized by separation from the mother and ending of the symbiotic union and formation of a new type of relationship. These BPM's play an important role and given a fundamental basis for further experiences on psycho-dynamic levels; for instance "bad and good wombs" seem to give, on perinatal level, an experiential grounding of the later ex-perience of "bad and good breast". They are also described in other words by Frederick Leboyer (30) in his experience of non-violent birthing; he distinguishes the golden phase in which the fetus is smaller than the uterus, from the hell phase, in which the uterus is too small for the fetus.

Following our own experience, it seems that in all of these ex-periences, there is a duality: the fetus and the placental wall (32); it is for this reason, that we think that all kinds of unitive re-gressive experiences of this level, are still false cosmic and transpersonal experiences.

The true cosmic experience must be situated in some place of pre-uterine level of regression.

3. Pre-uterine Level

On level of fecundation there is still life; the spermatozoa is an alive microscopic fish in brotherhood competition with millions of other spermatozoa, for reaching the living ovule; some memories of these levels exist, like spermatozoal dreams (34). On this level, memory cannot be anymore of a neuronal nature, but of a cellular nature (ADN, ARN) like Mavens experiences (35), the electronic nature of Charon (7) or on the holographic nature of man (6), which we explained briefly in the beginning of this paper.

But the works of Ferenczi, Jung, Grof, Gesell (36), and Lupasco, admit the hypothesis of a life and memory continuum, which reaches not only organic but includes also inorganic levels. It is on the levels of potentialisation of energy that we may situate the true unitive transpersonal experience; it seems that it is on this level that all boundaries are dissolved. It may correspond to what John Lilly named the "Metaprogramme" (37).

Perinatal Regression and Transpersonal Experiences

Our own experience in Group Psychotherapy and Psychodrama, even without any psychodelic drug, confirms the work of Stanislaw Grof;

parapsychological phenomena like telepathy, precognition, retro-
cognition or clairvoyance, and transpersonal ones, occurs especially
when the individual or the whole group enter into perinatal regression. We discovered this principle very slowly, and it took
years of observation before we became totally aware and convinced
of this fact (32).

In particular the "enlightenment" phenomenon, in which people
see themselves as pure light or perceive a ineffable light with
closed eyes, occurs after description of inner travelling in a dark
space, sometimes in a tunnel. This enlightenment is followed by a
state of deep bliss, grace and peace; generally, we observe that
we are very close to the end of the therapeutical process. Some time
is necessary to work through this new dimension, and to adapt the new
values which emerge in this step, to daily life.

Time, Regression, Evolution and the Self

After this explanation we can see that not only the ontogenetic
past but also the phylogenetic and cosmogenetic one is "written" in
some place or places of everybody. If we change our state of consciousness, an operation which progressively eliminates the barrier
of our mentally conditioned concept of three dimensional time, regression to all these levels may occur; even progression to future
events is observed. In the Cosmic state of consciousness, the distinction of regression and evolution has no more meaning, because
time does not exist anymore.

This new approach to human regression, has serious consequences
on our daily practice of therapy; the knowledge and adequate understanding of what we in transpersonal psychology name the "maps of
consciousness", helps not only to situate and make an accurate
diagnosis of what level or levels of regression is occurring in the
patient, but also to guide him in his inner "voyage" or "trip", till
he reaches the realm of holistic planes of experience. This is also
the unexpressed aim of every human being; it is the purpose of
transpersonal psychology to give the support to reach such levels
of consciousness, through such specific methods as meditation, and
other methods.

If there are no frontiers of regression and if life has no
beginning, we may say the same in relationship to evolution and
death; if there is an "end" of human evolution, we will find it in
the realm of cosmic consciousness. Then, we can experience inner
peace, beauty, truth and love, which constitute some of the typical
values of the "end" of this evolution (38).

If we follow the theoretical model of the process of regression
and evolution, we can see that the origin and end of human Self is the
same; what we name the Ego, is perhaps some universal Self which

identifies itself, provisionally, with the body, emotion, mind and conditioned roles; this Self may have no beginning and no end. We should compare the self to a programme of television; millions of TV receptors receive the programme; they are the individual self which is perceived as unique; if we destroy the TV apparatus the programme continues in the air.

Let us end this too brief explanation of so broad a matter, by a little story which came to our mind.

Once a wave met another wave of the same sea. "Who are you? "asked the first one. "I am a wave", was the answer. "And you, who are you?". "I am the Sea".

REFERENCES

1.   LUPASCO, S., "Les trois matieres".   Julliard.   Paris.

2.   SNYDER, Reger D., "Holographic Theory and PSI".   Proceedings.
     IV International Conference on Psychotronic Research. Vol.
     II. p.435-38.   Sao Paulo 1979.

3.   DEAN, E. Douglas. "Psychotronics and the Holographic Model of
     Brain".   Proceedings.   IV International Conference on Psycho-
     tronic Research.   Vol. II. p.430-34.   Sao Paulo 1979.

4.   GABER, D. "Holography".   Address to the Nobel Committee.
     Science. Dec. 1, 1971.

5.   BOHN, D. "Quantum Theory as an Indiciation of a New Order in
     Physics.   Part A and B. Foundations of Physics 1 and 3 1971
     and 1973.

6.   COLEMAN, D. "Karl Pribram, chercheur et neuro-chirurgien"
     Psychologie. p.47-52.   Retz.   Paris 1979.

7.   CHARON, J.E. "L'Esprit cet Inconnu".   Albin Michel.   Paris
     1977.

8.   PIAGET, J. "La construction du Reel".   Delachaux et Niestle.
     Neuchatel.

9.   WEIL, P. "COSMODRAMA; an Experiential Approach of Relation-
     ship between Consciousness and Reality".   Proceedings.   IV
     International Congress of Transpersonal Psychology".   Boston
     1979.

10. TART, Ch.T. Altered States of Consciousness.   Wiley, New York,
     1969.

11. TART, Ch. "Scientific foundations for the Study of Altered States of Consciousness". The Journal of Transp. Psychol. 1971, No. 2, p. 93-124.

12. BUCKE, R.M. Cosmic Consciousness. Dutton, New York, 1969.

13. JAMES, W. The Varieties of Religious Experience, New York, Random House, 1962.

14. DEIKMAN, A.J. "Deautomatization and mystic experience". Psychiatry, Vol. 29, p.324-338, 1966.

15. PRINCE, R. and SAVAGE Ch. "Mystical States and the concept of regression", in The highest state of consciousness. Anchor, New York 1972, p.114s.

16. PAHNKE, W.H. "Drugs and mysticism", in The highest state of consciousness. Anchor, New York 1972, p.257s.

17. WEIL, P. "Content. Analysis of Reports obtained in a State of Cosmic Consciousness" Conep. 1978 and Psicol. Clinica e Psicoterapia Belo Horizonte. Interlivres. 1 (2): 55-32- 1977.

18. WHITE, R.A. "Surveys in Parapsychology" Scarecrow Press. Metuchen, N.J. 1976.

19. DEVEREUX, G. "Psychoanalysis and the Occult", New York, International University Press. 1970.

20. ELIADES, M. "Le Chamanisme et les techniques archaiques de l'extase", Paris, Payot, 1968.

21. JUNG, C.G. "Psychology of the Occult". p.5. Bollingen Paperbacks. Princeton 1977.

22. ASSAGIOLI, R. The act of will. Penguin books. Baltimore 1973.

23. RAMA, Ballentine R., Ajaya. "Yoga and Psychotherapy". Himalayan Institute, Glenview, Illinois 1976. Chapter 5.

24. FREUD, S. "Introduction a la Psychanalyse". Payot, Paris 1917, p.367.

25. LAPLANCHE et PONTALIS. "Vocabulaire de la Psychanalyse". PUF. Paris 1967.

26. WEIL, P. "Fronteiras da Regressao". Vozes. Rio-Petropolis 1977.

27. WEIL, P. "A Consciencia Cosmica". Vozes. Rio-Petropolis 1978.

28. RANK, D. "O Traumatismo do Nascimento" Estudo Psicanalitico,
     Rio, Marisa, 1934, p.168.

29. FERENCZI, S. "Thalassa. Psychanalyse des origines de la vie
     sexuelle", Paris Payot, 1962.

30. LEBOYER, F. "Pour une naissance sans violence", Paris, Le
     Seuil, 1974.

31. GROF, S. "Theorical and empirical Basis of Transpersonal
     Psychology and Psychotherapy; Observations from LSD Research".
     The Journal of Transpersonal Psychology, n. 1, p. 15s, Stan-
     ford, 1973.

32. SCHUTZENBERGER, A.A. and WEIL, P. "Psychodrama Triadique".
     Interlivres. Belo Horizonte, 1978.

33. ORR, L. and RAY, S. "Rebirthing in the New Age". Celestial
     Arts. Millbrae, 1977.

34. SILBERER, "Spermatozoentraume" and "Zur Frage der Spermato-
     zoentraume", Jahrbuch IV, 1972 (cit. Otto Rank).

35. MAVEN, A. "The Mystic Union: a suggested biological inter-
     pretation" The Journal of Transpersonal Psychology, Spring
     1969, Palo Alto.

36. GESELL, A.Y., Amatruda, C. "Embriologia de la Conducta".
     Buenos Aires, Paidos, 1972.

37. LILLY, J.C. "The Center of the Cyclone", New York, Julian
     Press, 1973.

38. WEIL, P. "Fronteiras da Evolucao e da Morte". Vozes.
     Rio-Petropolis 1979.

39. WEIL, P. and SCHUTZENBERGER, A.A., "Filobacia, Ocnofilia e
     Metodos de Regressao Intra-uterina". Estudos de Psicanalise,
     no. 6, Belo Horizonte, 1973.

40. JUNG, C.G. "Ma Vie". Gallimard, Paris 1966, p. 332-340.

41. WEIL, P. COUTO, L.F., CUNHA, S.E. "Analise fetorial de une
     questionario de Consciencia Cosmica" in Medida la Consciencia
     Cosmica. Vozes. Petropolis 1978.

ARCHITECTURAL BOUNDARIES AND THEIR IMPACT ON SOCIAL ORGANISATION

Imre Szecsödy, M.D.

Stockholm Mental Health Center

Maria Hansson, Marie Hessle, Ulf Nordahl

University of Stockholm

Background, assumptions, realization

In the beginning of the 70's Swedish Mental Health Care Services were mainly centered around services given in hospitals. Each hospital had a catchment area, from which people, defining themselves as sick (or given that definition by others) could turn to the hospital. They could visit the hospital directly on an emergency basis, or where referred to it or to its out-patient clinics by a physician. Waiting lists at the out-patient clinics were enormous, the hospitals were over-populated. Private practice was also scarce, psychiatrists had very long waiting lists - 2 to 4 years was not unusual to wait for psychoanalysis or long term individual psychotherapy. Inpatient care was mostly initiated by the emergency units - where people came with all kinds of problems, of recent or long lasting duration. Compulsory admission to mental hospitals varied from region to region, from 4-30%. In short - people had difficulties in receiving adequate treatment at the beginning of their career as patients, at least as outpatients. If they decompensated, they often became inpatients. After-care was almost non-existent, or badly organized. At a meeting of the Swedish Psychiatric Association, Dr. Bengt Bergren (chief of Psychiatric Care Services of the Southern Stockholm Region) described the organisation as a sausage: caregivers and patients were concentrated in time and space before and after patients would enter hospitals (sausage). His vision and recommendation was likened to an hour-glass - where resources should be concentrated in time and space before and after patients would enter hospitals. Some changes and projects were initiated at different places in the country - beginning from the 60's. These included day-hospitals. more organized after-.

care, patient clubs, more effective outpatient services with short-
time and focal psychotherapies, more extensive use of group-therapy
and by establishing therapeutic communities.

In the beginning of the 70's, Dr. Bengt Bergren and some others,
who had visited and studied in Holland, England, the U.S.A., started
to plan for vast changes in the organisation of mental health care
services. Coinciding with certain administrative and economic
changes the "Nacka Project" was started in 1974. The primary task
of the project was formulated as follows: to find and establish
efficient and decent alternatives to hospitalization. Secondary to
"efficient" was the registration, evaluation and reporting of the
experiment period of three years (SPRI-report). Secondary to "decent"
was the follow-up with patients, nonpprofessional caregivers and the
public in general. The initiator and leader was Dr. Bengt Bergren;
responsible team leaders were Dr. John Cullberg, Dr. Per Stenfelt and
Dr. Imre Szecsödy.

The "Nacka Project" was run by three psychiatric teams, located
in three Mental Health Centers, which were to provide psychiatric
services for a catchment area in the Great Stockholm region. Each
Center had to serve a population of about 22,000 to 25,000. The main
goals were the following: the teams would give direct and immediate
service (evaluation, counselling, treatment) to anybody who visited
the Mental Health Center. No waiting lists were allowed. After
office hours and on holidays, the three teams had a common emergency
service, that could be reached by telephone. Those on duty would
answer calls, try to give help in the first place through the telephone. For many this was appropriate, more so as they could get an
appointment the following day. If necessary, people could be visited
in their home, mostly those who could not make use of their own resources or those of others. Some patients came directly to the emergency unit of a near-by General Hospital. Personnel on duty could
also provide consultation to this Hospital, mainly for intoxicated
or suicidal patients. This way the project wanted to make itself
available to people as soon as they felt they needed psychiatric
services. The aim was to establish methods and work with patients
and their families at the beginning of their "patient-career" and
also to decrease the need for hospitalization. If absolutely
necessary, one could use the facilities of a mental hospital, to which
the project was linked administratively.

Other than direct services, the project also planned to co-op-
erate with other institutions and organisations in the catchment area.
Resources were allocated for Mental Health Consultation and preventive work.

Each team was composed of professionals, who usually worked within
the hospitals. One of the reasons for this composition was stated in
the primary task: to find alternatives to hospitalization. Hospital

staff should have the opportunity to test and develop their expertise under non-hospital conditions. The director of each Center was an experienced, psychoanalytically trained psychiatrist, with interest and knowledge in social psychiatry. Each team was composed of two psychiatrists (at the beginning and towards the end of their post-graduate training in psychiatry and most of them also in psycho-analytic training), two clinical psychologists (some of them very experienced, also having analytic and/or group-analytic training), two social workers; two psychiatric nurses and two nurses aides. Each team had also a secretarial staff who also worked as reception-ists.

The psychiatric team that was to work in the Mental Health Cen-ter of Saltsjobaden had also the opportunity to influence the plan-ning done by the architects who designed the localities of the Center. In doing so, we discussed the ideas, the theories, the values that were underlying the activities of the team. We saw individual development in the context of mutual interaction between the person - with his constitutional and psychological endowments - and his physical and social environment. The mutual interpretation of this interaction defines and directs the individual, his inten-tions, what meaning he gives to himself and others and forms his personality. To express his needs, intentions and ambitions he has to interact with his environment in a meaningful way. This capacity is called by social-anthropologists "cultural competence". This competence is related to the perons's social status. The systematic organisation of social relations, such as the ways people approach and use institutions, services etc. - as well as how space is used in a symbolic and psychical sense, represented in architectonic forms.

The Saltsjobaden Mental Health Center wanted to present itself to the community in a way that emphasized openness, availability and that mutual goals and limits between clients and staff should be clarified and be the basis of interaction. These ideas were con-veyed architecturally in the following ways:

The premises were divided conspicuously and with clear bound-aries into four territories, operationally called the Hall, the Plaza, the Cells, and the Back Stage. Each territory had thus defined functions and characteristics.

People were to enter the Center into the Hall, from where they could overlook the localities and activities therein. They could sit down, read the papers, look, listen, turn and leave - without being approached by the staff. They were to make their own appeal for help "autonomously". Between the Hall and Plaza there is a soft bench; its back about 120cm., symbolizing the boundary towards the Center. Between the bench and the reception desk there is a small passage. Anybody who wanted to make contact with the staff, had to enter through this passage. At that point he would ask and

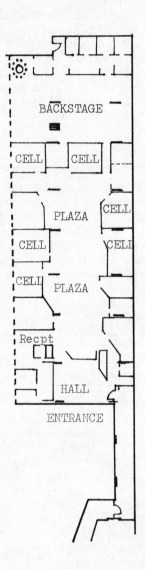

BACKSTAGE

CELL   CELL

PLAZA   CELL

CELL   CELL

CELL   PLAZA

Recpt

HALL

ENTRANCE

SALTSJÖBADENS PSYKIATRISKA
MOTTAGNING

Figure 1. The Plaza viewed from the Hall

Figure 2. The Plaza showing the Hall, Reception/Entrance and Niches

Figure 3. A Niche with entrance and view into an office, i.e. Cell

Figure 4. Back Stage - the conference room

had to answer questions. If he wanted to meet someone of the staff,
the therapist on duty was called. All members of the team were on
duty alternately. The staff member and the visitor would then choose
one of the "niches" of the Plaza. Here the purpose of the visit was
discussed in more detail. The visitor then could be recommended to
apply for the services of another agency - such as a general practitioner, social-welfare office, lawyer, etc. If his problems were
considered to be emotional or psychiatric, a contract was made. Only
at this point would client and therapist enter into one of the offices
- called the Cells - that surrounded the Plaza. These offices were
used for functions, to conduct individual, pair, family or grouptherapy in. They were not the private territory of any staff member.

One had to use the office that was available at the moment. All
the rooms were furnished similarly, with the same high quality
Scandinavian type furniture and had no desks in them, only writing
pulpits. The office of the secretaries was divided from the Plaza
with the help of glass walls. This way work there could be observed
by visitors without disturbing the - often confidential - work
done there. The main idea was to use boundaries to divide functions
according to the defined tasks of the Center. In the beginning much
openness and little seclusion was offered. As involvement between
clients and staff deepened, the higher were the walls of intimacy
and confidentiality raised around them. At the same time it was
emphasized that clients and staff would meet on "neutral" territory
with shared responsibility all the time. Competence was related to
tasks, not to pre-arranged status.

On the other hand, the staff wanted to use resources in a task
oriented way. When not engaged in therapeutic work, the staff was
assembled "Back-Stage" on the fourth territory, a conference room,
where no patient could enter. In this room the daily conferences were
held, discussing and giving information about whatever happened during
the past 24 hours. Among these were information about emergency
calls during the night, about new patients, planning of therapies,
progress of ongoing therapies. Information was shared also about
mental health consultations done in the area as well as other types of
co-operative and preventive activities within the community. There
were also administrative staff meetings, supervisory and theoretical
seminars. The staff did paperwork, dictations, calls in the conference room though they could use any of the offices that were available if they needed more privacy.

The team leader (medical director of the Center) occupied one
of the corners of the conference room. There he had his office to
do all administrative work and was available for short consultations,
to discuss if medication, sick-leave certificates or other questions
arose where his qualifications as an MD or experienced psychotherapist were needed. For supervision, to meet clients, to do psychotherapy he used the same offices - Cells - as the other staff members.

The office in the corner helped to do leadership work adequately, to
have a general overview of the activities of the team, to aid and
control the staff. By leadership work I mean, to clarify the primary
tasks and to allocate resources towards these, define functions and
delegate responsibilities.

The conference room was considered as the "revir" (common territory) of the team. Here the staff could receive support from peers,
immediate consultation as well as feedback. It was hoped that this
arrangement would help to develop a common ideology and understanding
of functions. One wanted to increase competence by defining clear
boundaries around functions - that were open for discussion and
control. It was also hoped, that staff would derive confidence and
security from this closeness, the availability of others who had
greater experience and competence. Concern was expressed that lack
of privacy could be a strain for many. Offices could be used to
"close the door behind one" and there was also a specific rest room
available for the staff. From the beginning it was planned to provide moveable desks on wheels for everybody. These could be used to
keep papers, personal belongings and "transitional objects".

A few years after the Center was opened, three psychologists
(as a masters paper) did an investigation to find out how the staff
used the localities. It was half a year after the original medical
director had left the Center and about the time when desks for private
use for each member were put into the conference-room (Back-Stage).

Imre Szecsödy, M.D.

Socio-psychology Study

Summary of the Socio-psychological Study

Three years after the Mental Health Center of Saltsjöbaden was
opened changes in the functional design were initiated by the staff.
They decided to put in desks for each team-member in the "Conference
Room". This innovation was experienced as new and contrary to the
basic ideas by the participants.

We used this development - the use of personal desks in the
Conference Room - as a starting point for our study. We wanted to
see:

1) did the original ideas, expressed in the Center's architecture and design persist after this change ?

2) what kind of processes were responsible for this change ?

Some theoretical aspects

When human beings interact, they communicate with words, gestures and other different kinds of expressions for feelings, moods and intentions. This interaction takes place in a physical context to which little attention is paid. Altman (1971) claims that people actively use the physical surroundings as an aid in organising the social processes. The physical space of a room is a reflection of the interpersonal relations which take place there. The physical environment created by man is an addition to other forms of communication.

The physical design of space is thus our starting point. Research in the field in question is extensive but diffuse. In short, there are no good theories in the field, but lots of concepts. We have used two theoretical concepts to cover our questions, the widely used terms privacy and territoriality.

To begin with Altman (1971) defines privacy as "the capacity of controlling human interaction - it is the possibility to decide which kind of information you want to communicate to the surrounding world and under which circumstances."

Privacy is sought not only by the individual, but also by all kinds of groups. Privacy is a dialectic process regulating interaction between people. The two poles in this process are the need for personal integrity and the need for other people including togetherness. People strive for a balance between these poles and mobilize all available resources to maintain this balance, and react with stress and anxiety if the limits become too difficult to maintain. Loneliness and isolation are the price for not daring to communicate. All kinds of communications are used to obtain optimal privacy: language, gestures, ways of moving towards or away from people and objects. The physical space is, of course, used as one of many ways of setting limits between oneself and others. The term personal space defines the limits the individual sets in different situations, depending on which kind of contact he seeks - or seeks to avoid.

Territoriality Sommer ( ) contends that the function of territorial behaviour is to limit aggressivity between individuals because they avoid intruding upon each other's territories to avoid being involved in conflicts. Sommer also claims that the hierarchical structure in society has the same function: it is determined beforehand who is the strongest. People in prison or in isolation react by creating a territory of their own. This is an adaptive behaviour, that is to say, those who fail to do this are not able to cope with the situation as well. Altman also showed that people who are not

able to set up a functioning power structure find territoriality an
important means of relating to each other. Territorial behaviour is
an important means of relating, prior to the establishment of social
relations.

The design of the localities of the Mental Health Center of
Saltsjöbaden was intended to convey the basic ideas and primary
tasks of the project. One intention was to influence the social
processes in the staff, as well as between staff and clients, to be
optimal for the task. The conference room was to become the territory of the staff to gather resources there and to facilitate mutual
support and aid in facing the difficulties in work. It should also
enable a democratic work-distribution as well as permit mutual insight and control between team-members.

Method
We devised a questionnaire which we distributed to those six
team members who had been working in the team from the start and
were still working with the project.

Results and Discussion
From the responses to the questionnaire, it is obvious that all
members of the team experienced a conflict between working discipline
and the need for an emotional "green house". It was also very common
that the members felt disturbed in the large conference room and for
that reason sometimes wished to be left in peace. This situation
can be described rather well in terms of "privacy". Privacy is, in
fact, defined as the need to achieve optimal balance between personal
integrity and togetherness with other people. Altman (1976) points
out that the group also has a need for privacy in relation to the
surrounding world and that he can compensate for the individual need
if the group need is desired strongly enough. The physical design of
the premises had as a clearly formulated goal, to provide a "territory" for the therapists where they could relax from demanding client
relations and where they could give each other confidence and support.
The responses to the questionnaire gave us the impression that the
conference room was really used in this way.

Social Structure and Territoriality
Further examining the responses we find a clear expression of a
wish by the majority to have individual territories in the conference
room from the beginning of the project. In spite of that the only
person who had (or took) a place of his own was the medical director
and no one else. It seems obvious, that everybody perceived this to
be the (implicit) policy dictate by the medical director.

Our hypothesis is that the way the team members acted, not establishing places of their own in the conference room, was an expression
of a conflict within the team. It is hard to believe that the question of personal space was such a "hot" question that they were not

able to tackle it. We suppose that the way the members of the team
acted had the purpose of avoiding a more serious conflict which would
have surfaced if they had begun to fight for seats of their own.

This hidden conflict is that of hierarchy of social status
positions in the team. The policy of the Nacka Project was to obliterate the status differences related to basic training and profession.
Instead, the plan was to form a new structure, with a high level of
equality in rights and responsibilites. Differences in position
should be based on personal experience, relevant knowledge and training.

With the exception of the direct references to the importance of
the medical director, we find in the responses to the questionnaire
three types of reasons for not forcing the issue dealing with the
design of the premises. One reason is, in some cases, a sense of
being new and not feeling secure in the team. This is, without a
doubt, linked to the uncertainty regarding the individual's status
within the team. It is not difficult to imagine that those who felt
most insecure in the situation were threatened by the possibility of
starting discussions about roles and positions in the group.

Another reason is that the issues regarding the premises were
deemed of lesser importance. We do not doubt the face validity of
this judgement, but in the light of our hypothesis, this attitude
seems to be a defense. The same interpretation can be given to the
third reason, i.e. a general preparedness to try something new. Behind this kind of reasoning we can surmise the force of group pressure.
If someone would insist on going back to a more "conservative" way of
using working areas he would thereby lower his social position. This
could inhibit raising any questions. This way of reasoning expresses
already the idea that there is a connection between social hierarchy
and use of physical environment.

We could also see a direct and explicit expression of this connection. The medical director was the only one in the team who had,
or did take a defined position in social organisation of the team and
it was he alone who had, or did take, a defined place in the conference room. The other team-members had no distinct or defined
roles or positions in the team, neither did they take any defined
place in the conference room.

The physical arrangements seem to be a direct reflection of the
social structure. Bearing this in mind, it is possible to interpret
the response of individual members of the team to our questionnaire:
the stronger the desire to have a personal working space, the greater
the need to have a defined position in the team which, in turn, could
point to a relatively greater uncertainty regarding one's "place" in
the group. It is interesting in this connection to note that the two
physicians among the respondents generally gave us the impression of

being the least emotionally committed to these questions. We think
that this is related to the professional roles of the physicians.
They were the only ones to have a clearly defined competence area, which
which means that they assumed the medical responsibility. This gave
them certain possibilities to gain power and control over the other
team members.

Our hypothesis regarding the group dynamics concerning individual working areas and positions in the group could also be connected
with the concept of territoriality.

Altman assumes that the possibility of realizing territorial
strivings facilitates the formation of stable social structure. Thus,
to counteract the establishment of territories, would be to maintain
an unclear social structure in the team. Even though this was felt
burdensome, it was accepted and even encouraged as long as any other -
than a traditional - structure could not be established. Viewed in
this perspective, the stubborn resistance against any territorial
behaviour from the medical director was important. His open stance
for his position and authority (that he also expressed territorially)
was a precondition for the establishment of a new, social structure
in the team.

It has been exciting to follow the dynamic conflict between the
needs of the individuals and the need of the group as expressed by
their privacy and territorial behaviour during these years.

The solution chosen by the team to give each of the members a
place of his own is a concession to the needs of individuals. Is it
a development from natural individual territorial strivings or is it
an indication of internal stability of the team? Perhaps a new non-
hierarchical structure will develop from these experiences or the
group efforts lose strength when the individuals are permitted to
gain territory?

Maria Hansson, Marie Hessle, Ulf Nordahl

Summary

As the reader could see, the researchers used two concepts, that
of privacy and territoriality to investigate how and why the localities were used by staff in the described way. It is interesting to
learn why the staff did not use "private territories", not even introducing the use of moveable desks, as was planned from the beginning.
They seemed to experience a "taboo" against territoriality. This was
not exactly the stated policy, nor the intention of the team-leader.
He took his "place" in a corner of the conference-room. He could do

it, as he had a clear function and status in concordance with the
primary task. Within the staff there was a hidden rivalry. Status
was not to be related to previous professional roles (except for M.D.s
who had a special legal responsibility and also had to serve the team
with specific functions of a physician). Everybody had to find a new
profession, role and status; to work as a therapist and consult with
social-psychiatric aims. In the beginning this increased an insecurity, that favoured a "dependency-basic-assumption climate" (Bion),
where rivalry is experienced as dangerous.

An open hierarchy within the team was not allowed to form, and
so also was occupying personal territories counteracted. This was
often painful and not very practical in doing work that needed
personal space: a desk, storing of papers, privacy when dictating,
thinking, etc. On the other hand this, in a constructive way, prevented a premature closure of the social organisation of the team.
Slowly more stratification of competence was established. At the
beginning it was only those who had a clear and well defined function
who were also free to use and feel comfortable with the architecture
of the Center. The more identity and integrity a person had in his
social role, the less he needed territorial privacy.

To give one example how the organisation of the team was internalized I want to relate an episode that happened one year after
the team started to work in its premises. During a weekend a fire
broke out in the basement of the building below the Center. We had
to move, without preparation and share the localities of another
team, that worked in another office-building. Our team established
a conference room in the kitchen of this Center and for contact with
clients shared rooms with the other staff. The team functioned well
almost from the beginning. Our hosts were concerned and inconven-
ienced. They felt restricted and confused; our team worked efficiently and without observable stress.

Three years after the Center opened, the formal exhibition of
desks in the conference room shows the use of private territories
on a "work-group-level" (Bion). Social status is now openly confirmed, related to primary task, experience and competence, and not
to formal location of desks.

Imre Szecsödy, M.D.

References

Altman, I., Ecological Aspects of Interpersonal Functioning, in:
     Esser, A.H., (ed), Behaviour and Environment. The use of Space
     by Animal and Man. N.Y. Plenum (1971).

Altman, I., Privacy: A conceptual analysis. Environment and Behaviour. 1976, 8

Bexton, H., The architect and planner: change agent or scapegoat. Group Relations Reader, A.K. Rice Institute Series, 1975, Calif.

Brookes, M.H., & Kaplan, A., The office environment. Space planning and affective behaviour. Human Factors, 1972, 14.

Cheyne, A.J., & Efran, M.C., The effects of spatial and interpersonal variables on the invasion of group controlled territories. Sociometry, 1972, 35.

Cheyne, A.J., & Efran, M.C., Affective concomitant of the invasion of shared space. Behavioural psychological and verbal indicators. J. Personality and Social Psychology, 1974, 29.

Colman, A., Irrational aspects of design. Group Relations Reader, A.K. Rice Institute Series, 1975, Calif.

Edney, J.J., Human Territoriality. Psychological Bull., 1974, 81.

Moss R.H., Conceptualizations of human environments. Amer. Psychol., 1973, 28.

Sivadon, P., Baker, A., & Davies, R.L., Psychiatric services and architecture. Public Health Papers, W.H.O., 1954.

Sommer, R., Spatial Parameters in Naturalistic Social Research, in: Esser, A.H. (ed), Behaviour and Environment. The use of Space by Animal and Man. N.Y. Plenum (1971).

Sommer, R., Further studies of small group ecology. Sociometry, 1965, 28.

SPRI Rapport: Psykiatri i omvandling. Stockholm, 1978-79.

Szecödy, I., Rapport om och utvärdering av Saltsjöbadens Psykiatriska Mottanings lokaler - dess arkitektoniska utformning och utnyttjande. Intern rapport, Nackprojektet 1977.

A NUCLEAR CONFLICT AND GROUP FOCAL CONFLICT MODEL FOR INTEGRATING INDIVIDUAL AND GROUP-LEVEL PHENOMENA IN PSYCHOTHERAPY GROUPS

Dorothy Stock Whitaker

Department of Social Administration and Social Work
University of York
Heslington
York, YO1 5DD

Taken together, the models to be described here constitute a way of conceptualizing total group events and individual dynamics in readily comparable terms.   Conceptualizing the individual in nuclear conflict terms and the group in group focal conflict terms can help one to understand persons in groups: the ways in which a person enters into, engages with and influences a group, and the ways in which a group forms, evolves, and has its impact on persons. These models can be used to help one to see how individual and group resonate with and challenge one another, and to see the complex patterns of mutual influence.

Before describing the models and their uses in any detail I would like to make some very simple statements about psychotherapeutic groups and the persons in them:

First, a group is nothing more and of course nothing less than a number of persons interacting together.   The kind of group I shall be discussing is a small, face-to-face group, usually six to nine patients and a therapist, or sometimes two therapists.   Usually, the members begin as strangers to one another.

Second, in a group, things happen which do not happen or do not happen in the same way in either pairs or in larger collections of persons.   For example, in a small face-to-face group norms become established, belief systems develop which are shared and special to the group, emotional contagion may occur, and internal structures develop in which different positions are occupied by different persons. Pairs and sub-groups may emerge.   None of this is static but continually shifts and evolves.   Preoccupations surface in groups which

are carried by all members or different sub-sets.   These preoccupations may be expressed explicitly or in a more hidden way.
They change over time, building up and then dissolving and giving
way to something else.

Third, the person pre-dates the group.   In a stranger-group,
each person entering the group has a personal history of his or her
own and has already developed a "personality".

Fourth, when a person enters a group he or she brings that
personality along into the new interactive situation.   There is no
way to leave it behind.   However, "personality" is complex.   Not
everything of the person is displayed in every situation.   Every
new situation, including of course a group, is in some sense unique.
The person sizes up the situation in some way and in some sense
"decides" how to present himself and what to say and do.   The person
is a meaning-maker, and on the basis of the meanings he makes of the
group he acts in some ways and not in others.   More than this: the
situation is powerful: it presents the person with stimuli and events
which may be easy or difficult for him to handle.   A further point:
the person himself has some influence over the situation, through what
he initiates and how he responds or doesn't respond to unfolding
events.

These basic points suggest that if we wish to understand the
person in the group, or a group which acquires its character from the
interaction of persons in it (however one wishes to put it) then we
need ways of conceptualizing persons and ways of conceptualizing
groups which can be expected to help us to see the interrelations
between the two.

Conceptualizing the person in nuclear conflict and focal conflict terms

I shall start with the person and how he may be described at
the point of entering a therapeutic group.   Everyone knows that a
person can be described in many ways.   We need to use one which
serves our purposes, which is to see what goes on for this person
in this group.   The formulation of the person I have come to prefer
is called a nuclear conflict model.

Nuclear conflict theory was developed by Thomas French, an
American psychoanalyst who presented his ideas in a multiple volume
work called "The Integration of Personality" (French, 1952, 1953).
The essentials of the theory can be described briefly.   (I must say
here, parenthetically, that I have long since internalized French's
model, and can no longer be certain that I am presenting it exactly
as he did or would.   I do not think that the following account does
serious violence to French's views).

All persons have and under some circumstances display certain impulses, needs or wishes which require some response from or co-operation with the environment in order to be dealt with or satisfied. Negotiations with the environment--which mainly means other people but also includes things--begins as we all know very early. The infant or young child presses its environment to meet its needs. The environment responds, or doesn't respond, or partially responds. Sometimes the infant or young child meets with a serious block. Perhaps the infant who seeks closeness through body contact with the mother is met by a depressed mother who cannot and does not respond in the way the infant "wishes". French uses the term "disturbing motive" to describe these basic impulses--in this example the impulse toward (or the wish for) closeness. The motive is "disturbing" in the sense that it "disturbs" the organism into seeking a response. Sometimes the satisfaction of the disturbing motive is blocked by something: in this example it is the preoccupied or depressed mother. So far, there is nothing that can be called an internalized conflict. The disturbing motive is in conflict with a reality factor. However, if such a situation repeats itself (or some might argue occurs before the infant negotiates a separation between self and mother) then the block which in the first instance occurs in reality, outside the person, becomes represented internally, as what French calls a "reactive motive". This takes the form of some fear or sense of guilt. In our example, the child might develop an abiding fear of being rejected, or a guilty sense of being intrinsically unworthy of love. The disturbing motive and the reactive motive together are the nuclear conflict. The state of being enmeshed in such a conflict is unsatisfying and distressful and the child will seek a way out of it. In attempting to deal first with the reality factor and later with the internalized fear or guilt the child will seek what French calls "solutions" to his dilemma. A three year old in this situation might become a clown, because in this way he penetrates his mother's depression and gains something of what he seeks; or he might find solace in material objects and give up trying to gain closeness from persons. He might, and usually does, adopt more than one solution to the same nuclear conflict.

To summarize, nuclear conflict theory puts forward three concepts which are related in a particular way: the disturbing motive, which is an impulse or wish in conflict with the reactive motive, a fear or guilt, and the solution, which in some way seeks to deal with the disturbing and reactive motives. The model can be shown in the form of a diagram:

Nuclear Conflict:

    disturbing motive   X   reactive motive

                   ↓

           Solution(s)

It is in a person's best interests if the solution or set of
solutions can alleviate the reactive motive or fear whilst at the
same time allowing for satisfaction of the disturbing motive or wish.
Sometimes it does this.   Sometimes, however, it does not: the
solution alleviates the fear but requires the person to give up the
wish, (as when the disappointed child turns to solace from objects)
or it may partially satisfy the wish but bring other disadvantages
(as when the child who becomes a clown gets mother's attention under
certain circumstances only and carries his clownishness inappropriately
and unnecessarily into other situations and relationships).

French used two terms to apply to the individual: "nuclear
conflict" and "focal conflict".   To understand the relationship
between the two one must hold on to the idea that while a person
carries a nuclear conflict and associated solutions around with him
into all situations, the situation will influence and colour whether
and how it is expressed.   Variations in expression occur because
some situations resonate strongly, in particular ways, with the kind
of situation which generated the conflict in the first place whilst
others resonate weakly or not at all.   Depending on the nature of
the resonance, some part or degree of the nuclear conflict will be
experienced in a particular situation, and some portion of the
individual's repertory of solutions will be displayed.   The nuclear
conflict becomes focal;   that is, the conflict as expressed in a
particular situation is a variant of the underlying nuclear conflict,
influenced by the character of current circumstances.   Thus our
young boy who learns to become a clown builds being a clown into his
personal repertory of solutions.   It is not the only thing in his
repertory, but it is there.   When he enters a situation which
resonates with the earlier one--that is, a situation in which he is
not sure of being accepted or of gaining a response--he may resort
to clownishness.   When he goes to school as a young boy, for
example, he amuses his classmates (but not necessarily his teacher)
by his antics.   When he grows older and more sophisticated, perhaps
he becomes a raconteur.

The person does not lose the nuclear conflict (or as sometimes
occurs the several closely related nuclear conflicts) developed early
in life.   The disturbing and reactive motives are largely lost to
consciousness and the functional character of the solutions is
unrecognized.   However, behaviours which express solutions may be
noted by the person and either desired or disliked, but in any case
they are likely to be seen as "the way I am".   Solutions include
but are not restricted to defences as usually defined.   A solution
might be a defence, but it might also be a preferred way of
presenting the self, or a characteristic inter-personal pattern
which requires other participants (the clown requires an audience).
A solution might even be expressed as a particular life style (for
example, the dedicated self-sufficiency expert whose need not to
need others finds expression in a self-sufficient life style).

It should be noted that particular solutions are not necessarily
noxious or disadvantageous to the person concerned.   A solution may
indeed be advantageous in that it makes it possible for the person
to achieve life goals without doing harm to self or others. Usually
one sees that a person has developed and seeks to operate on three
or four or five different solutions, all functionally related to the
same underlying nuclear conflict.   Some of these solutions are
disadvantageous from the person's point of view, and some are not.

A nuclear conflict model for conceptualizing the person has
several advantages.   It allows one to define "pathology" as holding
to disabling solutions which work against the individual's own
interests and life goals.   The model helps one to see a person's
strengths, for it calls attention to a range of solutions, only some
of which are pathological in the sense just described.   Further, the
model is not restricted to persons defined as patients.   Psychologically distressed persons can be described in these terms, but so
can ordinary, reasonably well-functioning persons.   In this paper I
shall discuss the model only as it may be useful to group psychotherapy, but it has other uses.   For example, it can be used to help
one to understand the impact of certain transitions and life crises
on persons, in terms of the disruption of established and necessary
sets of habitual solutions.   It can help one to understand how
persons may link together, each complementing the other in maintaining
certain preferred solutions of an interpersonal character--as in
marriage.   The nuclear conflict model cannot be applied to everyone,
in particular to those who cannot plausibly be regarded as having
developed internalized conflicts.   However, it can be applied to
most persons who become members of therapeutic groups which rely
mainly on talk as the route to personal gain.

As I have already said, a person can be expected to carry the
nuclear conflict(s) and habitual solutions into any new situation.
The therapeutic group is one such situation.   Within the therapeutic
group the nuclear conflict and some of the solutions can be expected
to emerge in a transformed, or "focal conflict" form, which takes on
some of its character from the current situation in the group.

Conceptualizing the group in group focal conflict terms

Group focal conflict theory is an extension of French's ideas
to the level of the group as a whole.   This model has been described
in detail elsewhere (Whitman and Stock, 1958; Whitaker and Lieberman,
1964).   Briefly, it is based on the recognition that the successive
comments and behaviours by different persons have a free-associational
quality, and that these associations build into themes.   The themes
are expressed partly in what is said, partly in the "how" of what is
said, partly in gesture and posture, and partly in pace and timing.
A group focal conflict approach asserts that these evolving and

shifting themes can be expressed in terms of a <u>shared</u> wish (analagous
to French's disturbing motive) which is in conflict with a <u>shared</u>
fear (analagous to French's reactive motive); that the shared wish
and fears constitute a <u>group focal conflict</u>; and that events can be
observed within the group which are efforts to deal with the group
focal conflict by establishing shared <u>solutions</u>. The shared
solution fulfils the same function for the group as it does for the
individual - that is, it diminishes or holds at bay reactive fears,
sometimes also allowing for the expression of the shared wish, sometimes not. The model can be shown diagrammatically as:

Group focal conflict:

Disturbing Motive	X	Reactive Motive
(shared wish)	↓	(shared fear or guilt)
	Solution(s)	

A distinction is made between <u>enabling solutions</u>, which allow for
the relief of fears and expression of the shared wish, and <u>restrict-
ive solutions</u>, which allow for the relief of fear but not for the
recognition or expression of the shared wish. From the point of
view of participants in the group, all solutions are functional in
that they operate to alleviate fears. From the point of view of
the therapist, enabling solutions are preferred to restrictive
solutions because they allow for exploration of both the wishes and
the fears involved. In contrast, restrictive solutions limit areas
of exploration.

Having provided this brief account of the theoretical models,
I shall move on to a discussion of some of the implications and uses
of the model, organizing my comments under four headings: how the
model can help one to understand the person-in-the-group and the
therapeutic process; how a therapist may go about forming an understanding of person and group in these terms whilst at the same time
conducting a group; how the model guides practice; and how
practice can guide research and research inform practice.

How the model can help one to understand the person-in-the-group and the therapeutic process

In the course of the free-associational process already referred
to, shared themes emerge which can be conceptualized in group focal
conflict terms. In and among this process, individual patients
participate, contribute, react to, withdraw from these evolving
events in ways which are related to individual nuclear conflicts
and preferred personal solutions.

Particularly when he or she first enters the group, a person
can be expected to try to establish in this new setting habitual,
"preferred" solutions linked to nuclear conflicts established early

in life and since maintained in derived but related forms. The
person seeks to do this because he or she experiences (but does not
explicitly recognize) habitual solutions as necessary to psychological
survival. Thus, the person can be expected to seek to place himself
in certain positions in the group, cue others to perceive and respond
to him in particular ways, establish alliances which support
preferred solutions, and seek to create conditions and a climate in
the group which allow his habitual solutions to operate.

All of the persons in the group seek to do this. Sometimes
their interests mesh together or are compatible, and then one sees
instances of mutual support and cooperation which work toward
establishing particular group conditions and/or instances where two
or more persons play parts in maintaining one another's preferred
solutions. Frequently the interests of individuals collide, and
then one sees instances where a person is prevented from (or
prevented from fully) establishing particular preferred solutions.

Beyond this, whatever the particular character of each person's
nuclear conflict(s) and habitual solutions, each is likely to
experience the group as a potentially threatening place. Patients
know or soon find out that in the group they are expected to express
and reveal feelings and experiences ordinarily concealed. They
themselves wish to do this in so far as they recognize self-
revelation and self-exposure as routes to personal gain. Yet the
risks--of exposure to criticism and rejection from others, of self-
disgust, of own feelings possibly getting out of control, and the
like--are great. Because all have such hopes and fears (although
they vary of course in detail) patients have a mutual interest in
rendering this potentially very risky situation viable--that is,
safe enough to remain in it and secondarily safe enough for self-
exposure to occur.

To summarize the argument so far, the associative process
occurring in the early sessions of a group can be seen in part as
efforts, manouverings and negotiations on the part of the patients
to establish preferred personal solutions in the new setting of the
group, and in part as collaborative efforts to make the group viable.
The associative process, influenced as it is by both individual and
mutual motivations, is likely to generate, early on in the group, a
shared group focal conflict something like the following:

Disturbing Motive:		Reactive Motive:
wish to be helped by revealing own feelings and problems	X	fear of criticism (or ridicule, or rejection or abandonment from other patients (or the therapist) or fear

REACTIVE MOTIVE (continued):   of being overwhelmed
                                                by own feelings or
                                                of being made more
                                                stressed or ill through
                                                exposure to the
                                                problems of others)

In response to and along with such a group focal conflict patients
are likely to generate such shared solutions as talking about
problems in abstract terms, or talking about the problems of persons
known to them but not in the group, or demanding that the therapist
help by providing advice or guidance as to how to proceed, or talking
about issues which are outside the group altogether, or expressing
shared fears in symbolic terms, etc.   All these possibilities have
in common the fact that they are restrictive in character, i.e. they
relieve reactive fears whilst at the same time precluding expression
of the associated disturbing motive or wish.   Initial solutions are
likely to be restrictive in character because nothing has happened
as yet to alleviate reactive fears or show them to be exaggerated in
character.

    The initial group focal conflict, or the initial solution, can
be expected to give way to others.   Perhaps the group initially
presses for the therapist to provide advice.   If he declines to
cooperate in this then a subsequent group focal conflict might be:

    Disturbing Motive: Reactive Motive:

      anger at the therapist   fear of abandonment
      for not providing help   X   by the therapist
                                              should he detect
                                              this anger (or other
                                              possible fears)

Again, a restrictive solution might become established: for example
expressing anger at others not present whom one has expected to provide
help but who have behaved disappointingly (teachers;   government);
or finding a person in the group who is prepared to offer advice
and thus be the kind of therapist the group is seeking.   Such
solutions provide relief of reactive fears but either preclude
expression of the associated wish or impulses or allow expression
in partial and disguised ways only.   Another possible sequence is
that the group moves to an enabling solution related to the initial
group focal conflict: for example, the patients might agree that
everyone has problems and therefore no one need feel ashamed.
Such a shared view is an enabling solution because it reduces
reactive fears and at the same time allows the patients to begin to
reveal themselves.   As some sort of sharing of personal feelings
and experiences begins to occur, further themes emerge which again
can be understood in group focal conflict terms.

There is much more to say about these processes and related ones--for example, the two possibilities that shared solutions could involve all patients behaving in the same way (all denying; all being silent) or that shared solutions could involve role differentiation within the patient group (one acting as patient and the others acting as therapist or one standing for the therapist and functioning as scapegoat in the group). There is also the phenomenon of the solutional conflict, where the group engages in a power struggle as to which of several solutions shall be established, or where one person holds out against a solution which could otherwise become established, thus becoming a deviant in the group. These specifics, and others which for reasons of space cannot be developed here, are all part of the complexity of the group.

The precise way in which each group moves will be different and cannot be predicted, since the course of events will be influenced by the composition of the group (in terms of individual nuclear conflicts and preferred solutions) and the manner in which the therapist participates in the early sessions.

Whatever the detailed development, according to this model the continuing process of the group can be seen in terms of an initial group focal conflict, the establishment of a solution or several successive shared solutions to that conflict, then the emergence of further group focal conflicts as movement becomes necessary or possible in consequence of the thwarting of initial solutions or the successful establishment of enabling solutions. This continually evolving situation is the context for therapy, although one needs to remember that the context is always being created and influenced by the persons in the group, who take an active and not a passive role in generating it.

What does all this have to say about the group becoming a therapeutic environment generally, and becoming an environment in which persons may undergo the highly particular experiences likely to be required to enable them to yield up their disadvantageous but firmly established habitual solutions? Moving toward becoming an environment which generally supports therapeutic change is, in group focal conflict terms, a shift toward the establishment of enabling solutions. The model recognizes that a well-functioning group will not operate consistently on enabling solutions. However, if periods of recourse to restrictive solutions can be limited, and the group helped to operate most of the time on enabling solutions, then the group is likely to be a generally facilitating context for therapeutic change. If such is the case, the boundaries of the group widen, and a wide range of human affects, relationships and situations can be experienced and explored, in terms of here-and-now experiences, current outside relationships, past personal relationships, and connections amongst these. Opportunities for more pointedly relevant therapeutic experiences occur if and when resonances develop between group focal conflicts and individual nuclear conflicts.

In a therapeutic group there is a high likelihood that many or some of the group focal conflicts which successively emerge will resonate with individual nuclear conflicts. The reason for this is that the affects involved in disturbing motives are the basic human ones of yearnings for closeness, intimacy and support; rages; jealousies. The affects involved in reactive motives are the equally basic ones of fear and guilt. In a group of six to eight persons it is unlikely that only one person will be concerned about needs for intimacy, say, or that only one person will experience guilt about angry impulses. It is far more likely that many, not a few, will be so concerned. As the associative process builds up, then, these basic affects can be expected to emerge in the form of successive group focal conflicts. Typically, certain themes recur repeatedly in different ways and forms. If the solutions associated with these successive group focal conflicts are largely restrictive in character, then nothing much in the way of useful experience or exploration will occur. But if the group, or the group with the help of the therapist can come to work for a substantial part of its time on enabling solutions, then explorations will occur in areas which can be expected to resonate with individual concerns. As this occurs, so also does the potential for personal change. As in other models which seek to understand the therapeutic process, this model takes the view that corrective emotional experiences need to occur, possibly but not necessarily supported by insight. In the terms of this model, the corrective emotional experience can be seen as the reality testing of reactive fears and through this their diminution and a lessened need to cling to habitual personal solutions heretofore experienced as essential to the survival and integrity of the person. In other words, as reactive fears diminish solutions may be yielded up: the solutions likely to be yielded up, once the person has choice, are those which operate dysfunctionally for him, interfering with personal life goals or generating secondary unwanted problems.

There are a number of ways in which resonances may occur and be positively exploited for the benefit of the individual. For example, as enabling solutions emerge in the group explorations of the under-lying impulses and fears can occur. An individual participating in such explorations is exposed to opportunities to reality-test his own fears. Another possibility is that if reactive fears involved in a shared group focal conflict can be alleviated, then a person whose own fears are in resonance with these may also experience alleviation and hence feel able to try out new behaviours which involve the tentative yielding up of established habitual solutions. Or, a person may be pulled along through processes of contagion into experiencing affects which feel to him highly risky: by so doing he sees that he survives what he has previously held to be unsurvivable. Here again reactive fears are diminished and the attendant necessity to maintain some associated dysfunctional habitual solution begins to give way. Sometimes a person collides with others in the group in ways which

make it impossible for him to maintain preferred solutions. If this
happens then underlying fears emerge and with this emergence the
opportunity to face the fears and test their current reality or the
patient's current capacity to cope with them. Sometimes a person
may not participate overtly yet observe that others dare the undare-
able without disastrous consequences. This may encourage and em-
bolden the person to make test-outs of his or her own. It is by such
means and by such routes, all of which involve an interaction between
group level and individual level events and experiences, that therapeutic gain can occur. Some examples of forms of resonance can be
found in an early paper (Whitman, Lieberman and Stock, 1960), although
the term was not used at that time.

Before moving on, I wish to make a comment about transference,
a term which does not appear in the above discussion. While I do
not find it necessary to use this term, I hope that it will be evident
that resonance between group focal conflicts and individual nuclear
conflicts as experienced in derived forms is transference and that
there are good reasons to expect that such resonances will occur in
the group. As the nature of the resonances varies, so also does the
nature of the transferred feelings, which may be expressed in terms
of experiences with or assumptions about the group therapist, other
patients individually or in clusters or the group as a whole. The
model thus accommodates the idea of transference, but prefers to refer
to such phenomena in other terms, specifically, in terms of the
particular character of the resonance.

How a therapist may go about forming an understanding of person and
group in nuclear and group focal conflict terms

Developing an understanding of persons and groups, and persons
in groups, is an ongoing and evolving process.   It can begin before
a group starts, but for the most part it goes on while a group is in
session when events may be moving very quickly and when a therapist
is a part of those events.

A therapist can develop an understanding of a person in nuclear
conflict and individual focal conflict terms by two routes which
complement one another: information provided directly by the patient,
as in preparatory individual interviews; and observations made during
the course of group sessions. A wide range of information gained
directly from the patient in individual interview can form the raw
materials for a formulation in nuclear conflict terms. These include
remembered events from childhood, which frequently operate like screen
memories, revealing aspects of the nuclear conflict and early personal solutions; subsequent events and experiences occurring in a variety
of settings with persons inside and outside the primary family,
affording opportunities to identify consistencies and recurrences;
responses to fortuitous events and transitions, which tend to reveal
what it is a person does and feels in response to the unexpected or

the unsought; choices about jobs, marriage partners, even general
life style (when choice has been possible), which suggest what sorts
of niches a person seeks to create for himself.   One tries to see
how all of this information, taken together, might fit or be accounted
for in terms of the nuclear conflict model. What recurring behaviours,
characteristic ways of interacting, favoured defences might be
functioning as solutions?   To what abiding underlying conflicts
might these be related?   Preliminary ideas about solutions and
associated conflicts may thus be generated.

Such a formulation is a start-point for one's understanding of
the person.   As soon as group sessions begin, rich opportunities
come into being for building, amplifying and correcting initial
formulations.   In the group one can see how the person presents
himself, with whom he chooses to engage, what he seeks from others,
how he reacts to the stimuli which the group presents.   One begins
to see both the range of his behaviour and consistencies in it.
One builds from observations of concrete instances to inferences
about the nature of the nuclear conflict and preferred solutions.
Further content which the individual reveals about his current and
past life helps to fill out the picture.

Developing a sense of the group focal conflict and related
solutions as these gradually emerge during the course of group
interaction requires close attention to the free-associational
process in the group.   As in individual psychoanalysis, one tries
to listen in a free-floating way, sometimes seeing directly and
sometimes sensing the communalities and linkages which begin to be
evident, often making use of one's own internal feelings and
reactions as a guide.   Both manifest and latent levels need to be
taken into account, so one tries to catch not only the obvious,
likely to appear in the content, but the not so obvious as conveyed
by shifts in topic, intonation, non-verbal behaviour, shifts in who
is in the forefront of the interaction, and the like. Often, it is
the solutions which first come to one's attention, as these tend to
be relatively more visible.   One notices, for example, that the
patients are complaining about the hospital food, or scrupulously
taking turns in the group, or blaming one patient for his lack of
interest in the group.   Having noticed some pattern or theme gain
hold in the group, one might then ask oneself some questions about
it: "Why?"   "To what underlying wishes and fears might this be a
response?"   Then: "What fears are being hinted at or symbolically
expressed?"   "What are the patients acting as if they want?"   One
gets hints from the content, the sequence, which bits of a complex
contribution get picked up and responded to and which do not, what
gets interrupted, the mood of the group, how the patients seek to
involve the therapist, what they demand from him, and so on.   It is
through sensitivity to all these aspects of the ongoing situation
that hypotheses about the import of what is occurring can be
established.   It is important to hold loosely to any notions one

might develop, looking to subsequent events to confirm, disconfirm or modify.   Hypotheses about the group focal conflict are always working hypotheses: on the basis of a current hypothesis one might intervene in a particular way.   On the basis of what happens next one might revise or hold to one's hypotheses.   One needs to recognize that in the fast-moving fluid group situation it is not always possible to formulate explicitly to oneself hypotheses about the possible significance of successive events.   During such periods one might be in touch intuitively, or one might simply be confused and lost in the complexity of the situation or invaded by own feelings.   If the former is the case, then a therapist may find that he intervenes spontaneously in just the best way.   If the latter is the case, he may make errors or miss opportunities.   To increase the likelihood of participating usefully in a group it seems to me worth striving toward making one's own assumptions explicit to oneself (knowing that one cannot always manage it) so that these assumptions can be checked against actually occuring events.

How a nuclear and group focal conflict model can guide practice

This model can constitute a guide to practice in three main ways.   First, it suggests what to aim for in composing a group, in order to maximize the likelihood that potentially useful resonances will occur and to minimize the likelihood of a group getting stuck in restrictive solutions.   Second, it suggests that one of the therapist's aims should be to encourage the establishment and maintenance of enabling rather than restrictive solutions in the group, since the former support the therapeutic process in ways that the latter do not.   Third, it points to interventions which can be expected to support useful therapeutic experiences for the various individuals in the group in specific ways.

Composition.   Morton A. Lieberman and I, in our book "Psycho-therapy through the Group Process" argued that potentially useful compositions are those which are heterogenous with regard to preferred defence and preferred affective mode and at the same time homogeneous with regard to what we called "level of vulnerability". These preferences with regard to composition can be understood in group focal conflict terms.   If there is substantial variation in level of vulnerability then some persons will need to operate on restrictive solutions far longer than others and will either be damaged by being pulled along by the others into areas which they cannot yet handle (their own needed defences or required solutions over-ridden) or else they will continually interfere with the establishment of enabling solutions for which the rest of the group is ready.   The group gets out of balance with respect to the pace at which patients can move toward establishing enabling solutions: some persons get hurt; some get held back.   With respect to

Supporting therapeutic experiences for individuals.   A
therapist who has built up a reasonable picture of the persons in
his group in nuclear/focal conflict terms and who tries to be in
touch with the evolving group focal conflict is in a position to
realize when something is happening in the group which may be of
special significance to particular patients.   If he knows or
suspects that an individual is terrified when witnessing a quarrel
he can ask directly "How did you feel when Fred and Sue were
quarreling just now?"   Or he could make a general observation
with that person and others in mind: "Fred and Sue seemed to be
just as angry as they can get just a little while ago.   I am
wondering how all this felt to them and to others".   Such interventions are based on hypotheses about likely resonances between
the individual nuclear/focal conflict and the group focal conflict.
They seek to call to the attention of individual patients the
possibility that reactive fears are unrealistic, exaggerated or
inappropriate to the current situation.   Experiencing and seeing
this is a corrective emotional experience and is the route to being
able to relinquish unwanted or dysfunctional personal solutions.

Note that elaborate interpretations are not necessarily required.
There seems to be a widespread view amongst group psychotherapists
that interpretations, and the deeper the better, are the preferred
form of intervention.   If properly timed, such interpretations can
certainly be useful, but if interpretations are at all premature
they can lead patients to feel "the therapist is on to us, be
careful", or "he is criticizing us".   In terms of the group focal
conflict model, existing reactive fears may be intensified or new
ones stirred up.   If this happens the group is likely to establish
some restrictive solution, a move which works against the therapeutic
process.   Such risks are lessened if the therapist proceeds by
steps which stay fairly close to the material of the session, such
that the patients themselves come to do the work of confronting
their impulses and fears and making their own interpretations.

One final point: adopting this model does not mean that the
therapist always directs his comments to the group and never to the
individual (I find this to be a common misunderstanding).   In the
first place, classifying interventions according to target sets up
an artificial distinction.   In a group, interventions focussing on
the group level are never only that but also have particular import
for specific individuals.   Conversely, interventions directed toward
one person rarely have significance for that person alone, but mean
something to others and to the group as a whole.   Sometimes it is
appropriate to direct a comment to the group as a whole, as when one
is trying to encourage all those present to examine shared fears, or
when one judges that a direct statement to the person one has in mind
would be excessively threatening.   Sometimes it is appropriate to

heterogeneity of preferred defences and affective mode, consider what
is likely to happen if these are the same: if <u>everyone</u> flees from
conflict, then everyone supports everyone else in establishing shared
solutions which preclude explorations in this area.   If everyone is
fearful of closeness, then a shared solution involving mutual withdrawal becomes established quickly, and there is no one in the group
amongst the patients who can take the risk of approaching others.
This matters on two grounds: first, if restrictive solutions of
whatever character become firmly established in the group, then the
group is bound to have limited value.   The boundaries within which
exploration can occur are too narrow and too much is ruled out.
Second, not enough collision will take place amongst the patients;
not enough contrast is represented in the composition.   If such is
the case, challenges to preferred personal solutions will not occur;
demonstrations that one need not be afraid of anger, or jealousy, or
whatever, will not occur.   So, a group focal conflict model provides
theoretical support for the notion that composition is important and
suggests guidelines for the therapist who is at the stage of composing
a group.

   <u>Encouraging the establishment and maintenance of enabling rather
than restrictive solutions.</u>   To avoid misunderstanding I must mention
that maintaining a sense of safety in a group is of overriding
importance.   If patients do not feel minimally safe in a group they
can be expected to do little other than flee or render the group
innocuous.   As already suggested, groups can be expected to start
by operating on restrictive solutions and are likely to return to
them from time to time.   Yet in general it is in the patients' best
interests that the group comes to operate on enabling solutions as
soon as possible and for as much of its time as possible.   Lieberman
and I argued that the best way to influence the group toward
relinquishing restrictive solutions is usually not to attack the
solution directly but to encourage the diminution of reactive fears.
A therapist who monitors, internally, the group's state with respect
to prevailing shared group focal conflicts and solutions will have
some sense of what it is that is feared.   With this in mind he can
look for openings to alleviate fears.   There are many possibilities.
He can state directly his own feelings and intentions ("I intend to
stick with this group no matter what").   He can call to the patients'
attention events which have actually occurred and which if explicitly
recognized would show the needlessness of their fears ("When John got
angry just now no one jumped on him").   He can encourage the group
to acknowledge and explore and test their fears ("What would happen
if someone criticized someone else in this group?").   I am of course
offering only a few illustrative suggestions.   Much more could be
said about the range of situations which may occur, types of interventions, and the grounds on which a therapist should, for the moment,
leave well enough alone (in the interests of safety) and not intervene
at all.

direct a comment to the group as a whole, as when one is trying to
encourage all those present to examine shared fears, or when one
judges that a direct statement to the person one has in mind would
be excessively threatening.   Sometimes it is appropriate to direct
a statement to an individual patient, as when one judges it may be
crucial to underline and name features of a corrective emotional
experience.

Research, Theory and Practice

When working with groups one becomes curious about certain
aspects of them and may wish to investigate these through systematic
research.   One hopes that the research will prove to be relevant
both to theory-building and to practice.   Two research efforts come
to mind as examples:

While working in an in-patient setting some colleagues and I
noticed that in several groups episodes occurred in which a particular
patient became the focus of attention.   During such times the others
spent substantial time trying to persuade him that he felt or believed
something that he clearly did not feel or believe, or that he should
behave in some way other than the way he was behaving.   A study was
undertaken which systematically examined several such episodes in
terms of the behaviour of the person concerned, the circumstances
under which he came to occupy this special position, how others
successively responded to him, and the consequences for the person
and the group.   (Stock, Whitman and Lieberman, 1958).   The findings
showed that such persons held to their positions in the face of
considerable pressure from others, and that in the end the group
often yielded by changing its views about what was acceptable.   In
terms of theory, the findings suggested that a group could become
engaged in periods of "solutional conflict", where most were pressing
for the establishment of a particular shared solution while one person
resisted.   The study also pointed to one form of resonance between
group and individual, in which a group solution could threaten an
essential personal solution.   From a practice point of view it
showed that such episodes could benefit a group by forcing a move
toward a more enabling solution.   It also showed that such episodes
could be utilized for the benefit of the individual by pressing into
awareness the nature of the preferred personal solution, why it was
experienced as so important to retain and how it might have become
established in the primary family.

Another study was sparked by an interest in how it is that some
patients seem to benefit substantially from the therapeutic
experience whilst others benefit little.   Four patients who were
members of the same therapy group (two high-gain, two low-gain) were
followed closely through their group experience.   For both of the
high-gain patients, episodes could be identified which constituted

corrective emotional experiences. For one of the patients this was
accompanied by indications of insight; for the other, not.
Preparatory work leading up to the corrective emotional experience
could be seen to occur, as could subsequent working through.
(Whitaker, 1964). From the point of view of building theory the
study suggested that insight may be an integral feature of the
corrective emotional experience for some persons but not others.
It also demonstrated how group-level phenomena could trigger such
critical experiences for individuals. From a practice point of view
the study might sensitize practitioners to the rather subtly expressed working-toward processes which seem to precede corrective
emotional experiences.

In what they regard as worth investigating and in how they choose
to investigate it, researchers are influenced both by their experiences as practitioners and by the theoretical models which they use
in thinking about their experiences. For example, practitioner one
might become concerned about early drop-outs. Group focal conflict
theory suggests that persons may be likely to drop out when insufficient levels of safety exist in a group or where (to put it
another way) early solutions are sensed as potentially undermining
of essential personal solutions. Such might occur either in consequence of the composition of the group or of how the therapist
handled events during the early sessions. The flow of events during
early sessions and the position of individuals with respect to them
could be examined systematically. To take another example: every
therapist has the experience of realizing that some of his interventions seem exactly right while others have consequences other than
those intended. Theory suggests that interventions could be classified according to how they are located within evolving group focal
conflicts, and how they pertain to resonances between group and individual focal conflicts. The consequences of different kinds of
interventions could be identified. Such studies can be expected both
to expand theory and feed in to practice.

In this paper I shall refer only briefly to procedures which can
be employed in research. One such is a scheme for assessing the
"affective message" of successive comments in a group and from this
identifying and characterizing larger units of interaction (Stock
and Lieberman, 1964). This procedure has been used to identify initial and later personal repertories of affective behaviour and interpersonal instigators of and responses to affective behaviour. When
applied to the therapist, it can identify features of a therapist's
style, and the interpersonal events to which he is and is not inclined to respond. For getting at other aspects of individual behaviour or perception content analysis, adjective check-lists and
Q-sorts have been employed. The best procedure found to date for
formulating events in group focal conflict terms has been to specify
as explicitly as possible the steps involved and the nature of
supporting evidence (Stock and Lieberman, 1962). In general, method

should follow purpose, and once purposes are defined, methods can be
found or invented. The above should be taken only as examples.

                        *   *   *   *   *

     There are many routes to model-building. In this case the nuclear
conflict/focal conflict model as applied to persons had been developed
by Thomas French from his clinical experience with patients in
psychoanalysis. Once the idea emerged of testing the possible
application of this model to groups, the next step was a long series
of seminars in which tapes and protocols of group therapy sessions
were examined in detail in the light of French's model. Those
principally concerned in these seminars were Dr. French, Dr. Roy M.
Whitman, Morton A. Lieberman and Dorothy Stock Whitaker. This group
soon became convinced of the potential usefulness of the model as
applied to groups, and began to see that certain modifications and
extensions were required. It was only after this essentially
clinical approach to model-building was well under way that systematic
research began to be undertaken and bit by bit led to further
elaboration of the model.

Stock, D. and Lieberman, M.A. (1962) "Methodological Issues in the
        Assessment of Total-Group Phenomena in Group Therapy"
        International Journal of Group Psychotherapy, 12, 312-325.
Stock, D. and Lieberman, M.A. (1964) "Assessing Interpersonal
        Behaviour in Group Therapy" Perceptual and Motor Skills,
        18, 763-764.
Stock, D., Whitman, R.M., and Lieberman, M.A. (1958) "The Deviant
        Member in Therapy Groups" Human Relations, 11, 341-372.
Whitaker, D.S. (1964) "The Processes by which Change Occurs and the
        Role of Insight" Paper presented at the Sixth International
        Congress of Psychotherapy, London. Psychother. Psychosom.
        13: 126-141 (1965).
Whitaker, D. and Lieberman, M.A. Psychotherapy through the Group
        Process New York: Atherton Press, and London: Tavistock
        Press.
Whitman, R.M., Lieberman, M.A. and Stock, D., (1960) "The Relation
        between Individual and Group Conflicts in Psychotherapy"
        International Journal of Group Psychotherapy, 10, 259-286
Whitman, R.M. and Stock, D. (1958) "The Group Focal Conflict",
        Psychiatry, 21, 269-76. Reprinted in S. Scheidlinger,
        (ed.), Psychoanalytic Group Dynamics: Basic Readings
        New York: International Universities Press, 1980.

INDIVIDUAL BEHAVIOR, GROUP AND ORGANIZATIONAL PROCESSES:

AN APPLICATION OF A PRELIMINARY MODEL*

Siv Boalt Boëthius

Department of Psychology, University of Stockholm

S-113 85 Stockholm, Sweden

Group activities have always formed an integral part of
human life. Working in a group is generally regarded as both
stimulating and rewarding but it also poses certain problems. In
a group situation the thoughts, feelings and actions of individual
members are influenced by a number of factors inherent in the
structure of the group and in the task of the group. Some of
these factors can make individual members inhibited, bored or
anxious, thus preventing them from using their full capacity.
Other factors will increase the performance of some members.

When members in a group become deskilled the efficiency of
the group work may decrease. A lack of efficiency can often be
related to inhibition processes. Therefore it is important to
study inhibition systematically but also to screen processes which
lead to constructive behavior and allow the individual to use his
full capacity. Theoretically these phenomena have been dealt with
both for psychotherapeutic groups in terms of, e.g., resistance
and oppression (Bion, 1961; Gustafson & Cooper, 1979), and work
organizations in terms of efficiency (Tubbs, 1978; Zander, 1977).

Previous studies on individual reactions in groups suggest
that individuals seek stimulation and want to behave construc-
tively. It seldom happens that people prevent each other or that
they destroy a group discussion on purpose. A constructive behavior in a group implies a balance between gratification of personal wishes, e.g., to talk, ask questions or give suggestions,

---

*This study was supported by grants from the Bank of Sweden
 Tercentenary Foundation and the Swedish Work Environment Fund.

and the coordination of this activity with other members in the
group. In order to function well the individual has to be able
to express his thoughts and ideas. If an individual holds back
too much he feels inhibited. Previous studies (Zander, 1977) have
shown that members hold back because they are apprehensive about
being disapproved by others. The apprehension is more frequent,
if the things they hold back are unpleasant for other members and
if they are deviant from the established views of the group.
Another cause for constrained participation is when tension
among members is high.

Previous investigations on group activity have been concerned
with analyses of whole groups or organizations disregarding the
characteristics' of the individual members. A number of studies
are based on theories in social psychological or organizational
theory. Their aim has been to investigate interaction processes
in small groups such as problem solving and group cohesion (Bales,
1970; Hare, 1976), or organizational processes such as effects of
different types of leadership and formal and informal structures
in organizations (Katz & Kahn, 1978; Schein, 1970; Zander, 1977).
Other studies are based on group analytic theory and have been
focused on unconscious processes influencing the work in groups
(Bion, 1961; Whitaker & Lieberman, 1964) or in organizations
(Menzies, 1970; Rice, 1970).

In order to study inhibition and stimulation it is necessary
to study both the behavior of the individual and the behavior of
the group. The analysis of the individual member is necessary in
order to find out when and how he is inhibited. The analysis of
the group has to be done in order to assess processes which cause
the inhibition in the individual. If the group is a part of a
larger system as in the case of most work groups it is also necessary to analyze organizational processes directly related to the
conditions for work in the group.

The present study describes reactions of inhibition and
stimulation for individual group members in relation to group and
organizational processes. A preliminary model is formulated in
a psychoanalytic and an interactionistic frame of reference. The
model is then applied to four group situations which were video-
taped. The analysis of individual behavior was performed with
the aid of interviews and observations of manifest behavior in
terms of coping and defense. The analysis of group behavior was
performed according to a modified version of Bion's (1961) model
for describing group processes. The analysis of organizational
processes was done with the aid of interviews. In the following
the model and some preliminary results are presented.

A preliminary model

The behavior of an individual member is determined by the interplay between the personalities of different members in a group and the group situation (Endler & Magnusson, 1974). In order to describe the behavior of a group member it is necessary to study the individual member, the group situation including the organizational setting to which the group belongs and the interaction between these factors.

The individual member. The interaction between the individual and the group situation implies that individual members interpret the situation in relation to personal motives and situational demands. The interpretation of the situation differs between members in the same group situation and is a function of (1) the selection of cues, on which the perception of the situation is based, (2) the goals, (3) the strategies the member formulates and finally (4) the actions he undertakes in order to reach his goals (c.f. Björkman, 1978)

The concepts of situation perception, strategies and actions are relevant for describing each member. By asking members in the group to describe their interpretation of various aspects of the group, it is possible (1) to get their situation perceptions, strategies and actions, and (2) to relate the differences in situation perception for the individual members to the degree of distality or degree of physical or emotional distance to the situation (Björkman, 1978).

The group. A group is defined as "a number of individuals with a common task who interact in an attempt to influence one another" (Tubbs, 1978, p. 7). In the present article the group situation is defined as the total situation of a group thus interacting. A group situation is known to be characterized by two properties: task activity or work and social or emotional activity. A large amount of theoretical and experimental work has demonstrated that these two aspects of group activity must be present for optimal function. Indeed, it seems impossible, e.g., to have groups which produce only work and allow no time for emotional behavior (Bales, 1970; Bion, 1961; Hare, 1976).

The organization. An organization can be defined as "the rational coordination of activities of a number of people for the achievement of some common explicit purpose or goal, through the division of labour and function, and through a hierarchy of authority and responsibility" (Schein, 1979, p. 9). Processes of interest for the present study are the effect of explicit and implicit goals, the hierarchical structure of the organization and "norms" associated with these factors.

Methods

The study was performed on four small groups with members
employed at day care centers for children. The group members all
worked in the same organizational setting. In one group (no.1)
the members did not know each other before the discussion while
the other groups were staff groups that previously had worked regularly together (see table 1).

Table 1. Description of the groups.

| Group | Size | Sex | | Age | Prof. training | | | Employment time in years | |
		F	M	Range	1	2	3	Actual inst.	Total time
1	5	4	1	28-55	3	2	-	1/2-4	4-10
2	5	5	-	25-40	2	2	1	1/4-4	1-10
3	4	4	-	20-50	1	3	-	1/4-4	1/4-12
4	3	3	1	20-40	1	1	1	1-3	1-3

1 = preschool teacher
2 = nurse
3 = no formal training

In order to observe manifest behavior, group discussions
during one to two hours were videotaped. The task in group 1, was
to discuss how to introduce new children in a day care center.
Group 2, 3 and 4 had planning discussions (group 2 discussed planning for Lucia, a traditional festural, group 3 a meeting with the
parents of the children and group 4 preparation for Christmas.)

The behavior in the groups was categorized during three observation periods during ten minutes in the beginning, middle and
the end of the discussion. Individual activity, coping reactions
and defensive reactions were judged according to a category system
based on a method described by Haan (1977). By coping is meant
reactions which "involve purpose, choice and flexible shift, adhere
to intersubjective reality and logic and allow and enhance propor-
tionate affective expression". Defensive reactions are defined as
reactions which are "compelled", negating, rigid, distorting of
intersubjective reality and logic, allow covert impulse expression
and embody the expectancy that anxiety can be relieved without
directly addressing the problem" (Haan, 1977, p. 134).

The behavior in the group as a whole was judged with the aid
of a category system based on a modified version of Bion's (1961)
model. For the judgement of manifest behavior we used three
categories of "work". A high degree of work was characterized by

three conditions: (1) the members in the group were concentrating on the task, (2) their activity was co-ordinated and (3) the general climate in the group was creative. A medium degree of work was characterized by the first two conditions, and a low degree of work the first condition only.

Emotionally oriented manifest behavior was classified according to the following four categories: dependency, fight, flight and pairing, according to Thelen's (1959) definitions. A fifth category, splitting, included projection of feelings which could not be contained by individual members (Bion, 1961).

All participants were interviewed before and after the group discussions. The interviews were recorded. The pre-interviews aimed at getting information about the formal and informal organization of the daily work within the staff group and about the working situation of individual members. The post-interviews aimed at information about how the participants had felt and reacted during the videotaped discussions. The content of the post-interviews was analyzed in respect to a) situation perception, b) strategies and c) action propensity and action.

By situation perception was meant judgements of "objective" and "subjective" circumstances in the situation, such as reports about the content of the discussion and feelings connected to this content. The strategies or intentions individual members formulated in order to reach certain goals were categorized in terms of approach or avoidance, and either as coping or defense, indicating the degree of rationality. Approach strategies are directed towards a situation, e.g. trying to get the group to continue with a task. Avoidance strategies aim at avoiding certain situations. An example of an avoidance strategy is the intention to withhold information which could prolong a discussion. The third category action propensity/action was defined as actions the individual reported he had performed and impulses to actions which had been withheld.

A detailed study was done on three episodes in each group session using the technique of stimulated recall. This technique implies that individual members together with the interviewer study and discuss some parts of a recorded session. However, the results from this study are not reported here.

The general procedure for group 2, 3 and 4 is shown in Fig. 1. Due to the fact that the members in group 1 had not met before the group discussion, the information about the project and their task was given individually. Otherwise all groups followed the same procedure as outlined below.

Week		Procedures	Collected data
1	Preparation	Recruiting of groups	
2		Confirmation of groups	
4		Information I	
5		Information II	
6		Videorecording	
7-9	Research phase	Pre-interview	Personal data Working conditions General experiences of groups
9		Group work	Behavior observations of individuals and of the group
		Post-interview	Introspective data concerning the group
		Stimulated recall	Individual comments to the episodes on the videotape Behavior observations of individuals and of the group
34	Follow up	Feed back of the results to the groups	
35-38		Individual interviews	
39		Group discussion	

Fig. 1. Design for groups 2, 3 and 4.

Results

The results for observational data were analyzed according to manifest behavior of (a) individuals, (b) the group and (c) comparison between individuals and group behavior. Introspective data were analyzed according to (a) situation perception, (b) strategies and (c) action propensity and action.

Observation of manifest behavior of individuals. Coping and defense reactions were observed for all members during the group discussions. Common coping reactions were to give support, to release tension by joking, to ask direct questions and to express opinions openly. The most prominent defense reactions were a marked indirect way of talking and listening to each other (e.g., manifested in indirect questions), withdrawal and preoccupation with details.

The typical individual reaction during the first part of the
group discussion was characterized by more coping than defense in
all groups except group 1 (where there were more defense than
coping reactions). In the middle of the discussion the members of
group 1 had shifted to more coping than defense while the others
showed the opposite pattern. Towards the end of the discussion
the members of all groups except group 4 showed more coping than
defense (see Table 2).

Observed manifest behavior of the group. The observation
periods categorized as work oriented were slightly more than those
categorized as emotionally oriented or both work and emotionally
oriented. The first period, the beginning of the discussion, was
categorized as work oriented in all groups. Two groups (no.1 and
no. 3) functioned on a fairly good level; they were concentrated on
the task and the activity in the groups was well coordinated. The
other two groups (no. 2 and no.4) were categorized as work oriented
but on a lower level since they were ambitious but lacked coordination. Towards the middle of the discussions, all groups had shifted
to more emotionally oriented activity and two groups (no.2 and no.
3) shifted towards the end of the discussion back to work oriented
activity. The two groups (no.1 and no.4) who retained an emotionally oriented activity ahd shifted type of emotional orientation
or were about to do it (see Table 2).

Observed group and individual behavior. A comparison between
individual behavior, in terms of coping and defence, and behavior in
the group as a whole, in terms of work an emotionality, showed that
there were no distinct relations between the amount of coping reactions and the degree of work in the group. Individuals with dominating coping reactions, e.g., outnumber individuals with dominating defence reactions both under more work oriented and more emotionally oriented activity (see Table 2).

Introspective data. The analysis of introspective data includes the way individual members perceived the group, the strategies they formulated and their reported manifest and latent actions.
The analysis of individual interpretation of the group was based on
two types of situation descriptions. The first concerned general
descriptions of the group, based on questions about the atmosphere
in the group, the work with the task, the relations in the group,
the degree of "individual autonomy" and effects of the research
situation. The second contained more detailed descriptions of the
group, based on specific situations that individual members perceived as crucial for their judgement of the group and their own
behavior.

Analysis of the general descriptions showed that the answers
from the members in three groups (no 1, 2 and 4) were very similar
within each group. In groups 1 and 4 all members were very positive

about most aspects of the grcup work, whereas in group 2 questions about the way the group started to work and how they solved their problem were met by all participants with similar and rather nega- tive reactions. The members of group 3 did not follow this general pattern. Instead all members gave individualized and different accounts of their experiences.

Table 2. Individual behavior and group behavior.

Phase	I		II		III	
Judgement	Individual	Group	Individual	Group	Individual	Group
group 1	$c < d$	W_m	$c > d$	$E_{Bfl}\ E_s$	$c > d$	E_{BP}
group 2	$c > d$	W_l	$c < d$	$W_l E_{Bf} E_s$	$c > d$	$E_{Bfk}\ W_l$
group 3	$c > d$	W_m	$c < d$	$W_l\ E_{Bd}$	$c > d$	W_m
group 4	$c > d$	W_l	$c = d$	$W_l\ E_{Bd}$	$c < d$	$E_{Bd}(E_{Bf})$

c   coping
d   defense
W   work (m medium, l low)
E   emotionality (B basic assumption, d dependency, f fight,
                  fl flight, p pairing, s splitting)

When the members were asked to give detailed descriptions based on specific situations the previous consensus of groups 1 and 4 vanished completely. Instead each member gave a personal and char- acteristic description, the general tenor of which varied according to the member's personality and position in the group. Group 2 showed a somewhat similar pattern but less pronounced. Group 3 which had displayed a lack of consensus already when giving the general description of the group retained this pattern also for the detailed descriptions.

Analysis of the detailed descriptions was done in terms of situation perception, strategies and action propensity/action and showed that all members in the groups had used different situations as cues to build their judgements. The situations each person had chosen as cues were interwoven in such a way as to give a coherent and, from a personal point of view, understandable and meaningful picture of the group discussion. (For an illustration of detailed descriptions of the group given by individual members in one group, group 2, see Table 3).

Table 3. Detailed descriptions of the group situation (group 2)

Frida	Gunnel	Hanna	Inga	Jonna
Felt unsatisfied with the work in the group. Thought the planning was loose and not thought through. Found the discussion about whether one should have wine or not for the party was unsatisfactory. Felt inflexible and obstinate and that much of the discussion took part between her and two of the others, the rest were fairly silent. Did not like that so few said what they really thought but instead alluded to other sectors and persons. (Judgement negative).	Felt fairly pleased with the discussion and thought they had done a good job. Thought the discussion had been a bit vague but otherwise good. Found herself and others free to say what they wanted, but that Frida as usual had been able to express herself more freely than the others. (Judgement positive).	Did not think that the work in the group was sufficient for a final plan but might do for a rough one. Thought Gunnel and Frida were the most active members and that Frida was as dominant as usual. Did not bring forward her own opinions concerning for instance whether or not to have wine. Felt that she now, as frequently before, got into a defensive position and had difficulties making herself understood. At the same time she felt overwhelmed by the arguments and opinions of the others. (Judgement in between).	Felt disappointed with the discussion. Found the discussion dull but that they were more concentrated than otherwise and would have preferred a more careful planning. Thought the interaction was the usual one dominated by Frida and Gunnel. Inga felt herself to be rather unimportant and that some of the participants at times talked as if she was not there. (Judgement negative).	Thought the discussion was more to the point than otherwise but that most people brought up unimportant matters. She felt off key and uninterested and thought the others were in the same mood. Found the arguments about the wine too lengthy but that the result was good. She did not dare to participate in the discussion herself but was satisfied that the majority shared her opinion. Was disturbed by her impression that Frida was in a bad mood. (Judgement in between).

Table 3 shows how individual members saw the group situation.
Two members (Frida and Inga) felt disappointed with the group discussion whereas one (Gunnel) was satisfied. The remaining two
(Hanna and Jonna) were somewhat ambivalent. Those who were dis-
satisfied were so for different reasons. Frida was angry and
irritated with herself because she had lost her temper and with
the others because they had been too silent. Inga felt that she
was unimportant in the group and that no one listened to her.

The individual members had formulated different strategies in
relation to their work in the groups. The result showed that
avoidance strategies (n = 37) were more common than approach strategies (n = 25). Nearly all approach strategies were coping oriented and the majority of avoidance strategies were defensive. The
most common avoidance strategies were to avoid criticism, confrontations and quarrels (19%), to avoid dominating behavior, taking responsibility or leadership (11%), and avoiding over-involvement (10%).
The most common approach strategies were to remain with the task and
to focus on the discussion (10%) and to give suggestions, to take
notes and to be helpful (8%).

For reported manifest and latent activity in terms of action
propensity/action, the result showed the opposite tendency. Approach
activity (n = 49) was more common than avoidance activity (n = 37)
in the reports in all groups except in group 2 where the amounts of
approach and avoidance activity were equal. About two-thirds of the
approach activity was coping oriented. The rest was defensive
activity. The most common approach activities were to remain with
the task (10%), to be active and give suggestions (10%) and to wait
for and link up with others (7%). The most common avoidance activities were to withhold criticism and irritation (10%) and to hold
back opinions and thoughts (7%).

The analysis of organizational processes, which was based on
interview data, showed that most members found the goals of the work
in day care centers difficult to define and unco-ordinated. They
also perceived the job demands as high and at the same time diffuse.
As to the organization of staff groups it was clearly demonstrated
that the members perceived contradictions in the way they were expected to work. On one hand the groups were composed of persons
with different levels of professional training indicating a clear
hierarchical order. On the other hand the instruction for the staff
was that everybody should do the same job, regardless of differences
in training and experiences. Several pre-school teachers reported
that they felt as if they "hid extra knowledge" they had obtained,
in order not to be criticized by other members in the group.

Discussion

The present study aimed at describing manifestation of inhibition and stimulation in small groups and to try to explain these
reactions in terms of psychological theory.   Manifestations of inhibition and stimulation were analyzed for individual members in
terms of coping and defense and for the group in terms of work and
emotionality.   Observations of manifest behavior of individual members showed that there were slightly more coping than defense reactions in most groups and that the behavior in the group as a whole
tended to be more work oriented than emotionally oriented in two
groups and vice versa in two groups.   A comparison between observed individual behavior and the group behavior showed that there
was no distinct relationship between, e.g., the amount of coping
behavior and the degree of working orientation in a group.   On the
contrary, a good level of work in the group as a whole could be
combined with defense behavior for single members, and emotionally
oriented phases contained a substantial proportion of individual
coping behavior.

As to the second question, why individuals become inhibited
or stimulated in a small group, reactions of inhibition and stimulation were related to the way individual members judged the group
situation. The way individuals saw the group was categorized in
three categories: situation perception, strategies and action
propensity/action. As for the individuals'perspectives on the group
discussions there was a marked tendency for the members to answer
in the same way about how they perceived the group discussions on a
general level. This tendency was valid for the three groups where
there are reasons to believe that the members had felt insecure
with each other (groups no. 1, 2 and 4). In the fourth group (group
3) whose members declared that they had felt fairly accepted by each
other, all members gave different, personally relevant and coherent
descriptions of the group work already on the general level. These
results support the findings reported by Zander (1977).

When individual members were asked to give more detailed descriptions of their groups, there were no longer any similarities between members in the same group. All members in the four groups
gave different but personally relevant and coherent pictures of their
groups. Strategies they had formulated were to a large extent
different types of avoidance. When asked about their acitivty,
various kinds of approach activities were more often mentioned than
avoidance activities, but a large proportion of the approach activity
was defense oriented.

The analysis of how the individuals saw the organisation showed
that the nature of the work involved in fostering other people's
children and the organization of sub-groups within the staff in-

volved problems that could be related to inhibition and stimulation.

The results of this study show that the methods and concepts
which were suggested for relating individual behavior to processes
in a group within an organization can be used for analysis of the
problems outlined above.   As has been pointed out by some authors
(e.g., Ekehammar, 1974), a disadvantage with using different concepts for describing the individual and the group situation is that
predictions and comparisons between the two systems become more
difficult.   Although this is relevant from a methodological point
of view, the use of the same concept implies a risk of underesti-
mating the complexity of the processes involved.   Both methods are
therefore needed in order to approach this complex area.

Three aspects of the result will be discussed in this paper.
The first one concerns the lack of distinct relations between the
amount of individual coping reactions and the degree of work in
the group.   It seems that for a group to function effectively, it
is not sufficient that its members are concentrated on the task,
thereby exhibiting coping behavior.   In addition, individual members have to exert a certain degree of co-operation and their
strivings have to be directed towards roughly the same goal. Some
capacity to express aggression and to deal with anxiety and conflict is also needed.   The present groups did not achieve this.   On
the individual level most members were ambitious and concentrated
on their task, but they did not communicate effectively with each
other nor did they co-ordinate their activity towards a common goal.
We explain this as an expression of a dominating wish for individual
members to establish their own identity in the group rather than to
develop the task of the group.   This wish was manifested in the
interaction, in dominance of others, submission in the form of
seeking support and acceptance, or as withdrawal.

The second point concerns the tendency to conform to what individual members had thought would be the accepted behavior in the
group and consequently also a general tendency of avoidance.   It
was evident that pronounced forms of this general behavioral pattern
only occured in those groups where the members felt insecure and
defensive.   In addition, all groups demonstrated a general inclination to avoid situations which could evoke aggression or
criticism and tended to withhold a large part of their ideas, thoughts
and feelings.   The interview data suggest that the members held
open disputes in such abhorrence that they would often not express
their opinions or try to get support for their point of views.   It
thus seems that when divergent intentions, strategies and goals inherent in a group cannot be expressed or dealt with openly a group
has problems with inhibition.   Inhibition in the groups was manifested e.g., through tendencies to get stuck in very detailed discussions about unimportant matters and through difficulties in
keeping at work.

The third point concerns the nature of the work in a day care center which makes staff members especially vulnerable to inhibition and stimulation.   The unstructured goals for the work and the high and at the same time diffuse demands on the staff made it difficult to evaluate good job performance.   The strong conforming tendencies, that means strong wishes to feel accepted, could be one way for members in insecure groups to compensate for the above mentioned work aspects.   The wish to be accepted was also manifested in the denial of differences in personal skill due to professional training.   Staff members with more professional training than the majority of members in a group, tended to withhold their extra knowledge, which meant that a lot of competence was unused.   The members showed a general trend to adapt their behavior to a kind of "minimal common denominator".   The same type of phenomenon has been reported by Yalom (1970). He describes how individual members in psychotherapy groups tend to adapt their behavior to the member with the lowest tolerance of anxiety, thus preventing the group from working efficiently.

The demonstrated strong tendency to conform to what was believed to be the most acceptable way of behaving, and thereby to restrict one's personality to a limited sector, has implications, e.g., in relation to the use of group interpretations (Bion, 1961). As has been argued by Gustafson & Cooper (1979), it seems reasonable to assume that there are usually fairly large discrepancies in personal strategies and goals between the members in a group. If the group is confronted with a group interpretation which assumes that all members have the same intentions and wishes, it will inhibit the creativity and curiosity of some members and thus also the development of the group.   The kind of group interpretations which seem to be helpful are those where differences in goals and strategies can be recognised and yet related to each other in a way which allows for the variations in situation perceptions, strategies and actions which are manifested in the group.

REFERENCES

Bales, R.F. Personality and Interpersonal Behavior.   Holt
      Rinehart & Winston, New York (1970).

Bion, W.R. Experiences in Groups and Other Papers.   Tavistock
      Publications, London (1961)

Björkman, M. Ekologisk psykologi.   Almqvist & Wiksell Förlag AB,
      Stockholm (1978)

Ekehammar, B.   Interactionism in personality from a historical
        perspective. Psychological Bulletin. 81:1026-1048 (1974).

Endler, N.S., and Magnusson, D. Interactionism, trait psychology,
        psychodynamics, and situationism.   Reports from the
        Psychological Laboratories, the University of Stockholm,
        Stockholm (1974).

Gustafson, J.P., and Cooper, L. Unconscious Planning in Small
        Groups. Human Relations. 32:1039-1064 (1979).

Haan, N., Coping and Defending. Academic Press. Inc. New York (1977).

Hare, A.P. Handbook of Small Group Research (Second Edition).   Free
        Press, New York (1976).

Harre, R., and Secord, P.F. The Explanation of Social Behaviour
        Basil Blackwell, Oxford (1972).

Katz, D., and Kahn, R.L. The Social Psychology of Organizations
        2ed. John Wiley & Sons, Inc., New York (1978).

Menzies, I.E.P. The Functioning of Social Systems as a Defence
        Against Anxiety. The Tavistock Institute of Human Relations
        (1970).

Rice, A.K. Individual, Group and Intergroup Processes.   Human
        Relations. 22:565-584 (1970).

Schein, E.H. Organizational Psychology. Prentice-Hall, Inc.,
        Englewood Cliffs, New Jersey (1970).

Thelen, H.A. Work-emotionality theory of the group as organism.
        In S. Koch (Ed), Psychology: a study of a science, McGraw
        Hill, New York (1959)

Tubbs, S.L. A systems approach to small group interaction.
        Addison-Wesley Publishing Company, London (1978)

Whitaker, D. Stock and Lieberman, M.A. Psychotherapy through the
        group process. Prentice-Hall, New York (1964)

Zander, A. Groups at work. Jossey-Bass Publishers, London (1977)

Yalom, I.D. The Theory and Practice of Group Psychotherapy.
        Basic Books, Inc., New York (1970).

GROUP PERSONALITY AND GROUP BEHAVIOR: AN EXPANSION OF BION'S MODEL

Bengt-Åke Armelius, Ph.D.

Department of Applied Psychology

University of Umeå, S-901 87 Umeå, Sweden

PURPOSE AND POINT OF DEPARTURE

The purpose of this paper is to present some methods for study-ing some aspects of group personality and some ideas about determi-nants of the culture of a group. The research project is inspired by Bion's ideas about groups and we will use the concepts he has described. In particular we feel that his descriptions of the group culture in terms of basic assumptions fight, flight, dependency and pairing in addition to the work aspect are useful. We will use these terms as our descriptive concepts throughout the paper. We will focus on two questions in this paper.

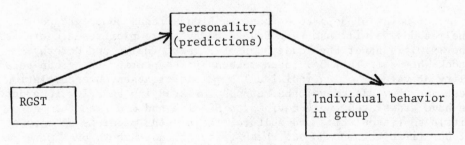

Figure 1. Schematic illustration of prediction of group behavior.

The first is concerned with individual behavior in groups and our aim is to formulate a theory of group personality that allows

prediction of group behavior in different types of group situations.
For this purpose we have borrowed Bion's concept of valency, which
means the individuals tendency to combine with other individuals to
maintain or introduce a certain basic assumption in the group. By
means of a projective test, RGST, we formulate a picture of
group personality of a certain individual and then we make predictions about his probable group behavior. These predictions are then
compared to the actual group behavior of the same individual.

The second question we will focus on is concerned with certain
aspects of the group as a whole. We will try to look at the importance of two factors for creating a certain group culture (see Figure
2).

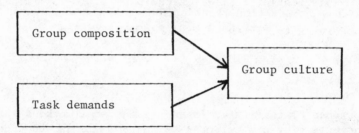

Figure 2. Group composition and task demands as determinants of
          the group culture.

The two factors are group composition or the importance of the
group personalities and the second factor is the influence of task
demands on the group culture.

Our point of departure then, is Bion's ideas about groups and
the methods we will use were developed by a group of researchers in
the 1950:ies under the leadership of Herbert Thelen and Dorothy
Stock-Whitaker. They developed methods for capturing the group personality or valency of an individual by means of a sentence completion
test and they also developed methods for studying behavior in groups.
We have translated these devises to Swedish and modified them a
little to fit our time and culture. The present paper is an account
of our first attempt to use these research instruments on a more
serious basis.

GROUP PERSONALITY

I will now go into some detail about our attempts to predict
individual behavior in a group.

Bion uses the concept valency to account for the individual's tendency to combine with other people in the group to introduce or maintain a certain basic assumption. We have modified this to mean each individual's tendency to behave in a mood characteristic of a certain basic assumption. Thus valency is a pattern of relatively stable reactions to various group situations. We think of them as historically learned reactions that may take the form of transference reactions in relation to other people. These reactions will be released by a variety of situations with a common denominator that can be described as one of the basic assumptions. The Reaction to Group Situation Test is projective in the sense that the situations described by the items are representative of a certain basic assumption and this causes the individual to respond in his typical mood. Therefore a detailed analysis of the reactions to the different test items gives a picture of the group personality. The analysis of the answers to RGST are made both quantitatively and qualitatively.

Type of situation

Type of response		Dependency	Pairing	Fight	Flight	Work
	Dependency					
	Pairing					
	Fight					
	Flight					
	Work					

Figure 3. Scoring matrix from RGST.

First, we count the number of reactions related to each basic assumption that the subject gives for each type of situation. (See Figure 3.) Then we classify the reactions according to whether they are cognitive, emotional or activity oriented. This gives us an idea about the form of the reaction and what the typical reaction will be for each basic assumption. (See Figure 4.)

The second step is to make a detailed analysis of the typical behavior within each basic assuption. Here we may find that a person is more active and comfortable in one basic assumption than in another or that he uses one basic assumption to escape from another that is more loaded with conflict or discomfort. Thus a person might prefer to operate in a pairing culture in order to

Type of situation

Type of reaction		Dependency	Pairing	Fight	Flight	Work
	Action					
	Emotion					
	Cognition					

Figure 4. Scoring of typical reactions to RGST.

avoid feelings of dependency. The last step is to form a clinical
opinion about the whole person and his probable reactions in
different group situations. These guesses about probable behavior
are translated into quantitative form by means of a Q-sort technique.
The devise for quantification was borrowed from Thelen and Stock-
Whitaker and consists of 100 items describing a piece of behavior.
Each item is keyed to one of the basic assumptions and an observer
sorts the 100 items into nine piles according to a normal frequency
distribution. The piles are arranged so that the end piles are least
and most descriptive of the person or group being studied and the
pile in the middle is considered irrelevant or neutral. This
technique is known as the Q-sort technique and allows for quantification of qualitative verbal statements about persons as well as
groups.

THE EXPERIMENT

    In order to test our possibilities for prediction of group
behavior we asked a group of five students to participate in a
small group experiment. We asked them to fill in the RGST and scored
their results according to the procedure I just described and we
ended up with a set of figures describing their probable behavior
in terms of the basic assumptions. Then we asked them to work with
certain group tasks. The first task was to rank order a list of
items to bring with them after a crash landing on the moon. This
is a group dynamic excersise called the astronauts and it is done
first individually and then by the group as a whole. The second
task was to discuss student-teacher relations based on their experience as students of psychology. The third task was to talk about
feelings and ideas about working together in this group, both here
and now and during previous tasks. We introduced a group leader for
the last task. His role was to help keep to the task and intervene
at a group level.

We expected the first task to stimulate fight tendencies in the
group and the last task to stimulate dependency, both due to the introduction of the leader and to the unstructured nature of the task.
Each task lasted for about 45 minutes and the second task was used
merely as a distractor between the first and third task. We also
used it for establishing reliability estimates and for training of
judges. The whole experiment was video-taped for later analysis. The
behavior of each subject was described for each task with the Q-sort
keyed to the various basic assumptions. Thus, we got an index of the
degree to which each person expressed the various basic assumptions
during the two tasks. This could be directly compared to our predictions based on RGST since the same Q-sort was used for both measurements. The reliability of the measurements were around .40 - .60
for the predictions and a little higher for observations of group
behavior, around .55 on the average. These are correlations between
two judges. Retest reliability after 3 months on the observations of
group behavior had an average of about .75. In summary it seems
possible to get satisfactory measurements of both personality and
observations of behavior if the judges are trained to use a common
frame of reference.

The central question now is whether the predictions of group
behavior are valid or not. The correlations between predictions and
actual behavior in the two tasks are given in table 1. As you can

Table 1. Validity; correlations between predictions and actual
behavior.

	Subject				
Task	1	2	3	4	5
1	.22	.44	.46	.10	.14
2	.26	.55	.41	.15	.04

see there is some validity in the predictions for subjects 2 and 3
and a fair amount for some of the others. These correlations are
on the item level of analysis, and a better picture is given
by the analysis on the level of basic assumption. We will now go
into some detail about that for two subjects. I will give you a
brief account of the qualitative analysis of the RGST protocol and
a short description of the actual behavior for two subjects in the
two tasks. In addition I will show you the quantitative results of
both predictions and actual behavior.

SUBJECT 2

Prediction from RGST

   This is an agreeable person who does not show very much of herself, but who supports whatever the others do. A typical dependency
person who waits for others to take the initiative. She has a lot of
valency for fight, but it is never shown in the group since it is
held at a feeling level of response. Strong conflicts over dependency.

Actual group behavior

   She is high on dependency and flight in both tasks. Shows very
little fight and does not take part in the discussions in task 1.
In task 2 the group chose her as the central person and she got

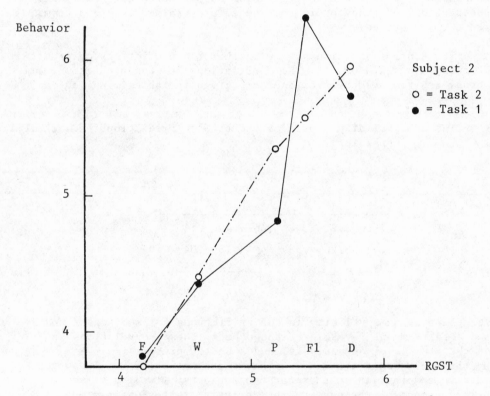

Figure 5. Behavior plotted against RGST for subject 2.

a much more active role when the group started to talk about her
silence during the group work. She agreed to this role and assured
the group that she had had a good time and that this was her typical behavior.

If we look at the figure you will see that our RGST results are
shown on the X-axis and actual group behavior on the Y-axis. We have
one curve for each task. If the predictions were perfectly correct
all observations would fall on the diagonal between the two axis.
For this person you can see that the highest scores on RGST are
Dependency and Flight, then comes Pairing, Work and Fight last. Her
behavior in the first task was mostly Flight and Dependency and in
the second task it was Dependency and Flight. This person is relatively consistent in her behavior, independently of the task. Her
activity may vary, but she always exhibits the same pattern of basic
assumptions.

The second person we will look at, subject 5, is expected to
vary her behavior dependent on the situation or task that is set
before her.

SUBJECT 5

Predictions from RGST

A person who follows others in the group. Fight and work will
dominate in task oriented groups and flight will be the modality
if the situation becomes more personally intimate. Pairing is avoided by either fight or flight. The basic conflict is with intimacy
and not dependency.

Actual group behavior

This person is high on fight and work in task 1 and shows great
interest in the task. She fights for leadership and is a dominant
person during this task. However in task 2, the dependency task she
withdraws and does not take part in the discussion. Typical flight
behavior. The degree of intimacy was very high during this task.
Especially in relation to subject 2.

If we look at the figure 6 you can see that she is high on
fight in task 1 and low on flight, in task 2 the reverse is true.
The important thing about this person is that her behavior is dependent on the task. This could be predicted althought not translated into quantitative form unless two separate Q-sorts had been
made for her. In our study 2 out of the 5 subjects behaved in this
way. Another two were consitent in what basic assumptions they
showed, but their degree of involvement or activity was different
for the two tasks (e.g. subject 2). The fifth person did not behave
in the way expected from RGST.

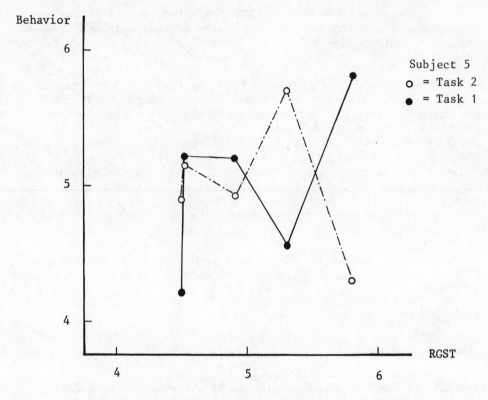

Figure 6. Behavior plotted against RGST for subject 5.

Group composition and tasks as determinants of group culture

Our next question is concerned with two possible determinants of the group culture. We define group culture as the pattern of basic assumptions that exist in the group during each task. It is measured in the same way as individual behavior in the group, i.e. by means of a set of 100 descriptive statements of the group as a whole. The statements are keyed to the various basic assumptions and are sorted into piles by observers. The reliability is about the same as for observations of individual behavior – around .55.

First we asked ourselves whether the group culture is a mirror
of the valency pattern the persons bring into the group. If this
is the case it should be possible to predict the group culture by
taking the average of the valency patterns of all individuals in the
group.

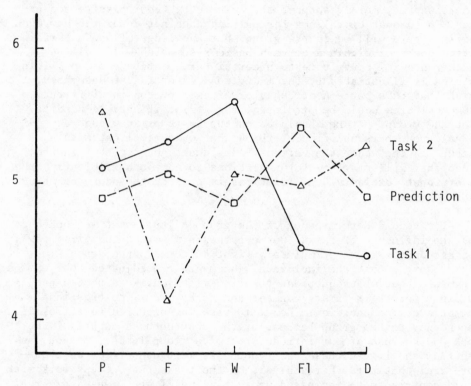

Figure 7. Group culture in the two tasks and predicted from RGST.

As you can see from this figure the valency patterns sum up to
a Flight group basically. However, in task 1 there is a strong tendency towards a fight-work group and in task 2 a pairing-dependency
group. Therefore we may conclude that the group culture is not equal
to the average of the valency patterns or the sum of the personalities in the group. Surely, it would be a most surprising result if
the personalities determined the group culture in such a simple way.
It would mean that there would be no shift in the group culture over

time or across different tasks. A more adequate role for the group
composition has been described by Bion, I think. He describes in
his writings how a certain group culture puts pressure on different
individuals to take certain roles. Thus, the fight group requires a
fighting leader etc. In this sense, the group composition can be
considered as the resources that the group has. Dependent on the
group culture that exists the behavior of each individual will vary.
Some people are more likely to act in a pairing culture than others
and these people will contribute more to that culture than the
others who may merely support the culture by their passive acceptance. The amount of valency for pairing does not determine how much
pairing there will be in the group, but knowledge of how a certain
person operates within a certain basic assumption will tell us
whether he will contribute to a certain group culture or not. This
is clearly illustrated by the individual cases I just described. I
think that this pattern of behavior of each person in different
group cultures could be predicted, but I find it hard to predict
what the group culture should be on the basis of knowledge of individual group personalities. I think that what complicates this
picture is that once the various individuals get together in the
group they will start to form relations to each other. Clearly, the
determinant of individual relations is outside the scope of this
paper.

The second determinant of the group culture that we looked at
was the influence of tasks. Our hypothesis was that the first task,
the astronauts would stimulate a fight culture in the group. The
task requires that the individual judgments are adjusted to a common
judgment about what equipment to bring with you. We expected people
to fight for their first judgment and to have difficulties in arriv-
ing at a common decision. The last task was expected to stimulate
dependency in the group because of the unstructured nature of the
task and because of our introduction of a group leader. As you can
see from the figure these two hypotheses were confirmed. We therefore feel that a further analysis of the tasks that groups work with
would contribute to increased understanding of what causes a certain
group to develop a certain group culture. The problem is to arrive
at a good typology of tasks. What dimensions should you use to describe the difference between various tasks and how should you
build a theory connecting task characteristics to actual group
processes? Our choice has been to argue that certain tasks will
stimulate certain basic assumptions, but this is not quite satisfactory since the tasks are defined by their expected influence
on the group process. We would like to have an independent classification of the tasks.

The fact that tasks are important is also illustrated by the
individual case stories. As already mentioned most individuals
changed their behavior between the two tasks. Either they changed

from active to passive or they changed their dominant basic assumption, e.g. from flight to fight. This calls for a theory of group personality that takes this interaction between behavior and tasks into account.

In conclusion, we feel that tasks are most important for what behavior a certain person will exhibit. Tasks are also powerful determinants of the group culture, yet, the research efforts that are directed towards the interaction between tasks and group phenomena and individual behavior in groups are hard to find.

REFERENCES

Bion, W. F., 1961, Experiences in groups and other papers, Tavistock, London.

Thelen, H. A., and Stock, D. S., 1954, Methods for studying work and emotionality in group operation. Unpublished paper, University of Chicago.

LARGE GROUP PERSPECTIVES

Patrick de Mare, MRCPSYCH, Consultant Psychotherapist
(rtd), St. George's Hospital, London, Founder Member
of the Institute of Group Analysis (London) and The
Group Analytic Society, and Robin Piper, Senior Social
Worker, Marlborough Hosp, London, Dip.Soc. Work Studies,
L.S.E. and Ass. Member of British Assoc. of Psychotherapy.

"The Chronicles of King Arthur relate
how King Arthur with the help of a Cornish
carpenter invented the marvel of his Court,
the miraculous Round Table at which his
Knights would never come to blows.
Formerly, because of jealousy, skirmishes,
duels and murders had set blood flowing
in the most sumptuous feasts.

"The carpenter says to Arthur: "I will
make thee a fine table, where sixteen
hundred may sit at once, and from which
none need be excluded and no knight will
be able to raise combat, for there the
highly placed will be on the same level
as the lowly". ("The Gift" by Marcel Mauss).

The authors, Robin Piper and Patrick de Mare, have worked together for the past five years covering a weekly median-sized group
averaging twenty people, both professionals and patients on a fee-
paying basis under the auspices of the Institute of Group Analysis.
Encouraged by Freud's prophesy 'that one day someone will venture
to embark upon a pathology of cultural communities' - we have recorded each meeting from which we have been able to arrive at the
following theoretical implications.

As long ago as 330 B.C. Aristotle wrote: "Man is a creature
by nature adapted for life in the polis, or city state". In the same
vein, over two thousand years later, Foulkes wrote that "group therapy

365

was an altogether desirable contribution to people's education as responsible citizens".   Professor Halsey, in the Reith Lecture of 1978, similarly argued for the "constant need for alert and know-ledgeable citizenry to protect itself against oppression and to pre-vent the public services disintegrating into organisations which serve the private interest of public servants (viz. bureaucracy)."

When Foulkes first introduced small group psychotherapy to Northfield in 1944, he also developed a group approach to the whole hospital but in the form of small groups involving activities of various kinds, painting, drama, sport, journalism, and a co-ordination group. He himself acted as the link between these various groups but there were no inter-group or large group meetings per se: that is the small groups did not meet together and therefore Foulkes (like a Shaman) himself represented the large group in his own person. He represented the whole of Northfield and to that extent Northfield did not get around to representing itself.   The next step was self-evident, namely to consider setting up a large group and to apply his small group principles to this larger situation.   These principals are essentially that there are no directives given, no task, no goal, no programme other than to meet and talk.   The convener does not lead; he adopts the interpretive attitude of the analyst in psycho-analysis. He sees communication as anything that can be observed and as constituting the network or group matrix. He encourages group associations as equivalent to the free associations of psychoanalysis in the form of free floating discussion.

We suggest that these principles be applied to the larger situation but with modifications, since large groups begin where small groups break off, and are in many ways antithetically distinct, for instance, rather than determining the group culture, as Foulkes described, the convener's function is to draw attention to the pre-vailing cultural assumptions that the group has already made.   The circular face to face seating remains the same and group discussion takes the form of a free floating dialogue.

Social psychology, takes the group (as distant from the individual) as its basic unit.   It is tilted towards the socio-cultural as opposed to the small group, which reflects the psycho-analytic and biological family level.   Citizenship is only adequately observable in a larger setting since the small group, by its very nature, displays only the most rudimentary evidence of social dynamics.   To apply a psycho-analytic or small group model hook, line and sinker to the large group is like trying to "play Ludo on a Chess board".   For intance, imprinting a family culture on the social context produced Freud's Primal Horde construct, which, as Freud wrote, is a mythical caricature.   (In any case he overlooked the antithetical relationship between family and horde as established by Espinas in 1877).

In 1972, at the Second European Symposium held at the Maudsley,
Lionel Kreeger and Pat de Mare suggested they apply a more formal
structure to the meetings of large groups, similar to the rigour
adopted in psychoanalysis and in small groups. De Mare, for instance,
recommended daily meetings of fifty to a hundred people for one and a
half to two hours, for a duration of two or more years.   It is important to realise that a large group technique had not till that
time been seriously suggested. There was little recognition that
this powerful, but unpredictable chaotic structure is sensitive and
potentially intelligent, and requires more structuring, more not
less.   In this situation group dynamics are in the foreground, and
become more clearly definable. Attitudes, ideas, ideologies,
assumptive worlds, value systems, freed of social and community
considerations, make themselves evident not as cloudy, idealistic non-
sequitors, but as definite cultures which can be observed as either
impeding or promoting information flow.   At this symposium it was
arranged for the membership which totalled about a hundred people
to meet in a single circle. It stimulated considerable interest and
in 1975 Kreeger edited a book entitled "The Large Group".

Despite the initial interest not a great deal was done subsequently to implement this enthusiasm; there was in fact a curious
lack of response. It was not till 1975 that Robin Piper and de Mare
finally launched a median-sized group of forty people, which rapidly
fell to thirty and eventually stabilised at twenty, and which met
weekly for one and a half hours.

It became evident that certain features of the large situation
were specific to it.   These features can again be appropriately
classified under the headings of structure, process, content and
metastructure:

1.   The structure refers to context of the larger group itself.

2.   Process refers to the dialogue, to the text that arises as a
     result of members being placed in this context.

3.   Content refers to the subject matter, themes and topics.

4.   Metastructure refers to the changing cultural patterns which
     ensue, the dialectic between individual and group bringing
     about culture, the meaning of the structure to the individual
     member.

1. Structure or Context

This consists of the characteristically increased number of
Members. It constitutes less an instinctual and more a learning
situation, and involves meaning as distinct from gratification,

matters of head rather than of heart, the touch-stone of citizenship.
We have yet to learn how to achieve successful citizenship as distinct from the instinctive imprintation of a flock of birds or hive
of bees. To increase the size of the group from twenty to let us say
thirty members could take several years to learn. Unlike the small
group whose size is deliberately and exclusively limited to eight
to twelve members it is conceivable that a large group slowly expands
and can grow to a number that has yet to be arrived at. Our median
group, after meeting for five years, has yet to establish sufficient
friendliness or Koinonia to affirm the advent of new members, and
to differentiate them from the intrusion of a new born infant, to
learn to expand from the familocentric constraints to an appreciation
of world citizenship, to change from the war of all against all to a
'pan-human science of society' (Marvyn Harris).

     Whichever way you look at it, the striking feature of the
larger group in its size; group factors are in the foreground. It
is altogether much more of a group. It goes in the opposite direction
to that of psychoanalysis, for instead of excluding context, context
is central.

     As a result of these experiences we become interested in the
way of thinking known as structuralism involving ideas about surface
and deep structure, not simply as a uniform system of social relationships abstracted from concrete behaviour but as a two level
model, an extrinsic system with a special intrinsic purpose. For
Levi Strauss, communication is based on an underlying bar on incest.
People learn to talk and exchange because they are not permitted the
more direct expression of incest. Society, exchange, social
elaboration, is created by this prohibition. Incest is natural but
anti-social. Sisters, instead of being objects of desire for brothers
become a form of currency or exchange for bondings of increased size
with other families, creating larger and more powerful social units.

     Some writers have described Marx, Durkheim, Freud and de
Saussure as first generation structuralists since they share a conviction that surface events, structure or context are to be explained
in terms of deep structure, that is, infrastructures or sub-texts.
This first generation helped to set the study of human behaviour on
a new footing, human behaviour could not be treated as a series of
events as in the physical world, but only in relation to a deeper
dimension of subjective instinct, that events take place in relation
to their function in a general social framework. These deep
structures, however, are unconscious even though they constitute
the biological basis for culture and unconsciously subtend our every
thought. Piaget describes structuralism as systems of transformation
in dynamic relation to each other, in a state of motion. He sees
the key ideas of structuralism as wholeness, self-regulation and
transformation. For us self-regulation belongs only to system
thinking and transformation is the hallmark of structuralism.

In psychoanalysis context is excluded as far as possible and the roots or subtextual instinctual themes suggested by the text of free association are explored. In small groups context is judiciously introduced in the form of the network of matrix formulated through the text of group association; in the large group the context plays a more evident role through the text of dialogue.

The process of relating sub-text to context through the text of dialogue presents us with a fuller and more comprehensive picture. This cross fertilisation provides us with a cultural superstructure or metastructure. For instance, the implication of the atom bomb or of the micro electronic revolution can no longer be ignored by simply repeating what is done, what is already structured.

2. Process or text

Turning to process we see that in psychoanalysis text takes the form of free-association, in group therapy that of group-association, and in the larger group that of dialogue. People have to learn dialogue, because of the learning process a feature of the larger situation is its frustrating nature. The hate generated by this constitutes the basis for mental, psychic or ego energy, as distinct from instinctual energy. It becomes the driving force of thought through dialogue. The situation is all the more frustrating to begin with, since the network of communication is rudimentary. Whilst the thinking agency in the individual is mind, the equivalent of this in the larger group is culture. Culture is the dialectic and dialoguic outcome of the contradiction between individual and social structure. Together they constitute a cultural system. The social theorist, T.H. Marshall, makes it clear that today there is a double thrust in society between the politico-economic structure on the one hand, and cultural status on the other. The culture of citizenship involves levelling, affiliation and free speech as distinct from the monologue of hierarchical structures. The individual therefore comes up against a structure that, as we have said is often neither realistic nor gratifying, and it is this that generates the mental or ego energy of hate, and constitutes the basis for thinking and dialogue. As we have said, dialogue is a learning, not an instinctual process, in fact it is anti-instinctual, 'the supreme art' as Plato termed it, which gives rise to the impersonal fellowship of Koinonia. People have to learn how to talk to each other. "Opposition is the Friendship" as William Blake wrote in "The Marriage of Heaven and Hell".

In the larger situation the process of thinking has therefore two dimensions, the one-to-one, which is 'vertical' and the other which is lateral and takes into account the presence, the minds, the experience of other people. In narcissistic disorders this lateral dimension is undeveloped and the on-to-one vertical takes precedence. When limitation of lateral awareness is disguised by

a superficial conformity or conventionality, it is not always at
first recognised. Unexpectedly the therapist may be landed with all
the fascination of a primary instinctual narcissistic attachment
unmodified by the social, lateral, dimension, termed the psychotic
transference. Freud considered people suffering from narcissistic
disorders are incapable of developing relationships, including the
transference. This distinguished the psychoses from the transference
neuroses. It later emerged, however, that some psychotics are
capable of the most passionate one-to-one relationship. These have
the characteristic of being linear and of excluding lateral attachment to others, and therefore of being impervious to social implications. They can be very strikingly displayed in the larger
group as a disregard for others, as for example, saying the right
thing at the wrong time, or in the wrong place, i.e., to the wrong
person.

3. Content

     Out of dialogue and a fog of disconnected and fleeting topics
emerge content and meaning, linking personal style to cultural
patterns. These can be classified as pre-oedipal, oedipal, familo-
centric, and sociocentric. Dreams, metaphors and myths link up to
produce decipherable sub and micro-cultures; the assumed is no
longer assumed in the sense that it is examined instead of being
left as an invisible preverbal assumption. As Timothy Woolmer
quoted from Ella Freeman Sharpe, "The activity of speaking is substituted from the physical activity previously restricted to other
openings of the body". To give an example, a member ejaculated
"Fucking women!" and "Filthy wogs!" This could be looked on as a
preoedipal attack on the breast or as a primal scene fantasy, or as
the expression of peer group hatred, or as a chauvinistic political
onslaught which provoked the retort "Bloody yobbo!"

     We have tried to classify these themes and quickly realised that
this alone presented an enormous undertaking; for instance, one conclusion we reached related to peer group levelling and gave rise to
an interesting observation about bonding. The blood relation of
siblings is the closest and most incestuous, and therefore the most
repressed of all. The blood relatedness between parent and child is
only fifty per cent separated by a generational gap, whilst the
blood relationship of brother and sister is a hundred per cent and
is therefore the more deeply repressed and frustrated by the social
structure.

     In Levi-Strauss terms, siblings have to choose between incest
and exchange, biologically natural incest versus an artificial socio-
cultural currency. Whether to symbolise rather than reify, whether
to transform hate and fratricide into the Koinonia of fellowship, into impersonal friendship and tenderness which is not erotic since

Eros is libidinal and friendship arises from anti-libidinal energies.
If this relationship is successfully transformed, it constitutes the
powerful tie binding people together in groups; if it is not
successfully transformed it falls between two stools and results in
the psychotically cruel manifestations of unstable political situations. The wolf-pack scape-goat response is a simplistic reduction
of the social lateral response into a one-to-one linear relationship;
as Freud put it "Hypnosis is a group of two".

In this connection it is interesting to recall a variation in
the story of Narcissus. Pavsanias, a second century Greek scholar
reports that Narcissus, to console himself on the death of his
twin sister, his exact counterpart, sat gazing into a pool to recall
her features by his own; he rejected the nymph Echo and his lover
Amenias, who pined away, drawing upon himself the vengence of the
Gods and finally drowning himself (14th Edition Encyclopaedia
Britannica). Fraser, in The Golden Bough, reports the widely held
superstition that it is unlucky, even fatal, to see one's own
reflection.

This reflection was therefore not of himself but that of his
sister. Echo calls him, but he cannot respond since the echo is
even fainter than the reflection. The tale is the most poignantly
nostalgic of all the Greek myths.

Essentially the problem we pose and for which we recommend a
possible operational solution, is that today we suffer not from
lack of thoughtfulness generated by individual minds, but from the
shattering of such intelligence and mindfulness by effete pathological cultures. Culture we regard as the equivalent of group
mind, group culture is group mind.

We are troubled by the discrepancy between individual mind and
culture; how effectively to hasten a reciprocity between them?
We pose the possibility that culture can more adequately be explored
in a setting that is larger than the small group, and note that
Walter Schindler (1980) models his small groups on family interpretations. Family conflicts of the past are resolved in the proxy
small group of the present. The dimension that is more social he
suggests, should be considered under a separate heading, namely
that of political psychology.

We posit that the latter level, the political adult peer
cultural level cannot appropriately, technically or operationally
be contained or generated in the small group setting, but demands
a larger setting of more people. So far our experience of five
years has confirmed this suggestion. As we have remarked, psychoanalysis and small group analysis manifest pre-oedipal, oedipal and
family constellations. The median group attempts to approach the

community. Perhaps at a later date a larger group technique will
be practised for more global political situations. Freud cited one
source of human suffering as the inadequacy of our methods of regulating human relationships in the family, in the community and in
the State. To quote him, "It is impossible to ignore the extent
to which civilisation is built up on renunciation of instinctual
gratification" - "Culture ... exerts a heavy toll of aim inhibited
libido in order to strengthen communities by bonds of friendship
between its members", - "The stranger has more claim to my
hostility, even to my hatred" - "Civilised society is perpetually
menaced with disintregration through this primary hostility of
men towards one another".

     The question is whether this hate is primary and instinctual or
secondary? To quote Freud "The assumption of the evidence of the
death instinct or a destructive instinct has raised opposition".
For us as evidenced in the median group,whilst instinct is a form
of physical energy, hate is endopsychic energy and in no way instinctual since it is epiphenomenal and anti-instinctual. As we
see it, hate comes before guilt but after Eros. It is a form of
ego energy which is neither creative nor destructive per se, not to
be subdued or denied but to be affirmed, cultivated and transformed.
We make no apology for using the word 'hate'. We see it, like
hunger, as a psychological absence and not as a biological presence
such as aggression. What we are talking about is the anti-instinct
occasioned by what Freud termed Ananke, a Greek word meaning
external reality, necessity or fate. Freud describes ego instinct
as libidinal; but for us this is a contradiction. Guilt is a
secondary consideration which denies hate and renders it invisible,
an anti-anti-instinct. Freud wrote "Eros and Ananke are the parents
of human culture .... Again, "But we know the power which forced
a development of this kind upon humanity and maintains its pressure
in the same direction today. It is once again, frustration by
reality or if we are to give into its true grand name the pressure
of vital needs, necessity and Ananke".

     The construct of a primal horde of brothers bonded by a homo-
sexual tie could be restated as a band of brothers bound, not by a
homosexual tie, but by a deeply repressed incestuous instinct transformed into hate, alias mental energy, and as a result of frustration
by Ananke or external influences, into the bending of groups by the
impersonal fellowship of Koinonia which indeed has to be learned as
much as does the handling of external reality. The crucial feature
then of the median group is to transform the sub-cultural mode of
the pregenital or the micoculture of the oedipal familo-centric group
into the framework of its socio-cultural equivalent, previously
rendered invisible by being ignored. The Kleinian quality of large
group behaviour is often very clear as if the whole group culture
symbolises the world of the breast as posited by Bion or the mother's

body into which these fantasies are projected and transformed into
cultural themes, e.g. when two members become a combined parental
figure. Whilst St. Paul saw the church in terms of a family group,
Christ preached that such ties be abandoned in favour of a more
universal linking.

Another Greek word which relates to Koinonia was introduced
to us by Beaumont Stevenson. It is Eutropelia, literally meaning
"good turning" or "versatility of mind", seeing things in divergent
rather than convergent ways when the familiar becomes strange and
the strange familiar and tickles our sense of humour, provoking
laughter.

We concluded that the very size of the group could provide
a sufficient cohesiveness to act as ballast, as cement, to contain
the destructive individual attacks (which were often between two
members) instead of surrendering as victims or retaliating in kind
or colluding like a pack of wolves, and could present a powerful
front; this absorbed thse violations by a steady pressure of persistent negotiating, an example of "ego training in action", acting
as a good match, as Foulkes remarked, for the ancient super ego, in
the form of the group matrix, a network response. In the larger
situation the network is of course potentially in greater evidence.
The cementing process of dialogue gives us a technique for treating
the schizoid friability of groups in early stages.

The pre-genital and oedipal qualities display characteristic
sub and micro cultures which undergo transformations as a result of
frustration, starting with the sub-culture of the breast of which
Freud wrote it is the "unmatched" prototype of every later sexual
gratification.

4. Metastructure

In an attempt to disguise their inappropriate and infantile
nature these sub-cultures are rendered invisible both by projection
and by having stemmed from an incoherent preverbal level into the
culture of the group as a whole producing thereby one of Freud's
"pathological cultural communities". It is this aspect of content
that we have referred to as metastructure, which corresponds to
the 'superstructure' of structuralism and is essentially cultural.
It concerns the varied meanings that the context of the larger group
holds for the individual.

Since the large group presents us with a broader span, a pano-
rama ranging from the inner world at one end to being a citizen of
the world at the other, if offers us a setting to understand the
different transformations in which cultural patterns emerge from
pregenital preverbal sub-cultures and oedipal microcultures. These

patterns range, as we have said, from the instinctual pre-oedipal
Kleinian (oral-anal) level at one end, proceeding through the
Oedipus (phallic) complex of parents and siblings, family centric
culture, with its small group micro-cultural systems, to the socio-
culture at the other in transformations than can therefore be looked
at in relationship to each other. Class distinction, racialism,
economic status, professionalism, assumptions of attitudes in
general, humorous, hostile, destructive, creative, promotive,
nurturing, can all be explored; the relationship, for instance,
between incest on the one hand and marital status on the other. There
is much in marriage that is a successful transformation of incest,
since it is universal, powerful, repetitive, exclusive and if disturbed results in primitive, even psychotic responses. The larger
group, in manoeuvering a cultural transformation from hate to friendliness, plays a major role in affirming genital primacy. Genitality
not only expresses an instinct involving a relationship, but a total
social learning situation, the outcome of the latency period at
puberty. Hence perhaps the reputed success of sexual dysfunction
clinics.

    Whilst psychotherapy treats mind and the small groups handles
the group matrix, the larger group involves the equivalent of group
mind in the form of culture. The small group has to learn how to
express feeling, the latter how to express thought. Assemblages
losing cultural metastructures erupt with into mob violence (hate)
or fragment into chaos (panic) or stultify into states of in-
stitutionalisation which strangle or demand to be anaesthetised, e.g.
drug addiction. Culture, therefore, is at the interface between
individual and social context: it is the outcome of the dialectic
between them just as agriculture is the cultivation by the individual
of the soil, or science, art, philosophy and religion by mankind of
the universe. The larger group can therefore serve as a situation
for exploring and discovering its own projected sub and micro-
cultures, "anthropology in the making". We do not need to go to
Africa. The median group functions as a traditional object or a rite
of passage. It presents itself as a possible technique for the
treatment of the traumatic neuroses of contextual catastrophy, war,
mob violence which induce panic embedded in the mind like splinters
of a mirror, as in the eye of the boy, Kay, in "The Snow Queen".
It offers itself as a potential technique for the renegotiation of
earlier contextual traumata; for instance, leaving from home for
boarding school, from school to university, from university to
employment, from the single to the marital state, or for inter-
disciplinary and inter-cultural splits such as expatriation. Ronald
Fairbairn has written that the core of neurosis is the panic of
separation anxiety. Marie Stride, in the journal "Group Analysis"
wrote that the origin of narcissism lies not so much in self love
as in the symptomatic feelings of acute dread of the outside world.

We have seen that the individual threshold of panic was notably
raised in the course of the meetings, and people made successful
changes in their external lives which previously had been un-
thinkable. In the split with reality of psychosis, the larger group,
by creating through dialogue, an extremely powerful, undeniable
ballast of context, establishes a reality which cannot be side-
stepped, but at the same time is open to negotiation. Whilst
psychoanalysis faced inward reality and is intrinsic in that sense
denying context in favour of a total focussing on relationship, the
large group looks out extrinsically at the surrounding culture and
society. The one then is biologically determined and the other is
sociological and has to be learned. So the former, you might say,
is a system and the latter a structure. Koinonia, citizenship, impersonal fellowship, is not an instinctual by-product of sublimated
Eros; on the contrary, it has to be learned as a sociogenic process of civics, and if it is a sublimation of anything, it is a
transformation of hate.

To underplay the cultural context of metastructure in any way
is to overplay a crucial dimension of social reality. Unfortunately
it is often ignored as part of our social heritage; it comes in with
the milk and is therefore disregarded. Taken out of the cultural
context and pushed into individual terms, culture often looks like
insanity. Culture can render personal insanity invisible by
camouflaging it behind its own peculiarities. Negative response
to a vindictive national tyrant may be interpreted as personal
transference. To the individual he might be interpreted and explained away, when in social terms he remains an unadulterated
monster who has failed to undergo a successful transformation but
remains as a disastrous projection of psychotic internal objects,
untransformed, uninterpreted, and regarded as an inevitable expression of social reality or of 'human nature', as part of any
undeniable status quo, that is completely denied, however crazy.
Fortunately metastructure, through dialogue, contains the seeds of
its own potential restructuring. Having placed people together in
the collective situation, the individual is involved in the text
of an infinite surface diversification of dialogue which is a
creative process. Basic themes similar to the twelve notes on the
chromatic scale can give rise to an infinitude of melodic arrangements. The frustrated biological energy flow of the collective
situation constitutes the driving power to unfold and to proliferate
in the form of a projection into the cultural context. It is a
reflection of the inner world providing a decipherable meaning which
is also at the same time translation. This spans the entire range
from the inner world to the total cultural context in a gigantic
transformation. The fourth member of the tetrad then is the metastructure, or cultural context. This in turn starts off a new cycle
of events resulting in further transformations.

Twenty members, as distinct from eight, is correspondingly a more powerful and a more complex situation which is distinguished primarily by this cultural texture. So that whilst membership in a small group may generate an infinitude of familocentric micro-cultures, twenty may enable us to experience a wide range of social cultures, literally untenable in the smaller group.

The world today is dominated by oligarchy; we have still to learn the praxis of assemblages, the intermediation between in-dividual citizen and society through the tree trunk of larger groups of which oligarchies are the mere twigs. We have conveyed some of our thoughts concerning group analytic principles being applied to a median sized group of 20. A similar approach to a large or global group of let us say 100 people has yet to be explored.

The following diagram is an attempt to present these thoughts schematically.

SYSTEM (Diachronic) →

STRUCTURE (Synchronic)

Structure (Context)	Energy	Process (Text)	Content	Meta-Structure, Culture or Code (Sub-Text or Meaning)
I Psychoanalytic (Two Person)	Libidinal	Free Association	Transference	Psycho-biological
No context Relational Dyadic	Desire & gratification		Intrapersonal and binary 'digital' matrix Imaginary (Lacan)	Egocentric Progenital Narcissistic
II Small Group (8 people)	Psychic Energy	Group Association	Transposition	Biosocial
Oligarchic Hierarchic Bureaucratic	Frustration & Hate		Inter-personal discursive group matrix Symbolic (Lacan)	Familocentric Oedipal
III Large Group (20 people or more)	Socio-Cultural Cathexis	Dialogue	Transformation	Socio-Cultural
Affiliative Polygarchic	Power		Transpersonal 'analegic' social matrix Real. (Lacan)	Sociocentric Genital

Conclusion: Pathological cultures arise wherever confusion between the three structural levels occur (i.e. between I, II or III). For example: where a large group is treated as a family, or a small group as a transference situation, or a large group as a two-person relationship (horde or pack) or a two person as a large group ("Hypnosis is a group of two" Freud).

PSYCHODRAMA AS TECHNIQUE OF THE

PSYCHOANALYSIS OF INSTITUTIONS

Didier Anzieu

Université de Paris-X Nanterre

7 bis, rue Laromiguière - 75005 Paris

INTERVENTION REQUEST COMING FROM AN INSTITUTION

The experiment that I shall report is about the children section of a psychiatric hospital. Some fifteen children are hospitalized in it : they are psychotic. The staff includes about thirty treating persons.

From one period of sessions to another, the number of partici-pants has varied from 18 to 24. The purpose of the intervention, that I was asked for, was a severe crisis in the working-team follo-wing the "dismissal" of two educators (in fact, a male nurse had been transfered into another ward after professional faults and a female nurse, rather closely bound to him, had resigned soon after : but these two departures had been lived by the team as dismissals). The staff meetings were very silent and inefficient, the general atmos-phere was heavy. The team members, loosing their motivations, faced with difficulty the unavoidable difficulties of psychotic children and hoped, in agreement with the medical ward-chief, both to benefit from a professional training and to have the general institutional problem treated.

The terms of the intervention were settled as follows : for the treating-persons, including the ward-chief, three sets of intensive psychodrama sessions a year, lasting two days each, at the rate of four one hour-and-a-half sessions a day. I chose to operate as only psychodramatist, but accompanied by a non-participating female obser-ver, in charge of taking down notes and able to help me to analyse my counter-transference, to keep up my narcissism, to fix the first names and places of the participants, to remember their interventions and to gather   material making possible a further theoretic elabo-

379

ration. Moreover, the image of a heterosexual couple happened to be
useful to maintain the presence of a genital level among the group
of participants called to meet along the psychodrama sessions their
anxieties facing the children's psychosis and the regression down
to their own psychotic nucleus.

There were sessions without any acting, sessions with one, two
or three plays, sessions where, in fact, plays were sometimes defensive discussions, and some other time, of great emotional intensity.
The participants, anxious of the internal dissensions of the department, would not have accepted to be separated into two groups. They
wanted to live together the same experience. I then had to work on
a large group of about twenty persons : it posed particular technical
problems.

TERNARY SPATIAL SETTING IN THE LARGE GROUP PSYCHODRAMA

Every day, participants were invited by me to divide themselves
into two or three sub-groups. Only one of them went in the middle of
the room and acted the psychodrama. The rest of the participants
remained at the periphery and instruction was given to them to refrain from any intervention in discussions and games. A little
before the end of the session, the sub-group which had discussed
and played, returned to the external large circle and all participants commented with me on what this sub-group had said and done.
At the next session, it was the turn of the second sub-group to
take up the central position. Once a day, there was a plenary meeting
and general discussions took place about the ward department. Incidentally it happened that a member played alone (in a dumb show).

How was the splitting into sub-groups carried out ? At the
beginning, I arbitrarily imposed it : all those who sat on my right-
hand formed the sub-group A ; those on the left, the sub-group B.
Later on, the experiment progressing, I could let it go more spontaneously. Sometimes, I arranged five to eight chairs in the middle
of the acting-hall and invited the willing persons to go and sit down;
some other time, I would go and sit down myself in the middle and
waited that some of the protagonists join me (which always happened).

In short, space was divided into three zones :
- one big external circle of spectators (9 to 13), compelled to silence and inaction and to which belonged the observer ;
- one small inner circle of participants-observers (three to ten)
who attended to the plays, who could freely intervene and who
participated to the discussions preceding and following the acting ;
I always took part in them during the five first session periods ;
during the sixth and last one, the small circle had to do without
me ;
- a central nucleus of volunteer actors (one to six) who played a
scenario to which I too could belong if I was asked for.

The small inner circle was almost always closed and narrowed :
the members welded to one another, forming continuous circumference,
reacting to the menace of being encircled and to the multiple intruding gazes coming from the external larger circle.

As for the large external circle, it was sparser, its members
not being numerous enough to fill all places and not feeling the
need for solidarity. They would generally form rather an arc of a
circle.

These topographical differentiations revealed particular psychic
properties.

PSYCHIC PROPERTIES OF THE CENTRAL ZONE

In the centre, two types of phenomena developed: cathartic
events during certain plays ; a symbolization work and the mental
elaboration during some discussions.

First example : the central sub-group carries on a discussion
on the general subject of leadership and on the role, in the ward-
department, of the nurse-responsible-of (it is the report of one of
them to the general manager of the hospital which caused the shifting
of the dismissed male-nurse). Suddenly, transgressing the rule of
abstention of speech, Andrée, a nurse, sitting in the outer circle,
stands up and vehemently expresses her disagreement about the words
said in the center. Immediately, Jacques, a resident medical student,
also of the external circle, gets angry and blames Andrée of being
against any authority. I step in to underline that, if the rule has
not been respected, it is on account of the acuteness of the problem
raised.

I invite Andrée and Jacques to come with me in the central position. One, two and three other participants join us. Andrée explains
that when a little girl, she couldn't even then bear the authority
of the teacher. She breaks down in tears : "I have never been ...
responsible", she says. Then, after I had suggested it, we play two
sequences of a teacher in his classroom. The first time, I am a severe
and punishing school-master. The second time Andrée is a school-mis-
tress, "as it doen't exist" (she says), who is totally understanding
but she is rapidly overwhelmed by rowdy children. A double catharsis
takes place, an individual and a collective one. Collective : at the
following whole large group meeting, after the pause, Andrée and
Jacques can return with several others to the debate on what it is
to be "responsible" (in the two senses of the word) and on the necessity and the limits of the authority in the ward : the atmosphere
is dense, attentive and naturally controlled. It is a sociodrama that
has just happened : the agressivity, latent since the "dismissal" of
the two educators and which paralysed the working of the department,
has, at last, burst into the open, and the crisis which had been

therefore opened, could begin to be overcome. Furthermore I will
learn during the next session-period, several weeks after, that
Andree had started a personal psychotherapy (there has therefore
been an individual catharsis).

The central zone, in the psychodramatic space, as I have
structured it, gives itself as a scene for the dramatisation of the
conflicts internal to the institution by means of representation
between two spokesmen of the underlying antagonistic orientations
(here the pro- and anti-authoritarians).

The second example is the one of an important and grave discussion: the anxiety of the nursing persons in face of the children's
psychosis, the death anguish when a violent adolescent assaults
you, anguish of being led, against one's will, into a too emotional
too symbiotic relation (how must one react when a psychotic adolescent girl asks her male nurse to masturbate here?), anguish caused
by the inability of the psychotic patient to communicate, anguish to
keep silent and anguish to talk during the staff meeting of one's own
anguishes, anguish of being persecuted by the other treating persons
if we state about our uncertainties, our weaknesses, anguish of
wounding them if we express our disagreement on their way to do. I
then interpret the projective-identification's mechanism: if we show
to others the good object that we keep inside us, they will envy it
and destroy it; if we expel on them a bad inner object, they send
it back on us with hate. It is the first time, so say the participants, that they can talk together of the real feelings they experience during their work. The large outer circle listened to them
with unremitting attention, in exceptional silence and immobility.

PSYCHIC PROPERTIES OF THE SMALL INNER CIRCLE

It constitutes a transitional space between the most internal
psychic reality represented in the center (the inter-subjective
conflicts, intricated in inter-personal antagonisms) and the external
reality, the institution under these circumstances, materialized by
the large open circle. It fills the role of a container of the
sensation-affect-images which have not, up to now, been subject to
the work of symbolization and collective elaboration and the function
of an auxiliary-Ego supplying a backing to the psychic edges of the
psychodrama actors to exert their inhibited or still undeveloped
mental functions.

This little inner circle indeed figures the body-Ego, double-
sided as Freud has described it; one side turned towards the unconscious and the drives, the other side forming a screen and a fil-
ter towards the external world. It is, again, the skin-Ego as I have
conceptualized it; the place where symbolization, starting from the
interface of the skin, can start functioning, establishing differences
and links between the objects and the fantasies, between the inside

and the outside, between the unconscious and the institution.

It is there, in psychodrama sessions, that theme which obeyed
more precisely to a ternary coding, were invented : they symbolized,
at the same time, the institutional structure (with its hierarchies
of persons and activities), the group   fantasies dynamics as it
was here and now in the on-going psychodrama session and also certain
personal problems. For example, at the second session of the second
period, the psychodrama's theme is the admission of a new child in
the ward. Janine and Nicole, who couldn't or wouldn't come at the
first session and thus who are newcomers, play their own situation
transferring it on the child : Janine takes the role of the child
to be admitted ; Nicole who has had the initiative of the theme which
has been accepted, through this, feels herself being accepted by
the group ; she plays a child already admitted into the ward.

This play unlatches a lively discussion about the ward's life
and on how each of them experiences it. One can locate there, in
the story of the psychodramatic intervention on this institution
what René KAES has called the buildup of the psychic group   apparatus.
The newcomers' admission theme has symbolized :
- at the institution's level, the admission of a child to the section,
admission which is, in reality, effected collectively by a sub-group
of doctors and educators or nurses.
- at the psychodrama's group level, the new participants' admittance
to the session and also the B sub-group's admission in the inner
small circle after the A sub-group had acted in it ;
- at the individual level, the "admission" of the "other" in me and
of me in the "other", represent the interplay of identifications and
projections ;
- finally, at the transferential level, which constitutes the driving
force of the three-fold preceding process, the theme of the newcomers'
admission has symbolized the admission to the group's life and to the
real problems of the section, of the couple formed by the psychodramatist (he has already played in a psychodrama at the first session :
the accepted child figures him in the play) and by the observer (she
doesn't play and doesn't speak : this overdetermines the fact that the
to-be-accepted child is represented in the play as mute).

PSYCHIC PROPRIETIES OF THE OUTER LARGE CIRCLE

It is restricted to a part of a circle of the persons sitting
and occupying the cap's same partial and lateral position through
which Freud represents the Super Ego on his diagram of the psychic
apparatus in "The Ego and the Id" and, later, in the "New Introductory Lectures".

The observing outer sub-group is, effectively, resented by the
central sub-group's members as a Super-Ego. Its members experiment with
the advantages and the disadvantages of the observer's position.

They can see others expose themselves without being in turn exposed.
But, they are obliged to keep their reactions for themselves until
the end of the session. This obligation to listen without expressing anything of oneself proved to be, at the same time, frustrating
and useful.   If, in the centre, the participants feel themselves
put into the role of the analysed persons, at the periphery, they
have the difficult experience of being in the psychoanalyst's position
and they realize how much, in the ward-section, they lack, miss even
more listening to others than to express themselves.

I will give an example of a scene, symbolizing this ternary
organisation of the psychodramatic space. The proposed, and accepted,
theme is the one of a dormitory. Actors, including me, lean down in
all directions in the central space. One starts a row, one other
snores, a third one dreams, a fourth has a nightmare and howls.
The actors belong in reality to both but in the play all are
boys (the girls, in the following discussion will recognize here
the accomplishment of their virile desires). Another girl plays
apart from others ; she's in the room next door, in the girls'
dormitory, she cannot get to sleep and she waits for the coming of
a boy ; in vain, none of them will come, the incest's taboo is a
necessity, if not in the institution, at least it is in the group.

Six actors lean down, separated but united in the same transitional space. The three other persons are not there by accident.
They are the ward-director and the two male nurses in-charge. They
condense three meanings : the Super-Ego's role in the psychic apparatus, their own role in the institution, the role of the outer
large circle in regard to the psychodrama's central group. They
watch the regression.

The male-nurse-in-charge has chosen to be the dormitory's superior. He grumbles, for he cannot sleep on account of the noise,
he goes around to calm down and reassure but also to forbid sexuality :
"put your hands over the sheets !". These allusions signify to the
group to pass on to less professional and more personal psychodra-
mas, this means the staging of sexual fantasies. I see there the
confirmation of my hypothesis that primal fantasies (here a primal
scene fantasy) constitute one of the unconscious group organizers.

The group-therapist, by his interventions (which are not limited to interpretations) expresses his presence in the three places.
In the center, by playing, he makes himself the ally of the inhibited
or repressed drives' liberation. In the small inner circle, he takes
upon himself and helps it to be taken upon oneself, the settling of
the transitional area's function (Winnicott), of the double support
and multiple anaclisis (R. Kaës), of the Skin-Ego (D. Anzieu). In
the big external circle, he is the Super-Ego that states the rules
and guarantees their respect. He is apart, he takes his meal at a
separate table. At the same time, the animator is present by his

glances, his postures, his eventual words, his physical and psychic
proximity : the group makes the paradoxal experience of being alone
but next to him as a reassuring mother (Winnicott).

GROUP'S EVOLUTION

     The group's evolution went from a set of roleplayings with
professional character, towards a more cathartic psychosociodrama.
The aim of the beginning (which was a training of the treating persons as well as an intervention in the institution) more and more
gave place to a brief psychotherapy of certain interpersonal and
intra-psychic conflicts. A psychoanalytic type process came into
action in the group, in close interaction with the transference on
the group analyst as a psychoanalyst and on the couple he formed
with his collaborator.

     This psychoanalytic process essentially consisted in bringing
into the psychodrama group, the anxieties of the psychotic children.
The participants firstly reproduced in the plays the ward's real
life's scenes, whether it were scenes with children (meal, baths,
parent's visits) or treating persons' meetings where the children
were in question (for instance the shifting-team meeting when the
afternoon team takes over from the morning one). Later, a part of
the group presented itself as a mute, obstinate, disordely, ununders-
tandable and destructive child who waited for but refused to be cured
by the psychodramatist and his assistant as well as by the non-psy-
chotic part of the goup. This transference culminated in a very
dramatic play where a mother gave birth to a monstrous child. In
the end, the participants partly disengaged from their identifications
to the psychotic child by laying it down before the group and the
team constituted by the psychodramatist and the observer, were able
to start using the psychodrama group for their own individual personal therapy. But the problem was then posed of whether such a large
group composed of persons who worked together was the proper formula
to reach this new goal. This awareness entailed the decision, shared
at the end of the sixth period by the group therapist, to put an
end to the psychodramatic intervention in this institution and to
leave each person get through into training or personal therapy by
other ways.

     The interpretation work mainly laid on the defence mechanisms
in action : splitting, projective identification, disavowal, attacks
against links (intra-psychic links, links between treating persons),
attacks against the individuals' and the group's natural growth and
against the participants' formation's progress through psychodrama.
The splitting's analysis (between the psychodrama-good-group and the
bad-mother-institution, between the doctors and the psychologists who
possess the psychoanalytical speech and the nurses who have it not)
was essential at the beginning. The language differences (in the
vocabulary, in the abstraction's level, in the implicit references)

often strengthen in the institutions the hierarchical differences
and conflicts. It was the case here. Most of the doctors made constant references but always implicitly to the psychoanalytic theory.
The nurses were then excluded with a feeling of ignorance and
powerlessness and the hate which it entails. On the opposite side,
the nurses' spontaneous references concerned the body's language,
gestures, postures, language which the ward doctors didn't listen
and didn't decipher for it was not verbal.

The analysis of the alternation of idealisation and depression
followed and allowed a certain clearing related to persecutory anxieties. The more the setting adopted for the large group psychodrama
gave the "illusion" (in the sense of Winnicott) of unity, the more
the breaking up anxieties kept fixed to the institution. These
anxieties seemed to me to constitute one of the main resistance
sources of the personel to a better organized work and, on the part
of the managing persons, to a more clear and coherent care policy
Resistance also to better horizontal and vertical communications
in the ward. It is, it seems, when the participants gave up asking
of the psychodrama the magic solution of all their professional and
institutional difficulties, that is to live it as their grandiose
self, that they were able to take in charge together the organization of their own work (this organization was until then determined
by the chief-nurse with the agreement of the ward-chief).

EVOLUTION OF THE INSTITUTION

What has been the evolution of the atmosphere in the institution ? The first series of sessions brought up a rather quick improvement of the institutional functionings , overcoming of the trau-
matism created by the "dismissal" of two staff members, greater
involvement in the ward-meetings, better mutual tolerance of the
colleagues' anxieties, spontaneous resignings of treating persons
discovering themselves the inability to work with psychotic children,
more invigorated and euphoric atmosphere. Then, after the illusion
that the group would be a perfect mother continuously filling up
all the gaps, came the disillusion, the depression, the return into
inertia, in the : "what's the use", the : "its hopeless", the : "we
listen one another less than ever". This sentence has been the most
challenging for the therapist's counter-transference. Finally, it
is through the analysis of the idealizing/persecuting transference
towards me, through the systematic research of a psychoanalytic work
in the group and through the depositing of the participants' psychotic
part into the therapist-observer couple that the disillusion, and the
destructive and self-destructive hate have been able to be overcome.
A common wording, between both languages of the body and of psychoanalysis could be found/created. The staff then considered to take
itself in charge more actively in the institution. The ward-chief
has organized for them a series of lectures on the psycho-analytic
psychopathology of the child and small supervision groups of psychotic

children cases posing peculiar problems to the nurses, small groups
animated by the ward's psychologist/psychotherapist. Finding that
his ward team now worked normally, the ward chief informed me of it
and decided not to take part in the sixth psychodrama session set.
I verified, during this same period, as I said earlier, that the
participants also didn't feel anymore the need for an external intervention and I inferred that I had to put an end to my intervention.

INDIVIDUAL EVOLUTIONS AND THEIR LIMITS

The studying of the individual slips on which had been noted all
the verbal and psychodramatic interventions of each person, session
after session (at least those which could have been noted), brought
up a surprise; many things had changed in the group, some had in the
institution; on the other hand, each person, when intervening, had a
tendency to deliver the same speech, the same declarations, the same
demands, complaints or problems, the same compulsive language habits,
the same type of play in the psychodrama scenes. The persons who
showed a noticeable change from one set of sessions to another were
those who already were following a psychoanalysis or had meanwhile
undertaken an individual psychotherapy or, finally, had got involved
in a very personal psychodrama which had had a cathartic effect.

These facts lead us to revise certain taken for granted ideas.
When many staff members undergo an analysis, an institution does not
necessarily work better. Psychoanalysis leads to priviledged
realization of personal goals and sometimes to favour wild interpretations in the institution.

Another conclusion to draw is that it is not necessary for an
institution to change, that individuals change in their psychic
functioning. They must, on the other hand, while keeping their own
same psychic apparatus, build together an homorphic (and not isomorphic) group psychic apparatus which gives to each of them the
freedom of being themselves but which creates between them a group
mentality able to guide or organize their collective behaviours.
Such a build-up happens to be facilitated by the establishment of
an object and a space identical to what Winnicott has termed
"transitional object" and "transitional space" between the child and
his mother. The psychoanalytic psychodrama group can constitute,
between the individuals and the institution to which they belong, a
transitional object and a transitional space, provided the psychoanalyst that leads it fulfils not only the interpretative function,
but also the one of a container, of an auxiliary Ego, and of the
container, for the participants, of the psychotic part.

This large group technique represents a particular aspect of a
broader method which René Kaës has called, for this reason, "transitional analysis". It is the extension to the adult and to the
group of Winnicott's discovery for the child. It seems to me an
essential tool of the psychoanalysis applied to institutions.

ARCHAIC PROCESSES IN ORGANIZATIONS :

FLUID BOUNDARIES BETWEEN INDIVIDUALS AND GROUPS

Jean Claude Rouchy   Vice-Président ARIP

Association pour la Recherche et l'Intervention
Psychosociologiques
6 bis rue Bachaumont   75002 Paris France

When I am called upon to consult an organization, I find
myself in the presence not of the whole of the organization, but of individuals, groups, and sub-groups who
speak to me about the organization. These are discussions
about what's going on in the organization, these are
imagos of the organization and not the organization per
se which are being communicated to me. These are individuals, groups, or sub-groups trying to use my presence in
the organization for their own purposes or strategies,
consciously or not, and it's through the way they are
trying to use me that I can work through, with them, what
is going on in the organization.

The second point raised by my presence is to know
who is speaking to me, who is the subject ; are they individuals who are speaking in the context of the organization, or is it the organization, or rather certain sub-
groups that one identifies with the organization, which
is speaking through individuals ? At this moment the organization would speak through them or they would be spoken
through by the organization. We are thusly faced with the
question of identity and conflicts of identity, of mechanisms which develop within the groups and organizations
and which are present in any process of change. This
poses, through identification, the question of alienation
and even of depersonalization within the organization when
individuals are brought to identify themselves no longer
with people but to interiorize, in bureaucratic systems,
impersonal rules which take their place within them.

The internalization by individuals of the values of
the organizations in which they find themselves, of which
they belong, has long led us to believe that all consulting work in a company, in a school or a hospital, in any
social group cannot only aim at the structure of the organization external to people, but in the way that it is
internalized by the individuals, because the structure of
the organization becomes a part of the individuals themselves and any change brings us to consider a rearran-
gement of both the individual and collective structures.

It is in this way that I spoke in the title of this
presentation of the fluidity of boundaries between individuals and groups which forms the space in which the
analyst works in an organization at the junction of these
boundaries which fluxuate and change. Therefore the boundaries of an organization are not a given. In a hospital,
for example, do these boundaries include the physicians,
the nurses, the staff, the administration, the unions,
in-patients, out-patients, medical equipment suppliers,
maintenance people, the area in which the hospital is
situated, etc ? So the boundaries designating the inside
and the outside of an organization are in perpetual
motion for organization members according to the time,
the place, and the problem, and the consultant who is
said to be "on the outside" can be at once within and
without just as all the other people normally considered
to be within the organization can be within it or without
it.

I will try to clarify this question of identity and
boundaries by citing two of my consultations, one concerning the French National Education System which has been
going on for fourteen years, and the other, which has
been going on for two and a half-three years in a foreign
textile company. These are examples where an identity is
negated and this process of negation is very indicative
of the conflicts we see both on a personal and organizational level.

First of all I will speak about the textile company
in which the executives denied the fact that it was a
family enterprise and always said, "Yes, we know that
there are two families in charge of this company and
possessing most of the capital but the firm is sufficiently large, more than five thousand people, that this
family situation has a relatively small influence". This
denial of family identity in the enterprise had, in fact,
all the more repercussions on the structure of the company. There was not only a total cleavage between the

production sector and the commercial sector as in many
firms, notably those with a charismatic structure, but
these departments acted as if they were two separate com-
panies, two citadels. It seems as though this structuring
by opposing couples was caracteristic on all levels of the
company, it structured many of the relationships between
different departments and it was also possible to find
this structuring between individuals of different levels.
It seemed to reproduce the antagonistic alliance between
the two owning families, a dualistic conflict from the
president and the general director on down. This duality
was transfered to the consultation itself since a few
months after I had started consulting this company, another consultant was called in who started to put into place a new hierarchical structure by product and whose way
of working was radically opposed to mine although the
idea was to have us work together.

Therefore, in the consultation itself, was reproduced what was fundamentally denied about the identity of
members of the organization and of the organization
itself. I will come back to the internalization of these
values which are put into place unconsciously and structure both the reality of the individuals and the organization.

Before beginning the second example, I would like to
describe the modalities by which the values of organizations are internalized by individuals subjected to them,
who undergo them and also the way in which individuals
project, as we have just seen, their own internal reality
in the context of the organization and the way they structure this reality in terms of own history. This double
movement of introjection and projection is completed by
phenomena perhaps less known and more archaic, such as
incorporation, of which I will speak more specifically
from two angles ; one in making reference to two psychoanalysts, Nicolas Abraham and Marika Torok, who worked
to distinguish introjection from incorporation and to
give back to introjection the meaning that Ferenzi had
originally given to it, that is to say, situating introjection as an extension of auto-erotic interests and an
enlarging of the ego, that is, a process which establishes
a coming and going between narcissism and the object relationship and which is, at once, both auto- and hetero-
erotic.

On the contrary, the fantasy-like mechanism by which
the object is incorporated does not cooperate with the
growth of the ego, since it is hidden and when it appears

it will be in manner close to hallucinatory experiences.
In incorporation desire is forbidden and this constitutes
an insurmountable obstacle to introjection. Desire then
appears in compensatory behavior and by shiftings to the
oral zone, although other zones of the body are aimed at ;
it is thusly that we can open the refrigerator after a
stress, which has no great effect on the situation itself
and does not cooperate with the growth of the ego. The
incorporation of objects therefore, does not aid in the
enrichment of the ego but rather exerts a very great influence on behavior.

I would draw together this form of incorporation and
another process which to me seem linked, as these analysts
have indicated, to an unconscious to unconscious communication and not to the repression of the subject himself.
This makes me think of the work of E.T. Hall concerning
the importance of the incorporation process in social
culture. The texture seems made up by an unconscious to
unconscious communication inscribed directly in the body
which conditions ones relation to space. From the very
first moments of life, in the relationships established
between the mother and the baby through care for the
body, the holding, skin contact, voice, rhythms, there is
a cultural and social conditioning of the gestures, bodily
attitudes, the distance of others sensed as either welcoming or aggressive, the expression of emotions, and so
on, and this in a fundamental way by the fusion of the
body and the psyche. In a society it is also possible to
identify the social class of people and even to know their
socio-professional categories, not only by the way they
dress and speak, but also in the way they handle themselves, move, situate themselves in space, and in many
other ways. This brings us to a notion introduced by
Winnicott concerning the relationships between the mother
and the baby when he says that in what preceeds the object
relationship it is not the individual who is the cell but
the structure constituted by the environment and the individual, the center of gravity of the being is not constituted for him by the individual, but rather in this whole
formed by the mother/baby couple.

This permits us to situate the individual's history
not only within the latent structures of the family but
opens the path to research into the individual and social
origins of the identity, which is, at once, both singular
and individual but also always similar since the fantasies, incorporated thusly, can well be shared at least by
a family, by a group, by an organization, by a culture,
by a social class, or by a society. It is obvious that

the somatic, the gesture, the relation to the body, is
present in the interaction between members of an organization. This situates all the more the problems of change
and evolution as a work for the organization members to
do on themselves with a sufficient working through time
to treat all the anxiety felt by the reactivation of internal, interpersonal, and intra psychic conflicts having
such archaic roots and which put directly into play both
the identity of the person as an individual and as a
member of the organization in an inseparable manner.

My second example of identity denial takes place in
a consultation done in the French National Education
System since 1966. After the events of May 68 there was an
agreement between the Ministry of Education and the FOEVEN,
a Federation of Educators Organizing Vacations for children in the National Education System. This Federation
was created after the war with the idea of taking children
on vacation ; and since has been more and more interested
in pedagogical concerns and what goes on in the classroom, and is now very interested in the structure of the
school itself.

In the agreement the two parties had settled on three
types of activities : firstly, group dynamics sessions
with four or five educators including the director from
ten schools, making about fifty people who divided up
into four or five workshop groups ; secondly, the educators, once back in their own schools could request a
consultation to deal with the particular problems of their
school ; and thirdly, a training program for the educators
so that, little by little, they could replace us by doing
the consulting job themselves.

I had therefore written an article at the start of
the consultation, about 1971 or 1972, in which I underlined the bonds between this organization and the French
National Education System. This little sentence provoked
some very negative reactions from those concerned since
it was precisely these bonds which were denied by them,
completely denied, even though they were all educators,
their association in each school district was presided
over by the district superintendant, and that they only
intervened within the framework of the French National
Education System, and finally that in the name of their
federation, FOEVEN, the last two letters stand for
"National Education". This denial of identity explained
the resistance which had a great effect on the consultation, this resistance being dammed up jointly by a strong
desire for innovation and evolution. Concerning the

sensitivity sessions, there was a bureaucratic phenomenon
which conformed very well to the normal procedures of the
French National Education System. The members of FOEVEN
had become the organizers of these sessions and we were
working for them, a little like teachers work for the
administration. This traditional division of labor had a
tendancy to place us in the service of their own aims and
we regarded them as administrators. A certain number of
decisions which were linked, in the spirit of the project,
to a request by the participants became thusly automatic
from an administrative point of view. For example, after
the sessions, it had been decided that the participants,
once back in their own school, could ask for a consultant,
if they wished, to come work with them on the problems
posed within the framework of their school. This was rapidly transformed by the members of FOEVEN into a bureaucratic obligation, that is, a consultant was sent, automatically, into each school where a group of five people
had done the session. After some budget cuts, the number
of days of the consultations had to be diminished and in
the same way, this reduction was equally applied to all
the schools without regard for what happened in these
consultations, whereas in some schools there were problems
to be dealt with but in others practically nothing.

Apparently organizational, such decisions had obvious
effects and very strongly limited the possiblities of evolution in all the schools. Afterwards, there were other
examples of this nature of which I haven't the time to
speak to you.

Concerning projections, I will simply say that they
often provoke feelings of persecution when they are attributed, as usual, to entities such as the Organization
with a capital "O" or the Administration with a capital
"A", but this will serve us as a transition to go on to
what could be titled "Organization and Depersonalization",
that is to say, to processes which are rather intense in
that what happens is very personalized through interpersonal conflicts, or success attributed to individuals
rather than groups, phenomena of leadership, or scape-
goating, and at the same time everything which happens in
these organizations is conceived of as a collective des-
tiny from which it is all the more difficult to escape
since the individuals don't have the impression that they
are involved in the organization as subjects but rather
are operated by remote-control as if they could do
nothing : strings are pulled as if their actions were
programmed by a system, and we could imagine that, despite

the impression of a personal life, they would have no thoughts of their own.

A concept used by the psychoanalyst François Roustang, that of expropriation and ballast, describes the sensation of being empty or emptied and lived in by another's ideas. This constitutes an absolutely fundamental part of the experience of each person with archaic relationships which govern the system of relation and the collective structures in the organizations.

It's here that lies the interest of incorporation and of formations of the unconscious which would directly take on things from the unconscious of another. There would be unconscious formations placed in the individuals and which could be shared in the context of the organization.

The feeling that our thoughts are guessed, that they don't belong to us, that they've been stolen, or that they've been imposed upon us, as if prompted by the will of another, of an external object, of the Organization, on the Administration is certainly reinforced by the current organization of hospital, industrial, and commercial entities as well as by the society at large, by the fundamental separation found between those who think and those who execute. Alienations seem to proceed by the incorporation of repressed ideas or desires which are not ones own but those of the dominant group or class.

This would not only involve the replacement of the ego ideal by the same object which has as a consequence the identification of their own ego as Freud suggests to explain the processes of identification in groups of a neurotic register, it seems that it is rather question of what we could call a psychotic position as in crowd movements where the actions are surprising by their demented characteristics ; collective panics, fears sensed in social situations, the inability to take the floor at a discussion, or being paralyzed, seem much more fundamentally governed by the process that we could qualify as primitive, the subjects being expropriated from themselves and undergoing impulses which seem to come from the outside. This reminds us of Victor Tausk's "influencing machine" and of the famous little note in which he indicated that in the course of the debate Freud had insisted upon the importance of secrecy for the child with regards to his parents in the formation of the ego, since the child's belief that the others know his thoughts

"comes from his experience in learning to speak. The
child receives the thoughts of others... he has the
impression that the others have made his speech and with
it they have made his thoughts..." That such a process be
reactivated on the occasion of situations of new belonging which come to form the identity and during the new
internalizations of the ego is more than probable. Part
of the resistance encountered in consulting work thusly
concerns, paradoxically enough, the fear of losing ideas
which are not ones own but with which the individual is
loaded. These ideas constitute a form of security for the
individuals, they are not empty. When one imagines new
forms of organization, other structures, other forms of
society, other social relationships, one of the fears is
that of emptiness and of senselessness, of a crazy language in which individuals stray out of the paths laid
out which serve them as protection even if they suffer
from the situation in which they find themselves.

I'm going to go back to the textile company in which
they had a habit of fielding questions two by two. Several months after the start of the consultation, a meeting
was organized grouping twelve directors and department
heads with the general director. This meeting was opened
with these words : "We have taken advantage of the presence of Mister Rouchy to meet together", as if this were
really the motive and not just a pretext for this first
meeting. So why say it like that ? This sentence covered
up the anxiety felt by each and every one and served as
a common identity which unified what was separated. The
idea of this meeting caused such malaise that the personnel head, on his way to the meeting room, jokingly whis-
pered to me : "I'd like to make myself very small so I
could hide under the table and know what's going to happen"
In fact, the uneasiness he spoke of was shared by everyone, and once in the meeting they seemed to undergo,
unable to speak, this situation of which they weren't
susceptible of exploring the causes, a little like in the
Exterminating Angel by Bunuel where the guests had to
come, bound by an exterior force which isolated them from
the rest of the world. In this situation they were invaved
by this force and adhered to it without any distancing
between themselves and with themselves. There was the
idea of a catastrophe that my presence permitted to con-
jure up but of a catastrophe expected for several meetings.

I said that part of the resistance encountered was
linked to fear of emptiness. And now to close I'd like to
make a second proposition which refers, by the way, to that
of Elliott Jaques when he considers structures as defenses

against primary anxieties since perhaps we haven't taken
his proposition literally enough, that is, that part of
the defenses on an individual level and the resistance on
the structural level of the organization are mingled and
in an anaclitic situation up to the choice of a profession
and also that the regrouping of what was separated, dis-
jointed, the presence of individuals face to face, over-
throws the imaginary territories of individuals and of
groups in their complementary representations from the
inside and the outside for both themselves and for the
organization. This would certainly be the origin of
anxieties felt and of the fear that a catastrophe is in
the making. It is their own identity as an individual and
as a group which is endangered in its internal organization and they are confronted with a test of reality with
the environment on which and within which take place a
certain number of projections and to which they have
attributed, sometimes in a hallucinatory way, constraints
and persecutions which come in part from themselves. No
one is sure he won't be taken far away from his territorial waters which were relatively well established.

The hope of being liberated from the weight of des-
tiny with the help of the presence of the consultant
coexists with the fear of losing ones ideas, of foreign
objects which live in us, of finding oneself face to face
with emptiness, of senselessness, change throws positions
into confusion, mixing what was separate. The meeting
confronts not only the social actors one with another but
with themselves in the way they use their rationality. It
serves them as a railing against madness. If a consultant
is called it is probably to change this dangerous situation by exorcising the bad object and put a stop to these
influences seen as coming from the outside. The assimilation of this situation to a transference is not without
several problems though it could be said that it is essentially from the way different individuals and groups try
to use the presence of the consultant that the consultant
can help bring about an analysis of the situation.

PSYCHIC AND POLITICAL CONSTRAINTS ON THE GROWTH OF INDUSTRIAL

DEMOCRACIES

W. Gordon Lawrence, M.A.
    and
Eric J. Miller, M.A., Ph.D.

Consultants
The Tavistock Institute of Human Relations
120 Belsize Lane
London NW3 5BA

The particular version of group relations training that has been developed in the Tavistock Institute and is associated with the Leicester Conferences on Authority and Organization (or some version of that title) has informed the parallel practice, in action research and consultancy, of the scientific staff who have been responsible for sponsoring them. Apart from the development of a heuristic framework for understanding groups and institutions, there has been the identifying of such issues as the politics of relatedness (Lawrence, 1979a; Miller, 1979a).

The heuristic framework is familiar enough. It is grounded partly in the work of Wilfred Bion (1961) which, in turn, owes much to object-relations theory, and partly in the concept of groups and enterprises as open systems (Rice, 1958, 1963, 1965; Miller and Rice, 1967; Miller, 1976, 1979b).

There are three identifiable outcomes of this framework and the accumulated experiences of the Tavistock conferences in group relations training. One is the value of seeing all individuals in an enterprise as being managers in the sense that they exercise authority to manage their task activities and their relations with other role-holders. (This is irrespective of the title of "manager" - and in the English language the status and process of management are confused.)

The second outcome is the view that action research or consultancy projects should be seen as open-ended, rather than guided by a particular notion of what the results ought to be (Miller, 1977).

The third outcome is the view that a project in industrial democracy must itself start from democratic principles, i.e., there must be an opportunity for people to express deep feelings as well as conscious thought. These should not be a forced choice offered to the potential participants in a project, say, on industrial enterprise.

Essentially, we are pointing to the close tie between the work of the Group Relations Training Programme and the practice of action research. One activity illuminates the other. At the same time, it should be said that it is not a matter of literally matching one to the other but rather of "making", i.e., seeing the differences between the two activities as well as their similarities.

In thinking about industrial democracy we have kept all this in mind, together with some ideas of D.W. Winnicott.

Following him, we can postulate that 'a democratic society is "mature", that is to say that it has a quality of individual maturity which characterises its healthy members. Democracy is here defined, therefore, as society well adjusted to its healthy individual members' (Winnicott, 1950, pp.175-176).

Any enterprise, such as a work and employment institution, could be expected to have similar characteristics if its members have aspirations for democracy.

Material From Two Case Studies

Because of space we have to be selective. Both cases are industrial. The first concerns an enterprise we shall call "Omicron". It was a failing company within a group called "Omega". Internal consultants for the firm devised a diagnostic questionnaire which was given to all employees - nearly 1000. The 70% response allowed the strengths and weaknesses of the firm to be identified. Among these were the "splits" in the firm between managers and workers and the expending of energy on inter-department rivalries that were not helping the attainment of the overall objectives of the firm. In turn, people were confused about the various objectives of the firm and their departments.

The strategy of intervention that arose out of these conclusions started from the assumption that it was necessary to establish the implicit "rules" that were guiding people's behaviour in the firm. Here it is worth stating that an organization has no independent existence as an entity. It 'is a product of the actions and interactions, beliefs and assumptions; of people located inside it and outside' (Miller, 1977).

This led to the development of the "People Programme" which was
seen as an open-ended experiment which might have unknown and radical
outcomes and not as a controlled device for providing token worker
participation. The main element in this programme was the provision
of educational experiences for employees that derived from the group
relations training programmes: small group, intergroup and large
group events. Initially, these were provided for managerial,
supervisory and technical staff; later for any employee who wished
to attend.

Moreover, the consultant group, from its position on the
organizational boundary, attempted to interpret unconscious
processes in the system as a whole. An early outcome was the
development of problem-solving groups spontaneously created by
employees. A large self-selected group which met each week for
over two years became used as "container" for the feelings of
anxiety and doubt people were experiencing as well as for the debate
of larger issues about industrial democracy. It was also a Forum
for airing of "crazy" ideas - a place where the organization could
have its dreams, as it were.

These experiences resulted in people becoming more aware of
which boundaries they were managing. Some remained aloof or
antagonistic; many others reported that they now had greater
confidence to speak out and interpret what was taking place within
the firm as a system, i.e., the programme had provided opportunities
for people to gain insight and the authority to use it.

In the end the programme was stopped by management. Although
it could be shown that by business criteria Omicron was now the most
successful company in its division of Omega, having previously been
the worst, management disbanded the consultant group because they
were not certain as to where the programme might lead people in
their aspirations. We have to postulate, however, that they were
also expressing anxieties on that score for some employees within
Omicron itself.

The other case study is more recent. At the invitation of an
enterprise a project in industrial democracy was launched. The
consultant team from the Tavistock negotiated money and other
resources from the management of the firm to establish what was
called "System Future". The primary task of this system was to
provide opportunities for people to explore what it was like to
work in the firm and how they wished it to be in the future.

Each employee was invited to take part, but the choice was
theirs. A corollary to this decision was that there was no
negotiation with trade unions before the project was launched.
Employees were invited to exercise their freedom to choose for
themselves.

While people did come and talk about their experiences to the consultant team there was, on the whole, a denial of the team's existence. Essentially, the main struggle was with the unions who oscillated between wanting to cooperate and wanting to get rid of the team.

Using their experiences as these occurred, the team formulated working hypotheses which were offered to the local trade union leaders for testing. The central hypothesis was that trade union representatives were used by other employees to act as a buffer between them and management. Furthermore, they were being used to contain the feelings of anxiety that employees might hold about disorder and change. In addition, they had to hold the feelings of disillusionment and anger that all employees were denying. This led them into having to hold a "basic assumption fight" culture vis-a-vis management. This has to be contrasted with overt conflict, which can be a politically sophisticated method of gaining ends.

The resultant formulation was that the firm was characterised by the politics of dissociation, i.e., the majority dissociated themselves from the political processes and exported their feelings onto a minority (shop stewards). Management, equally, were also colluding in the same process.

One hypothesis is that the maintenance of a basic assumption fight culture is a defence against the anxiety of examining real conflicts of interests between management and workers.

The present state of the project is that the team is continuing to make attempts to have the working hypotheses explored by those concerned.

Both these projects in industrial democracy have been arrested in their development. Why?

One postulate is that increasingly in enterprises employees (whether managers or workers) are taking up a position of schizoid withdrawal. The reasons for this are complex and have been argued in a number of papers (Lawrence, 1979b, 1979c, 1979d). Essentially, the argument is that conditions in which employment is conducted cause the employee to regress into a less than adult position. In particular, the authority structures of employing institutions are directly reminiscent of the authority relations the individual experienced in childhood. One outcome is a feeling of anger. The employee, however, is in an impossible fix. If he expresses the anger directly he runs the risk of destroying his employing institution. On the other hand, if he takes the anger back into himself and becomes depressed, for instance, he runs the risk of immobilising himself. Consequently, he can only take up the schizoid position, i.e., withdraw from involvement with his feelings. He finds his satisfaction from within his sentient groups and not in the task organization.

Another way of describing this is to recognize the futility that employees feel.

Both these cases illustrate some of the connectedness between group relations training and consultancy. They also show the nature of the resistances that such consultancy encounters. But they also point to the ultimate need to be able to interpret the unconscious social processes in the larger society that come to influence the psychic and political lives of individuals in enterprises.

REFERENCES

Bion, W.R., 1961, "Experiences in Groups", Tavistock Publications, London.

Lawrence, W.G., 1979a, A Concept for Today: The Management of Self in Role, in: "Exploring Individual and Organizational Boundaries", W.G. Lawrence, ed., John Wiley & Sons, London.

Lawrence, W.G., 1979b, Making Life at Work Have Quality. Tavistock Institute Document No. 2T 281 (unpublished).

Lawrence, W.G., 1979c, Some Psychic and Political Dimensions of Work Experiences. Tavistock Institute Document No. 2T 282 (unpublished)

Lawrence, W.G., 1979d, Citizenship and the Work Place: A Current Case Study. Tavistock Institute Document No.2T 296 (unpublished)

Miller, E.J. and Rice, A.K., 1967, "Systems of Organization", Tavistock Publications, London.

Miller, E.J., 1976, Introductory Essay: Role Perspectives and the Understanding of Organizational Behaviour, in: "Task and Organization", E.J. Miller, ed., John Wiley & Sons, London.

Miller, E.J., 1977, Organizational Development and Industrial Democracy, in: "Organizational Development in the U.K. and U.S.A. : A Joint Evaluation", C. Cooper, ed., Macmillan, London.

Miller, E.J., 1979a, The Politics of Involvement. Paper presented to Scientific Meeting of the A.K. Rice Instit., March (unpublished)

Miller, E.J., 1979b, Autonomy, Dependency and Organizational Change, in: "Innovation in Patient Care: An Action Research Study of Change in a Psychiatric Hospital", D. Towell and C. Harries, eds., Croom Helm, London.

Rice, A.K., 1958, "Productivity and Social Organization: The Ahmedabad Experiment", Tavistock Publications, London.

Rice, A.K., 1963, "The Enterprise and its Environment", Tavistock Publications, London.

Rice, A.K., 1965, "Learning for Leadership: Interpersonal and Intergroup Relations", Tavistock Publications, London.

Winnicott, D.W., 1950, Some Thoughts on the Meaning of the Word Democracy, Human Relations, 3:175-186.

PATHOGENIC LEADERSHIP IN ORGANIZATIONS

Galvin Whitaker, Director of Organizational Research

Dept. of Management Studies, The University of Leeds

Leeds LS2 9JT, England

GROUPS, DECISION-MAKING, REALITY AND LEADERSHIP

If it is to survive, any organization, or unit which is part
of an organization, must maintain net favourable exchanges with its
environment.   That is to say, it must draw in to itself from its
surroundings enough resources to make up for all that it consumes
and all that it puts out.   A firm, for instance, must draw in
through revenue and other channels enough to be able to pay for wages
and for the materials and services which it uses, or it will eventually be unable to continue producing services and products.   A
government department must secure the appropriations or grants of
money and other support which will enable it to keep operating.   A
voluntary organization must generate such services or satisfactions
as will bring in sufficient voluntary workers for it to function.

Whether this will happen depends partly on the efforts of the
people who together are the organizational unit.   What they choose
to do will depend on their estimates of the feasibility and likely
consequences of various courses of action.   Actions are more likely
to be effective in leading to intended outcomes if they and the intentions towards which they are directed are based upon "realistic"
information about the surrounding world than if they have been chosen
on the basis of error and illusion.   One might indeed define
"realistic" information as assertions or beliefs confirmed by ensuing
experience, or as whatever serves as basis for actions which turn
out to be effective in accord with intention.

For a group's actions to be efficient as well as effective,
the members of the group need to function in concert rather than at

405

cross-purposes. To be compatible in this way their actions need to be based on a common or at least a compatible body of information, and on common or compatible rules for using it to make and carry out and monitor decisions.

Developing and maintaining some such body of realistic and consistent information, or "model of reality", is thus fundamental both to a group's functioning and to its survival. Contributing to developing and maintaining this model of reality is one of the major functions of a group's leader.

Next let us apply to some of the functions performed by leaders a simple closed-loop systems model for decision and action. According to such a model an action has consequences, information about which can be fed back for comparison with plans and intentions. The outcome of the comparison is then used with other situation reports and with predictions about the occurrence and consequences of events, in processes of decision and planning which issue in further action. Further action generates more consequences, information about which enters again into further rounds of similar processes.

In several parts of this sequence of processes leaders are important:

(a) Leaders often make decisions as to what actions shall be taken.

(b) To decisions about action, leaders contribute crucial information and influence as to what is feasible and what consequences are to be expected.

(c) Leaders construct and/or maintain the structures and procedures by which deciding, planning, monitoring, evaluating and the other elements of the process-sequence outlined above are done. For instance, a leader may establish decision-rules, or ways of securing, channelling and using feedback information, situation reports and predictions, and estimates of resources and of the strengths and purposes of allies and opponents.

(d) Leaders allot meaning, in the sense of elucidating or declaring what shall be held to be valid and usable information, and what weight is to be given to reports, and what conclusions are to be drawn from and actions based upon evidence coming in from the outside world.

Any leader who performs these functions does much more than merely tell other people what to do; he goes far towards controlling how others in his group see and understand the surrounding world.

disorientation and unease about self where they belong,namely to
the credit of the pathogenic leader and his activities. This does
not make such feelings comfortably bearable, nor does it guarantee
that one can then dispel them. It does however make sense of them,
by crediting them to their proper source, and thus reduces the
feelings of helplessness which otherwise can keep a person
immobilised in the grip of the adverse feelings.

If the leadership is indeed intransigently pathogenic, there
are two solutions either of which is conclusive. Both of them are
highly risky. They both involve simple and radical change in the
organization. One is for the person or persons who have perceived
and are subject to the pathogenic leadership to leave their jobs.
The other is for them to get the leader out of his job, whether by
firing or promotion or transfer. It may be that neither of them is
possible. If either of them is unsuccessfully attempted, one can
end up worse off than ever.

There are palliative and partial solutions. Those recommended
here have in common that they involve taking initiatives to safeguard and to supplement sources and channels of information, and
particularly feedback information, to use instead of the misleading
information which comes from or through the leader. There are at
least three applications of this recommendation which may usefully
be distinguished. One is to take steps to arm oneself at the
intrapersonal level against the intrusions of the leader and their
disorienting and immobilising consequences. This is done by re-
suming charge of one's own processes of inference about onself, at
the same time seeking other sources of information than the leader's
opinions. It would be prudent to look to this solution first and
always, since a person's ability to deal realistically and effectively with the leader or indeed with anything else is severely hampered
by unrealistic concerns about being of low worth, and by being
disoriented about self.

The second is an organizational solution. It is to take
initiatives to explore and to use the channels and sources of information which are formally and legitimately available in and through
the organization, to make up for the paucity or misleadingness of
the information which the leader provides about the organization
unit itself, the larger organization, the surroundings, and their
relationships.

The third is to work within what is allowable by the organization, in such a way as to reduce the need one's working group of
peers or subordinates has for rumour-mongering and related activities,
by providing them instead with opportunities for dealing directly
with one another in terms of actual specifics. Both the second and
the third solutions can with advantage be augmented by resorting to
devices which give conventional sanction to distinguishing observed

evidence from inference and clarifying who has what preferences and
expectations and who is doing what, with what specific consequences.
These devices are, for instance, the use of agenda-formulation to
clarify purposes, of reporting-back to establish operational
definition in terms of specific actions and outcomes, and of minuting
to keep transactions visible rather than having them reported in
terms of the leader's inferences about them.

Finally, there is the solution of not appointing nor going to
work for a pathogenic leader. For this it is necessary to recognise
such a leader in advance. To do so of course is not easy. However,
the costs of involving oneself with a pathogenic leader are so high
and the likelihood of extricating oneself without loss so low that
it is nevertheless worth the attention and effort. As in the case
of being trapped in a sailing ship between a storm and a lee shore,
so with being involved with a pathogenic leader: the advice which
writers on seamanship used to proffer is still ultimately the most
useful, namely that the best course of action is by every effort to
avoid ever getting into such a predicament.

Amongst issues which it would now appear profitable to discuss
are: the question of early warnings of pathogenic leadership
proclivities; examination of how it is that pathogenic leadership
is likely to be self-sustaining, rather than self-limiting or self-
extinguishing; and a review of the factors peculiar to organizations which influence the likelihood of potential pathogenic leaders
being appointed to positions of command. These are the subject of
an article now in preparation.

It is for obvious reasons peculiarly difficult to gather information on instances of pathogenic leadership by the ordinary
means of, for instance, observation and comparison of instances and
non-instances in the field. I therefore wish to ask the help of
people who read this article. I should be grateful for reports of
cases, anecdotes, experiences, incidents and events bearing in any
way on the subject matter and the arguments here presented.

REFERENCES

Adams, D., The restaurant at the end of the universe, London: Pan
     Books, 1980.
Brown, J.A.C., The social psychology of industry. Harmsworth,
     Middlesex: Penguin Books, 1954.
Jahoda, M. Current concepts of positive mental health. New York:
     Basic Books, 1958.
Kindrey, C. The little mouse who didn't come home. London: Hamlyn,
     1968, (Adapted from Konezumi Choro Choro. Tokyo: Kaisei-sha,
     1967).

Langdon, S. (Transcribed & Trans.) Enûma Elish: the Babylonian
    Epic of Creation. Oxford: Oxford University Press, 1923.
Seligman, M.E.P., Helplessness: on depression, development and
    death. San Francisco: W.H. Freeman & Co., 1975
Sherwood, J.J. An introduction to organization development. In
    Pfeiffer, J.W. & Jones, J.E., The 1972 Annual Handbook for
    Group Facilitators. Iowa City: University Associates, 1972.
Silone, I. Fontamara. Milano: Mondadori, 1949. (Quoted passage
    trans. by G. Whitaker)
Stanislavsky, C. An actor prepares. (E.R. Hapgood trans.) London:
    Geoffrey Bles, 1937.
Tannenbaum, R. & Savis, S.A. Values, man and organizations.   In
    Eddy, W.B., Burke, W.W., Dupré, V.A. & South, O. (Eds),
    Behavioral science and the manager's role. Washington, D.C.:
    NTL Institute for Applied Behavioral Science, 1969. (Reprinted
    from Industrial Management Review, 1969, 10, pp. 67 - 83).
Von Neumann, J. & Morgenstern, O. Theory of games and economic
    behaviour. Princeton: Princeton University Press, 1947.
Westwood, J. Gilgamesh and other Babylonian tales. London: The
    Bodley Head, 1968.
White, R.W. The enterprise of living: growth and organization in
    personality. New York: Holt, Rinehart & Winston, 1972.

COMMUNITY MENTAL HEALTH AND PSYCHIATRY: THE ITALIAN EXPERIENCE

Franco Paparo M.D.,Ph.D. and Maurizio Bacigalupi M.D.

Mental Health Center, City of Rome

12 via Sabrata, Rome, Italy

The first problem we had in preparing our paper was the strong need for our account of the Community based Mental Health Service in Italy to be correctly understood by people of many other Countries. In order to be understood we shall try our best to give clear and simple information, but we have to emphasize that even trivial expressions as "community" and "mental health" acquire special nuances according to cross-cultural differences.

To start with, as the American Scholar of Psychiatry and Law Leonard Kaplan aptly puts it, "it is worthwhile to debunk the notion that the "community" in "Community treatment" has anything to do with the consensual and committed interpersonal bonding associated with the concept "community". This notion presupposes the existence of a cohesive community which often dces not, in fact, exist"[1].

Bearing in mind the general trends of psychiatry, we can affirm that in last twenty years there has been a tendency all over the world to shift from the public mental hospital approach to the concept that mental health treatment should be available locally and provide a comprehensive range of services (in-patient, out-patient, partial hospitalization and emergency services) with continuity of care[2].

However, the diversities of the starting situation, and of medical, sociocultural and political backgrounds in the various Countries were such that they resulted, notwithstanding the common general trends, in marked differences in the actual pattern and rationale of the psychiatric services.

We cannot go into detail, but by way of example we may mention here that there are many analogies but many more differences and discrepancies between the pattern, dimensions and efficacy of the Community Mental Health Centers created in the United States[3,4,5] after the Community Mental Act of 1963, and the community psychiatric services with the same name (Mental Health Centers) being set up in Italy mostly after 1970. To give another example the Swedish Nacka

Project[6], set up in an outer suburb of Stockholm in 1974 "to provide
an immediate and almost comprehensive psychiatric service with minimal reliance upon inpatient facilities", was designed as a community
based experiment and care was taken to ensure the presence of a research and evaluation group monitoring the new development. In Italy
Community Mental Health Services were established, mostly after 1978,
by a national Law with the same aim, however formulated in a rather
abstract way ("to eliminate any kind of discrimination and segregation and to provide favorable conditions for the recovery and social
reintegration of mental patients")[7] and in sharp contrast with the
Swedish project there was no provision of research to monitor the
possible consequences of the Law.

We shall come back to the vital problem of research and evaluation of results later. Now, in order to outline the developments in
recent years, we need to characterize the situation of public psychiatry in Italy in the early 60s, which really means to describe
the State Mental Hospitals (then the only resource available to
mental patients of the lower socio-economic strata) and the laws
governing admission.

As far as the Italian mental hospitals are concerned, we point
out that their structure and main regulations were about the same
as those described by Erving Goffman in his research[8], but in
addition the living conditions were extremely poor and the patients
were utterly abandoned.

The psychiatric law dated from 1904 and regulated compulsory
admission to the mental hospital of people, who were considered by
a single doctor (usually a general practitioner) to be "dangerous
to themselves or to others or creating public scandal".

In practice this formula allowed easy admission, not only of
mental patients, but also of young mentally handicapped (sometimes
children), patients with organic diseases, seniles, mild behaviour
disturbance cases, coming from the lower socio-economic strata.

Once in the Mental Hospital the patient was kept in an "observation ward" where he (or she) could stay up to one month. The only
treatments available were psychotropic drugs and E.C.T., which was
used very intensively (up to once a day) and without discrimination
(for instance E.C.T. was a routine practice in states of agitation).
The wards were crowded, under-staffed and the nurses had no psychiatric training.

The psychiatrists were generally strictly biologically minded
and very concerned about their legal responsibility in discharging
the patients: after one month, if any "dangerousness" was still
considered present the patient was not discharged and was transferred
to a common ward of the hospital. The same lack of definition of the
concept "dangerousness" and the fact that there was not a service
to give some support to the patients when discharged, meant that
underprivileged people, with no family or a poor background, were
kept for months, sometimes for years, even when mental pathology was
not relevant or absent.

In the common wards (the true Asylum) the patients were amassed, according to their clinical condition.

The buildings were squalid and dilapidated, and had practically no furniture, except beds, tables and benches. In particular there were no cupboards and the patients had no personal drawers, so they were obliged to carry with them their personal belongings in a plastic bag. The patient had poor and improper clothings and shoes and had no money from social Security. The doors were all locked. There was no program of rehabilitation.

The hierarchy of privileges between the patients was the same as in Goffman's research: at the apex of the pyramid were the patients working for the hospital for a miserable pay. In a study performed in the early 70s by one of us[9], during the hard work to transform one of these wards into a therapeutic community, it was observed that the dominant defensive mechanisms used by the staff against anxiety caused by the close contact with mentally disturbed people, were of a psychotic type (splitting, massive projections, scapegoating etc.). As symbolized by the lack of cupboards in the wards, the hospital had no function of "containment" of the patient's anxieties.

In such a horrible situation[10], Franco Basaglia, appointed director in 1961, found the Mental Hospital of Gorizia, a small town in the north-east of Italy, at the border with Yugloslavia. After many months of debate in the psychiatric staff two simple concepts emerged: (a) the mental hospital does not meet the needs of the patients and (b) the mental hospital is an end in itself. It was therefore decided that "the mental disease be initially disregarded" so that the patient's needs could be listened to and considered. In this initial stage the British Therapeutic Community was a model of cultural reference, even if criticized by Franco and Franca Basaglia: "what seems to be lacking in Maxwell Jones's argument is an analysis of the word social: social is considered a "fact" and not a "product", the political dimension being overlooked"[11].

Basaglia was on the other hand influenced by existentialism and antipsychiatry and proposed a "class" analysis of psychiatric emargination. So the Gorizia experience was characterized right from the start as opposition to the role of custody bestowed by the capitalist society on psychiatry.

With the publication in 1968 of "L'Istituzione Negata"[12], the so-called anti-institutional battle became a point of convergence of the students' movement and of the great workers' achievements in those years (the workers rights Statute, the admission into the factories of technicians chosen by the workers to control the health conditions, the broader sphere of action of the Unions in the factory etc.).

Starting from 1965 in Perugia, in the centre of Italy, severe criticism of the mental hospital had been made. This time the left-wing politicians responsible for local government join the enlightened psychiatrists to fight for de-institutionalization of the mental

hospital, crowned by the opening of ten Community Mental Health
Centers and the transfer of psychiatric care from the hospital to the
Community itself, in the period between 1970 and 1975.

On the other hand, in Gorizia, the absence of bonds between
Basaglia's team, the political powers and the workers movement, was
one of the main reasons for the resignation (in 1972) of the medical
staff, after the refusal by the local authorities of the proposal
to close down the hospital and transfer psychiatric care to the
Community.

After 1970 many Italian local authorities, impressed by the
cultural success of the New Psychiatry, called upon psychiatrists,
who had worked in Gorizia, to direct mental hospitals in the North
and Centre.

Prof. Franco Basaglia was appointed director of the Mental
Hospital in August 1971 by the Provincial administration of Trieste,
with a personal support of its President, who was anxious to change
the situation.

Dr. Douglas Bennet, consultant psychiatrist at the Maudsley
Hospital in London, acting as consultant of the W.H.O. visited
Trieste seven years after the initial transformations (August 21st-
September 9th 1978) "to make an assessment report on the organiza-
tion of psychiatric services in Trieste in the light of the recent
change in Mental Hospital policy".

Since the written appraisal by Dr. Bennet, recently published
by the regional office for Europe of W.H.O. in Copenhagen[13], is
very clear, simple and detailed we shall use it extensively, often
verbatim.

The province of Trieste (before the first world war part of
the Austro-Ungarian Empire) is situated in the north-east corner of
Italy. In 1969 the population was 300,304. In the hospital, built in
1908, there were 1,262 inmates. 1,210 patients were compulsory
admitted; only 52 were voluntary (in 1968 a limited psychiatric Law
had been passed introducing voluntary admission). 1,130 people were
admitted to the hospital during that year. The high bed ratio (4
beds per 1,000 inhabitants) reflects the psychiatrist's caution and
anxiety about discharging patients.

After his appointment as Director of the Mental Hospital in
1971, Basaglia recruited more social workers, some nurses and some
young psychiatrists to fill the vacant posts, to set in motion a
policy of abolishing the mental hospital and replacing it with other
services.

Reforms related to the (improper) custody and impoverishment
of patients were speedily undertaken. Ward doors were opened, the
number of compulsory patients reduced and financial benefit for
individual (discharged) patients mobilised. Those patients unable
to find a community placement were encouraged to live more independently as "guests" (i.e. relieved of some legal disadvantages and
entitled to the payment of the Social Benefit) in facilities of the
hospital site.

In 1974 three district mental health centers were opened. With the support of three teams, each based on a centre, the process of deinstitutionalization and discharge of the patients continued.

The number of residents was reduced to 810. 350 were voluntary patients, 360 guests and only 100 compulsory patients. In 1976-77 three more centers were opened in the Community and the first group apartments for discharged patients were set up. Hospital admissions, which had been reduced, could be discontinued; a single admission unit situated in the hospital site, but linked with the centers and having no connection with the hospital, was provided for those acutely ill patients, who needed overnight stay.

The most recent innovation was the emergency service, which provides consultations in the general hospital casualty department and arranges emergency admission. The emergency team screens referrals and seeks alternatives to hospital admission. In 1977 there were 1,144 consultations in the emergency service. There were 492 referrals to the admission ward; nobody was sent to the mental hospital.

In the mental hospital there were only 344 persons (262 guests, 41 voluntary and only 33 compulsory).

The apartments in town were 18.

As Douglas Bennet rightly remarks, the principal trends of the change we have barely outlined are in keeping with the more advanced trends in European psychiatric practices:

a) intense transformation of the hospital prior to its dissolution and continuing responsibilities for the patients;

b) comprehensiveness, variety and good integration of services.

But major theoretical principles and operational style are at variance. We shall list which are in our opinion the most important and debatable differences:

a) In Trieste there is little emphasis on "medical" treatment even in severe functional psychosis: apart from medication (used at moderate dosage and mostly as a means of establishing a relationship with the patients) no physical methods are employed;

b) There is no use of formal psychotherapeutic methods. The removal of institutionalizing influences and an active concern for patient's needs are more evident than any planned program of rehabilitation.

c) As in Gorizia, there is much use of group meetings (small and large) with a stimulation of the group resources by the leaders. The main focus in the group meeting is to promote sharing,mirroring and solidarity among the members in the process of "reconstructing the history" of their career as mental patients.

d) Much stress is laid upon team-work or group-work among the staff with insistence on role-blurring, hierarchy negation and equal sharing of responsibilities.

e) Little attention is dedicated to formal training of the nurses: the accent is on their human motivation, along with their involvement in political and social fights against inequality and discrimination of the underprivileged.

The deep change in Trieste demonstrated that with determination, enthusiasm and good integration of efforts by the politicians,local

administrators,and the psychiatrists involved, the mental hospital
could be dismantled with "staffing level not unduly high" and only
a real increase of 13.5% in the overall costs of the psychiatric
services.

These favourable results, and the ones obtained along the same
lines in other Provinces of North and Central Italy (Perugia, Arezzo,
Reggio Emilia, Parma) were extensively publicized in Italy and
abroad through the mass media. In this atmosphere,more than five
hundred thousand signatures had been collected to repeal the psychiatric Law of 1904 (considered outdated and against the most ele-
mentary civil rights); in order to avoid a national referendum of
uncertain outcome in May 1978 a new Law was passed by Parliament.

The new legislation was formulated under the pressure of the
Italian Society of Psychiatry (a professional association), of F.
Basaglia and "Psichiatria Democratica" (the association of the New
Psychiatry) and the political and social forces which in those years
had been working to renew psychiatric care.

The three main points of the new legislation (included afterwards in the Law 833 of December 1978 establishing in Italy the
National Health Service) were:

a) closing down of the Mental Hospital, where new patients
could not be accepted any more;

b) development of community care and near elimination of hospitalization, which would in any case be in general hospitals (in
psychiatric services of no more than 15 beds);

c) abolition of the concept of "dangerousness" of the mental
patient and introduction of rules further garanteeing individual
freedom, especially in case of compulsory medical treatment (which
must be the exception rather than the rule);

In essence the Law had the aim of extending the successful
experiences of Trieste and Perugia to all the Country, without any
due consideration to the real situation of the Mental Hospital and
to the phase of development of the alternative services, in the
different areas of Italy.

Now we shall see the data collected by the Italian National
Research Council (section of Psychology) more than one year after
the enforcement of the new Law and presented for the first time in
Arezzo at a Congress, devoted to the evaluation of the outcome of
the Law (Psychiatry and Good Government, October 1979).

	North	Center	South	Total
Compulsory admission 1977 (mental hospitals)	18,246	5,225	8,818	32,289
Compulsory medical treatments 1978-79 (general hospitals)	7,561	1,543	3,111	12,215
Percent of variation	-58.5	-70	-65	-63

The above figures show compulsory admissions one year before
(1977) and one year after (June 1978/May 1979) the new Law. We can

observe that in the North, Center and South of Italy there was a
very marked drop in the compulsory admissions. From a total of
32,289 compulsory admissions in 1977, there was a fall to 12,215
compulsory medical treatments from June 1978 to May 1979. The percent of variation was minus 63. Note the drop in the South from
8,218 to 3,111 with a percent of variation of minus 65.

The next figures show voluntary admissions one year before
(1977) and one year after (June 1978/May 1979) the new Law.

	North	Center	South	Total
Voluntary admissions 1977 (mental hospitals)	31,403	9,946	9,578	50,927
Voluntary admissions 78/79 (mental hospitals and general hospitals)	42,271	12,544	10,080	64,895
percent of variation	+ 34	+ 26	+ 5	+ 27.5

There is an increase in voluntary admissions in the North,
Center and South of Italy, with a total of 64,895 admissions in
mental Hospitals and general hospitals from June 1978 to May 1979
and a percent of variation, in comparison with 1977, of plus 27.5.
We have to stress the sharp difference between the figures for the
North (from 31,403 to 42,271: percent of variation + 34) and for
the South (from 9,578 to 10,080: percent of variation + 5). We shall
come back later to the meaning of these figures in the South. Let's
now consider the total number of psychiatric admissions in Italy
(compulsory and voluntary) from June 1978 to May 1979 (fig.1).

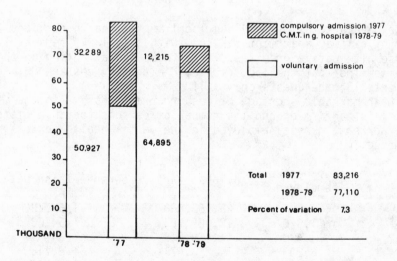

Fig.1 Total of admissions (compulsory and voluntary) during 1977
       and from 6.1st 1978 to 5.31st 1979).

In other words: we believe that a hierarchy of curative factors exists in any course of treatment. We do not contest that abreaction, affective reactions, catharsis, form important stages of the hierarchy, but the interpretation in the situation of transference appears in our opinion to be of even further importance. The situation of transference is fundamentally based on the biography of the patient, and an interpretation proves impossible without the therapist's knowledge of this biography and without his ability to place the interpretation within a theoretical frame of reference.

To the above rather rigorous demands of what could in our opinion be defined as psychotherapy we should like to add the following comments:

Various other forms of therapy other than the classical psychoanalytical ones or the psycho-analytically orientated ones deny a theoretical and biographical basis. Irrespective of this face we believe them to be therapeutically successful in many cases, in spite of themselves. In the first case, the therapist will unwittingly and unconsciously make use of biography and theory. In the second case, even if he consciously refuses this basis from a politico-ideological standpoint, he will still use it. In any case, we conclude that therapy can only be understood as processes complying with our demands mentioned above.

Finally we feel it is important to emphasize the necessity of the professionalism of the therapist. No matter how we turn matters over in our minds we feel that to be justified in calling yourself a therapist you should possess both education and professional training. The therapist should have experienced a certain form of self-therapy, he should master some basic theoretical knowledge, just as he should have had the opportunity of being supervised in his work.

As for the patient, he should be well-motivated, or it should be possible to make him motivated, just as he should be willing to work upon himself and acquire insight into his conflicts, so that he is able to take part in a lasting treatment together with his therapist. At the same time the therapist should endeavour to meet his patient on his own terms, so that the interaction between the two persons will result in the development of the patient from one stage to another, where this stage is already integrated in the mind of the therapist.

Here it is only natural to us here in Copenhagen to quote Søren Kierkegaard who wrote as early as well over one hundred years ago: That if real success is to attend the effort to bring a man to a definite position, one must first of all take pains to find HIM where he is and begin there. This is the secret of the art of helping others. Anyone who has not mastered this is himself deluded when he proposes to help others. In order to help another effectively I must understand more than he - yet first of all surely I must understand what he understands.

Does Christiania Constitute A Therapeutic Community?

In our efforts to make clear to ourselves what we mean by the term "therapy" we shall now have to look more closely at the concept of "The Therapeutic Community" and its connection to our view of Christiania.

The concept of the therapeutic community has existed for approximately thirty years, launched by Tom Main in 1948, and it has found immense dispersion in the treatment philosophy of the Western World. However, it is clear that the concept will hardly comply with our definition of "psychotherapy", e.g. the demands for biography and theoretical frames of reference. It is immediately obvious that the phenomenon contains certain therapeutic aspects, but for the sake of consistency we shall suggest that the term be changed, even though this will prove difficult.

Contriving to find a term that in our opinion is more appropriate than the Therapeutic Community we hit upon the term Freetown which has its roots in Danish history. The term Freetown is the designation of a town which was legitimized by the State as a refuge for outlaws, criminals and unwanted ethnic groups in the 17th and 18th centuries. Today Christiania calls itself a Freetown. In our view, all therapeutic communities are, in fact, freetowns of various kinds, each with its own subculture.

The Freetown of Christiania is relevant in this connection, because it presents numerous examples of active tolerance, as we have already suggested.

The sociologist, Ferdinand Tönnies made the distinction between the concept of Gemeinschaft and that of Gesellschaft. In the first case the interaction of the members of the community is characterised by a mechanical solidarity to be understood in the way the members see their immediate advantages in "being related to each other".

Opposed to this is the organization of the highly industralized Western society where solidarity between the members of the society is rooted in the structure of that society, as rules and statutory instruments which are not even felt to be immediately important to the existence of each individual.

In our opinion there is no doubt that the vast majority of the psychiatric patients that pass through the established psychiatric system are handicapped by the lack of close relationships, in other words the above-mentioned mechanical solidarity.

When we see a number of persons in Christiania who has been stigmatized as deviants by the established society and who have in many cases passed through numerous institutions for treatment, we find that they function much better in Christiania and as we suggested in case number three, this is because the Freetown provides mechanical solidarity and <u>Gemeinschaft-relationship</u> far more easily than the established society.

But Christiania does not always function "therapeutically" in the debased sense of that word. As mentioned in case number two at the beginning of this paper, it is of course possible in this type of community to find situations which may be mistaken for active tolerance, but which are in reality expressions of a laissez-faire attitude, or social apathy. In any event, this social apathy will have unfortunate consequences for each individual member of the society, and as mentioned earlier, the established clinical agencies will have more to offer than mere indifference.

Finally, as we saw in case number one, it should be mentioned that many of the Christianites have themselves undergone various forms of treatment and on this basis may be more sensitive to the needs of other deviants than most people in the established society.

To summarize it can thus be said:

That Christiania is not a "psychotherapeutic" agency in the rigorous definition of that term because it lacks the conditions necessary for the process of psychotherapy to take place that Christiania is not a "therapeutic community" in the debased sense of that term because of the high level of social apathy that is a necessary component of its existence, but that Christiania, like similar communities, is a Freetown because it is characterized by a blend of active tolerance, Gemeinschaft-relationships, and of social apathy as well.

Despite its psychotherapeutic limitations, the concept of the Freetown does provide a useful alternative to the established clinical agencies because it offers an oasis for suffering persons who do not at all belong in our psychiatric wards, but who will often end up there in default of a better solution. In a Freetown they might find a refuge where as law-abiding citizens together they could build up a new life or recuperate of their own free will. At the same time an openness should exist in the established agencies so that people who were unable to cope with life in a Freetown would be included in the system for a shorter or longer period, in order to return later either to the Freetown or to the established society whenever they feel prepared to do so.

SOLIDARITY AS A PROBLEM IN SOCIETY AND THERAPY

Horst-Eberhard Richter

Center of Psychosomatic Medicine
University of Giessen
D-6300 Giessen

Psychologists and psychotherapists are in general
reluctant to express their opinion on burning issues of
the day. The ethnopsychoanalyst Paul Parin (1978) has
investigated the reasons why psychoanalysts in particular behave in this way. Among other factors, he adduces:
analysts do not wish their identity to be threatened by
active external participation; the life of society has
no place in its social niche between armchair and couch;
the theme of psychoanalysis is the inner life of the
individual and not society; psychoanalysis envisages
adaptation to the conditions of capitalist society; the
insights of psychoanalysis mature only gradually and
usually come about only when it is much too late for
adopting a position to current events.

Developments in group therapy and family therapy
in addition to individual analysis have now changed some
of these limitations. Group therapy is no longer primarily concerned with the inner world of the individual
but with the relations between individuals and with
group processes. Thereby, it necessarily impinges on
the connexions between psychological processes and
social factors. But there is only a slow growth of
interest in using this expanded viewpoint to supply
contributions to the elucidation of burning issues of
the day. Only cautiously - too cautiously, in my opinion -
is any use made of the possibility of drawing practical
conclusions from recognisable relationships and analogies
between microsocial and macrosocial conflicts.

Many therapists base or rationalise their abstinence
in this context on the traditional delimitation of their
subject. They thereby deny that in every case treated by
them and in every treated family or group they have to
deal, not only with conflicts produced by those treated
themselves, but also, often and in decisive measure,
with the effects of social factors. On the other hand,
the problem clearly poses itself of clarifying the
effect of psychological conflicts on the political
posture of individuals, groups and institutions. The
noble self-effacing argument that one should not, for
Heaven's sake, inadmissibly psychologise political problems, completely ignores the fact that there exists no
superfluity, rather a striking deficiency, of contributions to the clarification of the motives involved in
regulating political conflicts and crises.

I should like to exemplify this in relation to the
common attitudes connected with nuclear weapons and the
problem of the prevention of war. This topic has once
again demonstrated its surpassing importance through
the critically sharpened general political situation in
the first half of this year. Anxiety about war has expressed itself in the many fantasies and dreams of our
patients and has repeatedly flared up in the discussion
of therapeutic groups. Not least we therapists ourselves
are seized by this unease. Thus, at the German Congress
of Psychotherapy in Lindau, prompted by a spontaneous
impulse a joint letter to the government was drawn up
with the demand for measures to safeguard peace. But
the general excitement is already gradually subsiding
again. The discussions that have taken place in contacts
beween politicians of east and west, so far so little
productive of concrete agreement, supply the desired
pretext for further massive regression of the existing
danger of war continuing with the escalation in armaments.
Enormous psychological defensive processes produce a
gigantic appeasing self-deception. Among other effects,
they prevent one from grasping that the prevailing
doctrine of the alleged guarantee of peace through
deterrence, which seems to sanction any escalation in
nuclear armaments - provided only that this takes place
in equilibrium - results in a constant increase in the
risk of catastrophe.

This denial implies a tremendous psychological
failure in face of the greatest threat to the survival
of humanity. "It is", wrote KARL JASPERS in 1958, "as
if this subject belongs to those about which one is
silent for decency's sake. For there is a danger that

it may render life intolerable. But it is this intole-
rableness alone that can lead to the event which changes
the very threatening state of affairs itself." "Overriding possibilities is opposed to reason."

Significantly, it was not psychologists but physi-
cists and philosophers who originally emphatically
postulated that without a thoroughgoing alteration in
human psychological attitudes an effective strategy for
the prevention of war can never be attained. Exactly
30 years ago ALBERT EINSTEIN warned: "The unleashed
power of the atom has changed everything except for our
way of thinking... We need an essentially new mode of
thought if humanity is to survive." And he added in
illustration: "Men must fundamentally change their
attitude to one another and their view of the future."
The German atomic physicist MAX BORN agreed with him:
"There is now no longer much time available; what
matters is that this our generation is prepared to
think anew. If it cannot do so, the days of civilised
man are numbered."

BORN and the British physicist P.M.S. BLACKETT,
indeed expresses great anxiety that the human psyche
might possibly offer not only an inadequate resistance
against atomic armament; rather, this armament, for
its part, threatens to evoke psychological reactions
which would, on the contrary, increase the risk of war
even further. As early as 1956 BLACKETT prophesied:
"Once a nation bases its security on an absolute
weapon (the atomic bomb), it becomes psychologically
necessary to believe in an absolute enemy." MAX BORN
underlined and substantiated this danger: "In order to
soothe the conscience of man towards military plans
which contemplate the slaughter of many tens and even
hundreds of millions of men, women and children of the
other side - and, which is however obscured, of their
own also - the other side must be thought of as depra-
ved and aggressive by nature."

Ladies and gentlemen, does not this year in
particular furnish us with massive evidence for the
accuracy of the pessimistic socio-psychological con-
jectures of BLACKETT and BORN? Is it not the belief in
the absolute enemy which, on either side and despite
the risk of selfdestruction, makes possible an ever more
dangerous mutual threat with the most terrible weapons
of massdestruction? Do not the majority of us participate unresistingly and even unconsciously in an archaic
and primitive delusion, in the projective fixation on

the picture of an absolute enemy, which spares us the
intolerable perception of our own shared responsibility
for an insane confrontation strategy which is falsely
labelled as politics of détente?

We psychologists and therapists have therefore
arrived at the paradoxical position that scientists and
philosophers have advanced with critical socio-
psychological hypotheses and analyses into a field that
most of us, for whatever reason, have all too long
neglected. For the moment I would prefer to continue
no further with the series of interpretations for our
abstinence advanced by PARIN, little as we may ultimately avoid this task of resolving our difficulties.
I would rather, for the time being, proceed to consider
where and how we analysts and therapists may engage in
significant fashion in order to contribute so overcoming the psychological conditions of serious abnormal
political attitudes.

It is cogent, for this scrutinizing reflexion, to
seize on the pre-eminent problem of personal attitudes
to the atomic armaments race. Actually, we need only
touch on the programmatic warning words of EINSTEIN,
BLACKETT, BORN and JASPERS for us to recognise, as
psychospecialists, that we are called on to cooperate.
Peace is only possible, as EINSTEIN explained, when men
fundamentally change their attitude to one another. Is
this not a theme of our daily therapy of relational
conflicts, to help men to alter their attitude to one
another in a positive sense? But we now know, however,
that men only seriously exert themselves towards constructive change if they suffer the consequences of their
previous behavior or fear such consequences in the future.
But the immutability of the masses with regard to the
danger of atomic warfare follows as a direct consequence
of the fact that they completely repress this danger.
The mere knowledge of the growing possibility of total
destruction is of no avail, wrote JASPERS, if this
knowledge is encapsulated. As he asserted: "We must consider it daily, if an item of knowledge is to engender
a response in us."

But this is precisely what does not happen. Great
citizen initiatives have been launched in many of our
western countries to campaign against ecological
nuisances and against the construction of atomic power
stations. But no comparable mass movement has so far
been concentrated on the even more urgent danger, in
scale exceeding all other, of reckless nuclear armament.

The reasons for this repression are easy to name. But yet nothing is changed by this.

What matters, then, is that ever more men learn to face their anxiety. But they can only do so if, at the same time, they find the possibility of discussing their anxiety with others. Thus, it does not suffice for experts to interpret this repression in public. Men must seek opportunities to unburden themselves to each other of the pressure under which they live. Anxiety can only be borne by sharing it.

From this motive a series of small initiatives have already developed which have dedicated themselves to working for peace. Groups of women, socialists, Christians or other variedly linked communal groups of citizens come together and concern themselves with how they can do something to lessen the danger of war. Thereby they usually rapidly acquire the experience that profits every single member in that he supports the others and the others support him in coming to terms with a constant menace which one believes himself capable of evading through this very repression and denial, if only in illusion. A first important step in such initiatives, therefore, consists in consciously and expressly taking the pressure of the burden on oneself; one must learn to accept it before all other activities.

When I here portray these processes in such initiative groups, this casts me in the role of an expert observer acquiring from outside a sympathetic understanding of what others do together. But I must say at this point that, as a therapist, I have the same difficulties as everyone else in coping with my anxiety in face of the ever-increasing danger of a nuclear war. I, too, am unable to reflect daily on the fearful possibility, as JASPERS demanded, without exchanging ideas with others and considering with them how we can best articulate our will to resist.

Thus it has arisen that I myself participate in such an initiative. I seek therein precisely the support of those others I would like to help, so that we may together become better able to defend ourselves against the oppression of a political development vitally threatening all of us. I therefore report on the works of these initiatives not as a superior scientific specialist, but as an involved and co-responsible member of such a group; as an engaged citizen, so to speak,

who can freely contribute with analytic and group
therapy experience to clarifying many internal and external conflicts of the initiative in its psychological
aspects. Persons from divers other vocations and disciplines are in a position to help the group forward in other
ways with essential information or practical suggestions.
The principle remains that one takes as one gives,
reciprocally, whereby all feel responsible for what is
to be jointly studied and executed.

Hitherto, such base initiatives, intended as
stated to serve the policies of peace, have still led
a relatively unpretentious existence. Their particular
difficulty lies in that they strive to deal with a problem that is of overwhelming dimensions, that is, further,
completely invisible, and finally more than any other
seems to be remote from the direct political influence
exerted by the base. Therefore, within such groups the
articulation of the anxiety and the portrayal of the
danger instantly combine with the concern as to whether,
and if so, what one can really do about it. All the
defence and escape impulses which are otherwise custo-
marily mobilised in the reductive repression of the fear
of atomic war also appear naturally in these initiatives,
even when their members have expressly banded together
in a common resistance.

Some persons soon disappear again. Others prefer
to concern themselves with nothing but the technical
organisation of events, resolutions and other measures
to do with peace policies. Others again soon return in
their discussion to the classical paranoid enemy perspectives with which the anxiety is habitually projectively
displaced also in the social environment. In doing so,
a reversal of the disparagement frequently occurs.
Again one takes refuge in a persecution theory, but in
one with reversed symptoms. The resistance against the
levelling pressure of the surrounding social majority
then ends up in a unilateral confrontation with one's
own party, because the tension of a superior mediating
position can be sustained only with difficulty.

Steadfast and constructive further work demands
that one accepts and sustains not only the anxiety of
the external danger of the atomic weapon threat, but
also the anxiety of the shared personal responsibility
for the creation and constant increase of this danger.
Only if one can tolerate the thought of personal implication may one relinquish the scapegoat projection which
MAX BORN has revealed as the obvious escape from
the conflict of conscience.

If such initiative groups can withstand the first trials of strength which result from the conflicts that inevitably arise within them, they find themselves confronted with the task of persevering in the pursuit of two parallel aims. On the one hand they will and must work in an outward direction. They must join together with similarly motivated groups, they must stir up public opinion, and they must exert a measurable pressure on the responsible political groups and institutions in order to prevent these from obstinately pursuing a paranoid policy of disparagement and armaments race. But they can only confidently make progress on this long path if the members of the groups keep in view, as their second aim, the alteration of their own modes of life and behavior according to the principles which must prevail in the macrosociety if this is to realise a genuine peace and not one guaranteed by a temporary stalemate of deterrence. This is precisely what EINSTEIN so rightly demanded: "Men must fundamentally change their attitude to one another and their view of the future." This is a task for every individual, at which he has to work perseveringly in discussion and in cooperation with others if he, or the groups, are to press credibly for a corresponding alteration in political principles and strategies.

The linkage of these two postulates, the demand for an alternative policy in combination with an equivalent alteration in personal modes of life and behaviour, characterises the self-understanding of a basic movement for peace that is as yet not very impressive but is convincingly founded as to its concept. Against the supremacy of the rigid bureaucrats, incapable of innovation, for whom the radical rethinking and realignment necessary to ensure peace is impossible, something can be most likely achieved, if at all by a flow of basic citizen initiatives which may possibly expand into a broad movement of self-help.

What has developed in many places, and especially by parts of critical youth, as a so-called alternative culture and is being further developed, makes plain the propulsive force of positive newer and more humane norms and behaviour patterns, which might be capable of seriously challenging in the long run the principles of a militantly rivalistic society which cannot exist without violence and war over a longer period.

This confidence in the prospects of basic initia-

tives, which may appear to many of you at least dubious
if not completely illusionary, is shared by me with a
range of colleagues with whom, for some 10 years, I
have been either studying divers variants of new self-
help organisations from the outside or experiencing
them from within. Some of you are possibly aware of our
Giessen studies on spontaneous parent-child groups and
on initiative group work in housing estates for the
homeless. Through the agency of M.L. MOELLER, at our
Center for Psychosomatic Medicine in Giessen, much has
been done for the promotion and study of therapeutic
self-help groups. In addition, we as therapists have
been cooperating for 7 years in our region in a particular self-help organisation known as the Psychosocial
Study Group. Psychologists, physicians, social workers,
home teachers, nurses, remedial educationists, family
counsellors, geriatric helpers, probation officers,
clergyman and lay helpers from over 50 institutions meet
together regularly, partly in plenary sessions, partly
in subgroups, in order to collaborate more closely in
our own field and act in common for improvement in the
organisation and coordination of the psychosocial care
of the population. The experience gained in these
various activities is that in all these self-help groups,
which stem from the distress of the socially disadvantaged
of patients, of marginal groups, of citizens who feel
themselves under threat or of vocational aid groups
considering themselves inefficient, there arises a latent
and important political potential that replenishes those
social forces which have already been rather widely
deployed in the so-called alternative youth culture. This
then expresses itself, in manifold variants, as something
like a social will to recovery. The advance of the
citizens' self-help organisations, from the base outwards,
follows precisely on the recognition that the established
social institutions, by virtue of their rigid structure
and rituals, deny the necessity of fundamental rethinking.
What can no longer be expected from above can only be
given impetus from below. And so the concept finally
develops that one should come together in a citizens'
movement for such general tasks as ensuring peace. For
it is worth stating, on the widest possible basis, that
men will not much longer acquiesce in a political
evolution which, in itself, and because of the accumulated
extent of barely controllable destructive energy , makes
reliable and truly peaceful coexistence of men and peoples
impossible. The vicious interaction between armaments
race, alarm and persecuation ideology, als BLACKETT and
BORN have pointed out, can presumably only be halted
when men venture to set so work to embody their opposi-

tion in the mighty expression of a mass movement.

Ladies and gentlemen, the far-reaching implications
of our psychological dealings with the risk of war and
the possible perspectives of a self-help society seem
remote from the professional field in which we move in
daily life when we are working with our clients in a
practice, clinic or advisory body. But I assert that
there nevertheless exists a much closer connexion in so
far as we should consider, whether we would not need a
radically new concept of psychosocial health, one that
reaches beyond or rather above purely medical criteria
to the capacity for that new attitude which EINSTEIN
demanded. Let us deal with this in more detail.

For long, psychiatry and psychotherapy have uncritically acquiesced in society's mandate to deal with
disorders of adaption as diseases in themselves, without
asking whether in the actual circumstances a smooth
adaption is truly reasonable. One is orientated towards
organic disease: adapted functioning quite simply counts
as healthy. The leading American army psychiatrist in
the last World War, WILLIAM MENNINGER, called for a
searching illumination of American education and family
structure because it appeared to him as an intolerable
danger for national health that fourteen per cent of
young Americans had been rejected as unfit for military
service on psychological grounds. In fact, the majority
of these were neither actually ill nor incapable of work.
The converse question, whether the capacity for psychologically or psychosomatically unimpaired functioning
within the homicidal machinery of a war is an obvious
aim of psychosocial prevention, remained long undis-
cussed in the postwar psychiatric literature. G.ELSÄSSER,
former director of a German psychotherapeutic institute,
in an article in 1961, expressed surprise that he had
found twenty per cent of "inconspicuous" characteristics
in 1400 so-called war neuroses in soldiers studied by
him in the Second World War, in his own words: "soldierly",
"orderly", "alert" and "matter-of-fact" men. Sooner he
had understood the medical decompensation of presumably
striking and deviant characters, in which he included,
among others, simple, weak, shiftless, aggressive and
self-willed persons. Whether one should not rather
regard as deviant and undesirable that psychological
disposition which permits a man to take part in the
annihilating activity of a war in an always alert,
matter-of-fact,orderly and efficient manner has been
only recently and occasionally, but still much too
rarely, considered.

Further, it was WILLIAM MENNINGER under whose direction group therapy was first established as standard
procedure. It first entered into American military
psychiatry in the last World War. MENNINGER wrote:
"It was impossible for the psychiatrist to spend much
time with individual patients. Consequently, physicians
treated many patients simultaneously, a method that had
been partly explored with children before the war.
Obviously, the newly introduced group therapy, together
with pharmacotherapy, narcoanalysis, electrotherapy and
various techniques, served exclusively for the purpose
of rendering soldiers with psychological or psychosomatic symptoms fit again as quickly as possible for
reentery into the homicidal machinery of the war.

The psychotherapist ELSÄSSER developed for this
purpose a very painful so-called electrosuggestive
therapy,with which he treated so-called chronic war
neurotics - admittedly predominantly against their will -
with powerful and extremely unpleasant electric shocks.
The anxiety to do with the war was expelled by the fear
of the electric shocks. Even 16 years after the end of
the war, the author, without critical reflexion, evaluated the fact that this was successful in eighty per cent
of cases as another medical success.

For the average approach of psychiatry and psychotherapy in wartime, what counts as specially significant
is merely the degree of automatic adaptation to which
self-understanding thrives in our discipline. Avowed or
unavowed, the aim of all prevention and treatment is the
pliable, utilisable man who tolerates even the most inhuman
and unreasonable demands prescribed from above and in
stable psychosomatic disposition, or should he decompen-
sate, allows himself to be desensitised to a certain
extent even against his will. Thus it may happen, quite
absurdly, that psychotherapy comes to include even
techniques which have as their aim the weakening of the
sensitivity and differentiated moral feeling that constitute in us the absolutely indispensable fundamentals for
the reliable control of ethical social behavior.

Without doubt, now as formerly, our western
psychiatry and psychotherapy carries predominantly conservative traits. Most of our congresses bear witness
that the need of revision of our concept of health hardly
appears as a burning problem. Thus, in family therapy,
if we are not altogether misled, those concepts gain the
upper hand which strive exclusively towards the overcoming of tension and the elimination of difficulties

of communication within the so-called family system,
independent of how sensitive, percipient and critically
the family relates with its social environment and of
the degree to which it is capable and ready of participation in the shared responsibility of shaping
communal life, and even of consciously sharing the
burden of superimposed political developments or of
steadfastly opposing these if necessary. But these
very criteria should find unconditional acceptance
in our therapeutic guidelines.

On the other hand, many psychotherapeutic colleagues
now as formerly adhere to the prejudice that the best
prerequisites for the development of an alert social
conscience and for a mature democratic attitude are
automatically provided in a family whose members get on
well together without striking neurotic, psychosomatic
or psychotic features. Experience, however, teaches that
e.g. many middleclass families hold themselves in just
that equilibrium by remaining aloof from all anxiety-
enhancing information about threatening political circumstances and also by avoiding all uneasiness that might
arise from active engagement in political affairs. I
have labelled this type of family as the "sanatorium
family". The art of avoidance of anxiety-provoking
external stimuli can, however, be so perfected by
such a family that the predisposition to anxiety, often
embodied or focussed in one family member, is kept latent
within the group as a whole. In critical perspective
such a family can and must certainly be designated as
phobic, but from a conservative viewpoint one may also
be inclined simply to idealise this family type as the
healthy model for a healthy society. In so doing, it
is actually not understood that this family achieves
its supposed health precisely and only via the phobic
uncoupling of the processes and conflicts of the social
environment. That is to say, what is actually involved
is, at bottom, an antisocial family type which develops
individuals who in no way serve in the mature collaborative moulding of society, let alone in the courageous
resistance to misguided political developments.

Not less dubious, there appears in this context
another widely spread family type which, under certain
circumstances, attracts still less attention than the
model of the sanatorium family according to conventional
clinical standards. This is the type of the paranoid
family. Ten years ago I described the dynamics of the
paranoid family, using the example of sectarian stubborn
outsider or minority families. At that time I overlooked

the possibility that a familial paranoia may form part
of a mass paranoia to which a large part, perhaps the
majority, of a society falls a victim. Under such
circumstances the delusional disturbance becomes converted into inconspicuousness, into average social norm.
If, in a phase of exacerbated world political tensions
or economic recession, all take refuge on all sides in
a persecution ideology and arm themselves for the pursuit
of the supposed creators of any trouble, then it is not
he who participates in this delusional reaction but he
who remains aloof from it who becomes the striking problem case and is likely to be driven into the hands of
the psychiatrist. Henceforth, the paranoid fellow-
conspirator families will count as normal and healthy,
those who suppress their anxiety towards external mis-
fortune as also their internal conflictual tensions with
the aid of the collective idea of the absolute enemy.
However, it is precisely this doom-laden family and/or
group dynamic which represents on a microsocial scale
those macrosocial motives which prevent a peaceful
coexistence in place of a constantly escalating armaments race.

Repeatedly to pose to ourselves the question of the
criteria of true psychosocial health is certainly irksome
and delicate, Ladies and Gentlemen. Therefore it is only
infrequently raised as a topic for discussion. It is, of
course, calculated in great measure to imperil harmony
in our discipline more widely than all the self-com-
placent and yet so embittered controversies over intraprofessional problems of concept and method. And further
it perpetuates the danger of burdening our image as an
expert elite reigning above all social conflicts and
polarisations with just that distrust which strikes all
persons and groups who occupy a critical position
particularly in phases of a tension-filled paranoid
climate. That a special loyalty is required of our
discipline in this context is generally recognised. Who-
ever rejects this, at least in our country, must arm
himself against a massive campaign of intimidation.

But, in my opinion, there is no other way: We must
accept the challenge. When we see how extensive a part
of youth strays away from established society in disillusion, precisely because it can no longer live
healthily and humanly therein in accordance with its
ideas, and we must realise that this youth is neither
sick in the conventional sense nor willing for treatment
nor treatable in the frame of our conventional means,
then we must either say: We are at our wits' end! or we

must summon up the courage to construct out of our
perceptions an appropriate contribution to the revision
of the principles of social coexistence, in order to
prevent the breaking away of many who should test their
essential alternative concepts not outside, but in and
with this society.

Our identitiy in this society is not exhausted by
our existence as therapists. The demands of the profession
are rather overruled by our duties as fellow-creatures
in a crisis-ridden and threatened society. Thus, we can
only adequately serve the great aim of acquiring another,
more human, relation if we combine our actions as helpers
with an awareness that, in common with all linked vocational groups and ultimately with all other citizens, we
form part of a social entity which must set to work energe-
tically as a kind of great self-help partnership to overcome the basically destructive attitude of will to power
and paranoid rivalry.

You will have noticed, Ladies and Gentlemen, that
I have not once employed the notion of solidarity in
the theme of my lecture. It is customary today, by the
inflationary listing of those values which one in
reality betrays, to persuade oneself that one watches
over them in the best way. Solidarity is thus something
which we precisely do not have, which we must first seek.
But I believe that you have understood that what I have
been speaking of throughout is that the development of
the capacity for a true, i.e. a unanimous solidarity
as the basic element of psychological health and as the
prerequisite of the capacity for peace, implies a
central task for us all.

Literature

Blackett, P.M.S., 1956: Atomic Weapons and East-West-
        Relations. cit. Born, M.
Born, M., 1960: Politk und Physik. Kleine Vandenhoeck-
        Reihe 93. Vandenhoeck u. Ruprecht, Göttingen
Einstein, A.: cit. Jaspers, K.
Elsässer, G., 1961: Erfahrungen an 1400 Kriegsneurosen.
        In: Psychiatrie der Gegenwart 3, 623. Springer,
        Berlin-Göttingen-Heidelberg
Jaspers, K., 1958: Die Atombombe und die Zukunft des
        Menschen. Piper, München
Menninger, W.C., 1967: Psychiatry and the War (1945).
        In: Selected Papers of W.C. Menninger: A
        Psychiatrist for a Troubled World. The Viking
        Press, New York

Moeller, M.L., 1978: Selbsthilfegruppen. Rowohlt, Reinbek
Parin, P., 1978: Warum die Psychoanalytiker so ungern
        zu brennenden Zeitproblemen Stellung nehmen.
        Psyche 32:385
Richter, H.E., 1972: Die Gruppe. Rowohlt, Reinbek
Richter, H.E., 1977: Randgruppenarbeit und "introspek-
        tives" Konzept. In: Jahrbuch der Sozialarbeit
        1978. F. Barabas ed. Rowohlt, Reinbek
Richter, H.E., 1978: Die Psychosoziale Arbeitsgemein-
        schaft Lahn-Dill. Erfahrungen mit einem selbst-
        organisierten Kooperationsmodell. In: Engagierte
        Analysen. Rowohlt, Reinbek
Richter, H.E., 1980: Lernziel: Verantwortung für den
        Nächsten. Speech - Theodor-Heuss-Price, München
        1.3.1980 / ZEIT No. 12, 14.3.1980
Richter, H.E., 1980: Unfähigkeit zum Frieden?
        Psychosozial 3, No. 4

THE INDIVIDUAL IN THE SOCIAL NETWORK

R.D. Hinshelwood, Consultant Psychotherapist

St. Bernard's Hospital, Southall, Middlesex

The concept of the social network was first exploited in the 1950's by Barnes (1954) when he moved from the study of tribal territorial groups to more amorphous non-territorial urban societies. Connectedness, density and other statistical patterns are described clearly by Mitchell (1969) and he shows their use in classifying social groups. But these are 'abstracted' features of a network and little use to the therapist who is concerned with the actual relationship that is existing in front of his eyes. Crocket (1979) has begun to study this 'real' network and he uses the term 'relationship network' to distinguish it from the sociologist's statistical abstractions.

In this paper I shall give two examples of actual interactions observed within the relationship network of a small institution. Its smallness was a help. Chains of personal interactions are implied in many descriptions of working institutions. For instance, Stanton and Schwartz (1954) noticed that disturbances broke out amongst the patients when there was uncertainty and anxiety amongst top management about financial arrangements. A pathway of some kind must have existed outside the formal command structure. They called it the informal structure. But they could not specify exactly how anxiety flowed through the human medium. My observations were serendipitous and show such pathways step by step.

The institution was a small clinic which contained a number of facilities for psychiatric and psychotherapeutic treatments - a day hospital run along therapeutic lines; a Children's Department which also ran a daily treatment programme for autistic children; and a weekly day-long 'school group' for primary school children who were disturbed.

The staff worked in a highly democratised team with a good deal of overlap between the departments. The social system was somewhat unusual for psychiatric institutions and a great deal of traditional authority was passed over to multi-disciplinary meetings.

Example One (see Fig. 1)

1. One morning Dr. A. arrived in the hospital building and found that the room she normally used was occupied by Dr. B. a new locum.

2. Dr. A. was annoyed with the newcomer but, unable to interrupt Dr. B. who was interviewing a patient, she tackled the receptionist, Mrs. C. blaming her for directing Dr. B. to the disputed room.

3. Mrs. C. was put in a bad humour. Now Dr. A.'s ten year old son, D, was away from school that day and she had brought him to the hospital. Mrs. C. displaced her anger when Dr. A. was not present, from the mother to the son, D. Mrs. C. criticised D, but he remained unabashed and disobliging.

4. Mrs. C. then made an accusation about D. to Miss E. Miss E. is one of the clinical staff and therefore has some responsibility to see that the behaviour of patients within the hospital remained within limits.   In effect this was an attempt to Mrs. C. to activate the authority structure.   Clearly it was easier for the receptionist to do this over D, a child, than over Dr. A.

5. However, Miss E. attempted to calm the situation by speaking to Dr. A. about her son D.   But since the trouble had arisen over Dr. B. this discussion seemed irrelevant to Dr. A.   So Miss E.'s efforts in this direction came to nothing.

6. She tried again.   This time Miss E.pursued the authority structure by informing Dr. F. the consultant with overall responsibility. She said D. had annoyed Mrs. C.

7. Dr. F. considered the problem. In his opinion the most troublesome children in the hospital were those who attended the weekly 'school group' for children with severe behaviour disturbances. They constituted something of a problem for him. He decided that Mrs. C.'s irritation was really derived from these children.

Dr. F. conveyed his anxiety about controlling this 'school group' to the weekly staff meeting which functioned as the final authority in the hospital.

8. The staff meeting discussed this and became concerned about

the impact of the children in the hospital as a whole. In particular
it was thought that there may be friction between the adult patients
and the children: and adults had often expressed anxiety about the
special group of autistic children (quite different from the 'school
group').

    9. The staff meeting resolved, that Miss G, the psychotherapist
in charge of the Autistic Unit, should give a talk to the adult
patients about the children in her unit. The end result of the
activation of the authority structure was action.

	Relationship	Transformation
1.	Dr. A. - Dr. B.	Rivalry
2.	Dr. A. - Mrs. C.	Argument
3.	Mrs. C. - D.	Complaint
4.	Mrs. C. - Miss E.	Alerting the authority system
5.	Miss E. - Dr. A.	Conciliatory attempt
6.	Miss E. - Dr. F.	Moving up the authority system
7.	Dr. F. - Staff Meeting	Problem-defining
8.	Staff Meeting - Miss G.	Decision-making
9.	Miss G. - Day Patients	Action taken

FLOW CHART

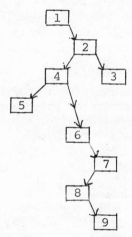

Figure 1.

Fig. 1 illustrated what is really a flow chart.   Something
arises in the social network, flows through formal and informal
channels and ends up at a point far removed from the source.   Let us
note some of the features of this flow.

The Medium.   The flow takes place in a series of relationships and
the diagram is a chain of them.   The chain has two dead ends (3 and
5) which are false starts in a random flow through the relationship
network of this social system.

Affects and transformations.   What is it that flows through the network?   It starts with the strong affect in Relationship 1 - rivalry
and anger.   However, when we come to Relationship 9, it is very
different.   Its content is a professional decision about a therapeutic action.

The content of one relationship is not the content of the next.
A transformation of the content takes place at each step. One affect
becomes another, becomes something else.

In the course of these transformations what starts out as
personal affect between two individuals ends up as an action in the
purpose of the institution.

Formal Structure.   The overall transformation from personal affect
to institutional purpose looks bizarre and inappropriate on the face
of it.   One can only smile that the action taken at the end is so
distant from the inflamed tempers of A and C at the start.

However, from the point of view of the institution something
appropriate has happened. Some sort of energy has come into the
organisation and prompted an activity which is useful in its own
right. Something that was once personal and individual has become
a depersonalised asset of the institution.

The means of this overall transformation is something to do
with the formal authority structure of roles and employment contracts
etc. The formal structure is designed for the primary purpose of
the institution as a whole and is organised on the principles of
division of labour, leadership command, responsibility, authority
etc.

The example shows how informal personal relationships live
alongside and feed into and out of the formal structure. The
organisation gains its energy from the personal affects of the individual members. The formal structure is a kind of energy gathering
system for the organisation.

Example two (see Fig. 2)

1. Dr. A. had advised one of his patients, Mr. B., to leave the hospital and return to work. This would entail Mr. B. having to accept that he was unable to continue his university career. As a student he had failed.

2. Mr. B.'s symptoms intensified. He believed that one of the occupational therapists, Miss C., was in love with him. He became abusive and threatening towards her when she did not admit to this. Here the imparting of a sense of failure to Mr. B. was transformed into a delusional love relationship with Miss C. Failure at university became success in love.

Stream (i)

3. Miss C. sought support from a fellow occupational therapist, Mrs. D. in maintaining her firmness with Mr. B. and his delusions. Miss C.'s anxiety over Mr. B. was transformed into a re-affirmation of the professional role alliance with Mrs. D.

4. Subsequently Mrs. D. tackled Dr. A. and attacked him for not giving sufficient support to the non-medical clinical staff.

5. The Hospital Staff Meeting later considered the occupational therapists' need for support in their relationships with patients. That between occupational therapists and doctors was formed into a secure alliance.

The hostility of the patients towards the staff had been a prominent feature of the hospital recently as a result of the staff's attempts to introduce a stiffer and more demanding programme for the community. The staff viewed many patients as self-indulgent and clinging to the hospital as a kind of paradise. (In a subsequent community meeting the staff re-asserted their view about the 'hospital Paradise' and the need for a stiffer programme - one contribution to Relationship 10).

6. Branching out separately after Relationship 5 was a reinforcement of Dr. A.'s attempt to discharge Mr. B. from the hospital. The alliance between occupational therapists and doctors was transformed back into the original relationship again (a further interview between Dr. A. and Mr. B.).

Stream (ii)

7. Branching out separately after Relationship 2 was a relationship of fear between Mr. B. and other patients alarmed by Mr. B.'s

aggressiveness. He had in fact shown some physical violence. He became isolated outside the boundary of the patients - a scape-goat.

8. The patients, in meetings, asserted the peaceful and pleasant nature of the hospital community. This transformation was another delusion formation that created the notion of a hospital paradise.

9. The contrast between the pleasant hospital 'paradise' and the unpleasant outside world was maintained - this relationship of fear and rejection emphasised the boundary of the hospital.

10. That feeds back into a relationship stream (i) again. Staff and patients going their separate ways, nevertheless are united in the view of the hospital as a 'paradise'. Though they have alternative reactions to that view both are engaged in the processes of boundary maintenance and internal cohesion.

FIGURE 2

Relationship	Transformation
1. Dr. A. - Mr. B.	Medical Interview
2. Mr. B. - Miss C.	Delusional "affair"
3. Miss C. - Mrs. D.	Role alliance
4. Mrs. D. - Dr. A.	Complaint
5. OT's - Drs.	Role demarcation and alliance
6. Dr. A. - Mr. B.	Medical Interview
7. Mr. B. - Patients	Fear and rejection
8. Patients - Hospital	Delusional "paradise"
9. Hospital - Outside World	Fear and rejection
10. Staff - Patients	Myth-making

FLOW CHART

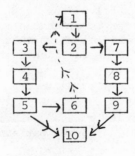

Stream i	Stream ii
(Staff)	(Patients)

In this second example there are frequent transformations which involve alliances, identifications and solidarity. The emphasis throughout is on boundaries, and who and what is inside the boundary. The institution polarises in its attitudes to itself (two streams), but is solidly united in a myth about its identity as a 'hospital paradise'.

The flow of affect has two outcomes. On the one hand, Relationship 6 is within the formal structure of the hospital, promoting the organisational purpose of the organisation (outcome as in Example 1). A's Relationship 6 and 1 are the same, there is a positive feedback loop within the network. This can therefore persist as a self-reinforcing mechanism which keeps the process going.

The second outcome is the creation (or really more properly the reinforcement) of a community or hospital myth about the paradise there. It would seem that the characterisation of the hospital as 'paradise' attracts the continuing identification with the institution and holds the members to it.

Mr. B. in this example was a chronic schizophrenic. He demonstrates his psychotic personality by substituting a favourable fantasy (that he is successful in love) for an unfavourable piece of reality (that he is a failure at university). In an analagous process on a community scale, the unfavourable reality of the hospital is denied and replaced by a favourable myth about it. (Staff also fail sometimes to appreciate reality fully.) It shows how in groups and institutions, psychotic processes can infect and dominate the individual members.

However, from an institutional point of view, there is again an appropriateness to this outcome. It serves the need of the institution to hold itself together, to maintain and emphasize its boundaries.

Discussion

Currently it is usual to view an institution as a system - either from a systems theory angle with emphasis on the homeostatic mechanisms; or as a culture employing a semiotic code (that is a system of meanings including values and attitudes). But these are static approaches aiming to encompass the "essence" of the institution - its form or its culture independent of time.

To see it as a network allows the introduction of a time scale and then we can analyse processes. Normally even process analysis brings static results. For example Miller & Gwynne (1972) describe the processes of four residential caring institutions simply in terms of input, conversion process and output. This level of

process is constant over time and between institutions. But the
process I have described and the observations noted by Stanton and
Schwartz (1954) occur in a time dimension.

It is clear that they also occur within the personal relationships of the people involved. They are barely conscious and are not
carried with the same symbolic clarity of the words that the formal
organisation uses.

"Affect flow" in a social network has a number of features that
contrast with systems theory. The system is not merely for
communication but for 'energy transmission' as well. Weiner (1948)
distinguishes the two kinds of electrical system - telecommunications,
in which the power is low but information is high; and the electri-
city grid system which transmits power but with no information. The
processes revealed in my observations are analogous to power transmission of affects. Boundary maintenance of the whole system may
depend on positive feedback loops,not negative feedback.

Human institutions are systems that transmit powerful affects.
The formal command structure represents the institutional control
system, attempting to mobilise the power that comes from personal
relationships.

The individual in the institution has his own personal object-
relationships. The way noxious affects are passed on in this network would be described in psycho-analytic work as pathological
forms of projection. We are familiar with these in large group work -
and Tom Main describes them well (Main 1975). What we have here is
evidence of a sequence of such projections. Each one is idiosyncratic for the persons involved. It would seem that such forms
of projection are a basic ingredient of an institution's achievements
and its survival.

There are implications for therapy. Such trains of projections
and of projective identifications, reveal the personal characteristics
of the individuals and can be analysed as such in therapeutic groups
or communities. If they are allowed to run unchecked the individual
may lose his own personal affects - become depersonalised and in-
stitutionalised - a common enough occurrence in our long term
institutions.

It is in the nature of institutions that their functioning and
their survival depends on mobilising spontaneous personal affects,
and transforming them into either (i) energy for planned action; or
(ii) myths for boundary maintenance. The transformations are brought
about by the talent of particular individuals as crucial mediators
who turn affects into energy or into myths. These examples suggest
that mobilising affects in this way depends on the mechanisms of

depersonalisation and delusion-formation. From the point of view of
the individual these features would be regarded as psychotic symptoms. From the point of view of the institution a certain degree of
'contained' psychosis seems to have adaptive advantage.

The psychotic experience of projection is that something is
actually transferred out of or into the mind - depending on whether
the projection is made or received. It is the concretisation of the
experience which lends the quality of a physical flow in the network.
Boissevin (1979) has noted that exchange theory (Heath 1976) is
particularly suited to provide a theoretical framework for social
network analysis. In fact a beginning has been made in a previous
article - "Supervision as an Exchange System" - (Hinshelwood 1979)
to describe exchange processes in which the exchange commodity is an
affect. The present paper records the rich variations and vicissitudes of the exchanges, as a quantity of affect flows through the
network. To conclude this paper I am tempted to define this quantity,
or quantum, of affect as an 'emotion'.

REFERENCES

Barnes, J.A., 1954 'Class and Communities in a Norwegian Island
    Parish' Human Relations 7 p.39
Boissevan, J., 1979 "Network Analysis: A Reappraisal" Current
    Anthropology 20 p. 392
Crockett, R., 1979 "Social Network Theory" in Hinshelwood and Manning
    (eds) Therapeutic Communities: Reflections and Progress
    (Routledge and Kegan Paul: London)
Heath, A., 1976, Rational Choice and Social Exchange (Cambridge
    University Press: Cambridge)
Hinshelwood, R.D., 1979 "Supervision as an Exchange System" in
    Hinshelwood and Manning (eds) Therapeutic Communities:
    Reflections and Progress (Routledge and Kegan Paul: London)
Main, T.F., 1975 "Some Psychodynamics of Large Groups" in Kreeger
    (ed) The Large Groups (Constable: London)
Miller, E.J.and Gwynne, G.V., 1972 A Life Apart (Tavistock: London)
Mitchell, C., 1969 (ed) Social Networks in Urban Communities
    (Manchester University Press: Manchester)
Stanton, A. and Schwartz, M. 1954 The Mental Hospital (Basic Books:
    New York)
Weiner, N., 1948 Cybernetics (Massachusetts Institute of Technology
    Press: Cambridge, Mass.)

INDIVIDUAL AND GROUP: A LATIN AMERICAN PERSPECTIVE

Bernardo Blay-Neto, M.D.

Fellow of the American Group Psychotherapy Association

Rua Henrique Monteiro, 14, Sao Paulo, Brazil

It is my intention in this paper, to give a brief overview of Brazilian group psychotherapy, relating it to the theme of this Congress, the group and the individual, describing also matters with a characteristic of psychoanalytic and group analytic thinking in Latin America.

Using as a reference the historical aspects of group psychotherapy to elaborate this study, I came across a difficulty: at the very beginning, the instrument of investigation used for this purpose; the informative source, when I studied the situation of group psychotherapy in the State where I live was one quite different from the source I had when I considered the whole Brazilian situation. In the first case I had at my disposal my own experience, whilst in the second, I had information that came through scientific activities transmitted by specialized journals.

The development of group psychotherapy in Brazil arose, in my point of view, as a consequence of the interplay of forces between the social group and the individuals who became sick in the same group. When this situation arose, the healthy group tried to put aside the sick individuals because they provoked disturbances in the balance of the social group, and thus, they were able to re-establish their equilibrium.

Therefore, the Brazilian group movement had its origin connecting to the relationship group-individual, as I will prove later on, the central theme of this Congress, that approaches the boundary issues between the individual and the group.

Using this conception as a reference, I began to study the interplay of relationships between the Brazilian social group of the years 1950 to 1960, and the individuals that constituted a menace to its stability. My interest in this period is justified, because in that period labour and social reforms appeared in Brazil, the workmen started to have stability in their jobs, and at the same time, free medical assistance was provided by the state.

The workmen, in view of those reforms, acquired the right of being treated, when before this, treatment was given as charity. Thus, the working classes began to demand instead of asking for attendance. To achieve this purpose, the state created institutions for physical and mental care. The institutions began to represent, in theory, a place where workers went for treatment, so as to be able to resume their places in the social group from which they were left out.

I say in theory, because in practice this did not happen: what really occurred was that the institutions began to be con-sidered as deposits, where two groups, the employees and the family, both started to send their sick people, trying most of the time to expel them from the limits of their group areas, instead of treating and recuperating them.

This tendency was principally shown when the patients were of the psychic or psychological kind. The institutions, when they were cured, had difficulties to reintegrate them into the groups from which they had been expelled, in view of the refusal from the employees as well as of the families to receive them back. Using as a model western films, the society deals with the sick people as the sheriff with the bandit. Putting him out of the limits of the city and advising him not to come back anymore, so as not to disturb the local peace.

It was on this occasion, that I and other colleagues were invited to participate in this new conception of mental health; the objective was to recover the workers and put them back to work. To each one of us was assigned a defined task: some to attend psychotics, others to work with drug addicts, as for myself I was assigned to work with alcoholics.

I will describe my experience in this activity because it is a personal testimony, and because as I came to know later on, it was similar to my colleagues' experiences.

At the time, I was in charge of a pavillion with the capacity for 80 people, but which really contained over 300. This number (300), was not stable, increased continually, because the number of discharges was less than the admissions. Due to all this, the situation began to become difficult, the patients were obliged to

sleep on the floor sheltering one another to keep warm. Despite this
situation we had very little time to spend with them. Sometimes I
could only review a patient one or two months after our first contact,
because I had no one to help me in this activity. The situation
came to such a point that the patients started to rebel against me.
They complained of everything and especially of my lack of attention.
The group pressure of the patients was so great, that I began avoiding to enter the pavillion. Sometimes they remained waiting at the
door and when they saw me, they surrounded me, demanding attention.

Hence, developed a relationship group-individual, where the
first was represented by the alcoholic patients and the individual -
myself. This pressure was so great, that I had to ask the management of the department to name more professionals to help me in my
work. I continued my work, each time more pressed by the rebelling
patients. One day, when coming to the pavillion, I found the door
closed and the patients hindering my entrance. I then perceived
that I had been expelled by the group. Now it was I who felt in my
own flesh, the pain of being outcasted by the group. Now I felt the
divorce between the group and myself. Like the bandit and the
sheriff I was also put out of the boundaries of the town.

The pressure that the group exercised over me, expelling me
from their midst, made me try to find means to get reintegrated.
For this purpose I talked with the group of alcoholics, proposing
them to divide them in groups, and so I could treat them as a team,
because individually it was impossible. They accepted my suggestion,
the door was opened and I joined the group again.

This is how I started my group therapy activities: the origin
of this activity was not to attend the alcoholic patients, so to
say, but, primarily, my efforts to reintegrate myself into the
group that had closed the door on me. Therefore, my activity as group
psychotherapist was the result of a group imposition, more than
a personal iniative.

On this occasion, other colleagues, all psychoanalysts, began
the same group activities in different places of the Country. We
only got to know each other and our mutual activities, in 1957,
during the Lo Latin American Congress of Group Psychotherapy, in
Buenos Aires, Argentina. This Congress had as its principal merit,
the gathering of the Brazilian group of psychotherapists, enabling
them to exchange experiences of group activities. In this Congress
the different schools and all group techniques were represented,
allowing the participants to have an idea of what was being done
in Latin America concerning group psychotherapy. Even then one
could observe the predominance of papers of psychoanalytical line
over the other techniques, and the evidence that Argentine was the
country that had the largest number of analysts working in this
field.

Congresses were held and it was thought that there should be a
selection of papers and participants as well.   This selection would
have to be based on the following judgement; a) only the papers
following analytical orientation should be accepted; b) only
colleagues with psychoanalytical training should be able to participate.   The studies coming to these points went on for about eleven
years and finally, between 1967 and 1968 the measures for the
selection of papers and participants were put into use.   The societies then assumed the obligation to add the term "analytical" to their
names and thus characterize the new position adopted.

At the time of this reformulation there were eight group societies in Latin America, thus distributed; one in Sao Paulo, two in
Rio de Janeiro, one in Porto Alegre, one in Uruguay, one in Buenos
Aires, one in Chile and one in Mexico.   Besides these, co-ordinating
the Brazilian Societies, we had the Brazilian Association of Analytical Group Psychotherapy, and co-ordinating all of them, the Latin
American Federation of Analytical Group Psychotherapy (FLAPAC).

Historically, I consider the years of 1967/68 as the time that
group psychotherapy in Brazil definately acquired it's identity
based on a technical and scientific concept.   With this outline I
only intend to point out an historical event, necessary to understand
the actual situation of group psychotherapy in our country.   I also
wish to emphasize again, according to my personal experience, that
the group movement in Brazil arose as a consequence of the pressure
carried out by patients in need of psychological help and deprived
from getting it by means of individual psychotherapy.

Letting aside the statistical, historical and genetical aspects
of this therapy, I shall now study several events that were considered by some as an expression of a crisis in group psychotherapy
in our country.   The ones that considered this situation as a
crtical one, came to this conclusion based upon the aloofness that
prevail among those that work with groups.   They point out still,
to emphasize their points of view, the small production of scientific
papers by our group psychotherapists and the dissolution of several
group societies.   On the other side, the validity of group psychotherapy as a therapeutic method was being questioned as well as the
abandonment of this therapy by some colleagues, contributed to the
idea that group psychotherapy might be ending.

I remember that in a recent Psychoanalytic Congress, the pre-
sumption that this modality of treatment could also be going through
a crisis was examined.   It seems to be fashionable to talk about
crisis without knowing exactly what the use of this word means.   This
definition is fundamental because if for some, it means the beginning
of the end, for others it means the end of the confusion.   I stay
with the last ones, that is to say, that the events by which group

psychotherapy is passing in our country represent a healthy evolution. My opinion is based on the fact that the actual difficulties
are directly connected with the measures taken to unify the selection
of group therapists. As a consequence of these measures all the
societies had to reformulate, as was just pointed out, their by-laws;
some of them even had to eliminate several members that did not fulfill the pre-qualifications to belong to the societies.   Thus, the
number of members diminished as well as the number of participants
to local or international Congresses. These difficulties in reality,
represented a reaction to the necessity to attend to the growth of
group psychotherapy and its uniformization, bringing an apparent confusion which was confounded with a disintegrating crisis. Let us
take as an example the Group Society of Rio de Janeiro; it had to
be dissolved in order to re-organize itself in accordance with the
by-laws.

On the other side, colleagues, some pioneers of this therapy,
stopped using it to dedicate themselves exclusively to psychoanalysis.
Some of them justified this attitude by expressing that they didn't
believe in group psychotherapy as an instrument of cure.   I won't
discuss this matter but just point out that these facts contribute
to give an unfavourable impression about group therapy not only
concerning the clients but among the colleagues as well. I add up
still the actual economical difficulties that Latin America, including Brazil, is going through, with direct consequences on individual activities particularly on psychoanalysis. Cost of living
allied to inflationary problems forced many clients that up to then
were undergoing individual analysis, to give it up due to economic
difficulties. Group psychotherapy, due to this economic pressure
became more intense than the demand for individual psychotherapy,
with economic as well as emotional consequences for the therapists.

This situation created a competitiveness between group
individual therapists due to the following: 1) - less patients,
decrease of income; 2) - loss of patients - emotional conflicts
among the therapists.

A paradoxal situation was developed on account of the above
mentioned conflict; some individual therapists began to work with
groups without mentioning it to anybody. They were ashamed of doing
it because they were once against and violently criticized it.

Still as a consequence of this economic situation another
difficulty arose: the increase of patients on the look out for group
therapy and the small number of analytical group psychotherapists to
attend to this demand. As a consequence, the clients on the waiting
lists of the most qualified colleagues, patients pressed by anxiety
and in need of immediate attention, looked for therapists less
qualified and with inadequate training. The results were not

always satisfactory, sometimes were even very harmful; this obviously produced a negative effect and discredit towards group psychotherapy.

The above-mentioned facts: economic situation, emotional conflicts on qualified professional, competitive situation, the emerging
of group societies with no scientific basis, contributed to involve
group psychotherapy in a wave of dermit which resulted that many
analysts, psychiatrists and even the public started a movement trying
to qualify it as bastard and a sub-product of psychoanalysis without
any therapeutic value; other colleagues went even further satirizing
group psychotherapy as one that attends more to the financial needs
of the therapists than to the emotional necessities of the patients.
However, despite the critics and all the above-mentioned situation,
the natural and secure growth of group psychotherapy could not be
stopped.

Let us take Sao Paulo as an example, where several faculties included the discipline "Group Psychotherapy" in their curriculum.
Group techniques are being used in some medical schools to stimulate
better relationship between students and teacher, students and
patients. I had the opportunity to write a paper concerning my experiences on this subject. Some Hospitals are using group activities
with alcoholics, drug addicts and even with mental patients.

Looking at group therapy today and comparing it with 25 years
ago, when it was just starting, we evidence its remarkable development and progress. The picture drawn about group psychotherapy in
Sao Paulo, reflects what is happening in Brazil today. In Rio de
Janeiro, group dynamics is being applied in institutions with a
social character. In Porto Alegre it was a great help for the
establishment of therapeutic communities.

We can thus conclude that group psychotherapy in Brazil, presents a condition that we can consider as the one that has the greatest penetrability and application in human groups.

There are not enough therapists to fulfill the demand. Group
Societies, aware of this situation, founded Institutes with the purpose to prepare new ones. In spite of this, the answer to this project was not as we expected. Few candidates applied due to the fact
that it is difficult to fulfill the Institute's requirements. I
personally, consider the Institute's requirements adequate, because
this solution helps to maintain the good level of group psychotherapists, to destroy the bad image that some have towards it.

Looking at group therapy today, we observe its remarkable
development and progress and we can also observe that group psychotherapy has nowadays reached a position of distinction and respect
in our community, despite the attempts to diminish and devaluate it.

I saw in Europe, a church that was built by a man who believed
that the human being has the same origin and the same creator. This
building was built with bricks with the very same shape and colour
so nobody can differ one brick from the other, to symbolize his
marvellous conception of mankind's unity.

Similarly, a group exists independent of men's desire, to prove
and to reassure their independence when they belong to a group.

So, I believe that theoretically I can speak about a Brazilian
group movement, a Danish one, or a French one, and so forth, but this
is artificial. Groups exist all over the world, and we must search,
like the man who built the church, what puts us together instead of
what separates us.

INTERPRETING ANALYTICAL GROUP PSYCHOTHERAPY, more specifically

THE INDIVIDUAL INTERPRETATION AND THE GROUP INTERPRETATION

Prof. P.-B. Schneider

University Psychiatric Policlinic

Rue Caroline 11 bis, 1009 Lausanne, Switzerland

1. INTRODUCTION

Analytical group psychotherapy - whereby I stress the word analytical - has certain characteristics which set it off distinctly from all other therapies or group therapies. It does have in common with the latter the phenomena which appear wherever men and women come together in a small group of 6-12 persons with the intention of reaching a common goal. These phenomena are described in a general way under the title group dynamics. The basic differences - resulting from its relationship to Freudian psychoanalysis - derive on the one hand from the fundamental rule which invites the patients to express what they think and feel without being selective and without omitting anything which comes into their mind, and on the other hand from the psychotherapist's neutrality in connection with the suspended attention which characterizes his therapeutic attitude. On the basis of the fundamental rule and the suspended attention of the therapist and other rules which I will not go into here, the psychoanalytical setting of the analytical group therapy is created.

In this setting - which is formed artificially due to the requirements of the therapy - the patients' understanding of the transactions going on between each other and between themselves and the psychotherapist will take place on two levels: on the level of groups dynamics and on the level of the psychoanalytical mechanisms per se. As a result of this complex situation, we can see that the interventions of the psychotherapist, including his interpretations, can also be located on two levels. This is an important problem which we will discuss later on. All the foregoing is well known, but perhaps it is beneficial to repeat it. In addition, it must also be

pointed out that the therapeutic objectives of group psychotherapy
above all pertain to changes in the psychic balance of the members
of the group, and not in the alteration of their existence or of
their relationship with others.   The latter effects can appear - as
they normally do - but they are secondary to the changes in the personal, psychodynamic equilibrium.

II. INTERPRETATION IN PSYCHOANALYSIS AND IN ANALYTICAL GROUP PSYCHO-THERAPY

Interpretation is one of the interventions undertaken by the
psychoanalyst or the group psychotherapist, all of which have their
own therapeutic purpose.   I will only cite a few of the other interventions which the psychoanalyst makes, such as encouraging the
patient to speak, reassurance, the explaining of a mechanism of a
symbol, injunctions, confrontations, underlining a patient's contribution and finally the reconstruction of a part of the patient's past.
Similarly to other factors of group therapy apart from the interventions of the therapist, we would point out the partial or complete identification of the patients with each other and with the
therapist which has the potential of introjecting a good parental image, certain learning mechanisms and corrective, interpersonal experiences between the participants.

What is interpretation in psychoanalysis?   It concerns something which is communicated to the patient in such a way that it tends
to give him access to the latent meaning of what he says and does.
In other words, to make his affects and eventually his desires pass
from the unconscious to the conscious or, from a topical point of
view, to permit the Id to reach the Ego.   By means of the interpretation of the therapist, the defensive conflict of the patient when
faced with his unconscious desires comes to the surface.

As we know, this defensive conflict comes alive against the
therapist in what is called the transference;   the greatest resistances to the interpretation of desires are the resistances to transference.   This is what makes what the psychoanalyst is and does
during the course of the treatment important.   Finally, one can also
say that interpreting (German "deuten") consists of determining the
meaning ("Bedeutung") of what is behind the defensive barrier.

All the above is also applicable to analytical group therapy,
but with some subtle and even some major differences.   For example,
the reconstruction used in the group - very close to interpretation -
which consists of encouraging the individual during individual treatment to relive parts of his childhood after he has evoked a memory,
takes on a new aspect which is the make-up of the history of the
group.

The psychotherapist as an indentification figure is not the only

one in the group; each patient can take on this function. Finally,
the group - by the sheer presence of its members - represents the
meeting of equals confronted with a person who exercises a different
function and who holds a different position: the therapist. This
gives them a feeling of belonging, for example, to a group or to a
fantasized family group, and thus allows them to experience something
similar to splitting. These factors can become therapeutic. They
are specific to the group, as well as is the face-to-face encounter
of the group members which allows their mutual exploration of each
other, as well as and above all the possibility of communicating in
a non-verbal manner (mimes, gestures, etc.). This is what is also
called the "analogical" language - an incorrect term - as opposed to
the "digital" language, the actual language expressed by the spoken
word. In fact, we are only dealing here with "analogical" communication and not with a language at all. However, interpretation requires
the spoken word and non-verbal communication is insufficient for this.
The latter does allow interaction, but not the expression of the
interaction being understood; the "why" - which is the enlightening
explanation found in the heart of the interpretation - simply does
not exist in this manner of communication without words.

III. CHARACTERISTICS OF INTERPRETATION IN ANALYTICAL GROUP PSYCHO-
THERAPY

    1. Interpretation and "group dynamics"

    We have already found that when people come together regularly,
group phenomena - which make-up group dynamics appear. If, furthermore, the framework of these meetings is clearly defined (in time and
space as well as the rules on what is done in the group), a process
starts unfolding - similarly to the analytical group psychotherapy -
which precisely permits conscious and unconscious phenomena between
the members of the group and within each one of these to be understood within the group itself.

    "Group dynamics" is the result of observed, conscious, apparent
phenomena which appear during the course of the group's life: group
cohesion, the creation of sub-groups, the feeling of belonging to the
group, the building of an atmosphere and of a group morale, the member who monopolizes the group, the scape-goat, etc. There is no
purpose in listing all the other group characteristics which are certainly interesting to know and of which the group psychotherapist
must take into account. But can he use these descriptive notions in
his interpretations? If the latter are analytical, a further dimension must be added to group dynamics, the simple observation of group
phenomena, a dimension which includes the unconscious background of
these phenomena and their defensive meaning, specifically as seen in
the transference.

    Let us take an example: group cohesion, the pleasure with which the members come and the joy that they feel from living together, can take on two almost diamentrically opposite meanings and it is advisable to first of all be able to distinguish them from each other, and then afterwards to understand their meaning. The joy of repeatedly coming together and of sharing a communal experience can mean for some members of the group - if not for all - the initiation to a life lived in relation with others which they had never known before and which is similar to the moments of elation in the family or within a group of equals. This is a positive experience which can be underlined by the group therapist. However seen from another angle, although the exterior signs of the group life seem to be the same, the cohesion and this feeling of belonging and of soldering with the other members of the group can be a very powerful, defensive action, generally directed unconsciously against the therapist and preventing the patients from experiencing negative feelings towards him through the perpetuation of a happy existence within the group, from which he is usually excluded. This unconscious and unformulated splitting if repeated and remaining unrecognised by the psychotherapist, can lead to the sterilisation of the analytical life of the group.

The result is that the interpretations which can be made within the analytical group by using the most simple language of everyday life can leave aside certain facts which may be of great interest concerning group dynamics because these facts do not conform to the interpretations and cannot be understood inside the dynamic movement of the group.

From the very first session of group therapy, one of the members will try to take over the most important role; to become the alpha element, according to R. Schindler's classification, or the monopolist or the co-animator. It is also clear that this very obvious action is experienced by the members of the group as a competition which will be played off within the group. Please note that if the meaning in unconscious language is not clear to the group therapist, it is with difficulty that he will be able to bring up these banal group phenomena which, however, become revealing as soon as they can be attributed a meaning on the same level on which place they take place, a meaning which takes into account their unconscious nature in respect to the psychotherapist, i.e. in the transference, which is precisely what is not clear when seen phenomenologically.

2. Individual interpretation and group interpretation

It seems to me that the discussions, confrontations and the polemics which have taken place in group psychotherapy circles concerning the actual essence of this form of psychotherapy have been quite fertile. What happens when a group of patients is analysed who are all being treated at the same time?   Can one act upon each one of them in a series of understandings and isolated interventions, and make individual interpretations within the group, or should one,

quite on the contrary, consider the group as a totality in the psychological sense and make group interpretations? It was through ardent
discussions on this subject that we have been able to go beyond the
extremist positions and find another point of view which is not merely
located in-between the two, but which is much more original; it takes
into account the real, dynamic situation which is being played off
within the structured group in order to allow the analytical processes to unfold.

Without going into detail and while refraining from pointing out
the opinions of various authors, we can describe the two extreme
positions. There are those who do what they call psychotherapy in a
group or psychoanalysis in a group and who treat individual patients
who are united in a group for practical reasons. The interpretations
which they make border on the psychodynamics of each individual and
his personal conflicts. On the other extreme, there is group psychotherapy or group psychoanalysis or rather psychotherapy or psychoanalysis of the group: the group of patients is seen and is considered as a whole whose common fantasys and common tension one tries
to discern. The interpretations affect the largest possible portion
of the members, if not all the members of the group.

My own position is different: it is not half-way between these
two conceptions, but it does allow that both are correct as long as
the evolution of the group and the phases of its development are
taken into consideration. In fact, when one closely studies the works
of those who uphold psychotherapy in a group, one can see that they
also make group interpretations and inversely, those who do psychotherapy of the group also give individual interpretations. Our
position is based on our experience and the conception which we have
concerning the objectives of group psychotherapy. Under no circumstances are we saying that we have a group "which works smoothly" and
which will continue its happy existence as a group after the treatment is over. Quite to the contrary, it is necessary that the group
can end in such a way that each one of the members of the group is
free to live his life after having undergone sufficient changes so
as to make it more balanced and that he need no longer take recourse
to the session where he felt at home. However, we feel that the
therapeutic qualities which the group has and which are partially expressed by group dynamics - but are also expressed by psychoanalytical concepts such as lateral transfer, partial or total identifications (the Hall of Mirrors), etc. - should be used. It is for this
reason that when we give an individual interpretation, we try to
make it in a way that the other members of the group can relate to
it and can also apply it to themselves through a partial identification throughout the length of the interpretation. We thus prefer
to give individual interpretations which can be generalized to other
members of the group.

However, we only use the individual interpretation during cer-

phases of the treatment. The beginning of a psychoanalytical group is characterized - as described in an earlier work - by the appearance of a negative transference which is strong enough to affect all the members of the group, a fact which unconsciously solders them against the unsuspected enemy present within the group, i.e. the therapist. The appearance of this negative transference is due to frustration, which is greater in group psychotherapy than it is in psychoanalysis and which the patients must bear up with and finally accept; it becomes the therapeutic catalyst. This frustration is connected with the fact that they share the therapist and with what Anzieu has called the "group illusion"; that is, the constantly renewed illusion, shared by the patients, that the group will act as the good guy, the "comforting mother" who will look after all the needs of her children. During this opening phase, we prefer group interpretations, whereas we will act through other interventions on certain group members by reassuring him or by re-integrating him into the group through an injunction or by bringing out what he has just said when other members have set it aside.

The group interpretations are based on this unconscious group tension - to use Ezriel's term - in fairly close connection with the negative and unconscious transference which, by the way, strengthens the bond between the members. Moreover, by leaving individual interpretations aside, the silent members - persons with a pregenital structure or else highly phobic patients - can gradually make a place for themselves inside the group without being rejected this time, by the therapist who only speaks to actively participating members, who are the only ones with whom he can intervene with the use of individual interpretations.

Let us take one example: at the end of the very first session of nine patients - which had been very animated from the beginning with exchanges appearing already between various members which could be understood as lateral transferences - three women and two men evoke "the bad mother" of their childhood at great length and with considerable emotion. During the course of this session, nothing in particular had been said about the psychotherapist apart from a comment from one of the members who I had previously treated. I pointed out to the group that without realizing it they already were trying to exclude me from their group as if I might become as baleful as most of the members' mothers. The question already confronting the group at this very first session was to decide whether they can include me among them or whether they will have to push me out of the group as an undesirable object.

From the second session onwards, the group got settled and continued to disregard me. The patients more or less explicitly decided to speak of their problems one after the other and to consecrate at least one session to each member. Despite the interpretations which I made on the defensive aspect of this decision, they

acted upon their decision until their patience ran out.   In this
group behaviour, we can see a well-organised, unconscious defence
consisting in a transgression of the rule of free speech which was
apparently agreed upon in the beginning of the group.   This defence
finally broke down by an interpretation on the tension common to all
members of the group and on the morale which it was obliged to set
up itself through fear of the maternal or paternal morale represented
by the therapist.   This was followed by very lively exchanges containing a series of lateral transferences and identifications, most
of them fusional.

This phase is again characterized by the psychotherapist being
pushed out by the group.   I made some interventions and interpretations on defences set up against impulses, at which time the problem of sexuality and the feelings of the members towards each other
were brought up.   However, the psychotherapist is once again relatively excluded from the discussion until the 23rd session, where
he pointed out very clearly through a group interpretation this excluding attitude and gave his own explanation in connection with
very negative feelings, hostility and even hate for him because he
did not sufficiently protect each of the members and, more particularly, because each of the group members only has the right to an
equal part of him and must apparently content himself with little
pieces of this immense love which he believes that the therapist,
the archaic mother, could have for him.

This interpretation is based on an unconscious group phantasy
("the psychotherapist neglects me: he prefers the others and pays
no attention to me").   I associate this interpretation with another
one, namely avoiding painful experiences within the group itself;
as if the treatment could unfold without each of the members experiencing the group, being completely committed and, in particular,
facing the competition existant from the group's being, i.e. who
would be the first violin and be the preferred one. Each member of
the group feels threatened by the others and all simultaneously experience the therapist's inability to completely protect them - a
belief which they had more or less consciously upheld.

This example shows that by grouping various episodes throughout
the therapy global interpretation tries to find a common denominator
i.e. the need to be protected and loved and the resulting disappointment because this does not happen often enough.

This is the point we have reached in this particular group, but
observation of other groups shows that when this topic is sufficiently interpreted, the internal development within each patient
allows them to reach another level in connection with the inter-
nalised parental imagos and allows them to start introjecting a good
imago in place of a bad imago. It is during this phase that in certain very precise circumstances we give personal interpretations.

In fact, as we have already stated, we generally prefer interpretations which are not directed to the group as a whole for all the
members are not on the same psychodynamic level of understanding at
each session; we prefer to speak to the majority of them, even if
the interpretation does not directly concern some members whose
problems are currently to be found in other sectors. However, it
does happen that one member remains completely untouched by these
regressive or progressive waves and just isn't able to follow and
regress with the group's fluctuations in order to reach a point
where the interpretation will be active and more constructive. I
feel that such slow members often need an "injection" i.e. a very
personalized interpretation, which helps them to get back on their
feet and keep up with the group.

We are quite happy to name this phase - which is the lengthiest
phase of group psychotherapy - the working through phase as it is
also called in individual psychoanalysis. The therapeutic alliance
is established after the negative transferences are converted first
into ambivalent and then into positive transferences at which time
the therapeutic work can set in in a more steady manner and with
greater continuity.

When it becomes obvious that the end of the group is approaching, it is important that the group phenomena common to all the
participants be taken under control again. At this time the interpretations concerning mourning, being neglected and the major regression which occurs during this final period once again become
group interpretations. On the other hand, the personal attitude of
the therapist vis-a-vis each of the members becomes much more individualized without all the while being interpreted; this in order
to put an end to the projection - internalization system which went
on for the duration of the therapy.

In conclusion, we can say that individual interpretations and
group interpretations are not mutually exclusive, but rather that
they are always complementary. The psychotherapist chooses one or
the other depending, on the one hand, on which phase the group is
(in opening phase, working through phase, or the final phase), it
thus depends on the timing as well as on the psychodynamic situation
of the group, i.e. in a sense, the shape in which the group is in
the hic et nunc of a session. These time and space parameters determine part of the setting of the analytic group psychotherapy.

3. The setting and its meaning for the interpretation

On the onset of the treatment, the psychotherapist states the
rules (i.e. the need to be present regularly, to speak openly, the
fact that meeting each other outside the session is unnecessary in
regards to the good functioning of the treatment, the respect of
utmost secrecy concerning what happens in the group, the discussion

of the question of the therapist's fees etc.). Under no circumstances does he lay down these rules to show his authority and power, but rather he does so to outline a particular setting. These rules include constraints, which immediately implies that the former will soon be broken, thus allowing the psychodynamics to flow and opening the way to interpretations. To repeat what certain authors have described, it is altogether possible to say that a "matrix" is created having dimensions in time and in space. This is where regression is possible and where a psychotherapeutic space appears, i.e. the exchanges of the patients between themselves and of the patients with the psychotherapist. This "matrix" essentially takes a symbiotic and maternal shape. Inside the group, the members re-discover and experience a very archaic pleasure as well as dependency which unites them and moreover allows the phenomena described by group dynamics (the feeling of belonging, of cohesion, and of group morale) to arise. In Great Britain and France, Malcolm Pines and Didier Anzieu have described this "matrix" very accurately and Anzieu in particular describes the influence this can have on the actual unfolding of group dynamics when he speaks of the "group illusion", i.e. the pleasure, accompanied with much elation which the patients feel at certain times and which can become - if unrecognized by the psychotherapist - an obstacle to the investigation of unconscious conflicts which must be grappled with and interpreted.

These fluctuations of the group as a whole, if recognised to be resistances, can be interpreted by group interpretations; this generally triggers off a depressive reaction coupled, however, with exchanges much nearer to the individual conflicts of each of the group's members - making it once again possible to structure the psychodynamics. These interpretations are based on the psychotherapist's perception of a common unconscious tension related on the one hand to dependency and fusional phantasys, and pleasurable phantasys entirely and completely shared, and on the other hand to the lack of differentiation of the members between themselves. In this sense, these interpretations have as a goal to prevent the group from seemingly functioning very well, with total cohesion and stability, a group illusion which, if not interpreted, will result in the breaking up of the group and finally in its dissolution due to the disillusionment and disappointment of not having been able to maintain this very primitive and regressive state. Thus there are forces hidden in the analytic group which do not exist in individual analytic psychotherapy or in psychoanalysis: these forces can abash beginner psychotherapists.

Group interpretation first of all brings out the pleasurable and dependent state which the members of the group experience (the "group illusion" or, according to Ezriel, the "required relationship"). It then shows that this is a resistance to another relationship between the group members which would call forward neurotic and thus more painful conflicts (Ezriel's "avoided relationship"). This re-

lationship is avoided because the members phantasize it on the basis
of their negative experiences which they feel are dangerous (Ezriel's
"catastrophic relationship"). Experience in the group itself shows
the positive affects of this type of interpretation which always provokes an transference situation.

Such interpretations are only necessary when the group unconsciously resists in this regressive manner, thus usually avoiding a
more oedipal type of structure which would imply more active interpretations. Although certain authors feel that the transference exclusively characterizes the one to one situation found in psychoanalysis and they designate what happens in a group as mere "relationships", from my point of view this differentiation is not of
prime importance.

4. Face-to-face contact, non-verbal communication and interpretation

As one of my collaborators, E. Gillieron, has very clearly shown,
individual analytic psychotherapy introduces the visible presence of
the psychotherapist and no longer permits the psychotherapist to be
visually "absent" as he is in the psychoanalytic setting. This absence creates a vague, undefined space which is "propitious to the
growth of phantasys" and encourages the patient to re-construct his
analyst from his own internal objects in the transference neurosis.
When sitting face to face with the patient, the therapist represents
an object of desire of the patient. The expectations of the patient
are concentrated on the therapist. Consequently, the patient - in
his need to make the person of the therapist correspond with his internal imagos - unconsciously exercises pressure on the therapist.
This is all the more accentuated in that to the verbal channel of
communication - which is the only such channel in psychoanalysis -
is added a non-verbal channel which is often of primordial importance, and which at times favours and at times very much hinders the
development of the psychotherapy.

How does this look in analytic group therapy? The face-to-face
contact is not the same as in individual psychotherapy. It is not
constraining and each patient can either merge with the group, more
or less stand apart, move forward or step back, indicate his presence
to the psychotherapist or, on the contrary, fade into the background,
make himself invisible. Non-verbal messages constantly intervene and
play a very important role; this is obvious and such communication
must be taken into account in the psychotherapist's interpretations
in order to allow the meaning behind gestures, glances, expressions
of the body as a whole, and above all visual expression to be verbal-
ized.

Non-verbal communication is always ambiguous. "Were you smiling
at me, were you showing me your affection or were you making fun of

me?" This example is sufficient to clearly demonstrate that without
the intervention of the spoken word in order to try and resolve the
ambiguity, almost everything which is communicated through gestures,
smiles or expressions can signify the best and the worst, the good
and the bad, love and hate, without one being sure to have understood
properly. Interpretation requires this "because" which I have already spoken about as well as its communication through the spoken
word.

Nevertheless the group psychotherapist must pick up on precisely the non-verbal interactions of the members between each other and
with himself and be able to interpret them verbally whenever necessary.
For example, he must be able to understand the meaning of depressive
attitudes, but also the meaning behind the physical exaltation experienced at a particular moment inside the group. Once again, the
interpretations applying to the largest possible portion of the group
members, i.e. a group interpretation, allow conflictual, interpersonal situations inside the group to be untangled in an exemplary manner
revealing the convergence of impulses, and thus the convergence of
desires and defences when faced with these impulses.

On the other hand, I feel that it is incorrect to think that
once a message or a non-verbal communication is transmitted, its
meaning will become clear to the patient without recourse being taken
to the spoken word, which - although also ambiguous - is still less
so than gestures and mime. Finally, in a group of 8-10 patients, it
is not possible for the therapist to usefully note all the infra-
verbal exchanges which often occur in the "twinkling of an eye".

5. Who does the interpreting - the group psychotherapist or
the patients?

This question is worth asking. Due to the lateral transferences and the partial or complete identifications of the members
with each other, each patient can make very pertinent remarks on the
psychodynamics of the other patients; sometimes these remarks take
on the value of an actual interpretation. One of the members can
even exceptionally make a group interpretation. However, a group
member usually only starts it off and the psychotherapist must finish
it, i.e. by adding the enlightening causal explanation. Most often,
however, these rudimentary interpretations made by the group members
are individual interpretations; at times they are very valuable and
useful for the therapist who can thus leave the patients to work
with each other without often having to intervene.

However there is one major danger. Certain interpretative interventions are much too brutal or deep and do not correspond to the
psychodynamic level of the group members. A correction is called
for and by means of his intervention - which takes on an interpretative aspect - the psychotherapist must protect the attacked

member.   In every group, one or several members feel the inner, unconscious need to play the role of the psychotherapist, either in
order to protect him, or, on the contrary, in order to oust him. Such
members often become the group animator and take on the role of the
co-therapist.   The seemingly interpretative interventions of such
patients are often no more than intellectualisations which remain
without effect and are not harmful.   However, these same members
often might make premature, individual interpretations which are too
deep and perturbing for the functioning of the group or for certain
patients.

The conflicts experienced "here and now" within the group reflect the personal, intrapsychic conflicts and the interiorized
parental imagos which are very often projected on the group members
rather than on the therapist.   The interventions made by the group
members concerning each other often refer to these imagos but do
not include the interpretative connection which must therefore be
made evident by the group psychotherapist.   He completes the interpretation whose first two components have already been given, i.e.
the outgoing situation and the fear of the impulse: he brings out
the "why", which thus unveils the primordial, conflictual situation.
From this angle, the psychotherapist can intervene individually in
order to support certain members - either by reassuring interventions
or else by an individual interpretation similar to what is done with
a phobic patient who remains silent and who needs this interpretation.

IV. CONCLUSION

The foregoing presentation fits in very harmoniously into the
theme of this Congress.   By concentrating on a very specific, technical problem, i.e. that of the interpretation, I hope to have shown
how - at least in our own civilization - the individual never stands
up against the group, and that the group is not the only social
possibility of life in the West, as it is in a certain traditional
African civilization.   Analytic group psychotherapy enriches the
individual if it permits him to become free and to choose either to
live alone or else to join other groups, i.e. family, work, leisure,
and friendship groups.   In this sense, all that makes up the conscious dynamics and the unconscious phenomena which are played off
in a group are no more than the means in analytic group psychotherapy
in order to reach an improved, psychodynamic understanding which must
culminate in the dissolution and the death of the group.

UNCONSCIOUS PLANNING BY PATIENTS FOR GROUP THERAPY

James P. Gustafson

Department of Psychiatry
University of Wisconsin
Madison, Wisconsin 53792

Lowell Cooper

California School of Professional Psychology
Berkeley, California

CONTROL-MASTERY THEORY EXTENDED TO GROUP SITUATIONS

There have been some dramatic changes in recent years in psychoanalytic theory and technique which have influenced us very much and
which we have found powerful in our group work. This new framework
is based on concepts from psychoanalytic ego psychology which have
been synthesized into a theory of psychotherapy called control-mastery theory. This theory is being developed by Joseph Weiss, M.D.
along with his colleague Harold Sampson(Weiss, et al., 1977, 1980;
Sampson, 1976; Weiss, 1971). Both are on the faculty of the San
Francisco Psychoanalytic Institute as well as of Mount Zion Hospital
and Medical Center. Weiss and Sampson also head a large research
group which has been carrying out formal studies of the new theory
as contrasted to traditional psychoanalytic theory.(Weiss et al.
1977, 1980). They have made several crucial proposals about the
functioning of the patient's mind and his behavior in psychotherapy,
as follows:

The Planning Hypothesis

According to Weiss and Sampson's control-mastery theory the patient's chief motivation, both conscious and unconscious, is to solve
his problems. His relationship to the therapist is guided by the
wish to enlist the therapist as an ally in his struggle to solve his
problems. Through unconscious control over his mental life, the

patient is able to evolve an unconscious plan for how he will approach the therapy and use the therapist. While this process shares
many of the cognitive characteristics of planning as it has been discussed as a conscious higher level ego function(Miller, Galanter,
Pribram, 1960), the same unconscious decisions and evaluations, imag-
ing, etc., also occur unconsciously, and it is a crucial aspect of
the therapist's work to be able to understand the patient's plan
since it sets the overall goals for the treatment. Now when a set of
individuals come together in a psychotherapy group, each one is likely
to have a different plan from his fellow members. What emerges
very quickly in the awareness of members, however, is the existence
and power of their collective efforts to influence their mutual interaction. At first the group process might emerge with relatively
little planning or take advantage of a dramatic external event such
as seeing the leader in a sharply defined group-process role. What
is central at this point to note is that group process becomes a
vehicle for individuals to work collaboratively to develop and clarify plans which will be of collective benefit, along with whatever
individual benefit might accrue. In our prior writing in this area
it has been demonstrated that the planning process is observable at
a group level as well as within individuals in a group.(Gustafson &
Cooper, 1979; Cooper & Gustafson, 1979a; Cooper & Gustafson, 1979b)

Testing

     The individual operationalizes plans for getting better, i.e.,
mastering developmental traumas which have stood as obstacles to
progressive development, through tests. Tests refer to unconscious
decision-making processes through which a patient in psychotherapy
proceeds to use the therapist to assure and reassure himself that
he will not be traumatized by the therapist as he had been traumatized in childhood. As Weiss and his colleagues describe for individual therapy, the patient tempts the therapist to do "the very
things which his parents had done and which he had experienced as
traumatic, hoping that the therapist will not react as his parents
had"(1977, p.5).

     For instance, a male patient came to therapy with considerable
unconscious guilt about separating from a clinging mother and with
the presenting difficulty of being close with a woman. In the course
of the treatment he found a new girlfriend and began to come late
and miss therapy hours, using as an excuse being with the girlfriend.
He got into conflict with the therapist about not getting extra time
and having to pay for missed hours. The therapist might feel quite
annoyed about continued difficulty in regular scheduling and he might
be tempted to take the position that the patient is being stubborn
and resisting the treatment. In the control-mastery view such a
position would be a repetition of the childhood trauma in which the
parent was critical of the patient's independence. In this greatly

over-simplified example, a control-mastery position would focus on
the transference conflict as a reflection of difficulties in attaining sought after independence. Here it is important to note that
this kind of therapeutic challenge is unconsciously mounted through
unconscious decisions on the part of the patient to test the therapist's capacity to tolerate the patient's independence without either
capitulating to patient demands or retaliating.

In the group, of course, such individual testing is also prominent, in relationship to the group analyst but also between members. Because of the possibility of the individuals working collectively, it is also quite likely to see shared group testing which
might take the form of a subgroup, factional conflict within the
group. For instance, in a group with which I worked, a dramatic
argument emerged between a subgroup of two members who believed
that there should be total openness in the group and who were disappointed in the wariness of other individuals, and another large
faction who wanted to move slowly. While there were important individual plans unfolding and being worked towards here, for the
group collectively there was an important test for the therapist as
to which direction he wanted the group to go in and whether he
would take sides. Rather than siding with either faction, the
difficult leadership dilemma (what Dr. Gustafson and I have called
a "steering contradiction" in a recent paper, Gustafson & Cooper,
1979) was exposed to the group, worked on in subsequent sessions,
and was eventually connected with family group difficulties in
which side-taking parents consistently traumatized particular
family members. The main point to note here is the emergence of a
theme relevant to both subgroups through their clashing in the group
and the consequent transference dilemma.

Ways Of Working In Psychotherapy

The two major ways in which the patient works in individual and
group psychotherapy, the modes in which the testing appears, are (a)
directly transferring and (b) turning passive into active. (a) In
directly transferring the individual treats the therapist as a
direct transference figure - the usual transference situation - and
is testing to see whether the therapist will respond as the traumatizing parent. The patient is essentially the childhood version of
himself, the adult with the childhood trauma. This would very much
follow the format of the example given above in which the therapist
can be made to feel like he controls the fate of the patient and
the treatment in a very powerful way. (b) In working by turning
passive into active the patient creates a situation in which he
takes the part of the parent (and has actually identified with a
traumatizing parent) and relates to the therapist as if the therapist
were the patient as a child. Here the testing gives the therapist
the same treatment which he (the patient) received as a child in

order for the therapist to provide a more mature way of dealing with
the parent than the patient had, for instance maintaining self-control rather than identifying with an out-of-control parent. The
therapist is expected to be a direct growth model for identification.
Such passive into active tests can be quite difficult.

For instance, an individual whose therapy was supervised by me
came to treatment frantic about not being able to complete her Ph.D.
dissertation. She was very agitated, paced continually, tearfully
demanding immediate suggestions and curative recommendations from
the therapist. This patient had a very labile mother who repeatedly
had dramatic and hysterical crying episodes whenever the patient had
gone away from the home and initiated independent activity. While
the patient had pursued an independent course, she felt quite guilty
about driving the mother to states of hysteria and had, through
identification, taken her mother with her. Being hysterical instead
of writing was quite debilitating in her current situation. The
therapist was being tested to provide a more stable and mature way
of dealing with such maternal lability in the face of independence,
such as disregarding it, and interpretations to this point were
very useful for the patient.

Both directly transferring and turning passive into active are
ways patients work individually and collectively within the group
therapy process. With a relatively non-directive therapist, it is
quite common for a group to act helpless, as if to test for permission for independent functioning from a transferential adult. Turning passive into active also occured powerfully, for instance, in a
therapy group led by me in which for several sessions members had
great fun picking out an article of my clothing and making fun of it
rather mercilessly while having a·very good time together. This
was invariably followed by concerns about hurting my feelings and
worries about either depressing me or courting retaliation. The
turning passive into active test here was interpreted in terms of
the patients feeling ridiculed themselves and worried about its impact on me and what emerged over the weeks during which this issue
was worked were many reports of family incidents in which individuals
were unprotected from siblings and underestimated by parents, with
consequent feelings that they should become socially withdrawn in
order to be safe with people. They were very uplifted by my not
withdrawing from them as they had withdrawn in the family.

What greatly complicates the analysis of the group levels of
collaborative tests is the likelihood that in any one incident some
individuals might be transferring directly and others turning passive
into active. At some rare moments, probably more typical of the
group dramas described in Bion's (1959) basic assumption life, the
group can be seen exclusively as a whole. In the therapy situation
in which members have succeeded in articulating their individual

plans, a collective effort can serve several purposes concurrently. As with other therapeutic endeavors, the therapist must focus on what seems most primary and salient, recognizing that behaviors are planned on multiple levels for varied if not contradictory therapeutic purposes.

The Family-Group

I would like to focus on aspects of planning in family-group development for a few moments, especially as it relates to individual plan differences and conflicts. Managing plan differences and contradictions is a very major part of group therapist role functioning.

To take family group development seriously has tremendous implications for the social life experiences of adults. We are really talking about a situation in which the person carries images and makes plans which include experiences and problems stemming from the family network. So when an individual joins an adult group, such as a psychotherapy group, his/her group behavior is directly affected by the family-group object-relations.

Three aspects of plan differentiation can be distinguished as they bear on group analysis. First, at crucial points for individuals specific plan differences become contradictions (Gustafson and Cooper, 1979). Here we are talking about children whose plans contradict the plans of other family members or the plans of the family as a whole. At these times the child begins to sense that certain other people in the family seem disturbed by or unable to cope with his plans and he must take them into account in order to manage any semblance of plan accomplishment. So, for instance, an individual's plans for being big by being very smart in school might have the following impact on the family: the mother worries about this assertiveness and is concerned about losing control, the father is very cold and business-like and offers little support to mother and little encouragement to the child with whom he feels competitive, and a sibling who is considerably more compliant and placid is given more unconflicted positive response from both parents. The child's being big is interfered with by a family-group stage which limits certain kinds of assertiveness and is guilt-arousing and unsupportive. The child could either hold back, develop bigness in secret out of view of the family, try to become more placid, etc. The resolutions are myriad, but the nature of the plan contradiction in the family group dynamic is itself crucial and could be followed as it re-emerges in other developmental challenges highlighting assertiveness.

Secondly, it can be important to note for individuals the developmental stage in which the plan contradiction emerges. Following

the example given it is also possible to see a range of depth of
disturbance around assertiveness as a developmental issue. For instance, assertiveness might not be a problem for the family until
the child is about to go off to college and surpass the family ed-
ucationally and thereby be seen as putting the family in a bad light,
or the plan contradictions could begin at a earlier and more damag-
ingly influential age, as when the child is learning to walk, when
the conflict around independence could take a more dire form. The
importance of stage of emergence, early vs. late family-group problems, is that difficulties occurring earlier in life could point to
a greater degree of psychological disturbance for the social adult.

   Thirdly, individuals differ in their capacity to <u>expose</u> and <u>work</u>
on their plans in <u>dyads</u> <u>vs.</u> <u>groups</u>. For reasons likely to be connected to family configuration and how plans are handled in the
family, some individuals are better prepared psychologically for
dyad or group involvement. Of course, this has considerable impact
on the comfort with which the individual works on plan contradiction
problems in a group, how inviting or psychologically safe the group
is as a helpful change agent. If a person feels dramatically traumatized by the family-group configuration, he/she may become a loner,
preferring to accomplish things out of view of potential worriers
who have been nonsupporters in competition. In this case, an individual might not make himself available to group work at all; the
family group may have been too traumatizing. For such an individual,
the plan encouragement may have come from a parental figure in dyadic
relationship when, for instance, mother and son were alone and away
from the family group. In such a case, dyadic treatment might be
more effective. Pushing this point even further, this kind of reaction is frequent in individual psychotherapy in which a person is
truly so damaged by earlier dyadic relationships that he/she is incapable of making plans for his/her own development prominent and
working on them even in a dyad without tremendous anxiety, guilt,
and psychological disruption.

   It is also quite clear that, for some, the group milieu can
facilitate plan exposure and development. For others in a group
it is important to provide supportive dyads in order for them to
feel safe enough to use the group. Individuals might feel strong
and safe enough inside themselves when in a group to approach the
group by testing carefully and indirectly the safety of being big
relative to its impact on members and leader. Others might well be
able to do so only with strong support from an influential companion.
Is assertiveness a plan which can be worked on? Is the leader receptive or rejecting? How do the peers stand up under the competition? Where are the allies for this plan? and with whom does this
plan conflict? Each group question raises an issue for each individual for which extended analysis of the whole family-group constellation is necessary, as well as more usual partial aspects of
familial transference.

I would now like to give the floor to Dr. Gustafson, who will continue from the summary of theory and move through some of the practical, technical implications of our theory for group therapy intervention.

JUDGING NEW THEORY

In hearing Dr. Cooper's account of our essential concepts, you, the listener, undoubtedly have the problems which arise in judging any new theory. New theory always builds on previous concepts, which have had some usefulness and some shortcomings. The existing concepts then are taken up as special cases of the new theory. Since you recognize these older and familiar elements in what we are saying, you might wonder whether it is merely the old theory put in different language. Indeed, it could be so, and this is for you to judge. On the other hand, the new theory could only appear to be a restatement in new language, when in fact a major shift in theory is taking place. This is also up to you to judge. In order to clarify what is indeed new and surprising in our idea of unconscious planning for group therapy, I will take up the two major problems of the clinical practice of group therapy, to inquire how they are altered by our theory. First, how is the technique of conducting group therapy sessions changed by our theory? Second, how is the selection of patients for group therapy changed by our theory?

HOW DOES THIS THEORY CHANGE TECHNIQUE?

First, how does this theory change technique? As the field of group therapy is now arranged, each school of theory implies certain "therapeutic conditions" which are, undoubtedly, helpful to helping some patients solve their problems, yet most of these pose as universal theories of group therapy. In practice, patients who need the therapeutic conditions favored by a given school do well in their particular groups. Thus Yalom finds that successful outcome correlates only with "group cohesion" and group "popularity". We interpret this result to mean that the "popular" patients have gotten the group conditions most favorable to their own development. Those who do not benefit from this particular set of conditions remain on the fringe and do not benefit. For example, a group theory which promotes an atmosphere of mutual congratulation will draw out and encourage narcissistic patients, who require a full supply of mirroring, but it may be very discouraging to patients who need help in being skeptical, critical and mindful of the ugly backside of getting along with the narcissistic members. The show offs will flourish, and the skeptics will recede. This may be the unwitting consequence of a psychodrama theory of group therapy.

Our theory predicts that this clash of developmental needs be-

tween group members is to be expected in every group. For example
Mrs. C. will join a group needing to develop her assertive capacities
at first, because she is in danger of being taken advantage of at
close quarters. She will need therapeutic conditions in the group
which support her assertions, i.e., not only encouragement for it,
but other members who can take it without getting hurt by her or
without retaliating unfairly. Mr. D., however, will join a group
needing first to be reassured of being taken care of, because he is
in danger of feeling he doesn't matter at all and having to leave.
He will need therapeutic conditions in the group which support his
dependency, not only encouragement but also other members who are
not unduly frightened by his need to attach nor having to attack
him harshly for his attachment seeking. But here is the typical
problem. Mrs. C. will be inclined to assert herself with Mr.D.,
needing to feel free to push him away and criticize him. He is apt
to be frightened and hurt by her behaviour, since he wants to start
by attaching. His negative reaction is going to block her feeling
free to continue her assertion. Conversely, Mr. D. is inclined to
reach out for nurturance to Mrs. C., scaring her about coming close
before she is ready. She is apt to panic and push him away, blocking his effort to set up the conditions of dependency he needs.
This is a typical way in which the developmental plans of two patients may cancel each other out.

Since group therapists are continually on the defensive when
their medium, the group, is compared with individual psychotherapy,
their theories tend to deny that patients can cancel one another out.
They think as if people were essentially <u>alike</u> in what they need
from their therapy. <u>We</u> <u>believe</u> <u>this</u> <u>assumption</u> <u>of</u> <u>like</u> <u>needs</u> <u>is</u>
<u>false</u>. Mrs. C. will need group conditions favorable to aggression,
while Mr. D. will need group conditions favorable to dependency.

If a given theory of group therapy assumes that joining is
brought about by initial dependency culture, Mr. D. is likely to
join and advance, while Mrs. C. is a likely dropout. If a given
theory of group therapy assumes that assertiveness is the first
order of business, Mrs. C. will be encouraged, and Mr. D. is likely
to quit. The theories which pretend that Mrs. C. and Mr. D. are
alike in their "therapeutic needs", we predict, will be likely to
lose one of them or the other. In fact, we believe it is common
for these groups based on theories of alikeness of members to lose
<u>both</u> Mrs. C. and Mr. D., because each is inherently traumatic for
the other! They knock each other out.

The unconscious planning theory allows the therapist to control
this ubiquitous phenomenon of patients canceling one another, in
several ways. First, it alerts him to avoid being captured as an
advocate of a particular set of conditions, instead, e.g., to support
the dependency conditions of some members, while supporting the
aggressiveness conditions of others. Each subgroup then has at least

one ally, in the therapist, for its necessary conditions. Once he
takes up this position of steering between these contradictory conditions, the patients may fully join in a battle for what the group
conditions will be. The most important issue and the most intense
feeling will emerge over whose interests are being served by any
particular line of discussion. The Mrs. C's and the Mr. D's, <u>given</u>
<u>at least</u> the understanding and alliance of the group therapist, are
reassured that at least some of the time some of their optimal conditions will prevail. For example, in one of my groups, the women
tend to bring up problems of demanding more from their men, without
losing the nurturance and sexual interest they may have been getting.
They push the group toward a feminist culture. On the contrary, the
men tend to bring up problems of looking for nurturance from their
women, without losing their masculinity, their self respect. They
push the group towards a culture of male honor. Capture of the
therapist by either subgroup deadens the other subgroup, while
demonstrated solidarity with both allows both to engage intensively.
The result is a series of spirited compromises between the two sets
of conditions.

<u>HOW DOES THIS THEORY CHANGE SELECTION</u>?

     According to the present theories of selection, it is useful
to consider what Yalom(1975) calls both "exclusion" and "inclusion"
factors. For example, Yalom has a list of exclusion factors, based
on empirical research in which patients who dropped out of group
therapy gave their reasons for quitting. Of course, it may be useful
to pose to therapist and patient the most common obstacles, but most
candidates for group therapy qualify for at least several of the
problems on the Yalom list. For example, the patient may have a
"fear of intimacy." What Yalom admits in his book is altogether
commonplace: it is hard to know if this patient's "fear of intimacy"
means he <u>needs</u> group therapy all the more to solve it, <u>or</u> that he
<u>needs to avoid</u> group therapy because the intimacy required will be
intolerable.

     In regard to inclusion factors, most discussions center on "mot-
ivation." The trouble with judging motivation, from dyadic pre-
group interviews, is that it is very difficult to judge how the motivation will hold up under the usual stresses of groups. The critical question becomes: Will motivation remain high once the trouble
begins: Is there motivation to interact under stress? Given the
patient apparently motivated to face his "fear of intimacy," will
he fold with the first problems of being approached by other members
or will he persist in the interaction? No theory has been able to
show the solution to this most common dilemma of selection in group
therapy.

     The unconscious planning theory offers the following clarifica-

tion. Consider again Mrs. C., who is afraid of intimacy, because
she submits to men when involved with them, making intimacy into a
dangerous form of self-sacrifice for her. Thus she must avoid it.
How will she do in group therapy? Our theory predicts that Mrs. C.
will do well in group therapy, if her need to learn self assertion
prior to any intimacy is supported by conditions in the group. She
will provoke others with bits of assertion, hoping that some of
them will tolerate her assertion without defensiveness, without
being hurt or retaliating. Of course, our theory also predicts
that, inevitably, some members will be defensive, will be hurt, will
retaliate. The question we need an answer to is: How resilient
is Mrs. C. when her therapeutic conditions temporarily fail? These
"anti-plan" conditions, antagonistic to her unconscious plan for
solving her problems, are sure to arise, according to our theory.
If she has this resilience, she will be able to push the group back
to the conditions necessary to her progress.

How then can you read resilience in advance of the group, in the
period of selection? Our method is to induce the emotional conditions of actual groups, by a series of drawings we have designed,
which are called the Wisconsin Projective Test (WP). The test procedure is analagous to the TAT, or Thematic Apperception Test, in
which the patient is asked to make up stories as vivid as possible
about the cards he is shown. (Let us have Slide 1, a situation
between 2 persons, about dependency and fear of it/now Slide 1A, in
which we retained the figure of the 2 persons, while changing the
ground, adding a neutral group of onlookers. Let us now have Slide
2...and 2A, etc.) From the typescript of 16 stories, we are able to
predict: the recurrent problem which the patient is trying to solve,
how this patient will provoke others to see if they can provide the
right conditions, and what happens when others are provoked to do
what is harmful to the patient. The most interesting and critical
judgement, however, is how resilient the subject is when he represents being failed in these provocative tests. Subjects who can
bounce back and deepen their revelations, after describing harmful
reactions, seem to have the necessary resilience in the actual situations of group therapy. This, is at least, is our present working
hypothesis, confirmed to date by our empirical study which is in
progress.

TRANSITION TO THE QUESTION PERIOD

Given our available time, we have been able only to give you
the faintest sketch of our concepts and their surprising implications
for clinical practice of group therapy. We certainly invite all of
you to attend our Workshop tomorrow afternoon from 2 to 4 p.m. in
Room 13-1-59 called, "The Theory of Unconscious Planning Applied
to Technique and Selection" where we will go through a complete set
of stories by one of the twenty-four subjects whom we have studied

and followed in group therapy, and also discuss the research and its results and problems as they now stand. Also, we will demonstrate further our ideas of technique in a videotape of a group by Dr. Cooper.

For now, we think that a useful discussion here might take us in several possible directions. Perhaps, how other present theories might engage this same material? Surely you have your own ways of thinking about this, which you might compare with ours. Secondly, we might get into the research problems, of how to decide between this and its rival theories, how we would know which is more useful.

REFERENCES

Bion, W.R., 1971, "Experiences in Groups," Basic Books, New York.
Cooper, L., and Gustafson, J.P., 1979a, Planning and mastery in group therapy: A contribution to theory and technique, Human Relations, 32:689.
Cooper, L., and Gustafson, J.P., 1979b, Towards a general theory of group therapy, Human Relations, 32:967.
Gustafson, J.P., and Cooper, L., 1979, Unconscious planning in small groups, Human Relations, 32:1039.
Miller, G.A., Galanter, E., Pribram, K.H., 1960, "Plans and the Structure of Behavior," Holt, Rinehart and Winston, New York.
Sampson, H., 1976, A critique of certain traditional concepts in the psychoanalytic theory of therapy, Bull. Menninger Clinic, 40:255.
Weiss, J., 1971, The emergence of new themes: A contribution to the psychoanalytic theory of therapy, Int. J. Psa., 52:459.
Weiss, J., Sampson, H., Caston, J., Silberschatz, G., and Gassner, S., 1977, Bulletin #3, Psychotherapy Research Group, Department of Psychiatry, Mount Zion Hospital and Medical Center. Available on request from Ms. Janet Bergman, San Francisco Psychoanalytic Institute, 2420 Sutter Street, San Francisco, CA 94115.
Weiss, J., Sampson, H., Gassner, S., Caston, J., 1980, Bulletin #4, Psychotherapy Research Group, Department of Psychiatry, Mount Zion Hospital and Medical Center.
Yalom, I., 1975, "The Theory and Practice of Group Psychotherapy." Basic Books, New York.

FAILURES IN GROUP THERAPY AND THE POTENTIAL FOR GROWTH THROUGH THE STUDY OF SUCH FACTORS

Saul Tuttman, M.D., Ph.D.

New York University School of Medicine
Department of Psychiatry
170 East 77th Street
New York, New York 10021

In evaluating any therapeutic method (whatever the malady requiring care and treatment), one crucial issue involves failure - the
cause and nature of failure to achieve the goals of patient or therapist. This is an important subject because failure may reflect limitations in our theory or concept of practice and the study of failure
may help us enhance our understanding. Such considerations led to my
proposal that the American Group Psychotherapy Association devote a
session of the February 1980 Los Angeles meeting to a study of failures in group therapy.

Dr. Fern Azima chaired a colloquium at which Normund Wong,
Isaiah Zimmerman and I explored this matter. I will summarize the
viewpoints expressed there and I will offer my current thoughts on
the subject.

Dr. Azima[1] observed that there is a general reluctance of therapists to disclose their failures, especially when personal factors are
involved. An accepting atmosphere among colleagues can help to
facilitate further inquiry into this delicate and important area.

Dr. Normund Wong[2] described some of the difficulties in defining
failure. For example, increased symptomatology appearing in the
course of treatment need not reflect failure. We would need to know
about the patient's prior psychic state before group therapy began.
Without such data, it is difficult to attribute whatever emerges as
a direct consequence or result of group therapy.

Hadley and Strupp[3] used the phrase negative effect which may be
preferable to "failure" or "casualty" since it more specifically
refers to the patient's condition deteriorating in response to the

511

group situation. Whether or not a negative effect in a particular
instance is a lasting result or a normal vicissitude in treatment
which is on the pathway to successful outcome must also be considered.
For example, I - and others - in the tradition of Balint have published papers on the place of regression in treatment; describing
how often regression, manifested in the course of treatment, turns
out to be conducive to good long range positive therapeutic results. [4]

Wong reminded us that Galinsky and Schopler[5] classified three
types of casualties in group therapy. One type relates to intrapsychic factors in the patient: that is, when personal pathology
involves ego weakness, inappropriate, negativistic or disruptive
behavior. Such patients often become casualties or induce casualties
depending upon their ability to subvert the group. In such cases,
the outcome will also depend upon the group's capacity to tolerate
the particular pathology of such individuals. Often, the therapist's
skill is crucial to developing a therapeutic group milieu wherein
potential hazards become productive challenges and opportunities.

This point brings us to the second factor in failure: the
qualities and skill of the group leader. Hadley and Schopler[6]
reported that group leaders with high casualty rates tended to be
extreme (that is, either impersonal and inactive or highly charismatic and over-stimulating). Leaders who are inexperienced and who
lack psychodynamic and group training are not equipped to diagnose
and contend with unconscious factors and have high casualty rates.

Failure factor three is the group characteristics. For example,
a group which lacks structure may be unable to help bind some
patients' anxieties and provide the necessary order and delineation
which is essential for that individual's growth. In other instances,
group pressure to participate, ventilate or probe defenses before
a particular patient is motivated or secure enough may prove catastrophic. Personally I conceive of this variable in terms of Bion's[7]
basic concepts. When the group "acts out" one of these archaic
patterns and does not become a "working group, there will probably
be a failure to achieve therapeutic goals.

Related to this variable, Wong also examined the influence of
group composition: heterogeneity versus homogeneity, the presence of
enough spontaneous, active participants, the impact of too many passive or negativistic, severly depressed or hallucinating psychotics.

Wong stressed that crises in the life of the leader can be
detrimental to group therapy, especially since the therapist becomes
susceptible to the pressure of so many patients interacting at the
same time in this kind of treatment, and there are innumerable
opportunities for the many patients to mirror the therapist's feelings
and problems. I do not completely agree with this. I have seen group
therapy sometimes enhanced by the visible humanity and vulnerable,

yet coping, integrity and engagement of the therapist. Of course, as in all psychodynamic matters, the specific variables and the details of a particular instance require individual evaluation of the forces at play.

In summary, Wong attributes much importance to the personalities and pathology of the group members and to the style and skill of the group therapist. I will discuss my hypotheses about this later.

At this California meeting[8] Dr. Isaiah Zimmerman presented examples of failure and casualties from his personal practice and his function as administrator and supervisor. He concluded that the following variables are most influential in determining therapeutic failure. (1) Therapists' problems due to unconscious motives, "acting out" and countertransference were illustrated in some of his examples which stressed the difficulties of inexperienced, insecure therapists, especially when serving in the complex role of co-thera-pists. (2) Failure in patient selection for the group, either on the basis of disruptive pathological factors or clashing philosophical world views between patient and group or between patient and therapist. Such confrontations of value systems often detract from each parti-cipant's therapeutic task of searching inward, facing internal motives and conflicts and working them through. Instead failures or casualties result from acting out and displacing issues and affects onto a political or religious cause celebre. Zimmerman offered a third cluster of failure factors: that is, the overall societal pressures at work. The administrative forces in clinic, institute, or hospital may so affect the atmosphere and the reality conditions that any group therapeutic intent is seriously compromised, if not doomed! Personally, I consider these issues (of the overall organis-mic forces in which a therapy group would be immersed) to be but a part of the larger organization in the context of general system theory.

Finally, Zimmerman spoke of group dynamics which may in them-selves cause negative results. Policies of selectivity, degrees of homogeneity, open versus closed admission, patient preparation, flex-ibility versus rigidity, structure versus ambiguity - such possibili-ties may prove crucial to outcome for a patient under particular circumstances. Zimmerman concluded that success or failure of a group may sometimes depend upon the support system available from outside the therapy group to the trainee or even experienced group therapist. It is important for the therapist that he be permitted to function in the context of a working climate where he or she is safe to expose and explore problems and errors and "work through" whatever might inter-fere with effective group leadership.

My Los Angeles comments on failure were based upon experience as group therapist, teacher and supervisor who functions within a psycho-analytic framework wherein I stress object relations theory and deve-

lopmental ego psychology along with a group dynamics orientation. I
take the "middle road" as described by E. James Anthony[9].

   I see the group modality as inherently different from individual
treatment in certain ways. Failure may be related to the treatment
modality. Some of these differences may be exploited to great advantage by particular kinds of patients. For others, the group treatment mode is more difficult. I have summarized these factors in a
paper recently published in the Journal of the American Academy of
Psychoanalysis[10]. A similar viewpoint was eloquently expressed by
Malcolm Pines in his paper "Group therapy with 'Difficult' Patients'[11]
and by J. H. Rey in "Intrapsychic Object Relations: The Individual
and the Group"[12].

   In Los Angeles I presented anecdotal reports illustrating factors
I relate to failure[13]. An example: the special vulnerability of narcissistic personalities and certain borderline patients. These people
dread disclosure and intimacy as much as they hunger for it. Here the
talents and the sensitivity of the group therapist are put to the test
in his efforts to encourage a group atmosphere whcih generates trust
and offers members both the space and flexibility in timing which is
so necessary if deeper levels of productive communication are to
develop and failure is to be avoided.

   I reported a condition which can portend failure if not understood and worked through; certain individuals whose early life history involved specific traumas in a context of group situations, or
those whose chaotic, archaic early life experiences did not permit
them sufficient integrative experience. These personalities did not
have the opportunity to develop intact self and object intrapsychic
representations. These patients are particularly frightened by and
resistant to the group situation. Primitive malevolent, assaultive
attributions are symbolically assigned to any group automatically and
this can predispose such patients to profound resistances and failure
unless such factors are recognized and responded to appropriately.
Here the skill and experience of the group therapist are crucial.

   In my opinion, even in less difficult patients, the group
therapist's countertransference problems and "acting out" behavior
are the most frequent and important cause of unsuccessful group
therapy. One needs the capacity to cope with intense transferences
both from the group as a whole and from each individual patient. It
is not realistic to expect our patients to come for treatment free
from resistances and "acting out" symptoms. Of course, we endeavor
to select promising trainees and to develop programs geared to providing opportunities to resolve the personality problems of students
which can interfere with effective therapeutic leadership.

   Nevertheless, I appreciate my colleagues' reports of failure
as related to the emotional difficulties on the part of therapists.

This may be a crucial consideration, not only because the therapist's
personality is his most valuable instrument, but also because therapist failure can give us important clues about the therapeutic process. And, perhaps even more important, we must be able to design
studies which separate therapist failure per se from other sources of
therapeutic failure so that we can test our theories of group therapy
aside from our evaluation of therapists' techniques and problems!

In general, I am not comfortable about the quality of research
data we have regarding several group therapy issues. Which pathology
responds best to which treatment modality or combination? What about
the endless questions on the pros and cons of homogeneity and heterogeneity? Should there be preparation and selection of patients for
groups? Should there be matching of personality and value systems
of patients and therapist? When does cautious control of group factors encourage success? When does contrived pre-structure interfere
with treatment?

My hunch is that although these issues need more carefully controlled study, these matters become decisive primarily when the skill
and expertise of the therapist is the limiting variable; that is, when
the group therapist is inexperienced and understandably insecure. If
the group therapist is poised, sophisticated theoretically, personally genuine and able to respond therapeutically, I do not believe that
other variables are of such great importance. In my opinion, the
best of the group modality potential operates when there is opportunity for greater spontaneity of interaction and a situation emerges
in which group and leader cope together in the presence of a variety
of life styles and perceptual contrasts. The capacity to tolerate
and reconcile the wide range of internal worlds and perceptual styles
provides the most growth-conducive potential inherent in the group
situation. Of course, this could not occur if rigidities, anxieties,
narcissistic needs or autocratic exploitations are part of the therapist's problems.

A "good enough" group leader (to use Winnicott's phrase[14])
usually can generate a facilitating, good enough group environment.
In this setting the group will become an instrument both of containment and of experimentation. Within such a framework, the structure
and boundaries offered make play and fantasy safe enough to share.
Each individual member will probably eventually share his private
world, including traumatic memories; and the projection of personal
self and object representations can be expressed, re-engaged - the
past has an opportunity to awaken - first in the form of acting out
expression when other group members can serve as containers, surro-
gates, advocates, substitutes, critics, observers, confronters,
mirrors and contrasts. The helpful therapist catalyzes the therapeutic potential of the group by facilitating the development of a
poignant instrument.

We concluded again and again that a special kind of therapeutic
community, as an intensive short-term therapy, is far superior to
all other treatments. At first, this was not our expected finding
and our professional pride was hurt. After all we were spending
about 20 hours a month in psychoanalytic treatment of one patient.
There in the village of Lobetch, the therapeutic community was run
by two female therapists without formal training. We visited Lobetch
only once a week, spending one hour per patient a month of our time.

We believe that Fig. 1 describing the outcome of treatment
in Lobetch in the 50's (with those improved, not improved and worse)
underrates rather than overrates the outcome. In 2 - 5 years
follow-up 75% of the patients felt happier in life than before treatment. More sophisticated was our study in Canada (Knobloch, Reith,
Miles, 1973; Reith, Knobloch, Miles, 1974; see Knobloch et al 1979)
where we compared 3 equalized groups of neurotic patients in a ward
of a University hospital with traditional treatment, in an impro-
vised therapeutic community of a day care, and a residential therapeutic community in a Haney Forestry Camp with physical work in the
forest. The results based on multivariate analysis showed that
there existed consistent symptomatic improvement in the invariant
order: Haney Forestry Camp - day care - (both significant on most
measures) - and Hospital treatment (no significant changes). The
same order of improvement was found in measures of anxiety, self-
acceptance, self-confidence, and hopefulness. The costs of the
treatment were in reverse order to the efficiency: if the costs of
in-patient treatment is taken as 100%, the cost of day care was 32%
and of Haney Forestry 18%. Of 118 patients followed, 84 could be
reached after 2 years, and the order of improvement was the same,
that is: Haney Forestry, day care, hospital.

Neither this study is without flaws, typical of psychotherapeutic research. We still regard it only as a support for our clinical observations. The better results in the Haney Forestry camp,
a residential therapeutic community, were certainly not caused by
better skills of therapists are of theoretical interest. It seems
that living close together for 24 hours made the difference, with
intense feeling of belonging to a group, sometimes for the first
time in the patient's life.

Are we perhaps too uncritically enthusiastic about the therapeutic community ? We do not think so - after all, we have stakes in
several kinds of psychotherapy including psychoanalysis, which we
continue to practice. We have recognized the limits of the therapeutic community. First, in our experience, the improvement the
patients achieve in 6 - 8 weeks is rarely surpassed by longer stay
in the therapeutic community. Second, a minority of patients cannot
achieve their therapeutic goals in the therapeutic community, but
can achieve it in subsequent individual therapy. But invariably
any further improvement takes a long time, sometimes years. We

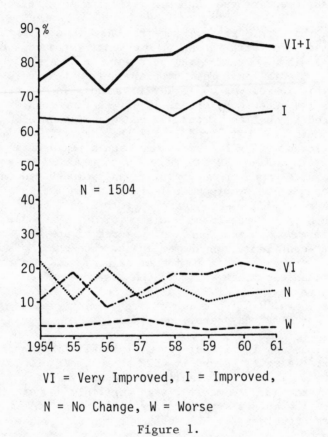

VI = Very Improved, I = Improved,

N = No Change, W = Worse

Figure 1.

conclude, therefore, that no person with serious neurotic difficulties should go into long-term individual treatment, without going
first through therapeutic community of a special kind. This is of
particular importance for countries with nationalized health services
since extended individual treatment without preceeding therapeutic
community treatment is not economical. For example, in Canada, one
day of treatment in the Day House costs about 3/5 of the costs of
one hour of individual psychotherapy. However, even disregarding the
treatment costs completely, the therapeutic community is in our
experience superior in effectiveness to any individual psychotherapy
of the same duration.

Our therapeutic community may be different from that of M. Jones
- he said (1956) that the therapeutic community should "have a single
therapeutic goal, namely adjustment of the indivual to social and
work conditions outside - without any ambitious psychotherapeutic
program". We fail to see the dichotomy: our therapeutic community
is an ambitious psychotherapeutic program and its criterion of
success is the patient's adjustment to social conditions - in Freud's
words, capability to love and work. Here, M. Jones may have been
influenced by Robert Rapoport who in his study of the Henderson
Hospital (Rapoport, 1960) stressed the differences between psychotherapy or treatment (intrapsychic integration) and rehabilitation
or sociotherapy (adjustment to social reality). Similarly Marshall
Edelson (1970) distinguished strictly between psychotherapy and
socio-therapy, and while he sees the processes as complementary, the
intrusion of psychotherapy in a therapeutic community can according
to him be confusing, obstructive and harmful. He sees psychotherapy
and sociotherapy as taking the patient in two opposite directions.
Stuart Whiteley (1979) seems to vacillate: "The distinction between
psychotherapy and sociotherapy is conceptually helpful, but a skillful blend would seem more in keeping with the original therapeutic
community ideology..." He sees psychotherapy and sociotherapy as
two different ways to the same goal. He says (1979):

"An understanding and modification of human behaviour can
  be reached through investigating intrapersonal processes,
  and this is called psychotherapy. A similar goal can be
  arrived at through exploring interpersonal activity and
  this is called sociotherapy. While the pathways taken
  and the aids applied differ in many respects the general
  direction and ultimate goal are the same, so that a rigid
  division between sociotherapy and psychotherapy seems
  artificial. Understanding the differences and appreci-
  ating what each approach has to offer in the large group
  setting, however, leads to a more profitable application
  of either technique."

If they are so different, why is the division artificial ? Our

position is that the division is artifical, because it is based on
incorrect distinction between intrapsychic and interpersonal. We
would not squabble about words, if this would not be a perpetuation
of myths about psychoanalytic treatment as opposed to other treatments. In our view, therapeutic community, group and family therapy
throw new light on psychodynamics and individual therapy. The time
has come for radical reconceptualization of the whole field. Our
attempt at reconceptualization is rather complex and goes counter
to ingrained habits of dualistic thought and language - so we do
not expect to convince anyone with our brief remarks, and can refer
those interested to our book "Integrated Psychotherapy" (Knobloch
and Knobloch, 1979a, 1979b). Briefly, the human group is a natural
behavioural unit or system and an individual can be understood only
as a sub-system of the group system. Even if alone, an individual is
is surrounded by a fantasy group (which we call a group schema) and
his behaviour is influenced by imaginary interactions with group
schema figures. In other words, so-called intra-psychic processes
are interpersonal processes in fantasy group, and psychodynamics can
be formulated as sociodynamics. If social exchange theory talks
about the balance of rewards and costs between reciprocating group
members, we extend this idea to imaginary reward-costs exchange an
individual has with his group schema figures. Freud's great innovation was to design powerful rewards for patients in transference
relationships, combined with costs of abstinence. In a therapeutic
community, we have to analyse how the rewards-costs of all patients
fit together, and to watch for hidden rewards which divert the patients from their therapeutic goals. Neurotics are virtuosos at
failing to achieve their major goals and rewards, but obtaining
hidden substitute rewards instead. We formulate the postulates
underlying therapeutic community in the following way:

Postulate 1. Arrange the distribution of rewards and costs to
intensify the striving towards therapeutic goals!

We regard this rule as basic for all kinds of psychotherapy and
in fact we formulated it at first, as a "rule of motivational balance," for family therapy (Knobloch et al., 1954). In family therapy, the task is to assess rewards-costs balance among all family
members, and then step-by-step to initiate the reshuffling of
rewards-costs, till a more mature state of the family group is
reached. Only later an orientation in social psychology developed,
best known as "social exchange theory", developed particularly by
G.C. Homans (1961) and Thibaut, J.W., and Kelley, H.H. (1959), and
Kelley, H.H. and Thibaut, J.W. (1978). In a therapeutic community
a greater variety of rewards and costs is available than in any
other treatment, and their full utilization promises a sharp rise
in effectiveness of the therapeutic community in the future.

Here, each postulate will point to different aspects of rewards-
costs economy in the therapeutic community.

Postulate 2. Form a closed socio-ecological system.

This means that therapeutic community is relatively isolated, so that the uninterrupted interpersonal vicious circlés of each individual can be studied. In neurosis, the persistence of mal-adaptive behaviour despite the apparent lack of rewards is of central importance. It was described by Freud so masterfully, and explained so poorly, by repetition compulsion. H. Schulz-Hencke (1942) was the first psychoanalyst to describe it as an interpersonal vicious circle. Therapeutic community, as a closed system for rewards and costs, is a unique place to analyse vicious circles of behaviour. The maximum number of patients for intensive treatment is 30 in a residential therapeutic community, 20 in the Day House. It will be obvious that although we stress the closed system and Max Jones the open system, there is likely no difference of opinion - he uses the term rather broadly.

Postulate 3. Therapeutic Community admits those who make contract about personal and group goals, and about norms.

Our community is homogeneous in the sense that all patients are capable and willing to make a contract. We do not admit patients such as schizophrenics, since we are not certain about their capability to adhere to strict norms. However, another therapeutic community with relaxed rules may be useful for them. In fact, we established such a Day Care - separate from the Day House - at the University Hospital in Vancouver. A group heterogenous in regard to capability to make contracts is not rewarding enough for anyone. This is one of the reasons for general demoralization in many day care centres we witness too often, both of patients and staff.

The norms and sanctions for breaking rules and social approval for following them are an extremely important part of the therapeutic community.

Postulate 4. Share leadership and responsibility with the patients! Shift executive power to them as much as possible, and keep expert power!

There are rewards for patients sharing leadership, and training for leadership roles. The patients can encourage each other in ways in which the therapists cannot, and the way they do it is itself valuable material for psychotherapy.

Postulate 5. Include the significant persons of the patient in the therapy.

One night each week, significant persons (parents, spouses, sexual partners, friends, co-workers, bosses) join the group. If the husband of our patient Sylvia fears that the patients will side

with her against him, he will likely be pleasantly surprised. She
created similar tension with some male patients, as with her husband,
similar rewards-costs patterns. These patients may facilitate expression of his complaints about her - by what we call amplified
family technique. Her marital situation was role-played in psychodrama from many aspects before her husband came, which made many
patients involved in Sylvia's case during the Visitor's night. Although we do not include both partners in the therapeutic community
(generally, not two people who are interdependent in life outside),
no good psychotherapy can leave the natural groups aside, without
exploring and utilizing the levers of their mutual rewards and costs.
It is not unusual that parents come across the Continent or even from
Europe for Visitor's night, and it is invariably worthwhile. Both
the patient and the parent often go through a unique corrective experience of reconciliation.

Postulate 6. Make the group a model of natural groups!

The therapeutic community, to be effective, must have far-
reaching similarities with real life. In Lobetch, the existence of
the centre depended for years upon the work of patients in the State
Farm, including strenuous work in the fields. In Haney, the patients
worked in forestry. In Lobetch and the Day House, the patients,
under their own work instructors, work for money which goes to the
patients' fund. Strangely, the importance of work is rarely stressed
- with some exceptions as M. Jones and Cumming and Cumming. We know
that many therapists shy away from the real work of patients, hoping
erroneously that it can be replaced by occupational therapy. Yet
real work with stress is an opportunity to study personalities of
patients second to none. The ability to overcome obstacles in
strenuous physical work supports self-confidence in an unexpected
way, and enhances the powerful experience of belonging to the group,
as if touching deep biological strata of personality. In the Day
House, the patients remodel the house and clean it, maintain a
garden, and operate a car wash. But, as in real life the work on
a group task creates difficulties and frustrations, which incite
the patient to initiate his characteristic neurotic vicious circles.
A hike to the mountains shows tolerance to stress, giving up easily,
whining, helping, or not caring about others.

Therapeutic community can create a broad range of similarities
with real life, such a group tasks, challenge to overcome obstables
competition, relatively strict norms, and roles including leadership. Quasi-professional and quasi-familial relations develop
since every patient is likely to find complementary roles of boss,
friend, girlfriend or boyfriends, father, mother and every complementary role is likely to be represented by several patients in the
community.

The potential of the therapeutic community to assess personality in detail is so tremendous that one is astonished to read M.F. White's Obit milieu (1972a) and the Descent of Milieu Therapy (1972b) "a critique of the maxims and traditions of milieu therapy". White says: "The imitation of 'real life' suffers because of its setting and from certain practical constraints. It is a very costly way to provide a patient with practive for a social task. 'Real life' situations can be reconstructed only in the crudest fashion and staff who do no appreciate the gross defect of this facsimile world are liable to be seriously misled when assessing problems. The attractive assumption is made that in this comprehensive social context a diagnostic appraisal results which is superior to the standard across-the-desk office impression."

We do not know whether White wrote his essays just from the desk, or whether he observed one of the caricatures (admittedly widespread) of therapeutic community. Comparing for decades behaviour assessments of patients with information from close persons, co-workers, etc., we are again and again surprised how the therapeutic community with its very rough imitations of real life, elicits similar reactions.

There is a widespread belief among psychiatrists that psychoanalytic treatment is the only treatment which can achieve structural personality changes. We were pleased to read that Dr. Kernberg retreats from this point of view in his book on "Object Relations", and acknowledges the "possibility of obtaining change in these intrapsychic structures by means of particular therapeutic functions of the hospital" in severely regressed (borderline and psychotic) patients. On the basis of our experience, therapeutic community is the most suitable place for initiating personality changes in neurotics. Even in our patients who improve sufficiently only after individual therapy, we would not have been able to achieve these personality changes without preceding treatment in a therapeutic community. But even during the individual treatment, we still utilize observations from the time the patient spent in the therapeutic community. Individual therapy - including psychoanalysis - gives only fragmentary opportunity for personality study.

Postulate 7. Differences from real life in certain areas are as important as similarities.

If the therapeutic community would be a perfect model of reality, everybody would be led by his vicious circles to an unhappy outcome reached before again and again. Obviously, the differences are also essential. First of all, the patient's behaviour has no long-term consequences other than therapeutic ones. Unlike in real life, no one is promoted or fired for not liking the foreman. It is easier than in real life to give sympathy, care, to forgive and have training in these activities. Some discover for the first time the rewards of altruism. The difference from real life is extremely

important. It gives the patient freedom to experiment with attitudes
and relationships, in a creative atmosphere of play and fantasy. The
therapeutic community creates its surplus reality, to use the term of
J.S. Moreno. The world of fantasy is created through the use of
plays, games, dramatization of fantasies, dreams and fairy tales,
and further by psychodrama, psychomime, group painting and clay
modelling and musical improvization. These activities are an integral part of psychotherapy and led by the same therapist. They
stimulate the creativity so necessary for seeking new life solutions.
In this atmosphere, the multiple transferences develop quickly and
corrective experience with both emotional and cognitive aspects
takes place with speed not known in individual therapy. This is
possible precisely because the patients are not interdependent as in
real life, and their behaviour does not have real-life consequences.

Besides working with transferences, psychodrama and abreactions
help to establish direct interactions with group schema figures,
particularly those of the father and mother. Although this surplus
reality and the trust in the community is extremely useful for
corrective experience and new social learning, our patients do not
expect this in real life. We help them to recognize the differences.

Our paper started with positive aspects of utopias. They are,
no doubt, a native soil of creativity. However, at a certain point
of inquiry we have to draw a sharp line between reality and fantasy.
Many years ago, Stanton and Schwartz analyzed the misleading dream,
"fantasy of life as one great psychotherapeutic hour". It seems
that some would like to see the whole world as one therapeutic
community. You may ask: What's wrong with it ? Don't we want to
have everywhere the openness, closeness and caring which is so moving
in therapeutic communities ? Sure, we want it; but if the continuity between the therapeutic community and society is utopistic,
we obfuscate and not foster whatever society can learn from therapeutic communities. M. Jones, as a pioneer of the therapeutic
community, has more right to utopias than we do. However, we cannot
follow him when he conceives of a therapeutic community as "a model
of social organizations in general". We find it misleading to
connect the idea of the therapeutic community, as M. Jones does in
his "Maturation of the Therapeutic Community" (1976) with counter-
culture as interpreted by its prophets of his choice. As late as
1976 he says (Jones, M. 1976): "There is reason to believe that in
the United States a counterculture... is already leading to a new
value system, particularly apparent in the youth of America." He
further praises Charles A. Reich's "Greening of America", and Jean-
Francois Revel who sees this world revolution already starting in
the United States. He says: "Political theory and systems theory
are hard to reconcile but what Reich calls "consciousness three" and
Revel calls "the second world revolution" can, at least in part, be
understood in terms of the systems theory..."

Well, according to Charles A. Reich, to achieve consciousness three is "to be deeply suspicious of logic, rationality, analysis, and of principles". The central thesis of these prophets of counterculture is the belief that consciousness controls history, objective conditions count for little. "Consciousness is prior to structure... The whole corporate state rests on nothing but consciousness". This is a typical bias of idealistic orientation, disregarding statistical distribution of hierarchies of human needs. Involved is also an inappropriate extrapolation from group to society and vice versa, a typical idealistic bias. Freud speculated about society and wars on the basis of observing individuals. Group theorists and therapists in the past speculated inadmissably about society as a big group. A therapeutic community is not a miniature of society, and society and natural groups are very different from therapeutic communities. In our view, the broad therapeutic potential of therapeutic communities lies precisely in their planned mixture of similarities and differences from real groups, in other words, in their artificiality. From the six categories of the resources of social exchange, goods, services, money status, love, and information, only the last three are exchanged in the therapeutic community and only temporarily. Not to see it could obfuscate the direction of research on therapeutic communities. And it is the research of therapeutic communities which is needed most badly now - and has been so far neglected. Here, M. Jones gave us a great example when he opened the door of the Henderson Hospital for research of Robert Rapoport and his team as early as 1953.

The systems theory, which M. Jones mentions and which is talked about in this congress, does not exist yet, that is, in behaviour sciences. The prestige it has is borrowed from the achievements in mathematics and physics underlies the present-day technology of communications systems, computers and servomechanisms. It helped the development of physiology, but for psychotherapy is mainly a promise for the future. So far those who talk about systems theory, are mainly translating their assumptions, sometimes trivial, into fashionable slang. This is regrettable for two reasons. One, an erroneous impression is created that a new knowledge is gained. Second, tentative theories coupled with systems theory gain undeserved prestige. (In our opinion, also Dr. O. Kernberg is guilty of making speculative constructs such as internalized object relations, id-ego-super-ego, subsystems of personality and of group, as discussed in Knoblosch and Knobloch, 1979a).

We do not want to be misunderstood. We are confident that systems research will become important in the future and that it will meet its crucial criterion of usefulness, that is to help us to predict processes in a group and therapeutic community. We are thrilled by the close connections between systems research, social exchange theory and the theory of games. We will end with a thought of Bartos (1967) recommending game - theoretical approach to the study

of groups. Game theory assumes that each game is self-contained in
the sense that utility function completely describes the preferences
of a player. "But what is the utility of learning which is separated
from real-life problem solving ? What is going to motivate the
trainees to learn ? In the training period there are no real-life
rewards...and therefore substitute rewards have to be found. One
of the universal and usually the least expensive of these substitutes
is fun, having a good time. Children learn how to solve serious
adult problems by playing games that are fun. An autoelic activity
is one which is self-rewarding, which needs no additional reward
beyond the pleasure derived from the very performance of the activity.
"Having fun" does have properties of a simple utility function as
assumed by the Theory of Games, since having fun is autoelic. Music,
poetry, and drama all may be viewed as culturally formalized devices
enriching man's emotional life, and perhaps, enlarging his repertoire
of emotional responses..."

Fun and good time is, beside social approval, important as a
resource of rewards in the therapeutic community, compensating for
all the suffering and tears.

We end with an apology. A friend who read our paper before
the meeting said there were four papers in one. We agree, yet we
wanted to raise issues we regarded important for further development
of therapeutic communities, even in a fragmentary way. Our only
excuse is that we tried to do it more fully in our publications.

Bibliography

Bartos, O.J., 1967, Simple Models of Group Behaviour, New York:
     Columbia University Press.

Edelson, M., 1970, Psychotherapy and Sociotherapy, Chicago:
     University of Chicago Press.

Jones, M., 1956, The Concept of a Therapeutic Community, American
     J. Psychiatry, 112.

Jones, M., 1976, The Maturation of the Therapeutic Community,
     New York: Human Sciences Press.

Knobloch, F., Knobloch, J., 1979a, Integrated Psychotherapy,
     New York: J. Aronson.

Knobloch, F., Knobloch, J., 1979b, In Search of a New Paradigm of
     Psychoanalysis, J. American Academy of Psychoanalysis, 7:4,
     499-524, John Wiley & Sons, Inc.

Knobloch, F., Sefrnova, 1954, Prispevek K technice rodinne psycho-
      therapie, (A contribution to the Technique of Family Psycho-
      therapy), Neurologie a psychiatrie ceskoslovenska, Prague,
      17:218-224.

Rapoport, R.M., 1960, Community as Doctor, London: Tavistock
      Publications.

Schultz-Hencke, H., 1942, Der gehemmte Mensch Leipzig: G Thieme.

White, N.F., 1972a, Reappraising the Inpatient Unit: Obit Milieu,
      Can. Psychiatric Ass. J., 17: 51-58.

White, N.F., 1972b, The Descent of Milieu Therapy, Can. Psychiat-
      ric Ass. J., 17: 41-49.

Whiteley, J. Stuart, The Large Group Dynamics and Therapy: ed.
      Kreeger, L., 1975, Constable and Co. Ltd., London, p.193-
      The Large Group as a Medium for Sociotherapy.

ADVANTAGES AND LIABILITIES OF THE THERAPEUTIC COMMUNITY

Professor Otto F. Kernberg

The New York Hospital - Cornell Medical Center

Westchester Division, White Plains, N.Y. 10605, U.S.A.

1. Definition, Basic Theory and Assumptions of Therapeutic Change

More than a decade of experience with therapeutic communities in hospital settings makes it appropriate for me to evaluate them. I have been in a position to observe the therapeutic effectiveness and the potential damaging effects of the treatment methods. The therapeutic community has deeply transformed the more traditional types of hospital milieu treatment, opened new roads to the in-patient treatment of severe character pathology, and shed new light on the optimal administrative requirements for psychiatric hospitals. Some of these new insights were not only unforeseen, but unintended.

Whitely and Gordon (1979), after pointing out that the term therapeutic community is one of the most misused and misunderstood terms in modern psychiatry, offer the view that it "is a specific, specialized treatment process utilizing the psychological and socio-logical phenomena inherent in the large, circumscribed and residential group. In this respect it is an intensified extension of milieu therapy (as described by these authors in an earlier chapter) "which has more general implications and applications for patients of all categories in the mental hospital community." In the course of their excellent chapter reviewing the history and recent developments of therapeutic community models, Whiteley and Gordon introduce an additional dimension to their concept of the therapeutic community, namely, that of an ideology. In fact, both T.F. Main and Maxwell Jones - key originators of therapeutic community models - stressed their conviction in the value of a democratization of treatment pro-cesses, in the desirability of a "therapeutic setting with a spon-taneous and emotionally structured (rather than medically dictated) organization in which all staff and patients engage" (Main, 1946), or

of the flattening of the hierarchical pyramid, role blurring, and
open communication as an expression of a democratic therapeutic environment (Jones 1953).

It is my basic thesis that it is from this combined technical
ideological conception of the therapeutic community, the conception
of the therapeutic community as a treatment modality and as a democratization of the treatment process (in contrast to a hierarchical
and authoritarian social organization of the hospital), that the new
findings, therapeutic advantages, as well as the shortcomings and
problems of this approach emerge.

Therapeutic community concepts may also be defined by contrasting
them with the "team approach" to diagnosis and treatment that is so
prevalent in contemporary psychiatry. Whereas both use the participation and collaboration of various types of mental health professionals in the treatment process, the team approach distributes
decision-making authority functionally among various disciplines
according to the tasks involved. In the therapeutic community, in
contrast, the opposition to hierarchical distribution of authority
goes beyond that functionally required by any concrete tasks. In
the typical therapeutic community the aim is to minimize hierarchical
levels stemming from professional expertise, degrees, and titles and
to maximize a democratic decision-making process. In addition, the
emphasis on the psychotherapeutic advantage of the patient's treatment by and within the therapeutic community transcends the ordinary
team approach.

Stanton and Schwartz (1954), in their classic study of the
effects of breakdown in morale of staff and of covert disagreement
of staff on pathological excitement of patients, particularly the
activation of the "special case" syndrome, highlighted the impact of
the social and administrative structure of the hospital on individual
patients' functioning: social pathology reinforces individual
psychopathology. Caudill (1958) illustrated how the isolation of
patients from staff encouraged by the hierarchical hospital structure
contributes to the crystalization of a culture of the patient group,
which has powerful effects on the treatment of individual patients
as well as on the functioning of patients as a group. He describes
how the induction of the patient role, the patient peer pressures
for socialization and for accepting the doctors' value system - together with a general opposition on the part of patients to authority
(particularly that of nursing staff) - fosters mutual ignorance of
patients and staff, stereotyping, and alternations between permissiveness and restriction in the form of cultural "ground swells"
that strongly influence all treatment carried out in the hospital.
Belknap (1956) and Goffman (1968) stressed even more sharply the regressive and degrading effects of the traditional hierarchical system
in large hospital settings, where the deterioration of patients'
self-respect and a general prison atmosphere were the complement

to aribtrary and authoritarian control exerted by the lowest echelons
of the hierarchically organized staff.

T.F. Main's paper "The Ailment" (1957) provided a crucial counter
part to all these findings; it was in particular a theoretical and
clinical complement to Stanton and Schwartz's work. Main concluded
that the "special case" may induce a pathological activation of conflicts among staff that reflect, in the interpersonal field, the
activation and projection of the unconscious conflicts of the
patient's internal world. This finding, I think, represents the single
most important bridge between the understanding of the hospital as
a social system, on the one hand, and the understanding of the activation of pathology of internalized object relations of patients in
that social system, on the other.

The concept of therapeutic community treatment emerged as a
direct challenge to the regressive and antitherapeutic effects of
the traditional psychiatric hospital functioning which was along a
hierarchical medical model. Although various authors might describe
the essential aspects of this approach in somewhat different ways,
the basic orientation stemming from Jones and Main emphasized the
following features: (1) Community treatment; staff and patients
functioning jointly as an organized community carry out the treatment of the patient population; patients actively participate in
and are co-responsible for their own treatment, not passive recipients. (2) Therapeutic culture: all activities and interactions
should relate to the goal of re-educating and socially rehabilitating
patients. The optimal functioning of patients in the therapeutic
community would be the first phase in promoting their optimal
functioning in the external community. (3) Living-learning-con-
frontation: an open flow of communication between patients and staff
provides immediate feedback regarding observed behaviors and reactions to them. An exploration of the functions of these behaviors
in the "here and now" and of alternative, new, experimental behaviors
would help the patients to cope in the therapeutic community and in
the external community.

The methods used to carry out these aims of therapeutic community
treatment call for group meetings - small group, large group, and
task group - to facilitate open communication, to generate pressures
in the direction of socialization and rehabilitation, and to foster
a democratic - in contrast to authoritarian - process of decision
making.

Three particular types of meetings are common to therapeutic
community models, apart from the category of small, large, and task
group meetings. (1) The community meeting, which includes all
patients and all staff. This meeting aims to examine the total
social environment in which staff and patients participate, the distortions and interferences with a free flow of communication from

whatever source, and the development of antidemocratic or authoritarian processes and their possible resolution. (2) Patient government:
regardless of the specific form such government takes, therapeutic
community models tend to foster patients' organization for the purpose of having the patients participate in the social and decision-
making processes. (3) Staff meeting: this meeting complements
patient government, expresses the concept of democratic decision
making among staff and allows staff to study how they are influenced
by administrative and other pressures, as well as by their interaction with patients. The staff meeting allows for democratic distribution of authority regarding tasks to be done, in contrast to
hierarchical decisions from above.

A number of assumptions regarding therepeutic change are implied
in therapeutic community concepts. First, it is assumed that
patients as individuals and as a group are able to help each other.
Second, patients functioning in a group setting may react in "normal"
appropriate and responsible ways, in contrast to the effect of individual patients' psychopathology on particular interactions outside the group setting. Third, by the same token, staff as a group
may function pathologically and antitherapeutically, in contrast to
the individual maturity and skills of staff. In fact, in agreement
with these assumptions, I think that the pathology and social
effectiveness of groups does not coincide with the pathology and
social effectiveness of their individual members, and that clinical
experience has confirmed these assumptions in very definite ways.

Fourth, it is assumed that authoritarianism is anti-therapeutic,
and that decisions made on the basis of power rather than reason
militate against patients' best interests. I believe that this
assumption is correct if one defines authoritarianism as taking responsibility for making decisions beyond what is functionally warranted.
I am suggesting that there exists a functional, in contrast to an
excessive or inappropriate or non-functional, authority, and that
therefore the antinomy is not of authoritarian versus democratic
decision-making, but of authoritarian versus functional decision-
making. With this qualification, I agree with the general assumption,
abundantly documented in the literature, of the negative, sometimes
devastating effects of authoritarian treatment systems on patients'
welfare and improvement. Even an authoritarian organizational
structure that apparently affects only the upper echelon of staff
cannot but affect all participants in the therapeutic community.
Authoritarianism is transmitted by complex psychological mechanisms
along the hierarchical ladder, particularly by means of submission
to and identification with the aggressor, and it tends to erode the
authenticity of patient/therapist relationships throughout the entire hospital system. An authoritarian hospital administration may
transform treatment arrangements, distorting them so that they will
utterly confound the therapeutic team trying to diagnose them. Such
distortions in treatment arrangement can promote a pseudo-adaptation

of the patient to the hospital system and militate against the
development of his autonomy and growth. An authoritarian hospital
structure, almost by definition, interferes with an open, ongoing
evaluation of the hospital as a social system, and practically
eliminates the possibility of expanding hospital milieu treatment by
the therapeutic use of the hospital as a social system.

Fifth, in contrast to authoritarian treatment systems, therapeutic community concepts imply that democratization of the treatment process is therapeutic per se. Democratization increases the
patient's self-esteem, the effectiveness of his functioning, the
honesty of his communications, and is directly growth promoting. In
the light of experience, I believe that this assumption can be
challenged. The results of democratization of the decision-making
processes in hospitals have often been complex, unforeseen, a mixture
of therapeutic and antitherapeutic effects. More about this later.

Sixth, collective decision making in an open setting at public
meetings is assumed to be therapeutic because it fosters democratic
in contrast to authoritarian processes. Later, I shall examine the
illusions implied in this assumption.

Seventh, patients are assumed to be able to help each other as
individuals and, in the process, to develop interpersonal skills,
creativity, as well as ego, strength. On the basis of my experience,
I think this is remarkably true; by the same token, however,
patients can also have very destructive effects upon each other,
and for every David and Lisa who help each other one can find a
psychopath potentially driving another patient to suicide.

2. The Therapeutic Community as a Threat to Traditional Organization
of Psychiatric Care in Hospital Settings.

The most important precondition for the development of a therapeutic community is that it be functionally integrated with the
administrative structure of the psychiatric or general hospital within which it operates. This precondition might seem trivial if it
were not that, in practice, leaders of therapeutic communities are
so often innocent regarding the full implications of administrative
structures, boundaries, and constraints of their institution. They
are frequently equally innocent regarding a general theory of administration or institutional management that would permit a full
analysis of administrative feasibilities and constraints for a
therapeutic community within that particular setting. The problem
is that even the literature on the therapeutic community does not
sufficiently consider the relationship between the therapeutic
community structure and the overall institutional organization.

Thus, for example, Marshal Edelson in Sociotherapy and Psychotherapy (1970), while explicitly describing the administrative and

professional implications of the relation between hospital administration and the director of sociotherapy, in fact presents models of
organizational functioning in which there is no clear administrative
structure linking, say, the authority vested in the therapeutic
community with that of overall hospital administration. While he
acknowledges the potential for strain and conflicts in his model,
his proposed solution is a consultative one, not organizational/
administrative. I mention this example because Edelson seems to me
one of the most sophisticated theoreticians in this field, not prone
to replace a study of administrative constraints with a declaration
of ideological convictions.

    If the therapeutic community is to explore openly the social
system actualized by the patient/staff community, it cannot but
activate as well all stress and latent conflicts in the system,
with consequent influences on the political dimension of the decision-
making process in the institution. The assumption that a purely
observational, clarifying, and informative approach to conflicts in
the social system, couched in technical and neutral interpretive
terms can be carried out without, in turn, implying an active participation in the conflicts involving hospital administration is an
illusion. The proof is the frequency with which one encounters the
following scenario: An enthusiastic group develops a therapeutic
community model in a sector of the hospital; an "ideal society" is
formed that generates gratification, excitement, hope and perhaps
a messianic spirit contaminating both staff and patients, to be
followed by a later phase of bitter disappointment because of the
"lack of understanding" and apparent rejection of this ideal society
by the institution within which it has developed. A final stage of
disappointment follows, with abandonment of the task, collapse of the
therapeutic community, the leaders emigrating either into a different
system to start the cycle all over again - or into the private
practice of a mental health profession.

    In practice, a therapeutic community setting has a necessary
limit as to size; the patient/staff community should number probably
somewhere between 80 or 100 participants as a maximum. This means
that therapeutic communities can be established only in very small
psychiatric hospitals or in relatively small services within a
larger hospital. It is no coincidence that some of the more successful models have operated within small psychiatric hospitals where
the complexities of relating to larger administrative structures are
less evident. But even under such optimal circumstances, the
following considerations do apply.

    When the leader of the therapeutic community is fully aware of
the organizational structure of the institution, of the degree and
stability of the authority delegated to him, and therefore to the
therapeutic system he is in charge of, then the limits of the authority vested in the entire community as well as in its individual

members can be diagnosed, spelled out, and considered when the conflicts within the therapeutic system and across the boundaries of the
therapeutic community are studied. An authentic boundary function
of the leader of the therapeutic community requires clear administrative arrangements linking the community to its environment; and
the community leadership should have the capacity to spell them out.

In the last resort, the ideological - in contrast to the technical - convictions about democratic political organization often
influence leaders of therapeutic communities - and the staff members
who share their convictions - to operate as if they constituted a
minority party in a state governed by an authoritarian leadership.
Unconsciously or unwittingly they confuse the exploration of the
social system with a political means for changing it. The therapeutic community becomes condensed with the political aim of democratization of a health care institution. Eventually, both staff
and patients pay the price for this confusion between a technical-
therapeutic setting and a political system without clearly defined
tasks or differentiated boundaries.

The support of the administrative structure for the therapeutic
community system needs to be worked out by the leadership of the
therapeutic community, and constantly redefined and renegotiated.
This implies an additional precondition for establishing a therapeutic community, namely,the leader's ability to carry out a
political function in terms of boundary negotiations - that is, not
in terms of democratic concepts, but in terms of effective ways of
influencing individuals and groups across task determined boundaries
in the institution. This precondition can be broadened into a
definition of the basic skills required for leadership of the therapeutic community, such as a solid knowledge of small group, large
group, and task group functioning and management; a solid knowledge
of individual psychopathology, of the influence of individual
psychopathology in distorting small group processes in the environment, and a solid grasp of psychotherapeutic principles. These
basic skills required for leadership of a therapeutic community
point to the problems involved in training appropriately skilled
leadership.

Still another precondition for the development of a therapeutic
community is the clear definition of authority, of roles and
functions of all individual staff members as well as of formally
organized, interlocking groups carrying out the therapeutic community
functions. The implication is that the authority delegated to the
therapeutic community must in turn be distributed within it in
functional ways. The danger is that group processes may permit
shared decision making, but may also blur the clarity of whose
responsibility it is to carry out the decisions made in group settings, as well as the nature of the system of inspection control,
and monitoring of the community functions. Another danger is the

possibility that traditional roles and expertise that have been
"imported" into the therapeutic community are underutilized or that
authority is delegated to those who do not have appropriate technical
skills.

In the last resort, an egalitarian approach that neglects the
differences in capacity, skills and training of individuals may prevail, with a consequent inefficiency and waste in utilizing available human resources. The deskilling that occurs in small and large
groups under the effect of regression into basic- assumption-group
functioning is greatly amplified by the failure to use available
skills caused by a lack of administrative clarity within the therapeutic community.

In this connection, as A.K. Rice pointed out (1969), there is
an advantage in maintaining a dialectic tension between task groups
and task sentience, on the one hand and professional sentience
groups (represented by the loyalties within each particular group
of mental health professionals that have consolidated into a team)
on the other, as a protection against the regressive features that
develop when task and sentience systems coincide.

Therapeutic communities have often been perceived as a threat
by the traditional administrative and professional leadership
structure of psychiatric hospitals. Insofar as the authority vested
in the medical profession was being challenged in the name of a
doctrine of egalitarianism, the threat was real enough. Beyond that,
the functional analysis of the relation between actual expertise and
skills required by various professions, on the one hand, and the
amount of authority distributed to medical and non-medical personnel,
on the other, highlighted authoritarian distortions and, by implication, threatened traditional power structures in the hospital.
Another threat posed by the therapeutic community was the open
examination of the functioning of the hospital as a social system,
which could not but highlight, ever-present problems in the hospital's
administrative structure and functioning. An open examination of
the hospital as a social system cannot but become a monitoring process of the adminisrative process, with all the political implications and challenges implied. It may be argued, of course, that this
is a very healthy development for some petrified hospital systems,
but, the proponents of therapeutic communities should not be surprised by the active or subtle opposition they evoke in the hospital
administration.

The therapeutic community is also a threat to the traditional
patient/doctor relation, and the traditional relations among inter-
disciplinary staff. In terms of democratizating life in a psychiatric hospital this is of course an advantage; but in terms of the
optimal utilization of all therapeutic resources, it has had unforeseen, partly negative consequences. Relatively uneducated staff in

the lower echelons of the hospital hierarchy may find themselves
invested with more authority but at the same time with a more direct
scrutiny of their functioning. Consequently, their relations with
their adminiatrative and professional supervisors will become more
uncertain. The contradictions between social inequality, inequality
in salaries, and work expectations, dictated by the environment within which the hospital functions,and the development of an egalitarian
atmosphere in the therapeutic community sharpen the awareness of
social conflicts and contradictions that are real and beyond the
therapeutic community's ability to resolve satisfactorily. Simmering
resentment and unresolved guilt feelings at various heirarchical
levels may increase tensions among staff and further complicate the
analysis, let alone resolution, of tensions in the social system of
the therapeutic community. All of this increases the danger of
diminishing professional efficiency on all sides.

     Therapeutic communities can also become a real or experienced
threat to the patients treatment. Because of the number of individuals involved and the effort to maintain a relatively open flow of
communication owing to a desire to reduce the formalities at meetings
to a minimum, patient meetings, staff meetings, and particularly
the community meeting itself easily acquire characteristics of large
group processes; the regressive effects of large group processes may
affect individual patients' developments in the community in anti-
therapeutic ways. Elsewhere (Kernberg, 1976, Chapter 9; 1980, Chapter
11) I have pointed to the danger of regression of patients as a
group to basic assumptions group functioning when functional, task-
centered leadership is not available, when the tasks carried out by
patients are not meaningful but trivial, when the delegation of
authority from staff to patient is ambiguous, and when their own
leadership is ineffective. Under such regressive circumstances,
patient groups may become intolerant of individuals, establish a
dictatorship of the group that acquires characteristics of a
primitive morality, and foster the ascendence of personalities with
narcissistic and antisocial features to leadership positions. Staff
may contribute to this regression by an ideologically determined
denial of differences among individual patients, an implicit expectation that all patients have the same needs and should be expected to react or participate in similar ways. Patient and staff
groups may enter into unconscious collusion in interfering with the
autonomous development of individual patients and in fostering an
uncontrolled invasion of privacy that corresponds to the total group's
acting out of aggression against individual members.

     The understanding that regressive group processes may produce
a worsening of symptoms in individual patients, however, may also
give rise to the mistaken assumption that all patient pathology
corresponds to group processes, thus denying that psychopathology
can be individual in nature. Such an attitude promotes a defensive
idealization of group processes which feeds into patients' magical

expectations of treatment ("if the group functions well, patients
will get better....")

In addition, groups may develop an exaggerated need for formalities and rituals as a defense against violence (which large groups
in particular tend to generate), a defense that may be functional
for the group but restrictive to individual patient needs. The control of unstructured group processes by the most regressed patients,
the chronic monopolizers, highly effective manipulators, or simply
the most violent patients, may significantly distort the content
of meetings first, and total allocation of resources later, thus reducing many patients' treatment time.

Unacknowledged and dissociated sadistic tendencies of individuals may infiltrate the group process in the form of accentuation
of bureaucratic rigidities, which serve to control violence while yet
expressing it in subtle ways: this excessive formalization of group
processes, combined with rigid conventionality (particularly regarding sexual issues) may result in throwing the therapeutic
community back to restrictive group processes of latency and early
adolescence.

Under the conditions of Bion's (1961) basic-assumptions-group
developments, all the negative effects of group processes increase.
The very concepts of egalitarianism, democracy, and trust in the
beneficial effects of open communication may feed into the messianic
expectations inherent in the "dependent" or "pairing" basic assumption group's development, thus fostering an unrealistic hospital
environment which militates against the functional re-entry of
patients into the external world. Under regression into "fight-
flight" conditions, the exacerbation of social struggles within the
hospital derived from intrastaff tensions may naturally blend with
patients' search for ad hoc "parties" and militant ideologies that
rationalize violence.

3. Further Comments on the Theoretical Limitations and Problems of Therapeutic Communities

As mentioned before, some of the literature and clinical
approaches to the therapeutic community clearly favor democratic in
contrast to authoritarian decision making. The assumption seems to
be that the ultimate authority for decision making should reside
within the temporary community constituted by all patients and staff.
This assumption fails to consider the difference between political
processes and administrative structures. It confuses decision making
in an open community without fixed institutional boundaries by means
of political elections and negotiations among political parties with
the functional requirements of therapeutic institutions with a
limited number of boundaries, tasks and constraints that codetermine
their survival, and that dictate a need for decision making regarding

the investment of resources and priorities, that is, a functional
organizational structure. To put it simply, what is needed for optimal functioning of a psychiatric institution is a functional administration, not a democratic one. In fact, the replacement of a
functional by a democratic organization may easily lead into distortions of the relation between authority, responsibility, and
accountability, thus ending up re-creating an authoritarian structure
as opposed to a functional one.

Consequences of this basic misunderstanding include a neglect of
the need for clarity of decision making, for clear definition of individual responsibility and accountability, and, particularly, the
loss of concern for quality control. Thus, quality of staff may
deteriorate, and, in the long run, the patients' right to expect a
staff with optimal expertise and capabilities is denied them.

Another theoretical problem with therapeutic community concepts
is their implication that society at large contains no intrinsic
contradictions. Proponents of therapeutic communities are often
unaware that building up an "ideal society" within a hospital can
easily merge with patients' needs to deny their own conflicts - both
intrapsychic and interpersonal - and the real contradictions in the
external world to which they must eventually return. Hence the
patients adapt to hospital life but fail to prepare for re-entry into
the external environment. At a different level, there may be a
subtle assumption that all people are essentially good, and that open
communication permits the elmination of distortions in perceptions
of self and others that are the ultimate cause of pathological conflict and pathological psychic structure. This philosophical concept
denies the existence of unconscious intrapsychic sources of aggression
a striking contradiction to what staff and patients themselves can
observe in patients in a psychiatric hospital.

Jones (1953, 1956) recommends therapeutic communities for
patients with severe character pathology who require hospitalization;
he conceives the re-education and resocialization effected by the
therapeutic community as the main, if not exclusive treatment modality
for such patients. He conveys the impression that he sees these
patients as social casualties who require educational support and
pressures to provide them with new social and vocational roles. This
view neglects the importance of intrapsychic determinants for psychopathology and supports the illusion that a healthy social atmosphere
in the hospital, the activation of group processes toward resocialization can replace psychotherapy and produce fundamental personality
change. I believe this concept confuses a psychotherapeutic atmosphere geared to developing intensive individual and group treatments
with the treatments themselves. To assume that patients are victims
of irrational social forces and, are in fact, expressing them, and
that a rational society (one obviously without intrinsic contradictions) will permit a full restoration to health is appealing but

naive.   It is probably not a coincidence that the idea of the therapeutic community had particular appeal for the counter-culture of the
1960's.   Today, in the 1980's, the utopian quality of the ideas and
assumptions of many of the models is more transparent.

The failure to differentiate the social from the intrapsychic
factors influencing psychopathology may promote a faulty application
of systems theory to the psychotherapeutic situation.   The assumption
that patients' psychopathology directly reflects contradictions in
the environment, can result in locating the etiology exclusively in
the social system.   Here Main's approach and Bion's description of
group processes diverge sharply from Jones and the focus on social
psychopathology in some community psychiatry applications of the
therapeutic community that were fashionable in the United Sates in
the 1970's.

Practical consequences of this failure to differentiate the
intrapsychic from the interpersonal - while still studying the relations between the two - include a failure to clearly define the
indications and limitations of group treatment modalities and techniques, and a failure to critically evaluate the effects of combining
and overlapping various treatments.   It is easy, for example, for
group methods to proliferate in a psychotherapeutic community, so
that eventually the same issues and problems are discussed from
different perspectives at different places without regard to the
economy of human resources involved.   There is, further, the ubiquitous possibility for splitting mechanisms to be activated by the
simultaneous discussion of the same issues in different settings.
In theory, of course, all information flows together in the community,
staff, and patient meetings;   in practice, however, overflowing
agendas and increasing diffusion of information militate against integration of information.   In the long run, the loss of privacy may
be a lesser evil than the waste of time and human resources brought
about when treatment modalities and techniques are not differentiated
from each other.

Edelson (1970) attempted to solve the problem of the relation
between sociotherapy and psychotherapy by keeping them completely
separate. In my view, that solution artificially isolates the
patient's dynamics as manifest in his psychotherapy from observations
of the patient's dynamics in the therapeutic community, and im-
poverishes both psychotherapy and social modalities of treatment.

To neglect the relation between therapeutic community concepts
and the theory of administration has important clinical consequences
for the functioning of the therapeutic community.   If the leader of
the therapeutic community lacks administrative skills, the system
might break down.   In practice, the leader's lack of administrative
skill can be seen in his failure to monitor therapeutic functions,
to distribute resources adequately, and particularly to establish

priorities at various meetings. The consequences of the leader's
administrative inadequacies will be reflected in a lowering of staff
morale. Staff will feel overworked, overwhelmed with responsibility
and as if drowning in a flood of information. The "gate-keeping"
function of group leaders deteriorates when no clear set of priorities
has been established for the administrative aspects of the therapeutic community. This internal chaos may be the counterpart of the
breakdown of communication between the therapeutic community and
hospital administration at large that is a consequence of the neglect
of administrative knowledge in the negotiation of the external
boundaries of the therapeutic community.

4. Some Illustrative Clinical Observations

     What follows results from observations made in three different
settings at three different periods of time. The first setting, the
C.F. Menninger Memorial Hospital in Topeka, Kansas, shifted from a
fairly traditional hospital model to one experimenting with modified
therapeutic community approaches during the years 1969-1973 when I
was Medical Director there. The second setting was the General
Clinical Service of the New York State Psychiatric Institute where,
as Director of that service, I developed an experimental therapeutic
community model from 1973-1976. The third setting is the Westchester
Division of the New York Hospital-Cornell Medical Center where, as
Medical Director since 1976, I have had the opportunity to evaluate
different types and degrees of therapeutic community models in
various services, and to compare them with more traditional approaches
in other units. The administrative organization of the hospital
within the broader complex of the Department of Psychiatry of the
Cornell University Medical College and the New York Hospital-Cornell
Medical Center, covering several geographic locations, also has permitted the observation of additional facets of how actual clinical
practice of therapeutic communities reflects on the cost effectiveness of program developments throughout the entire therapeutic system.

     To begin, the time element is of crucial importance in deter-
mining the success of failure of therapeutic community settings. In
units for acutely regressed patients, with a rapid turnover related
to a short length of stay and acute medical problems requiring urgent
attention all the time, therapeutic community approaches seem to
work least well. In contrast, for patients with chronic characterological difficulties, in units of slow turnover and extended length
of stay, the benefits of therapeutic community approaches become
maximal. This is in agreement with Jones, who had originally stressed
that therapeutic community approaches were indicated for these
patients.

     In addition, again relating to the dimension of time, the short-
term (one to six months) effects of therapeutic communities may be
strikingly different from the long-term effects, with the advantages

of therapeutic communities strongly predominating over a shorter
period of time, and the problems generated by them in the long run.
In the short term, the activation of patients' potential for helping
each other, the highlighting of internal contradictions of the social
treatment system that often can be resolved as part of this diagnosis,
the exciting and exhilarating effects of group processes strengthen
the bonds between patients, among staff, and between patients and
staff, and increase rapidly the knowledge gained about patients that
can be used for therapeutic purposes. In the long-term (six months
to years) treatment setting, however, the following phenomena make
their appearance.

The agendas of community meetings and all decision-making groups
tend to become overloaded. Efforts to stimulate patients and staff
to participate freely typically result in the emergence of group
resistances and basic assumptions groups, in the development of
passivity among patients and staff alike, long silences and waste of
time, or else, in the eruption of such an abundance of primitive
material that sorting it out in terms of priorities for the community
takes up inordinate time. Efforts to solve these problems by making
the meetings more formal create the danger of bureaucratization, of
slowing down the decision-making process - and once more the agenda
becomes overloaded. Gradually, the very need for administrative
decision-making, and the negoations between the therapeutic community
and the external environment that give rise to reality pressures
foster a new informal network of decision making. This ad hoc administrative structure may, paradoxically, be optimally functional,
but it may also be perceived as running counter to the idea of shared
decision making and thus will require further analysis and lengthy
negotiations of otherwise rather obvious community needs.

Patients with a strong manipulative and violent potential, who
are impelled to test the limits of their power and control, frequently
present another problem. What are the responsibilities of staff to
protect these patients as well as the rest of the community from inordinate violence? For example, the practically unavoidable power
struggles that evolve around patients with anorexia nervosa or
patients who use suicide attempts to control the environment create
agonizing conflicts for the nursing staff, and sharpen the contradictions between the efforts to protect the idea of permissiveness on
the service and yet maintain control over life-threatening acting
out. What for individual cases may look like functional decision-
making - in the sense of a gradual, painful process of rational
analysis, explanation, outlining, and implementation of a treatment
plan - may combine with similar processes involving other patients
to create impossible time constraints.

Patients' efforts to split the medical group - who are (rightly)
perceived as having the ultimate real power from the nurses - who
are (rightly) perceived as having real immediate power, may reduce

the efficiency of the nursing staff and induce breakdown of morale on the service. More frequently, however, the staff group manages to restore its boundaries, but with the practical consequence of an increase of staff's shared decision-making with a consonant decrease of permissiveness on the service, which may antagonize the leadership of the therapeutic community. The counterpart of this development is the tendency of the medical staff to delegate increasing authority to patients, which in fact corresponds to a decrease in authority to nursing staff (intermediary management pays the price for democratization). Finding compromise solutions requires even further time for analysis and resolution of conflicts.

All of these features may bring about an exhaustion among staff, an exhaustion that is at first masked by the messianic spirit, the excitement, and high morale that therapeutic communities trigger off in the short run, thus obscuring the dangerous overstretching of staff for some time. Eventually, however, staff exhaustion, particularly nursing staff exhaustion may bring requests for increased staffing, a need for the senior medical staff to spend more time with nursing, the development of passivity among staff - who continue to attend all meetings but with an increasing passivity - and a curious ascendance of staff and patients with narcissistic personality features to leading positions in the therapeutic community. The lack of commitment in depth of narcissistic personalities to any real convictions, their lack, therefore, of perception of intrapsychic stress and conflicts under such trying circumstances, and the ease with which they superficially adapt to group processes - particularly when they are in the center of a group's interest and admiration - powerfully impels them to a leadership function that promotes a thrilling pseudo-intimacy and tends to erode deep feelings as well as quality control on the service (Kernberg, 1980, Chapter 11).

One other manifestation of staff exhaustion and regression is the growth in staff's self-absorbtion. An outside observer of the development of therapeutic communities over a period of time is always surprised by the gradual decrease of the proportion of time directly spent with patients, and the increase of group meetings involving staff only. At the same time, a "burning out" frequently occurs among the leadership of therapeutic communities, so that after three to five years there is a strong tendency for service chiefs who are interested in and committed to therapeutic communities to abandon their positions.

A question that usually tends to be avoided is the cost/benefit ratio of the therapeutic community in comparison with traditional psychiatric hospital treatment. The simultaneous development of alternative models in autonomous services, while their utilization of resources can be compared from the outside, permits some typical findings. Earlier findings indicated that, when insufficient staff

is available to treat patients in the first place - such as in
severely neglected large state institutions (where some of the
studies of the damaging social effects of traditional mental hospitals
were first studies), the use of group methods permits an increase
of patient/staff contacts, and a humanization of hierarchically
rigidified channels of communication between patients and staff.
However, the need for individualization of treatment of patients is
not resolved by such an organizational shift, and a natural selection
takes place by which some patients with severe character pathology
can be helped while other patients drop out even further from therapeutic involvements.

In contrast, in a modern psychiatric hospital setting with
adequate patient/staff ratios, multidisciplinary approaches, and an
adequate complement of senior psychiatric staff, therapeutic communities permit intensifying the individual treatment of patients, and
enrich enormously the understanding of him gained on the unit and the
treatment modalities and techniques geared to helping him. This
positive effect, however, tends to be neutralized in the long run
because the time of the most experienced members of the staff is
taken up in group meetings, which reduces their availability for individual contacts with patients; furthermore, the least skilled
members of staff sit in group meetings rather passively, without
participating or necessarily learning much, while their skills in
relating to individual patients are underutilized. There develops,
in short, an irrational and uneconomical distribution of resources.

This phenomenon is made worse by the neglect of and withdrawal
from the external institutional environment of the hospital unit,
a development commonly encountered in connection with therapeutic
communities. Work in the therapeutic community generates an
emotionally intense yet protected atmosphere, so that staff wants
to stay together with its patients, in contrast to an open flow
of other staff and trainees through the unit for limited periods
of learning and eventual export of knowledge of the new treatment
modality.   Therapeutic community settings are sometimes the most
reluctant ones in tolerating students and trainees who have to leave
after a limited period of time.

The previously mentioned fact that some of the most violent
and manipulative patients manage to draw attention to themselves
consistently in dramatic ways and absorb inordinate treatment resources is one of the most permanent features of therapeutic
community functioning. In theory, all patients are presented with
the same model of social treatment; in practice, inappropriate
behavior may be rewarded by increased attention, while other patients
fade into the background without any compensating mechanisms in
operation due to the chronic overloading of all agendas.

There is a danger of a lack of accountability of individual

staff members to what happens to patients between group meetings, maximized when so many decisions regarding individual patients are arrived at in such group meetings. Neglect of individual patients also stems from the neglect of the analysis of the external circumstances surrounding a patient's treatment. A patient's family is often perceived as an intrusive outside force, and communications with family members may decrease while staff is totally engaged in the internal world of the therapeutic community. Thus, patients' re-entry into society may suffer.

One feature is the treatment of families, increasingly in the hands of psychiatric social workers, who may compensate the inward stance of the therapeutic community by intense family treatment. The problem is that this solution is achieved by investing even further resources, so that at some point most families may end up in intensive family therapy rather than in reality oriented psychiatric case work, a development that can be rationalized in terms of the psychosocial conception of emotional illness implied in therapeutic community models ("the patient is a product of his family circumstances") - but that also increases the complement of social workers required to carry out boundary function. In more general terms, over a long time, the professional sentience of staff may reassert itself in unconscious ways by developing new professional functions and the corresponding request for more positions on the part of each discipline, and the demand for increasing financial rewards on the part of originally unskilled staff (such as nursing aides) who have acquired more specialized functions as part of the "functional" redistribution of tasks.

Quality control tends to suffer when staff members are so intimately involved with one another that the senior staff members find it awkward to make decisions regarding promotions, firing, and the like. By the same token, evaluation of whether sufficient learning is occurring also suffers. Over a period of time, one would expect that relatively junior or inexperienced staff should be able to take over the therapeutic community functions, thus permitting senior staff to dedicate its time to individual work with patients and/or research and educational activities. This optimal redistribution of time and functions tends to be neglected.

In the intitial enthusiasm and excitement of staff and patients working together, personality conflicts among staff tend to be submerged in the strivings for common goals. In the long run, however, such personality issues reassert themselves, often cannot be included in the analysis of conflicts among staff - because the theory of the therapeutic community and of democratic decision-making has no room for unsolvable personality clashes, and, for the sake of peace, distortions in the administrative process may evolve. Paradoxically, personality issues now may become more important than would be true in the hierarchical model of hospital administration, where strict

rules, regulations, and bureaucratic hierarchical expectations tend
to decrease the direct impact of personality functioning.

I earlier mentioned the stress between the leadership of the
therapeutic community and the hospital administration that derives
from the failure to integrate therapeutic community and administrative theories. In practice, these conflicts evolve into a fantasy
structure on the part of the therapeutic community staff of a protected, ideal island within the total institution, an island where
staff and patients help each other, where staff members protect each
other from acknowledgement of shortcomings, mistakes, and outside
criticism, with a concomitant transformation of community boundaries
into barriers (Robert Michels, personal communication). By projection, the critical concern for the effectiveness of the functioning of the therapeutic community re-emerges as a sense of attack
from outside forces, who, in reality, have to carry out the analyses
of cost effectiveness, staff performance, and staff morale. From
the viewpoint of social resources provided for treatment purposes,
the therapeutic community may now appear geared more to fulfilling
the needs of staff than those of patients. The shortcomings of the
therapeutic community are first diagnosed from the outside, rather
than from within, which perpetuates the myth of an ideal world
crushed by an envious, materialistic, and autocratic organizational
environment.

5. Some Proposed Solutions

The problem is, how to preserve the eminent advantages of the
therapeutic community: its therapeutic utilization of the hospital
as a social system; the activation of patients' potentials for
contributing to their own treatment; the development of skills and
responsibilities of staff at lower echelons; the increasing knowledge about the interaction between the internal world of patients
and the structured conflicts in the environment; the corrective
emotional experiences provided by the therapeutic community; and
the increase in staff morale without falling prey to the serious -
sometimes devastating - disadvantages of this powerful therapeutic
tool.

Above all, the indications for the therapeutic community
settings need to be sharpened. Long-term hospital treatment of
severe character pathology, of borderline personality organization,
of patients with severe, chronic regressive features, who, while
not psychotic, would not be able to sustain a psychotherapeutic
process outside the hospital, all present an optimal indication for
therapeutic community treatment. I think there is an enormous advantage for specialized services treating such patients to adopt
therapeutic community models. The usefulness of such models for
chronically regressed schizophrenic patients is more questionable
and certainly would require careful experimental comparison with

more traditional ways of intensive psychotherapeutic hospital treatment of schizophrenia, a pressing research question at this time.
In contrast, the use of the therapeutic community for acute psychotic
illness requiring hospitalization is questionable, and probably con-
traindicated for hospitalization of less than one month. In broader
terms, I think that there is a need for highly specialized services
treating specific subgroups of patients populations, in contrast to
the traditional mixing of all kinds of patients requiring hospitalization in the same unit. The question of whether the therapeutic
community can absorb patients of different degrees of regression
and type of illness seems less important: the real issue is what is
the optimal treatment structure for different types of patients.

By the same token, the use of interdisciplinary teamwork and
of group processes for diagnostic and therapeutic purposes is indicated for all hospital treatment modalities and should not be
linked exclusively to therapeutic community approaches.

The organization and implementation of a therapeutic community
must include a clear administrative structure, a clear link to the
administrative structure of the psychiatric institution within which
the therapeutic community functions, and a clear definition of tasks,
authority, responsibility, and accountability of all involved. Staff
should be utilized for its specific expertise and professional background, periodically evaluated regarding its performance and learning,
and role diffusion should be avoided.

All staff members have a common, nonspecific human function in
interacting with patients, namely, that of utilizing their personality to resonate with patients' personalities, to understand their
emotional reactions to patients, and to use that understanding for
the diagnosis of the total pattern of patients' internal world and
the activation of their intrapsychic conflicts in the interpersonal
field. This nonspecific function, however, must be complemented with
a differentiated, specific function that varies from discipline to
discipline and corresponds to the professional skills required for
the total treatment of patients. At a different level, the team
spirit (task sentience) should never completely override the loyalty
within the various professions: it is important to protect the
dialectic of task sentience and professional sentience.

One implication of the proposals I have offered so far is that
the hierarchical structure of lines of authority has to be preserved for the benefit of functional decision making, allocation of
responsibilities, accountability, and for the evaluation of staff
performance, program effectiveness, and alternative treatment
modalities and administrative arrangements. Staff should be expected either to learn and become more independent in its functioning,
or else be reduced to relatively nonskilled functions, less involved
in complex discussions about patients and the community's dynamics.

Working relations between staff members should respect boundaries
of privacy, in contrast to the exciting, eroticized, and exhausting
stripping that may become part of the intimacy and staff self-
evaluation in the therapeutic community. By the same token, hierarchical leadership has to preserve its internal freedom for critical
evaluation of staff instead of an automatic defense of "inside" staff
against "outside" criticism. The contradiction between shared
decision making, on the one hand, and preservation of hierarchical
lines of authority, on the other, reflects the healthy preservation
of a real dynamic tension of the world at large, in addition to
essential administrative requirements.

For practical purposes, it is extremely helpful to differentiate
what Rice (1963) has described as executive conferences from executive
meetings. Executive conferences include all those providing information fundamental for decision making as well as the decision makers
themselves; executive meetings include only those who functionally
should make decisions. This clarification can be crucial in preventing regressive processes, particularly in the community meetings
and in other large group meetings. If, in the process of discussing
any issue, it is clarified whether the final decision will be taken
at that meeting or elsewhere, unnecessary expectations and disappointments can be prevented, and rational choices protected regarding who is the functionally appropriate authority to make any
particular decision.   This eliminates embarrassing deteriorations
of therapeutic community settings, such as when a group of patients
participates in a "vote" of whether a potentially suicidal patient
should be permitted a weekend pass.

By implication, I think that democratic - in contrast to
functional decision making - has a very small place within optimal
therapeutic communities.

Regarding the actual functioning of group processes, it is indispensable to set clear priorities for the subject matters to be
discussed, and to be willing to drop the lowest priority issues once
allocated time limits have been reached. One reason for delegating
certain decision making authority to individual staff members -
rather than subjecting the issue to a broader - and lengthy - discussion, is its low priority. By the same token, strict limits
should be set to time allocated for all activities, and this means a
merciless reduction of all group meetings, including that of the
community at large, to the minimum necessary to carry out high-
priority functions. Charting of all the meetings in which patients
spend their time may highlight unnecessary overlap of treatment
methods.

More generally speaking, it is important to review systematically the individual developments of all patients, and to evaluate
to what extent patients are really obtaining a fair share of total

treatment time – in contrast to over-involvement of staff with
"special cases."   One indication for restricting patients is to
free staff time for other activities that are esential for patients
in general, and there is a need for a clear consciousness throughout
the therapeutic community that staff time is the most valuable
commodity and needs to be carefully rationed.   To illustrate the
opposite trend: staff members are often only too happy to talk
individually with patients who feel they must communicate at that
moment with a staff member.   Such intense individual contacts lend
themselves to splitting processes, to a distortion of utilization
of staff time, and should be included in the overall evaluation of
time dedicated to individual patients.

     Each patient requires, at all times, one staff member with final
authority, responsibility, and accountability for the treatment
development of that patient in the system.   That authority and responsibility may be flexibly delegated to other individual and even
group processes, but the accountability cannot be delegated.   This
necessarily restricts the scope of decision making in the community
regarding each individual patient.   In general, decisions arrived
at by staff and patients in group meetings regarding individual
patients should be an exception.

     It is important to clearly separate the inservice training pro-
gram legitimately required for staff development and as part of
overall educational programs from the satisfaction of irrational
dependency needs of staff that can be powerfully activated as part
of basic assumption group functioning as a consequence of regressive
group processes.   In the last resort, staff is there to treat
patients and not itself, and there must be necessary limits to staff
gratifications as well as to the demands put on staff.

     One of the greatest potential strengths of the therapeutic
community is the analysis of functional task requirements for optimal
treatment of patients, so that tasks can be redistributed from a
functional viewpoint.   This functional decision making should and
can be carried out within the context of an administrative analysis
of what patients' total needs are, what the total available resources
are, and how to utilize them optimally.   For example, an activity
therapist may be more interested in doing group therapy (under the
heading of resocialization or living-learning experiences) than in
teaching specific skills to patients;   or a psychiatric social
worker may be more interested in intensive family therapy than in
participation in the patient's rehabilitative efforts with various
community support systems.   All staff should be encouraged to shift
to functions needed by patients rather than functions reflecting
preferences of staff.

     The relative proportion of staff from various disciplines should
depend on a functional allocation of tasks, in contrast to the

internal, intraprofessional hierarchical time-allocation preferences
of various disciplines. In addition, it is helpful for the administrative leader of each professional group to have a clear understanding and knowledge of the actual time distribution throughout
the week of at least two levels of staff functioning within his area
of authority. Such information, combined for the entire therapeutic
community, may highlight surprising maldistribution of staff time
hidden underneath the surface of overlapping group meetings and
reflect the subtle but effective reassertion of independent professional priorities. However, I have also stressed the importance
of maintaining professional sentience. The various professions
should be able to openly struggle for their interests in the distribution of resources, in contrast to the subterranean distortion
of allocation of resources that is the consequence of a chaotic role
diffusion and the condensation of therapeutic community task
sentience with the sentience of the professional groups involved.

I think that each therapeutic community system should have a
leadership with capabilities in the following areas: (a) administrative expertise as illustrated in the requirements mentioned;
(b) expertise in the leadership of groups, particularly the conducting of small and large groups, so that an optimal balance can
be maintained between a necessary focusing on processes that interfere with optimal group functioning and focusing on the major tasks
of each group meeting; (c) a clear theory of therapeutic change
and of corresponding therapeutic methods that will permit a conceptual and clinical integration of individual and group psychotherapy with the use of task groups and the therapeutic community
process themselves. Such an integrated theory seems to me indispensable for the analysis of the mutual influences of the social
system and of individual psychopathology, and for the use of that
knowledge for management of both social regression and individual
psychotherapeutic needs.

What is involved here, really, is an integrated theory of
human behavior and psychopathology that includes the relationship
between social and intrapsychic dissociation and regression, a major
requirement that necessarily will set therapeutic community leadership apart from the more limited knowledge and expertise of individual psychotherapists and all other professionals on the unit.
Here I am pleading for professional expertise to replace political
doctinairism and naive enthusiasm. Such expertise will necessarily
require a senior clinician and administrator as the leader of the
therapeutic community. A major task is to protect the very survival
of such a senior leader by helping him to develop a viable therapeutic system that will not bring exhaustion upon him and his staff.
A major educational task of therapeutic communities is to facilitate
the development of such leadership.

Finally, I think there is a great advantage in having alternative, competing therapeutic systems sponsored by the same institution. In contrast to a monolithic doctrine which promotes a basically similar treatment model throughout all the units of a hospital, there is an enormous advantage in developing highly specialized, relatively autonomous units that can experiment with different treatment philosophies and arrangements, thus facilitating the study of therapeutic effectiveness, cost effectiveness, and the creative development of new treatment models. This implies building a research function into therapeutic community models, a research function that should include both consideration of therapeutic-effectiveness and cost-effectiveness studies. A study of pure cost effectiveness often neglects optimal treatment methods that require time and high specialization of care; a neglect of the financial and administrative constraints of treatment methods often leads to a concept of treatment that loses its relation to social reality.

REFERENCES

Belknap, I. (1956) Human Problems of a State Mental Hospital. New York: McGraw-Hill
Bion, W.R. (1961) Experiences in Groups. New York: Basic Books.
Caudill, W.A. (1958) The Psychiatric Hospital as a Small Society. Cambridge: Harvard University Press.
Edelson, M. (1970) Sociotherapy and Psychotherapy. Chicago: University of Chicago Press.
Goffman, E. (1968) Asylums: Essays on the Social Situation of Mental Patients and Other Inmates. Harmondsworth: Penguin.
Jones, M. (1953) The Therapeutic Community: A New Treatment Method in Psychiatry. New York: Basic Books.
Jones, M. (1956) The concept of the therapeutic community. American Journal of Psychiatry, 112:647-650
Kernberg, O. (1976) Object Relations Theory and Clinical Psychoanalysis. New York: Jason Aronson, 9:241-275
Kernberg, O. (1976) Internal World and External Reality. New York: Jason Aronson, 11:211-234.
Main, R.F. (1946) The hospital as a therapeutic institution. Bulletin of the Menninger Clinic. 10:66-70
Main, T.F. (1957) The ailment. British Journal of Medical Psychology, 30:129-145
Rice, A.K. (1963) The Enterprise and It's Environment. London: Tavistock.
Rice, A.K. (1969) Individual, Group and Intergroup Processes. Human Relations, 22:565-584.
Stanton, A.H. and Schwarz, M.S. (1954) The Mental Hospital. New York: Basic Books.
Whitley, J.S. and Gordon, J. (1979) Group Approaches in Psychiatry, London: Routledge & Kegan Paul.

THE THERAPEUTIC COMMUNITY IN NORWEGIAN PSYCHIATRY

Jarl Jørstad, M.D.

Medical Director
Psychiatric Department 6 B
Ullevål Hospital
Oslo 1, Norway

The concept of the therapeutic community was introduced from England in Norwegian psychiatry rather early in the late fifties and early sixties. In contrast to the situation in Denmark and Sweden, psychiatrists also tried to develop and practise these ideas in many variations all over the country. This is from one point of view rather astonishing as we Norwegians, from historical and geographical reasons, are experienced as quite individualistic , may be quite idealistic also! We are lacking the social training which you in Great Britain have in the large cities and in the pubs. Traditionally, however, Norway more than Denmark and Sweden has been western oriented, towards Great Britain and USA. The last war strengthened these ties and lessened the German influence, also in Norwegian psychiatry.

Another difference, may be connected with these historical events, is that psychodynamic understanding and psychotherapy were integrated in general psychiatry in Norway after the last war. To some extent this development was brought about by some pioneers in Norwegian psychiatry. Two more characteristics are important, namely the keen engagement among young psychiatrists and psychiatric residents, and the great influence of the Norwegian Psychiatric Association on this process. Some of the most influencing pioneers of psychiatry in our country combined the strong engagement and interest in psychotherapy with social psychiatry, including the concepts of milieu therapy and therapeutic community.

I will particularly mention two names Herluf Thomstad, the leader of the Psychiatric Department at Ullevål General Hospital in Oslo (Oslo City Hospital), and Harald Frøshaug, the Director of

Dikemark Hospital outside of Oslo (Oslo City Mental Hospital), the
largest psychiatric hospital in Norway. He was later Medical Director at Department II at the same hospital.

None of these collegues had academic positions, but they were
strong and idealistic leaders, future-oriented and openminded, with
particularly good relations to British psychiatry. Both were much
influenced by Maxwell Jones and his Belmont experiences, - the
Ullevål department also had much impact from Tom Main at Cassel
Hospital; - Dikemark from David Clark and American writers like
Caudill, Goffman, Stanton and Schwarz, the Cummings and the Menning-
ers.

These two hospitals attracted many young colleagues who had
their residency training there, and also many nurses and members
from other professional groups. A school for psychatric nursing at
Dikemark Hospital also contributed to spreading the ideas to other
places.

From 1956, we also had regularly 3 days seminars 2-3 times a
year for all psychiatrists in Norway, arranged by the psychotherapy
section in the Norwegian Psychiatric Association. There we met a.o.
Maxwell Jones, Tom Main and David Clark as invited speakers, and
quite a number of psychiatrists also visited their therapeutic
communities in Britain. Some also went to USA and learned about the
experience with therapeutic communities there. Maxwell Jones additionally had the genious idea to use young female therapists from
Norway at Bellmont, - some of them trained and worked later as nurses
and social workers in psychiatry when they came back.

It was thus the British model of the therapeutic community which
we tried to apply in a rather wide scale in Norway, and about 1970
it reached the peak of popularity. At that time it had almost been
a matter of mode, most psychiatric clinics and many mental hospitals
advertized with concepts like: advanced milieu therapy or therapeutic
community. The real substance behind the word were not always that
convincing. Often the hospital administration and medical directors
could accept vague ideas about milieu therapy, but they were not at
all convinced about the usefulness of the more radical therapeutic
community model. They showed their ambivalence particularly when
there were crises, or demands about more staff resources, or more
influence and power from other staff members.

The strongest force in this area through the last decade has
however been the young doctors and nurses who believed in the therapeutic community, and who tried to develop the model on psychiatric
wards and clinics in spite of difficulties and more or less open
resistance.

Some effects have been remarkable in most of our psychiatric

institutions. On most places the staff works in interprofessional
teams with regularly meetings in teams and staffs, and most places
there are patient groups and ward meetings. Still more important
is the development of more open communication, more decisions through
consensus, and at many places a flattening in the hierarchical organization of the institution.

In these years we also used much energy in public relation
work, and a couple of TV programs were made from the more advanced
therapeutic communities and were sent on our only TV channel.

Critical voices came more to the surface the last 6-8 years.
The gap between the ideals and the realities of many hospitals has
repeatedly been expressed. The uncritical use of the therapeutic
community-ideology as a general therapeutic panacea for all sorts
of patients, have many of us realized can be harmful, particularly
for the most seriously disturbed patients. Some of these patients,
i.e. with acute schizophrenic break-downs or melancholic depressions,
are in need of a more individualized and sheltered therapeutic setting in the beginning. They should not necessarily have to face a
huge community meeting the very first day after their hospitalization.

Our verbal methods and reality-confrontations in groups, and
the aim to give "insight", are not good for all patients either. In
an increasing degree we are confronted with new groups of patients
in our psychiatric clinics; individuals who are more undeveloped,
non-verbal and early stigmatized. Some of them are called borderline or narcissistic personalities, some addicts or alcoholics. They
often don't fit in our verbal groups and psychotherapy methods, and
are a growing challenge in our therapeutic communities.

Gradually we also realized that it is not necessarily an advantage to mix all patient categories together, and that certain patient groups, like schizophrenics or young drug abusers, may profit
on different types of therapeutic communities.

The so called "democratic" structure of the therapeutic community necessarily also create periods of role diffusion and crises,
with confusion about leadership, competance and decision making
process, pseudodemocracy and double-communication. There have been
examples in Norway where this kind of problems have been used in a
devastating way, both from the side of the leader/doctor, and from
political fractions in the staff. One therapeutic community had to
be closed of the authorities for such reasons.

We also still may have critics from outside about the timecon-
suming effect and ineffectivity of all the staff meetings and group
settings in our therapeutic communities. I think some of these are
shooting over the head, but we also from inside have to ask ourselves

if the teams and groups can be used too much for gratification of
dependency needs of the staff, with the concequence that the primary
task of treating the patients is coming in the background.

We have in Norway already at an early stage worked with a multi-
dimensional approach in our psychiatric institutions, trying to combine psychodynamic and sociodynamic approaches. The therapeutic community has been the most concequent model for organizing a psychiatric ward, the communication system, the teams and the milieu work.
But still we look upon individual psychotherapy, family therapy,
occupational therapy, social work, schools and rehabilitation, as
important aspects of every psychiatric treatment program, which
should also be integrated in a therapeutic community. More and more
of the patients who once were treated in our therapeutic communities
are now treated at an out-patient-basis.

From 1961 we have a mental health legislation which gives every
psychiatric institution responsibility for both pre-care, institutional treatment and after-care. The last 6 years we also have re-
structured the whole psychiatry in Norway into a comprehensive mental
health system, giving most hospitals and clinics responsibility for
a certain catchment area. In every sector we have to organize an
emergency service, out-patient clinics, and both short and long term
day- and night service for psychiatric patients from the district.
A spesial problem is the increasing shortage of trained nurses in
the whole psychiatric field, and an increasing turnover of all staff
members, particularly at the mental hospitals where the critical
level already is reached.

This development has of course influenced the existing therapeutic communities. Even the pioneer departments at Ullevål and
Dikemark have been facing a new reality, and this also have had an
effect on our therapeutic community.

As I mentioned in my previous paper today, the ideology of the
therapeutic community, as all ideologies and systems, after a time
tend to be formalized and frozen, changing in closed systems where
there are little or no living/learning and further development.
Then the ideology is used as a defence against anxiety, and as a
safe bastion for established power positions and routines. Both
for old and new leaders of therapeutic communities, and the staff
members, this constitutes a very serious challenge.

Many of us in Norwegian psychiatry feel that we constantly need
an open and critical self-reflection, to see how we can change our
therapeutic communities in accordance with the changing environment
and different needs of our patients. We also feel an increasing need
to evaluate the outcome, i.e. in more systematic ways examine what
happen with our patients during their stay in our therapeutic communities, - and further: what are the assets and what the limitations

of the system. A clinical research on these subjects has developed
in Norway now, - and some of the preliminary results were presented
by the Norwegian group at this congress. Still many of us think that
there will develop new and different therapeutic communities in
Norway, and we look to the future with a certain degree of optimism.

THE PSYCHOANALYTIC ORIENTED APPROACH TO THERAPEUTIC COMMUNITY

TREATMENT IN THE NETHERLANDS

Dr. Peter Bierenbroodspot

Psychiatrist-psychotherapist, Psychotherapeutic Community

"Rijnland", Santpoort, Holland

I. Introduction

The Dutch therapeutic communities, united in the Association of Workers in Psychotherapeutic Communities (V.W.P.G.), call themselves psychotherapeutic communities (in contrast for instance to the 'drug-free' or sociotherapeutic communities) for a good reason. With this name they want to stress their aim to provide clinical psychotherapy in the special setting of the TC, the main goal of treatment being to achieve structural personality changes as intensively as possible for those coming to treatment.

Though all are psychotherapeutically oriented only a few have a definite psychoanalytic approach. This is of special value for the treatment of patients with a more severe pathology, the borderline and psychotic patient. In this paper, I shall refer to this kind of treatment to which I am most familiar.

David Clark (1965) has already made a distinction between the therapeutic community "in general", which was an ideological change of attitude in the psychiatric hospital as a whole, started as early as about 1850 (Pinel, Connolly, Dorothy Linde Dix), and the therapeutic community "proper", a "small face-to-face intensive treatment facility with extensive social restructuring", started since 1945.

Peter van der Linden (1979) distinguished three models of TC: reconstructive, aiming at personality changes, re-educative, aiming at improving the social interactional competence of the patient, and supportive, which simply focused on relieving symptoms in crisis situations with the use of supportive measures. He pointed out

that the Dutch TC's (or PC's) especially adhere to the reconstructive
model.

Their aim is to extend psychotherapy to the clinical setting
for those who are unable to benefit from out-patient treatment because of the severity of their symptoms and pathology.   TC methods
are primarily seen as the best way to counteract unfavourable
hospital conditions and tendencies (such as regression) and also as
an excellent way of using group dynamics to get in touch with the
deeper layers of the personality structure.   The model of TC provides the necessary and optimal therapeutic milieu for clinical
psychotherapy.   To make optimal use of the clinical setting a clear
differentiation of roles and positions of staff members (the
professionals) and group members (the patients) in the community becomes necessary to avoid role-blurring.

The characteristics of the therapeutic community are well-known.
They are usually formulated by way of 'principles', such as
Rapoport's (1960) famous principles: democratization, permissiveness,
communalism and reality confrontation.   Such principles describe the
social field of interaction or the preferred therapeutic attitudes
in the TC, but they say little or nothing about therapeutic aims or
processes.

Therefore it is pertinent to develop better ideas about the
therapeutic process itself.   What is therapeutic in the therapeutic
community?   I think we cannot take that question for granted.

Given that the central idea of therapeutic community is "to
bring about the optimal use of (therapeutic) potential within staff,
patients and their relatives, for the betterment of the patient
population", as Maxwell Jones put it (Maxwell Jones 1967), then it
is vital to have more insight into the therapeutic process itself,
the goal of treatment.   If our goal is to promote clinical psychotherapy, more reflection is necessary about this ultimate goal and
thus an overall therapeutic frame of reference is needed.   In my
opinion TC ideology or TC principles do not and cannot give that
frame of reference.

In recent years theoretical steps have been taken to formulate
such a frame of reference.   Unfortunately they have not proven satisfactory.   For instance one TC some years ago had developed a so-
called 'pressure-cooker model':   the idea is that interactional
processes in the TC develop under optimal social 'pressure'.   When
the pressure is too low not much happens therapeutically usually.
The low pressure results from too much staff intervention with the
group process.   On the other hand too high a pressure in the TC
intervenes with the general feeling of safety, in which case more
staff intervention is necessary.   This model certainly gives the
staff some guide-line, but again little is said about the process
going on inside the therapeutic pressure-cooker.

These processes may be better understood, in my opinion, within
a psychoanalytic frame of reference. In the clinical setting we have
generally to deal with patients who have disturbances in their object
relations that result from early developmental problems of a psycho-
traumatic nature. Kernberg's object relations theory (1976), explaining ego identity formation, early identificational and intro-
jectional processes etc., is particularly helpful to such an analysis.

Object relations theory however should be supplemented with
attention to the family system at work during treatment. This has
been made very clear by the work of Theodor Lidz cs. (1959, 1965,
1973). Patients with early disturbances in their object relations,
especially borderline and psychotic patients, are often kept in that
position (of patient) by ongoing symbiotic relations with their
relatives, symbiotic relations of a very pathological nature,
thoroughly opposing the therapy. So the family system, just as much
as the "identified patient" himself, should be involved in therapy.

II. Clinical Psychotherapy

In 1972, in a paper about the therapeutic value (or lack of
value) of democratization, I formulated the essential characteristic
of clinical psychotherapy as follows: - "In neurosis perception of
reality is obscured and distorted by the memory of events the patient
went through in the past. To get rid of these memories the patient
should become aware of their distorting effects. It means that he
must be capable not only of perceiving his inner-self, but also the
outside world of here-and-now, the present in which he lives. A
comparison between this inner and outer world leads to the so-called
corrective emotional experience and thus to recovery. A too regressed Ego is not capable of so doing. Reducing regression by making the patient feel his own responsibilities improves Ego-function
and is the basis of recovery". (Benedetti 1965, Bierenbroodspot
1972). What during out-patient treatment usually is not worked
through extensively - daily life in the reality outside treatment
sessions - comes into focus in the clinical setting with its special
aim to reduce regression and to promote Ego-functioning by reality
confrontation.

Though not absolutely wrong this statement obviously is too
simple: the perception of the objects (reality) and of the inner
self needs further exploration. Time does not permit me to go into
Kernberg's theories in much detail, nor into our clinical observations that confirm his theory. Object relation theory has in my
opinion however strong implications for clinical psychotherapy:

1.   New is the idea that self and object images are by no means
     integrated in the case of patients with early developmental
     disturbances. The images are perceptive ideas and feelings
     of the inner self and self-ideals (what I am and what I should

or want to be) and the objects (what I think them to be
or want them to be). The phenomenon of splitting as a
defence mechanism, keeping apart positive and negative
feelings and images (later to be followed by represssion)
plays an important role in keeping the archaic and scattered
amounts of libidinal and aggressive energy separated as a
defence against overwhelming anxiety, especially the fear
of destruction of loved or loving objects. Splitting is
in many ways a common phenomenon in TC treatment, splitting
of the staff team for instance may confirm the patient's
ideas about a split world of objects.

2.   Early parental images (object images) and corresponding
      self images are not integrated images of the parents or
      the self as such, but are fragments of early emotional ex-
      periences, mostly of a non-verbal nature, which makes access
      to them difficult. (Glover speaks of early Ego nuclei,
      which keep the Ego split). (Glover 1956).

3.   Images of reality are always an approach to reality, closer
      or farther away from reality, more or less distorted by
      projections of inner feelings. This concept certainly is
      not new: two thousand years ago Plato made his famous par-
      able of the Cave, in which people only see the shadows on
      the wall of what is happening outside - because they have
      never seen the outside world they hold these projected
      shadows for reality itself. It makes us think of the human
      eye: the image on the retina is upside-down, but we do not
      realize this fact because we are only familiar with one
      particular situation.

4.   A well-known Dutch poet wrote the following lines:

      " - I am a God in the deepest of my thoughts
          And sit on my throne at the inner of my soul...." (Kloos)

He was of course not familiar with the concept of the grandiose self, but described it in his way. It seems to me
that when this God, who is little in touch with reality,
or these Gods (Kernberg's images), are very strong, the Ego
comes into great difficulty having to serve them and at
the same time the just as strong demands of reality itself.
Under certain conditions psychotic reactions may occur when
the ties with reality are left behind and the Gods prevail.

The nature and origin of the grandiose self is a matter of
much controversy, however we may encounter gradiosity in
clinical psychotherapy in many ways, not only in psychosis,
but also in neurotic character disorders and - I must add -
also in staff interaction in many ways.

5.   In object relation theory both psychotherapeutic intervention
     (aiming at the inner world) and sociotherapy (representing
     the object world by reality confrontation) come into one frame
     of reference, explaining to the staff the different roles
     and activities within the staff-team.

     In sociotherapy for instance the patient is confronted with
     reality as it is in the living situation and his images of
     reality, projected into the outside world, blurring his
     perception of reality objects and thus hindering him in his
     social contacts. It must be clear to the sociotherapist
     what his therapeutic intervention really means, when he
     confronts the patient with the present reality of here-and-now.

6.   In the TC, in the group, in the family, in interaction with
     the staff members and with the hospital setting as a whole,
     early archaic images, contrasting with reality, but never-
     theless determining the distorted self and object relations,
     come into focus and can be changed by growth and integration.

     As I said objects relation theory as a psychoanalytic theory of
early developmental stages primarily deals with intrapsychic processes, the personality structure as it has been formed, the fixation
at or the regression to certain developmental points. The 'time-
table' of intrapsychic development is seen as the main explanation
for pathological personality structures. I think this is the weak
point of the theory: too little attention is paid to intrapsychic
symbiotic processes in the present between members of the family
system: the nature of traumatic events and the pathological identifications within the family also play an important role in determining the final outcome of the personality structure.

     Schizophrenia for instance can be seen as stemming from fixation
points at some crucial developmental stage, but also as a function
of the schizophrenogenic family with its peculiarities such as
schism, withdrawal and, above all, family irrationality. Lidz,
who extensively studied these families, wrote:

     " - If a major aspect of psychotherapy with schizophrenic
     patients involves the patient's recognition that the parents'
     ways of perceiving are distorted, and having the patient
     free himself from their stultifying influence, the patient
     usually needs to be in a setting in which he can gain dis-
     tance and begin to regard his family from a different
     perspective. -" (Lidz 1973).

     We think of Freud's analysis of Schreber's case and his con-
clusions about the basic passive-feminine attitude of Schreber's
personality structure as an explanation of his symptoms and patho-

logy, together with Niederland's study of Schreber's father with his
highly sadistic and seductive educational methods. (Freud 1909-1913,
Niederland 1959). Freud and Niederland supplement each other in a
way that has vital implications for clinical psychotherapy.

    To summarize we can conclude that we should regard as crucial
in the clinical psychotherapeutic process the integration of various
self and object images into a well-balanced image of the self and
the object reality, in which there remains place for the ambivalence
of feelings towards these objects.

    In clinical treatment within the TC both the perception of the
inner self and the object world - reality - come into focus as a
result of the many different tasks, roles and groups within the
community.

III. Theoretical application to the clinical setting

    Thus far we have only spoken about the individual patient in the
community. We may now say something more about therapeutic processes
in the community itself:

1.   The group

    "Open-system" groups, groups without a special task or
    agenda (as in a meeting) enable the free play of group
    dynamic forces.   This kind of groups, as you all know,
    brings easily to the surface early self and object images.
    Kernberg calls this phenomenon, to which everybody is
    susceptible, regression. To me this seems inaccurate.
    Rather we must say that the presented social field of
    interaction poses to everybody the primacy of early
    developmental stages as the main basis for social contact.

    By setting limits in time and frequency of exposure to
    the group process, as is done in group psychotherapy,
    this "regression" is easily reversed. In the small
    psychotherapy groups the group focal conflict circles
    around the problems of early object relations and self
    perception. (Whitaker and Lieberman 1965) Focal Conflict
    theory focuses more on unconscious counteracting forces
    in the group as a structural-dynamic model (comparable
    to the psychoanalytic ideas about symptom-formation)
    and less on transference phenomena of the group as a whole:
    to look upon the group as if it were a person with person-
    like qualities seems to be highly questionable.

2.   The therapeutic community

    TC as a whole also functions more or less as an open-

system group. However, much more organization and
differentiation of tasks and roles takes place. Through
reality confrontation, by the necessity of living together
and having to take decisions as an independent group,
object reality is stressed.

We think it is important to make at least a clear distinction in the organisation between:

- the community: the daily life, decision-making, etc.
(the reality aspects of here-and-now)

- the verbal and non-verbal psychotherapeutic group
activities: group psychotherapy, psychodrama, psycho-
motor therapy, creative therapy, non-verbal expression
therapy, etc. (the inner world)

- social work activities (a go-between): work, family,
the problem of living outside the clinical setting etc.
(a bridge-function between the outside world of the past
and the future, and between the family system and the
clinical system).

3.   Transference reactions to the hospital

Of course many transference and countertransference reactions and feelings play a role in community life
amongst the members of the patient group and staff. Important is the ever-present double orientation Szasz
(1963) described: reality and transference aspects are
judged over and over again by the partners in the interaction. Maxwell Jones' social learning is a good example
of this process. (1968) Of course this therapeutic
process is as fragmented as the patient's Ego: image
after image is in this way worked through until at last a
more integrated and consistent picture arises.

But besides these transference reactions within the group
there also exist transference reactions of a primitive
nature to the group as a whole or to the hospital or institute. (Van Eck 1972, 1978). The institute is felt
as a primitive mother, sometimes in a rather oral-
aggressive form. "If you come to the hospital you will
never get out of it anymore", says a patient and it
becomes a self-fulfilling prophecy.... Talbot and Miller
(1966) speak of "magic mountain fantasies", following
Thomas Mann's description of the Magic Mountain.

The fact that different personalities react differently
to this magic mountain gives important information about

early object relations. The schizoid patient, for instance,
fears to be manipulated,his fusion anxieties arise at the
start of treatment and have to be worked through. The
depressive patient, with his overdependent attitude, loves
to be mothered, his separation anxiety becomes evident
towards the end of treatment.

These considerations of course have strong implications
for the course and strategy in treatment.

IV. Conclusion

Much more could be said about the desired clinical setting in
accordance with our theoretical frame of reference and about the
possibilities of clinical psychotherapy in a Psychotherapeutic
Community. Elsewhere I have described in more detail our organizational model - the Rijnland model - and the three co-ordinated stages
of treatment (the psychotic, borderline and neurotic stage).
(Bierenbroodspot 1978, 1980).

For the moment I hope I have made clear to you our psychoanalytic approach to TC treatment.

Summary

The ultimate psychotherapeutic aim of structural personality
changes in the individual makes interactional considerations in the
therapeutic community subordinate to the theoretical and technical
aspects of treatment. Both therapist and patient have a double
orientation within therapy towards the transference and reality
aspects of their interrelation. In the therapeutic community setting
these aspects both come into focus. The ultimate goal of promoting
reality orientation and object relations of the individual in treatment is facilitated by this setting. The individual, group, family,
staff and institutional interrelations constitute modalities of
treatment of a complex nature, giving access to the deeper layers of
personality that are otherwise difficult to reach. A clearly formulated all-encompassing frame of reference to rationalize treatment
is therefore necessary. Psychoanalytic theory of personality
development can give that frame of reference. In the Dutch (psycho)
therapeutic communities stress is laid upon the formulation of such
frames of reference, sometimes psychoanalytical oriented, serving
to understand the significance of the various verbal and non-verbal
techniques being applied.

LITERATURE

Benedetti, G., Die Handhabung der Regression in der individuellen
        Psychotherapie schizophrener Psychozen. Proc. VIth
        Int. Congress Psychother. London 1964. Karger 1965.

Bierenbroodspot, P., Democratization in the Mental Hospital as
        a Therapeutic Vehicle. Psychother. Psychosom.
        20:130 (1972).

Bierenbroodspot, P., The Rijnland Model. Paper for the U.K.-
        Netherlands Workshop on Therapeutic Communities,
        Windsor 18-21 Sept. 1978.

Bierenbroodspot, P., Klinische psychotherapie van de psychotische
        patient: theoretische en technische aspecten.
        To be published T.v.Psychother. 1980.

Clark, D.H., The therapeutic Community - concept, practice and
        future. Brit J. Psychiat. 111:974 (1965).

van Eck, L.A.J.M., Transference Relation to the Hospital. Psycho-
        ther. Psychosom. 20:135 (1972).

van Eck, L.A.J.M., Transference to the Hospital. Paper for the UK-
        Netherlands Workshop on Therapeutic Communities, Windsor
        18-21 Sept. 1978.

Freud, S., Psychoanalytische Bemerkungen uber einen autobiographisch
        beschriebene Fall von Paranoia (Dementia Paranoides).
        G.W. 8:241. Imago/Fischer 1945.

Glover, E., On the early development of the mind. New York: Int.
        University Press (1956).

Jones, M., Beyond the Therapeutic Community - Social Learning and
        Social Psychiatry. Yale Univ. Press (1968)

Jones, M., Therapeutic Community Principles within the Hospital
        and in the Outside Community. Proc. VIIth Int. Congress
        Psychother., Wiesbaden 1976 - Karger (1979).

Kernberg, O., Object Relations Theory and Clinical Psychoanalysis.
        Jason Aronson Inc. New York (1976).

Lidz, Th. cs., Zur Famileinumwelt des Schizophrenen. Psyche 13:243
        (1959).

Lidz, Th. cs., Schizophrenia and the Family. Int. Univ. Press,
        New York (1965)

Lidz, Th. cs., The origin and treatment of schizophrenic disorders.
      Basic Books New York (1973).

van der Linden, P., Various Models of Therapeutic Communities. Paper
               UK-Netherlands Workshop on Therapeutic Communities,
               Windsor 18-21 Sept. 1978.

Niederland, W.G., The miracled-up world of Schreber's childhood.
               PASC 14:383 (1959)

Rapoport, R.N., Community as Doctor. Tavistock Publ. (1960)

Szasz, Th. S., The Concept of Transference. Int. J. Psa. 44:432
        (1963)

Talbot, E. and Miller, S.C., The struggle to create a sane society
        in the psychiatric hospital. Psychiatr. 29:165 (1966).

Whitaker, D.S. and Lieberman, M.A., Psychotherapy through the Group
        Process. Tavistock Publ. London (1965).

RECURRING CRISIS IN THERAPEUTIC COMMUNITIES

Saul S. Kutner, Ed.D., ACSW

Associate Professor

University of Connecticut, School of Social Work

Recurring crisis is a well-known theme to anyone who has spent a significant amount of time working in a therapeutic community. It is a pheonomenon which takes a heavy toll on both patients and staff. Nevertheless, very little has been written about it and still less regarding a theory as to its cause. The basic premise of this paper is that the egalitarian ideology of the therapeutic community and the manner in which it is applied is at the very heart of the problem in that it prevents participants from dealing with the vital issues confronting them, viz., group process and community development. This has its greatest impact on how authority, control and influence issues present themselves and are resolved. In this paper I will first describe the phenomenon of recurring crisis. Then I will devote my attention to the limited but related literature. Finally, I will present my theory of recurring crisis and the need for further research in this area.

The concept of recurring crisis was first developed by Rapoport (1960) while doing research in the therapeutic community organized by Maxwell Jones in Belmont, England. He observed that a therapeutic community goes through a series of four "oscillatory phases" which has a distinctive impact on the behavior of the staff and the patients during each phase. Essentially, his theory suggests that a therapeutic community moves from a period marked by equilibrium and co-operation to a period marked by disorganization, crisis and conflict. This leads to a re-organization phase during which the therapeutic community repairs itself and the cycle begins again.

Phase A represents the period of greatest equilibrium and integration in the therapeutic community, i.e., conforming behaviour, relaxed, free, decision by consensus, etc. During Phase B the potential for disorganization mounts as constructive patients are discharged and are replaced by new patients. This leads to an increase in deviant behavior, tension, staff anxiety and disagreement in the therapeutic community. The crescendo is reached in Phase C as deviant behavior peaks and the latent authority of the staff emerges. Phase D is the reorganization phase as the therapeutic community attempts to repair itself, i.e. through discharge of disruptive patients, staff leadership, return to conformity, freedom, agreement, reduction of tension, etc.

Hobson (1979) describes a condition which he calls "the therapeutic community disease" which closely resembles Rapoport's oscillatory phases. He describes it as follows:

> Recurrent disturbances occur within the group, after the extrusion of members, patients or staff, or by acting-out the unresolved persecution and destructiveness in diverse ways such as violence, suicide attempts and secret sexual relationships. Relief follows the departure of irritant members but only for a time. The ritual of the 'scapegoat' needs to be repeated (p.235).

As indicated earlier, it is my contention that the roots of these problems are to be found in the egalitarian ideology of the therapeutic community but it appears that no one has made that direct connection. However, it is important to note the concerns and criticism levelled at the ideology and how it creates problems in the area of authority, control and influence. Morrice (1972) contends that the model of the democratic process in the therapeutic community contains three major myths:

a. No system of authority is needed ("A therapeutic community requires no leader").

b. Everyone makes an equal contribution to the therapeutic process.

c. Only group techniques can help.

The author concludes that although democratic approaches have advantages over dynamic conservatism of traditional institutions, myths about therapeutic communities have to be examined and dealt with. Myths are used as an aid for survival and should be abandoned for more truthful and useful concepts.

Hoffman and Singer (1977) discuss the incompatibility of the medical model and the therapeutic community model. The concept of the therapeutic community is thoroughly imbedded in the theory and

practice of hospital psychiatry. They argue that the inevitable
in-hospital amalgamation of the agenda of the medical model and the
agenda of the therapeutic community results in anti-therapeutic
double messages to patients. On the one hand, they are given the impression that they are adults who are responsible for their own lives.
On the other hand, they are given the impression that they are to
understand that their actions are beyond their control since they
are manifestations of "illness." A variety of specific ramifications
of the mixing of these contradictory agenda are described by the
authors. The medical agenda is often a covert one. A double de-
ception is involved. In the first place, the rhetoric of the therapeutic community conceals the prescriptions of medical authority.
In the second place, the prescriptions of the medical authority
conceal the imposition of the social values of the staff on the
patients. They conclude that a true therapeutic community has a
chance to develop only outside the hospital setting.

Mawson (1979) points out that the therapeutic community model
may have as its professed aim the liberation of its patients from
the limitations and constraints of neurotic illness or personality
disorder, in order that they may be able to return to the world and
live a freer, more effective and richer life. He goes on to say
that:

Closer examination of how such a community actually
operates (in terms of social organization, values,
rituals, behavior and attitudes it reinforces) may
show it to be directing more energy to satisfying the
staff's need to be needed and the patient's desire
for a professionally sanctioned retreat from the
stress and responsibility for themselves and others.
In other words, a contemporary therapeutic community
may operate the same sort of defensive-collusive system
that characterized the old-style asylum, differing only
in that the system is dressed up in a new set of socio-
political attitudes and is tricked out with a different
set of rituals, (p. 169).

He devotes much attention to the inconsistencies between the abstractions regarding leadership and authority and what actually takes
place in most therapeutic communities.

The premise of this paper is that the basic problem of the
therapeutic community is imbedded in unresolved authority issues and
is reflected in the recurring crisis scenarios which inevitably
develop. The seemingly permissive environment of the therapeutic
community helps to develop many of the conditions which prevail in a
T group.   In its development a T group moves from preoccupation with
authority relations to preoccupation with personal relations.   The

assumption is that before the members of the group can become interdependent, they have to deal with the issues regarding authority,
power and influence (Bennis, 1964).

The therapeutic community model with its focus on developing an
egalitarian ethos provides the group with the climate for allowing
authority issues to surface. However, the therapeutic community is
unable to deal with these issues adequately and results in recurring
crisis. It is important to note that periods of crisis are marked
by a high degree of deviant acting-out behavior which frequently en-
dangers the lives of individual patients and the therapeutic community
itself. The enormity of the crisis brings the latent authority of
the staff to the fore and prevents the community from ever dealing
with the authority issue adequately. Dissident members are discharged and the remaining group is exhorted to "save the community."
Thus the mythical harmony of the egalitarian community is allowed
to persist and the cycle begins again until the next crisis.

It is my firm belief that if the therapeutic community is to
maintain its vitality as a treatment model it will have to deal with
the crippling effects of recurring crisis. There are three things
which can be done to affect this situation. First, there is a need
to re-examine the ideology of the therapeutic community and perhaps
change it; specifically, as it relates to issues regarding control,
authority and influence. Perhaps egalitarianism does not promote
the environment where these issues can be dealt with effectively.
Secondly, there is a need for research in this area in order to get
a firmer grasp of what leads up to a crisis. It might be desirable
to first begin with post facto, retrospective studies. A second
stage for research could be to utilize this information to begin to
predict and deal with a crisis before it occurs by either preventing
it from occurring or dealing with it more effectively. Another area
which needs further investigation is the influence of the organizational environment. I am referring specifically to the "Stanton-
Schwartz phenomenon" which addresses itself to the impact of staff
conflicts on the acting-out behavior of patients (Bradshaw, 1972).
Even though this phenomena can occcur in any therapeutic setting it
may be a more prevalent phenomenon in a therapeutic community.

The therapeutic community model has proven itself to be a very
powerful tool for dealing with a variety of human problems. If there
is to be any further progress with this model, the issue of recurring crisis will have to be dealt with in a more effective way.
This paper has addressed itself to the dynamics of recurring crisis
and a theory as to its cause. Several areas for further investigation and research have been suggested.

REFERENCES

Bennis, W.G., Patterns and Vicissitudes of T-Group Development, In
      T-Group Theory and Laboratory Method. (Edited by Bradford,
      L.P., Gibb, J.R. and Benne, K.D.) pp. 248-278 John Wiley,
      New York, 1964.

Bradshaw, W.H., Jr., The Coffee-Pot Affair: An Episode in the Life
      of a Therapeutic Community. Hospital and Community
      Psychiatry. 23(2), pp.33-38, 1972.

Hobson, R.F., The Messianic Community. In Therapeutic Communities:
      Reflections and Progress. (Edited by Hinshelwood, R.D. and
      Manning, N.) pp. 231-244, Routledge and Kegan Paul, London
      1979.

Hoffman, I. and Singer, P.R., The Incompatibility of the Medical
      Model and the Therapeutic Community, Social Science and
      Medicine, Vol. II (6-7), pp. 425-431, 1977.

Morrice, J.K.W., Myth and the Democratic Process, British Journal
      of Medical Psychology, 45(4) pp. 327-331, 1972

Mawson, A., The Role of the Consultant in a Therapeutic Community.
      In Therapeutic Communities: Reflections and Progress.
      (Edited by Hinshelwood, R.D. and Manning, N.) pp. 166-169,
      Routledge and Kegan Paul, London, 1979.

Rapoport, R.N., Community as Doctor: New Perspectives on a Thera-
      peutic Community. Thomas, Springfield, Ill., 1960.

CHANGING LEADERSHIP IN DEVELOPING A THERAPEUTIC COMMUNITY

Edgar Heim

Psychiatrische Universitätspoliklinik
Murtenstrasse 1
CH - 3010 Bern

Usually, the traditional concept of hospital organization distinguishes between the actual medical services with its specific diagnostic and therapeutic requirements, and the administrative services
with infrastructural and economic responsibilities. Frequently, only
the latter are expected to conform to the laws of management, while
as far as the medical sphere is concerned such aspects are considered to be of secondary importance and consequently often badly neglected.

However, in the Therapeutic Community Movement therapeutic and organizational aspects have been integrated from the very beginning to
such an extent that it was often no longer clear whether the Therapeutic Community should be regarded as an organizational model or
as a therapeutic instrument. As far as the theoretical system is
concerned the two aspects are inseparable: as a subsystem of the
politically highly complex health system the hospital organization
remains related to analogous systems (other types of hospitals),
and comprises itself a number of subsystems. This pattern exists
independently of the specific character of a given Therapeutic Community, its proclaimed principles and its progress in the direction
of an open system.

In the hospital organization leadership depends essentially on these
conditions and the following controlling factors can be discerned
(1):

a) The personality characteristics of the leader
b) The nature of his technical and conceptual skills

c) The adequacy of task definitions, availability of human and material resources and priority settings of the institution.
d) The adequacy of the administrative structure to the task requirements.

The above circumscription includes on the one hand the role aspect
as determined by the imposed tasks; but it also refers to the self-
understanding, i.e. the influence of a task on the leader's self,
on his own identity. What really matters, however, is the fact that
role-understanding and self-understanding are not simply static elements, but are subject to changes as a result of the constant interaction between clinic organization and leader. Klerman (2) attempted
to define 7 tasks which are conferred upon the "Clinician Executive"
in the course of his activity:

1) Mapping, developing a conception of the organization.
2) Translating knowledge into action while learning organizational
   intervention (cognitive and tactical mastery).
3) Acceptance of responsibility for authority in the social system.
4) To relate to mental health professions and interfaces between
   professional groups and training and research and service-
   subsystems.
5) Cardinal competence for boundary maintenance: negotiation between
   the different system and subsystems.
6) To ensure organizational adaptation, promoting organizational
   growth and renewal.
7) Achieving and claiming new identity (role versus self).

On the basis of earlier studies I propose in this paper to describe
the changing requirements in leadership as experienced in the development of a Therapeutic Community. The phases presented here as
well as their background have been explained elsewhere in greater
detail (3, 4). They correspond to certain laws which are well known
from industrial organization studies, which can also be traced in
the relevant literature, at least there where the process character
of the Therapeutic Community is at all taken into account. Nevertheless, my evaluation of this process remains highly subjective,
since I was involved neither as a detached, critical observer nor
as a participant observer, but on the contrary as the fully responsible leader. However, I tried constantly to reflect on the process
with all staff members involved. In addition, I resigned 3 years
ago from my position as superintendent to take on other responsibilities.

The situation concerned here is the Psychiatrische Klinik Schlössli,
Oetwil a.S., Zürich, Switzerland, a teaching hospital of 400 beds
serving a catchment area close to the City of Zürich; it is State
supported but of independent financial structure (5).

1. INFORMATION AND RETRAINING

Therapeutic Community casuistics refer repeatedly to the importance of a charismatic leader. In fact, without their capacity for enthusiasm, such pioneers as Maxwell Jones, David Clark, Dennis Martin, Tom Main, Harry Wilmer etc. would not have been able to overcome the resistance which they encountered. Even 10 or 15 years ago, when the Therapeutic Community model was not yet as widely known and accepted as it is today, the leader's power of persuasion was an essential prerequisite.

His first task is to observe and assess situations. In this manner, he tries to define the existing concepts of leadership and therapy - which are in many cases only known by implication - to recognize their deficiencies, and to deduce the given needs.

From a colleague, who had fairly recently been appointed head of an university clinic, I had a very impressive account of his starting period in the new position: during the first 3 months he listened as much as possible to his staff, and deliberately refrained from taking any decisions that could be postponed (6).

Only then follows the conceptualization of the Therapeutic Community with specific goals. Clearly and intelligibly, the leader has to instruct first of all his closest staff, then those who cling to traditional ideas, and only at the end his enthusiastic young staff members, motivating them for the new task. Although the technical approach may vary, it should always incorporate meaningful retraining in the sense of in-service-training. Personally, I only found out afterwards how very important retraining is, because of something the matron told me some years later - and I would like to point out that our work relationship had always been excellent. She confessed that for a long time she herself, as well as her staff, although very much open to the change, had not understood the actual purpose of the Therapeutic Community; and that the confusion caused by this had been a certain handicap in her own leadership. I was very much taken aback by her remark, in particular since from the very beginning I had made a point of explaining time and again, in writing and verbally, the principles of the Therapeutic Community.

In this phase the leader's attitude should be unequivocal, prudent, determined, yet balanced. He must make it clear that he is exercising his full authority and consequently making full use of the existing hierarchical structure to promote the new goal. But at the same time he has to respect the inertia of the clinic as a social organism and therefore should refrain entirely from trying to overcome a possible resistance by force. He must beware of shocking his staff with excessive missionary zeal or of devaluing or untimely changing of established values.

At no time must he leave room for any doubt regarding his basic approach which gives first priority to the therapeutic task for the patient.

2. CREATING MODELS

The next stage is particularly critical: the leader has to look for suitable, motivated staff members who will put the new therapeutic model into practice in a pioneer-ward. They must be stimulated and encouraged; he has constantly to reflect on the process together with them, protect them against attacks by the envious and give them due praise for even the slightest success. In my experience of reorganization it is perfectly feasible, in this manner, to restructure several wards at the same time (7). As a rule, however, anything new will have to spread slowly, while the leader tries to make the rest of the staff interested and to strike the spark that ignites; but at the same time he will be open to criticism and remove any fears that might arise. I recall that in particular the administrative sphere tends to see itself as the guardian of tradition, distrusting any changes; while the superintendent's position in terms of the hierarchical structure is apparently accepted, innovations will be obstructed by 1000 pinpricks. There is no need to stress how important it is for the leader, especially at this stage, to establish sound relationships with the key figures of the hospital organization (administration, head nurses, chief resident) to disarm any resistance in advance. From the publications in this field it appears that many Therapeutic Community models failed unfortunately in this phase and surrendered to the manifold resisting forces encountered.

3. GROUP DYNAMICS AND ROLE CHANGE

But wherever, protected by the leader, the pioneer ward has become firmly established, it is bound to enhance the dynamics of the hospital as a whole. Since at that stage only very few staff members are adequately prepared for the various group processes in the ward team, in the professional group and in their work with the patients, crises and disappointments will be frequent. Here, the leader has to exert a stabilizing influence in terms of crisis intervention. And since, as a rule, his intervention takes place within a group, his leadership serves at the same time as a model for those whose own functions already imply responsible leadership. An analogous situation applies in particular to those teams for whom he acts as a natural leader. I remember that young residents, and also young nurses, integrate quite easily into these group processes while head nurses and older members of the nursing staff in executive (senior) positions find it difficult to readapt themselves from the two-way relationship to the group process. In fact, it took all of 2 years until head nurses and chief residents had finally come together to form a true leading team. In this phase the individual staff members' understanding of their roles is undergoing a change, which, however, will not be discussed in this context (8, 9).

4. WARD AUTONOMY

The third phase leads to increasing autonomy of the ward. Thus, the therapeutic action as well as the responsibility for this action are delegated to those who are working closest with the patients. It is the leader's task to settle the allotment of tasks by constant discussions, to define clearly the responsibilities and to strive for a control of events only as far as his own responsibility requires this. Systematically speaking, the leader controls the boundaries to the subsystems. Whenever staff members are afraid to take a greater initiative in reorganizing their own wards he has to assist and encourage them. In my own experience this concerns as a rule hospital areas which are by definition less privileged, such as chronic and geriatric wards.

The more dynamic acute wards must be reminded by the leader that there exist also centripetal requirements besides the centrifugal forces which are striving for autonomy. Still, as long as ward egotism does not become excessive in relation to the concerns of the clinic as a whole, some healthy competition between the various wards should be positively encouraged. As the representative of the total system the leader is aware of the important impulses which he receives from the subsystems for further transmission.

5. INTEGRATION

Now follows, inevitably, a reintegration process opposing the centrifugal forces of ward autonomy. I still remember vividly my fear and my anger when after approximately 4 years of hard development work we had a team session of the total staff where all of a sudden everything looked as if the Therapeutic Community experiment had at last failed. This black Wednesday, where young and old team members had seriously quarrelled, assumed symbolic value for the further development of the Therapeutic Community. Only from then onwards were all staff members fully aware that their solidarity was needed primarily for the clinic as a whole with its patient-oriented tasks, only secondly for the individual wards and functional groups, and thirdly for their own professional group.

For this purpose the leader has to assert his authority clearly but proportionately. He has to point out that communication must be a two-way process (from the hospital management to the ward and vice versa). He has to insist on administrative duties which are important for the clinic as a whole. I learned a precious lesson, when on one occasion I was told by the residents that they much preferred an angry boss who insisted clearly on the administrative jobs (such as case histories, anamneses, discharge reports) to a depressive

one whose disappointment in them gave them feelings of guilt which
had to be repressed. The result was a mutually important lesson in
open communication, shared responsibility and decision-making processes.

Yet, this example proves also that conflicts are unavoidable in a
Therapeutic Community – and quite a number of unreflected tensions
are due to the fact that this is often not realized. It is not conflicts as such that matters but the manner in which they are solved. The approach to the solution of conflicts and also the deci-
sions-making process depend on whether administrative problems or
relationship difficulties are concerned. Furthermore, the manner
in which a conflict is solved serves always as a model for the work
at ward level, both within the team and particularly where patients
and team members are involved (particularly in the relations between patients and team members). Again and again the leader will
have to try to prevent two potential errors on each level: it is
impossible to use administrative procedures for therapeutic purposes and it is equally not feasible to solve administrative tasks
by therapeutic methods. In some cases Therapeutic Communites failed
precisely because of their excessive permissiveness. And very often
they had reached that stage because therapeutic freedom had been confused with an administrative vacuum.

6. NEW ORIENTATION OF THE MEDICAL LEADERSHIP

In his effort to restructure the various elements of the clinic the
leader risks neglecting his actual leading team, i.e. chief residents, head nurses, and perhaps some other leading executive staff
members. I myself at any rate, realized one day that the head nurses,
for instance, were delegating an increasing amount of responsibility
to the periphery, i.e. the wards. But during the sessions of the medical leading team they showed a tendency to look at me – the superintendent – as a kind of "super head nurse". Most likely, this reflected the feelings of insecurity experienced by the head nurses
whose authority had been based on their traditional position in the
hierarchy, and who now had to learn to accept the relativity of their
authority. Consequently they felt the need to prove to the wards
that their position and decisions were based on technical competence.
Obviously, this produced their almost regressive tendency to look to
the superintendent for reassurance.

But at the same time, this was an alarm signal calling for increased
participation by the leading team itself in overall and partial
responsibilities. Outwardly, all participants acted in turn as chair-
men of the sessions of the leading team which were held twice a week.
Decisions were clearly stipulated, recorded and as general information communicated to all staff members in a weekly bulletin. Tensions
within the leading team were discussed openly in special retreats
until emotional understanding to continue the difficult task was reach

With subtle authority which by then is based on his competence to overlook the overall dynamics of the hospital rather than on his hierarchical position, the leader is now instructing his closest collaborators
to supervise the wards with their increased autonomy. At the same time
he encourages them to act as clearly and firmly as necessary in times
of crisis or when general tasks are neglected. He has to be aware of
the danger that unpopular decisions are pushed on him as the officially responsible leader while for example his deputy or closest
staff member might find himself unwittingly in the role of the popular leader who confines himself to give sound technical advice but
fails to exercise his administrative responsibility and authority.

7. INCORPORATION OF ADMINISTRATION AND SUPERIOR AUTHORITIES

According to an unfortunate tradition prevailing in the whole of the
medical world the superintendent, who lacks the appropriate training,
tends to regard his administrative work as an unpleasant but necessary duty. Nevertheless the leader should always be aware of the considerable indirect effect on patient care of competent planning,
satisfactory management, well-conceived programmes and balanced bud-
gets. During the golden 60ies medical therapists were but little
handicapped by financial restrictions. But the cost awareness of the
70ies resulted in countless new regulations, cost control, personnel
freezes and a critical public approach to medicine in general. It is
an essential responsibility of the leader not to lose sight of these
dimensions, also, or particularly so, in the Therapeutic Community,
which in fact is often in danger to develop into a kind of subculture
that is unaware of important aspects of the external reality. In this
respect the leader has to act as a kind of translator for his medical
staff, making them gradually aware of these correlations. For instance,
we had often difficulties in convincing our staff members of the importance of satisfactory bed occupation. Only after more extensive
information regarding the budget and its implications was provided
did the staff realize that in a self-supporting establishment all of
their material requirements were also related to the earnings, i.e.
indirectly to the bed occupation. From then onwards this aspect was
much more spontaneously taken into consideration when patients were
admitted.

Furthermore, the superintendent derives his function as an intermediary from the fact that he does not accept the traditional ladder
game. According to common practice, the medical staff's request have
to be passed up the hierarchical ladder before reaching the superintendent by whom they are transmitted to the administrator who in
turn will pass them down along his hierarchical ladder. But a system
with open communication like that of the Therapeutic Community implies
that the staff members or patients concerned whenever possible present their wishes and requests directly to the competent authorities
or answer to the administration. In our clinic we gradually developed
a routine for some ward problems to be solved directly with the admi-

nistration and others to be decided by the actual administrative and medical responsible staff. These multiple interrelations contributed considerably to a better mutual understanding between administration and medical services which led to a more relaxed collaboration of the administrative and medical leaders.

Equally important is the intermediary function of the leader to the superior authority, which as a rule knows little about hospital routine but which as a kind of Superego authority is extremely sensitive to the slightest criticism regarding the image of the hospital. It is common knowledge that occasionally the operational methods employed by the Therapeutic Community may seemingly superficially affect "law and order", and this invites various attacks. And it is a very central responsibility of the leader to do the necessary explaining, and also make the superior authority aware of the meaningfulness of the therapeutic activities. Only then will he succeed in preventing obstruction by those on whose political power depends the survival of the Therapeutic Communities.

8. OPEN SYSTEM AND PARTICIPANT LEADERSHIP

Working together in an open system under participant leadership of staff and patients may well be regarded as the optimal goal which the leader can hope to attain as far as leadership organization is concerned. Depending on the subject matter the share of the various participants in the decision-making process varies, however, considerably. The leader has the important task of defining areas of competence and of stipulating where actual shared decision making and where only consultation are appropriate. In fact, misunderstood or excessively applied democratization leads to a backlash causing the leadership structure to relapse into rigidity.

At ward level "decision making by consensus" as advocated by Maxwell Jones is doubtlessly appropriate. Where the clinic as a whole is concerned the leader has to accept and advocate that ultimate responsibility and authority - especially regarding administration - rest with him. He has to resist the danger of paralyzing important processes by excessive postponement of decisions. He must be aware of the limitations of "multiple leadership", but vice versa he has to see to it that the various areas of competence are by the respective leading staff members represented directly towards the outside and the top level. Participant leadership is important in personnel decisions. In our case it was introduced consistently at all levels in the course of the years. Even when I resigned as superintendent it was possible to concede to the staff members participation in decisions regarding the complicated processes of succession, which was certainly something new in the Swiss hospital world.

The maintenance of communication processes constitutes a decisive aspect of the open system. Continuous information on all internal

hospital concerns must become a routine. It should not be possible
to demonstrate power by controlling information - this applies as
much to the ward staff's ways with auxiliary nurses or patients as to
the administrator who conceals certain budget items. In practice we
tried to guarantee communication by team-meetings at all levels, by
continuous information regarding the administrative area (budget,
decisions by the board of governors etc.), by a bulletin issued by
the medical executive team and by the plenary clinic assembly. In
this context a biannual internal hospital seminar assumed central
importance, since it provides a kind of supervision of the clinic
as a whole. Under the competent guidance of a Norwegian colleague
small and large groups discussed at these occasions a variety of
topics which concerned the activities of the clinic as a whole.

In this phase the leader also tries to delegate responsibilities
wherever possible. This applies to the rather autonomous wards as
well as to personnel matters, and problems relating to organization
and training. We were thus able to develop, at different levels, representations of the personnel to the superior authority, to initiate
working groups - which organized for example permanent in-service-
training, maintained, in various fields, public relations and external contacts - and always did useful work when new operational
and therapeutic aspects had to be clarified.

But at this stage of the development in particular the leader has
to act as the guardian of the basic principles of the Therapeutic
Community. He must realize that now, when the Therapeutic Community
is getting on in age, the original enthusiasm might flag excessively,
new rigid forms might develop, and that in particular the idealization of the work by outsiders might easily cause depressive stal-
ling, because an open system is not at all immune against failures,
mistakes, setbacks etc. This elicits readily harsh criticism by
outsiders and/or insiders. If the leader does not intervene to correct and to support, he will not be able to prevent disappointment
and resignation from spreading primarily among the young and initially enthusiastic members of his staff.

9. OPENING TO THE OUTSIDE

Although in the first years of the development of the Therapeutic
Community some degree of self-absorption is unavoidable, the leader
must be constantly aware how essential external contacts are both
for therapy and leadership; because the real task consists obviously
in the treatment and rehabilitation of the patients.

We were fortunate in having been able to set up psychiatric services
for an autonomous region parallel to the internal development of the
Therapeutic Community. We were able to link the gradually developed
social psychiatric services to a corresponding therapeutic network.
Simultaneously it was necessary to establish contacts with regional

social organizations, i.e. somatic hospitals, welfare institutions,
municipal authorities etc. Finally, we launched intensive public
activities in collaboration with the media, professional groups and
village communities. Thus, the opening to the outside aims at a
psychiatric approach at community level.

The leader has the task of controlling this movement, initiating
activities but also checking them. As an initiator he constantly
prepares his staff members for the externally oriented work, encouraging and supporting them where his collaborators themselves are
in charge. On the other hand he has to check the inflation of external
contacts, supervise the effects of public activities on patient care
and reflect on misplaced idealization and the ensuing disappointment.

Particularly the organization of an international symposium on the
aspects of milieu therapy showed us that such an opening can be highly
rewarding, since we had the opportunity for a critical review of our
own work, discussing it with others and comparing it with the efforts
of other clinics (10).

10. SCIENTIFIC EVALUATION

Finally, this critical review is also the essence of what has so far
been the last phase. However, it is extremely difficult to evaluate
scientifically such a highly complex model as that of a Therapeutic
Community, both in respect of organization and medical therapy (ct 11).
It hardly lends itself to a proper outcome research procedure involving comparisons with traditional institutions, which at any rate
would be extremely costly. But a number of other research methods
would appear to be feasible, and improve at the same time the quality
of the therapeutic work:

- examination and description of work effectively carried out by comparison with the postulated principles;
- elaboration of principles as working hypotheses, in particular regarding the therapeutic process;
- study of the therapeutic process and its different modalities
  respectively.

In the past years our hospital has been engaged in scientific evaluation projects in terms of the above strategy, which have been the subject of earlier publications (12, 13, 14, 15). Our reasons were partly
the search for external recognition as a response to the not always
unbiassed criticism from colleagues with a traditional outlook. But we
were equally motivated by our desire to examine what the hospital had
achieved. Here it is the leader's responsibility to face the critics,
to question constantly the activity of his institution, encourage and
guide scientific projects or to advocate and enforce them at least
among his own staff. I know from experience that this is not always
easy because many staff members tend to overidentify themselves with

their own work and are therefore little inclined to accept any restrictions of their work by scientific procedures which are often
complicated and costly and sometimes also irritating.

CONCLUSIONS

Occasionally, the Therapeutic Community is accused of depending exclusively on the charismatic leader. In the relevant literature we
find indeed numerous indications that after the original leader's
departure the principles of the Therapeutic Community were neglected
or watered down or even opposed by a custodial counter-movement.
Probably, this applies in particular to those Therapeutic Communities
who for their development relied excessively on their originator's
enthusiasm. Consequently the hour of truth comes only with the departure of the original initiator of the Therapeutic Community. Only if
he succeeds in introducing the principles in question successively at
all staff levels to ensure that they will be equally observed and
developed in his absence, his concept and he himself as leader will
have really stood the test of truth.

It is important to note that the original leader of the Therapeutic
Community shares with the ongoing development more and more of the
leadership with many of his coworkers. This and an unavoidable personal development allow for constantly adjusting on the changing tasks
of leadership.

Therapeutic Communities appear to impose themselves like a kind of
force majeur in keeping with contemporary social tendencies. We can
only hope that after a while it will also spread beyond the actual
institution itself to the outside. As a result of such a development,
psychiatric hospitals would no longer constitute a target of projected,
collective, magic anxieties, but accepted pacemakers of mental health.

REFERENCES

1) O.F. Kernberg, "Leadership, personality and organizational
functioning", (a psychoanalytic study of some emotional conflicts of
leaders in organizations), Part I: Regressive pressures within the
organization. Part II: Regressive pressures within the personality
of the leader, Manuscript presented at the Sterling Forest Conference,
and 31st annual Conference, American Group Psychotherapy Association,
New York, 19174.
2) G.L. Klerman, "The joys and vicissitudes of life as a clinician
executive", in: R.G. Hirschowitz and B. Levy, "The changing mental
health scene", Spectrum Publications, New York, 1976, Chap. 18.
3) E. Heim, "Phasen und Widerstände im Aufbau der therapeutischen
Gemeinschaft im psychiatrischen Krankenhaus". Hrsg. H.J. Haase:
Sozialpsychiatrie, Schattauer-Verlag, Stuttgart, 1977, pp. 63-84.
4) E. Heim, "Aufbauschritte der therapeutischen Gemeinschaft in
der Psychiatrischen Klinik", Psychiatrische Praxis, Bd 5, Heft 1, 1978.

5) E. Heim, "Therapeutische Gemeinschaft in Praxis", Huber, Bern, in preparation.

6) W. Böker, personal information.

7)   "   "   "

8) E. Heim, "Therapeutische Gemeinschaft: Verändertes Rollenverständnis", Psychiatrische Praxis 3, Heft 1, 1976, pp. 15-31.

9) E. Heim, "Das Rollenverständnis von Patienten und Team auf einer Aufnahme- und Rehabilitationsstation", Psychiatrische Praxis 3, Heft 1, 1976, pp 31-36.

10) E. Heim, "Milieu-Therapie", Huber, Bern, 1978.

11) N. Manning, "The politics of survival: the role of research in the therapeutic community" and " Evaluating the therapeutic community", in R.D. Hinshelwood and N. Manning " Therapeutic communities", reflections and progress, Routledge and Kegan Paul, London, 1979, chap. 27 and 29.

12) C. Lilienfeld, H.N. Stauffacher, P. Wirz, "Die therapeutische Gemeinschaft in ihrer praktischen Anwendung - empirische Untersuchung in einer psychiatrischen Klinik", Lizentiatsarbeit unter Anleitung von E. Heim.

13) E. Heim, E. Johnsen, C. Lilienfeld, H. Stauffacher, P. Wirz, "Application of the principles of the therapeutic community with the participation of schizophrenics", V. International Symposium on the psychotherapy of schizophrenia, Oslo, 1975.

14) R. Isele, E. Schmid, "Milieu-Skala WAS",Lizentiatsarbeit unter Anleitung von E. Heim.

15) E. Heim, E. Bernstein, "Interaktionsprozesse im therapeutischen Milieu", Manuskript VII. International Congress of Group Psychotherapy, Copenhagen, 1980.

PSYCHOANALYTIC CONTRIBUTIONS TO THE

UNDERSTANDING OF GROUP PROCESS

Peter Kutter, Prof. Dr. med.

Inst. of Psychoanalysis
Senckenberganlage 15
6000 Frankfurt/M. 1

I. THE PSYCHOANALYTIC METHOD

According to Merton M. Gill's (1954) definition
the essentials of the psychoanalytic method are (1)
the neutral attitude with its characteristic balance
of attachment and detachment (2) the regressive formation of a transference neurosis and its resolution
and (3) interpretation as its exclusively technical
instrument. With this method psychoanalysts are able
to make conscious what was unconscious, to overcome
resistances by interpretation and to resolve an opposing transference. Traumatic infantile experiences
are reactivated, can be remembered and worked through
with both the analyst and the patient finally gaining
insight into the unresolved problems and conflicts.
This holds true in regard to the classical psychoanalytic situation of a two-persons-relationship.

II. PROBLEMS OF APPLYING THE PSYCHOANALYTIC METHOD TO
    THE GROUP SETTING

Within a group situation psychoanalysts usually
have problems in applying their method to the unusual
setting: A group is characterized by a plurality of
persons, not by a dyadic or two-persons-relationship.
But there are two ways in which psychoanalysts can
transform the group setting into a situation which is
familiar to them:

611

(1) by psychoanalysis of the individual in the
group (A. Wolf and E. K. Schwartz, 1962): According
to this model each group member is seen as involved
in a dyadic relationship with the analyst. The only
difference is that the leader is not facing one but
several persons in one and the same situation. Theoretically each individual member can be analysed in
the same way as in the dyadic relationship with which
the psychoanalyst is familiar with. In practice, however, the multiplicity of the transferences get in the
way of a straightforward application of this method.
There are two disadvantages of this method: On the
one hand it may easily happen that during analysis
of an individual participant the rest of the group
feels boring, and on the other hand simultaneous
analysis of all members at the same time is beyond
the conductor's capacity.

(2) by psychoanalysis of the group as a whole
(H. Ezriel, 1952; W. R. Bion, 1961; H. Argelander,
1972): This model views the group as if it would be
an individual. The group leader behaves exactly as
in the classical analytical dyadic situation. He
listens to the associations of the group members as
if these associations came from one and the same
person. In practice a psychoanalyst can work well
with this dyadic group concept. The situation is
easily managable, he is handling a familiar object,
and the method corresponds exactly to psychoanalysis
as a dyadic process.
Within this transformed psychoanalytic model psychoanalysts are able to look at the group like a structure
consisting of a group ego, group super ego and group id.
In fact, group structures can develop in the same way
as structures known from individual analysis. We can
see hysterical, or obsessional (H. Argelander, 1968)
or other classical neurotic structures. In the view of
W. R. Bion (1961), it seems to me, there are structures
which are close to psychotic characteristics, with
boundaries between the individuals becoming blurred,
with archaic anxieties of being swallowed, and with
primitive defence mechanisms, such as denial, splitting,
introjection, not to forget projective identification
(M. Klein,1946).

Groups can also develop a structure corresponding
to a narcissistic personality disorder as described by
H. Kohut (1971). It seems to me, that such a structure
is most likely to establish itself when the majority

of the group members are as a matter of fact suffering from narcissistic personality disturbances. In
this case we may speak of a "narcissism theory" of
the group (P. Kutter, 1976, page 57). If a group
has a majority of patients with borderline personality structure we can see how the group often very
rapidly is developing a group structure characterized
by sub-groups containing 'all good' parts and other
sub-groups containing 'all bad' parts. We may call
this view a sort of "borderline theory" of the group
(P.Kutter, 1976, page 67).

Looking at these two methodological devices of
solving the problem of applying the dyadic psychoanalytic method to a group situation we might conclude:
Neither of both devices do justice to the group as
context for a different research and treatment strategy.
In reality the group constitutes a situation which is
entirely different from the familiar dyadic setting.
Therefore, the psychoanalyst's instrument, which has
proved effective in the classical dyadic relationship,
is not appropriate for the group. For this reasons
there have been more than a few attempts at trying to
solve this problems.

Group dynamics as a theory of rules and regulations
pertaining to groups may fit much better to what is
going on during the group process. Substantial contributions to this kind of group dynamics were made by
sociology with its theory of small groups, by psychology concerning the changed behaviour of people in
groups and especially by Kurt Lewin. But it holds true
that these group dynamic theories have nothing common
with psychoanalysis. (For this reasons they are, by the
way, studied and taught in the other professional circles
or societies).

Group analysis in the sense of S. H. Foulkes (1948,
1975) is another attempt at solving the methodological
problem of applying psychoanalysis to the group. In
this method transference and resistance are taken into
account as the neutral psychoanalytic attitude and the
use of psychoanalytic interpretation. But at the same
time group specific aspects as the group situation with
its plurality of persons, their relationships to each
other, and their "transpersonal" communication are also
seen. This group analysis is a procedure of a specific
kind, that cannot be equated with psychoanalysis proper.

As a result group dynamics and group analysis are
for methodological reasons more adequate methods in
regard to group situation and group process than either
of the first-mentioned devices (psychoanalysis of the
individual in the group or psychoanalysis of the group
as a whole).

But we are asking for other, especially psychoanalytic contributions to the understanding of group-
process. My answer is: Let us look at the following
possibilities of applying the psychoanalytic method
in groups:

(1) With Freud's description of the church and
the army in "Group psychology and Ego-Analysis" (1921),
in my view, a very "patriarchal" interpretation of the
group is given: According to Freud, the group is regressed in the sense that like a child each group
member unconsciously submits to the leader replacing
his ego ideal with the leader and also identifying
with each other. In regard to another similar theory
(T. Adorno et al., 1950) the group is authority-bound
and that means: at the individual's expense. Thus each
member buys his advantage in the group with a certain
loss of his individuality. But in this view each participant may feel well because in phantasy the leader
will free every one from all his sufferings and will
lead his "chosen people through the desert into the
promised land where milk and honey are flowing".
Phantasies of this kind may be called "monotheistic
group phantasies", refering to Freud (1937).

(2) With the "group as a family pattern", first
described by Walter Schindler (1951), we have a concept,
which can explain the group symbolically as mother and
the leader as father. With siblings added we have a
sort of"family model" of the group in which each group
participant experiences the other group members unconsciously as representations of his own childhood
family.

(3) W. R. Bion (1961) sees in groups a pronounced
regression of all participants, together with a preva-
lence of the primary process and a simultaneous re-
ceding of the secondary process. There are primitive
anxieties of one's own greed and of archaic envy.
These and other primitive anxieties cause each partici-

pant unconsciously to take refuge into dependance on
the conductor (first basic assumption), to defend
against reactivated incestuous impulses (pairing, -
second basic assumption) or to escape the threatening
early mother-child-relationship (fight/flight, - third
basic assumption). In opposite to Freud's "patriarchal
theory" Bion's view of the group may be seen as a sort
of "matriarchal theory" because of its emphazising
the early mother-child-relationship in the sense of
Melanie Klein (1932).

(4) In addition to his group analytic method
S. H. Foulkes (1948, 1975) views the group as a sort
of "network" in which each member is a "nodal point",
the network consisting of externalisations of each
group member's internalized representational world.
This model, together with the group analytic method,
is in my view a very good synthesis of what psychoanalysis can contribute to the understanding of group
process, and of what has additionally to be seen in a
more group dynamic view and with a better sociological
foundation.

III. OWN PRACTICAL EXPERIENCES

My first practical experiences in a group process
are stemming from an experimental group which met
intermittently (between 1961 and 1971) led by the
late Erich Lindemann (1979). Problems of sexuality,
jealously between sisters and brothers and rivalry in
reactivated infantile longings connected with being
loved especially by the leader played an important part
in the group. Since the group met only intermittently,
separation and mourning because of repeated separation
were also central to this group's work. The group
process occured in a typical course: oedipal and pre-
oedipal conflicts were re-lived regressively, but in
reverse order to their original appearance (W. Reich,
1933, I. Lampl-Le Groot, 1952; P. C. Kuiper, 1962/1963;
P. Kutter, 1971). As a result the group process could
be approached quite well in a manner comparable to the
dyadic process in psychoanalysis.

In regard to the therapy groups I conducted in my
private practice I am aware of the great differences
between the several groups: Group I, was composed of
somewhat older participants, all of whom had sexual

problems. Similar to the group process in which I was
involved as member, difficulties in male and female
relationships constituted the most frequent and persistent "common denominator" among participants. In this
group it was again psychoanalytic theory of sexuality
resp. of oedipal conflicts which made it relatively
easy to understand what went on during the group process.

In group II, composed of somewhat younger participants, narcissistic problems of worth and worthlessness
prevailed. Thus in this group it was very helpful to
understand and to interpret the group's behaviour in
the light of Heinz Kohut's narcissism theory (1971).

The climate in group III - another group I should
like to mention - was entirely different. This group
was composed of students who previously had been involved in drug abuse and the formation of communist
political groups (some of them later on acquired dubious
fame as terrorists). The childhood of these participants
was characterized by severe traumas, such as having
been born out of wedlock, having overburdened mothers,
absent or weak fathers, and being brought up by foster
parents or in children's homes. These participants
proved unable to admit their dependency needs hidden
behind their acting out in political activities. The
group developed split   transferences characterized
by 'all bad' parts, filled with archaic destructive
aggressiveness and also 'all good' parts consisting
of omnipotent possibilities to change even the whole
society. It is therefore obvious that one should consider this group as having a structure parallel to a
borderline case as described by Otto F. Kernberg (1975).
In other words the group's central problem was its
inability to reach the "depressive position" as outlined by Melanie Klein (1946).

In a further group IV, a couples' group - varying
patterns of sado-masochistic object relationships dominated the picture. In this sequence of the group process desires from early infancy with the abandoned
children's longing for their parents appeared.
Through continuing analysis of the resistance and
the predominant transference the participants were
more and more able to free themselves from their close
ties with parents. As a result it was very useful in
working with this couples' group to understand the
group process not only as compulsion repetition of
drive impulses but also in the light of modern psychoanalytic object relations theory (O. F. Kernberg, 1976).

IV. CRITICAL EVALUATION

Summing up, to my point of view, the following psychoanalytic contributions to the understanding of group process are useful:

(1) Merton Gill's essentials of psychoanalysis as initially mentioned holds true also in group analysis, although in a group-specific modified manner.

(2) Neither psychoanalysis of the individual in the group nor psycho-analysis of the group are sufficient methods of solving the methodological problems of applying psychoanalysis to the group setting. However, it is possible to understand some group formations just as an individual personality structure, for instance like a neurotic structure, a narcissistic personality, a borderline case or even a psychotic patient.

(3) Each of the following concepts can be used as specific psychoanalytic contributions to the understanding of group process:

(3.1.) Freud's 'Group Psychology' helps us to understand the nature of identifications and substitutions occuring in groups dominated in phantasy by an authority figure with projections of ego ideals onto the leader and with mutual introjections of the participants between themselves.

(3.2.) Walter Schindler's family model which corresponds to an oedipal concept of the group together with observing siblings relationships.

(3.3.) Bion's model of group dynamics consisting of the well known basic assumptions which is at the same time within psychoanalytic theory and beyond of it when stressing pairing as a subgroup formation.

(3.4.) But only Foulkes' concept with its definition of the group matrix and of the group network is, in my opinion, a nearly optimal synthesis of what psychoanalysis can contribute to the understanding of group process and of what has to be added from sociology and group dynamics because of the specific group situation with its plurality of persons.

Additionally the following psychoanalytic theories proved to be useful according to my own experience working with groups as psychoanalyst: The psychoanalytic

theory of sexuality and its disturbances, the psychoanalytic concept of narcissism, the psychoanalytic
theory of borderline personality organisation and modern
psychoanalytic object relation theory; of course, not
to forget the psychoanalytic method itself using resistance and transference continiously during the
group process for interpretation.

But besides these advantages of using analytic
concepts in working with groups I also registerd some
disadvantages especially when handling groups composed
of severe disturbed patients, for example narcissistic
personality disorders, borderline cases, patients with
psychosomatic diseases, with drug abuse, and with
delinquent behaviour.

In groups of this kind it easily happens that
individual members were forced into specific roles
in which they become fixated, even when interpreted
repeatedly. This is definitely a disadvantage for the
participant who should as far as possible learn and
practice variant roles corresponding with his latent
predispositions.

In groups of this kind also the reactivated emotions
corresponding to the predominant early object relationships were of such an intensity that is was difficult
for the participants to gain insight into the current
group process at the same time. In such phase of the
group process the intensified affectivity of the group
prevented the neccessary distance to the immediate
experience of the single group member. This result is
confirming Freud's early description of the 'horde' or
'mob' in his famous papers 'Totem and Taboo' (1913/1914)
and 'Group Psychology and Ego-Analysis' (1921).

Another disadvantage in groups of this kind can be
the very rapid succession of the reactivated scenes that
arise through externalisation of early traumatic experiences within the developing group. In some phases
of the group process there is even a sort of competition
between various traumatic scenes, one outstripping the
other, and sometimes leading to a chaotic situation.

In regard to these undoubted disadvantages working
with therapy groups composed of severe disturbed persons
it seems to be an overestimation of the effectiveness
of the group when only the group is seen as an instrument

for help in any case; for instance like H. E. Richter
(1972). All the described contributions of psychoana-
analytic method and theory to a better understanding of
what is going on during the group process are not
sufficient to avoid the disadvantages which I have
mentioned refering to the main goal of psychoanalysis
namely to gain insight by experience and by understanding of what has been experienced.

V. CONCLUSIONS

With reference to this critical evaluation I would
like to suggest that a 'two-phase model' of psychotherapy especially in regard to the therapy of severe
disturbed persons should be welcomed:

The first phase occuring in a group setting in
which each participant experiences himself at the same
time on a level reliving his traumatic infantile conflicts and on another level making new relationships
with other persons of whom the conductor is the most
significant one against whom one can revolt, with whom
one has to come to terms, and with whom one identifies.
This first phase in the group setting offers a framework for the reactivation of past traumatic experiences,
and it creates space for growth and development for
each participant.

Now, in my opinion, it seems to be a good recommendation to add to the first place of psychotherapy in the group setting, especially of group analysis,
a
second phase of psychoanalysis in a dyadic setting
in which the many scenes experienced during the first
phase can be remembered, repeated in phantasy and
finally "worked through" in the sense of Freud (1914).
This aim can much easier be realized within a dyadic
relationship because only under these circumstances
the required balance of 'attachment' and 'detachment'
as imperative preposition for insight is taken for
granted.

Therefore, in conclusion, it is recommended to
adopt this two-phase-model with its first "experience-
orientated" phase in the group setting - that is:
group analysis - and its second insight-orientated
phase in a dyadic setting - that is: psychoanalysis
proper.

In this recommendation on the one hand the
advantages of both methods - psychoanalysis and group-
analysis - may be used in the best manner and the
disadvantages can be prevented and by this way also
better therapeutic results can be realized.

REFERENCE LIST

Adorno, T., et al, 1950, The Authoritarien Personality,
        Studies in Prejudice, New York.
Argelander, H., 1968, Gruppenanalyse unter Anwendung
        des Strukturmodells, Psyche, 22: 913-933.
Argelander, H., 1972, Gruppenprozesse, Wege zur Anwen-
        dung der Psychoanalyse in Behandlung, Lehre
        und Forschung, Rowohlt, Reinbek bei Hamburg.
Bion, W. R., 1961, Experiences in Groups and other
        Papers, Tavistock Publs., London.
Ezriel, H., 1952, Notes on psychoanalytic Group therapy
        II, Interpretation and Research, Psychiatry 15:
        119-126.
Foulkes, S. H., 1948, Introduction to Group-Analytic
        Psychotherapy, Heinemann, London.
Foulkes, S. H., 1975, Group-Analytic Psychotherapy,
        Method in Principles, Gordon and Breach, London.
Freud, S., 1912/13, Totem and Taboo, St.E. 13., Imago,
        London.
Freud, S., 1914, Remembering, Repeating, Working through,
        St. E. 12: 145-156.
Freud, S., 1921, Group Psychology and Ego-Analysis, St.
        E. 18: 65-143.
Freud, S., 1937, Moses and Monotheism, St. E. 23: 1-137.
Gill, M. M., 1954, Psychoanalysis and exploratory
        Psychotherapy, J. Am. Psychoanal. Asscn. 1:
        771-797.
Klein, M., 1932, The Psychoanalysis of children, Hogarth,
        London.
Klein, M., 1946, Notes on some schizoid mechanism, Int.
        J. Psychoanal. 27.
Kernberg, O. F., 1975, Borderline conditions and patho-
        logical Narcissism, Aronson, New York.
Kernberg, O. F., 1976, Object relations theory and clini-
        cal Psychoanalysis, Aronson, New York.
Kohut, H., 1971, The Analysis of the Self. A Systematic
        Approach to the Psychoanalytic Treatment of Nar-
        cissistic Personality Disorders, Int. Univ. Press,
        New York.

Kuiper, P. C., 1962/63, Probleme der psychoanalytischen
        Technik in Bezug auf die passiv-feminine Ge-
        fühlseinstellung des Mannes, das Verhältnis der
        beiden Ödipus-Komplexe und die Aggression,
        Psyche 16, 321-344.
Kuiper, P. C., 1969, Psychoanalytische Gruppentherapie,
        Social Psychiatry, 4: 120-125.
Kutter, P., 1970, Aspekte der Gruppentherapie, Psyche,
        24: 721-738.
Kutter, P., 1976, Elemente der Gruppentherapie, Vanden-
        hoeck & Ruprecht, Göttingen. In English:
        Basic concepts of Psychoanalytic group therapy,
        to be published by Routledge & Kegan Paul,
        London, 1981.
Lampl-de-Groot, J., 1952, Re-Evaluation of the Role
        of the Oedipus Complex, Int. J. Psychoanal. 33.
Lindemann, E., 1979, Beyond Grief, Aronson, New York.
Reich, W., 1933, Charakteranalyse, Selbstverlag, Wien.
Richter, H. E., 1972, Die Gruppe, Hoffnung auf einen
        neuen Weg, sich selbst und andere zu befreien,
        Rowohlt, Reinbek bei Hamburg.
Schindler, W., 1951, Family Pattern in Groupformation
        and Theory. Int. J. Group-Psychother. 1:
        100-105.
Wolf, A. a. E. K. Schwartz, 1962, Psychoanalysis in
        Groups, Grune and Stratton, New York a. London.

DIFFERENCES AND INTER-RELATIONS BETWEEN PSYCHO AND GROUP ANALYSIS

Leonardo Ancona

Via Nemea 21, Roma, Italy

It is a truism to say that group analysis, although born from psychoanalysis, is totally different and can't be reduced to it. As a matter of fact, the differences between the setting and the methodology in psycho and group analysis have been repeatedly emphasized, the epistemology of their nature still remaining to be clearly resolved. Some authors consider indeed the group analysis as a psychoanalysis carried out in a group, a sort of rotatory psychoanalysis.

On the contrary, in this paper an effort will be made in order to show that group analysis is an autonomous approach to psychotherapy, that it uses psychoanalytic contents only as basic structures, a sort of an alphabet, building a new language, the language of the social roots of many psycho-neurosis and psychosis: therefore that group analysis has a methodology of its own, and only through a continuous and faithful adherence to its way of working is it possible to decode the languages in question and to achieve optimal therapeutic effectiveness.

The premise from which the idiosyncratic nature of group analysis arises is clinical and belongs to the unique experience of being part of an autocentered group, where no more than a dozen persons are collected together in a face to face setting, in order to work on the very fact of their presence "here and now", outside any external goal or any dramatic action and with the aim of a mutual sharing of mental fields, above all the aim of new knowledge, the psychological transformations and the symptomatic changes deriving from this work.

The peculiar experience of being a member in a group analytic group is an event variously scattered all along the life of the group, but it is acutely felt in some recurring circumstances: as it is before the holidays,approaching Christmas or Easter breaks, and returning from summer holidays. They are critical points of difficulty, for everyone of the group or at least for the majority of the members, strictly in agreement with the observations by D. Meltzer in the chronological phenomenology of individual psychoanalysis.

In these instances of group analytic situation membership is enhanced, there is general grief and individual protests before the breaks, fears, anxieties, feelings of disgust and multi-faceted defences when the moment to recommence the group work is approaching;   these kind of reactions in their variety indicate un-animously that the group is lived as a reality deeply different from that everyday life, a reality either protecting or menacing.

It is experienced indeed as "group-space" alienated from the "mundane-space" (Pines), lying beyond a mysterious barrier which in some instances protects, terrifies in some others, anyway always fascinating as good or bad. It is clearly for these reasons that Kurt Levin first defined that the group does exist as a gestalt, a dynamic whole based on the inter-dependance of its components;   and that the late Michael Foulkes spoke in terms of unified mental field.

Of paramount importance, at this regard, seems to be the fact that in the group gestalt the individual does not lose his identity; Solomon Asch, a pupil of K. Lewin, did a lot of work for defending this point of view, and Foulkes emphasized the fact that the group should be researched as a network in which the multi-personal hypothesis of the mind is reflected;   therefore as a reality in which both the whole, the group, and the components, its members, should be simultaneously considered, and where the treatment should continously oscillate between the orientation to the individual and the orientation to the group. Just as in the Rubin figure, which is the emblem of this Congress, the figure and the background are to be simultaneously taken into account.

With this assumption in mind, it is possibly clearer that psychoanalysis, as an instrument of transformation and knowledge devised for the individual, is not tuned for the group work;   but it should also be clear that, because the individual is not lost in the group, its personal dynamics always remain of no little importance, that it cannot be dismissed and that only the way to deal with it should be changed, from the way peculiar to psychoanalysis.

One of the possibilities to pursue this point is considering the dreams told in a therapeutic group;   let us begin this reflection by reminding that group dreams are substantially different from those recurring in individual psychotherapy and this for more than one reason.

First of all, the group setting may be viewed as a pre-sleep
event, expected to be incorporated into the dream of group members,
just as the day residue is present as raw material in the manifest
content of the dream (S. Freud, 1900). Secondly,the group setting
enhances to a maximum the motivations of group members in terms of
expectation from the situation or from the relationship to the other
presences and this too facilitate the incorporation, in the dream,
of group events or of their symbolic constructs (Breger et al., 1971).
Thirdly, altered states of consciousness foster the reprsentation of
the social setting in the dream content (Whitman et al., 1962).
Fourthly, group members projections, identifications, transferences
and interactions enter directly into the dream vicissitudes, because
the group transferences produce less anxiety than in individual
therapy and hence less need for repression.   (Locke, 1957).

Finally, subjects who dream are those who experience most clearly
and most intensively the emotional situation which the group is undergoing (Zimmerman, 1967).   Therefore, the group dream is an unconscious reflection of events of the group (Foulkes, 1964), as well
as an helpful instrument in analyzing either the phenomenon occurring
in the group viewed as a whole, or the individual dynamics triggered
by social events. All this means that in a group where the emotional
emphasis rests in the group itself as it is in the group analytic
group, the manifest or the hidden content of the member's dreams will
be naturally shaped in collective terms: not only the group components will be present in the dream and the day residues will frequently be events of group life, but these dreams will also express
something not reducible to the instinctual unconscious of the dreamer.
As a matter of fact, the group dream shows a network dynamic: interpersonal relationships and conflicts, interactions and transactions
not pertaining to the unconscious private communications, either
inter-systemic (between Ego, Ed, Super-Ego) or intra-systemic (inside
each of these areas).   In the group dreams we detect a new language,
and an emotional network, expressing the social roots of the neurotic
and psychotic ailments. The very duty of the group leader should
therefore be to enhance the intelligibility of this language, and to
decode it on everybody's behalf.

In this respect an important consideration for the clinical work
comes now: in individual psychoanalysis the emphasis of interpretation is of course systematically centered on the transference
relationship; that is, even if social contents enter in the manifest
or hidden content of dreams, an effort is made for their interpretation in the transferential frame of reference. In such a way the
psychoanalytic dreams more and tend more to correspond to the program tuned by the analyst, becoming an increasing expression of the
transference.

More generally there is no doubt that in psychoanalysis the
mental setting of the analyst is continously communicated to the

analysand, therefore that ways of thinking and the dreams of the
latter are "trained", "educated", to be in agreement with those of
the analyst.   This transmission of psychological modalities is
evident when one considers the contents of dreams in different
settings: in classical psychoanalysis they tend to be freudian, in
analytical psychology, jungian, in individual analysis, adlerian;
moreover, when the psychoanalyst works in the frame of reference
of the development aspect of psychoanalysis, the dream content tends
to reflect the oral, anal, phallic levels of the theory; when the
transference countertransference is the main referent, the content
shifts to parental relationships; when the Kleinian aspects are on
the fore, there tend to prevail in the content the primitive aspects
of the mind, fragmentations, projections, envy and death dynamics.
And, last but not least, when working in sympathy with Dr. Matte
Blanco's way of thinking, it is possible to hear patient's dreams
unequivocally expressed in terms of "infinite sets".

Now if this is the basic condition of the dream in classical
analytic treatment it follows that in an analytic group the leader,
acting as a catalyzer of the whole dynamics, has the unique possibility to foster the collective dimension of the member's dreams,
that is the dimension of their inter-personal unconscious; or, on
the contrary, to stop it: we have the first case when the interpretations are suggested in terms of collective dynamics, the second
one when they are offered in terms of personal unconscious. The
very aim of a therapeutic group's leader, and of the group itself,
is therefore that to educate more and more each group member to feel,
to live and to dream in a collective dimension; the failure consists
in disregarding or in ignoring this clinical reality.

Although these statements do define the epistemological distance of psychoanalytic and group analytic treatment, they don't
enter as yet in the very nature of the group situation, from which
it should be possible to disentangle the technique to be followed
in group analysis. In order to arrive at this goal I refer to a
paper presented to the first Italian Congress on Analytical Group
Psychotherapy, held in Rome in the beginning of this year, Dr.
Menarini demonstrated with clinical and anthropological material
that the setting of an auto-centered therapeutic group allow for a
collective regression; through the same, the group situation promotes a sort of dream-state because the single components find themselves submerged in a field of transpersonal expressivity, losing
thereby their personal differentiation: as it happens in the
natural dreams.

Dr. Menarini emphasized the fact that in this particular
situation the "sleep-instinct", outlined by S. Freud in his "Summary
of Psychoanalysis" in order to explain transference dynamics and
dream-work is activated; and advanced the hypothesis that "to be
in group" means "to be sleepy", that both the situations are pheno-

menotogically and dynamically inter-connected, two processes of the
same level of articulation both representing a sort of primary
socialization: for which the relationship between the individual
and his group becomes homogeneous to that between the child and his
mother;   finally, according to Dr. Menarini, the sleep-state of the
group is responsible for dreams, representing collective events,
group events that have happened or are on the point of happening.
The group dreams are therefore the perceptual transcription of the
group sleep-state and correspond to the manifest content of the
group discussion, that Dr. Foulkes related to the unconscious contents of the group matrix.

     With this hypothesis in mind it is possible to say that in an
analytic group the work of the group, that is it's specific methodology, should consist in being continously tuned to the group sleep-
state, in fostering it when yet present and in refraining to disturb it through improper manners: the more dangerous of them being
represented by pervasive psychoanalytic interpretations, shaped in
terms of personal unconscious drives,of individual sexuality, of
transference, and of family dynamics.   If the very nature of an
analytic group is to be a network, a matrix, therefore its methodology should necessarily be one of emotional unconscious communications, either of libidinal or aggressive nature expressed as
actual relationships going on in the group, as a reflection/pro-
jection in the group setting of the most archaic inter-actions buried
in the unconscious of the components, not qua individuals but qua
elements of a primitive social network.

     This means for instance that the sexual sequences, either
hetero or homosexual and of perverse nature, when they are part of a
group dream, as well as of a discussion in the group, should not be
primarily or exclusively interpreted in the frame of reference of
the individual sexuality, but in that what is metaphorically expressed by sexuality: association, inclusion, meeting and fusion,
as against collision, exclusion, impact and alienation.   This also
means that when the "mother" is present in a group dream or phantasy,
she doesn't primarily refer to a person, but to the functions of
the mythic mother, better to the group as a matrix, able to accept,
to nurse, to make warm, but also to reject, to close, to cool and
to starve.   The "father" in its part is the mythic one, who begins,
drives, carries and creates and who on the contrary stops, hurts,
punishes and blames.

     This perspective holds also for the processes of transference
(through which the leaders are seen as the father and/or as the
mother);   moreover it holds for any trend to refer to the others
in the group as brothers and sisters, to see the newcomers as newborn babies, the group as a family, which indeed it is not, and in
general for considering events as marriage, birth, death, pregnancy
in instinctual terms.

expressed conditions of identity - especially sexual identity - uncertainty of the group by inconsistent transference manifestations
relating to the analyst. The observation of the analyst is also
concentrated on the registration of the latent uniform phantasized
transference wish of the group and it is thought also to be the aim
of interpretation.

In a psychoanalytic group process, which doesn't differ in it's
duration from a classical psychoanalytical process and which can
last by all means four or five years, several typical phases of group
transference can be recognized: The oral-symbiotic, the anal, the
oedipal, the narcisstic and the separation phase.   One can see
that these typical transference phases and constellations are
organized like a pattern of psycho-sexual development phases of the
individual.   Indeed it is seen, that a psychoanalytic group goes
through all "classical" psycho-sexual development phases, re-activates
in the transference and works through. However there is no in-
variable sequence - but we see a strong tendency for early regression
phases to stand at the beginning of an analytical group process,
while riper development phases can be reached closer to the end. In
every case we can say that the phases mentioned occur steadily in
each psychoanalytic group process and stand there for interpretation
and working through.

I repeat: all group members take part in these regression and
transference phases.   Such members become a "speaker" who expresses
or verbalizes a certain transference constellation with particular
strength, whose individual problems and biography most depend on
the temporary transference phase.

The oral transference phase, which mostly occurs in the first
group hours, is determined by intense clinging and feeding wishes.
The transference object - the analyst - is interpreted as an overwhelming, providing mother - and at the same time there exists the
disappointment or the fear of disappointment, of perceiving the
analyst with his limited opportunities, with his solely verbal
"feedings", a steady source of disappointment.   The goal of the
working through of this transference phase is the "no more nursing"
and this means separation from fusion, the symbiosis with the mother
object: the individuation of the group as a whole, which then seems
to be a limited, a separate individual, no longer fusing with the
analyst.

As we know from classical psychoanalysis, the anal transference
phase goes along with intense annihilation of the analyst as well as
with fears of being annihilated or of being punished by the analyst.
Empirically the narcissistic part of the anal problem in an analytic
group is especially evident. But of course problems of respectability
and diligence are re-activated here, not least in connection to the
payment of the fee. The goal of the working through lies in a new

experience of autonomy, of independence. It represents another step
of the separation, of the individuation, of the assignment of the
symbiotic fusion with the transference object.

In the oedipal transference phase there is especially the clear
sexual attachment of the transference object in the foreground and
herewith also the clearness in seeing his own sexuality in the group.
Here the group divides itself into a male and a female part, it
differentiates itself in clear distinguishable - even male and
female - parts. Reaching the oedipal transference phase signalizes
also the approaching successful end of the group process.

The narcissistic phase is harder to determine from the process
and seems to accompany the total group process: in particular it
is activated close to the end of the group, but also by eliminating
single members of the group during the group process. As a theme
it is characterized by intense phantasies of ruin and destruction of
the group members, which often can be felt in the physical part.
The participants suffer from major fears of having a severe illness,
such as cancer or heart attack and often feel a sudden physical illness. In a group setting it was remarkable for me to observe how
all the group members believed in having broken and weakened bones
and this was interpreted as major narcissistic anxieties.

Especially at the end of a group process each group is engaged
with separation and mourning problems, which often lead to depressive
interferences. It might sound a little bit pedagogical, if it is
mentioned as the goal of the working through of this separation
phase, that here the finiteness and limitation of the life process
is meant and thereby also that of the therapeutic process, the
acceptance of the fact that many wishes must be given up, i.e. those
for total safety and neutralization, for endless therapy - that at
least a renunciation of a durable happy life must be done.

Group psychoanalysis consists in working through the group
transference neurosis with its specific phases and that with the aid
of interpretations, which always deal with the group as a whole. In
comparison to the classical individual psychoanalysis this treatment
is "rougher", since the individual problems of each member cannot
be treated as thoroughly - but it is clearer in accordance with the
emotional intensity and the characteristic constellation of developmental forms of regression and resistance.

The observation of the counter transference, it's diagnostic use
for each transference phase and also it's - careful - use in the
interpretation technique is even more important in group analysis
than in classical psychoanalysis. The intensity of the emotions,
the total regressions are larger and deeper in a group.   The
psychoanalyst experiences the regressions of his patients more
intensely than in classical psychoanalysis; he identifies himself

with the group as a whole and becomes part of it.   Therefore it is
even more important, in these circumstances that he can withdraw his
identification with the group in favour of a distance: a separation
from the object.   Also for a group analyst separation and individuation in a group analytical process is a "main task".

First of all there may be his counter transference difficulties.
The group analyst often has to be cautious not to glide out of the
identification with the group and to agitate and thus to leave the
analytical distance.

Finally, we want to think about the psychoanalyst, who likes to
work or mainly works with groups.   The group analyst must ask himself, whether his own resistance to classical psychoanalysis leads
him to the practice of another setting, even the group setting.
Should this be the situation then his acting would mean to avoid the
necessary abstinence, the temporary suspension of the outer reality
in favour of the transference interpretations.   The group setting
could seem seductive, to make outer reality "directly present" as
well "to unpersonify" transference and resistance with the aid of a
more-person-situation, so that the analyst must not be the only
target of these procedures.

The "submission" to these rules of a classical psychoanalytical
situation could be felt as a narcissistic insult by some analysts,
as a limitation of their "broader effect", i.e. their grand interpretations - but also as a frustration of their personal needs by
the oddities of the transference analysis.   Such a misunderstanding
of the psychoanalytical situation also corresponds to the reproaches
against psychoanalysis such as have been made in connection with
the student revolt since 1968:   It "separates" who can be understood
entirely socially, weakens and deprives him and reproduces his
exploitation and suppression and puts himself into the service of
social repression mechanisms;   but also it doesn't deal with the
necessary emancipation efforts,since it doesn't take the meaning of
the outer, direct inter-personal reality already in it's "artificial"
double-setting into account.   If one accepts such ideas, the group
situation seems to offer such a practicable, almost releasing
solution: analytical work beyond the couch (Wolf and Schwartz, 1970)
considers changed social goals as well as technical innovations.
Here there could be a narcissistic satisfaction for the group
analyst, who is willing to go out of his "beyond-couch-situation" -
by means of social action as if it were modern psychoanalysis.   By
these forms of group therapy he would escape the strict conditions of
psychoanalytical work, which engages in the analysis of transference
neurosis and compliance with strict technical rules.

There is the question, whether the protection of the classical
psychoanalytical position means an insult for the analyst, for instance experienced as an undesired submission to a rule-system, as

a limitation of his grandiose needs, perhaps his therapeutic consciousness and his social political goals. Thereby he would forget -
or avert - that psychoanalytical work is possible, not by compliance
with the specific modalities of observance and techniques of interpretation, which can be achieved especially by a limitation of the
field of work and a renunciation of grand interpretation, "to be
able to do everything".

I want to emphasize, that also the group setting is and must be a
psychoanalytical setting, that it is a requirement also in the
changed conditions (several patients at one time, face-to-face
situation), the psychoanalytical observation and interpretation work,
the working through of transference and resistance by the means of
a group transference neurosis.

Another difficulty with which a psychoanalyst might be confronted
within a group, seems to be the plethora of postulated "group conceptions" in the past. The development of ever new conceptions and
methods could also have a touch of avoidance: it could mean an
evasion of the treatment of psychoanalysis by itself. Indeed, it
might be difficult and burdensome "to withstand" the multiplicity
and intensity of emotions and transference interpretations - moreover from face-to-face and lasting 90 to 100 minutes. Besides this
the abundance of the material recorded in a group setting can exhaust
the capacity of observation of the analyst. Fear and insult of the
analyst could result in the working out of a new, better handling,
easier surveying conception, which is not oriented on psychoanalytical
theory and practice, but takes refuge in the social psychological
for instance.

Also personal problems and conflicts could influence the analyst
to enter "new land" with a group: the analyst must ask himself,
whether he wants to satisfy his own "common needs" with a group and
to escape from his fear of loneliness, also the fear of intimacy and
responsibility of the psychoanalytical work could lead to an "escape
into publicity", such as the one of the group; finally the large
number of people present could give narcissistic gratification by the
means of popularity and indispensability.

I'm conscious that my remarks sound a little bit warning, even
imploring. But just theoretical thoughts don't seem to be enough on
this theme. The setting of the group is also seductive and this then
leads to warning and imploring - and in doing so theoretical arguments often come too short. To be an analyst is to encounter dangers
and hindrances; these are encountered in psychoanalytic work with
groups and have steadily to be reflected.

TRANSITIONAL PHENOMENA AND THE MATRIX IN GROUP PSYCHOTHERAPY

D. Colin James

51 Courthope Road

London NW3 2LE

This is a very simple paper; in fact I feel somewhat embarrassed in presenting such an obvious link which I think most people who know about Winnicott's work and who work with groups are aware of.

My aim is to examine what I think is an important link between Winnicott's description of transitional phenomena, emanating from the initial separation-individuation elements of mother and child, on the one hand, and Foulkes' work on the matrix in groups, on the other.

I do not wish to suggest that these areas are identical, but that there are overlaps. There are areas in the repetition of earlier phenomena, in the life and therapy of adults, both individual and group, where what happens in the potential space between individuals is what matters most.

Nevertheless, there are links, and these need to be stated and to be examined, and understood, in great detail.

It is my contention that a knowledge of Winnicott's work, will deepen our understanding of Foulkes, and will heighten our ability to use our understanding of the matrix, therapeutically, especially with the ever-increasing proportion of patients who present for therapy, (or to use a Winnicottian phrase - "who present themselves for mending") who have borderline or frankly psychotic problems.

Winnicott paid particular attention to the earliest phases of human development and maintained throughout his professional career that the events in the earliest period of development influence profoundly the organisation and development of the personality,

particularly in relation to the development of the capacity for
separation and individuation, and to the ability to develop a true
sense of self, and from there to be able to relate to other selves.

I shall review what I think are the essentials of the Transitional Phenomena concept, but let me say at the outset, that I think
it is imperative to be aware that Winnicott's paper on transitional
phenomena was published at the same time as another paper, entitled
"Psychosis and Child Care". This second paper emphasises some of
the important elements of the concept of transitional phenomena, and
in which he likens the events during analysis of small children, to
those of regressed adults, or of psychotics of all ages, or of
relatively normal people who make temporary, or even momentary regressions. He likens these events to those which are occurring in
the very earliest stages of human development, when the infant is
being introduced gradually to external reality.

"It is generally acknowledged that a statement of human nature
in terms of interpersonal relationships is not good enough even when
the imaginative elaboration of function and the whole of phantasy
both conscious and unconscious including the repressed unconscious
are allowed for.

........of every individual who has reached to the stage of
being a unit with a limiting membrane and an outside and an inside,
it can be said that there is an inner reality to that individual,
an inner world that can be rich or poor and can be at peace or in a
state of war."

Winnicott emphasized that while being able to differentiate between an inner and an outer reality there was also a need to recognise a third area. He referred to the need for a triple statement.
The third part of the life of a human being is an intermediate area
of experiencing, to which inner reality and external life both contribute. It is this statement which forms for me the linking of
Winnicott's ideas to those of Foulkes.

In his transitional object paper Winnicott elaborates the nature
of the intermediate area, one that is not challenged because no
claim "is made on its behalf except that it shall exist as a resting
place for the individual engaged in the perpetual human task of
keeping inner and outer reality separate yet interrelated." He goes
on to describe the way in which this intermediate area might become
represented by a concrete transitional object such as the teddy bear,
and emphasizes the mother's important role in providing for the infant, such an object that can be partly his own and partly a representation of the mother. I will not pursue here the special
characteristics that he attributed to transitional objects, but in-

stead I will go back to the paper on psychotic and child care to
look at the nature of the illusory shared area or experience.

Winnicott traces the way in which the individual is affected by
environmental tendencies. He stresses that forces within the individual enable him to make a spontaneous movement towards the environment
and that this environment is best discovered without loss of a sense
of self.   This is the main theme of this paper and the distortions
which can occur in the earliest phases underscore Winnicott's theory
about the origins of psychosis.

He goes on to say that the creative potential of the individual
arising out of need produces a readiness for hallucination and
stresses that the mother's identification with her infant make her
aware of the infant's need to the extent that she proves something
more or less in the right place and at the right time, and that this
process, much repeated, starts off the infant's ability to use
illusion, without which no contact is possible between the psyche
and the environment.

We might be mistaken, in thinking of the transitional object
paper as talking about just teddy bears, that sort of thing, but a
re-reading and understanding of what all this is about is well
worthwhile.

Winnicott introduced the term "transitional objects and transitional phenomena" for designation of the intermediate area of experience between the thumb and the teddy bear, between the oral
erotism and the true object relationship, between the primary creative
activity and projection of what has already been introjected, between
primary unawareness or indebtedness and the acknowledgement of indebtedness.

"By this definition an infant's babbling and the way in which
an older child goes over a repertory of songs and tunes while preparing for sleep come within the intermediate area as transitional
phenomena, along with the use made of objects that are not part of
the infant's body yet are fully recognised as belonging to external
reality."

I will illustrate some of Winnicott's ideas about these early
stages of development by using a few diagrams which I hope will focus
our attention on to my theme which is a comparison of these events
with Foulkes' ideas about the matrix in groups. I would draw attention to Edgar Rubin's mandala, which emphasises the constant interplay between figure and ground, and which, as we all know epitomises
the Congress theme of "The Individual and the Group".

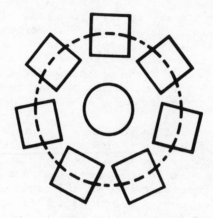

Figure 1.

Figure 1 shows Foulkes' mandala of group analysis, which will
help us to begin together to alter our focus from the individual to
the group and back again.

We might think of the transitional phenomena, and the illusory
space as something that happens in infancy; with little or nothing
to do with us adults.   The reality, from Winnicott's point of view
in his technical writings certainly from the phase of his work
covered by the two papers that I have already mentioned "Transitional
Objects and Transitional Phenomena" and "Psychoses and Child Care",
up to and including that most important paper of his "The Use of an
Object and Relating through Identifications", is that these phenomena permeate our experiences throughout life and they have a considerable impact on our work as therapists and as group therapists.
I hope to be able to demonstrate that they have a bearing on the extension of these phenomena from the life of the infant to the very
actual life of a patient experiencing himself and others in a group
analytic setting.

Before I make the jump I would like to remind us of the object
relations bias throughout all of this material and to do this I shall
quote Henry Rey (1975).   I will summarise this in a table (table 1).

"The individual can be considered as having an inner space in-
habited by inner objects in intrapsychic relationships.   Inner objects
are constructs of the subject corresponding to various levels of de-

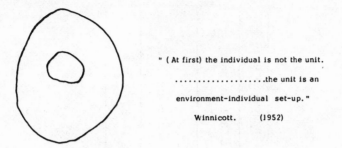

" (At first) the individual is not the unit.

....................the unit is an

environment-individual set-up. "

Winnicott.   (1952)

Figure 2.

velopment from the most primitive to the most sophisticated stages."

"The subject tends to interpret and structure his environment in terms of these groups of internal objects. The more pathological the early stages of structuration of the inner world, the more autonomous primary groups will be and the more they will impose their structure on the external environment."

Winnicott's contention, and one which influenced his clinical and theoretical work, at least from 1952 onwards, was

"At first the individual is not the unit. As perceived from outside the unit is an environment-individual set-up" (figure 2).

"The outsider knows that the individual psyche can only start in a certain setting. In this setting the individual can gradually come to create a personal environment. If all goes well the environment created by the individual becomes something that is like enough to the environment that can be generally perceived, and in such a case there arrives a stage in the process of development through which the individual passes from dependence to independence".

I would like here to acknowledge my gratitude to Mrs. Claire Winnicott for discussion of some of this paper, particularly for her permission to use Winnicott's own original diagrams for the figures which accompany this paper.

Winnicott's own diagram of the theoretical first feed (figure 3) can be modified to delineate the area of illusion, which facilitates contact between the psyche and the environment (figure 4). Incidentally, as Winnicott said, if in place of the word illusion we put the thumb or that bit of blanket or that soft rag doll that some infants employ for giving consolation or comfort then one sees what he described under the term "transitional object" (figures 5 and 6).

TABLE 1.

OBJECT RELATIONS THEORY	Notes
Considers the individual in its interaction with its surroundings	
Focuses on the subject's mode of relation to his world	
A model directly related to clinical data and to social interaction	
Central position of Subject's need to relate to Objects	Contrast, instinct theory: Subject's need to reduce instinctual tension
Object relation(ship) is the relation of the Subject to his Object	Different from Interpersonal Relationship = relation between subject and object
Ultimate aim of libidinal striving	
ORT: Relationship with the Object	Instinct theory: Gratification of the impulse
Cross-roads where instinct and social systems meet	
Outer objects tend to be perceived and responded to in terms of inner objects.	
"The subject tends to interpret and structure his environment in terms of these groups of internal objects" (Rey)	
The individual is considered as having an inner space 'inhabited' by inner objects in intrapsychic relationships.	
Inner objects are constructs of the subject at various levels of development: primitive to sophisticated.	
Therefore a word of caution: the object relationship has to be studied essentially in terms of phantasy based on past relationships that are constantly likely to intervene upon real relationships in the present.	

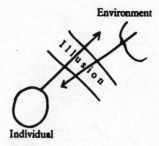

Figure 3. Theoretical first feed.

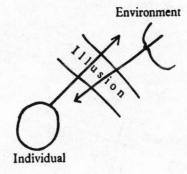

Figure 4.

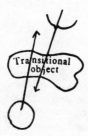

Figure 5. Positive value of illusion. The first possession
    equals transitional object.

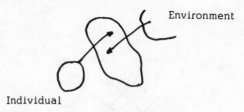

Individual

Figure 6.

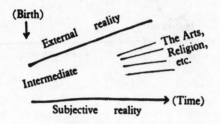

Figure 7. Intermediate area of primary madness.

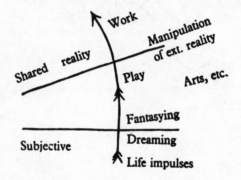

Figure 8.

By the next diagram (figure 7) one can again examine the intermediate area of illusion which in infancy is an agreed area, un-
challenged in respect of its being created by the infant or accepted
as a bit of perceived reality. We allow the infant this 'madness'
and only gradually ask for a clear distinguishing between the subjective and that which is capable of objective or scientific proof.

This can be further elaborated (figure 8).

I would like to take a look at these phenomena when seen in a
group setting and to use them to try and understand further Foulkes'
concept of the matrix.

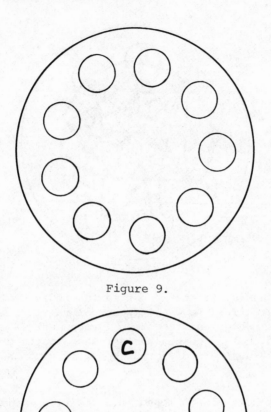

Figure 9.

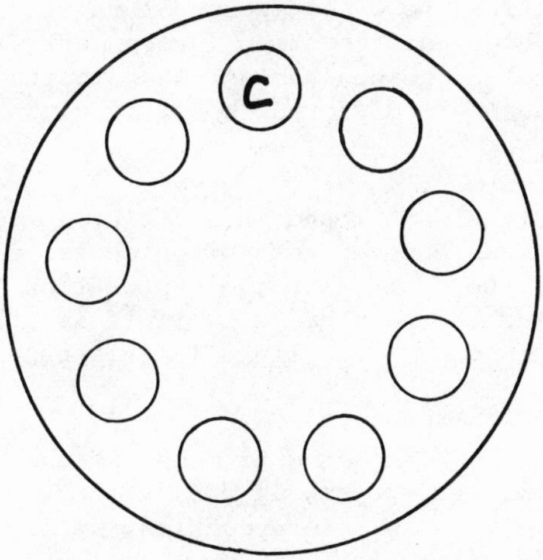

Figure 10.

For some time I have been aware of a close link between Winnicott's work and Foulkes' work and it was therefore with a great deal of pleasure that Malcolm Pines' (1978) paper on the Contribution of S.H. Foulkes to Group Analytic Therapy led me to read Foulkes' paper "On Introjection" (1937) where he points out the importance for psychoanalysis of understanding the process of psychic differentiation of the infant from the infant mother-relationships.

Here is a diagramatic representation of a group (figure 9).I am assuming that this is a stranger group, that has seven or eight persons in it.......and a conductor (figure 10).

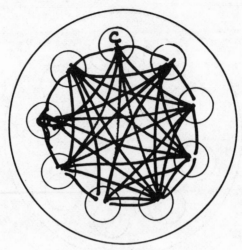

Figure 11.

Foulkes' emphasis was that "Just as the individual's mind is a complex of interacting processes (personal matrix), mental processes interact in the concert of the group (group matrix)". The interacting psychological processes taking place in the group matrix involves the individuals in different specific ways and constellations (figure 11).

I personally have always found this easier to follow in relation, for example, to the dependency that often occurs at the beginning of a group towards the conductor, the expectation that he is going to be the leader and the teacher, etc. This is shown in figure 12. This, by the way, is one of the links in this paper to the descriptions of Bion.

The next step which I am going to make, is the most difficult step in the whole of this paper, if not in the whole of the theory of groups. When we make an interpretation, we might say, "It seems that what the group is saying....." or when our trainees report a session they might say "This group, such and such....."

Now, what do we mean by this? I am under no illusion, that the way in which I conceptualise the next step, nor the manner in which I have chosen to represent it, in any way minimises the conceptual difficulty.

I have tried to represent the complicated structure of the matrix, with all that that implies, in a simple fashion, and we must bear in mind that this is a complex structure. A great deal of work is still necessary, in trying to describe and conceptualise the matrix, but for brevity I have chosen to represent the matrix as a sort of precipitate within the group, of something representing the lines of force, the communications, the emotional links etc. (figure 13).

Figure 12.

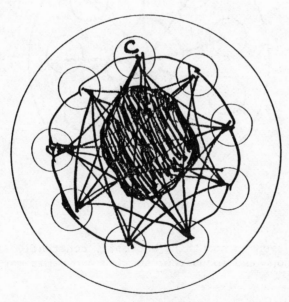

Figure 13.

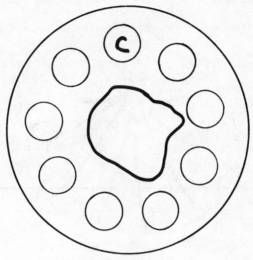

Figure 14.

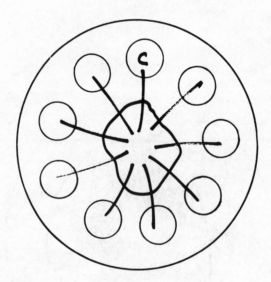

Figure 15.

This can be seen as something amoeboid, constantly fluctuating and changing shape and focus representing a dynamic matrix (figure 14).

Each individual is related to the matrix and to each other via the matrix (figure 15).

Let us review our previous diagram from Winnicott (figure 16).

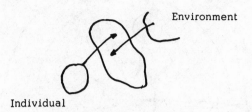

Figure 16.

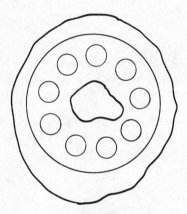

Figure 17.

The matrix encompasses the whole group and extends to relationships and settings outside the group. It extends beyond the boundary
of the group. (Figure 17).

Each individual, through this external matrix is related to the
outside, to the community and to society, at large. (Figure 18).

At this point let us remind ourselves of Winnicott's extension of
the area of illusiory space, beyond the confines of the mother - infant pair, and the family, to the outside world (see figure 8).

Let us further remind ourselves of Winnicott's idea of the manner
in which the individual relates to the environment and the people
in it through a shared space, a shared piece of reality (see figure 6).

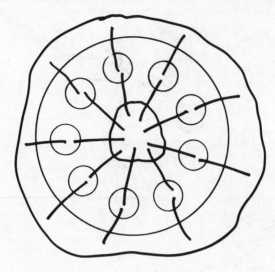

Figure 18.

According to Foulkes, inside this network of communications, the individual is conceived as a nodal point and not as a close system but as an open system relating to Foulkes' analogy, borrowed from Goldstein, of the neuron being the nodal point in the total network of the nervous system which always reacts and responds as a whole "as in the case of the neuron in the nervous system so is the individual suspended in the group matrix".

The individual is seen as a nodal point in a network of relationships (figure 19).

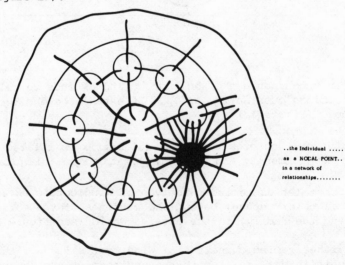

Figure 19.

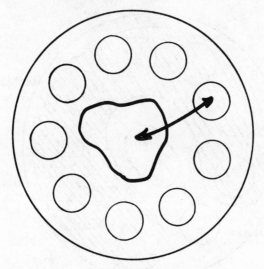

Figure 20.

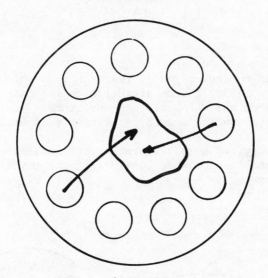

Figure 21.

The individual relates to others in the group via the shared space via the matrix (figure 20).

Individuals relate to each other via the matrix and in the context of the matrix (figure 21).

From the diagram of Winnicott's conceptualisation of the manner in which the individual relates to the environment (see figure 6), I have attempted to represent this, as it occurs in a group, in figure 22.